Rail Guide

2012

Colin J. Marsden

Ian Allan
PUBLISHING

First published 2010
Reprinted 2010, 2011
This Third Edition first published 2012

ISBN 978 0 7110 3649 9

© Ian Allan Publishing Ltd 2012

Published by Ian Allan Publishing.

An imprint of Ian Allan Publishing Ltd, Hersham, Surrey KT12 4RG.
Printed in England by Ian Allan Printing Ltd, Hersham, Surrey KT12 4RG.

Visit the Ian Allan Publishing website at www.ianallanpublishing.com

Distributed in the United States of America and Canada by BookMasters Distribution Services.

Front Cover Top: *The established 'Flying Scotsman' name was resurrected to the East Coast timetable with a new 'fast'
Edinburgh to London service from the 2011 summer timetable. To mark the event, No. 91001 was repainted and branded in a
special Flying Scotsman livery, carrying a huge Flying Scotsman name along the bodyside. On 23 May 2011, the loco is seen
leading the 16.30 King's Cross to Edinburgh past Colton near York.* **Robin Patrick**

Front Cover Bottom: *Operator London Midland has been upgrading Birmingham and West Midlands local services in 2011
by the introduction of two batches of Class 172 diesel-mechanical DMU, based on the Bombardier 'Turbostar' family. Twelve
2-car Class 172/2 sets are allocated to Tyseley. These units are gangwayed throughout and have been well accepted by the
travelling public. On 15 August 2011, two-car set No. 172211 and three-car set No. 172345 depart from Henley in Arden.*
John Binch

Back Cover Top: *Colas Rail operated Plasser & Theurer 08-16/4x4C100 tamper No. DR73931 passing Newport.* **CJM**

Back Cover Bottom: *Royal saloon No. 2923, one of the purpose-built vehicles of the 1970s.* **CJM**

Acknowledgement – The Author would like to record his thanks to the many railway staff who have provided
invaluable information for the production of this book. Also to the many photographers, especially
Nathan Williamson, Tony Christie, Stacey Thew, John Binch and Brian Morrison, for providing many of the
images. I would also like to express my thanks to Jean Marsden, and Keith Ewins for reading the updated
manuscript. **CJM**

The success of the return of the Ian Allan ABC loco and rolling stock number book in 2010 seems to have rekindled the minds of many platform-end enthusiasts, with what appears to be a rise in the number of people collecting train numbers, observing rail operations and recording images of trains. Now in its third year of publication, Rail Guide 2012 brings together in one volume the locomotive, multiple-unit and coaching stock fleets seen throughout mainland UK.

Last year for the first time we included Network Rail certified track machines and engineering plant. This proved to be very popular and has been included again in this year's publication. We are very grateful to the builders and operators of this 'on-track plant' for providing detailed information.

Over the past 12 months we have seen a number of significant changes to our rail system. The closure of the Wrexham & Shropshire Railway in early 2011 was sad, but has enabled sister operator Chiltern to further develop its plans to operate a premier service over the Chiltern Line between London Marylebone and Birmingham.

In terms of new stock, 2011 has seen the completion of Class 379 'Electrostar' deliveries for the East Anglia franchise, final delivery of Class 378s to London Overground and the completion of Class 172 DMU orders for Chiltern, London Overground and London Midland. These deliveries of new stock have allowed significant cascading of older stock, especially Class 150s in various sub-classes from London Midland to First Great Western to increase capacity, while also allowing the transfer away to Northern of the remaining Class 142 'Pacer' sets.

First Great Western has also been successful in receiving Government funded transfers of stock, including five Class 180s to supplement services on the London to Worcester route, and authorisation to convert a significant number of off-lease HST buffet cars into standard class day saloon vehicles enabling selected FGW HSTs to be increased to 2+8 formations.

Few new train orders have been placed in the past year, the most significant being the order for a derivative of the Siemens Desiro build as the replacement 'Thameslink' stock. The official order for the Intercity Express or HST replacement stock has still to be placed.

The Editor and production team hope you enjoy the pages of Rail Guide 2012, and we are now hard at work in producing the 2013 edition. If you have any suitable illustrations for this edition, we look forward to seeing them.

Colin J. Marsden
Dawlish, January 2012

Information in Rail Guide 2012 is correct to 20 January 2012

Painted in Aggregate Industries livery, ex-Foster Yeoman Class 59/0 No. 59005 Kenneth J Painter passes over Fairwood Road Junction on 12 April 2011 with a Merehead to Acton via Westbury loaded stone service. **Antony Christie**

Train Operators, The Association of Train Operating Companies, and Network Rail welcome rail enthusiasts and photographers, but in today's safety led railway and with the continued concerns about possible transport terrorism, guidelines are very important and we encourage all to follow these published guidelines as much as possible. They are available to view and download from the National Rail and ATOC websites, but are reproduced in full below to assist you with this information. ■

The Official Railway Enthusiasts Guidelines

■ Network Rail welcomes rail enthusiasts to our stations.
■ The following guidelines are designed to help you to have a safe and enjoyable experience. Please keep them with you when you are at Network Rail managed stations.
■ You may also wish to take a copy of the Railway by-laws which are available from the Office of Public Sector Information website.

Before you enter the platform

■ When you arrive at a station, please let the staff at the Network Rail Reception Desk know that you are on the station. This will help keep station staff informed so that they can go about their duties without concern as to your reasons for being there.
■ You may require a platform ticket to allow access to platforms.

While you are on the platform

■ You need to act safely & sensibly at all times.
- Stay clear of the platform edge and stay behind the yellow lines where they are provided.
- Be aware of your surroundings.

Please DO NOT:
- Trespass on to the tracks or any other part of the railway that is not available to passengers.
- Use flash photography because it can distract train drivers and train despatch staff and so is potentially very dangerous.
- Climb on any structure or interfere with platform equipment.
- Obstruct any signalling equipment or signs which are vital to the safe running of the railway.
- Wear anything which is similar in colour to safety clothing, such as high-visibility jackets, as this could cause confusion to drivers and other railway employees.
- Gather together in groups at busy areas of the platform (e.g. customer information points, departure screens, waiting areas, seating etc.) or where this may interfere with the duties of station staff.

■ If possible, please try to avoid peak hours which are Monday – Friday 6:00am (06.00) – 10:30am (10.30) and 3:30pm (15.30) – 7:30pm (19.30).

Extra Eyes and Ears

■ If you see anything suspicious or notice any unusual behaviour or activities, please tell a member of staff immediately.
■ For emergencies and serious incidents, either call:
The British Transport Police on 0800 40 50 40.
The Police on 999.
■ Your presence at a station can be very helpful to us as extra "eyes and ears" and can have a positive security benefit.

Photography

■ You can take photographs at stations provided you do not sell them. However, you are not allowed to take photographs of security related equipment, such as CCTV cameras.
■ Flash photography on platforms is not allowed at any time. It can distract train drivers and train despatch staff and so is potentially very dangerous.

■ Tripod legs must be kept away from platform edges and behind the yellow lines. On busy stations, you may not be allowed to use a tripod because it could be a dangerous obstruction to passengers.

Railway By-laws

For safety & ease of travel on the railway system (which includes passengers, staff, property and equipment), the by-laws must be observed by everyone. A copy of the by-laws can be obtained at stations or downloaded from the Office of Public Sector Information website.

General

Train operators must put the safety of their passengers and staff first.   You may very occasionally be asked by station staff to move to another part of the station or to leave the station altogether. Station staff should be happy to explain why this is necessary. If you are travelling by train, they may ask you to remain in the normal waiting areas with other passengers. If this occurs, please follow their instructions with goodwill as staff have many things to consider, including the safety & security of all passengers, and are authorised to use judgement in this regard.

Below: *Painted in Children's Cancer Trust light blue livery, DBS Class 60 No. 60074* Teenage Spirit *passes Cardiff Central on 27 July 2011 powering train 6H24, the 11.21 Llanwern Exchange Sidings to Margam Yard.* **CJM**

Contents

Arriva Wales: 8, c2c: 14, Chiltern: 17, CrossCountry: 22, East Coast: 28, East Midlands: 34, Eurostar: 40, FCC: 44, FGW: 51, FSR: 64, FTP: 73, Grand Central: 76, Heathrow: 78, Hull Trains: 80, IOW: 81, LM: 82, London Overground: 89, Merseyrail: 92, Greater Anglia: 95, Northern: 107, SWT: 116, SET: 127, Southern: 137, Virgin: 146.

Colas: 152, DB Schenker (EWS): 153, Euro Cargo Rail: 167, Direct Rail Services: 168, Royal Mail: 172, Europorte GBRf: 173, Freightliner: 176, Mendip Rail: 182.

Eurotunnel: 184

Network Rail: 186, Royal Train: 189, Track Machines: 192, Balfour Beatty: 207.

Alstom: 208, Bombardier: 208, Electro-Motive Diesels: 209, General Electric: 209, Hitachi: 209, Knights Rail Services: 210, Pullman Group: 210, Railcare: 211, RVEL: 211, Siemens Transportation: 212, Wabtec: 212.

Siemens Transportation: 214.

Europhoenix Ltd: 215, Porterbrook: 215.

Angel Trains: 216, British American: 216, Cargo-D: 218, Electric Traction Ltd: 219, Eversholt: 219, HNRC: 220, Nemesis Rail: 222, Porterbrook: 223, Transmart Trains: 223.

Bo'ness: 224, Flying Scotsman: 224, GSWR: 224, Hastings: 224, Riley: 225, Mid-Hants: 225, NYMR: 225, Railfilms: 225, Ridings: 225, Riviera: 226, SRPS: 229, Stratford 47: 229, VSOE: 229, Vintage: 231, West Coast Railway: 231, Loco Support: 236.

Loco, DMU, EMU, Coaching Stock: 237.

Locomotives: 239, Diesel Units: 242, Electric Units: 244.

Class 03 - Class 66: 246, Class 86 - Class 87: 247.

Diesel & Electric: 248, Steam: 249.

Standard: 250, Drop Head: 250, Dellner: 251, Tightlock: 252, HST (emergency): 253.

London Underground: 254, Docklands Light Railway: 256, Croydon Tramlink: 256, Manchester Metrolink: 256, Nottingham Express Transit: 259, Midland Metro: 259, Sheffield Super Tram: 260, Tyne & Wear: 260, Glasgow: 261.

Livery Codes: 262, Pool Codes: 264, Preserved Site Codes: 265, Depot Codes: 266, Operator Codes: 268, Owner Codes: 269, Station Codes: 270, DMU & EMU Vehicle Codes: 278, Number Cross-Link: 279.

Arriva Trains Wales

Address: ✉ St Mary's House, 47 Penarth Road, Cardiff, CF10 5DJ
 ⌨ customer.relations@arrivatrainswales.co.uk
 ☎ 0845 6061 660
 ⓘ www.arrivatrainswales.co.uk

Managing Director: Tim Bell
Franchise Dates: 7 December 2003 - 6 December 2018
Principal Routes: Cardiff to Swansea and West Wales
 Cardiff Valleys
 Cardiff - Hereford - Shrewsbury - Crewe - Manchester Piccadilly
 Cardiff - Hereford - Shrewsbury - Chester - Bangor - Holyhead
 Manchester - Crewe - Bangor - Holyhead
 Shrewsbury - Pwllheli/Aberystwyth
 Swansea - Shrewsbury
Depots: Cardiff Canton (CF), Chester (CH), Holyhead* (HD)
 Machynlleth (MN), Shrewsbury* (SX) * Stabling point
Parent Company: Deutsche Bahn AG (DB Regio)

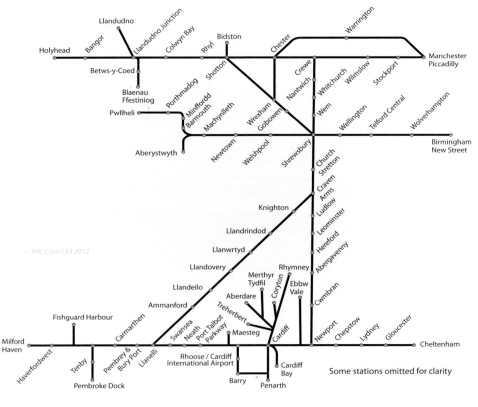

Class 57/3

	Vehicle Length: 63ft 6in (19.38m)	Engine: EMD 645-12F3B
	Height: 12ft 10⅛in (3.91m)	Horsepower: 2,750hp (2,051kW)
	Width: 9ft 2in (2.79m)	Electrical Equipment: Brush

Number	Depot	Pool	Livery	Owner	Operator
57313 (47371)	MA	ATTB	BLU	PTR	ATW/VWC
57314 (47372)	MA	ATTB	ATE	PTR	ATW
57315 (47234)	MA	ATTB	ATE	PTR	ATW
57316 (47290)	MA	ATTB	BLU	PTR	ATW/VWC

Right: *One of the two Arriva Trains Wales-liveried Class 57/3s No. 57314 at Newport in July 2011. The No. 1 end of the loco is nearest the camera.* **CJM**

■ Class 57/3 locos owned by Porterbrook and on lease to Virgin Trains, sub-leased to Arriva Trains Wales. These locos are due to return to Virgin Trains in early 2012.

Class 67

	Vehicle Length: 64ft 7in (19.68m)	Engine: EMD 12N-710G3B-EC
	Height: 12ft 9in (3.88m)	Horsepower: 2,980hp (2,223kW)
	Width: 8ft 9in (2.66m)	Electrical Equipment: EMD

Number	Depot	Pool	Livery	Owner	Operator
67001	CE	WATN	ATW	ANG	DBS/ATW
67002	CE	WATN	ATW	ANG	DBS/ATW
67003	CE	WATN	ATW	ANG	DBS/ATW

Right: *Three DBS Class 67s are allocated to Arriva Trains Wales for use on North-South Wales main line services. All three were outshopped in Arriva Trains blue livery in autumn 2011. This view shows No. 67001 at Doncaster without Arriva bodyside branding applied.* **Derek Porter**

■ The locos are scheduled to take up service between Cardiff and Holyhead, with trains formed with Mk2/3 stock and a DVT from May 2012.

Class 121

	Length: 64ft 6in (19.66m)	Engine: 2 x Leyland 150hp
	Height: 12ft 8½in (3.87m)	Horsepower: 300hp (224kW)
	Width: 9ft 3in (2.81m)	Seats (total/car): 65S

Number	Formation DMBS	Depot	Livery	Owner	Operator	Note
121032	55032	CF	ATW	ATW	ATW	Previously Departmental No. 977842

■ Operated exclusively on Cardiff Queen Street to Cardiff Bay 'shuttle' service.

Right: *Arriva Trains Wales still operates one vehicle of heritage traction on its Cardiff Queen Street to Cardiff Bay, 'shuttle' service. The Class 121 No. 55032, originally built by Pressed Steel and introduced in 1960, later went into Departmental stock and after withdrawal from that role was fully refurbished and taken over for Welsh capital operation. The vehicle is painted in full Arriva Trains Wales livery and allocated to Cardiff Canton.* **CJM**

Arriva Trains Wales

Class 142

Vehicle Length: 51ft 0½in (15.55m)
Height: 12ft 8in (3.86m)
Width: 9ft 2¼in (2.80m)

Engine: 1 x Cummins LTA10-R per vehicle
Horsepower: 460hp (343kW)
Seats (total/car): 90S, 46S/44S

Number	Formation DMS+DMSL	Depot	Livery	Owner	Operator
142002	55543+55593	CF	ATW	ANG	ATW
142006	55547+55597	CF	ATW	ANG	ATW
142010	55551+55601	CF	ATW	ANG	ATW
142069	55719+55765	CF	ATW	ANG	ATW
142072	55722+55768	CF	ATW	ANG	ATW
142073	55723+55769	CF	ATW	ANG	ATW
142074	55724+55770	CF	ATW	ANG	ATW
142075	55725+55771	CF	ATW	ANG	ATW
142076	55726+55772	CF	ATW	ANG	ATW
142077	55727+55773	CF	ATW	ANG	ATW
142080	55730+55776	CF	ATW	ANG	ATW
142081	55731+55777	CF	ATW	ANG	ATW
142082	55732+55778	CF	ATW	ANG	ATW
142083	55733+55779	CF	ATW	ANG	ATW
142085	55735+55781	CF	ATW	ANG	ATW

Name applied
142072 Myfanwy

Left: *Cardiff Canton has an allocation of 15 Class 142s; used in conjunction with Class 143s, these sets can be found on the Cardiff 'Valley' line services. In July 2011, set No. 142082 is seen arriving at Radyr with a Cardiff-bound service.* **CJM**

Class 143

Vehicle Length: 51ft 0½in (15.55m)
Height: 12ft 2¼in (3.73m)
Width: 8ft 10½in (2.70m)

Engine: 1 x Cummins LTA10-R per vehicle
Horsepower: 460hp (343kW)
Seats (total/car): 92S, 48S/44S

Number	Formation DMS+DMSL	Depot	Livery	Owner	Operator
143601	55642+55667	CF	ATW	BCC	ATW
143602	55651+55668	CF	ATW	PTR	ATW
143604	55645+55670	CF	ATW	PTR	ATW
143605	55646+55671	CF	ATW	PTR	ATW
143606	55647+55672	CF	ATW	PTR	ATW
143607	55648+55673	CF	ATW	PTR	ATW
143608	55649+55674	CF	ATW	PTR	ATW
143609	55650+55675	CF	ATW	CCC	ATW
143610	55643+55676	CF	ATW	BCC	ATW
143614	55655+55680	CF	ATW	BCC	ATW
143615	55657+55682	CF	ATW	PTR	ATW
143622	55663+55688	CF	ATW	PTR	ATW
143623	55664+55689	CF	ATW	PTR	ATW
143624	55665+55690	CF	ATW	PTR	ATW
143625	55666+55691	CF	ATW	PTR	ATW

Name applied
143609 Sir Tom Jones

Left: *To operate alongside the Arriva Trains Wales Class 142 fleet, are 15 Class 143s. All have been refurbished in the same way as the Class 142s and operate as a common pool of 'Pacer' sets. Set No. 143601 is pictured at Radyr with a service bound for Cardiff in July 2011.* **CJM**

Class 150/2

Vehicle Length: 64ft 9¾in (19.74m)
Height: 12ft 4½in (3.77m)
Width: 9ft 3⅛in (2.82m)

Engine: 1 x NT855R5 of 285hp per vehicle
Horsepower: 570hp (425kW)
Seats (total/car): 128S, 60S/68S

Number	Formation DMSL+DMS	Depot	Livery	Owner	Operator
150208	52208+57208	CF	ATW	PTR	ATW
150236	52236+57236	CF	ATW	PTR	ATW
150240	52240+57240	CF	ATW	PTR	ATW
150241	52241+57241	CF	ATW	PTR	ATW
150242	52242+57242	CF	ATW	PTR	ATW
150245	52245+57245	CF	ATW	PTR	ATW
150250	52250+57250	CF	ATW	PTR	ATW
150251	52251+57251	CF	ATW	PTR	ATW
150252	52252+57252	CF	ATW	PTR	ATW
150253	52253+57253	CF	ATW	PTR	ATW
150254	52254+57254	CF	ATW	PTR	ATW
150256	52256+57256	CF	ATW	PTR	ATW
150258	52258+57258	CF	ATW	PTR	ATW
150259	52259+57259	CF	ATW	PTR	ATW

150260	52260+57260	CF	ATW	PTR	ATW		150280§	52280+57280	NR	ATW	PTR	NXA
150262	52262+57262	CF	ATW	PTR	ATW		150281	52281+57281	CF	ATW	PTR	ATW
150264	52264+57264	CF	ATW	PTR	ATW		150282	52282+57282	CF	ATW	PTR	ATW
150267	52267+57267	CF	ATW	PTR	ATW		150283	52283+57283	CF	ATW	PTR	ATW
150278	52278+57278	CF	ATW	PTR	ATW		150284	52284+57284	CF	ATW	PTR	ATW
150279	52270+57279	CF	ATW	PTR	ATW		150285§	52285+57280	NH	ATW	PTR	NOR

§ 150280 on loan to Abellio East
    Anglia.
  150285 on loan to Northern.

Right: *A total of 26 Class 150s are on
the books of Arriva Trains Wales. At
the end of 2011, 24 were working for
the operator and two were on long term
lease to Northern and National Express
East Anglia. Set No. 150259 is viewed
from its DMS end at Gloucester.* **CJM**

Class 153

Vehicle Length: 76ft 5in (23.29m)		Engine: 1 x NT855R5 of 285hp	
Height: 12ft 3⅛in (3.75m)		Horsepower: 285hp (213kW)	
Width: 8ft 10in (2.70m)		Seats (total/car): 72S	

Number	Formation DMSL	Depot	Livery	Owner	Operator							
						153323	52323	CF	ATW	PTR	ATW
153303	52303	CF	ATW	ANG	ATW	153327	52327	CF	ATW	ANG	ATW
153312	52312	CF	ATW	ANG	ATW	153353	57353	CF	ATW	ANG	ATW
153320	52320	CF	ATW	PTR	ATW	153362	57362	CF	ATW	ANG	ATW
						153367	57367	CF	ATW	PTR	ATW

Right: *For longer distance lighter used
routes, mainly in west Wales, a fleet
of eight Class 153 single-car vehicles
are operated. Based at Cardiff Canton,
all are painted in Arriva Trains
livery. These vehicles were formerly
marshalled as two-car sets classified
as 155. Single car No. 153367 is
illustrated at Blaenau Ffestiniog.*
Murdoch Currie

Class 158

Vehicle Length: 76ft 1¾in (23.21m)		Engine: 1 x Perkins 2006-TWH of 350hp per vehicle	
Height: 12ft 6in (3.81m)		Horsepower: 700hp (522kW)	
Width: 9ft 3¼in (2.82m)		Seats (total/car): 134S, 66S/68S	

Number	Formation DMSL+DMSL	Depot	Livery	Owner	Operator							
						158829	52829+57829	MN	ATW	ANG	ATW
						158830	52830+57830	MN	ATW	ANG	ATW
158818	52818+57818	MN	ATW	ANG	ATW	158831	52831+57831	MN	WAL	ANG	ATW
158819	52819+57819	MN	WAL	ANG	ATW	158832	52832+57832	MN	ATT	ANG	ATW
158820	52820+57820	MN	ATT	ANG	ATW	158833	52833+57833	MN	ATT	ANG	ATW
158821	52821+57821	MN	ATT	ANG	ATW	158834	52834+57834	MN	ATT	ANG	ATW
158822	52822+57822	MN	ATT	ANG	ATW	158835	52835+57835	MN	WAL	ANG	ATW
158823	52823+57823	MN	ATW	ANG	ATW	158836	52836+57836	MN	WAL	ANG	ATW
158824	52824+57824	MN	ATW	ANG	ATW	158837	52837+57837	CF	ATT	ANG	ATW
158825	52825+57825	MN	WAL	ANG	ATW	158838	52838+57838	CF	ATT	ANG	ATW
158826	52826+57826	MN	WAL	ANG	ATW	158839	52839+57839	CF	ATT	ANG	ATW
158827	52827+57827	MN	ATT	ANG	ATW	158840	52840+57840	CF	ATT	ANG	ATW
158828	52828+57828	MN	ATW	ANG	ATW	158841	52841+57841	CF	WAL	ANG	ATW

Arriva Trains Wales

■ All sets are fitted with operational European Rail Traffic Management System (ERTMS) equipment for operation on the Cambrian Line.

Left: *Displaying the latest Arriva Trains Wales livery, applied to refurbished Class 158s, set No. 158838 is illustrated near Newport.*
Jamie Squibbs

Class 175/0
Coradia 1000

Vehicle Length: 75ft 7in (23.06m)
Height: 12ft 4in (3.75m)
Width: 9ft 2in (2.80m)

Engine: 1 x Cummins N14 of 450hp per vehicle
Horsepower: 900hp (671kW)
Seats (total/car): 118S, 54S/64S

Number	Formation DMSL+DMSL	Depot	Livery	Owner	Operator
175001	50701+79701	CH	ATW	ANG	ATW
175002	50702+79702	CH	ATW	ANG	ATW
175003	50703+79703	CH	ATW	ANG	ATW
175004	50704+79704	CH	ATW	ANG	ATW
175005	50705+79705	CH	ATW	ANG	ATW
175006	50706+79706	CH	ATW	ANG	ATW
175007	50707+79707	CH	ATW	ANG	ATW
175008	50708+79708	CH	ATW	ANG	ATW
175009	50709+79709	CH	ATW	ANG	ATW
175010	50710+79710	CH	ATW	ANG	ATW
175011	50711+79711	CH	ATW	ANG	ATW

Left: *Allocated to Chester depot and used mainly in the northern Wales area, as well as on longer distance North-South Wales services, are a fleet of Class 175 'Coradia 1000' units. These come in both a two- and three-car formation. Two-car set No. 175003 is seen at Newport on 27 July 2011. All sets carry Arriva Trains Wales livery.*
CJM

Class 175/1
Coradia 1000

Vehicle Length: 75ft 7in (23.06m)
Height: 12ft 4in (3.75m)
Width: 9ft 2in (2.80m)

Engine: 1 x Cummins N14 of 450hp per vehicle
Horsepower: 1,350hp (1,007kW)
Seats (total/car): 186S, 54S/68S/64S

Number	Formation DMSL+MSL+DMSL	Depot	Livery	Owner	Opt'r
175101	50751+56751+79751	CH	ATW	ANG	ATW
175102	50752+56752+79752	CH	ATW	ANG	ATW
175103	50753+56753+79753	CH	ATW	ANG	ATW
175104	50754+56754+79754	CH	ATW	ANG	ATW
175105	50755+56755+79755	CH	ATW	ANG	ATW
175106	50756+56756+79756	CH	ATW	ANG	ATW
175107	50757+56757+79757	CH	ATW	ANG	ATW
175108	50758+56758+79758	CH	ATW	ANG	ATW
175109	50759+56759+79759	CH	ATW	ANG	ATW
175110	50760+56760+79760	CH	ATW	ANG	ATW
175111	50761+56761+79761	CH	ATW	ANG	ATW
175112	50762+56762+79762	CH	ATW	ANG	ATW
175113	50763+56763+79763	CH	ATW	ANG	ATW
175114	50764+56764+79764	CH	ATW	ANG	ATW
175115	50765+56765+79765	CH	ATW	ANG	ATW
175116	50766+56766+79766	CH	ATW	ANG	ATW

Left: *A total of 16 Class 175/1 three-car 'Coradia 1000' sets are in traffic, sharing duties from Chester with the two-car Class 175/0 units. No. 175103 is seen passing Llandudno Junction signalbox while operating over the North Wales Coast route.*
Antony Christie

Class AC2E / TSO

Vehicle Length: 66ft 0in (20.11m)
Height: 12ft 9½in (3.89m)
Width: 9ft 3in (2.81m)
Seats (total/car): 62S

Number	Type	Depot	Livery	Owner	Operator
5853	TSO	CF	ATW	ATW	ATW

Number	Type	Depot	Livery	Owner	Operator
5869(S)	TSO	LM	ATW	ATW	-

Class AC2F / TSO

Vehicle Length: 66ft 0in (20.11m)
Height: 12ft 9½in (3.89m)
Width: 9ft 3in (2.81m)
Seats (total/car): 60S

Number	Type	Depot	Livery	Owner	Operator
5913(S)	TSO	CF	ATW	ATW	-
5965	TSO	CF	ATW	ATW	ATW
5976	TSO	CF	ATW	ATW	ATW
6013(S)	TSO	LM	ATW	ATW	-
6035(S)	TSO	LM	ATW	ATW	-
6119	TSO	CF	ATW	ATW	ATW
6137	TSO	CF	ATW	ATW	ATW
6162(S)	TSO	LM	ATW	ATW	-
6170(S)	TSO	LM	ATW	ATW	-
6183	TSO	CF	ATW	ATW	ATW

Class AE2E / BSO

Vehicle Length: 66ft 0in (20.11m)
Height: 12ft 9½in (3.89m)
Width: 9ft 3in (2.81m)
Seats (total/car): 60S

Number	Type	Depot	Livery	Owner	Operator
9503	BSO	CF	ATW	ATW	ATW
9509	BSO	CF	ATW	ATW	ATW

Class AE2F / BSO

Vehicle Length: 66ft 0in (20.11m)
Height: 12ft 9½in (3.89m)
Width: 9ft 3in (2.81m)
Seats (total/car): 60S

Number	Type	Depot	Livery	Owner	Operator
9521	BSO	CF	ATW	ATW	ATW
9524(S)	BSO	LM	ATW	ATW	-
9539	BSO	CF	ATW	ATW	ATW

Class AJ1G / RFM

Vehicle Length: 75ft 0in (22.86m)
Height: 12ft 9in (3.88m)
Width: 8ft 11in (2.71m)
Bogie Type: BT10

Number	Type	Depot	Livery	Owner	Operator
10249 (10012)	RFM	CF	ATW	DBR	ATW
10259 (10025)	RFM	CF	ATW	ATW	ATW

Mk3 Hauled Stock (NPCCS)

Vehicle Length: 75ft 0in (22.86m)
Height: 12ft 9in (3.88m)
Width: 8ft 11in (2.71m)
Bogie Type: BT7

NZAG - DVT

Number	Depot	Livery	Owner	Operator
82306 (82144)	CF	ATW	ATW	ATW
82307 (82131)	CF	ATW	ATW	ATW

Below: *Arriva Trains Wales operates a small fleet of Mk2 and Mk3 loco-hauled vehicles. All are based at Cardiff Canton and used on the loco-hauled services linking Cardiff with Holyhead. Trains are usually four-car formation and until the spring of 2012 were powered by hired-in Class 57/3 locos. From spring 2012 traction will be provided by hired-in DBS Class 67s with rebuilt Mk3 DVTs. Mk3 RFM No. 10259 is illustrated at Newport.* **CJM**

c2c

Address: ✉ 10th Floor, 207 Old Street, London, EC1V 9NR
🖰 c2c.customerrelations@nationalexpress.com
✆ 0845 6014873
ⓘ www.c2c-online.co.uk

Managing Director: Julian Drury
Franchise Dates: 26 May 1996 - 26 May 2013
Principal Routes: London Fenchurch Street - Shoeburyness
Barking - Pitsea via Purfleet
Ockendon branch
London Liverpool Street - Barking (limited service)
Depots: East Ham (EM), Shoeburyness*
* Stabling point
Parent Company: National Express

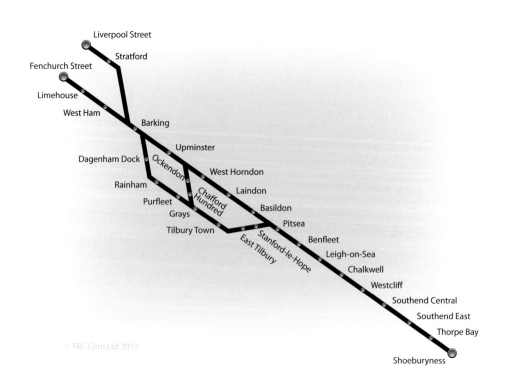

Class 357/0
Electrostar

Vehicle Length: (Driving) 68ft 1in (20.75m) Width: 9ft 2½in (2.80m)
(Inter) 65ft 11½in (20.10m) Horsepower: 2,011hp (1,500kW)
Height: 12ft 4½in (3.78m) Seats (total/car): 282S, 71S/78S/62S/71S

Number	Formation DMSO(A)+MSO+PTSO+DMSO(B)	Depot	Livery	Owner	Opt'	Name
357001	67651+74151+74051+67751	EM	NE2	PTR	C2C	Barry Flaxman
357002	67652+74152+74052+67752	EM	NE2	PTR	C2C	Arthur Lewis Stride 1841-1922
357003	67653+74153+74053+67753	EM	NE2	PTR	C2C	Southend City on Sea
357004	67654+74154+74054+67754	EM	NE2	PTR	C2C	Tony Amos
357005	67655+74155+74055+67755	EM	NE2	PTR	C2C	
357006	67656+74156+74056+67756	EM	NE2	PTR	C2C	
357007	67657+74157+74057+67757	EM	NE2	PTR	C2C	
357008	67658+74158+74058+67758	EM	NE2	PTR	C2C	
357009	67659+74159+74059+67759	EM	NE2	PTR	C2C	
357010	67660+74160+74060+67760	EM	NE2	PTR	C2C	
357011	67661+74161+74061+67761	EM	NE2	PTR	C2C	John Lowing
357012	67662+74162+74062+67762	EM	NE2	PTR	C2C	
357013	67663+74163+74063+67763	EM	NE2	PTR	C2C	
357014	67664+74164+74064+67764	EM	NE2	PTR	C2C	
357015	67665+74165+74065+67765	EM	NE2	PTR	C2C	
357016	67666+74166+74066+67766	EM	NE2	PTR	C2C	
357017	67667+74167+74067+67767	EM	NE2	PTR	C2C	
357018	67668+74168+74068+67768	EM	NE2	PTR	C2C	
357019	67669+74169+74069+67769	EM	NE2	PTR	C2C	
357020	67670+74170+74070+67770	EM	NE2	PTR	C2C	
357021	67621+74171+74071+67771	EM	NE2	PTR	C2C	
357022	67672+74172+74072+67772	EM	NE2	PTR	C2C	
357023	67673+74173+74073+67773	EM	NE2	PTR	C2C	
357024	67674+74174+74074+67774	EM	NE2	PTR	C2C	
357025	67675+74175+74075+67775	EM	NE2	PTR	C2C	
357026	67676+74176+74076+67776	EM	NE2	PTR	C2C	
357027	67677+74177+74077+67777	EM	NE2	PTR	C2C	
357028	67678+74178+74078+67778	EM	NE2	PTR	C2C	London, Tilbury & Southend Railway 1854-2004
357029	67679+74179+74079+67779	EM	NE2	PTR	C2C	Thomas Whitelegg 1840-1922
357030	67680+74180+74080+67780	EM	NE2	PTR	C2C	Robert Harben Whitelegg 1871-1957
357031	67681+74181+74081+67781	EM	NE2	PTR	C2C	
357032	67682+74182+74082+67782	EM	NE2	PTR	C2C	
357033	67683+74183+74083+67783	EM	NE2	PTR	C2C	
357034	67684+74184+74084+67784	EM	NE2	PTR	C2C	
357035	67685+74185+74085+67785	EM	NE2	PTR	C2C	
357036	67686+74186+74086+67786	EM	NE2	PTR	C2C	
357037	67687+74187+74087+67787	EM	NE2	PTR	C2C	
357038	67688+74188+74088+67788	EM	NE2	PTR	C2C	
357039	67689+74189+74089+67789	EM	NE2	PTR	C2C	
357040	67690+74190+74090+67790	EM	NE2	PTR	C2C	
357041	67691+74191+74091+67791	EM	NE2	PTR	C2C	
357042	67692+74192+74092+67792	EM	NE2	PTR	C2C	
357043	67693+74193+74093+67793	EM	NE2	PTR	C2C	
357044	67694+74194+74094+67794	EM	NE2	PTR	C2C	
357045	67695+74195+74095+67795	EM	NE2	PTR	C2C	
357046	67696+74196+74096+67796	EM	NE2	PTR	C2C	

Right: *Still identified as the UK's most reliable train fleet are the two sub-classes of Class 357, operated from East Ham on c2c services. 46 Porterbrook-owned Class 357/0s are in traffic. All are painted in National Express white livery. Set No. 357015 is illustrated.*
Antony Christie

Passenger Train Operating Companies - c2c

c2c

Class 357/2
Electrostar

Vehicle Length: (Driving) 68ft 1in (20.75m)	Width: 9ft 2½in (2.80m)	
(Inter) 65ft 11½in (20.10m)	Horsepower: 2,011hp (1,500kW)	
Height: 12ft 4½in (3.78m)	Seats (total/car): 282S, 71S/78S/62S/71S	

Number	Formation DMSO(A)+MSO+PTSO+DMSO(B)	Depot	Livery	Owner	Operator	Name
357201	68601+74701+74601+68701	EM	NE2	ANG	C2C	Ken Bird
357202	68602+74702+74602+68702	EM	NE2	ANG	C2C	Kenny Mitchell
357203	68603+74703+74603+68703	EM	NE2	ANG	C2C	Henry Pumfrett
357204	68604+74704+74604+68704	EM	NE2	ANG	C2C	Derek Flowers
357205	68605+74705+74605+68705	EM	NE2	ANG	C2C	John D'Silva
357206	68606+74706+74606+68706	EM	NE2	ANG	C2C	Martin Aungier
357207	68607+74707+74607+68707	EM	NE2	ANG	C2C	John Page
357208	68608+74708+74608+68708	EM	NE2	ANG	C2C	Dave Davis
357209	68609+74709+74609+68709	EM	NE2	ANG	C2C	James Snelling
357210	68610+74710+74610+68710	EM	NE2	ANG	C2C	
357211	68611+74711+74611+68711	EM	NE2	ANG	C2C	
357212	68612+74712+74612+68712	EM	NE2	ANG	C2C	
357213	68613+74713+74613+68713	EM	NE2	ANG	C2C	Upminster IECC
357214	68614+74714+74614+68714	EM	NE2	ANG	C2C	
357215	68615+74715+74615+68715	EM	NE2	ANG	C2C	
357216	68616+74716+74616+68716	EM	NE2	ANG	C2C	
357217	68617+74717+74617+68717	EM	NE2	ANG	C2C	Allan Burnell
357218	68618+74218+74618+68718	EM	NE2	ANG	C2C	
357219	68619+74719+74619+68719	EM	NE2	ANG	C2C	
357220	68620+74720+74620+68720	EM	NE2	ANG	C2C	
357221	68621+74721+74621+68721	EM	NE2	ANG	C2C	
357222	68622+74722+74622+68722	EM	NE2	ANG	C2C	
357223	68623+74723+74623+68723	EM	NE2	ANG	C2C	
357224	68624+74724+74624+68724	EM	NE2	ANG	C2C	
357225	68625+74725+74625+68725	EM	NE2	ANG	C2C	
357226	68626+74726+74626+68726	EM	NE2	ANG	C2C	
357227	68627+74727+74627+68727	EM	NE2	ANG	C2C	
357228	68628+74728+74628+68728	EM	NE2	ANG	C2C	

Below: *The 28 Class 357/2 sets are owned by Angel Trains, but operate as one common pool with the Class 357/0 sets. All sets are painted in National Express white livery. A number of sets carry cast nameplates; these are applied behind the driving cab at cant rail height. Set No. 375215 is illustrated.* **Antony Christie**

Chiltern Railways

Address: ✉ 2nd floor, Western House, Rickfords Hill, Aylesbury, Buckinghamshire, HP20 2RX

🖰 Via website (www.chilternrailways.co.uk)

✆ 08456 005165

ⓘ www.chilternrailways.co.uk

Managing Director: Rob Brighthouse

Franchise Dates: 21 July 1996 - 1 March 2022

Principal Routes: London Marylebone - Birmingham Snow Hill

London Marylebone - Aylesbury

Hatton - Stratford-upon-Avon

Depots: Aylesbury (AL), Wembley*

* Stabling point

Parent Company: Deutsche Bahn AG (DB Regio)

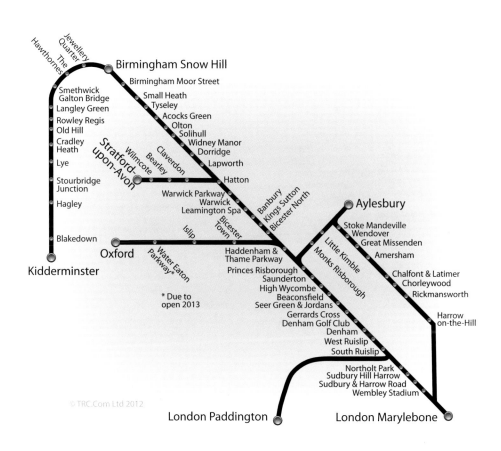

Chiltern Railways

Class 121

Length: 64ft 6in (19.66m)	Engine: 2 x Leyland 150hp
Height: 12ft 8½in (3.87m)	Horsepower: 300hp (224kW)
Width: 9ft 3in (2.81m)	Seats (total/car): 65S

Number	Formation DMBS	Depot	Livery	Owner	Operator
121020	55020	AY	BLU	CRW	CRW
121034	55034	AY	GRN	CRW	CRW

Left: *Chiltern Railways are another of the operators who still retain heritage traction. Two Class 121 'bubble' cars are based at Aylesbury for use on the Aylesbury to Princes Risborough line. Vehicle No. 55020 is painted in Chiltern blue, while No. 55034 (illustrated) has been restored to 1960s BR green. Both vehicles have modern central door locking.* **Colin Cooke**

Class 165/0 (2-car)
Networker Turbo

Vehicle Length: (Driving) 75ft 2½in (22.91m), (Inter) 74ft 6½in (22.72m)	
Height: 12ft 5¼in (3.79m)	Engine: 1 x Perkins 2006 TWH of 350hp per vehicle
Width: 9ft 2½in (2.81m)	Horsepower: 700hp (522kW)
Seats (total/car): 183S, 89S/94S	

Number	Formation DMSL+DMS	Depot	Livery	Owner	Operator
165001	58801+58834	AL	CRW	ANG	CRW
165002	58802+58835	AL	CRW	ANG	CRW
165003	58803+58836	AL	CRW	ANG	CRW
165004	58804+58837	AL	CRW	ANG	CRW
165005	58805+58838	AL	CRW	ANG	CRW
165006	58806+58839	AL	CRW	ANG	CRW
165007	58807+58840	AL	CRW	ANG	CRW
165008	58808+58841	AL	CRW	ANG	CRW
165009	58809+58842	AL	CRW	ANG	CRW
165010	58810+58843	AL	CRW	ANG	CRW
165011	58811+58844	AL	CRW	ANG	CRW
165012	58812+58845	AL	CRW	ANG	CRW
165013	58813+58846	AL	CRW	ANG	CRW
165014	58814+58847	AL	CRW	ANG	CRW
165015	58815+58848	AL	CRW	ANG	CRW
165016	58816+58849	AL	CRW	ANG	CRW
165017	58817+58850	AL	CRW	ANG	CRW
165018	58818+58851	AL	CRW	ANG	CRW
165019	58819+58852	AL	CRW	ANG	CRW
165020	58820+58853	AL	CRW	ANG	CRW
165021	58821+58854	AL	CRW	ANG	CRW
165022	58822+58855	AL	CRW	ANG	CRW
165023	58873+58867	AL	CRW	ANG	CRW
165024	58874+58868	AL	CRW	ANG	CRW
165025	58874+58869	AL	CRW	ANG	CRW
165026	58876+58870	AL	CRW	ANG	CRW
165027	58877+58871	AL	CRW	ANG	CRW
165028	58878+58872	AL	CRW	ANG	CRW

Left: *The principal rolling stock used for Chiltern local services is a fleet of Class 165 units, introduced in the days of Network SouthEast as 'Networker Turbos'. All sets have now been refurbished. Class 165s come in both two- and three-car formations. In this view we see two-car set No. 165006 departing from London Marylebone.* **Antony Christie**

Class 165/0 (3-car)
Networker Turbo

Vehicle Length: (driving) 75ft 2½in (22.91m), (inter) 74ft 6½in (22.72m)	
Height: 12ft 5¼in (3.79m)	Engine: 1 x Perkins 2006 TWH of 350hp per vehicle
Width: 9ft 2½in (2.81m)	Horsepower: 1,050hp (783kW)
Seats (total/car): 289S, 89S/106S/94S	

Number	Formation DMSL+MS+DMS	Depot	Livery	Owner	Operator
165029	58823+55404+58856	AL	CRW	ANG	CRW
165030	58824+55405+58857	AL	CRW	ANG	CRW
165031	58825+55406+58858	AL	CRW	ANG	CRW
165032	58826+55407+58859	AL	CRW	ANG	CRW
165033	58827+55408+58860	AL	CRW	ANG	CRW
165034	58828+55409+58861	AL	CRW	ANG	CRW
165035	58829+55410+58862	AL	CRW	ANG	CRW
165036	58830+55411+58863	AL	CRW	ANG	CRW
165037	58831+55412+58864	AL	CRW	ANG	CRW
165038	58832+55413+58865	AL	CRW	ANG	CRW
165039	58833+55414+58866	AL	CRW	ANG	CRW

Passenger Train Operating Companies - Chiltern Railways

Class 168/0
Turbostar

Vehicle Length: 77ft 6in (23.62m)
Height: 12ft 4½in (3.77m)
Width: 8ft 10in (2.69m)
Engine: 1 x MTU 6R 183TD13H 422hp per vehicle
Horsepower: 1,688hp (1,259kW)
Seats (total/car): 278S, 60S/73S/77S/68S

Number	Formation DMSL(A)+MSL+MS+DMSL(B)	Depot	Livery	Owner	Operator
168001	58151+58651+58451+58251	AL	CRW	PTR	CRW
168002	58152+58652+58452+58252	AL	CRW	PTR	CRW
168003	58153+58653+58453+58253	AL	CRW	PTR	CRW
168004	58154+58654+58454+58254	AL	CRW	PTR	CRW
168005	58155+58655+58455+58255	AL	CRW	PTR	CRW

Right: *Chiltern Railways were the first operator to order the 'Turbostar' product range from Adtranz (later Bombardier). Classified as '168', these sets sport an earlier design of front end, less streamlined than subsequent 'Turbostar' builds. Set No. 168002 is seen departing from London Marylebone.* **Antony Christie**

Class 168/1
Turbostar

Vehicle Length: 77ft 6in (23.62m)
Height: 12ft 4½in (3.77m)
Width: 8ft 10in (2.69m)
Engine: 1 x MTU 6R 183TD13H of 422hp per vehicle
Horsepower: 3/4-Car 1,266hp (944kW)/1,688hp (1,259kW)
Seats (total/car): 3-car - 208S, 59S/73S/76S, 4-car - 284S, 59S/73S/76S/76S

Number	Formation DMSL(A)+MS+MS+DMSL(B)	Depot	Livery	Owner	Operator	Notes
168106	58156+58756§+58456+58256	AL	CRW	PTR	CRW	§ is a MSL vehicle
168107	58157+58457+58757§+58257	AL	CRW	PTR	CRW	§ is a MSL vehicle
168108	58158+58458+58258	AL	CRW	PTR	CRW	
168109	58159+58459+58259	AL	CRW	PTR	CRW	
168110	58160+58460+58260	AL	CRW	PTR	CRW	
168111	58161+58461+58261	AL	CRW	EVL	CRW	58461 was originally 58661
168112	58162+58462+58262	AL	CRW	EVL	CRW	58462 was originally 58662
168113	58163+58463+58263	AL	CRW	EVL	CRW	58463 was originally 58663

Right: *By the time the production orders for 'Turbostar' stock was placed, the train builders had standarised on the more streamlined front end, as shown on set No. 168106 at Blackthorne Hill. This is one of only two Class 168/1s formed of four carriages, the remainder have just three.* **John Stretton**

Class 168/2
Turbostar

Vehicle Length: 77ft 6in (23.62m)
Height: 12ft 4½in (3.77m)
Width: 8ft 10in (2.69m)
Engine: 1 x MTU 6R 183TD13H of 422hp per vehicle
Horsepower: 3/4-Car 1,266hp (944kW)/1,688hp (1,259kW)
Seats (total/car): 3-car - 204S, 59S/76S/69S, 4-car - 277S, 59S/73S/76S/696S

Number	Formation DMSL(A)+MS+MS+DMSL(B)	Depot	Livery	Owner	Operator
168214	58164+58464+58264	AL	CRW	PTR	CRW
168215	58165+58465+58365+58265	AL	CRW	PTR	CRW
168216	58166+58466+58366+58266	AL	CRW	PTR	CRW
168217	58167+58467+58367+58267	AL	CRW	PTR	CRW
168218	58168+58468+58268	AL	CRW	PTR	CRW
168219	58169+58469+58269	AL	CRW	PTR	CRW

Passenger Train Operating Companies - Chiltern Railways

Chiltern Railways

Class 172/1

Vehicle Length: 73ft 4in (22.37m)		Engine: MTU 6H1800 of 360kW
Height: 12ft 4½in (3.77m)		Horsepower: 965hp (720kW)
Width: 8ft 8in (2.69m)		Seats (total/car): 121S, 53S/68S

Number	Formation DMS+DMS	Depot	Livery	Owner	Operator		Number						
172101	59111+59211	AL	CRW	ANG	CRW		172103	59113+59213	AL	CRW	ANG	CRW
172102	59112+59212	AL	CRW	ANG	CRW		172104	59114+59214	AL	CRW	ANG	CRW

Left: *In 2011, Chiltern Railways introduced four two-car Class 172/1 sets to supplement their 'Turbostar' fleet. The sets were largely different from previous deliveries having MTU power units and a diesel-mechanical transmission rather than hydraulic. A six-car formation of Class 172 stock formed of sets Nos. 172101, 172102 and 172104 is seen approaching Bicester North on 28 June 2011.* **John Binch**

Class 67

Vehicle Length: 64ft 7in (19.68m)		Engine: EMD 12N-710G3B-EC
Height: 12ft 9in (3.88m)		Horsepower: 2,980hp (2,223kW)
Width: 8ft 9in (2.66m)		Electrical Equipment: EMD

Number	Depot	Pool	Livery	Owner	Operator	Name
67010	CE	WNTR	CRG	ANG	DBS/CRW	
67012	CE	WAWN	CRG	ANG	DBS/CRW	*A Shropshire Lad*
67013	CE	WNTR	CRG	ANG	DBS/CRW	*Dyfrbont Pontcysyllte*
67014	CE	WAAN	CRG	ANG	DBS/CRW	*Thomas Telford*
67015	CE	WAWN	CRG	ANG	DBS/CRW	*David J. Lloyd*

Left: *Following the demise of Wrexham & Shropshire Railway in January 2011, the rolling stock and Class 67s passed to Chiltern Railways for their developing main line fast services between London Marylebone and Birmingham. Shorn of its Wrexham & Shropshire branding, No. 67013 Dyfrbont Pontcysyllte is seen at Marylebone with a five passenger vehicle formation and a Mk3 DVT at the far end.* **Antony Christie**

Mk3 Hauled Stock (Passenger)

Vehicle Length: 75ft 0in (22.86m)	
Height: 12ft 9in (3.88m) Width: 8ft 11in (2.71m)	
Bogie Type: BT10	

AJ1G - RFM *Seating 30F*

Number	Depot	Livery	Owner
10208 (40517)	AL	CRG	DBR
10230 (10021)	AL	CRG	DBR
10236 (10018)	AL	CRG	DBR
10255 (10010)	AL	CRG	DBR

AC2G - TSO *Seating 72S*

Number	Depot	Livery	Owner		Number	Depot	Livery	Owner
12048	AL	CRG	DBR		12145	AL	CRG	DBR
12059	AL	CRG	DBR		12169	AL	CRG	DBR
12069	AL	CRG	DBR		12173 (11042)	AL	CRG	DBR
12072	AL	CRG	DBR		12174 (11050)	AL	CRG	DBR
12117	AL	CRG	DBR		12175 (11052)	AL	CRG	DBR
12127	AL	CRG	DBR					
12131	AL	CRG	DBR					

Passenger Train Operating Companies - Chiltern Railways

Right: *In mid-2011 the former Wrexham & Shropshire Mk3s entered traffic with Chiltern, having only a minimal change to their recently applied silver grey livery. Looking very smart in two-tone grey, off-set with the Chiltern Railways logo, car TSO No. 12174 is seen at Birmingham Moor Street on 2 September 2011.*
John Binch

Mk3 Hauled Stock (NPCCS)

Vehicle Length: 75ft 0in (22.86m)
Height: 12ft 9in (3.88m)
Width: 8ft 11in (2.71m)
Bogie Type: BT7

NZAG - DVT

Number	Depot	Livery	Owner
82301 (82117)	AL	CRG	DBR
82302 (82151)	AL	CRW	DBR
82303 (82135)	AL	CRG	DBR
82304 (82130)	AL	CRG	DBR
82305 (82134)	AL	CRG	DBR

Class 960 - Service Units

Class 121
Length: 64ft 6in (19.66m)
Height: 12ft 8½in (3.87m)
Width: 9ft 3in (2.81m)
Engine: 2 x Leyland 150hp
Horsepower: 300hp (224kW)
Seats (total/car): None

Class 117
Length: 64ft 0in (19.50m)
Height: 12ft 8½in (3.87m)
Width: 9ft 3in (2.81m)
Engine: 2 x Leyland 150hp
Horsepower: 300hp (224kW)
Seats (total/car): None

Number	Formation	Depot	Livery	Owner	Operator	Notes
960014	977873	AL	BLG	CRW	CRW	Ex-Class 121 55022, Route Learning/Sandite
960301	977987+977992+977988	AL	GRN	CRW	CRW	Ex-Class 117, 51371/51375/51413 - used for water jetting

Right: *The 11.13 Rail Head Treatment Train (RHTT) from West Ruislip to Aylesbury approaches Saunderton on 23 October 2008, formed of ex-Class 117 DMU set No. 960301. This set remained in use during the 2011 leaf fall season.*
Brian Morrison

Class 01.5 (0-6-0)

Number		Depot	Pool	Livery	Owner	Operator	Name
01509	(433) RH468043	AL	MBDL	BLU	CRW	CRW	Lesley

Right: *To provide depot pilotage for its fleet at Aylesbury depot, Chiltern has one diesel shunter, a Ruston & Hornsby 0-6-0 No. 01509, built as R&H No. RH468043. The loco, named Lesley, is restricted to the depot at Aylesbury.* **Antony Christie**

CrossCountry Trains

Address: ✉ Cannon House, 18 The Priory, Queensway, Birmingham, B4 6BS
☏ info@crosscountrytrains.co.uk
✆ 0870 0100084
ⓘ www.crosscountrytrains.co.uk

Managing Director: Andy Cooper
Franchise Dates: 11 November 2007 - 1 May 2016
Principal Routes: Penzance/Paignton -
Manchester/Edinburgh/Aberdeen
Bournemouth - Manchester/
Edinburgh/Aberdeen
Birmingham - Stansted
Nottingham - Cardiff
Depots: Central Rivers (CZ),
Tyseley (TS),
Craigentinny (EC)
Parent Company: Deutsche Bahn AG
(DB Regio) / Arriva

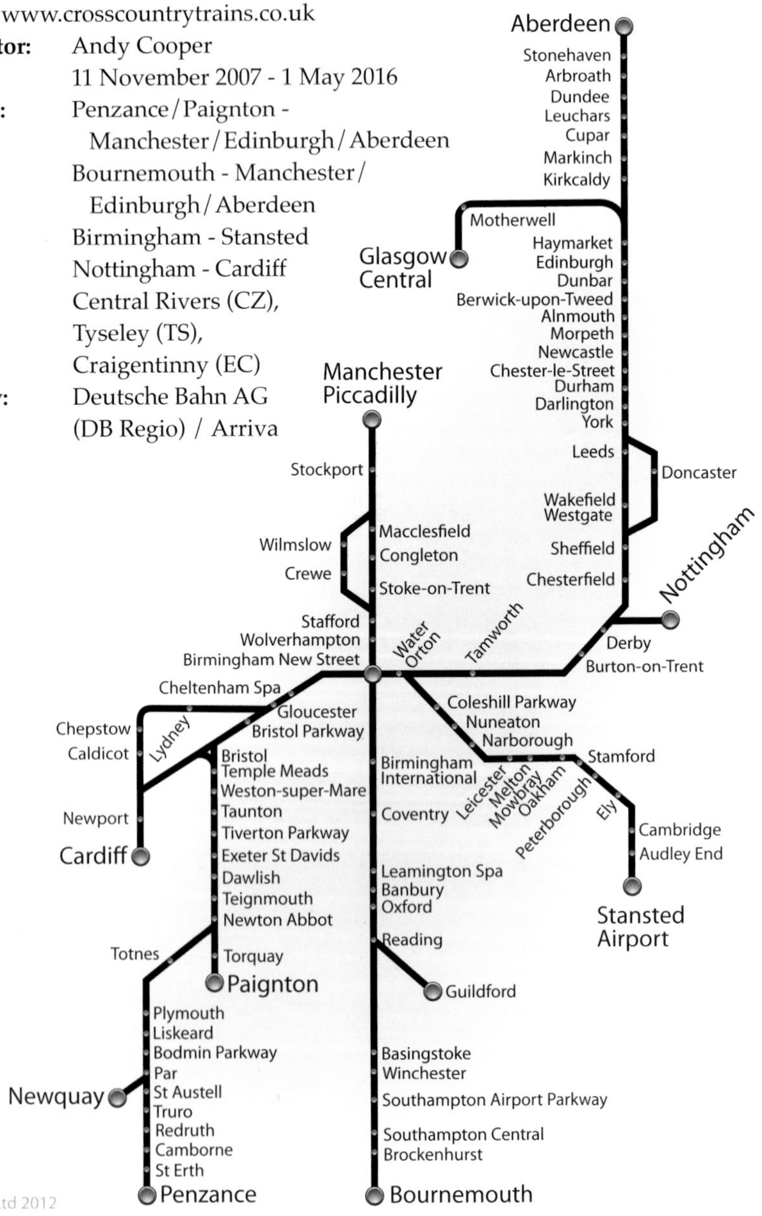

Aberdeen
Stonehaven
Arbroath
Dundee
Leuchars
Cupar
Markinch
Kirkcaldy
Motherwell
Glasgow Central
Haymarket
Edinburgh
Dunbar
Berwick-upon-Tweed
Alnmouth
Morpeth
Newcastle
Chester-le-Street
Durham
Darlington
York
Manchester Piccadilly
Leeds
Stockport
Doncaster
Wakefield Westgate
Macclesfield
Wilmslow
Congleton
Sheffield
Crewe
Stoke-on-Trent
Chesterfield
Nottingham
Stafford
Wolverhampton
Birmingham New Street
Water Orton
Tamworth
Derby
Burton-on-Trent
Cheltenham Spa
Gloucester
Coleshill Parkway
Chepstow
Bristol Parkway
Nuneaton
Caldicot
Lydney
Narborough
Bristol Temple Meads
Birmingham International
Stamford
Weston-super-Mare
Leicester
Melton Mowbray
Oakham
Newport
Taunton
Coventry
Peterborough
Ely
Cardiff
Tiverton Parkway
Cambridge
Exeter St Davids
Audley End
Dawlish
Teignmouth
Leamington Spa
Newton Abbot
Banbury
Oxford
Stansted Airport
Totnes
Torquay
Reading
Paignton
Guildford
Plymouth
Liskeard
Bodmin Parkway
Par
Basingstoke
St Austell
Winchester
Newquay
Truro
Southampton Airport Parkway
Redruth
Camborne
Southampton Central
St Erth
Brockenhurst
Penzance
Bournemouth

© TRC.Com Ltd 2012

CrossCountry Trains

Class 43 – HST

Vehicle Length: 58ft 5in (18.80m)			Engine: MTU 16V4000 R41R		
Height: 12ft 10in (3.90m)			Horsepower: 2,250hp (1,680kW)		
Width: 8ft 11in (2.73m)			Electrical Equipment: Brush		

Number	Depot	Pool	Livery	Owner	Operator		Number	Depot	Pool	Livery	Owner	Operator
43207 (43007)	EC	EHPC	AXC	ANG	AXC		43321 (43121)	EC	EHPC	AXC	PTR	AXC
43285 (43085)	EC	EHPC	AXC	PTR	AXC		43357 (43157)	EC	EHPC	AXC	PTR	AXC
43301 (43101)	EC	EHPC	AXC	PTR	AXC		43366 (43166)	EC	EHPC	AXC	ANG	AXC
43303 (43103)	EC	EHPC	AXC	PTR	AXC		43378 (43178)	EC	EHPC	AXC	ANG	AXC
43304 (43104)	EC	EHPC	AXC	ANG	AXC		43384 (43184)	EC	EHPC	AXC	ANG	AXC

Above: *CrossCountry Trains has a fleet of up to five HST formations at its disposal, but usually only a maximum of four are in traffic at one time. The sets are used on the core North East/Scotland to Devon and Cornwall routes, providing more seats than a 'Voyager' formation. On 3 June 2011, No. 43207 approaches Teignmouth Docks leading the 12.23 Plymouth to Edinburgh Waverley service.* **CJM**

HST passenger fleet

Vehicle Length: 75ft 0in (22.86m)		Width: 8ft 11in (2.71m)		
Height: 12ft 9in (3.88m)		Bogie Type: BT10		

GH1G - TF *Seating 40F*

Number	Depot	Livery	Owner			Number	Depot	Livery	Owner	
41026	EC	AXC	ANG			42372 (12055)	EC	AXC	PTR	
41035	EC	AXC	ANG			42373 (12071)	EC	AXC	PTR	
41193 (11060)	EC	AXC	PTR			42374 (12075)	EC	AXC	PTR	
41194 (11016)	EC	AXC	PTR			42375 (12113)	EC	AXC	PTR	
41195¤ (11020)	EC	AXC	PTR	¤ = TFD		42376 (12085)	EC	AXC	PTR	
						42377 (12102)	EC	AXC	PTR	
						42378 (12123)	EC	AXC	PTR	
GH2G - TS *Seating 82S*						42379* (41036)	EC	AXC	ANG	*=TSD
Number	Depot	Livery	Owner			42380* (41025)	EC	AXC	ANG	*=TSD
42036	EC	AXC	ANG							
42037	EC	AXC	ANG							
42038	EC	AXC	ANG			**GJ2G - TGS** *Seating 67S*				
42051	EC	AXC	ANG			Number	Depot	Livery	Owner	
42052	EC	AXC	ANG			44012	EC	AXC	ANG	
42053	EC	AXC	ANG			44017	EC	AXC	ANG	
42097	EC	AXC	ANG			44021	EC	AXC	ANG	
42234	EC	AXC	PTR			44052	EC	AXC	PTR	
42290	EC	AXC	PTR			44072	EC	AXC	PTR	
42342 (44082)	EC	AXC	ANG							
42366 (12007)	EC	AXC	PTR			**GH3G - TCC** *Seating 30F/10S*				
42367 (12025)	EC	AXC	PTR			Number	Depot	Livery	Owner	
42368 (12028)	EC	AXC	PTR			45001 (12004)	EC	AXC	PTR	
42369 (12050)	EC	AXC	PTR			45002 (12106)	EC	AXC	PTR	
42370 (12086)	EC	AXC	PTR			45003 (12076)	EC	AXC	PTR	
42371 (12052)	EC	AXC	PTR			45004 (12077)	EC	AXC	PTR	
						45005 (12080)	EC	AXC	PTR	

Passenger Train Operating Companies - CrossCountry Trains

CrossCountry Trains

Left: *All CrossCountry Trains HST stock has been fully refurbished and sports a two-tone grey livery, off-set by bright pink passenger doors and CrossCountry branding. In this view taken at Exeter St Davids, we see Trailer Guards Standard (TGS) No. 44012, from the guard's van end.* **CJM**

Class 170/1
Turbostar

Vehicle Length: 77ft 6in (23.62m)
Height: 12ft 4½in (3.77m)
Width: 8ft 10in (2.69m)

Engine: 1 x MTU 6R 183TD13H 422hp per vehicle
Horsepower: 1,266hp (944kW)
Seats (total/car): 9F/191S 52S/80S/9F-59S

Number	Formation DMS+MS+DMCL	Depot	Livery	Owner	Operator
170101	50101+55101+79101	TS	AXC	PTR	AXC
170102	50102+55102+79102	TS	AXC	PTR	AXC
170103	50103+55103+79103	TS	AXC	PTR	AXC
170104	50104+55104+79104	TS	AXC	PTR	AXC
170105	50105+55105+79105	TS	AXC	PTR	AXC
170106	50106+55106+79106	TS	AXC	PTR	AXC
170107	50107+55107+79107	TS	AXC	PTR	AXC
170108*	50108+55108+79108	TS	AXC	PTR	AXC
170109*	50109+55109+79109	TS	AXC	PTR	AXC
170110	50110+55110+79110	TS	AXC	PTR	AXC

Vehicle Length: 77ft 6in (23.62m)
Height: 12ft 4½in (3.77m)
Width: 8ft 10in (2.69m)

Engine: 1 x MTU 6R 183TD13H 422hp per vehicle
Horsepower: 844hp (629kW)
Seats (total/car): 9F-111S 59S/9F-52S

Number	Formation DMS+DMCL	Depot	Livery	Owner	Operator
170111*	50111+79111	TS	AXC	PTR	AXC
170112	50112+79112	TS	AXC	PTR	AXC
170113	50113+79113	TS	AXC	PTR	AXC
170114	50114+79114	TS	AXC	PTR	AXC
170115	50115+79115	TS	AXC	PTR	AXC
170116	50116+79116	TS	AXC	PTR	AXC
170117	50117+79117	TS	AXC	PTR	AXC

* Fitted with passenger counters

Left: *The original Class 170/1 sets which started out working for Midland Main Line are now operated by CrossCountry Trains, allocated to Tyseley depot. The design comes in both two- and three-car formation and all sets have now been refurbished, with the original buffet car facility removed. At Gloucester and sporting bodyside advertising, we see three-car set No. 170104. Note that the top marker light still has a Midland Main Line turquoise surround!* **CJM**

Class 170/3
Turbostar

Vehicle Length: 77ft 6in (23.62m)			Engine: 1 x MTU 6R 183TD13H 422hp per vehicle			
Height: 12ft 4½in (3.77m)			Horsepower: 1,266hp (944kW)			
Width: 8ft 10in (2.69m)			Seats (total/car): 9F-191S 59S/80S/9F-52S			

Number	Formation	Depot	Livery	Owner	Operator
	DMSL+MS+DMCL				
170397	50397+56397+79397	TS	AXC	PTR	AXC
170398	50398+56398+79398	TS	AXC	PTR	AXC

Below: *Two of the 170/3 sub-class operate for CrossCountry and are now set out as standard units. Viewed from its DMCL end, No. 170397 is seen at Gloucester.* **CJM**

Class 170/5
Turbostar

Vehicle Length: 77ft 6in (23.62m)			Engine: 1 x MTU 6R 183TD13H 422hp per vehicle			
Height: 12ft 4½in (3.77m)			Horsepower: 844hp (629kW)			
Width: 8ft 10in (2.69m)			Seats (total/car): 9F-111S 59S/9F-52S			

Number	Formation	Depot	Livery	Owner	Operator
	DMSL+DMCL				
170518	50518+79518	TS	AXC	PTR	AXC
170519	50519+79519	TS	AXC	PTR	AXC
170520	50520+79520	TS	AXC	PTR	AXC
170521	50521+79521	TS	AXC	PTR	AXC
170522	50522+79522	TS	AXC	PTR	AXC
170523	50523+79523	TS	AXC	PTR	AXC

Class 170/6
Turbostar

Vehicle Length: 77ft 6in (23.62m)			Engine: 1 x MTU 6R 183TD13H 422hp per vehicle			
Height: 12ft 4½in (3.77m)			Horsepower: 1,266hp (944kW)			
Width: 8ft 10in (2.69m)			Seats (total/car): 9F-191S 59S/80S/9F-52S			

Number	Formation	Depot	Livery	Owner	Operator
	DMSL+MS+DMCL				
170636	50636+56636+79636	TS	AXC	PTR	AXC
170637	50637+56637+79637	TS	AXC	PTR	AXC
170638	50638+56638+79638	TS	AXC	PTR	AXC
170639	50639+56639+79639	TS	AXC	PTR	AXC

Below: *Viewed from its first class or DMCL end, two-car set No. 170520 stands at Newport on 27 July 2011 with a Nottingham to Cardiff service.* **CJM**

CrossCountry Trains

Passenger Train Operating Companies - CrossCountry Trains

Class 220
Voyager

Vehicle Length: 77ft 6in (23.62m)	Engine: 1 x Cummins 750hp per vehicle
Height: 12ft 4in (3.75m)	Horsepower: 3,000hp (2,237kW)
Width: 8ft 11in (2.73m)	Seats (total/car): 26F/174S 42S/66S/66S/26F

Number	Formation DMS+MS+MS+DMF	Depot	Livery	Owner	Operator
220001	60301+60701+60201+60401	CZ	AXC	HBS	AXC
220002	60302+60702+60202+60402	CZ	AXC	HBS	AXC
220003	60303+60703+60203+60403	CZ	AXC	HBS	AXC
220004	60304+60704+60204+60404	CZ	AXC	HBS	AXC
220005	60305+60705+60205+60405	CZ	AXC	HBS	AXC
220006	60306+60706+60206+60406	CZ	AXC	HBS	AXC
220007	60307+60707+60207+60407	CZ	AXC	HBS	AXC
220008	60308+60708+60208+60408	CZ	AXC	HBS	AXC
220009	60309+60709+60209+60409	CZ	AXC	HBS	AXC
220010	60310+60710+60210+60410	CZ	AXC	HBS	AXC
220011	60311+60711+60211+60411	CZ	AXC	HBS	AXC
220012	60312+60712+60212+60412	CZ	AXC	HBS	AXC
220013	60313+60713+60213+60413	CZ	AXC	HBS	AXC
220014	60314+60714+60214+60414	CZ	AXC	HBS	AXC
220015	60315+60715+60215+60415	CZ	AXC	HBS	AXC
220016	60316+60716+60216+60416	CZ	AXC	HBS	AXC
220017	60317+60717+60217+60417	CZ	AXC	HBS	AXC
220018	60318+60718+60218+60418	CZ	AXC	HBS	AXC
220019	60319+60719+60219+60419	CZ	AXC	HBS	AXC
220020	60320+60720+60220+60420	CZ	AXC	HBS	AXC
220021	60321+60721+60221+60421	CZ	AXC	HBS	AXC
220022	60322+60722+60222+60422	CZ	AXC	HBS	AXC
220023	60323+60723+60223+60423	CZ	AXC	HBS	AXC
220024	60324+60724+60224+60424	CZ	AXC	HBS	AXC
220025	60325+60725+60225+60425	CZ	AXC	HBS	AXC
220026	60326+60726+60226+60426	CZ	AXC	HBS	AXC
220027	60327+60727+60227+60427	CZ	AXC	HBS	AXC
220028	60328+60728+60228+60428	CZ	AXC	HBS	AXC
220029	60329+60729+60229+60429	CZ	AXC	HBS	AXC
220030	60330+60730+60230+60430	CZ	AXC	HBS	AXC
220031	60331+60731+60231+60431	CZ	AXC	HBS	AXC
220032	60332+60732+60232+60432	CZ	AXC	HBS	AXC
220033	60333+60733+60233+60433	CZ	AXC	HBS	AXC
220034	60334+60734+60234+60434	CZ	AXC	HBS	AXC

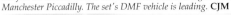

Below: *The backbone of CrossCountry main line services is maintained by a 'Voyager' and 'Super Voyager' fleet of four and five-car sets. Class 220 No. 220028 is seen arriving at Southampton on 8 June 2011, forming the 10.45 Bournemouth to Manchester Piccadilly. The set's DMF vehicle is leading.* **CJM**

Class 221
Super Voyager

Vehicle Length: 77ft 6in (23.62m)	Engine: 1 x Cummins 750hp per vehicle
Height: 12ft 4in (3.75m)	Horsepower: 3,750hp (2,796kW)
Width: 8ft 11in (2.73m)	Seats (total/car): 26F/236S 42S/66S/66S/62S/26F

Originally fitted with tilt system to allow higher speeds over curves. Equipment now isolated

Number	Formation DMS+MS+MS+MS+DMF	Depot	Livery	Owner	Operator	
221119	60369+60769+60969+60869+60469	CZ	AXC	HBS	AXC	
221120	60370+60770+60970+60870+60470	CZ	AXC	HBS	AXC	
221121	60371+60771+60971+60871+60471	CZ	AXC	HBS	AXC	
221122	60372+60772+60972+60872+60472	CZ	AXC	HBS	AXC	
221123	60373+60773+60973+60873+60473	CZ	AXC	HBS	AXC	
221124	60374+60774+60974+60874+60474	CZ	AXC	HBS	AXC	
221125	60375+60775+60975+60875+60475	CZ	AXC	HBS	AXC	
221126	60376+60776+60976+60876+60476	CZ	AXC	HBS	AXC	
221127	60377+60777+60977+60877+60477	CZ	AXC	HBS	AXC	
221128	60378+60778+60978+60878+60478	CZ	AXC	HBS	AXC	
221129	60379+60779+60979+60879+60479	CZ	AXC	HBS	AXC	
221130	60380+60780+60980+60880+60480	CZ	AXC	HBS	AXC	
221131	60381+60781+60981+60881+60481	CZ	AXC	HBS	AXC	
221132	60382+60782+60982+60882+60482	CZ	AXC	HBS	AXC	
221133	60383+60783+60983+60883+60483	CZ	AXC	HBS	AXC	
221134	60384+60784+60984+60884+60484	CZ	AXC	HBS	AXC	
221135	60385+60785+60985+60885+60485	CZ	AXC	HBS	AXC	
221136	60386+60786+60986+60886+60486	CZ	AXC	HBS	AXC	
221137	60387+60787+60987+60887+60487	CZ	AXC	HBS	AXC	
221138	60388+60788+60988+60888+60488	CZ	AXC	HBS	AXC	
221139	60389+60789+60989+60889+60489	CZ	AXC	HBS	AXC	
221140	60390+60790+60990+60890+60490	CZ	AXC	HBS	AXC	
221141	60391+60791+60991+--+60491	CZ	AXC	HBS	AXC	(Four-car set)

● A proposal has now been formulated for Class 220 and 221 sets to receive an additional intermediate pantograph vehicle, allowing dual diesel-electric operation. The project calls for the building of 57 new pantograph carriages and the rebuilding of other existing intermediate vehicles to pass train-line power. No agreement for this project has yet been reached. If the project goes ahead, vehicle construction would be undertaken by Bombardier at Derby.

Below: *CrossCountry operate a fleet of 23 Class 221 'Super Voyager' sets; all but one are five-car formations. These sets were built with full tilting capability, but this has now been isolated. With its DMS coach nearest the camera, set No. 221119 is seen at Exeter St Davids with a Paignton to Manchester Piccadilly service in July 2011.* **CJM**

East Coast

Address: ✉ East Coast House, 25 Skeldergate, York, YO1 6DH

✏ customers@eastcoast.co.uk

☎ 08457 225225

ⓘ www.eastcoast.co.uk

Managing Director: Karen Boswell

Operation Started: 13 November 2009*

Principal Routes: London King's Cross - Aberdeen/ Inverness, Edinburgh, Glasgow Hull, Leeds, Bradford, Skipton and Harrogate

Depots: Bounds Green (BN), Craigentinny (EC)

Parent Company: DfT (Directly Operated Railways Ltd)

* The Government took over operation from 13 November 2009 and will continue to operate the franchise as a 'stopgap' measure using the in-place operational staff. A new franchise bid process is likely to be launched in 2012.

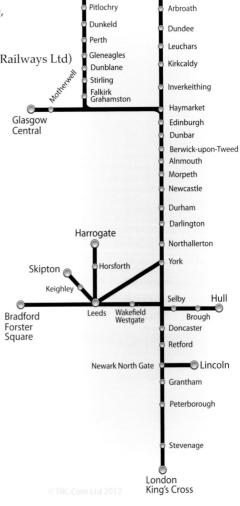

Inverness
Carrbridge
Aviemore
Kingussie
Newtonmore
Blair Atholl
Pitlochry
Dunkeld
Perth
Gleneagles
Dunblane
Stirling
Falkirk
Grahamston
Motherwell

Glasgow Central

Aberdeen
Stonehaven
Montrose
Arbroath
Dundee
Leuchars
Kirkcaldy
Inverkeithing
Haymarket
Edinburgh
Dunbar
Berwick-upon-Tweed
Alnmouth
Morpeth
Newcastle
Durham
Darlington
Northallerton
York

Harrogate

Skipton
Keighley
Horsforth

Bradford Forster Square

Leeds   Wakefield Westgate

Selby   Hull
Brough
Doncaster
Retford

Newark North Gate   Lincoln
Grantham
Peterborough

Stevenage

London King's Cross

© TRC.Com Ltd 2012

Class 43 – HST

Vehicle Length: 58ft 5in (18.80m)
Height: 12ft 10in (3.90m)
Width: 8ft 11in (2.73m)

Engine: MTU 16V4000 R41R
Horsepower: 2,250hp (1,680kW)
Electrical Equipment: Brush

Number		Depot	Pool	Livery	Owner	Operator	Name
43206	(43006)	EC	IECP	ECT	ANG	ICE	*Kingdom of Fife*
43208	(43008)	EC	IECP	NXE	ANG	ICE	*Lincolnshire Echo*
43238	(43038)	EC	IECP	NXE	ANG	ICE	
43239	(43039)	EC	IECP	NXE	ANG	ICE	
43251	(43051)	EC	IECP	ECT	PTR	ICE	
43257	(43057)	EC	IECP	NXE	PTR	ICE	
43272	(43072)	EC	IECP	SCE	PTR	ICE	
43274	(43074)	EC	IECP	SCE	PTR	ICE	
43277	(43077)	EC	IECP	ECT	PTR	ICE	
43290	(43090)	EC	IECP	NXE	PTR	ICE	*MTU Fascination of Power*
43295	(43095)	EC	IECP	NXE	ANG	ICE	
43296	(43096)	EC	IECP	ECG	PTR	ICE	
43299	(43099)	EC	IECP	NXE	PTR	ICE	
43300	(43100)	EC	IECP	ECG	PTR	ICE	*Craigentinny*
43302	(43102)	EC	IECP	ECG	PTR	ICE	
43305	(43105)	EC	IECP	NXE	ANG	ICE	
43306	(43106)	EC	IECP	NXE	ANG	ICE	
43307	(43107)	EC	IECP	NXE	ANG	ICE	
43308	(43108)	EC	IECP	ECG	ANG	ICE	
43309	(43109)	EC	IECP	NXE	ANG	ICE	
43310	(43110)	EC	IECP	ECG	ANG	ICE	
43311	(43111)	EC	IECP	ECG	ANG	ICE	
43312	(43112)	EC	IECP	ECT	ANG	ICE	
43313	(43113)	EC	IECP	ECT	ANG	ICE	
43314	(43114)	EC	IECP	ECG	ANG	ICE	
43315	(43115)	EC	IECP	ECG	ANG	ICE	
43316	(43116)	EC	IECP	NXE	ANG	ICE	
43317	(43117)	EC	IECP	NXE	ANG	ICE	
43318	(43118)	EC	IECP	ECT	ANG	ICE	
43319	(43119)	EC	IECP	NXE	ANG	ICE	
43320	(43120)	EC	IECP	NXE	ANG	ICE	
43367	(43167)	EC	IECP	NXE	ANG	ICE	*Deltic 50 1955 - 2005 v*

*With East Coast branding on the former National Express grey and white livery, East Coast Class 43 No. 43314 departs from Edinburgh Waverley on 11 April 2011. **Ron Cover***

East Coast

Class 91

Vehicle Length: 63ft 8in (19.40m)   *Power Collection: 25kV ac overhead*
Height: 12ft 4in (3.75m)   *Horsepower: 6,300hp (4,700kW)*
Width: 9ft 0in (2.74m)   *Electrical Equipment: GEC*

Number	Depot	Pool	Livery	Owner	Operator	Name
91101 (91001)	BN	IECA	ADV	EVL	ICE	Flying Scotsman (branding)
91102 (91002)	BN	IECA	ECG	EVL	ICE	City of York
91103 (91003)	BN	IECA	ECW	EVL	ICE	
91104 (91004)	BN	IECA	NXG	EVL	ICE	
91105 (91005)	BN	IECA	ECW	EVL	ICE	
91106 (91006)	BN	IECA	ECS	EVL	ICE	
91107 (91007)	BN	IECA	ECS	EVL	ICE	
91108 (91008)	BN	IECA	ECW	EVL	ICE	
91109 (91009)	BN	IECA	ECW	EVL	ICE	Sir Bobby Robson
91110 (91010)	BN	IECA	ECS	EVL	ICE	
91111 (91011)	BN	IECA	NXE	EVL	ICE	
91112 (91012)	BN	IECA	NXG	EVL	ICE	
91113 (91013)	BN	IECA	NXG	EVL	ICE	
91114 (91014)	BN	IECA	NXG	EVL	ICE	
91115 (91015)	BN	IECA	NXG	EVL	ICE	
91116 (91016)	BN	IECA	NXG	EVL	ICE	
91117 (91017)	BN	IECA	ECG	EVL	ICE	West Riding Limited
91118 (91018)	BN	IECA	NXG	EVL	ICE	
91119 (91019)	BN	IECA	NXG	EVL	ICE	
91120 (91020)	BN	IECA	ECW	EVL	ICE	
91121 (91021)	BN	IECA	NXG	EVL	ICE	
91122 (91022)	BN	IECA	ECG	EVL	ICE	
91124 (91024)	BN	IECA	ECG	EVL	ICE	
91125 (91025)	BN	IECA	NXG	EVL	ICE	
91126 (91026)	BN	IECA	NXG	EVL	ICE	
91127 (91027)	BN	IECA	ECS	EVL	ICE	
91128 (91028)	BN	IECA	ECG	EVL	ICE	
91129 (91029)	BN	IECA	NXG	EVL	ICE	
91130 (91030)	BN	IECA	ECW	EVL	ICE	
91131 (91031)	BN	IECA	NXG	EVL	ICE	
91132 (91023)	BN	IECA	ECG	EVL	ICE	

The established 'Flying Scotsman' name was resurrected to the East Coast timetable with a new 'fast' Edinburgh to London service from the 2011 summer timetable. To mark the event, No. 91001 was repainted and branded in a special Flying Scotsman livery, carrying a huge Flying Scotsman name along the bodyside. On 23 May 2011, the loco is seen leading the 16.30 King's Cross to Edinburgh past Colton near York. **Robin Patrick**

Mk3 HST Stock

Vehicle Length: 75ft 0in (22.86m)   Width: 8ft 11in (2.71m)
Height: 12ft 9in (3.88m)   Bogie Type: BT10

GK1G - TRFB *Seating 17F*

Number	Depot	Livery	Owner
40701	EC	NXE	PTR
40702	EC	NXE	PTR
40704	EC	NXE	ANG
40705	EC	NXE	ANG
40706	EC	NXE	ANG
40708	EC	ECT	PTR
40711	EC	NXE	ANG
40720	EC	NXE	ANG
40735	EC	NXE	ANG
40737	EC	NXE	ANG
40740	EC	NXE	ANG
40742	EC	NXE	ANG
40748	EC	NXE	ANG
40750	EC	NXE	ANG
40805	EC	NXG	ANG

GH1G - TF *Seating 48F*

Number	Depot	Livery	Owner
41039	EC	NXE	ANG
41040	EC	NXE	ANG
41043	EC	ECS	ANG
41044	EC	NXE	ANG
41058	EC	NXE	PTR
41066	EC	NXE	ANG
41083	EC	NXE	PTR
41087	EC	NXE	ANG
41088	EC	NXE	ANG
41090	EC	NXE	ANG
41091	EC	NXE	ANG
41092	EC	NXE	ANG
41095	EC	NXE	ANG
41097	EC	NXE	ANG
41098	EC	NXE	ANG
41099	EC	NXE	ANG
41100	EC	NXE	ANG
41115	EC	NXE	PTR
41118	EC	NXE	ANG
41120	EC	ECT	ANG
41150	EC	ECT	ANG
41151	EC	NXE	ANG
41152	EC	NXE	ANG
41159	EC	NXE	PTR
41164	EC	NXE	ANG

Number	Depot	Livery	Owner
41165	EC	NXE	PTR
41170(41001)	EC	NXE	ANG
41185(42313)	EC	NXE	PTR
41190(42088)	EC	NXG	PTR

GH2G - TS (*TSD) *Seating 76/62*S*

Number	Depot	Livery	Owner
42057	EC	NXE	ANG
42058	EC	NXE	ANG
42059	EC	NXE	ANG
42063	EC	NXE	ANG
42064	EC	NXE	ANG
42065	EC	NXE	ANG
42091*	EC	ECT	ANG
42106	EC	NXE	ANG
42109	EC	NXE	PTR
42110	EC	NXE	PTR
42116*	EC	NXE	ANG
42117	EC	NXE	PTR
42127*	EC	NXE	ANG
42128*	EC	NXE	ANG
42130	EC	NXE	PTR
42134	EC	NXE	ANG
42146	EC	ECT	ANG
42147	EC	NXE	PTR
42150	EC	ECT	ANG
42154	EC	ECT	ANG
42158	EC	NXE	ANG
42159*	EC	NXE	PTR
42160	EC	NXE	PTR
42161*	EC	NXE	PTR
42163	EC	NXE	PTR
42171	EC	NXE	ANG
42172	EC	NXE	ANG
42179	EC	NXE	ANG
42180	EC	NXE	ANG
42181	EC	NXE	ANG
42182	EC	NXE	ANG
42186	EC	ECT	ANG
42188*	EC	NXE	ANG
42189*	EC	NXE	ANG
42190	EC	NXE	ANG
42191	EC	NXE	ANG
42192	EC	NXE	ANG
42193	EC	NXE	ANG

Number	Depot	Livery	Owner
42198	EC	NXE	ANG
42199	EC	NXE	ANG
42215	EC	ECT	ANG
42219	EC	NXE	ANG
42226	EC	NXE	ANG
42228	EC	ECT	PTR
42235	EC	NXE	ANG
42237	EC	NXE	PTR
42238*	EC	NXE	ANG
42239*	EC	NXE	ANG
42240	EC	NXE	ANG
42241	EC	NXE	ANG
42242	EC	NXE	ANG
42243	EC	NXE	ANG
42244	EC	NXE	ANG
42286	EC	ECT	PTR
42306	EC	NXE	PTR
42307	EC	NXE	PTR
42322	EC	ECT	PTR
42323	EC	NXE	ANG
42326	EC	NXE	PTR
42330	EC	NXE	PTR
42340	EC	NXE	ANG
42352(41176)	EC	NXE	PTR
42354(41175)	EC	ECT	ANG
42355(41172)	EC	NXE	ANG
42357(41174)	EC	NXE	ANG
42363(41082)	EC	NXE	ANG

GJ2G - TGS *Seating 65S*

Number	Depot	Livery	Owner
44019	EC	NXE	ANG
44031	EC	NXE	ANG
44045	EC	NXE	ANG
44050	EC	ECT	PTR
44056	EC	NXE	ANG
44057	EC	NXE	PTR
44058	EC	NXE	ANG
44061	EC	NXE	ANG
44063	EC	NXE	ANG
44075	EC	NXE	PTR
44077	EC	NXE	ANG
44080	EC	NXE	ANG
44094	EC	ECT	ANG
44098	EC	NXE	ANG

Right: *Although the present East Coast operator is only a temporary one and a new franchise bid process will soon start, the operator has applied its distinctive branding to the National Express white/grey body colours. On passenger vehicles openable doors are in blue, while those in buffet cars which are for emergency use are painted body colour. TRFB No. 40805 is recorded at Doncaster.* **Nathan Williamson**

East Coast

Mk4 Stock

Vehicle Length: 75ft 5in (23m)   Width: 8ft 11in (2.73m)
Height: 12ft 5in (3.79m)   Bogie Type: BT41

Passenger Train Operating Companies - East Coast

AJ2J - RSB *Seating 30S*

Number	Depot	Livery	Owner
10300	BN	ECS	EVL
10301	BN	NXG	EVL
10302	BN	ECS	EVL
10303	BN	ECS	EVL
10304	BN	NXG	EVL
10305	BN	NXG	EVL
10306	BN	NXG	EVL
10307	BN	ECS	EVL
10308	BN	ECS	EVL
10309	BN	NXG	EVL
10310	BN	NXG	EVL
10311	BN	NXG	EVL
10312	BN	NXG	EVL
10313	BN	NXG	EVL
10314	BN	NXG	EVL
10317	BN	NXG	EVL
10318	BN	NXG	EVL
10319	BN	NXG	EVL
10320	BN	ECS	EVL
10321	BN	NXG	EVL
10323	BN	ECS	EVL
10324	BN	ECG	EVL
10325	BN	NXG	EVL
10326	BN	ECS	EVL
10328	BN	NXG	EVL
10329	BN	NXG	EVL
10330	BN	NXG	EVL
10331	BN	ECS	EVL
10332	BN	ECG	EVL
10333	BN	ECG	EVL

AD1J - FO *Seating 46F*

Number	Depot	Livery	Owner
11201	BN	ECG	EVL
11219	BN	ECS	EVL
11229	BN	NXG	EVL
11237	BN	NXG	EVL
11241	BN	NXG	EVL
11244	BN	NXG	EVL
11273	BN	NXG	EVL
11277(12408)	BN	ECS	EVL
11278(12479)	BN	ECS	EVL
11279(12521)	BN	NXG	EVL
11280(12523)	BN	ECS	EVL
11281(12418)	BN	NXG	EVL
11282(12524)	BN	ECS	EVL
11283(12435)	BN	ECS	EVL
11284(12487)	BN	ECG	EVL
11285(12537)	BN	NXG	EVL
11286(12482)	BN	NXG	EVL
11287(12527)	BN	NXG	EVL
11288(12517)	BN	ECG	EVL
11289(12528)	BN	NXG	EVL
11290(12530)	BN	NXG	EVL
11291(12535)	BN	NXG	EVL
11292(12451)	BN	NXG	EVL
11293(12533)	BN	NXG	EVL
11294(12529)	BN	NXG	EVL
11295(12475)	BN	NXG	EVL
11298(12416)	BN	ECS	EVL
11299(12532)	BN	ECS	EVL

AL1J - FOD *Seating 42F*

Number	Depot	Livery	Owner
11301(11215)	BN	ECS	EVL
11302(11203)	BN	ECS	EVL
11303(11211)	BN	ECS	EVL
11304(11257)	BN	ECS	EVL
11305(11261)	BN	ECS	EVL
11306(11276)	BN	NXG	EVL
11307(11217)	BN	ECS	EVL
11308(11263)	BN	NXG	EVL
11309(11262)	BN	NXG	EVL
11310(11272)	BN	ECS	EVL
11311(11221)	BN	ECS	EVL
11312(11225)	BN	ECG	EVL
11313(11210)	BN	NXG	EVL
11314(11207)	BN	ECG	EVL
11315(11238)	BN	NXG	EVL
11316(11227)	BN	NXG	EVL
11317(11223)	BN	ECG	EVL
11318(11251)	BN	NXG	EVL
11319(11247)	BN	NXG	EVL
11320(11255)	BN	NXG	EVL
11321(11245)	BN	NXG	EVL
11322(11228)	BN	NXG	EVL
11323(11235)	BN	NXG	EVL
11324(11253)	BN	NXG	EVL
11325(11231)	BN	NXG	EVL
11326(11206)	BN	NXG	EVL
11327(11236)	BN	NXG	EVL
11328(11274)	BN	NXG	EVL
11329(11243)	BN	NXG	EVL
11330(11249)	BN	NXG	EVL

AD1J - FO *Seating 46F*

Number	Depot	Livery	Owner
11401(11214)	BN	ECS	EVL
11402(11216)	BN	ECS	EVL
11403(11258)	BN	ECS	EVL
11404(11202)	BN	ECS	EVL
11405(11204)	BN	ECS	EVL
11406(11205)	BN	NXG	EVL
11407(11256)	BN	ECS	EVL
11408(11218)	BN	NXG	EVL
11409(11259)	BN	NXG	EVL
11410(11260)	BN	ECS	EVL
11411(11240)	BN	ECS	EVL
11412(11209)	BN	ECG	EVL
11413(11212)	BN	NXG	EVL
11414(11246)	BN	ECG	EVL
11415(11208)	BN	NXG	EVL
11416(11254)	BN	NXG	EVL
11417(11226)	BN	ECG	EVL
11418(11222)	BN	NXG	EVL
11419(11250)	BN	NXG	EVL
11420(11242)	BN	NXG	EVL
11421(11220)	BN	NXG	EVL
11422(11232)	BN	NXG	EVL
11423(11230)	BN	NXG	EVL

11424(11239)	BN	NXG	EVL
11425(11234)	BN	NXG	EVL
11426(11252)	BN	NXG	EVL
11427(11200)	BN	NXG	EVL
11428(11233)	BN	NXG	EVL
11429(11275)	BN	NXG	EVL
11430(11248)	BN	NXG	EVL
11998(10314)	BN	NXG	EVL
11999(10316)	BN	NXG	EVL

AI2J - TSOE *Seating 76S*

Number	Depot	Livery	Owner
12200	BN	NXG	EVL
12201	BN	ECS	EVL
12202	BN	ECS	EVL
12203	BN	ECS	EVL
12204	BN	NXG	EVL
12205	BN	NXG	EVL
12207	BN	ECS	EVL
12208	BN	NXG	EVL
12209	BN	ECS	EVL
12210	BN	NXG	EVL
12211	BN	NXG	EVL
12212	BN	ECG	EVL
12213	BN	NXG	EVL
12214	BN	ECS	EVL
12215	BN	NXG	EVL
12216	BN	NXG	EVL
12217	BN	NXG	EVL
12218	BN	NXG	EVL
12219	BN	NXG	EVL
12220	BN	NXG	EVL
12222	BN	NXG	EVL
12223	BN	ECG	EVL
12224	BN	NXG	EVL
12225	BN	NXG	EVL
12226	BN	NXG	EVL
12227	BN	NXG	EVL
12228	BN	NXG	EVL
12229	BN	ECG	EVL
12230	BN	NXG	EVL
12231	BN	ECS	EVL
12232	BN	ECS	EVL

AL2J - TSOD *Seating 68S*

Number	Depot	Livery	Owner
12300	BN	ECS	EVL
12301	BN	ECS	EVL
12302	BN	ECS	EVL
12303	BN	ECG	EVL
12304	BN	NXG	EVL
12305	BN	ECS	EVL
12307	BN	ECS	EVL
12308	BN	NXG	EVL
12309	BN	NXG	EVL
12310	BN	NXG	EVL
12311	BN	NXG	EVL
12312	BN	ECG	EVL
12313	BN	NXG	EVL
12315	BN	ECS	EVL
12316	BN	NXG	EVL

Number	Depot	Livery	Owner
12317	BN	NXG	EVL
12318	BN	NXG	EVL
12319	BN	NXG	EVL
12320	BN	NXG	EVL
12321	BN	NXG	EVL
12322	BN	NXG	EVL
12323	BN	NXG	EVL
12324	BN	NXG	EVL
12325	BN	NXG	EVL
12326	BN	NXG	EVL
12327	BN	ECS	EVL
12328	BN	NXG	EVL
12329	BN	ECS	EVL
12330	BN	ECG	EVL
12331(12531)	BN	NXG	EVL

AC2J - TSO *Seating 76S*

Number	Depot	Livery	Owner
12400	BN	NXG	EVL
12401	BN	ECS	EVL
12402	BN	ECS	EVL
12403	BN	NXG	EVL
12404	BN	ECG	EVL
12405	BN	ECS	EVL
12406	BN	NXG	EVL
12407	BN	NXG	EVL
12409	BN	NXG	EVL
12410	BN	ECG	EVL
12411	BN	ECS	EVL
12414	BN	ECS	EVL
12415	BN	ECS	EVL
12417	BN	ECS	EVL
12419	BN	ECS	EVL
12420	BN	NXG	EVL
12421	BN	ECS	EVL
12422	BN	NXG	EVL
12423	BN	ECG	EVL
12424	BN	NXG	EVL
12425	BN	NXG	EVL
12426	BN	ECG	EVL
12427	BN	ECG	EVL
12428	BN	NXG	EVL
12429	BN	NXG	EVL
12430	BN	NXG	EVL
12431	BN	ECG	EVL
12432	BN	ECG	EVL
12433	BN	NXG	EVL
12434	BN	NXG	EVL
12436	BN	ECS	EVL
12437	BN	ECS	EVL
12438	BN	ECS	EVL
12439	BN	NXG	EVL
12440	BN	NXG	EVL
12441	BN	NXG	EVL
12442	BN	NXG	EVL
12443	BN	ECS	EVL
12444	BN	ECG	EVL
12445	BN	NXG	EVL
12446	BN	NXG	EVL
12447	BN	NXG	EVL
12448	BN	ECS	EVL
12449	BN	NXG	EVL
12450	BN	ECS	EVL
12452	BN	NXG	EVL
12453	BN	NXG	EVL
12454	BN	NXG	EVL
12456	BN	NXG	EVL
12457	BN	NXG	EVL
12458	BN	NXG	EVL
12459	BN	ECS	EVL
12460	BN	NXG	EVL
12461	BN	NXG	EVL
12462	BN	NXG	EVL
12463	BN	NXG	EVL
12464	BN	NXG	EVL
12465	BN	NXG	EVL
12466	BN	NXG	EVL
12467	BN	NXG	EVL
12468	BN	NXG	EVL
12469	BN	NXG	EVL
12470	BN	NXG	EVL
12471	BN	NXG	EVL
12472	BN	NXG	EVL
12473	BN	NXG	EVL
12474	BN	NXG	EVL
12476	BN	NXG	EVL
12477	BN	NXG	EVL
12478	BN	ECS	EVL
12480	BN	ECS	EVL
12481	BN	NXG	EVL
12483	BN	NXG	EVL
12484	BN	ECS	EVL
12485	BN	NXG	EVL
12486	BN	ECS	EVL
12488	BN	ECS	EVL
12489	BN	ECS	EVL
12513	BN	NXG	EVL
12514	BN	NXG	EVL
12515	BN	NXG	EVL
12518	BN	ECS	EVL
12519	BN	NXG	EVL
12520	BN	ECS	EVL
12522	BN	ECS	EVL
12526	BN	ECG	EVL
12533	BN	NXG	EVL
12534	BN	NXG	EVL
12538	BN	NXG	EVL

NZAJ - DVT

Number	Depot	Livery	Owner
82200	BN	NXG	EVL
82201	BN	NXG	EVL
82202	BN	ECS	EVL
82203	BN	NXG	EVL
82204	BN	ECW	EVL
82205	BN	ADV	EVL
82206	BN	ECG	EVL
82207	BN	ECS	EVL
82208	BN	NXG	EVL
82209	BN	NXG	EVL
82210	BN	ECS	EVL
82211	BN	ECS	EVL
82212	BN	ECG	EVL
82213	BN	NXG	EVL
82214	BN	NXG	EVL
82215	BN	NXG	EVL
82216	BN	NXG	EVL
82217	BN	NXG	EVL
82218	BN	ECS	EVL
82219	BN	ECW	EVL
82220	BN	NXG	EVL
82222	BN	NXG	EVL
82223	BN	NXG	EVL
82224	BN	NXG	EVL
82225	BN	ECG	EVL
82226	BN	NXG	EVL
82227	BN	NXG	EVL
82228	BN	NXG	EVL
82229	BN	NXG	EVL
82230	BN	NXG	EVL
82231	BN	NXG	EVL

82205 carries Flying Scotsman advertising livery

Service Stock

HST and Mk4 Barrier Vehicles

Number	Depot	Livery	Owner	Former Identity
6340	EC	NEG	ANG	BCK - 21251
6344	EC	NEG	ANG	BG - 92080
6346	EC	NEG	ANG	BSO - 9422
6352	BN	NEG	ANG	SK - 19465
6353	BN	NEG	ANG	SK - 19478
6354	BN	NEG	ANG	BSO - 9459
6355	BN	NEG	ANG	BSO - 9477
6358	BN	NEG	EVL	BSO - 9432
6359	BN	NEG	EVL	BSO - 9429
9393	EC	PTR	PTR	BG - 92196
9394	EC	PTR	PTR	BG - 92906

Above: *Used to allow conventional coupling-fitted locos to attach to HST or MK4 stock, a fleet of barrier carriages are operated by East Coast. No. 6340, converted from BCK No. 21251 is seen at Doncaster.* **Derek Porter**

East Midlands Trains

Address: ✉ 1 Prospect Place, Millennium Way, Pride Park, Derby, DE24 8HG
 ✒ getintouch@eastmidlandstrains.co.uk
 ✆ 08457 125678
 ⓘ www.eastmidlandstrains.co.uk

Managing Director: David Horne
Franchise Dates: 11 November 2007 - 31 March 2015
Principal Routes: St Pancras - Sheffield/York/Leeds/Nottingham
Norwich/Skegness/Cleethorpes - Nottingham/Crewe/
Liverpool and Matlock
Depots: Derby (DY), Nottingham (NM), Neville Hill (NL)
Parent Company: Stagecoach

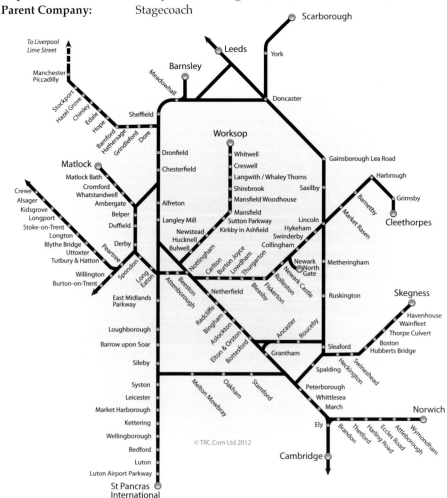

© TRC.Com Ltd 2012

Class 08

Vehicle Length: 29ft 3in (8.91m)				Engine: English Electric 6K		
Height: 12ft 8⅝in (3.87m)				Horsepower: 400hp (298kW)		
Width: 8ft 6in (2.59m)				Electrical Equipment: English Electric		

Number	Depot	Pool	Livery	Owner	Operator	Name
08525	NL	EMSL	EMT	EMT	EMT	Duncan Bedford
08690	NL	EMSL	EMT	EMT	EMT	David Thirkill
08899	DY	EMSL	BLU	EMT	EMT	
08908	DY	EMSL	EMT	EMT	EMT	Ivan Stephenson
08950	NL	EMSL	EMT	EMT	EMT	David Lightfoot

Right: *East Midlands Trains are one of the few operators to care for their shunting loco fleet and in recent times outshopped four of their charges in full East Midlands Trains livery, naming them after engineering staff. No. 08950* David Lightfoot *is seen inside the maintenance shed at Leeds Neville Hill on 3 February 2011.* **Ron Cover**

Class 43 – HST

Vehicle Length: 58ft 5in (18.80m)				Engine: Paxman VP185		
Height: 12ft 10in (3.90m)				Horsepower: 2,100hp (1,565kW)		
Width: 8ft 11in (2.73m)				Electrical Equipment: Brush		

Number	Depot	Pool	Livery	Owner	Operator
43043	NL	EMPC	SCE	PTR	EMT
43044	NL	EMPC	SCE	PTR	EMT
43045	NL	EMPC	SCE	PTR	EMT
43046	NL	EMPC	SCE	PTR	EMT
43047	NL	EMPC	SCE	PTR	EMT
43048	NL	EMPC	SCE	PTR	EMT
43049	NL	EMPC	SCE	PTR	EMT
43050	NL	EMPC	SCE	PTR	EMT
43052	NL	EMPC	SCE	PTR	EMT
43054	NL	EMPC	SCE	PTR	EMT
43055	NL	EMPC	SCE	PTR	EMT
43058	NL	EMPC	SCE	PTR	EMT
43059	NL	EMPC	SCE	PTR	EMT
43061	NL	EMPC	SCE	PTR	EMT
43064	NL	EMPC	SCE	PTR	EMT
43066	NL	EMPC	SCE	PTR	EMT
43073	NL	EMPC	SCE	PTR	EMT
43075	NL	EMPC	SCE	PTR	EMT
43076	NL	EMPC	SCE	PTR	EMT
43081	NL	EMPC	SCE	PTR	EMT
43082	NL	EMPC	SCE	PTR	EMT
43083	NL	EMPC	SCE	PTR	EMT
43089	NL	EMPC	SCE	PTR	EMT

Names applied

43048	T. C. B Miller MBE
43049	Neville Hill
43076	In Support of Help for Heroes
43082	Railway Children The Voice for Street Children Worldwide

Right: *East Midlands Trains main line services are shared operationally between HST formations and Class 222 unit formations. The HST fleet of Class 43 power cars and Mk3 trailer vehicles are based at Leeds Neville Hill, but also receive maintenance at Derby Etches Park depot. Painted in the distinctive Stagecoach Rail-based livery scheme, an EMT HST led by power car No. 43075 with No. 43082* Railway Children *on the rear, forms a charity special from St Pancras to the Mid-Norfolk Railway on 14 May 2011, travelling via Kettering, Leicester and Peterborough to Wymondham, and the Mid-Norfolk Railway to Dereham. It is seen at Hardingham on the Mid-Norfolk line.* **Brian Morrison**

East Midlands Trains

Class 153

Vehicle Length: 76ft 5in (23.29m)		Engine: 1 x NT855R5 of 285hp	
Height: 12ft 3½in (3.75m)		Horsepower: 285hp (213kW)	
Width: 8ft 10in (2.70m)		Seats (total/car): 66S	

Number	Formation DMSL	Depot	Livery	Owner	Operator
153302	52302	NM	EMT	ANG	EMT
153308	52308	NM	EMT	ANG	EMT
153310	52310	NM	EMT	PTR	EMT
153311	52311	NM	EMT	PTR	EMT
153313	52313	NM	EMT	PTR	EMT
153319	52319	NM	EMT	ANG	EMT
153321	52321	NM	EMT	PTR	EMT
153326	52326	NM	EMT	PTR	EMT
153355	57355	NM	EMT	ANG	EMT
153357	57357	NM	EMT	ANG	EMT
153374	57374	NM	EMT	ANG	EMT
153376	57376	NM	EMT	PTR	EMT
153379	57379	NM	EMT	PTR	EMT
153381	57381	NM	EMT	PTR	EMT
153383	57383	NM	EMT	PTR	EMT
153384	57384	NM	EMT	PTR	EMT
153385	57385	NM	EMT	PTR	EMT

Left: *East Midlands Trains is another operator which uses single Class 153 'bubble' cars on lesser used routes. All are now painted in full East Midlands blue livery and have been internally refurbished. No. 153326 (52326) is seen departing from Barnetby.* **Nathan Williamson**

Class 156

Vehicle Length: 75ft 6in (23.03m)		Engine: 1 x Cummins NT855R5 of 285hp	
Height: 12ft 6in (3.81m)		Horsepower: 570hp (425kW)	
Width: 8ft 11in (2.73m)		Seats (total/car): 148S, 72S/76S	

Number	Formation DMSL+DMS	Depot	Livery	Owner	Operator
156401	52401+57401	NM	EMT	PTR	EMT
156403	52403+57403	NM	EMT	PTR	EMT
156404	52404+57404	NM	EMT	PTR	EMT
156405	52405+57405	NM	EMT	PTR	EMT
156406	52406+57406	NM	EMT	PTR	EMT
156408	52408+57408	NM	EMT	PTR	EMT
156410	52410+57410	NM	EMT	PTR	EMT
156411	52411+57411	NM	EMT	PTR	EMT
156413	52413+57413	NM	EMT	PTR	EMT
156414	52414+57414	NM	EMT	PTR	EMT
156415	52415+57415	NM	EMT	PTR	EMT
156470	52470+57470	NM	NOR	PTR	EMT
156473	52473+57473	NM	NOR	PTR	EMT
156497	52497+57497	NM	NOR	PTR	EMT
156498	52498+57498	NM	NOR	PTR	EMT

Below: *For longer distance domestic services, East Midlands Trains operates a fleet of 15 Class 156 units, allocated to Nottingham Eastcroft depot. These sets carry standard Stagecoach blue livery with red/orange swirl ends and yellow passenger doors. All have been internally refurbished in a 2011-2012 contract. Set No. 156411 is shown at East Midlands Parkway in April 2011.* **Nathan Williamson**

Class 158

Vehicle Length: 76ft 1¾in (23.21m)
Height: 12ft 6in (3.81m)
Width: 9ft 3¼in (2.82m)

Engine: 158770-813 - 1 x Cummins NT855R5 of 350hp
Horsepower: 700hp (522kW)
Engine: 158846-862 - 1 x Perkins 2006TWH of 350hp
Horsepower: 700hp (522kW)
Engine: 158863-865 - 1 x Cummins NT855R5 of 400hp
Horsepower: 800hp (597kW)
Seats (total/car): 146S - 74S, 72S

Number	Formation	Depot	Livery	Owner	Operator
	DMSL+DMSL				
158770	52770+57770	NM	SCE	PTR	EMT
158773	52773+57773	NM	SCE	PTR	EMT
158774	52774+57774	NM	SCE	PTR	EMT
158777	52777+57777	NM	SCE	PTR	EMT
158780	52780+57780	NM	SCE	ANG	EMT
158783	52783+57783	NM	SCE	ANG	EMT
158785	52785+57785	NM	SCE	ANG	EMT
158788	52788+57788	NM	SCE	ANG	EMT
158799	52799+57799	NM	SCE	PTR	EMT
158806	52806+57806	NM	SCE	PTR	EMT
158810	52810+57810	NM	SCE	PTR	EMT
158812	52812+57812	NM	SCE	PTR	EMT
158813	52813+57813	NM	SCE	PTR	EMT
158846	52846+57846	NM	SCE	ANG	EMT
158847	52847+57847	NM	SCE	ANG	EMT
158852	52852+57852	NM	SCE	ANG	EMT
158854	52854+57854	NM	SCE	ANG	EMT
158856	52856+57856	NM	SCE	ANG	EMT
158857	52857+57857	NM	SCE	ANG	EMT
158858	52858+57858	NM	SCE	ANG	EMT
158862	52862+57862	NM	SCE	ANG	EMT
158863	52863+57863	NM	SCE	ANG	EMT
158864	52864+57864	NM	SCE	ANG	EMT
158865	52865+57865	NM	SCE	ANG	EMT
158866	52866+57866	NM	SCE	ANG	EMT

Right: *East Midlands Trains' longer distance 'local' services are operated by a fleet of 25 two-car Class 158s. This includes three sets (158863-865) fitted with the more powerful 800hp engine on each carriage. The '158' fleet, now refurbished, carries the Stagecoach-derived white livery, but is different from the similar South West Trains sets by having a ripple in the blue base colour band to the rear of the cab end doors. Set No. 158863 is illustrated. Note the '2' applied on the nose end, telling staff that it is the 52xxx vehicle of the formation.* **Antony Christie**

Class 222

Vehicle Length: 77ft 6in (23.62m)
Height: 12ft 4in (3.75m)
Width: 8ft 11in (2.73m)
Engine: 1 x Cummins OSK9R of 750hp per vehicle

Horsepower: 5,250hp (3,914kW)
Seats (total/car): 106F/236S
38S/68S/68S/62S/42F/42F/22F

Number	Formation	Depot	Livery	Owner	Opt'r	Name
	DMS+MS+MS+MSRMB+MF+MF+DMRFO					
222001	60161+60551+60561+60621+60341+60445+60241	DY	SCE	EVL	EMT	The Entrepreneur Express
222002	60162+60554+60562+60622+60342+60346+60242	DY	SCE	EVL	EMT	The Cutlers' Company
222003	60163+60553+60563+60623+60343+60446+60243	DY	SCE	EVL	EMT	Tornado
222004	60164+60554+60564+60624+60344+60345+60244	DY	SCE	EVL	EMT	
222005	60165+60555+60565+60625+60443+60347+60245	DY	SCE	EVL	EMT	
222006	60166+60556+60566+60626+60441+60447+60246	DY	SCE	EVL	EMT	The Carbon Cutter

Vehicle Length: 77ft 6in (23.62m)
Height: 12ft 4in (3.75m)
Width: 8ft 11in (2.73m)
Engine: 1 x Cummins OSK9R of 750hp per vehicle

Horsepower: 3,750hp (2,796kW)
Seats (total/car): 50F/190S
38S/68S/62S/28F-22S/22F

Number	Formation	Depot	Livery	Owner	Operator	Name
	DMS+MS+MSRMB+MC+DMRFO					
222007	60167+60567+60627+60442+60247	DY	SCE	EVL	EMT	
222008	60168+60545+60628+60918+60248	DY	SCE	EVL	EMT	
222009	60169+60557+60629+60919+60249	DY	SCE	EVL	EMT	
222010	60170+60546+60630+60920+60250	DY	SCE	EVL	EMT	
222011	60171+60531+60631+60921+60251	DY	SCE	EVL	EMT	

East Midlands Trains

(sidebar, rotated) Passenger Train Operating Companies – East Midlands Trains

Number	Formation	Depot	Livery	Owner	Operator	
222012	60172+60532+60632+60922+60252	DY	SCE	EVL	EMT	
222013	60173+60536+60633+60923+60253	DY	SCE	EVL	EMT	
222014	60174+60534+60634+60924+60254	DY	SCE	EVL	EMT	
222015	60175+60535+60635+60925+60255	DY	SCE	EVL	EMT	
222016	60176+60533+60636+60926+60256	DY	SCE	EVL	EMT	
222017	60177+60537+60637+60927+60257	DY	SCE	EVL	EMT	
222018	60178+60444+60638+60928+60258	DY	SCE	EVL	EMT	
222019	60179+60547+60639+60929+60259	DY	SCE	EVL	EMT	
222020	60180+60543+60640+60930+60260	DY	SCE	EVL	EMT	
222021	60181+60552+60641+60931+60261	DY	SCE	EVL	EMT	
222022	60182+60542+60642+60932+60262	DY	SCE	EVL	EMT	*Invest in Nottingham*
222023	60183+60541+60643+60933+60263	DY	SCE	EVL	EMT	

Left: *The Bombardier-built Class 222 units form the backbone of the main line East Midlands Trains operation, sharing duties on the St Pancras to Derby, Sheffield and Nottingham corridor with HST formations. The 222/0 fleet are a mix of seven and five-car formations. All have now been refurbished and sport a similar interior to the HST fleet. On 13 May 2011, set No. 222011 – a five car set – passes Cossington, north of Leicester, with a northbound express. Class 222s usually operate on Midland services with their first class end facing London.* **Antony Christie**

Class 222/1

Vehicle Length: 77ft 6in (23.62m)	Horsepower: 3,000hp (2,237kW)
Height: 12ft 4in (3.75m)	Seats (total/car): 33F/148S
Width: 8ft 11in (2.73m)	22F/11F-46S/62S/40S
Engine: 1 x Cummins OSK9R of 750hp per vehicle	

Number	Formation	Depot	Livery	Owner	Operator
	DMF+MC+MSRMB+DMS				
222101	60271+60571+60681+60191	DY	SCE	EVL	EMT
222102	60272+60572+60682+60192	DY	SCE	EVL	EMT
222103	60273+60573+60683+60193	DY	SCE	EVL	EMT
222104	60274+60574+60684+60194	DY	SCE	EVL	EMT

Left: *The four members of the Class 222/1 sub-class were originally built for First Hull Trains, but after Class 180s were deployed on this route, the Class 222s became redundant and were transferred to East Midland Trains. As four-car sets, these units are deployed on lessor used services and have recently been refurbished in line with the Class 222/0 fleet. The DMS from set No. 222102 is illustrated at Derby, awaiting departure with a semi-fast service to London St Pancras.* **CJM**

HST Passenger Fleet

Vehicle Length: 75ft 0in (22.86m) Width: 8ft 11in (2.71m)
Height: 12ft 9in (3.88m) Bogie Type: BT10

GK1G - TRFB *Seating 17F*

Number	Depot	Livery	Owner
40700	NL	SCE	PTR
40728	NL	SCE	PTR
40730	NL	SCE	PTR
40732	NL	SCE	PTR
40741	NL	SCE	PTR
40746	NL	SCE	PTR
40749	NL	SCE	PTR
40751	NL	SCE	PTR
40753	NL	SCE	PTR
40754	NL	SCE	PTR
40756	NL	SCE	PTR

GH1G - TF *Seating 46F*

Number	Depot	Livery	Owner
41041	NL	SCE	PTR
41046	NL	SCE	PTR
41057	NL	SCE	PTR
41061	NL	SCE	PTR
41062	NL	SCE	PTR
41063	NL	SCE	PTR
41064	NL	SCE	PTR
41067	NL	SCE	PTR
41068	NL	SCE	PTR
41069	NL	SCE	PTR
41070	NL	SCE	PTR
41071	NL	SCE	PTR
41072	NL	SCE	PTR
41075	NL	SCE	PTR
41076	NL	SCE	PTR
41077	NL	SCE	PTR
41079	NL	SCE	PTR
41084	NL	SCE	PTR
41111	NL	SCE	PTR
41112	NL	SCE	PTR

Number	Depot	Livery	Owner
41113	NL	SCE	PTR
41117	NL	SCE	PTR
41154	NL	SCE	PTR
41156	NL	SCE	PTR

GH2G - TS *Seating 74S*

Number	Depot	Livery	Owner
42100	NL	SCE	PTR
42111	NL	SCE	PTR
42112	NL	SCE	PTR
42113	NL	SCE	PTR
42119	NL	SCE	PTR
42120	NL	SCE	PTR
42121	NL	SCE	PTR
42123	NL	SCE	PTR
42124	NL	SCE	PTR
42125	NL	SCE	PTR
42131	NL	SCE	PTR
42132	NL	SCE	PTR
42133	NL	SCE	PTR
42135	NL	SCE	PTR
42136	NL	SCE	PTR
42137	NL	SCE	PTR
42139	NL	SCE	PTR
42140	NL	SCE	PTR
42141	NL	SCE	PTR
42148	NL	SCE	PTR
42149	NL	SCE	PTR
42151	NL	SCE	PTR
42152	NL	SCE	PTR
42153	NL	SCE	PTR
42155	NL	SCE	PTR
42156	NL	SCE	PTR
42157	NL	SCE	PTR
42164	NL	SCE	PTR
42165	NL	SCE	PTR

Number	Depot	Livery	Owner
42194	NL	SCE	PTR
42205	NL	SCE	PTR
42210	NL	SCE	PTR
42220	NL	SCE	PTR
42225	NL	SCE	PTR
42227	NL	SCE	PTR
42229	NL	SCE	PTR
42230	NL	SCE	PTR
42327	NL	SCE	PTR
42328	NL	SCE	PTR
42329	NL	SCE	PTR
42331	NL	SCE	PTR
42335	NL	SCE	PTR
42337	NL	SCE	PTR
42339	NL	SCE	PTR
42341	NL	SCE	PTR
42384¤	NL	SCE	PTR

¤ Modified from 41078

GJ2G - TGS *Seating 63S*

Number	Depot	Livery	Owner
44027	NL	SCE	PTR
44041	NL	SCE	PTR
44044	NL	SCE	PTR
44046	NL	SCE	PTR
44047	NL	SCE	PTR
44048	NL	SCE	PTR
44051	NL	SCE	PTR
44054	NL	SCE	PTR
44070	NL	SCE	PTR
44071	NL	SCE	PTR
44073	NL	SCE	PTR
44085	NL	SCE	PTR

Right: *The entire East Midlands Trains HST passenger fleet has now been refurbished by Leeds Neville Hill depot and all vehicles sport a derivative of the Stagecoach main line white livery, complete with red passenger doors. Car No. 42100, the lowest numbered TS in the EMT fleet, is illustrated.* **Tony Christie**

Service Stock

HST Barrier Vehicles

Number	Depot	Livery	Owner	Former Identity
6392	NL	PTR	PTR	BG - 81588/92183
6395	NL	PTR	EMT	BG - 81506/92148
6397	NL	PTR	PTR	BG - 81600/92190
6398	NL	MAI	EMT	BG - 81471/92126
6399	NL	MAI	EMT	BG - 81367/92994

Eurostar

Passenger Train Operating Companies - Eurostar

Address: ✉ Eurostar, Times House, Bravingtons Walk, Regent Quarter, London, N1 9AW

📠 new.comments@eurostar.com

✆ 08701 606 600

ⓘ www.eurostar.com

Managing Director: Nicolas Petrovic / Richard Brown

Principal Routes: St Pancras International - Brussels and Paris also serving Disneyland Paris, Avignon and winter sport service to Bourg St Maurice

Owned Stations: St Pancras International, Stratford International, Ebbsfleet

Depots: Temple Mills [UK] (TI), Forest [Belgium] (FF), Le Landy [France] (LY)

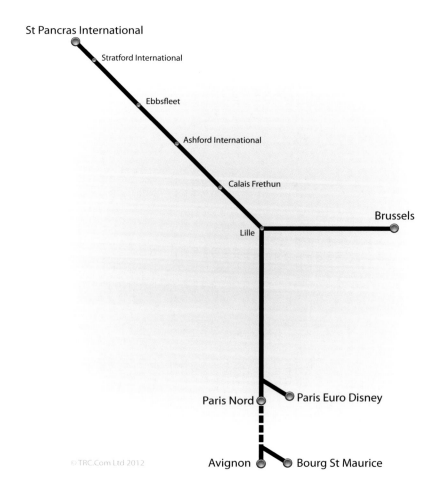

© TRC.Com Ltd 2012

Class 373

Vehicle Length: (DM) 72ft 8in (22.15m), (MS) 71ft 6in (21.84m)
(TS, TBK, TF, TBF) 61ft 4in (18.70m)
Height: 12ft 4½in (3.77m)
Width: 9ft 3in (2.81m)
Horsepower: 16,400hp (12,249kW)
Seats (total/car): 102F/272S, 0/48S/56S/56S/56S/56S/0/39F/39F/24F

Formation
DM+MSO+TSO+TSO+TSO+RB+TFO+TFO+TBFO

Number	Formation	Depot	Livery	Owner	Operator	Name
UK sets						
373001	3730010+3730011+3730012+3730013+3730014+3730015+3730016+3730017+3730018+3730019	TI	EUS	EUS	EUS	Tread Lightly
373002	3730020+3730021+3730022+3730023+3730024+3730025+3730026+3730027+3730028+3730029	TI	EUS	EUS	EUS	Voyage Vert
373003	3730030+3730031+3730032+3730033+3730034+3730035+3730036+3730037+3730038+3730039	TI	EUS*	EUS	EUS	Tri City Athlon 2010
373004	3730040+3730041+3730042+3730043+3730044+3730045+3730046+3730047+3730048+3730049	TI	EUS*	EUS	EUS	Tri City Athlon 2010
373005	3730050+3730051+3730052+3730053+3730054+3730055+3730056+3730057+3730058+3730059	TI	EUS	EUS	EUS	
373006	3730060+3730061+3730062+3730063+3730064+3730065+3730066+3730067+3730068+3730069	TI	EUS	EUS	EUS	
373007	3730070+3730071+3730072+3730073+3730074+3730075+3730076+3730077+3730078+3730079	TI	EUS	EUS	EUS	Waterloo Sunset
373008	3730080+3730081+3730082+3730083+3730084+3730085+3730086+3730087+3730088+3730089	TI	EUS	EUS	EUS	Waterloo Sunset
373009	3730090+3730091+3730092+3730093+3730094+3730095+3730096+3730097+3730098+3730099	TI	EUS	EUS	EUS	Remembering Fromelles
373010	3730100+3730101+3730102+3730103+3730104+3730105+3730106+3730107+3730108+3730109	TI	EUS	EUS	EUS	Remembering Fromelles
373011	3730110+3730111+3730112+3730113+3730114+3730115+3730116+3730117+3730118+3730119	TI	EUS	EUS	EUS	
373012	3730120+3730121+3730122+3730123+3730124+3730125+3730126+3730127+3730128+3730129	TI	EUS	EUS	EUS	London 2012
373013	3730130+3730131+3730132+3730133+3730134+3730135+3730136+3730137+3730138+3730139	TI	EUS	EUS	EUS	London 2012
373014	3730140+3730141+3730142+3730143+3730144+3730145+3730146+3730147+3730148+3730149	TI	EUS	EUS	EUS	
373015	3730150+3730151+3730152+3730153+3730154+3730155+3730156+3730157+3730158+3730159	TI	EUS	EUS	EUS	
373016	3730160+3730161+3730162+3730163+3730164+3730165+3730166+3730167+3730168+3730169	TI	EUS	EUS	EUS	
373017	3730170+3730171+3730172+3730173+3730174+3730175+3730176+3730177+3730178+3730179	TI	EUS	EUS	EUS	
373018	3730180+3730181+3730182+3730183+3730184+3730185+3730186+3730187+3730188+3730189	TI	EUS‡	EUS	EUS	
373019	3730190+3730191+3730192+3730193+3730194+3730195+3730196+3730197+3730198+3730199	TI	EUS	EUS	EUS	
373020	3730200+3730201+3730202+3730203+3730204+3730205+3730206+3730207+3730208+3730209	TI	EUS	EUS	EUS	
373021	3730210+3730211+3730212+3730213+3730214+3730215+3730216+3730217+3730218+3730219	TI	EUS	EUS	EUS	
373022	3730220+3730221+3730222+3730223+3730224+3730225+3730226+3730227+3730228+3730229	TI	EUS	EUS	EUS	
Belgian sets						
373101	3731010+3731011+3731012+3731013+3731014+3731015+3731016+3731017+3731018+3731019	FF[S]	EUS	SNB	EUS	
373102	3731020+3731021+3731022+3731023+3731024+3731025+3731026+3731027+3731028+3731029	FF[S]	EUS	SNB	EUS	
373103	3731030+3731031+3731032+3731033+3731034+3731035+3731036+3731037+3731038+3731039	FF	EUS	SNB	EUS	
373104	3731040+3731041+3731042+3731043+3731044+3731045+3731046+3731047+3731048+3731049	FF	EUS	SNB	EUS	
373105	3731050+3731051+3731052+3731053+3731054+3731055+3731056+3731057+3731058+3731059	FF	EUS	SNB	EUS	
373106	3731060+3731061+3731062+3731063+3731064+3731065+3731066+3731067+3731068+3731069	FF	EUS	SNB	EUS	
373107	3731070+3731071+3731072+3731073+3731074+3731075+3731076+3731077+3731078+3731079	FF	EUS	SNB	EUS	
373108	3731080+3731081+3731082+3731083+3731084+3731085+3731086+3731087+3731088+3731089	FF	EUS	SNB	EUS	
French sets						
373201	3732010+3732011+3732012+3732013+3732014+3732015+3732016+3732017+3732018+3732019	LY	EUS	SNF	EUS	
373202	3732020+3732021+3732022+3732023+3732024+3732025+3732026+3732027+3732028+3732029	LY	EUS	SNF	EUS	
373203¤	3732030+3732031+3732032+3732033+3732034+3732035+3732036+3732037+3732038+3732039	LY	SNT	SNF	EUS	
373204¤	3732040+3732041+3732042+3732043+3732044+3732045+3732046+3732047+3732048+3732049	LY	SNT	SNF	EUS	
373205	3732050+3732051+3732052+3732053+3732054+3732055+3732056+3732057+3732058+3732059	LY	EUS	SNF	EUS	
373206	3732060+3732061+3732062+3732063+3732064+3732065+3732066+3732067+3732068+3732069	LY	EUS	SNF	EUS	

Eurostar

Passenger Train Operating Companies - Eurostar

Number	Formation	Depot	Livery	Owner	Operator	Name
373207	3732070+3732071+3732072+3732073+3732074+3732075+3732076+3732077+3732078+3732079	LY	EUS	SNF	EUS	Michel Hollard
373208	3732080+3732081+3732082+3732083+3732084+3732085+3732086+3732087+3732088+3732089	LY	EUS	SNF	EUS	Michel Hollard
373209	3732090+3732091+3732092+3732093+3732094+3732095+3732096+3732097+3732098+3732099	LY	EUS	SNF	EUS	The Da Vinci Code
373210	3732100+3732101+3732102+3732103+3732104+3732105+3732106+3732107+3732108+3732109	LY	EUS	SNF	EUS	The Da Vinci Code
373211	3732110+3732111+3732112+3732113+3732114+3732115+3732116+3732117+3732118+3732119	LY	EUS	SNF	EUS	
373212	3732120+3732121+3732122+3732123+3732124+3732125+3732126+3732127+3732128+3732129	LY	EUS	SNF	EUS	
373213	3732130+3732131+3732132+3732133+3732134+3732135+3732136+3732137+3732138+3732139	LY	EUS	SNF	EUS	
373214	3732140+3732141+3732142+3732143+3732144+3732145+3732146+3732147+3732148+3732149	LY	EUS	SNF	EUS	
373215	3732150+3732151+3732152+3732153+3732154+3732155+3732156+3732157+3732158+3732159	LY	EUS	SNF	EUS	
373216	3732160+3732161+3732162+3732163+3732164+3732165+3732166+3732167+3732168+3732169	LY	EUS	SNF	EUS	
373217	3732170+3732171+3732172+3732173+3732174+3732175+3732176+3732177+3732178+3732179	LY	EUS	SNF	EUS	
373218	3732180+3732181+3732182+3732183+3732184+3732185+3732186+3732187+3732188+3732189	LY	EUS	SNF	EUS	
373219	3732190+3732191+3732192+3732193+3732194+3732195+3732196+3732197+3732198+3732199	LY	EUS	SNF	EUS	
373220	3732200+3732201+3732202+3732203+3732204+3732205+3732206+3732207+3732208+3732209	LY	EUS	SNF	EUS	
373221	3732210+3732211+3732212+3732213+3732214+3732215+3732216+3732217+3732218+3732219	LY	EUS	SNF	EUS	
373222	3732220+3732221+3732222+3732223+3732224+3732225+3732226+3732227+3732228+3732229	LY	EUS	SNF	EUS	
373223	3732230+3732231+3732232+3732233+3732234+3732235+3732236+3732237+3732238+3732239	LY	EUS	SNF	EUS	
373224	3732240+3732241+3732242+3732243+3732244+3732245+3732246+3732247+3732248+3732249	LY	EUS	SNF	EUS	
373225¤	3732250+3732251+3732252+3732253+3732254+3732255+3732256+3732257+3732258+3732259	LY	EUS	SNF	SNT	
373226¤	3732260+3732261+3732262+3732263+3732264+3732265+3732266+3732267+3732268+3732269	LY	EUS	SNF	SNT	
373227¤	3732270+3732271+3732272+3732273+3732274+3732275+3732276+3732277+3732278+3732279	LY	EUS	SNF	SNT	
373228¤	3732280+3732281+3732282+3732283+3732284+3732285+3732286+3732287+3732288+3732289	LY	EUS	SNF	SNT	
373229	3732290+3732291+3732292+3732293+3732294+3732295+3732296+3732297+3732298+3732299	LY	EUS	SNF	EUS	
373230	3732300+3732301+3732302+3732303+3732304+3732305+3732306+3732307+3732308+3732309	LY	EUS	SNF	EUS	
373231	3732310+3732311+3732312+3732313+3732314+3732315+3732316+3732317+3732318+3732319	LY	EUS	SNF	EUS	
373232	3732320+3732321+3732322+3732323+3732324+3732325+3732326+3732327+3732328+3732329	LY	EUS	SNF	EUS	

* Advertising livery - London Virgins. ‡ de Gaulle 70th branding ¤ Operated in France on domestic services.

Number Formation

DM+MSO+TSO+TSO+TSO+TSO+RB+TFO+TBFO

Regional sets

Number	Formation	Depot	Livery	Owner	Operator
373301	3733010+3733011+3733012+3733013+3733015+3733016+3733017+3733019	LY	EUS	EUS	SNF
373302	3733020+3733021+3733022+3733023+3733025+3733026+3733027+3733029	LY	EUS	EUS	SNF
373303	3733030+3733031+3733032+3733033+3733035+3733036+3733037+3733039	LY	EUS	EUS	SNF
373304	3733040+3733041+3733042+3733043+3733045+3733046+3733047+3733049	LY	EUS	EUS	SNF
373305	3733050+3733051+3733052+3733053+3733055+3733056+3733057+3733059	LY	EUS	EUS	SNF
373306	3733060+3733061+3733062+3733063+3733065+3733066+3733067+3733069	LY	EUS	EUS	SNF
373307	3733070+3733071+3733072+3733073+3733075+3733076+3733077+3733079	LY	EUS	EUS	SNF
373308	3733080+3733081+3733082+3733083+3733085+3733086+3733087+3733089	LY	EUS	EUS	SNF
373309	3733090+3733091+3733092+3733093+3733095+3733096+3733097+3733099	LY	EUS	EUS	SNF
373310	3733100+3733101+3733102+3733103+3733105+3733106+3733107+3733109	LY	EUS	EUS	SNF
373311	3733110+3733111+3733112+3733113+3733115+3733116+3733117+3733119	LY	EUS	EUS	SNF
373312	3733120+3733121+3733122+3733123+3733125+3733126+3733127+3733129	LY	EUS	EUS	SNF
373313	3733130+3733131+3733132+3733133+3733135+3733136+3733137+3733139	LY	EUS	EUS	SNF
373314	3733140+3733141+3733142+3733143+3733145+3733146+3733147+3733149	LY	EUS	EUS	SNF

Vehicle Length: (DM) 72ft 8in (22.15m), (MS) 71ft 8in (21.84)
(TS, TBK, TE, TBF) 61ft 4in (18.70m)
Height: 12ft 4½in (3.77m)
Width: 9ft 3in (2.81m)
Horsepower: 16,400hp (12,249kW)
Seats (total/car): 102F/272S, 0/48S/56S/56S/56S/56S/lOl
39F/39F/24F

■ These 14 short half-sets are loaned to SNCF for domestic duties for the forseeable future.

Above: *The Eurostar sets used on Anglo-French services still carry the same basic livery as they did when introduced in the mid-1990s. However, in 2011 a new Eurostar logo was applied on the cab sides of a blue stylised 'e' together with Olympic 2012 partner branding. UK sets Nos. (37)3019/20 are seen on HS1 near Rainham on 2 September 2011.* **Tim Easter**

Spare DM

Number		Depot	Livery	Owner	Operator
3999	(Spare vehicle used as required to cover for maintenance)	TI	EUS	EUS	EUS

● Ten new Eurostar e320 16-car sets have been ordered from Siemens; these will have a 200mph (320km/h) capability and seat 900. The sets, scheduled for delivery in 2014, will have the ability to operate throughout Europe. Length: 400m, Power: 16,000kW from 25kV ac and 1.5/3kV dc. Driving cars = 25.7m, Intermediate cars = 14.2m, 32 2-axle bogies per train.

Class 08

Vehicle Length: 29ft 3in (8.91m)
Height: 12ft 8⅝in (3.87m)
Width: 8ft 6in (2.59m)

Engine: English Electric 6K
Horsepower: 400hp (298kW)
Electrical Equipment: English Electric

Number	Depot	Pool	Livery	Owner	Opt'r
08948	TI	GPSS	TTG	EUS	EUS

Right: *This Sculfort battery-powered 'locotractor' based at the Temple Mills Eurostar depot is used to move and position Class 373 stock on the wheel lathe manufactured by the same company. The 'locomotive' is of type RBL-030-1200 and is numbered TM-FL-009. In this mid-2011 view the vehicle is seen in the yard at Temple Mills. It is not allowed outside the confines of the depot.* **Tony Christie**

First Capital Connect

Address:	✉ Hertford House, 1 Cranwood Street, London, EC1V 9QS
	📧 customer.relations.fcc@firstgroup.com
	✆ 0845 026 4700
	ⓘ www.firstcapitalconnect.co.uk
Managing Director:	Neil Lawson
Franchise Dates:	1 April 2006 - September 2013
Principal Routes:	London King's Cross - King's Lynn, Peterborough / Cambridge
	Moorgate - Hertford Loop and Letchworth
	Bedford - Brighton (Thameslink)
	Luton - Wimbledon /
	Sutton (Thameslink)
Depots:	Bedford Cauldwell Walk (BF),
	Hornsey (HE),
	Brighton (BI)*
	* Stabling point
Parent Company:	First Group PLC

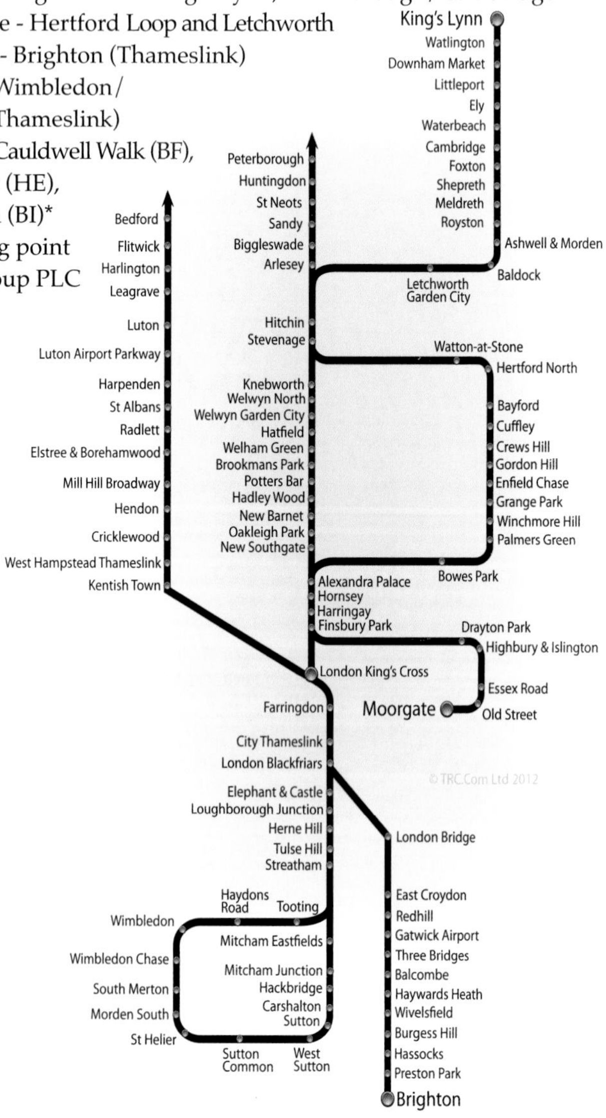

Passenger Train Operating Companies - First Capital Connect

King's Lynn
Watlington
Downham Market
Littleport
Ely
Waterbeach
Cambridge
Peterborough
Foxton
Huntingdon
Shepreth
St Neots
Meldreth
Bedford
Sandy
Royston
Flitwick
Biggleswade
Ashwell & Morden
Harlington
Arlesey
Baldock
Leagrave
Letchworth
Garden City
Luton
Hitchin
Luton Airport Parkway
Stevenage
Watton-at-Stone
Hertford North
Harpenden
Knebworth
St Albans
Welwyn North
Bayford
Radlett
Welwyn Garden City
Cuffley
Elstree & Borehamwood
Hatfield
Crews Hill
Welham Green
Gordon Hill
Mill Hill Broadway
Brookmans Park
Enfield Chase
Potters Bar
Grange Park
Hendon
Hadley Wood
Winchmore Hill
New Barnet
Cricklewood
Oakleigh Park
Palmers Green
New Southgate
West Hampstead Thameslink
Alexandra Palace
Bowes Park
Kentish Town
Hornsey
Harringay
Finsbury Park
Drayton Park
Highbury & Islington
London King's Cross
Essex Road
Farringdon
Moorgate
Old Street
City Thameslink
London Blackfriars
Elephant & Castle
Loughborough Junction
Herne Hill
London Bridge
Tulse Hill
Streatham
Haydons
East Croydon
Road
Tooting
Redhill
Wimbledon
Gatwick Airport
Mitcham Eastfields
Three Bridges
Wimbledon Chase
Mitcham Junction
Balcombe
South Merton
Hackbridge
Haywards Heath
Carshalton
Wivelsfield
Morden South
Sutton
Burgess Hill
St Helier
Hassocks
Sutton
West
Preston Park
Common
Sutton
Brighton

© TRC.Com Ltd 2012

Class 313/0 & 313/1

Vehicle Length: (Driving) 64ft 11½in (20.75m)		Width: 9ft 3in (2.82m)				
(Inter) 65ft 4¼in (19.92m)		Horsepower: 880hp (656kW)				
Height: 11ft 9in (3.58m)		Seats (total/car): 231S, 74S/83S/74S				

Number	Formation DMSO+PTSO+BDMSO	Depot	Livery	Owner	Operator	Name
313018	62546+71230+62160	HE	FCC	EVL	FCC	
313024	62552+71236+62616	HE	FCC	EVL	FCC	
313025	62553+71237+62617	HE	FCC	EVL	FCC	
313026	62554+71238+62618	HE	FCC	EVL	FCC	
313027	62555+71239+62619	HE	FCC	EVL	FCC	
313028	62556+71240+62620	HE	FCC	EVL	FCC	
313029	62557+71241+62621	HE	FCC	EVL	FCC	
313030	62558+71242+62622	HE	FCC	EVL	FCC	
313031	62559+71243+62623	HE	FCC	EVL	FCC	
313032	62560+71244+62643	HE	FCC	EVL	FCC	
313033	62561+71245+62625	HE	FCC	EVL	FCC	
313035	62563+71247+62627	HE	FCC	EVL	FCC	
313036	62564+71248+62628	HE	FCC	EVL	FCC	
313037	62565+71249+62629	HE	FCC	EVL	FCC	
313038	62566+71250+62630	HE	FCC	EVL	FCC	
313039	62567+71251+62631	HE	FCC	EVL	FCC	
313040	62568+71252+62632	HE	FCC	EVL	FCC	
313041	62569+71253+62633	HE	FCC	EVL	FCC	
313042	62570+71254+62634	HE	FCC	EVL	FCC	
313043	62571+71255+62635	HE	FCC	EVL	FCC	
313044	62572+71256+62636	HE	FCC	EVL	FCC	
313045	62573+71257+62637	HE	FCC	EVL	FCC	
313046	62574+71258+62638	HE	FCC	EVL	FCC	
313047	62575+71259+62639	HE	FCC	EVL	FCC	
313048	62576+71260+62640	HE	FCC	EVL	FCC	
313049	62577+71261+62641	HE	FCC	EVL	FCC	
313050	62578+71262+62649	HE	FCC	EVL	FCC	
313051	62579+71263+62624	HE	FCC	EVL	FCC	
313052	62580+71264+62644	HE	FCC	EVL	FCC	
313053	62581+71265+62645	HE	FCC	EVL	FCC	
313054	62582+71266+62646	HE	FCC	EVL	FCC	*Captain William Leefe Robinson VC*
313055	62583+71267+62647	HE	FCC	EVL	FCC	
313056	62584+71268+62648	HE	FCC	EVL	FCC	
313057	62585+71269+62642	HE	FCC	EVL	FCC	
313058	62586+71270+62650	HE	FCC	EVL	FCC	
313059	62587+71271+62651	HE	FCC	EVL	FCC	
313060	62588+71272+62652	HE	FCC	EVL	FCC	
313061	62589+71273+62653	HE	FCC	EVL	FCC	
313062	62590+71274+62654	HE	FCC	EVL	FCC	
313063	62591+71275+62655	HE	FCC	EVL	FCC	
313064	62592+71276+62656	HE	FCC	EVL	FCC	
313122	62550+71234+61614	HE	FCC	EVL	FCC	
313123	62551+71235+61615	HE	FCC	EVL	FCC	
313134	62562+71246+61626	HE	FCC	EVL	FCC	*City of London*

Right: *The Class 313 fleet, now operated by First Capital Connect, were the first production trains of the 1972-design high-density EMU which culminated from the PEP prototypes used on the Southern Region. Today's fleet of '313s' are allocated to Hornsey and operate the dual voltage Great Northern route into and from Moorgate. All sets are painted in First group livery. Set No. 313056 arrives at Gordon Hill on 27 April 2010 with a service from Hertford North to Moorgate.* **Brian Morrison**

Passenger Train Operating Companies - First Capital Connect

First Capital Connect

Class 317/3

	Vehicle Length: (Driving) 65ft 0¾in (19.83m)	Width: 9ft 3in (2.82m)
	(Inter) 65ft 4¼in (19.92m)	Horsepower: 1,000hp (746kW)
	Height: 12ft 1½in (3.58m)	Seats (total/car): 22F/269S, 74S/79S/22F-46S/70S

Number	Formation DTSO+MSO+TCO+DTSO	Depot	Livery	Owner	Operator	Name
317337	77036+62671+71613+77084	HE	FCC	ANG	FCC	
317338	77037+62698+71614+77085	HE	FCC	ANG	FCC	
317339	77038+62699+71615+77086	HE	FCC	ANG	FCC	
317340	77039+62700+71616+77087	HE	FCC	ANG	FCC	
317341	77040+62701+71617+77088	HE	FCC	ANG	FCC	
317342	77041+62702+71618+77089	HE	FCC	ANG	FCC	
317343	77042+62703+71619+77090	HE	FCC	ANG	FCC	
317344	77029+62690+71620+77091	HE	FCC	ANG	FCC	
317345	77044+62705+71621+77092	HE	FCC	ANG	FCC	*Driver John Webb*
317346	77045+62706+71622+77093	HE	FCC	ANG	FCC	
317347	77046+62707+71623+77094	HE	FCC	ANG	FCC	
317348	77047+62708+71624+77095	HE	FCC	ANG	FCC	*Richard A. Jenner*

Left: *Just 12 Class 317/3 sets are worked by First Capital Connect. Allocated to Hornsey and painted in First group corporate livery, the units operate longer distance outer suburban routes. Set No. 317340 is pictured arriving at Stevenage with a London King's Cross-bound service.*
Alex Martin-Brown

Class 319/0

	Vehicle Length: (Driving) 65ft 0¾in (19.83m)	Width: 9ft 3in (2.82m)
	(Inter) 65ft 4¼in (19.92m)	Horsepower: 1,326hp (990kW)
	Height: 11ft 9in (3.58m)	Seats (total/car): 319S, 82S/82S/77S/78S

Number	Formation DTSO(A)+MSO+TSO+DTSO(B)	Depot	Livery	Owner	Operator	Name
319001	77291+62891+71772+77290	SU	FCC	PTR	FCC	
319002	77293+62892+71773+77292	SU	FCC	PTR	FCC	
319003	77295+62893+71774+77294	SU	FCC	PTR	FCC	
319004	77297+62894+71775+77296	SU	FCC	PTR	FCC	
319005	77299+62895+71776+77298	SU	FCC	PTR	FCC	
319006	77301+62896+71777+77300	SU	FCC	PTR	FCC	
319007	77303+62897+71778+77302	SU	FCC	PTR	FCC	
319008	77305+62898+71779+77304	SU	SOU	PTR	FCC	*Cheriton*
319009	77307+62899+71780+77306	SU	SOU	PTR	FCC	
319010	77309+62900+71781+77308	SU	FCC	PTR	FCC	
319011	77311+62901+71782+77310	SU	SOU	PTR	FCC	*John Ruskin College*
319012	77313+62902+71783+77312	SU	SOU	PTR	FCC	
319013	77315+62903+71784+77314	SU	SOU	PTR	FCC	*The Surrey Hills*

Class 319/2

	Vehicle Length: (Driving) 65ft 0¾in (19.83m)	Width: 9ft 3in (2.82m)
	(Inter) 65ft 4¼in (19.92m)	Horsepower: 1,326hp (990kW)
	Height: 11ft 9in (3.58m)	Seats (total/car): 18F/212S, 64S/60S/52S/18F-36S

Number	Formation DTSO+MSO+TSO+DTCO	Depot	Livery	Owner	Operator	Name/Notes
319214	77317+62904+71785+77316	SU	SOU	PTR	FCC	
319215	77319+62905+71786+77318	SU	ADV	PTR	FCC	*(Visit Switzerland livery)*
319216	77321+62906+71787+77320	SU	SOU	PTR	FCC	
319217	77323+62907+71788+77322	BF	SOU	PTR	FCC	*Brighton*
319218	77325+62908+71789+77324	BF	SOU	PTR	FCC	*Croydon*
319219	77327+62909+71790+77326	BF	SOU	PTR	FCC	
319220	77329+62910+71791+77328	BF	SOU	PTR	FCC	

Class 319/3

Vehicle Length: (Driving) 65ft 0¾in (19.83m) Width: 9ft 3in (2.82m)
(Inter) 65ft 4¼in (19.92m) Horsepower: 1,326hp (990kW)
Height: 11ft 9in (3.58m) Seats (total/car): 300S, 70S/78S/74S/78S

Number	Formation	Depot	Livery	Owner	Operator	Name
	DTSO(A)+MSO+TSO+DTSO(B)					
319361	77459+63043+71929+77458	BF	FCC	PTR	FCC	
319362	77461+63044+71930+77460	BF	FCC	PTR	FCC	
319363	77463+63045+71931+77462	BF	FCC	PTR	FCC	
319364	77465+63046+71932+77464	BF	TLP	PTR	FCC	*Transforming Blackfriars*
319365	77467+63047+71933+77466	BF	TLP	PTR	FCC	*Transforming Farringdon*
319366	77469+63048+71934+77468	BF	FCC	PTR	FCC	
319367	77471+63049+71935+77470	BF	FCC	PTR	FCC	
319368	77473+63050+71936+77472	BF	FCC	PTR	FCC	
319369	77475+63051+71937+77474	BF	FCC	PTR	FCC	
317370	77477+63052+71938+77476	BF	FCC	PTR	FCC	
319371	77479+63053+71939+77478	BF	FCC	PTR	FCC	
319372	77481+63054+71940+77480	BF	FCC	PTR	FCC	
319373	77483+63055+71941+77482	BF	FCC	PTR	FCC	
319374	77485+63056+71942+77484	BF	FCC	PTR	FCC	*Bedford Cauldwell Walk TMD*
319375	77487+63057+71943+77486	BF	FCC	PTR	FCC	
319376	77489+63058+71944+77488	BF	FCC	PTR	FCC	
319377	77491+63059+71945+77490	BF	FCC	PTR	FCC	
319378	77493+63060+71946+77492	BF	FCC	PTR	FCC	
319379	77495+63061+71947+77494	BF	FCC	PTR	FCC	
319380	77497+63082+71948+77496	BF	FCC	PTR	FCC	
319381	77973+63093+71978+77974	BF	FCC	PTR	FCC	
319382	77975+63094+71980+77976	BF	FCC	PTR	FCC	
319383	77977+63096+71981+77978	BF	FCC	PTR	FCC	
319384	77979+63096+71982+77980	BF	FCC	PTR	FCC	
319385	77981+63097+71983+77982	BF	FCC	PTR	FCC	
319386	77983+63098+71984+77984	BF	FCC	PTR	FCC	

Class 319/4

Vehicle Length: (Driving) 65ft 0¾in (19.83m) Width: 9ft 3in (2.82m)
(Inter) 65ft 4¼in (19.92m) Horsepower: 1,326hp (990kW)
Height: 11ft 9in (3.58m) Seats (total/car): 12F/277S, 12F-54S/77S/72S/74S

Number	Formation	Depot	Livery	Owner	Operator	Name
	DTCO+MSO+TSO+DTSO					
319421	77331+62911+71792+77330	BF	FCC	PTR	FCC	
319422	77333+62912+71793+77332	BF	FCC	PTR	FCC	
319423	77335+62913+71794+77334	BF	FCC	PTR	FCC	
319424	77337+62914+71795+77336	BF	FCC	PTR	FCC	
319425	77339+62915+71796+77338	BF	FCC	PTR	FCC	*Transforming Travel*
319426	77341+62916+71797+77340	BF	FCC	PTR	FCC	
319427	77343+62917+71798+77342	BF	FCC	PTR	FCC	
319428	77345+62918+71799+77344	BF	FCC	PTR	FCC	
319429	77347+62919+71800+77346	BF	FCC	PTR	FCC	
319430	77349+62920+71801+77348	BF	FCC	PTR	FCC	
319431	77351+62921+71802+77350	BF	FCC	PTR	FCC	
319432	77353+62922+71803+77352	BF	FCC	PTR	FCC	
319433	77355+62923+71804+77354	BF	FCC	PTR	FCC	
319434	77357+62924+71805+77356	BF	FCC	PTR	FCC	
319435	77359+62925+71806+77358	BF	FCC	PTR	FCC	*Adrian Jackson-Robbins Chairman 1987-2007 Association of Public Transport Users*
319436	77361+62926+71807+77360	BF	FCC	PTR	FCC	
319437	77363+62927+71808+77362	BF	FCC	PTR	FCC	
319438	77365+62928+71809+77364	BF	FCC	PTR	FCC	
319439	77367+62929+71810+77366	BF	FCC	PTR	FCC	
319440	77369+62930+71811+77368	BF	FCC	PTR	FCC	
319441	77371+62931+71812+77370	BF	FCC	PTR	FCC	
319442	77373+62932+71813+77372	BF	FCC	PTR	FCC	
319443	77375+62933+71814+77374	BF	FCC	PTR	FCC	
319444	77377+62934+71815+77376	BF	TLP	PTR	FCC	
319445	77379+62935+71816+77378	BF	FCC	PTR	FCC	

Passenger Train Operating Companies - First Capital Connect

First Capital Connect

319446	77381+62936+71817+77380	BF	FCC	PTR	FCC	*St Pancras International*
319447	77431+62961+71866+77430	BF	FCC	PTR	FCC	
319448	77433+62962+71867+77432	BF	FCC	PTR	FCC	*Elstree Studios*
319449	77435+62963+71868+77434	BF	FCC	PTR	FCC	*King's Cross Thameslink*
319450	77437+62964+71869+77436	BF	FCC	PTR	FCC	
319451	77439+62965+71870+77438	BF	FCC	PTR	FCC	
319452	77441+62966+71871+77440	BF	FCC	PTR	FCC	
319453	77443+62967+71872+77442	BF	FCC	PTR	FCC	
319454	77445+62968+71873+77444	BF	FCC	PTR	FCC	
319455	77447+62969+71874+77446	BF	FCC	PTR	FCC	
319456	77449+62970+71875+77448	BF	FCC	PTR	FCC	
319457	77451+62971+71876+77450	BF	FCC	PTR	FCC	
319458	77453+62972+71877+77452	BF	FCC	PTR	FCC	
319459	77455+62973+71878+77454	BF	FCC	PTR	FCC	
319460	77457+62974+71879+77456	BF	FCC	PTR	FCC	

Left: *First Capital Connect are responsible for operating the present Thameslink service linking north and south London. For this the Class 319s and some 377s are used. Four different sub-classes of 319 exist; the different sub-groups refer to seating variants and some minor design changes. In this view we see a Class 319/3 No. 319361 calling at Bellingham with an afternoon service bound for Bedford on 12 October 2009.* **Brian Morrison**

Class 321/4

Vehicle Length: (Driving) 65ft 0¾in (19.83m) (Inter) 65ft 4¼in (19.92m)
Height: 12ft 4¾in (3.78m)
Width: 9ft 3in (2.82m)
Horsepower: 1,328hp (996kW)
Seats (total/car): 28F/271S, 28F-40S/79S/74S/78S

Number	Formation DMCO+MSO+TSO+DMSO	Depot	Livery	Owner	Operator	Name
321401	78095+63063+71949+77943	HE	FCC	EVL	FCC	
321402	78096+63064+71950+77944	HE	FCC	EVL	FCC	
321403	78097+63065+71951+77945	HE	FCC	EVL	FCC	*Stewart Fleming Signalman King's Cross*
321404	78098+63066+71952+77946	HE	FCC	EVL	FCC	
321405	78099+63067+71953+77947	HE	FCC	EVL	FCC	
321406	78100+63068+71954+77948	HE	FCC	EVL	FCC	
321407	78101+63069+71955+77949	HE	FCC	EVL	FCC	
321408	78102+63070+71956+77959	HE	FCC	EVL	FCC	
321409	78103+63071+71957+77960	HE	FCC	EVL	FCC	
321410	78104+63072+71958+77961	HE	FCC	EVL	FCC	
321418	78112+63080+71968+77962	HE	FCC	EVL	FCC	
321419	78113+63081+71969+77963	HE	FCC	EVL	FCC	
321420	78114+63082+71970+77964	HE	FCC	EVL	FCC	

Left: *Fleet changes in more recent years have seen a small number (13 units) of Class 321/4 operate for First Capital Connect. On 15 May 2011, set No. 321408 in full FCC livery passes Offord Cluny with a Peterborough to London King's Cross semi-fast service. All sets are allocated to Hornsey.* **Michael J. Collins**

Class 365
Networker Express

Vehicle Length: (Driving) 68ft 6½in (20.89m) Width: 9ft 2½in (2.81m)
(Inter) 65ft 9¼in (20.89m) Horsepower: 1,684hp (1,256kW)
Height: 12ft 4½in (3.77m) Seats (total/car): 24F/239S, 12F-56S/59S/68S/12F-56S

Number	Formation DMCO(A)+TSO+PTSO+DMCO(B)	Depot	Livery	Owner	Operator	Name
365501	65894+72241+72240+65935	HE	FCC	EVL	FCC	
365502	65895+72243+72242+65936	HE	FCC	EVL	FCC	
365503	65896+72245+72244+65937	HE	FCC	EVL	FCC	
365504	65897+72247+72246+65938	HE	FCC	EVL	FCC	
365505	65898+72249+72248+65939	HE	FCC	EVL	FCC	
365506	65899+72251+72250+65940	HE	FCC	EVL	FCC	The Royston Express
365507	65900+72253+72252+65941	HE	FCC	EVL	FCC	
365508	65901+72255+72254+65942	HE	FCC	EVL	FCC	
365509	65902+72257+72256+65943	HE	FCC	EVL	FCC	
365510	65903+72259+72258+65944	HE	FCC	EVL	FCC	
365511	65904+72261+72260+65945	HE	FCC	EVL	FCC	
365512	65905+72263+72262+65946	HE	FCC	EVL	FCC	
365513	65906+72265+72264+65947	HE	FCC	EVL	FCC	Hornsey Depot
365514	65907+72267+72266+65948	HE	FCC	EVL	FCC	Captain George Vancouver
365515	65908+72269+72268+65949	HE	FCC	EVL	FCC	
365516	65909+72271+72270+65950	HE	FCC	EVL	FCC	
365517	65910+72273+72272+65951	HE	FCC	EVL	FCC	
365518	65911+72275+72274+65952	HE	FCC	EVL	FCC	The Fenman
365519	65912+72277+72276+65953	HE	FCC	EVL	FCC	
365520	65913+72279+72278+65954	HE	FCC	EVL	FCC	
365521	65914+72281+72280+65955	HE	FCC	EVL	FCC	
365522	65915+72283+72282+65956	HE	FCC	EVL	FCC	
365523	65916+72285+72284+65957	HE	FCC	EVL	FCC	
365524	65917+72287+72286+65958	HE	FCC	EVL	FCC	
365525	65918+72289+72288+65959	HE	FCC	EVL	FCC	
365526(S)	65919+72291+72290+65960	ZN	NSE	EVL	¤	
365527	65920+72293+72292+65961	HE	FCC	EVL	FCC	Robert Stripe Passengers' Champion
365528	65921+72296+72294+65962	HE	FCC	EVL	FCC	
365529	65922+72297+72296+65963	HE	FCC	EVL	FCC	
365530	65923+72299+72298+65964	HE	FCC	EVL	FCC	The Interlink Partnership Promoting Integrated Transport Since 1999
365531	65924+72301+72300+65965	HE	FCC	EVL	FCC	
365532	65925+72303+72302+65966	HE	FCC	EVL	FCC	
365533	65926+72305+72304+65967	HE	FCC	EVL	FCC	
365534	65927+72307+72306+65968	HE	FCC	EVL	FCC	
365535	65928+72309+72308+65969	HE	FCC	EVL	FCC	
365536	65929+72311+72310+65970	HE	FCC	EVL	FCC	
365537	65930+72313+72312+65971	HE	FCC	EVL	FCC	Daniel Edwards (1974-2010) Cambridge Driver
365538	65931+72315+72314+65972	HE	FCC	EVL	FCC	
365539	65932+72317+72316+65973	HE	FCC	EVL	FCC	
365540	65933+72319+72318+65974	HE	FCC	EVL	FCC	
365541	65934+72321+72320+65975	HE	FCC	EVL	FCC	

¤ Set No. 365526 is stored at Wolverton Works with extensive collision damage sustained in the Potters Bar derailment.

Right: *In 2011 a fleet of 40 'Networker Express' Class 365 sets were operated by First Capital Connect on King's Cross line outer suburban services. On 21 July 2009, the 17.26 FCC service from Cambridge to King's Cross passes Welwyn Garden City, led by Class 365 No. 365538.* **Brian Morrison**

Class 377/5
Electrostar

Vehicle Length: (Driving) 66ft 9in (20.40m)	Width: 9ft 2in (2.80m)	
(Inter) 65ft 6in (19.99m)	Horsepower: 2,012hp (1,500kW) (ac), dual voltage sets	
Height: 12ft 4in (3.77m)	Seats (total/car): 20F-221S, 10F-48S/69S/56S/10F-48S	

Number	Formation DMCO(A)+MSO+PTSO+DMCO(B)	Depot	Livery	Owner	Operator
377501	73501+75901+74901+73601	BF	FCC	PTR	FCC *(Sub-lease from Southern)*
377502	73502+75902+74902+73602	BF	FCC	PTR	FCC *(Sub-lease from Southern)*
377503	73503+75903+74903+73603	BF	FCC	PTR	FCC *(Sub-lease from Southern)*
377504	73504+75904+74904+73604	BF	FCC	PTR	FCC *(Sub-lease from Southern)*
377505	73505+75905+74905+73605	BF	FCC	PTR	FCC *(Sub-lease from Southern)*
377506	73506+75906+74906+73606	BF	FCC	PTR	FCC *(Sub-lease from Southern)*
377507	73507+75907+74907+73607	BF	FCC	PTR	FCC *(Sub-lease from Southern)*
377508	73508+75908+74908+73608	BF	FCC	PTR	FCC *(Sub-lease from Southern)*
377509	73509+75909+74909+73609	BF	FCC	PTR	FCC *(Sub-lease from Southern)*
377510	73510+75910+74910+73610	BF	FCC	PTR	FCC *(Sub-lease from Southern)*
377511	73511+75911+74911+73611	BF	FCC	PTR	FCC *(Sub-lease from Southern)*
377512	73512+75912+74912+73612	BF	FCC	PTR	FCC *(Sub-lease from Southern)*
377513	73513+75913+74913+73613	BF	FCC	PTR	FCC *(Sub-lease from Southern)*
377514	73514+75914+74914+73614	BF	FCC	PTR	FCC *(Sub-lease from Southern)*
377515	73515+75915+74915+73615	BF	FCC	PTR	FCC *(Sub-lease from Southern)*
377516	73516+75916+74916+73616	BF	FCC	PTR	FCC *(Sub-lease from Southern)*
377517	73517+75917+74917+73617	BF	FCC	PTR	FCC *(Sub-lease from Southern)*
377518	73518+75918+74918+73618	BF	FCC	PTR	FCC *(Sub-lease from Southern)*
377519	73519+75919+74919+73619	BF	FCC	PTR	FCC *(Sub-lease from Southern)*
377520	73520+75920+74920+73620	BF	FCC	PTR	FCC *(Sub-lease from Southern)*
377521	73521+75921+74921+73621	BF	FCC	PTR	FCC *(Sub-lease from Southern)*
377522	73522+75922+74922+73622	BF	FCC	PTR	FCC *(Sub-lease from Southern)*
377523	73523+75923+74923+73623	BF	FCC	PTR	FCC *(Sub-lease from Southern)*

Below: *Officially on sub-lease from Southern, 23 Class 377/5s are currently operated by First Capital Connect on express services via the Thameslink route. All sets are painted in full FCC livery and allocated to Bedford depot. Following the introduction of new Thameslink stock and upon modernisation of the north-south route through London, these Class 377/5s are scheduled to return to Southern. Set No. 377505 is illustrated passing Harpenden on 18 June 2011.* **Tim Easter**

First Great Western

Address: ✉ Milford House, 1 Milford Street, Swindon, SN1 1HL
✎ fgwfeedback@firstgroup.com
✆ 08457 000125
ⓘ www.firstgreatwestern.co.uk

Managing Director: Mark Hopwood
Franchise Dates: 1 April 2006 - 31 March 2013
Principal Routes: Paddington - Penzance/Paignton, Bristol, Swansea
Thames Valley local lines
Local lines in Bristol, Exeter, Plymouth and Cornwall
Bristol - Weymouth, Portsmouth/Brighton
Depots: Exeter (EX), Old Oak Common (OO), Laira (LA), Landore (LE),
St Philip's Marsh (PM), Penzance (PZ), Reading (RG)
Parent Company: First Group PLC

Class 08

Vehicle Length: 29ft 3in (8.91m)	Engine: English Electric 6K	
Height: 12ft 8⅝in (3.87m)	Horsepower: 400hp (298kW)	
Width: 8ft 6in (2.59m)	Electrical Equipment: English Electric	

Number	Depot	Pool	Livery	Owner	Operator
08410	LA	EFSH	GWG	FGP	FGW
08483	OO	EFSH	GWG	FGP	FGW
08641	LA	EFSH	FGB	FGP	FGW
08644	PZ	EFSH	BLU	FGP	FGW
08645	LA	EFSH	GWG	FGP	FGW
08663(S)	PM	EFSH	GWG	FGP	FGW
08795	LE	EFSH	GWG	FGP	FGW
08822	LE	EFSH	GWG	FGP	FGW
08836	OC	EFSH	GWG	FGP	FGW

Names applied
08483 **Dusty - Driver David Miller**
08645 **Mike Baggott**

Above: *First Great Western currently has an allocation of nine Class 08 shunters on its books; these are based at the sites where HST or loco hauled stock might be required to be re-formed. The locos are air brake fitted and have either hinged or drop head knuckle couplers to provide an easy coupling to buck-eye fitted HST stock. No. 08644 painted in rail blue is seen at Long Rock depot in Penzance, where the resident '08' is frequently used to shunt the formation of the overnight sleeping car train, as well as haul the stock between Long Rock and Penzance station.* **Nathan Williamson**

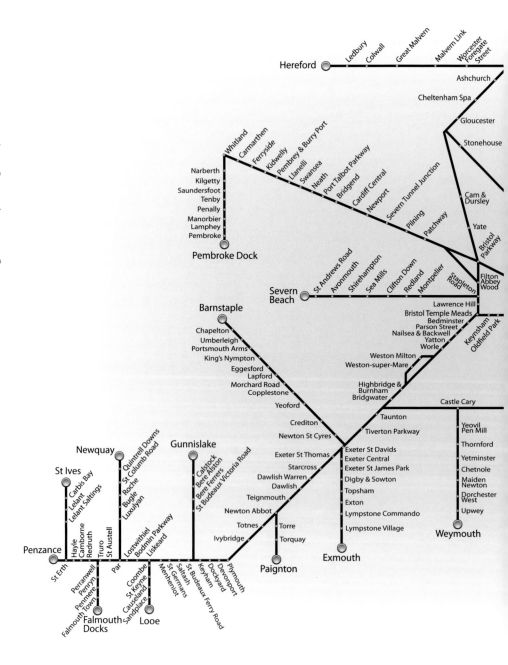

First Great Western

Class 43 – HST

Vehicle Length: 58ft 5in (18.80m)
Height: 12ft 10in (3.90m)
Width: 8ft 11in (2.73m)

Engine: MTU 16V4000 R41R
Horsepower: 2,250hp (1,680kW)
Electrical Equipment: Brush

Number	Depot	Pool	Livery	Owner	Operator		Number	Depot	Pool	Livery	Owner	Operator
43002	LA	EFPC	FGB	ANG	FGW		43134	LE	EFPC	FGB	ANG	FGW
43003	LA	EFPC	FGB	ANG	FGW		43135	LE	EFPC	FGB	ANG	FGW
43004	LA	EFPC	FGB	ANG	FGW		43136	LE	EFPC	FGB	ANG	FGW
43005	LA	EFPC	FGB	ANG	FGW		43137	LE	EFPC	FGB	ANG	FGW
43009	LA	EFPC	FGB	ANG	FGW		43138	LE	EFPC	FGB	ANG	FGW
43010	LA	EFPC	FGB	ANG	FGW		43139	LE	EFPC	FGB	ANG	FGW
43012	LA	EFPC	FGB	ANG	FGW		43140	LE	EFPC	FGB	ANG	FGW
43015	LA	EFPC	FGB	ANG	FGW		43141	LE	EFPC	FGB	ANG	FGW
43016	LA	EFPC	FGB	ANG	FGW		43142	LE	EFPC	FGB	ANG	FGW
43017	LA	EFPC	FGB	ANG	FGW		43143	LE	EFPC	FGB	ANG	FGW
43018	LA	EFPC	FGB	ANG	FGW		43144	LE	EFPC	FGB	ANG	FGW
43020	LA	EFPC	FGB	ANG	FGW		43145	LE	EFPC	FGB	ANG	FGW
43021	LA	EFPC	FGB	ANG	FGW		43146	LE	EFPC	FGB	ANG	FGW
43022	LA	EFPC	FGB	ANG	FGW		43147	LE	EFPC	FGB	ANG	FGW
43023	LA	EFPC	FGB	ANG	FGW		43148	LE	EFPC	FGB	ANG	FGW
43024	LA	EFPC	FGB	ANG	FGW		43149	LE	EFPC	FGB	ANG	FGW
43025	LA	EFPC	FGB	ANG	FGW		43150	LE	EFPC	FGB	ANG	FGW
43026	LA	EFPC	FGB	ANG	FGW		43151	LE	EFPC	FGB	ANG	FGW
43027	LA	EFPC	FGB	ANG	FGW		43152	LE	EFPC	FGB	ANG	FGW
43028	LA	EFPC	FGB	ANG	FGW		43153	OO	EFPC	FGB	FGP	FGW
43029	LA	EFPC	FGB	ANG	FGW		43154	OO	EFPC	FGB	FGP	FGW
43030	LA	EFPC	FGB	ANG	FGW		43155	OO	EFPC	FGB	FGP	FGW
43031	LA	EFPC	FGB	ANG	FGW		43156	OO	EFPC	FGB	PTR	FGW
43032	LA	EFPC	FGB	ANG	FGW		43158	OO	EFPC	FGB	FGP	FGW
43033	LA	EFPC	FGB	ANG	FGW		43159	OO	EFPC	FGB	PTR	FGW
43034	LA	EFPC	FGB	ANG	FGW		43160	OO	EFPC	FGB	PTR	FGW
43035	LA	EFPC	FGB	ANG	FGW		43161	OO	EFPC	FGB	PTR	FGW
43036	LA	EFPC	FGB	ANG	FGW		43162	OO	EFPC	FGB	ANG	FGW
43037	LA	EFPC	FGB	ANG	FGW		43163	OO	EFPC	FGB	ANG	FGW
43040	LA	EFPC	FGB	ANG	FGW		43164	OO	EFPC	FGB	ANG	FGW
43041	OO	EFPC	FGB	ANG	FGW		43165	OO	EFPC	FGB	ANG	FGW
43042	OO	EFPC	FGB	ANG	FGW		43168	OO	EFPC	FGB	ANG	FGW
43053	LE	EFPC	FGB	PTR	FGW		43169	OO	EFPC	FGB	ANG	FGW
43056	LE	EFPC	FGB	PTR	FGW		43170	OO	EFPC	FGB	ANG	FGW
43063	OO	EFPC	FGB	PTR	FGW		43171	OO	EFPC	FGB	ANG	FGW
43069	OO	EFPC	FGB	PTR	FGW		43172	OO	EFPC	FGB	ANG	FGW
43070	OO	EFPC	FGB	PTR	FGW		43174	OO	EFPC	FGB	ANG	FGW
43071	OO	EFPC	FGB	PTR	FGW		43175	OO	EFPC	FGB	ANG	FGW
43078	OO	EFPC	FGB	PTR	FGW		43176	OO	EFPC	FGB	ANG	FGW
43079	OO	EFPC	FGB	PTR	FGW		43177	OO	EFPC	FGB	ANG	FGW
43086	OO	EFPC	FGB	PTR	FGW		43179	OO	EFPC	FGB	ANG	FGW
43087	OO	EFPC	FGB	PTR	FGW		43180	OO	EFPC	FGB	PTR	FGW
43088	OO	EFPC	FGB	PTR	FGW		43181	OO	EFPC	FGB	ANG	FGW
43091	OO	EFPC	FGB	PTR	FGW		43182	OO	EFPC	FGB	ANG	FGW
43092	OO	EFPC	FGB	PTR	FGW		43183	OO	EFPC	FGB	ANG	FGW
43093	OO	EFPC	FGB	PTR	FGW		43185	OO	EFPC	FGB	ANG	FGW
43094	OO	EFPC	FGB	PTR	FGW		43186	OO	EFPC	FGB	ANG	FGW
43097	OO	EFPC	FGB	PTR	FGW		43187	OO	EFPC	FGB	ANG	FGW
43098	OO	EFPC	FGB	PTR	FGW		43188	OO	EFPC	FGB	ANG	FGW
43122	OO	EFPC	FGB	FGP	FGW		43189	OO	EFPC	FGB	ANG	FGW
43124	LE	EFPC	FGB	ANG	FGW		43190	OO	EFPC	FGB	ANG	FGW
43125	LE	EFPC	FGB	ANG	FGW		43191	OO	EFPC	FGB	ANG	FGW
43126	LE	EFPC	FGB	ANG	FGW		43192	OO	EFPC	FGB	ANG	FGW
43127	LE	EFPC	FGB	ANG	FGW		43193	OO	EFPC	FGB	PTR	FGW
43128	LE	EFPC	FGB	ANG	FGW		43194	OO	EFPC	FGB	FGP	FGW
43129	LE	EFPC	FGB	ANG	FGW		43195	OO	EFPC	FGB	PTR	FGW
43130	LE	EFPC	FGB	ANG	FGW		43196	OO	EFPC	FGB	PTR	FGW
43131	LE	EFPC	FGB	ANG	FGW		43197	OO	EFPC	FGB	PTR	FGW
43132	LE	EFPC	FGB	ANG	FGW		43198	OO	EFPC	FGB	FGP	FGW
43133	LE	EFPC	FGB	ANG	FGW							

Names applied

43003	*Isambard Kingdom Brunel*
43004	*First for the Future / First ar gyfer y dyfodol*
43009	*First Transforming Travel*
43020	*MTU Power Passion Partnership*
43021	*David Austin – Cartoonist*
43024	*Great Western Society 1961-2011*
	Didcot Railway Centre
43025	*The Institution of Railway Operators*
43027	*Glorious Devon*
43030	*Christian Lewis Trust*
43033	*Driver Brian Cooper 15 June 1947 – 5 October 1989*
43037	*Penydarren*
43040	*Bristol St Philip's Marsh*
43041	*Meningitis Trust Support for Life*
43053	*University of Worcester*
43056	*Royal British Legion*
43070	*The Corps of Royal Electrical and Mechanical Engineers*
43087	*11 Explosive Ordnance Disposal Regiment Royal Logistic Corps*

43097	*Environment Agency*
43127	*Sir Peter Parker 1924-2002 – Cotswold Line 150*
43132	*We Save the Children - Will You?*
43137	*Newton Abbot 150*
43139	*Driver Stan Martin*
	25 June 1960 – 6 November 2004
43142	*Reading Panel Signal Box 1965 - 2010*
43143	*Stroud 700*
43149	*University of Plymouth*
43156	*Dartington International Summer School*
43160	*Sir Moir Lockhead OBE*
43163	*Exeter Panel Signal Box 21st Anniversary 2009*
43165	*Prince Michael of Kent*
43169	*The National Trust*
43175	*GWR 175th Anniversary*
43179	*Pride of Laira*
43185	*Great Western*
43189	*Railway Heritage Trust*
43198	*Oxfordshire 2007*

Above: *Cast* University of Plymouth *nameplate and coat of arms as carried by No. 43149.* **CJM**

Right: *First Great Western operates by far the largest fleet of HSTs in the UK, with the fleet responsible for all main line services. All power cars are painted in FGW blue livery. No. 43144 is seen at Newport.* **CJM**

Class 57/6

Vehicle Length: 63ft 6in (19.38m)
Height: 12ft 10¹⁄₈in (3.91m)
Width: 9ft 2in (2.79m)
Engine: EMD 645-12E3
Horsepower: 2,500hp (1,860kW)
Electrical Equipment: Brush

Number	Depot	Pool	Livery	Owner	Operator	Name
57602 (47337)	OO	EFOO	FGB	PTR	FGW	*Restormel Castle*
57603 (47349)	OO	EFOO	FGB	PTR	FGW	*Tintagel Castle*
57604 (47209)	OO	EFOO	GWR	PTR	FGW	*Pendennis Castle*
57605 (47206)	OO	EFOO	FGB	PTR	FGW	*Totnes Castle*

Right: *FGW operates four Class 57s, which are deployed on the overnight sleeper services from Paddington to Penzance. If available a Class 57 could be used to power defective HST power cars or HST stock between depots. The FGW Class 57s are painted in standard FGW blue, with the exception of No. 57604 which is painted in mock Great Western green livery. No. 57602 is seen at Totnes on 21 May 2011 hauling power cars Nos. 43020 and 43124 to Laira depot.* **Nathan Williamson**

First Great Western

HST Passenger Fleet

Vehicle Length: 75ft 0in (22.86m)	Width: 8ft 11in (2.71m)
Height: 12ft 9in (3.88m)	Bogie Type: BT10

GN2G - TSRMB *Seating 70S*

Number	Depot	Livery	Owner
40101 (42170)	LA	FGW	PTR
40102 (42223)	LA	FGW	PTR
40103 (42316)	LA	FGW	PTR
40104 (42254)	LA	FGW	PTR
40105 (42084)	LA	FGW	PTR
40106 (42162)	LA	FGW	PTR
40107 (42334)	LA	FGW	PTR
40108 (42314)	LA	FGW	PTR
40109 (42262)	LA	FGW	PTR
40110 (42187)	LA	FGW	PTR
40111 (42248)	LA	FGW	PTR
40112 (42336)	LA	FGW	PTR
40113 (42309)	LA	FGW	PTR
40114 (42086)	LA	FGW	PTR
40115 (42320)	LA	FGW	PTR
40116 (42147)	LA	FGW	PTR
40117 (42249)	LA	FGW	PTR
40118 (42338)	LA	FGW	PTR
40119 (42090)	LA	FGW	PTR

GN1G - TRFB *Seating 23F*

Number	Depot	Livery	Owner
40204	LA	FGW	ANG
40205	LA	FGW	ANG
40207	LA	FGW	ANG
40210	LA	FGW	ANG
40221	LA	FGW	ANG
40231	LA	FGW	ANG

GK1G - TRFB *Seating 17F*

Number	Depot	Livery	Owner
40703	LA	FGW	ANG
40707	LA	FGW	ANG
40710	LA	FGW	ANG
40713	LA	FGW	ANG
40715	LA	FGW	ANG
40716	LA	FGW	ANG
40718	OO	FGW	ANG
40721	LA	FGW	ANG
40722	LA	FGW	ANG
40727	LA	FGW	ANG
40733	LA	FGW	ANG
40734	LA	FGW	ANG
40739	LA	FGW	ANG
40743	LA	FGW	ANG
40752	LA	FGW	ANG
40755	LA	FGW	ANG
40757	LA	FGW	ANG

GL1G - TRFB *Seating 17F*

Number	Depot	Livery	Owner
40801	OO	FGW	PTR
40802	OO	FGW	PTR
40803	OO	FGW	PTR
40806	OO	FGW	PTR
40807	OO	FGW	PTR
40808	OO	FGW	PTR
40809	OO	FGW	PTR
40810	OO	FGW	PTR
40811	OO	FGW	PTR

GN1G - TRB *Seating 23F*

Number	Depot	Livery	Owner
40900	LA	FGW	FGP
40901	LA	FGW	FGP
40902	LA	FGW	FGP
40903	LA	FGW	FGP
40904	LA	FGW	FGP

GH1G - TF *Seating 48F*

Number	Depot	Livery	Owner
41003	LA	FGW	ANG
41004	OO	FGW	ANG
41005	OO	FGW	ANG
41006	OO	FGW	ANG
41007	OO	FGW	ANG
41008	OO	FGW	ANG
41009	LA	FGW	ANG
41010	LA	FGW	ANG
41011	LA	FGW	ANG
41012	LA	FGW	ANG
41015	LA	FGW	ANG
41016	LA	FGW	ANG
41017	OO	FGW	ANG
41018	OO	FGW	ANG
41019	LA	FGW	ANG
41020	LA	FGW	ANG
41021	LA	FGW	ANG
41022	LA	FGW	ANG
41023	LA	FGW	ANG
41024	LA	FGW	ANG
41027	OO	FGW	ANG
41028	OO	FGW	ANG
41029	OO	FGW	ANG
41030	OO	FGW	ANG
41031	LA	FGW	ANG
41032	LA	FGW	ANG
41033	OO	FGW	ANG
41034	OO	FGW	ANG
41037	LA	FGW	ANG
41038	LA	FGW	ANG
41045	LA	FGW	FGP
41051	LA	FGW	ANG
41052	LA	FGW	ANG
41055	OO	FGW	ANG
41056	OO	FGW	ANG
41059	LA	FGW	FGP
41065	OO	FGW	ANG
41081	OO	FGW	PTR
41085	LA	FGW	FGP
41086	LA	FGW	FGP
41089	OO	FGW	ANG
41093	LA	FGW	ANG
41094	LA	FGW	ANG
41096	LA	FGW	PTR
41101	OO	FGW	ANG
41102	OO	FGW	ANG
41103	LA	FGW	ANG
41104	LA	FGW	ANG
41105	OO	FGW	ANG
41106	OO	FGW	ANG
41108	OO	FGW	PTR
41109	OO	FGW	PTR
41110	OO	FGW	ANG
41114	LA	FGW	FGP
41116	LA	FGW	ANG
41119	OO	FGW	PTR
41121	LA	FGW	ANG
41122	LA	FGW	ANG
41123	LA	FGW	ANG
41124	LA	FGW	ANG
41125	OO	FGW	ANG
41126	OO	FGW	ANG

Number	Depot	Livery	Owner
41127	OO	FGW	ANG
41128	OO	FGW	ANG
41129	LA	FGW	ANG
41130	LA	FGW	ANG
41131	OO	FGW	ANG
41132	OO	FGW	ANG
41133	LA	FGW	ANG
41134	OO	FGW	ANG
41135	LA	FGW	ANG
41136	LA	FGW	ANG
41137	OO	FGW	ANG
41138	OO	FGW	ANG
41139	OO	FGW	ANG
41140	OO	FGW	ANG
41141	LA	FGW	ANG
41142	LA	FGW	ANG
41143	LA	FGW	ANG
41144	LA	FGW	ANG
41145	LA	FGW	ANG
41146	LA	FGW	ANG
41147	OO	FGW	PTR
41148	OO	FGW	PTR
41149	OO	FGW	PTR
41153	OO	FGW	PTR
41155	OO	FGW	PTR
41157	LA	FGW	ANG
41158	LA	FGW	ANG
41160	LA	FGW	FGP
41161	OO	FGW	PTR
41162	LA	FGW	FGP
41163	LA	FGW	FGP
41166	LA	FGW	FGP
41167	LA	FGW	FGP
41168	OO	FGW	PTR
41169	OO	FGW	PTR
41176	OO	FGW	PTR
41179	OO	FGW	ANG
41180	OO	FGW	ANG
41181	OO	FGW	PTR
41182	OO	FGW	PTR
41183	OO	FGW	PTR
41184	OO	FGW	PTR
41186	OO	FGW	PTR
41187	OO	FGW	PTR
41189	OO	FGW	PTR
41191	OO	FGW	PTR
41192	OO	FGW	PTR

GH2G - TS *Seating 68-84S*

Number	Depot	Livery	Owner
42003	OO	FGW	ANG
42004	LA	FGW	ANG
42005 ●	LA	FGW	ANG
42006	LA	FGW	ANG
42007	LA	FGW	ANG
42008	OO	FGW	ANG
42009	LA	FGW	ANG
42010 ●	LA	FGW	ANG
42012	LA	FGW	ANG
42013	LA	FGW	ANG
42014	LA	FGW	ANG
42015	LA	FGW	ANG
42016	LA	FGW	ANG
42019 ●	LA	FGW	ANG
42021	LA	FGW	ANG
42023	LA	FGW	ANG
42024	OO	FGW	ANG

42025	OO	FGW	ANG	42138	OO	FGW	ANG	42275	LA	FGW	ANG
42026	OO	FGW	ANG	42143	LA	FGW	ANG	42276	LA	FGW	ANG
42027	OO	FGW	ANG	42144	LA	FGW	ANG	42277	LA	FGW	ANG
42028	LA	FGW	ANG	42145	LA	FGW	ANG	42279	LA	FGW	ANG
42029	LA	FGW	ANG	42166 ●	OO	FGW	PTR	42280	LA	FGW	ANG
42030	LA	FGW	ANG	42167	LA	FGW	FGP	42281	LA	FGW	ANG
42031	LA	FGW	ANG	42168 ●	LA	FGW	FGP	42283	OO	FGW	ANG
42032	LA	FGW	ANG	42169	LA	FGW	FGP	42284	OO	FGW	ANG
42033 ●	LA	FGW	ANG	42173	OO	FGW	PTR	42285	OO	FGW	ANG
42034	LA	FGW	ANG	42174	OO	FGW	PTR	42287	OO	FGW	ANG
42035	LA	FGW	ANG	42175	LA	FGW	FGP	42288	OO	FGW	ANG
42039 ●	OO	FGW	ANG	42176 ●	LA	FGW	FGP	42289	OO	FGW	ANG
42040	OO	FGW	ANG	42177	LA	FGW	FGP	42291	LA	FGW	ANG
42041	OO	FGW	ANG	42178 ●	OO	FGW	PTR	42292	LA	FGW	ANG
42042 ●	OO	FGW	ANG	42183	LA	FGW	ANG	42293	LA	FGW	ANG
42043	OO	FGW	ANG	42184 ●	LA	FGW	ANG	42294	OO	FGW	PTR
42044	OO	FGW	ANG	42185	LA	FGW	ANG	42295	LA	FGW	ANG
42045 ●	LA	FGW	ANG	42195	OO	FGW	PTR	42296	LA	FGW	ANG
42046	LA	FGW	ANG	42196	OO	FGW	ANG	42297	LA	FGW	ANG
42047	LA	FGW	ANG	42197 ●	OO	FGW	ANG	42299	LA	FGW	ANG
42048 ●	OO	FGW	ANG	42200	LA	FGW	ANG	42300	LA	FGW	ANG
42049	OO	FGW	ANG	42201	OO	FGW	ANG	42301	LA	FGW	ANG
42050	OO	FGW	ANG	42202	OO	FGW	ANG	42302	LA	FGW	FGP
42054 ●	LA	FGW	ANG	42203	OO	FGW	ANG	42303 ●	LA	FGW	FGP
42055	LA	FGW	ANG	42204	OO	FGW	ANG	42304	LA	FGW	FGP
42056	LA	FGW	ANG	42206	LA	FGW	ANG	42305	LA	FGW	FGP
42060	OO	FGW	ANG	42207	LA	FGW	ANG	42308 ●	OO	FGW	PTR
42061	OO	FGW	ANG	42208	LA	FGW	ANG	42310	OO	FGW	PTR
42062	OO	FGW	ANG	42209	LA	FGW	ANG	42315 ●	OO	FGW	PTR
42066	OO	FGW	ANG	42211	OO	FGW	ANG	42317	OO	FGW	PTR
42067	OO	FGW	ANG	42212 ●	OO	FGW	ANG	42319 ●	OO	FGW	PTR
42068	OO	FGW	ANG	42213	OO	FGW	ANG	42321	OO	FGW	PTR
42069	OO	FGW	ANG	42214	OO	FGW	ANG	42325 ●	LA	FGW	ANG
42070 ●	OO	FGW	ANG	42216 ●	OO	FGW	ANG	42332 ●	LA	FGW	ANG
42071	OO	FGW	ANG	42217	OO	FGW	PTR	42333	LA	FGW	ANG
42072	LA	FGW	ANG	42218	OO	FGW	PTR	42343 ●	LA	FGW	ANG
42073 ●	OO	FGW	ANG	42221 ●	OO	FGW	ANG	42344	OO	FGW	ANG
42074 ●	OO	FGW	ANG	42222 ●	OO	FGW	PTR	42345	LA	FGW	ANG
42075 ●	LA	FGW	ANG	42224	OO	FGW	PTR	42346	OO	FGW	ANG
42076 ●	LA	FGW	ANG	42231	LA	FGW	FGP	42347	OO	FGW	ANG
42077	LA	FGW	ANG	42232 ●	LA	FGW	FGP	42348	OO	FGW	ANG
42078	LA	FGW	ANG	42233	LA	FGW	FGP	42349 ●	OO	FGW	ANG
42079	OO	FGW	ANG	42236 ●	OO	FGW	ANG	42350 ●	LA	FGW	ANG
42080	OO	FGW	ANG	42245	LA	FGW	ANG	42351 ●	LA	FGW	ANG
42081	OO	FGW	ANG	42247 ●	OO	FGW	PTR	42353	LA	FGW	FGP
42083	OO	FGW	ANG	42250	LA	FGW	ANG	42356	OO	FGW	ANG
42085 ●	OO	FGW	ANG	42251	OO	FGW	ANG	42360 ●	LA	FGW	ANG
42087	OO	FGW	ANG	42252	LA	FGW	ANG	42361	LA	FGW	ANG
42089	OO	FGW	ANG	42253	LA	FGW	ANG	42362 ●	OO	FGW	ANG
42092	LA	FGW	FGP	42255	LA	FGW	ANG	42364	OO	FGW	PTR
42093	LA	FGW	FGP	42256	LA	FGW	ANG	42365	OO	FGW	PTR
42094	LA	FGW	FGP	42257	LA	FGW	ANG	42381 (41058)	OO	FGW	PTR
42095	LA	FGW	FGP	42258 ●	OO	FGW	PTR	42382 (12128)	OO	FGW	PTR
42096 ●	LA	FGW	ANG	42259	LA	FGW	ANG	42383 (12172)	OO	FGW	PTR
42098 ●	OO	FGW	ANG	42260	OO	FGW	ANG	42xxx (40208)		FGW	ANG
42099	OO	FGW	ANG	42261	OO	FGW	ANG	42xxx (40209)		FGW	ANG
42101	OO	FGW	PTR	42263 ●	LA	FGW	ANG	42xxx (40228)		FGW	ANG
42102	OO	FGW	PTR	42264	OO	FGW	ANG	42xxx (40709)		FGW	ANG
42103	LA	FGW	FGP	42265 ●	LA	FGW	ANG	42xxx (40712)		FGW	ANG
42105	LA	FGW	FGP	42266	OO	FGW	PTR	42xxx (40714)		FGW	ANG
42107	LA	FGW	ANG	42267	LA	FGW	ANG	42xxx (40717)		FGW	ANG
42108	LA	FGW	FGP	42268	LA	FGW	ANG	42xxx (40724)		FGW	ANG
42115 ●	OO	FGW	PTR	42269	LA	FGW	ANG	42xxx (40725)		FGW	ANG
42118	OO	FGW	ANG	42271	OO	FGW	ANG	42xxx (40726)		FGW	ANG
42126	OO	FGW	ANG	42272	OO	FGW	ANG	42xxx (40731)		FGW	ANG
42129 ●	LA	FGW	ANG	42273	OO	FGW	ANG	42xxx (40736)		FGW	ANG

First Great Western

42xxx (40738)		FGW	ANG
42xxx (40744)		FGW	ANG
42xxx (40747)		FGW	ANG

● Volo Television fitted

GJ2G - TGS *Seating 67-71S*

Number	Depot	Livery	Owner
44000	OO	FGW	PTR
44001	LA	FGW	ANG
44002	OO	FGW	ANG
44003	OO	FGW	ANG
44004	LA	FGW	ANG
44005	LA	FGW	ANG
44007	LA	FGW	ANG
44008	OO	FGW	ANG
44009	LA	FGW	ANG
44010	LA	FGW	ANG
44011	LA	FGW	ANG
44013	OO	FGW	ANG
44014	OO	FGW	ANG
44015	LA	FGW	ANG
44016	OO	FGW	ANG
44018	LA	FGW	ANG
44020	OO	FGW	ANG
44022	OO	FGW	ANG
44023	OO	FGW	ANG
44024	OO	FGW	ANG
44025	LA	FGW	ANG
44026	OO	FGW	ANG
44028	LA	FGW	ANG
44029	LA	FGW	ANG
44030	OO	FGW	ANG
44032	LA	FGW	ANG
44033	OO	FGW	ANG
44034	LA	FGW	ANG
44035	LA	FGW	ANG
44036	OO	FGW	ANG
44037	OO	FGW	ANG
44038	LA	FGW	ANG
44039	LA	FGW	ANG
44040	LA	FGW	ANG
44042	OO	FGW	PTR
44043	OO	FGW	ANG
44049	LA	FGW	ANG
44055	LA	FGW	FGP
44059	LA	FGW	ANG
44060	OO	FGW	PTR
44064	OO	FGW	ANG
44066	LA	FGW	ANG
44067	OO	FGW	ANG
44068	LA	FGW	FGP
44069	OO	FGW	PTR
44074	LA	FGW	FGP
44076	LA	FGW	FGP
44078	OO	FGW	PTR
44079	OO	FGW	PTR
44081	LA	FGW	FGP
44083	OO	FGW	PTR
44086	LA	FGW	ANG
44090	OO	FGW	PTR
44091	OO	FGW	PTR
44093	OO	FGW	ANG
44097	OO	FGW	PTR
44100	LA	FGW	FGP
44101	OO	FGW	PTR

Left: *The entire First Great Western Mk3 passenger fleet are painted in FGW blue with 'dynamic lines' branding. Viewed from its kitchen end, non-corridor side, TRFB No. 40757 is illustrated in a Paddington to Swansea formation at Newport in July 2011. The FGW HST fleet are usually formed of two first class vehicles at the London end, followed by the catering vehicle and standard class coaches.* **CJM**

Class 143

Vehicle Length: 51ft 0½in (15.55m)
Height: 12ft 2¼in (3.73m)
Width: 8ft 10½in (2.70m)

Engine: 1 x Cummins LTA10-R per vehicle
Horsepower: 460hp (343kW)
Seats (total/car): 92S, 48S/44S

Number	Formation DMS+DMSL	Depot	Livery	Owner	Operator
143603	55658+55689	EX	FGL	PTR	FGW
143611	55652+55677	EX	FGL	PTR	FGW
143612	55653+55678	EX	FGL	PTR	FGW
143617	55644+55683	EX	FGL	PTR	FGW
143618	55659+55684	EX	FGL	PTR	FGW
143619	55660+55685	EX	FGL	PTR	FGW
143620	55661+55686	EX	FGL	PTR	FGW
143621	55662+55687	EX	FGL	PTR	FGW

Left: *Eight Class 143 'Pacer' sets are based at Exeter depot to operate Devon branch line services. The fleet are fully refurbished and sport First Great Western 'local lines' livery with place names, businesses and structures applied on the bodyside in FGW 'dynamic lines' style. Set No. 143619 is seen departing from Dawlish in summer 2011 with an Exmouth to Paignton local service.* **CJM**

Class 150/0

Vehicle Length: (Driving) 65ft 9¾in (20.05m), (Inter) 66ft 2½in (20.18m)
Height: 12ft 4½in (3.77m) Engine: 1 x Cummins NT855R4 of 285hp per car
Width: 9ft 3⅛in (2.82m) Horsepower: 855hp (638kW)
Seats (total/car): 240S, 72S/92S/76S

Number	Formation DMSL+MS+DMS	Depot	Livery	Owner	Operator
150001	55200+55400+55300	RG	CTL	ANG	FGW
150002	55201+55401+55301	RG	CTL	ANG	FGW

Class 150/1

Vehicle Length: 64ft 9¾in (19.74m) Engine: 1 x NT855R5 of 285hp per vehicle
Height: 12ft 4½in (3.77m) Horsepower: 570hp (425kW)
Width: 9ft 3⅛in (2.82m) Seats (total/car): 141S, 71S/70S

Number	Formation DMSL+DMS	Depot	Livery	Owner	Operator
150101	52101+57101	PM	CTL	PTR	FGW
150102	52102+57102	PM	CTL	PTR	FGW
150104	52104+57104	PM	CTL	PTR	FGW
150106	52106+57106	PM	CTL	PTR	FGW
150108	52108+57108	PM	CTL	PTR	FGW
150120	52120+57120	EX	FGB	PTR	FGW
150121	52121+57121	EX	FGB	PTR	FGW
150122	52122+57122	PM	CTL	PTR	FGW
150123	52123+57123	PM	FGB	PTR	FGW
150124	52124+57124	PM	CTL	PTR	FGW
150125	52125+57125	PM	CTL	PTR	FGW
150126	52126+57126	PM	FGB	PTR	FGW
150127	52127+57127	EX	FGB	PTR	FGW
150128	52128+57128	PM	FGB	PTR	FGW
150129	52129+57129	EX	FGB	PTR	FGW
150130	52130+57130	PM	FGB	PTR	FGW
150131	52130+57130	EX	FGB	PTR	FGW

Names applied
150129 *Devon & Cornwall Rail*
Partnership
150130 *Severnside Community*
Rail Partnership

Right: *From the end of 2011 a fleet of 17 Class 150/1 non-gangwayed two-car sets were allocated to FGW for Devon and Cornwall local line use. These sets will soon all be painted in FGW blue livery, off-set by pink passenger doors. The sets retain 2+3 high-density seating. Set No. 150131 is seen from its DMS end.* **Antony Christie**

Class 150/2

Vehicle Length: 64ft 9¾in (19.74m) Engine: 1 x NT855R5 of 285hp per vehicle
Height: 12ft 4½in (3.77m) Horsepower: 570hp (425kW)
Width: 9ft 3⅛in (2.82m) Seats (total/car): 116S, 60S/56S

Number	Formation DMSL+DMS	Depot	Livery	Owner	Operator
150202	52202+57202	PM	CTL	ANG	FGW
150209§	57209+57212	EX	CTL	ANG	FGW
150216	52216+57216	PM	CTL	ANG	FGW
150219	52219+57219	PM	FGL	PTR	FGW
150221	52221+57221	PM	FGL	PTR	FGW
150232	52232+57232	EX	FGL	PTR	FGW
150233	52233+57233	PM	FGL	PTR	FGW
150234	52234+57234	PM	FGL	PTR	FGW
150238	52238+57238	PM	FGL	PTR	FGW
150239	52239+57239	PM	FGL	PTR	FGW
150243	52243+57243	PM	FGL	PTR	FGW
150244	52244+57244	PM	FGL	PTR	FGW
150246	52246+57246	PM	FGL	PTR	FGW
150247	52247+57247	PM	FGL	PTR	FGW
150248	52248+57248	PM	FGL	PTR	FGW
150249	52249+57249	PM	FGL	PTR	FGW
150261	52261+57261	PM	FGL	PTR	FGW
150263	52263+57263	PM	FGL	PTR	FGW
150265	52265+57265	PM	FGL	PTR	FGW
150266	52266+57266	PM	FGL	PTR	FGW

§ Set 150209 usually operates coupled to a Class 153; the 150 vehicles do not have toilet facilities.

Right: *Fleet changes in 2011 now see FGW with 19 Class 150/2 corridor-fitted 'Sprinter' sets in use. They are painted in FGW 'local lines' livery. Set No. 150249 is recorded near Ivybridge.* **Antony Christie**

First Great Western

Passenger Train Operating Companies - First Great Western

Class 153

Vehicle Length: 76ft 5in (23.29m)		Engine: 1 x NT855R5 of 285hp	
Height: 12ft 3⅛in (3.75m)		Horsepower: 285hp (213kW)	
Width: 8ft 10in (2.70m)		Seats (total/car): 72S	

Number	Formation DMSL	Depot	Livery	Owner	Operator
153305	52305	EX	FGL	ANG	FGW
153318	52318	EX	FGL	ANG	FGW
153329	52329	EX	FGL	ANG	FGW
153325	52325	EX	LMI	PTR	FGW
153333	52333	EX	LMI	PTR	FGW
153361	57361	EX	FGL	ANG	FGW
153368	57368	EX	FGL	ANG	FGW
153369	57369	EX	FGL	ANG	FGW
153370	57370	EX	FGL	ANG	FGW
153372	57372	EX	FGL	ANG	FGW
153373	57373	EX	FGL	ANG	FGW
153377	57377	EX	FGL	ANG	FGW
153380	57380	EX	FGL	ANG	FGW
153382	57382	EX	FGL	ANG	FGW

Left: First Great Western's Exeter depot is also the home to 14 single-car Class 153 units, rebuilt many years ago from two-car Class 155 sets. The '153s' are used on branch line services throughout Devon and Cornwall, frequently to strengthen two-car formations at busy periods. Sets frequently operate in pairs to provide accommodation in line with Class 150/2 or even 158 stock. All vehicles are painted in FGW 'local lines' livery. A two-car formation of '153' stock approaches Aller, west of Newton Abbot with a Penzance-bound train led by vehicle No. 153305.
Antony Christie

Class 158/0 (2-car)

Vehicle Length: 76ft 1¾in (23.21m)		Engine: 1 x Cummins NTA855R of 350hp per vehicle	
Height: 12ft 6in (3.81m)		Horsepower: 700hp (522kW)	
Width: 9ft 3¼in (2.82m)		Seats (total/car): 134S, 66S/68S	

Number	Formation DMSL+DMSL	Depot	Livery	Owner	Operator
158763	52763+57763	PM	FGL	PTR	FGW
158766	52766+57766	PM	FGL	PTR	FGW

Class 158/0 (3-car)

158798

Vehicle Length: 76ft 1¾in (23.21m)		Engine: 1 x Cummins NTA855R of 350hp per vehicle	
Height: 12ft 6in (3.81m)		Horsepower: 1,050hp (783kW)	
Width: 9ft 3¼in (2.82m)		Seats (total/car): 200S, 66S/66S/68S	

158950 - 158959

Vehicle Length: 76ft 1¾in (23.21m)		Engine: 1 x Cummins NTA855R of 350hp per vehicle	
Height: 12ft 6in (3.81m)		Horsepower: 1,050hp (783kW)	
Width: 9ft 3¼in (2.82m)		Seats (total/car): 204S, 66S/70S/68S	

Number	Formation DMSL+MSL+DMSL	Depot	Livery	Owner	Operator
158798	52798+58715+57798	PM	FGL	PTR	FGW

Number	Formation DMSL+DMSL+DMSL		Depot	Livery	Owner	Operator
158950	(158751/761)	57751+52761+57761	PM	FGL	PTR	FGW
158951	(158751/764)	52751+52764+57764	PM	FGL	PTR	FGW
158952	(158745/762)	57745+52762+57762	PM	FGL	PTR	FGW
158953	(158745/750)	52745+52750+57750	PM	FGL	PTR	FGW
158954	(158747/760)	57747+52760+57760	PM	FGL	PTR	FGW
158955	(158747/765)	52747+52765+57765	PM	FGL	PTR	FGW
158956	(158748/768)	57748+52768+57768	PM	FGL	PTR	FGW
158957	(158748/771)	52748+52771+57771	PM	FGL	PTR	FGW
158958	(158746/776)	57746+52776+57776	PM	FGL	PTR	FGW
158959	(158746/778)	52746+52778+57778	PM	FGL	PTR	FGW
158960	(158769/749)	57769+52769+57749	PM	FGL	PTR	FGW
158961	(158767/749)	57767+52767+52749	PM	FGL	PTR	FGW

Right: *To provide extra accommodation on longer First Great Western 'local lines' services, such as Cardiff/Bristol to Portsmouth Harbour, a batch of Class 158 two-car sets have been strengthened to three-car formation by adding a single '158' car at one end. As the sets are fully gangwayed no access restrictions are imposed. Three-car set No. 158957 is seen at Southampton forming a Bristol to Portsmouth service in July 2011. This unit is formed of set No. 158771 plus one car from 158748.* **CJM**

Class 165/1 (3-car)
Networker Turbo

Vehicle Length: (Driving) 75ft 2½in (22.91m), (Inter) 74ft 6½in (22.72m)
Height: 12ft 5¼in (3.79m) Engine: 1 x Perkins 2006TWH of 350hp
Width: 9ft 5½in (2.81m) Horsepower: 1,050hp (783kW)
Seats (total/car): 16F/270S, 16F-66S/106S/98S

Number	Formation DMCL+MS+DMS	Depot	Livery	Owner	Operator
165101	58953+55415+58916	RG	FGT	ANG	FGW
165102	58954+55416+58917	RG	FGT	ANG	FGW
165103	58955+55417+58918	RG	FGT	ANG	FGW
165104	58956+55418+58919	RG	FGT	ANG	FGW
165105	58957+55419+58920	RG	FGT	ANG	FGW
165106	58958+55420+58921	RG	FGT	ANG	FGW
165107	58959+55421+58922	RG	FGT	ANG	FGW
165108	58960+55422+58923	RG	FGT	ANG	FGW
165109	58961+55423+58924	RG	FGT	ANG	FGW
165110	58962+55424+58925	RG	FGT	ANG	FGW
165111	58963+55425+58926	RG	FGT	ANG	FGW
165112	58964+55426+58927	RG	FGT	ANG	FGW
165113	58965+55427+58928	RG	FGT	ANG	FGW
165114	58966+55428+58929	RG	FGT	ANG	FGW
165116	58968+55430+58931	RG	FGT	ANG	FGW
165117	58969+55431+58932	RG	FGT	ANG	FGW

Right: *Under the Network SouthEast modernisation of Thames lines, a sizeable fleet of 'Networker Turbo' Class 165 sets were introduced to replace heritage DMU stock on Paddington local services. The first 17 sets of Class 165/1 were three-car sets. Set No. 165116 is seen at Reading. All Class 165s are painted in FGW 'dynamic lines' livery and are allocated to Reading. Only 16 sets remain in operation; set No. 165115 was destroyed in the Ladbroke Grove collision.* **Antony Christie**

Class 165/1 (2-car)
Networker Turbo

Vehicle Length: 75ft 2½in (22.91m) Engine: 1 x Perkins 2006TWH of 350hp per car
Height: 12ft 5¼in (3.79m) Horsepower: 700hp (522kW)
Width: 9ft 5½in (2.81m) Seats (total/car): 16F/170S, 16F-72S/98S

Number	Formation DMCL+DMS	Depot	Livery	Owner	Operator
165118	58879+58933	RG	FGT	ANG	FGW
165119	58880+58934	RG	FGT	ANG	FGW
165120	58881+58935	RG	FGT	ANG	FGW
165121	58882+58936	RG	FGT	ANG	FGW
165122	58883+58937	RG	FGT	ANG	FGW
165123	58884+58938	RG	FGT	ANG	FGW
165124	58885+58939	RG	FGT	ANG	FGW
165125	58886+58940	RG	FGT	ANG	FGW
165126	58887+58941	RG	FGT	ANG	FGW
165127	58888+58942	RG	FGT	ANG	FGW

Passenger Train Operating Companies - First Great Western

First Great Western

165128	58889+58943	RG	FGT	ANG	FGW		165133	58894+58948	RG	FGT	ANG	FGW
165129	58890+58944	RG	FGT	ANG	FGW		165134	58895+58949	RG	FGT	ANG	FGW
165130	58891+58945	RG	FGT	ANG	FGW		165135	58896+58950	RG	FGT	ANG	FGW
165131	58892+58946	RG	FGT	ANG	FGW		165136	58897+58951	RG	FGT	ANG	FGW
165132	58893+58947	RG	FGT	ANG	FGW		165137	58898+58952	RG	FGT	ANG	FGW

Left: *As part of the 'Networker Turbo' order, 20 two-car Class 165/1s were obtained for London area Western Region services. Viewed from its first class end (DMCL) set No. 165137 is seen at Reading. Each two-car Class 165 seats 16 first and 170 standard class passengers.*
Nathan Williamson

Class 166
Networker Turbo Express

Vehicle Length: (Driving) 75ft 2½in (22.91m), (Inter) 74ft 6½in (22.72m)
Height: 12ft 5¼in (3.79m)   Engine: 1 x Perkins 2006TWH of 350hp per car
Width: 9ft 5½in (2.81m)   Horsepower: 1,050hp (783kW)
                              Seats (total/car): 32F/243S, 16F-75S/96S/16F-72S

Number	Formation DMCL(A)+MS+DMCL(B)	Depot	Livery	Owner	Operator
166201	58101+58601+58122	RG	FGT	ANG	FGW
166202	58102+58602+58123	RG	FGT	ANG	FGW
166203	58103+58603+58124	RG	FGT	ANG	FGW
166204	58104+58604+58125	RG	FGT	ANG	FGW
166205	58105+58605+58126	RG	FGT	ANG	FGW
166206	58106+58606+58127	RG	FGT	ANG	FGW
166207	58107+58607+58128	RG	FGT	ANG	FGW
166208	58108+58608+58129	RG	FGT	ANG	FGW
166209	58109+58609+58130	RG	FGT	ANG	FGW
166210	58110+58610+58131	RG	FGT	ANG	FGW
166211	58111+58611+58132	RG	FGT	ANG	FGW
166212	58112+58612+58133	RG	FGT	ANG	FGW
166213	58113+58613+58134	RG	FGT	ANG	FGW
166214	58114+58614+58135	RG	FGT	ANG	FGW
166215	58115+58615+58136	RG	FGT	ANG	FGW
166216	58116+58616+58137	RG	FGT	ANG	FGW
166217	58117+58617+58138	RG	FGT	ANG	FGW
166218	58118+58618+58139	RG	FGT	ANG	FGW
166219	58119+58619+58140	RG	FGT	ANG	FGW
166220	58120+58620+58141	RG	FGT	ANG	FGW
166221	58121+58621+58142	RG	FGT	ANG	FGW

Left: *As part of the 'Networker Turbo' order, a batch of 21 'Networker Turbo Express' sets were required for longer distance services, these were fitted with air conditioning and slightly improved interiors. The vehicles were immediately distinguishable from 165 stock by the mix of solid and quarter light fitted body side windows. All sets are allocated to Reading and carry standard First Great Western 'dynamic lines' livery. Set No. 166207 is illustrated at Oxford.* **Ron Cover**

Class 180
Adelante

Vehicle Length: (Driving) 75ft 7in (23.71m), (Inter) 75ft 5in (23.03m)
Height: 12ft 4in (3.75m)   Engine: 1 x Cummins QSK19 of 750hp per car
Width: 9ft 2in (2.80m)   Horsepower: 3,750hp (2,796kW)
Seats (total/car): 42F/226S, 46S/42F/68S/56S/56S

Number	Formation DMSL(A)+MFL+MSL+MSLRB+DMSL(B)	Depot	Livery	Owner	Operator
180102	50902+54902+55902+56902+59902	OO	FST	ANG	FGW (To be introduced 2012)
180103	50903+54903+55903+56903+59903	OO	FST	ANG	FGW (To be introduced 2012)
180104	50904+54904+55904+56904+59904	OO	FST	ANG	FGW (To be introduced 2012)
180106	50906+54906+55906+56906+59906	OO	FST	ANG	FGW (To be introduced 2012)
180108	50908+54908+55908+56908+59908	OO	FST	ANG	FGW (To be introduced 2012)

Right: From early 2012 First Great Western will be getting back five Class 180 'Adelante' five-car Alstom-built sets for use on the Paddington to Worcester corridor. The sets are likely to be fully refurbished before entering traffic with new seats, interior layout and full FGW livery. Set No. 180102 is seen when working on the Great Western route in 2004. **CJM**

Mk3 Hauled Stock

Vehicle Length: 75ft 0in (22.86m)   Width: 8ft 11in (2.71m)
Height: 12ft 9in (3.88m)   Bogie Type: BT10

AJ1G - RFB Seating 18F

Number	Depot	Livery	Owner
10219	PZ	FGW	PTR
10225	PZ	FGW	PTR
10232	PZ	FGW	PTR

AU4G - SLEP Comps 12

Number	Depot	Livery	Owner
10532	PZ	FGW	PTR
10534	PZ	FGW	PTR
10563	PZ	FGW	PTR

10584	PZ	FGW	PTR
10589	PZ	FGW	PTR
10590	PZ	FGW	PTR
10594	PZ	FGW	PTR
10601	PZ	FGW	PTR
10612	PZ	FGW	PTR
10616	PZ	FGW	PTR

AC2G - TSO Seating 45S

Number	Depot	Livery	Owner
12100	PZ	FGW	PTR

12161	PZ	FGW	PTR

AE1H - BFO Seating 36F

Number	Depot	Livery	Owner
17173	PZ	FGW	PTR
17174	PZ	FGW	PTR
17175	PZ	FGW	PTR

Right: A total of 18 Mk3 vehicles make up the First Great Western 'Night Riviera' fleet based at Long Rock, Penzance. All vehicles carry full FGW livery with the additional bodyside branding 'Night Riviera Sleeper'. All day vehicles have first class design 2+1 seating. 45-seat TSO No. 12161 is seen in a daytime stock transfer move passing Totnes. **Nathan Williamson**

Service Stock

HST Barrier Vehicles

Number	Depot	Livery	Owner	Former Identity					
6330	PM	FGB	ANG	BFK - 14084	6338	LA	FGB	ANG	BG - 81581/92180
6336	LA	FGB	ANG	BG - 81591/92185	6348	PM	FGB	ANG	BG - 81233/92963

Passenger Train Operating Companies - First ScotRail

First ScotRail

Address:	✉ Atrium Court, 50 Waterloo Street, Glasgow, G2 6HQ
	✎ scotrail.enquiries@firstgroup.com
	☎ 08700 005151
	ⓘ www.firstscotrail.com
Managing Director:	Steve Montgomery
Franchise Dates:	17 October 2004 - 30 November 2014
Principal Routes:	All Scottish services, plus ScotRail sleeper services
Depots:	Corkerhill (CK), Glasgow Shields Road (GW), Haymarket (HA), Inverness (IS)
Parent Company:	First Group PLC

Class 156

Vehicle Length: 75ft 6in (23.03m)
Height: 12ft 6in (3.81m)
Width: 8ft 11in (2.73m)
Engine: 1 x Cummins NT855R5 of 285hp
Horsepower: 570hp (425kW)
Seats (total/car): 142S, 70 or 72S

Number	Formation DMSL+DMS	Depot	Livery	Owner	Operator
156430	52430+57430	CK	FSS	ANG	FSR
156431	52431+57431	CK	FSS	ANG	FSR
156432	52432+57432	CK	FSS	ANG	FSR
156433	52433+57433	CK	FSS	ANG	FSR
156434	52434+57434	CK	FSS	ANG	FSR
156435	52435+57435	CK	FSS	ANG	FSR
156436	52436+57436	CK	FSS	ANG	FSR
156437	52437+57437	CK	FSS	ANG	FSR
156439	52439+57439	CK	FSS	ANG	FSR
156442	52442+57442	CK	FSS	ANG	FSR
156445	52445+57445	CK	FSS	ANG	FSR
156446	52446+57446	CK	FSR	ANG	FSR
156447	52447+57447	CK	FSR	ANG	FSR
156449	52449+57449	CK	FSR	ANG	FSR
156450	52450+57450	CK	FSR	ANG	FSR
156453	52453+57453	CK	FSR	ANG	FSR
156456	52456+57456	CK	FSR	ANG	FSR
156457	52457+57457	CK	FSR	ANG	FSR
156458	52458+57458	CK	FSR	ANG	FSR
156462	52462+57462	CK	FSR	ANG	FSR
156465	52465+57465	CK	FSR	ANG	FSR
156467	52467+57467	CK	FSR	ANG	FSR
156474	52474+57474	CK	FSR	ANG	FSR
156476	52476+57476	CK	FSR	ANG	FSR
156477	52477+57477	CK	FSR	ANG	FSR
156478	52478+57478	CK	FSR	ANG	FSR
156485	52485+57485	CK	FSR	ANG	FSR
156492	52492+57492	CK	FSR	ANG	FSR
156493	52493+57493	CK	FSR	ANG	FSR
156494	52494+57494	CK	FSS	ANG	FSR
156495	52495+57495	CK	FSS	ANG	FSR
156496	52496+57496	CK	FSS	ANG	FSR
156499	52499+57499	CK	FSR	ANG	FSR
156500	52500+57500	CK	FSR	ANG	FSR
156501	52501+57501	CK	FSS	ANG	FSR
156502	52502+57502	CK	FSS	ANG	FSR
156503	52503+57503	CK	FSS	ANG	FSR
156504	52504+57504	CK	FSS	ANG	FSR
156505	52505+57505	CK	FSS	ANG	FSR
156506	52506+57506	CK	FSS	ANG	FSR
156507	52507+57507	CK	FSS	ANG	FSR
156508	52508+57508	CK	FSS	ANG	FSR
156509	52509+57509	CK	FSS	ANG	FSR
156510	52510+57510	CK	FSS	ANG	FSR
156511	52511+57511	CK	FSS	ANG	FSR
156512	52512+57512	CK	FSS	ANG	FSR
156513	52513+57513	CK	FSS	ANG	FSR
156514	52514+57514	CK	FSS	ANG	FSR

Left: *First ScotRail's medium distance domestic diesel fleet is the Class 156, with 48 on the company books in early 2012. The sets are allocated to Corkerhill depot and are painted in a mix of First ScotRail and Scottish Saltire liveries. Set No. 156510 is illustrated showing the latest Scottish Saltire colour scheme, identified by the code FSS in the listing above.*
Alastair Blackwood

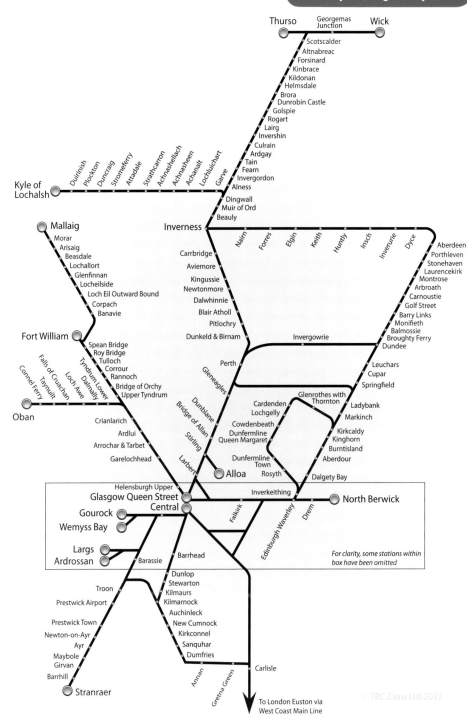

Passenger Train Operating Companies - First ScotRail

For clarity, some stations within box have been omitted

To London Euston via West Coast Main Line

© TRC.Com Ltd 2012

First ScotRail

Class 158

Vehicle Length: 76ft 1¾in (23.21m)
Height: 12ft 6in (3.81m)
Width: 9ft 3¼in (2.82m)

Engine: 1 x Cummins NTA855R of 350hp per vehicle
Horsepower: 700hp (522kW)
Seats (total/car): 14F/116S, 14F-46S/70S, * 138S, 68S/70S

Number	Formation DMCL/DMSL*+DMS	Depot	Livery	Owner	Operator
158701	52701+57701	IS	FSR	PTR	FSR
158702	52702+57702	IS	FSR	PTR	FSR
158703	52703+57703	IS	FSR	PTR	FSR
158704	52704+57704	IS	FSR	PTR	FSR
158705	52705+57705	IS	FSR	PTR	FSR
158706	52706+57706	IS	FSR	PTR	FSR
158707	52707+57707	IS	FSR	PTR	FSR
158708	52708+57708	IS	FSR	PTR	FSR
158709	52709+57709	IS	FSR	PTR	FSR
158710	52710+57710	IS	FSR	PTR	FSR
158711	52711+57711	IS	FSR	PTR	FSR
158712	52712+57712	IS	FSR	PTR	FSR
158713	52713+57713	IS	FSR	PTR	FSR
158714	52714+57714	IS	FSR	PTR	FSR
158715	52715+57715	IS	FSR	PTR	FSR
158716	52716+57716	IS	FSR	PTR	FSR
158717	52717+57717	IS	FSR	PTR	FSR
158718	52718+57718	IS	FSR	PTR	FSR
158719	52719+57719	IS	FSR	PTR	FSR
158720	52720+57720	IS	FSR	PTR	FSR
158721	52721+57721	IS	FSR	PTR	FSR
158722	52722+57722	IS	FSR	PTR	FSR
158723	52723+57723	IS	FSR	PTR	FSR
158724	52724+57724	IS	FSR	PTR	FSR
158725	52725+57725	IS	FSR	PTR	FSR
158726	52726+57726	HA	FSR	PTR	FSR
158727	52727+57727	IS	FSR	PTR	FSR
158728	52728+57728	IS	FSR	PTR	FSR
158729	52729+57729	HA	FSR	PTR	FSR
158730	52730+57730	HA	FSR	PTR	FSR
158731	52731+57731	HA	FSR	PTR	FSR
158732	52732+57732	HA	FSR	PTR	FSR
158733	52733+57733	HA	FSR	PTR	FSR
158734	52734+57734	HA	FSR	PTR	FSR
158735	52735+57735	HA	FSR	PTR	FSR
158736	52736+57736	HA	FSR	PTR	FSR
158737	52737+57737	HA	FSR	PTR	FSR
158738	52738+57738	HA	FSR	PTR	FSR
158739	52739+57739	HA	FSR	PTR	FSR
158740	52740+57740	HA	FSR	PTR	FSR
158741	52741+57741	HA	FSR	PTR	FSR
158782	52782*+57782	HA	FSS	ANG	FSR
158786	52786*+57786	HA	FSS	ANG	FSR
158789	52789*+57789	HA	FSS	ANG	FSR
158867	52867*+57867	HA	FSS	ANG	FSR
158868	52868*+57868	HA	FSS	ANG	FSR
158869	52869*+57869	HA	FSS	ANG	FSR
158870	52870*+57870	HA	FSS	ANG	FSR
158871	52871*+57871	HA	FSS	ANG	FSR

Name applied
158707 - Far North Line

Left: *The latest Scottish Saltire colour scheme is now being applied to Class 158s as they receive classified attention. Set No. 158871 is shown, the highest numbered Class 158 working north of the border.* **Tristan Smith**

Class 170/3
Turbostar

Vehicle Length: 77ft 6in (23.62m)
Height: 12ft 4½in (3.77m)
Width: 8ft 10in (2.69m)

Engine: 1 x MTU 6R 183TD13H 422hp per vehicle
Horsepower: 1,266hp (944kW)
Seats (total/car): 24F/140S, 12F-45S/43S/12F-52S

Number	Formation DMCL+MS+DMSL	Depot	Livery	Owner	Operator
170393	50393+55393+79393	HA	FSR	PTR	FSR
170394	50394+55394+79394	HA	FSR	PTR	FSR
170395	50395+55395+79395	HA	FSR	PTR	FSR
170396	50396+55396+79396	HA	FSR	PTR	FSR

Class 170/4
Turbostar

Vehicle Length: 77ft 6in (23.62m)
Height: 12ft 4½in (3.77m)
Width: 8ft 10in (2.69m)

Engine: 1 x MTU 6R 183TD13H 422hp per vehicle
Horsepower: 1,266hp (944kW)
(170431/432 have 3 x 483hp engines giving 1,449hp)
Seats (total/car): 18F/168S 9F-43S/76S/9F-49S

Number	Formation DMCL+MS+DMCL	Depot	Livery	Owner	Operator	Name
170401	50401+55401+79401	HA	FSR	PTR	FSR	*Sir Moir Lockhead OBE*
170402	50402+55402+79402	HA	FSR	PTR	FSR	
170403	50403+55403+79403	HA	FSR	PTR	FSR	
170404	50404+55404+79404	HA	FSR	PTR	FSR	

Passenger Train Operating Companies - First ScotRail

170405	50405+55405+79405	HA	FSR	PTR	FSR	*Riverside Museum*
170406	50406+55406+79406	HA	FSR	PTR	FSR
170407	50407+55407+79407	HA	FSR	PTR	FSR	*University of Aberdeen*
170408	50408+55408+79408	HA	FSR	PTR	FSR
170409	50409+55409+79409	HA	FSR	PTR	FSR
170410	50410+55410+79410	HA	FSR	PTR	FSR
170411	50411+55411+79411	HA	FSR	PTR	FSR
170412	50412+55412+79412	HA	FSR	PTR	FSR
170413	50413+55413+79413	HA	FSR	PTR	FSR
170414	50414+55414+79414	HA	FSR	PTR	FSR
170415	50415+55415+79415	HA	FSR	PTR	FSR
170416	50416+55416+79416	HA	FSR	EVL	FSR
170417	50417+55417+79417	HA	FSR	EVL	FSR
170418	50418+55418+79418	HA	FSR	EVL	FSR
170419	50419+55419+79419	HA	FSR	EVL	FSR
170420	50420+55420+79420	HA	FSR	EVL	FSR
170421	50421+55421+79421	HA	FSR	EVL	FSR
170422	50422+55422+79422	HA	FSR	EVL	FSR
170423	50423+55423+79423	HA	FSR	EVL	FSR
170424	50424+55424+79424	HA	FSR	EVL	FSR
170425	50425+55425+79425	HA	FSS	PTR	FSR
170426	50426+55426+79426	HA	FSS	PTR	FSR
170427	50427+55427+79427	HA	FSR	PTR	FSR
170428	50428+55428+79428	HA	FSR	PTR	FSR
170429	50429+55429+79429	HA	FSR	PTR	FSR
170430	50430+55430+79430	HA	FSR	PTR	FSR
170431	50431+55431+79431	HA	FSR	PTR	FSR
170432	50432+55432+79432	HA	FSR	PTR	FSR
170433	50433+55433+79433	HA	FSR	PTR	FSR	*Investor in People*
170434	50434+55434+79434	HA	FSS	PTR	FSR

Class 170/4
Turbostar

Vehicle Length: 77ft 6in (23.62m)
Height: 12ft 4½in (3.77m)
Width: 8ft 10in (2.69m)

Engine: 1 x MTU 6R 183TD13H 422hp per vehicle
Horsepower: 1,266hp (944kW)
Seats: 170450-170471 (total/car) 198S, 55S/76S/67S
170472-170478 (total/car) 200S, 57S/76S/67S

Number Formation   Depot Livery Owner Opt'r

DMSL+MS+DMSL

170450	50450+55450+79450	HA	FSR	PTR	FSR	170460	50460+55460+79460	HA	FSR	PTR	FSR
170451	50451+55451+79451	HA	FSR	PTR	FSR	170461	50461+55461+79461	HA	FSR	PTR	FSR
170452	50452+55452+79452	HA	FSR	PTR	FSR	170470	50470+55470+79470	HA	FSS	PTR	FSR
170453	50453+55453+79453	HA	FSR	PTR	FSR	170471	50471+55471+79471	HA	FSS	PTR	FSR
170454	50454+55454+79454	HA	FSR	PTR	FSR	170472	50472+55472+79472	HA	FSP	PTR	FSR
170455	50455+55455+79455	HA	FSR	PTR	FSR	170473	50473+55473+79473	HA	FSP	PTR	FSR
170456	50456+55456+79456	HA	FSR	PTR	FSR	170474	50474+55474+79474	HA	FSP	PTR	FSR
170457	50457+55457+79457	HA	FSS	PTR	FSR	170475	50475+55475+79475	HA	FSP	PTR	FSR
170458	50458+55458+79458	HA	FSR	PTR	FSR	170476	50476+55476+79476	HA	FSP	PTR	FSR
170459	50459+55459+79459	HA	FSR	PTR	FSR	170477	50477+55477+79477	HA	FSP	PTR	FSR
						170478	50478+55478+79478	HA	FSP	PTR	FSR

Right: *The Class 170 'Turbostar' now forms the backbone on longer-distance ScotRail services, as well as duties on the Edinburgh to Glasgow high speed link and domestic services in the Edinburgh and Glasgow areas. Various sub-classes exist, reflecting different seating configurations. Painted in First ScotRail colours, set No. 170395 is seen at Inverness. All ScotRail Class 170s are based at Edinburgh Haymarket depot.* **Brian Garrett**

First ScotRail

Class 314

	Vehicle Length: (Driving) 64ft 11½in (19.80m)	Width: 9ft 3in (2.82m)
	(Inter) 65ft 4¼in (19.92m)	Horsepower: 880hp (656kW)
	Height: 11ft 6½in (3.58m)	Seats (total/car): 212S, 68S/76S/68S

Number	Formation DMSO(A)+PTSO+DMSO(B)	Depot	Livery	Owner	Operator	Name
314201	64583+71450+64584	GW	FSP	ANG	FSR	
314202	64585+71451+64586	GW	FSP	ANG	FSR	
314203	64587+71452+64588*	GW	FSS	ANG	FSR	
314204	64589+71453+64590	GW	FSS	ANG	FSR	
314205	64591+71454+64592	GW	FSS	ANG	FSR	
314206	64593+71455+64594	GW	FSP	ANG	FSR	
314207	64595+71456+64596	GW	FSS	ANG	FSR	
314208	64597+71457+64598	GW	FSS	ANG	FSR	
314209	64599+71458+64600	GW	FSP	ANG	FSR	
314210	64601+71459+64602	GW	FSP	ANG	FSR	
314211	64603+71460+64604	GW	FSS	ANG	FSR	
314212	64604+71461+64606	GW	FSS	ANG	FSR	
314213	64607+71462+64608	GW	FSP	ANG	FSR	
314214	64609+71463+64610	GW	FSS	ANG	FSR	
314215	64611+71464+64612	GW	FSP	ANG	FSR	
314216	64613+71465+64614	GW	FSP	ANG	FSR	

* 64588 rebuilt from Class 507 car No. 64426 and seats 74S

Left: *Based on the 1972-design EMU fitted with end emergency doors for tunnel working, these 16 Class 314s are based at Glasgow Shields and operate suburban electrified services in the Glasgow area. Set No. 314201, painted in carmine and cream colours is seen at Gourock on a service from Glasgow Central.* **Murdoch Currie**

Class 318

	Vehicle Length: (Driving) 65ft 0¾in (19.83m)	Width: 9ft 3in (2.82m)
	(Inter) 65ft 4¼in (19.92m)	Horsepower: 1,328hp (996kW)
	Height: 12ft 1½in (3.70m)	Seats (total/car): 216S, 66S/79S/71S

Number	Formation DTSO(A)+MSO+DTSO(B)	Depot	Livery	Owner	Operator	Name
318250	77240+62866+77260	GW	FSP	EVL	FSR	
318251	77241+62867+77261	GW	FSP	EVL	FSR	
318252	77242+62868+77262	GW	FSP	EVL	FSR	
318253	77243+62869+77263	GW	FSP	EVL	FSR	
318254	77244+62870+77264	GW	FSP	EVL	FSR	
318255	77245+62871+77265	GW	FSP	EVL	FSR	
318256	77246+62872+77266	GW	FSP	EVL	FSR	
318257	77247+62873+77267	GW	FSP	EVL	FSR	
318258	77248+62874+77268	GW	FSP	EVL	FSR	
318259	77249+62875+77269	GW	FSP	EVL	FSR	Citizens' Network
318260	77250+62876+77270	GW	FSP	EVL	FSR	
318261	77251+62877+77271	GW	FSP	EVL	FSR	
318262	77252+62878+77272	GW	FSP	EVL	FSR	
318263	77253+62879+77273	GW	FSP	EVL	FSR	
318264	77254+62880+77274	GW	FSP	EVL	FSR	
318265	77255+62881+77275	GW	FSP	EVL	FSR	
318266	77256+62882+77276	GW	FSP	EVL	FSR	Strathclyder
318267	77257+62883+77277	GW	FSP	EVL	FSR	
318268	77258+62884+77278	GW	FSP	EVL	FSR	
318269	77259+62885+77279	GW	FSP	EVL	FSR	
318270	77288+62890+77289	GW	FSP	EVL	FSR	

Right: *Originally fitted with end gangways, the 21 members of Class 318 are allocated to Glasgow Shields depot. The sets currently operate on the Argyle line. Painted in carmine and cream colours, set No. 318270, the final set of the build, is seen near Lanark on 2 May 2011.* **Robin Ralston**

Class 320

Vehicle Length: (Driving) 65ft 0¾in (19.83m)		Width: 9ft 3in (2.82m)
(Inter) 65ft 4¼in (19.92m)		Horsepower: 1,328hp (996kW)
Height: 12ft 4¾in (3.78m)		Seats (total/car): 227S, 76S/76S/75S

Number	Formation	Depot	Livery	Owner	Operator	Name
	DTSO(A)+MSO+DTSO(B)					
320301	77899+63021+77921	GW	FSP	EVL	FSR	
320302	77900+63022+77922	GW	FSS	EVL	FSR	
320303	77901+63023+77923	GW	FSP	EVL	FSR	
320304	77902+63024+77924	GW	FSS	EVL	FSR	
320305	77903+63025+77925	GW	FSP	EVL	FSR	Glasgow School of Art 1845 – 150 – 1995
320306	77904+63026+77926	GW	FSS	EVL	FSR	
320307	77905+63027+77927	GW	FSP	EVL	FSR	
320308	77906+63028+77928	GW	FSP	EVL	FSR	High Road 20th Anniversary 2000
320309	77907+63029+77929	GW	FSP	EVL	FSR	Radio Clyde 25th Anniversary
320310	77908+63030+77930	GW	FSP	EVL	FSR	
320311	77909+63031+77931	GW	FSP	EVL	FSR	Royal College of Physicians and Surgeons of Glasgow
320312	77910+63032+77932	GW	FSP	EVL	FSR	Sir William A Smith Founder of the Boys' Brigade
320313	77911+63033+77933	GW	FSP	EVL	FSR	
320314	77912+63034+77934	GW	FSS	EVL	FSR	
320315	77913+63035+77935	GW	FSS	EVL	FSR	
320316	77914+63036+77936	GW	FSP	EVL	FSR	
320317	77915+63037+77937	GW	FSP	EVL	FSR	
320318	77916+63038+77938	GW	FSP	EVL	FSR	
320319	77917+63039+77939	GW	FSP	EVL	FSR	
320320	77918+63040+77940	GW	FSP	EVL	FSR	
320321	77919+63041+77941	GW	FSP	EVL	FSR	The Rt. Hon. John Smith, QC, MP
320322	77920+63042+77942	GW	FSP	EVL	FSR	Festival Glasgow Orchid

Right: *A start was made in 2011 to repaint the 22 members of Class 320 in the latest Scottish Saltire livery, as demonstrated on set No. 320315 at Springburn on a service to Dalmuir.* **Murdoch Currie**

Class 334
Juniper

Vehicle Length: (Driving) 69ft 0¾in (21.04m)	Width: 9ft 2¾in (2.80m)
(Inter) 65ft 4½in (19.93m)	Horsepower: 1,448hp (1,080kW)
Height: 12ft 3in (3.77m)	Seats (total/car): 183S, 64S/55S/64S

Number	Formation DMSO(A)+PTSO+DMSO(B)	Depot	Livery	Owner	Operator	Name
334001	64101+74301+65101	GW	FSP	EVL	FSR	*Donald Dewar*
334002	64102+74302+65102	GW	FSP	EVL	FSR	
334003	64103+74303+65103	GW	FSP	EVL	FSR	
334004	64104+74304+65104	GW	FSP	EVL	FSR	
334005	64105+74305+65105	GW	FSP	EVL	FSR	
334006	64106+74306+65106	GW	FSS	EVL	FSR	
334007	64107+74307+65107	GW	FSP	EVL	FSR	
334008	64108+74308+65108	GW	FSP	EVL	FSR	
334009	64109+74309+65109	GW	FSP	EVL	FSR	
334010	64110+74310+65110	GW	FSP	EVL	FSR	
334011	64111+74311+65111	GW	FSP	EVL	FSR	
334012	64112+74312+65112	GW	FSS	EVL	FSR	
334013	64113+74313+65113	GW	FSP	EVL	FSR	
334014	64114+74314+65114	GW	FSP	EVL	FSR	
334015	64115+74315+65115	GW	FSP	EVL	FSR	
334016	64116+74316+65116	GW	FSP	EVL	FSR	
334017	64117+74317+65117	GW	FSP	EVL	FSR	
334018	64118+74318+65118	GW	FSP	EVL	FSR	
334019	64119+74319+65119	GW	FSP	EVL	FSR	
334020	64120+74320+65120	GW	FSP	EVL	FSR	
334021	64121+74321+65121	GW	FSP	EVL	FSR	*Larkhill*
334022	64122+74322+65122	GW	FSP	EVL	FSR	
334023	64123+74323+65123	GW	FSP	EVL	FSR	
334024	64124+74324+65124	GW	FSP	EVL	FSR	
334025	64125+74325+65125	GW	FSP	EVL	FSR	
334026	64126+74326+65126	GW	FSP	EVL	FSR	
334027	64127+74327+65127	GW	FSP	EVL	FSR	
334028	64128+74328+65128	GW	FSP	EVL	FSR	
334029	64129+74329+65129	GW	FSP	EVL	FSR	
334030	64130+74330+65130	GW	FSP	EVL	FSR	
334031	64131+74331+65131	GW	FSP	EVL	FSR	
334032	64132+74332+65132	GW	FSP	EVL	FSR	
334033	64133+74333+65133	GW	FSP	EVL	FSR	
334034	64134+74334+65134	GW	FSP	EVL	FSR	
334035	64135+74335+65135	GW	FSP	EVL	FSR	
334036	64136+74336+65136	GW	FSP	EVL	FSR	
334037	64137+74337+65137	GW	FSP	EVL	FSR	
334038	64138+74338+65138	GW	FSP	EVL	FSR	
334039	64139+74339+65139	GW	FSP	EVL	FSR	
334040	64140+74340+65140	GW	FSP	EVL	FSR	

Left: *The 40 Class 334 'Juniper' sets, built by Alstom, are allocated to Glasgow Shields Road depot and are used on the North Clyde line. A start has been made of applying the latest Scottish Saltire colour scheme. Set No. 334006 shows this scheme at Drumgelloch.* **Murdoch Currie**

Passenger Train Operating Companies - First ScotRail

Class 380/0
Desiro

Vehicle Length: 77ft 3in (23.57m) *Horsepower: 1,341hp (1,000kW)*
Height: 12ft 1½in (3.7m) *Seats (total/car): 191S, 70S/57S/64S*
Width: 9ft 2in (2.7m)

Number	Formation	Depot	Livery	Owner	Operator
	DMSO(A)+PTSO+DMSO(B)				
380001	38501+38601+38701	GW	FSS	EVL	FSR
380002	38502+38602+38702	GW	FSS	EVL	FSR
380003	38503+38603+38703	GW	FSS	EVL	FSR
380004	38504+38604+38704	GW	FSS	EVL	FSR
380005	38505+38605+38705	GW	FSS	EVL	FSR
380006	38506+38606+38706	GW	FSS	EVL	FSR
380007	38507+38607+38707	GW	FSS	EVL	FSR
380008	38508+38608+38708	GW	FSS	EVL	FSR
380009	38509+38609+38709	GW	FSS	EVL	FSR
380010	38510+38610+38710	GW	FSS	EVL	FSR
380011	38511+38611+38711	GW	FSS	EVL	FSR
380012	38512+38612+38712	GW	FSS	EVL	FSR
380013	38513+38613+38713	GW	FSS	EVL	FSR
380014	38514+38614+38714	GW	FSS	EVL	FSR
380015	38515+38615+38715	GW	FSS	EVL	FSR
380016	38516+38616+38716	GW	FSS	EVL	FSR
380017	38517+38617+38717	GW	FSS	EVL	FSR
380018	38518+38618+38718	GW	FSS	EVL	FSR
380019	38519+38619+38719	GW	FSS	EVL	FSR
380020	38520+38620+38720	GW	FSS	EVL	FSR
380021	38521+38621+38721	GW	FSS	EVL	FSR
380022	38522+38622+38722	GW	FSS	EVL	FSR

Class 380/1
Desiro

Vehicle Length: 77ft 3in (23.57m) *Horsepower: 1,341hp (1,000kW)*
Height: 12ft 1½in (3.7m) *Seats (total/car): 265S, 70S/57S/74S/64S*
Width: 9ft 2in (2.7m)

Number	Formation	Depot	Livery	Owner	Operator
	DMSO(A)+PTSO+MSO+DMSO(B)				
380101	38551+38651+38851+38751	GW	FSS	EVL	FSR
380102	38552+38652+38852+38752	GW	FSS	EVL	FSR
380103	38553+38653+38853+38753	GW	FSS	EVL	FSR
380104	38554+38654+38854+38754	GW	FSS	EVL	FSR
380105	38555+38655+38855+38755	GW	FSS	EVL	FSR
380106	38556+38656+38856+38756	GW	FSS	EVL	FSR
380107	38557+38657+38857+38757	GW	FSS	EVL	FSR
380108	38558+38658+38858+38758	GW	FSS	EVL	FSR
380109	38559+38659+38859+38759	GW	FSS	EVL	FSR
380110	38560+38660+38860+38760	GW	FSS	EVL	FSR
380111	38561+38661+38861+38761	GW	FSS	EVL	FSR
380112	38562+38662+38862+38762	GW	FSS	EVL	FSR
380113	38563+38663+38863+38763	GW	FSS	EVL	FSR
380114	38564+38664+38864+38764	GW	FSS	EVL	FSR
380115	38565+38665+38865+38765	GW	FSS	EVL	FSR
380116	38566+38666+38866+38766	GW	FSS	EVL	FSR

Right: *These 38 Class 380 'Desiro' sets are allocated to Glasgow Shields Road and operate on the Ayrshire and Inverclyde lines, displacing Class 318 and 334 fleets to other routes. All sets were built in Germany and tested on the Siemens Wildenrath test track before rail delivery to the UK. Set No. 380101, formed as a three-car, is seen at Wildenrath while on test. All sets are painted in the latest Scottish Saltire livery.* **CJM**

Mk2 & Mk3 Hauled Stock

Mk2
Vehicle Length: 66ft 0in (20.11m)   Width: 9ft 3in (2.81m)
Height: 12ft 9½in (3.89m)   Seats (total/car): 60S

Mk3
Vehicle Length: 75ft 0in (22.86m)   Width: 8ft 11in (2.71m)
Height: 12ft 9in (3.88m)   Bogie Type: BT10

AN1F (Mk2) - RLO *Seating 28-30F*

Number	Depot	Livery	Owner
6700 (3347)	IS	FSS	EVL
6701 (3346)	IS	FSR	EVL
6702 (3421)	IS	FSR	EVL
6703 (3308)	IS	FSR	EVL
6704 (3341)	IS	FSR	EVL
6705 (3310)	IS	FSR	EVL
6706 (3283)	IS	FSR	EVL
6707 (3276)	IS	FSR	EVL
6708 (3370)	IS	FSR	EVL

AN1F (Mk2) - BUO *Seating 31U*

Number	Depot	Livery	Owner
9800 (5751)	IS	FSR	EVL
9801 (5760)	IS	FSR	EVL
9802 (5772)	IS	FSR	EVL
9803 (5799)	IS	FSR	EVL
9804 (5826)	IS	FSR	EVL
9805 (5833)	IS	FSR	EVL
9806 (5840)	IS	FSR	EVL
9807 (5851)	IS	FSS	EVL
9808 (5871)	IS	FSS	EVL
9809 (5890)	IS	FSR	EVL
9810 (5892)	IS	FSR	EVL

AU4G (Mk3) - SLEP *Comps 12*

Number	Depot	Livery	Owner
10501	IS	FSR	PTR

10502	IS	FSR	PTR
10504	IS	FSR	PTR
10506	IS	FSR	PTR
10507	IS	FSR	PTR
10508	IS	FSR	PTR
10513	IS	FSR	PTR
10516	IS	FSS	PTR
10519	IS	FSR	PTR
10520	IS	FSR	PTR
10522	IS	FSR	PTR
10523	IS	FSR	PTR
10526	IS	FSR	PTR
10527	IS	FSR	PTR
10529	IS	FSR	PTR
10531	IS	FSR	PTR
10542	IS	FSR	PTR
10543	IS	FSR	PTR
10544	IS	FSR	PTR
10548	IS	FSR	PTR
10551	IS	FSR	PTR
10553	IS	FSR	PTR
10561	IS	FSR	PTR
10562	IS	FSS	PTR
10565	IS	FSR	PTR
10580	IS	FSR	PTR
10597	IS	FSR	PTR
10598	IS	FSR	PTR
10600	IS	FSR	PTR
10605	IS	FSR	PTR
10607	IS	FSR	PTR
10610	IS	FSR	PTR
10613	IS	FSR	PTR
10614	IS	FSR	PTR
10617	IS	FSR	PTR

AS4G (MK3) - SLE *Comps 13*

Number	Depot	Livery	Owner
10675	IS	FSR	PTR
10683	IS	FSR	PTR
10688	IS	FSR	PTR
10690	IS	FSR	PTR
10693	IS	FSR	PTR
10703	IS	FSR	PTR

AQ4G (Mk3) - SLED *Comps 11*

Number	Depot	Livery	Owner
10648	IS	FSR	PTR
10650	IS	FSR	PTR
10666	IS	FSR	PTR
10680	IS	FSR	PTR
10689	IS	FSR	PTR
10699	IS	FSR	PTR
10706	IS	FSR	PTR
10714	IS	FSR	PTR
10718	IS	FSR	PTR
10719	IS	FSR	PTR
10722	IS	FSR	PTR
10723	IS	FSR	PTR

Left Upper and Left Below: *First ScotRail operate a limited loco-hauled service, being responsible for sleeping car services from Aberdeen, Inverness, Fort William, Glasgow and Edinburgh to London. The rolling stock is operated by ScotRail with locomotives hired in from DBS. A total of 73 Mk2 and Mk3 vehicles are based at Inverness. In the upper view we see Mk2 BUO No. 9805; these cars seat 31 unclassified and have a buffet position. In the lower view we see SLEP No. 10522, viewed from the corridor side.*
Both: **Antony Christie**

First TransPennine Express

Address: ✉ Floor 7, Bridgewater House, 60 Whitworth Street, Manchester, M1 6LT
✆ tpcustomer.relations@firstgroup.com
☎ 0845 600 1671
ⓘ www.tpexpress.co.uk

Managing Director: Nick Donovan
Franchise Dates: 1 February 2004 - between April 2014 & April 2015
Principal Routes: Newcastle, Middlesbrough, Scarborough, Hull, Cleethorpes to Manchester, Liverpool, Barrow, Carlisle, Edinburgh and Glasgow
Depots: Ardwick (AK) - Siemens operated, York (YK), Crofton (XW)
Parent Company: First Group, Keolis

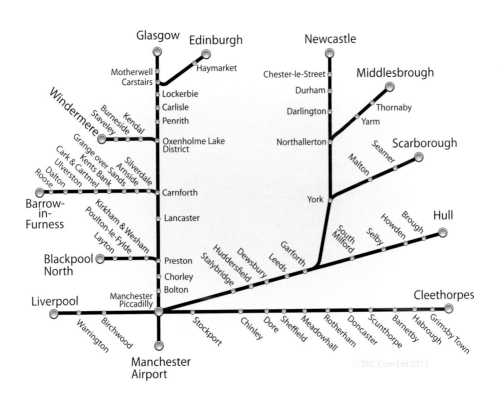

First TransPennine Express

Passenger Train Operating Companies - First TransPennine Express

Class 170/3
Turbostar

Vehicle Length: 77ft 6in (23.62m)
Height: 12ft 4½in (3.77m)
Width: 8ft 10in (2.69m)

Engine: 1 x MTU 6R 183TD13H 422hp per vehicle
Horsepower: 844hp (629kW)
Seats (total/car): 8F/108S 8F-43S/65S

Number	Formation DMCL+DMS	Depot	Livery	Owner	Operator
170301	50301+79301	XW	FTP	PTR	FTP
170302	50302+79302	XW	FTP	PTR	FTP
170303	50303+79303	XW	FTP	PTR	FTP
170304	50304+79304	XW	FTP	PTR	FTP
170305	50305+79305	XW	FTP	PTR	FTP
170306	50306+79306	XW	FTP	PTR	FTP
170307	50307+79307	XW	FTP	PTR	FTP
170308	50308+79308	XW	FTP	PTR	FTP
170309	50399+79399	XW	FTP	PTR	FTP

Above: *First TransPennine Express operate nine Class 170/3 units, allocated to Crofton, Wakefield. These are used on the Manchester to East Coast corridor. Set No. 170301 displaying full FTPE livery is seen at Barnetby in the summer of 2011.* **Nathan Williamson**

Class 185
Desiro

Vehicle Length: (Driving) 77ft 11in (23.76m), (Inter) 77ft 10¾in (23.75m)
Height: 12ft 4in (3.75m)
Width: 9ft 3in (2.81m)

Engine: 1 x Cummins OSK19 of 750hp per car
Horsepower: 2,250hp (1,680kW)
Seats (total/car): 15F/154S, 15F-18S/72S/64S

Number	Formation DMCL+MSL+DMS	Depot	Livery	Owner	Operator
185101	51101+53101+54101	AK	FTP	EVL	FTP
185102	51102+53102+54102	AK	FTP	EVL	FTP
185103	51103+53103+54103	AK	FTP	EVL	FTP
185104	51104+53104+54104	AK	FTP	EVL	FTP
185105	51105+53105+54105	AK	FTP	EVL	FTP
185106	51106+53106+54106	AK	FTP	EVL	FTP
185107	51107+53107+54107	AK	FTP	EVL	FTP
185108	51108+53108+54108	AK	FTP	EVL	FTP
185109	51109+53109+54109	AK	FTP	EVL	FTP
185110	51110+53110+54110	AK	FTP	EVL	FTP
185111	51111+53111+54111	AK	FTP	EVL	FTP
185112	51112+53112+54112	AK	FTP	EVL	FTP
185113	51113+53113+54113	AK	FTP	EVL	FTP
185114	51114+53114+54114	AK	FTP	EVL	FTP
185115	51115+53115+54115	AK	FTP	EVL	FTP
185116	51116+53116+54116	AK	FTP	EVL	FTP
185117	51117+53117+54117	AK	FTP	EVL	FTP

185118	51118+53118+54118	AK	FTP	EVL	FTP
185119	51119+53119+54119	AK	FTP	EVL	FTP
185120	51120+53120+54120	AK	FTP	EVL	FTP
185121	51121+53121+54121	AK	FTP	EVL	FTP
185122	51122+53122+54122	AK	FTP	EVL	FTP
185123	51123+53123+54123	AK	FTP	EVL	FTP
185124	51124+53124+54124	AK	FTP	EVL	FTP
185125	51125+53125+54125	AK	FTP	EVL	FTP
185126	51126+53126+54126	AK	FTP	EVL	FTP
185127	51127+53127+54127	AK	FTP	EVL	FTP
185128	51128+53128+54128	AK	FTP	EVL	FTP
185129	51129+53129+54129	AK	FTP	EVL	FTP
185130	51130+53130+54130	AK	FTP	EVL	FTP
185131	51131+53131+54131	AK	FTP	EVL	FTP
185132	51132+53132+54132	AK	FTP	EVL	FTP
185133	51133+53133+54133	AK	FTP	EVL	FTP
185134	51134+53134+54134	AK	FTP	EVL	FTP
185135	51135+53135+54135	AK	FTP	EVL	FTP
185136	51136+53136+54136	AK	FTP	EVL	FTP
185137	51137+53137+54137	AK	FTP	EVL	FTP
185138	51138+53138+54138	AK	FTP	EVL	FTP
185139	51139+53139+54139	AK	FTP	EVL	FTP
185140	51140+53140+54140	AK	FTP	EVL	FTP
185141	51141+53141+54141	AK	FTP	EVL	FTP
185142	51142+53142+54142	AK	FTP	EVL	FTP
185143	51143+53143+54143	AK	FTP	EVL	FTP
185144	51144+53144+54144	AK	FTP	EVL	FTP
185145	51145+53145+54145	AK	FTP	EVL	FTP
185146	51146+53146+54146	AK	FTP	EVL	FTP
185147	51147+53147+54147	AK	FTP	EVL	FTP
185148	51148+53148+54148	AK	FTP	EVL	FTP
185149	51149+53149+54149	AK	FTP	EVL	FTP
185150	51150+53150+54150	AK	FTP	EVL	FTP
185151	51151+53151+54151	AK	FTP	EVL	FTP

Below: *At present the core of FTPE passenger services is operated by a fleet of 51 three-car Class 185 'Desiro' diesel sets based at Manchester Ardwick depot. Set No. 185125 passes near Penrith on 9 April 2010, forming the 09.29 TransPennine service from Manchester Airport to Windermere.* **Brian Morrison**

■ 10 Desiro Class 350/3 four-car sets for First TransPennine Express are to be ordered in 2012 for delivery in 2013. These are likely to have a top speed of 110mph.

Grand Central

Address: ✉ River House, 17 Museum Street, York, YO1 7DJ
📠 info@grandcentral.com
✆ 0845 603 4852
ⓘ www.grandcentral.co.uk

Managing Director: Tom Clift
Franchise Dates: Private Open Access Operator
Principal Routes: London King's Cross - Sunderland/Bradford
Depots: Heaton (HT)
Parent Company: Arriva PLC

Below: *Following refurbishment of the trailer stock and power cars, including the fitting of MTU power units, the Grand Central HST fleet emerged in a distinctive black and orange livery, shown on power car No. 43468 passing Doncaster.* **Nathan Williamson**

Sunderland
Hartlepool
Eaglescliffe
Northallerton
Thirsk
York
Doncaster
London King's Cross

Bradford Interchange
Halifax
Brighouse
Wakefield Kirkgate
Pontefract Monkhill

© TRC.Com Ltd 2012

Class 43 – HST

Vehicle Length: 58ft 5in (18.80m)
Height: 12ft 10in (3.90m)
Width: 8ft 11in (2.73m)
Engine: MTU 16V4000 R41R
Horsepower: 2,250hp (1,680kW)
Electrical Equipment: Brush

Number	Depot	Pool	Livery	Owner	Operator
43423 (43123)	HT	GCHP	GTL	ANG	GTL
43465 (43065)	HT	GCHP	GTL	ANG	GTL
43467 (43067)	HT	GCHP	GTL	ANG	GTL
43468 (43068)	HT	GCHP	GTO	ANG	GTL
43480 (43080)	HT	GCHP	GTO	ANG	GTL
43484 (43084)	HT	GCHP	GTL	ANG	GTL

Name applied
43423 *'Valenta' 1972 - 2010*
43484 *Peter Fox 1942 - 2011*

Class 180
Zephyrs

Vehicle Length: (Driving) 75ft 7in (23.71m), (Inter) 75ft 5in (23.03m)
Height: 12ft 4in (3.75m)
Width: 9ft 2in (2.80m)
Engine: 1 x Cummins QSK19 of 750hp per car
Horsepower: 3,750hp (2,796kW)
Seats (total/car): 42F/226S, 46S/42F/68S/56S/56S

Number	Formation DMSL(A)+MFL+MSL+MSLRB+DMSL(B)	Depot	Livery	Owner	Operator	Name
180101	50901+54901+55901+56901+59901	HT	GTL	ANG	GTL	
180105	50905+54905+55905+56905+59905	HT	GTL	ANG	GTL	*The Yorkshire Artist Ashley Jackson*
180107	50907+54907+55907+56907+59907	HT	GTL	ANG	GTL	*Hart of the North*
180112	50912+54912+55912+56912+59912	HT	GTL	ANG	GTL	*James Herriot*
180114	50914+54914+55914+56914+59914	HT	GTL	ANG	GTL	

Above: *A total of five Class 180 sets are operated by Grand Central, who classify the design as 'Zephyrs'. All sets have been refurbished internally and now sport the operator's black and orange livery. Set No. 180112 James Herriot forms the 06.53 Grand Central service from Sunderland to London King's Cross on 17 October 2009 and is recorded passing Welwyn Garden City. It is a pity the original front hinged doors have been removed from these sets.* **Brian Morrison**

Mk3 HST stock

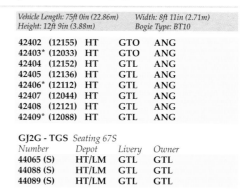

Vehicle Length: 75ft 0in (22.86m)	Width: 8ft 11in (2.71m)
Height: 12ft 9in (3.88m)	Bogie Type: BT10

GK2G - TRSB *Seating 33S*

Number		Depot	Livery	Owner
40424	(40024)	HT	GTO	ANG
40426	(40026)	HT	GTL	ANG
40433	(40033)	HT	GTL	ANG

GH1G - TF *Seating 48F*

Number		Depot	Livery	Owner
41201	(11045)	HT	GTO	ANG
41202	(11017)	HT	GTL	ANG
41203	(11038)	HT	GTL	ANG
41204	(11023)	HT	GTL	ANG
41205	(11036)	HT	GTL	ANG
41206	(11055)	HT	GTL	ANG

GH2G - TS *Seating 64S* ***TSD** *Seating 60S*

Number		Depot	Livery	Owner
42401	(12149)	HT	GTO	ANG

Number		Depot	Livery	Owner
42402	(12155)	HT	GTO	ANG
42403*	(12033)	HT	GTO	ANG
42404	(12152)	HT	GTL	ANG
42405	(12136)	HT	GTL	ANG
42406*	(12112)	HT	GTL	ANG
42407	(12044)	HT	GTL	ANG
42408	(12121)	HT	GTL	ANG
42409*	(12088)	HT	GTL	ANG

GJ2G - TGS *Seating 67S*

Number	Depot	Livery	Owner
44065 (S)	HT/LM	GTL	GTL
44088 (S)	HT/LM	GTL	GTL
44089 (S)	HT/LM	GTL	GTL

■ *Mk3 loco-hauled coaches 12058, 12104, 12165 owned by Grand Central stored at Long Marston.*

Grand Central also operate Mk2D BSO 9488 as a barrier vehicle.

Right: *The 21 HST passenger vehicles operated by Grand Central are based at Heaton depot in Newcastle. All carry the latest black and orange GC livery. TRSB No. 40426 is illustrated; note the grey passenger door with the catering symbol.* **Antony Christie**

Heathrow Express / Heathrow Connect

Address: ✉ 6th Floor, 50 Eastbourne Terrace, Paddington, London, W2 6LX
             ✆ queries@heathrowexpress.com or queries@heathrowconnect.com
             ✆ 020 8750 6600
             ⓘ www.heathrowexpress.com or www.heathrowconnect.com

Managing Director: Richard Robinson
Franchise Dates: Private Open Access Operator
Principal Routes: London Paddington - Heathrow Airport
Owned Stations: Heathrow Central, Heathrow Terminal 4, Heathrow Terminal 5
Depots: Old Oak Common HEX (OH)
Parent Company: Heathrow Express - British Airports Authority
             Heathrow Connect - British Airports Authority / First Group

Heathrow Express

© TRC.Com Ltd 2012

Heathrow Airport Terminal 5 — Heathrow Airport Terminals 1-3 — London Paddington

Heathrow Connect

Heathrow Airport Terminal 4 — Heathrow Airport Terminals 1-3 — Hayes — Southall — Hanwell — West Ealing — Ealing Broadway — London Paddington

Shuttle

Below: *The 30 minute interval stopping service between London Paddington and Heathrow Airport is operated by Class 360/2 sets, allocated to Old Oak Common. Usually sets Nos. 360201-204 are used, as set No. 360205 is dedicated to the Heathrow Airport internal shuttle between Heathrow Terminals 1-3 and Terminal 4. Set No. 360203 is illustrated at Acton Main Line.* **Nathan Williamson**

Class 332

Vehicle Length: (Driving) 77ft 10¾in (23.74m)
(Inter) 75ft 11in (23.143m)
Height: 12ft 1½in (3.70m)

Width: 9ft 1in (2.75m)
Horsepower: 1,876hp (1,400kW)
Seats 4-car (total/car): 26F-148S, 26F/56S/44S/48S
5-Car (total/car): 26F-204S, 26F/56S/44S/56S/48S

Number	Formation DMFO+TSO+PTSO+(TSO)+DMSO	Depot	Livery	Owner	Operator
332001	78400+72412+63400+ - +78401	OH	HEX	BAA	HEX
332002	78402+72409+63401+ - +78403	OH	HEX‡	BAA	HEX
332003	78404+72407+63402+ - +78405	OH	HEX	BAA	HEX
332004	78406+72406+63403+ - +78407	OH	HEX‡	BAA	HEX
332005	78408+72411+63404+72417+78409	OH	HEX‡	BAA	HEX
332006	78410+72410+63405+72415+78411	OH	HEX‡	BAA	HEX
332007	78412+72401+63406+72414+78413	OH	HEX‡	BAA	HEX

Vehicle Length: (Driving) 77ft 10¾in (23.74m)
(Inter) 75ft 11in (23.143m)
Height: 12ft 1½in (3.70m)

Width: 9ft 1in (2.75m)
Horsepower: 1,876hp (1,400kW)
Seats 4-car (total/car): 14F-148S, 48S/56S/44S/14F
5-Car (total/car): 14F-204S, 48S/56S/44S/56S/14F

	Formation DMSO+TSO+PTSO+(TSO)+DMFLO				
332008	78414+72413+63407+72418+78415	OH	HEX‡	BAA	HEX
332009	78416+72400+63408+72416+78417	OH	HEX‡	BAA	HEX
332010	78418+72402+63409+ - +78419	OH	HEX	BAA	HEX
332011	78420+72403+63410+ - +78421	OH	HEX‡	BAA	HEX
332012	78422+72404+63411+ - +78423	OH	HEX	BAA	HEX
332013	78424+72408+63412+ - +78425	OH	HEX	BAA	HEX
332014	78426+72406+63413+ - +78427	OH	HEX‡	BAA	HEX

‡ First class vehicles carry Vodafone advertising livery

Class 360/2
Desiro

Vehicle Length: 66ft 9in (20.4m)
Height: 12ft 1½in (3.7m)
Width: 9ft 2in (2.79m)

Horsepower: 1,341hp (1,000kW)
Seats (total/car): 340S, 63S/66S/74S/74S/63S
(360205 - 280S using 2+2 seats)

Number	Formation DMSO(A)+PTSO+TSO+TSO+DMSO(B)	Depot	Livery	Owner	Operator
360201	78431+63421+72431+72421+78441	OH	HEC	BAA	HEC
360202	78432+63422+72432+72422+78442	OH	HEC	BAA	HEC
360203	78433+63423+72433+72423+78443	OH	HEC	BAA	HEC
360204	78434+63424+72434+72424+78444	OH	HEC	BAA	HEC
360205	78435+63425+72435+72425+78445	OH	HEL	BAA	HEC

Below: *In 2011 a new advertising contract between British Airports Authority and Vodafone was struck with one driving car of each Class 332 branded in full Vodafone colours, plus advertising on all coaches.* **Nathan Williamson**

Passenger Train Operating Companies - Heathrow Express & Heathrow Connect

Train Operating Companies

Hull Trains

Address:	✉ Europa House, 184 Ferensway, Kingston-upon-Hull, HU1 3UT
	🖥 customer.services@hulltrains.co.uk
	✆ 0845 676 9905
	ⓘ www.hulltrains.co.uk
General Manager:	Cath Bellamy
Franchise Dates:	Private Open Access Operator, agreement to 2016
Principal Route:	London King's Cross - Hull
Depots:	Old Oak Common (OO) [Operated by FGW], Crofton (XW)
Parent Company:	First Group PLC

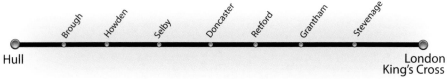

Hull — Brough — Howden — Selby — Doncaster — Retford — Grantham — Stevenage — London King's Cross

© TRC.Com Ltd 2012

Class 180
Adelante

Vehicle Length: (Driving) 75ft 7in (23.71m), (Inter) 75ft 5in (23.03m)
Height: 12ft 4in (3.75m)   Engine: 1 x Cummins OSK19 of 750hp per car
Width: 9ft 2in (2.80m)   Horsepower: 3,750hp (2,796kW)
                                  Seats (total/car): 42F/226S, 46S/42F/68S/56S/56S

Number	Formation DMSL(A)+MFL+MSF+MSLRB+DMSL(B)	Depot	Livery	Owner	Operator
180109	50909+54909+55909+56909+59909	OO/XW	FHT	ANG	FHT
180110	50910+54910+55910+56910+59910	OO/XW	FHT	ANG	FHT
180111	50911+54911+55911+56911+59911	OO/XW	FHT	ANG	FHT
180113	50913+54913+55913+56913+59913	OO/XW	FHT	ANG	FHT

Below: *First Hull Trains currently operate a fleet of four ex First Great Western Class 180 sets on their King's Cross to Hull service. All sets carry First Group 'dynamic lines' livery and are now devoid of front end coupling covers. Set No. 180110 is seen passing Gatehouse Farm, Marholm near Peterborough on 15 October 2010, forming the 09.48 King's Cross to Hull service.* **Brian Garrett**

Island Line

Address: ✉ Ryde St Johns Road Station, Ryde, Isle of Wight, PO33 2BA
📠 info@island-line.co.uk
✆ 01983 812591
ⓘ www.island-line.co.uk

Managing Director: Andy Pitt (South West Trains), **General Manager:** Andy Naylor
Franchise Dates: Part of SWT franchise 2 February 2007 - 28 February 2017
Principal Route: Ryde Pier Head - Shanklin
Owned Stations: All
Depots: Ryde St Johns (RY)
Parent Company: Stagecoach

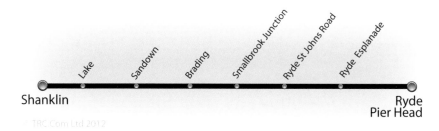

Class 483

Vehicle Length: 52ft 4in (15.95m)	Horsepower: 670hp (500kW)
Height: 9ft 5½in (2.88m)	Seats (total/car): 82S, 40S/42S
Width: 8ft 8½in (2.65m)	

Number	Formation DMSO+DMSO	Depot	Livery	Owner	Operator						
483002	122+224	RY	LUL	SWT	SIL	483006	126+226	RY	LUL	SWT	SIL
483004	124+224	RY	LUL	SWT	SIL	483007	127+227	RY	LUL	SWT	SIL
						483008	128+228	RY	LUL	SWT	SIL
						483009	129+229	RY	LUL	SWT	SIL

Below: *Six 2-car Class 483 units still form the only main line railway stock working on the Isle of Wight. Based at Ryde St Johns Road depot, usually two or occasionally three sets operate the daily service. In this view, set No. 008 (483008) stands at Ryde St Johns Road awaiting departure to Shanklin.* **Antony Christie**

London Midland

Address:	✉ 102 New Street, Birmingham, B2 4JB
	✍ comments@londonmidland.com
	☏ 0844 811 0133
	ⓘ www.londonmidland.com
Managing Director:	Patrick Verwer
Franchise Dates:	11 November 2007 - 19 September 2015
Principal Routes:	London Euston - Liverpool Lime Street, West Midlands routes to Stratford, Worcester, Hereford, Shrewsbury, plus Bedford and St Albans Abbey branches
Depots:	Northampton (NN)*, Soho (SI), Tyseley (TS), Stourbridge Junction (SJ) * Operated by Siemens
Parent Company:	Govia

Class 08

Vehicle Length: 29ft 3in (8.91m)	Engine: English Electric 6K
Height: 12ft 8⅝in (3.87m)	Horsepower: 400hp (298kW)
Width: 8ft 6in (2.59m)	Electrical Equipment: English Electric

Number	Depot	Pool	Livery	Owner	Operator
08616 (3785)	TS	EJLO	LMI	LMI	LMI
08805	SI	EJLO	BLU	LMI	LMI

Names applied
08616 *Tyseley 100*   08805 *Concorde*

Left: *London Midland have two Class 08s, one allocated to Tyseley and the other to Soho to shunt stock as required. The loco based at Tyseley, No. 08616, currently displays a version of London Midland livery complete with cast numberplate 3785 (the loco's pre-TOPS number) and is named* Tyseley 100. **John Stretton**

Class 139

Vehicle Length: 28ft 6in (8.7m)	Engine: 1 x MVH420 2.0ltr LPG, flywheel hybrid
Width: 7ft 8in (2.4m)	Seats (total/car): 18S

Number	Formation DMS	Depot	Livery	Owner	Operator		Number	Formation		Depot	Livery	Owner	Operator
139001	39001	SJ	LMI	LMI	LMI		139002	39002		SJ	LMI	LMI	LMI

Left: *The two Parry People Mover railcars used by London Midland on the Stourbridge Town - Stourbridge Junction 'shuttle' service are kept in a small single track 'depot' at Stourbridge Junction. The two vehicles painted in full London Midland livery with Stourbridge shuttle branding are not allowed off the branch. Vehicle No. 139002 is illustrated at Stourbridge Town.* **Stacey Thew**

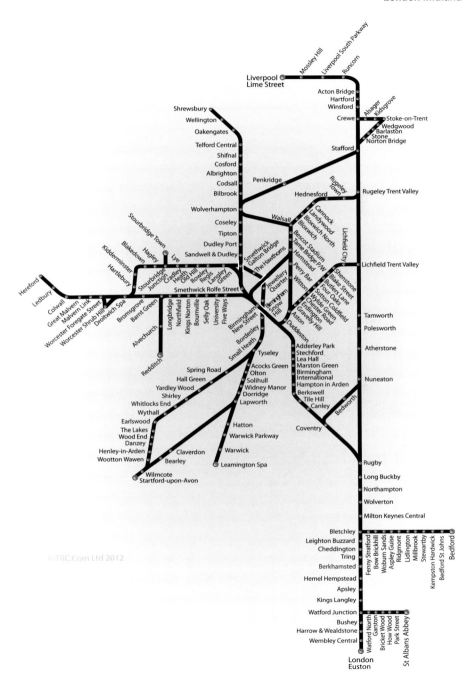

London Midland

Class 150/1

Vehicle Length: 64ft 9¾in (19.74m)
Height: 12ft 4½in (3.77m)
Width: 9ft 3⅛in (2.82m)

Engine: 1 x NT855R5 of 285hp per vehicle
Horsepower: 855hp (638kW)
Seats (total/car): 224S, 76S/76S/72S
*220S, 72S/72S/76S

Number	Formation DMSL+DMS	Depot	Livery	Owner	Operator
150105	52105+57105	TS	CTL	ANG	LMI
150107	52107+57107	TS	CTL	ANG	LMI
150109	52109+57109	TS	CTL	ANG	LMI

Class 153

Vehicle Length: 76ft 5in (23.29m)
Height: 12ft 3⅛in (3.75m)
Width: 8ft 10in (2.70m)

Engine: 1 x NT855R5 of 285hp
Horsepower: 285hp (213kW)
Seats (total/car): 72S

Number	Formation DMSL	Depot	Livery	Owner	Operator
153334	52334	TS	LMI	PTR	LMI
153354¤	57354	TS	LMI	PTR	LMI
153356	57356	TS	LMI	PTR	LMI
153364¤	57364	TS	LMI	PTR	LMI
153365	57365	TS	LMI	PTR	LMI
153366	57366	TS	LMI	PTR	LMI
153371	57371	TS	LMI	PTR	LMI
153375	57375	TS	LMI	PTR	LMI

¤ On loan to East Anglia at
Norwich Crown Point.

Left: *In early 2012, London Midland
operate a fleet of six Class 153 'bubble'
cars on lightly used services. All
vehicles carry London Midland livery
and are allocated to Tyseley depot.
Set No. 153354 (currently on loan
to National Express East Anglia) is
seen with Class 150 No. 170502 at
Bromsgrove.* **John Binch**

Class 170/5
Turbostar

Vehicle Length: 77ft 6in (23.62m)
Height: 12ft 4½in (3.77m)
Width: 8ft 10in (2.69m)

Engine: 1 x MTU 6R 183TD13H 422hp per vehicle
Horsepower: 844hp (629kW)
Seats (total/car): 122S 55S/67S

Number	Formation DMSL+DMSL	Depot	Livery	Owner	Operator
170501	50501+79501	TS	LMI	PTR	LMI
170502	50502+79502	TS	LMI	PTR	LMI
170503	50503+79503	TS	LMI	PTR	LMI
170504	50504+79504	TS	LMI	PTR	LMI
170505	50505+79505	TS	LMI	PTR	LMI
170506	50506+79506	TS	LMI	PTR	LMI
170507	50507+79507	TS	LMI	PTR	LMI
170508	50508+79508	TS	LMI	PTR	LMI
170509	50509+79509	TS	LMI	PTR	LMI
170510	50510+79510	TS	LMI	PTR	LMI
170511	50511+79511	TS	LMI	PTR	LMI
170512	50512+79512	TS	LMI	PTR	LMI
170513	50513+79513	TS	LMI	PTR	LMI
170514	50514+79514	TS	LMI	PTR	LMI
170515	50515+79515	TS	LMI	PTR	LMI
170516	50516+79516	TS	LMI	PTR	LMI
170517	50517+79517	TS	LMI	PTR	LMI

Class 170/6
Turbostar

Vehicle Length: 77ft 6in (23.62m)
Height: 12ft 4½in (3.77m)
Width: 8ft 10in (2.69m)

Engine: 1 x MTU 6R 183TD13H 422hp per vehicle
Horsepower: 1,266hp (944kW)
Seats (total/car): 196S 55S/74S/67S

Number	Formation DMSL+MS+DMSL	Depot	Livery	Owner	Operator
170630	50630+56630+79630	TS	LMI	PTR	LMI
170631	50631+56631+79631	TS	LMI	PTR	LMI
170632	50632+56632+79632	TS	LMI	PTR	LMI
170633	50633+56633+79633	TS	LMI	PTR	LMI
170634	50634+56634+79634	TS	LMI	PTR	LMI
170635	50635+56635+79635	TS	LMI	PTR	LMI

Right: *A total of 23 Class 170 'Turbostar' sets are operated by London Midland; 17 sets are formed of two carriages and six as three-car sets. All are allocated to Tyseley and have been refurbished internally by London Midland. All carry London Midland livery. Two of the two-car sets, with No. 170507 nearest the camera, are seen at Cosford.* **Antony Christie**

Class 172/2
Turbostar

	Vehicle Length: 73ft 4in (22.37m)	Engine: MTU 6H1800 of 360kW
	Height: 12ft 4½in (3.77m)	Horsepower: 965hp (720kW)
	Width: 8ft 8in (2.69m)	Seats (total/car): 121S, 53S/68S

Number	Formation DMS+DMS	Depot	Livery	Owner	Operator	Number	Formation	Depot	Livery	Owner	Operator
						172216	50216+79216	TS	LMI	PTR	LMI
						172217	50217+79217	TS	LMI	PTR	LMI
172211	50211+79211	TS	LMI	PTR	LMI	172218	50218+79218	TS	LMI	PTR	LMI
172212	50212+79212	TS	LMI	PTR	LMI	172219	50219+59219	TS	LMI	PTR	LMI
172213	50213+79213	TS	LMI	PTR	LMI	172220	50220+79220	TS	LMI	PTR	LMI
172214	50214+79214	TS	LMI	PTR	LMI	170221	50221+79221	TS	LMI	PTR	LMI
172215	50215+79215	TS	LMI	PTR	LMI	170222	50222+79222	TS	LMI	PTR	LMI

Right: *London Midland upgraded Birmingham and West Midlands local services in 2011 by the introduction of two batches of Class 172 diesel-mechanical DMU, based on the Bombardier 'Turbostar' family. Twelve two-car Class 172/2 sets are allocated to Tyseley. These units are gangwayed throughout and have been well accepted by the travelling public. On 15 August 2011, two-car set No. 172211 and three-car set No. 172345 depart from Henley in Arden.* **John Binch**

Class 172/3
Turbostar

	Vehicle Length: (Driving) 73ft 4in (22.37m)	Engine: MTU 6H1800 of 360kW
	(Inter): (76ft 7in 23.36m)	Horsepower: 1449hp (1080kW)
	Height: 12ft 4½in (3.77m)	Seats (total/car): 193S, 53S/72S/68S
	Width: 8ft 8in (2.69m)	

Number	Formation DMSO+MS+DMSO	Depot	Livery	Owner	Operator
172331	50331+56331+79331	TS	LMI	PTR	LMI
172332	50332+56332+79332	TS	LMI	PTR	LMI
172333	50333+56333+79333	TS	LMI	PTR	LMI
172334	50334+56334+79334	TS	LMI	PTR	LMI
172335	50335+56335+79335	TS	LMI	PTR	LMI
172336	50336+56336+79336	TS	LMI	PTR	LMI
172337	50337+56337+79337	TS	LMI	PTR	LMI
172338	50338+56338+79338	TS	LMI	PTR	LMI
172339	50339+56339+79339	TS	LMI	PTR	LMI
172340	50340+56340+79340	TS	LMI	PTR	LMI
172341	50341+56341+79341	TS	LMI	PTR	LMI
172342	50342+56342+79342	TS	LMI	PTR	LMI

Passenger Train Operating Companies - London Midland

London Midland

172343	50343+56343+79343	TS	LMI	PTR	LMI	
172344	50344+56344+79344	TS	LMI	PTR	LMI	
172345	50345+56345+79345	TS	LMI	PTR	LMI	

Left: *Three-car Class 172/3 set No. 172339 is seen at Stratford-upon-Avon station on 5 September 2011. Each three-car Class 172 seats 193 standard class passengers.* **John Binch**

Class 321/4

Vehicle Length: (Driving) 65ft 0¾in (19.83m)
(Inter) 65ft 4¼in (19.92m)
Height: 12ft 4¾in (3.78m)
Width: 9ft 3in (2.82m)
Horsepower: 1,328hp (996kW)
Seats (total/car): 28F/271S, 28F-40S/79S/74S/78S

Number	Formation DMCO+MSO+TSO+DMSO	Depot	Livery	Owner	Operator
321411	78105+63073+71959+77953	NN	LMI	EVL	LMI
321412	78106+63074+71960+77954	NN	LMI	EVL	LMI
321413	78107+63075+71961+77955	NN	LMI	EVL	LMI
321414	78108+63076+71962+77956	NN	LMI	EVL	LMI
321415	78109+63077+71963+77957	NN	LMI	EVL	LMI
321416	78110+63078+71964+77958	NN	LMI	EVL	LMI
321417	78111+63079+71965+77959	NN	LMI	EVL	LMI

Left: *A small fleet of seven Class 321/4s operate for London Midland, working alongside the Class 350 stock on semi-fast and stopping services over the Northampton-Euston route, mainly during peak hours. Set No. 321413 is seen departing from Watford Junction bound for Euston.* **Ron Cover**

Class 323

Vehicle Length: (Driving) 76ft 8¼in (23.37m)
(Inter) 76ft 10¾in (23.44m)
Height: 12ft 4¾in (3.78m)
Width: 9ft 2¼in (2.80m)
Horsepower: 1,565hp (1,168kW)
Seats (total/car): 284S, 98S/88S/98S

Number	Formation DMSO(A)+PTSO+DMSO(B)	Depot	Livery	Owner	Operator
323201	64001+72201+65001	SI	LMI	PTR	LMI
323202	64002+72202+65002	SI	LMI	PTR	LMI
323203	64003+72203+65003	SI	LMI	PTR	LMI
323204	64004+72204+65004	SI	LMI	PTR	LMI
323205	64005+72205+65005	SI	LMI	PTR	LMI
323206	64006+72206+65006	SI	LMI	PTR	LMI
323207	64007+72207+65007	SI	LMI	PTR	LMI
323208	64008+72208+65008	SI	LMI	PTR	LMI
323209	64009+72209+65009	SI	LMI	PTR	LMI
323210	64010+72210+65010	SI	LMI	PTR	LMI

323211	64011+72211+65011	SI	LMI	PTR	LMI
323212	64012+72212+65012	SI	LMI	PTR	LMI
323213	64013+72213+65013	SI	LMI	PTR	LMI
323214	64014+72214+65014	SI	LMI	PTR	LMI
323215	64015+72215+65015	SI	LMI	PTR	LMI
323216	64016+72216+65016	SI	LMI	PTR	LMI
323217	64017+72217+65017	SI	LMI	PTR	LMI
323218	64018+72218+65018	SI	LMI	PTR	LMI
323219	64019+72219+65019	SI	LMI	PTR	LMI
323220	64020+72220+65020	SI	LMI	PTR	LMI
323221	64021+72221+65021	SI	LMI	PTR	LMI
323222	64022+72222+65022	SI	LMI	PTR	LMI
323240	64040+72340+65040	SI	LMI	PTR	LMI
323241	64041+72341+65041	SI	LMI	PTR	LMI
323242	64042+72342+65042	SI	LMI	PTR	LMI
323243	64043+72343+65043	SI	LMI	PTR	LMI

Right: *A fleet of 26 Class 323 three-car electric sets operate on the London Midland Birmingham cross-city line linking Redditch with Lichfield via Birmingham city centre. The sets are all painted in London Midland livery and are allocated to Soho depot. Set No. 323215 is illustrated.* **Stacey Thew**

Class 350/1
Desiro

Vehicle Length: 66ft 9in (20.4m)
Height: 12ft 1½in (3.78m)
Width: 9ft 2in (2.7m)

Horsepower: 1,341hp (1,000kW)
Seats (total/car): 24F-209S, 60S/24F-32S/57S/60S

Number	Formation DMSO(A)+TCO+PTSO+DMSO(B)	Depot	Livery	Owner	Operator
350101	63761+66811+66861+63711	NN	LMI	ANG	LMI
350102	63762+66812+66862+63712	NN	LMI	ANG	LMI
350103	63765+66813+66863+63713	NN	LMI	ANG	LMI
350104	63764+66814+66864+63714	NN	LMI	ANG	LMI
350105	63763+66815+66868+63715	NN	LMI	ANG	LMI
350106	63766+66816+66866+63716	NN	LMI	ANG	LMI
350107	63767+66817+66867+63717	NN	LMI	ANG	LMI
350108	63768+66818+66865+63718	NN	LMI	ANG	LMI
350109	63769+66819+66869+63719	NN	LMI	ANG	LMI
350110	63770+66820+66870+63720	NN	LMI	ANG	LMI
350111	63771+66821+66871+63721	NN	LMI	ANG	LMI
350112	63772+66822+66872+63722	NN	LMI	ANG	LMI
350113	63773+66823+66873+63723	NN	LMI	ANG	LMI
350114	63774+66824+66874+63724	NN	LMI	ANG	LMI
350115	63775+66825+66875+63725	NN	LMI	ANG	LMI
350116	63776+66826+66876+63726	NN	LMI	ANG	LMI
350117	63777+66827+66877+63727	NN	LMI	ANG	LMI
350118	63778+66828+66878+63728	NN	LMI	ANG	LMI
350119	63779+66829+66879+63729	NN	LMI	ANG	LMI
350120	63780+66830+66880+63730	NN	LMI	ANG	LMI
350121	63781+66831+66881+63731	NN	LMI	ANG	LMI
350122	63782+66832+66882+63732	NN	LMI	ANG	LMI
350123	63783+66833+66883+63733	NN	LMI	ANG	LMI
350124	63784+66834+66884+63734	NN	LMI	ANG	LMI

Train Operating Companies

London Midland

350125	63785+66835+66885+63735	NN	LMI	ANG	LMI
350126	63786+66836+66886+63736	NN	LMI	ANG	LMI
350127	63787+66837+66887+63737	NN	LMI	ANG	LMI
350128	63788+66838+66888+63738	NN	LMI	ANG	LMI
350129	63789+66839+66889+63739	NN	LMI	ANG	LMI
350130	63790+66840+66890+63740	NN	LMI	ANG	LMI

Class 350/2
Desiro

Vehicle Length: 66ft 9in (20.4m)
Height: 12ft 1½in (3.78m)
Width: 9ft 2in (2.7m)

Horsepower: 1,341hp (1,000kW)
Seats (total/car): 24F-243S, 70S/24F-42S/61S/70S

Number	Formation DMSO(A)+TCO+PTSO+DMSO(B)	Depot	Livery	Owner	Operator
350231	61431+65231+67531+61531	NN	LMI	PTR	LMI
350232	61432+65232+67532+61532	NN	LMI	PTR	LMI
350233	61433+65233+67533+61533	NN	LMI	PTR	LMI
350234	61434+65234+67534+61534	NN	LMI	PTR	LMI
350235	61435+65235+67535+61535	NN	LMI	PTR	LMI
350236	61436+65236+67536+61536	NN	LMI	PTR	LMI
350237	61437+65237+67537+61537	NN	LMI	PTR	LMI
350238	61438+65238+67538+61538	NN	LMI	PTR	LMI
350239	61439+65239+67539+61539	NN	LMI	PTR	LMI
350240	61440+65240+67540+61540	NN	LMI	PTR	LMI
350241	61441+65241+67541+61541	NN	LMI	PTR	LMI
350242	61442+65242+67542+61542	NN	LMI	PTR	LMI
350243	61443+65243+67543+61543	NN	LMI	PTR	LMI
350244	61444+65244+67544+61544	NN	LMI	PTR	LMI
350245	61445+65245+67545+61545	NN	LMI	PTR	LMI
350246	61446+65246+67546+61546	NN	LMI	PTR	LMI
350247	61447+65247+67547+61547	NN	LMI	PTR	LMI
350248	61448+65248+67548+61548	NN	LMI	PTR	LMI
350249	61449+65249+67549+61549	NN	LMI	PTR	LMI
350250	61450+65250+67550+61550	NN	LMI	PTR	LMI
350251	61451+65251+67551+61551	NN	LMI	PTR	LMI
350252	61452+65252+67552+61552	NN	LMI	PTR	LMI
350253	61453+65253+67553+61553	NN	LMI	PTR	LMI
350254	61454+65254+67554+61554	NN	LMI	PTR	LMI
350255	61455+65255+67555+61555	NN	LMI	PTR	LMI
350256	61456+65256+67556+61556	NN	LMI	PTR	LMI
350257	61457+65257+67557+61557	NN	LMI	PTR	LMI
350258	61458+65258+67558+61558	NN	LMI	PTR	LMI
350259	61459+65259+67559+61559	NN	LMI	PTR	LMI
350260	61460+65260+67560+61560	NN	LMI	PTR	LMI
350261	61461+65261+67561+61561	NN	LMI	PTR	LMI
350262	61462+65262+67562+61562	NN	LMI	PTR	LMI
350263	61463+65263+67563+61563	NN	LMI	PTR	LMI
350264	61464+65264+67564+61564	NN	LMI	PTR	LMI
350265	61465+65265+67565+61565	NN	LMI	PTR	LMI
350266	61466+65266+67566+61566	NN	LMI	PTR	LMI
350267	61467+65267+67567+61567	NN	LMI	PTR	LMI

Left: The main train design operating for London Midland on the prime London Euston to West Midlands corridor is the Class 350 'Desiro', of which 67 four-car sets are in use based at Northampton. Porterbrook-owned Class 350/2 No. 350262 is shown from its DMSO(A) end. **Antony Christie**

■ Eight additional Class 350/3 four-car sets for London Midland are to be ordered in 2012 for delivery in 2013. These are likely to have a top speed of 110mph.

Passenger Train Operating Companies - London Midland

London Overground

Address: ✉ 125 Finchley Road, London, NW3 6HY
 ✏ overgroundinfo@tfl.gov.uk
 ✆ 0845 601 4867
 ⓘ www.tfl.gov.uk/overground

Managing Director: Steve Murphy
Principal Routes: Clapham Junction - Willesden, Richmond - Stratford
 Gospel Oak - Barking, Euston - Watford
 East London Line – Dalston - West Croydon
Depots: Willesden (WN) New Cross Gate (NX)
Parent Company: Transport for London

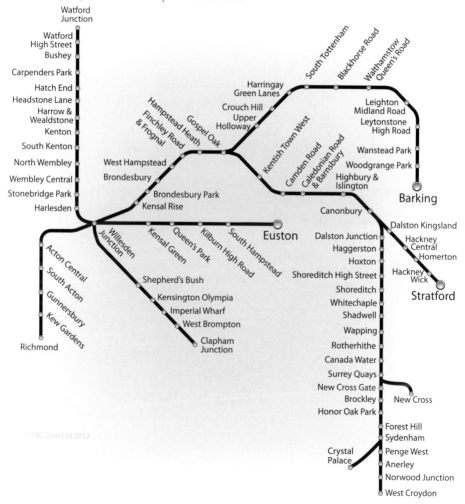

London Overground

Class 09/0

Vehicle Length: 29ft 3in (8.91m)			Engine: English Electric 6K		
Height: 12ft 8⅝in (3.87m)			Horsepower: 400hp (298kW)		
Width: 8ft 6in (2.59m)			Electrical Equipment: English Electric		

Number	Depot	Pool	Livery	Owner	Operator
09007	WN	-	LOG	LOL	LOL

Class 172/0
Turbostar

			Engine: MTU 6H1800R83 of 360kW (483hp)
Vehicle Length: 73ft 4in (22.37m)			
Height: 12ft 4½in (3.77m)			Horsepower: 965hp (720kW)
Width: 8ft 8in (2.69m)			Seats (total/car): 124S, 60S/64S

Number	Formation DMS+DMS	Depot	Livery	Owner	Operator		Number	Formation	Depot	Livery	Owner	Operator
							172004	59314+59414	WN	LOG	ANG	LOG
							172005	59315+59415	WN	LOG	ANG	LOG
172001	59311+59411	WN	LOG	ANG	LOG		172006	59316+59416	WN	LOG	ANG	LOG
172002	59312+59412	WN	LOG	ANG	LOG		172007	59317+59417	WN	LOG	ANG	LOG
172003	59313+59413	WN	LOG	ANG	LOG		172008	59318+59418	WN	LOG	ANG	LOG

Left: Eight two-car Bombardier-built Class 172/0 'Turbostar' diesel-mechanical sets were introduced on London Overground from the end of 2010 to operate over the Gospel Oak to Barking non-electrified route. The smart-looking units with 2+2 low-density seating do not have corridor ends and are likely to be displaced from London Overground once the Gospel Oak - Barking line is electrified. Set No. 172006 departs from Harringay Green Lanes station on 2 September 2011 with the 12.05 Gospel Oak to Barking service. **Tim Easter**

Class 378/1
Capitalstar

			Width: 9ft 2in (2.80m)
Vehicle Length: (Driving) (20.46m), (Inter) (20.14m)			
Height: 11ft 9in (3.58m)			Horsepower: 4-car (1,500kW)
750V dc sets			Seats (total/car): 146S, 36S/40S/34S/36S

Number	Formation DMSO+MSO+TSO+DMSO	Depot	Livery	Owner	Operator
378135	38035+38235+38335+38135	NX	LOG	QWR	LOG
378136	38036+38236+38336+38136	NX	LOG	QWR	LOG
378137	38037+38237+38337+38137	NX	LOG	QWR	LOG
378138	38038+38238+38338+38138	NX	LOG	QWR	LOG
378139	38039+38239+38339+38139	NX	LOG	QWR	LOG
378140	38040+38240+38340+38140	NX	LOG	QWR	LOG
378141	38041+38241+38341+38141	NX	LOG	QWR	LOG
378142	38042+38242+38342+38142	NX	LOG	QWR	LOG
378143	38043+38243+38343+38143	NX	LOG	QWR	LOG
378144	38044+38244+38344+38144	NX	LOG	QWR	LOG
378145	38045+38245+38345+38145	NX	LOG	QWR	LOG
378146	38046+38246+38346+38146	NX	LOG	QWR	LOG
378147	38047+38247+38347+38147	NX	LOG	QWR	LOG
378148	38048+38248+38348+38148	NX	LOG	QWR	LOG
378149	38049+38249+38349+38149	NX	LOG	QWR	LOG
378150	38050+38250+38350+38150	NX	LOG	QWR	LOG
378151	38051+38251+38351+38151	NX	LOG	QWR	LOG
378152	38052+38252+38352+38152	NX	LOG	QWR	LOG
378153	38053+38253+38353+38153	NX	LOG	QWR	LOG
378154	38054+38254+38354+38154	NX	LOG	QWR	LOG

Sets 378150-378154 fitted with De-icing equipment

Class 378/2
Capitalstar

Vehicle Length: (Driving) (20.46m), (Inter) (20.14m) Width: 9ft 2in (2.80m)
Height: 11ft 9in (3.58m)   Horsepower: 4-car 2,010hp (1,500kW)
Dual voltage - 750V dc third rail and 25kV ac overhead   Seats (total/car): 146S, 36S/40S/34S/36S

Sets built as 3-car units as Class 378/0, MSO added and reclassified as 378/2

Number	Formation DMSO+MSO+PTSO+DMSO	Depot	Livery	Owner	Operator
378201 (378001)	38001+38201+38301+38101	WN	LOG	QWR	LOG
378202 (378002)	38002+38202+38302+38102	WN	LOG	QWR	LOG
378203 (378003)	38003+38203+38303+38103	WN	LOG	QWR	LOG
378204 (378004)	38004+38204+38304+38104	WN	LOG	QWR	LOG
378205 (378005)	38005+38205+38305+38105	WN	LOG	QWR	LOG
378206 (378006)	38006+38206+38306+38106	WN	LOG	QWR	LOG
378207 (378007)	38007+38207+38307+38107	WN	LOG	QWR	LOG
378208 (378008)	38008+38208+38308+38108	WN	LOG	QWR	LOG
378209 (378009)	38009+38209+38309+38109	WN	LOG	QWR	LOG
378210 (378010)	38010+38210+38310+38110	WN	LOG	QWR	LOG
378211 (378011)	38011+38211+38311+38111	WN	LOG	QWR	LOG
378212 (378012)	38012+38212+38312+38112	WN	LOG	QWR	LOG
378213 (378013)	38013+38213+38313+38113	WN	LOG	QWR	LOG
378214 (378014)	38014+38214+38314+38114	WN	LOG	QWR	LOG
378215 (378015)	38015+38215+38315+38115	WN	LOG	QWR	LOG
378216 (378016)	38016+38216+38316+38116	WN	LOG	QWR	LOG
378217 (378017)	38017+38217+38317+38117	WN	LOG	QWR	LOG
378218 (378018)	38018+38218+38318+38118	WN	LOG	QWR	LOG
378219 (378019)	38019+38219+38319+38119	WN	LOG	QWR	LOG
378220 (378020)	38020+38220+38320+38120	WN	LOG	QWR	LOG
378221 (378021)	38021+38221+38321+38121	WN	LOG	QWR	LOG
378222 (378022)	38022+38222+38322+38122	WN	LOG	QWR	LOG
378223 (378023)	38023+38223+38323+38123	WN	LOG	QWR	LOG
378224 (378024)	38024+38224+38324+38124	WN	LOG	QWR	LOG

Sets 378216-378220 fitted with de-icing equipment

Number	Formation DMSO+MSO+TSO+DMSO	Depot	Livery	Owner	Operator	Name
378225	38025+38225+38325+38125	NX	LOG	QWR	LOG	
378226	38026+38226+38326+38126	NX	LOG	QWR	LOG	
378227	38027+38227+38327+38127	NX	LOG	QWR	LOG	
378228	38028+38228+38328+38128	NX	LOG	QWR	LOG	
378229	38029+38229+38329+38129	NX	LOG	QWR	LOG	
378230	38030+38230+38330+38130	NX	LOG	QWR	LOG	
378231	38031+38231+38331+38131	NX	LOG	QWR	LOG	
378232	38032+38232+38332+38132	NX	LOG	QWR	LOG	
378233	38033+38233+38333+38133	NX	LOG	QWR	LOG	Ian Brown CBE
378234	38034+38234+38334+38134	NX	LOG	QWR	LOG	
378255	38035+38235+38335+38135	NX	LOG	QWR	LOG	
378256	38036+38236+38336+38136	NX	LOG	QWR	LOG	
378257	38037+38237+38337+38137	NX	LOG	QWR	LOG	

Right: *The 'Capitalstar' product from Bombardier is based on the successful 'Electrostar' design family. When London Overground decided to modernise their electrified London network these were the most suitable trains on offer with a London Underground-style interior and wide end of vehicle connections. Although 24 sets were originally built as three-car units, all sets are now four-car form. Class 378/0 sets are dc (third rail) only, while the Class 378/2s are dual (25kV ac overhead and 750V third rail). Set No. 378226 is seen at Kensington Olympia.* **CJM**

Merseyrail

Address: ✉ Rail House, Lord Nelson Street, Liverpool, L1 1JF
📠 comment@merseyrail.org
☎ 0151 702 2534
ⓘ www.merseyrail.org

Managing Director: Maarten Spaargaren
Franchise Dates: 20 July 2003 - 31 July 2028
Principal Routes: All non-main line services in Liverpool area
Depots: Birkenhead North (BD)
Parent Company: Serco / Abellio

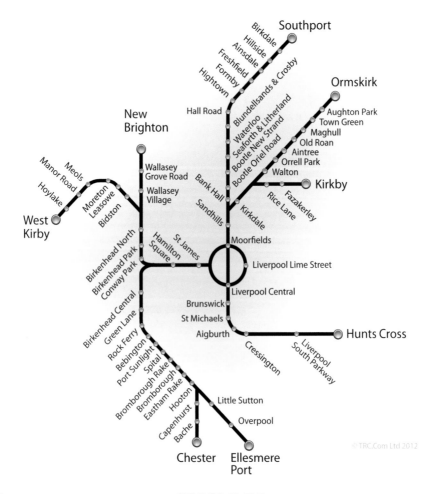

©TRC.Com Ltd 2012

Class 507

	Vehicle Length: (Driving) 64ft 11½in (19.80m)	Width: 9ft 3in (2.82m)
	(Inter) 65ft 4¼in (19.92m)	Horsepower: 880hp (656kW)
	Height: 11ft 6½in (3.58m)	Seats (total/car): 186S, 56S/74S/56S

Number	Formation DMSO+TSO+DMSO	Depot	Livery	Owner	Operator	Name
507001	64367+71342+64405	BD	MER	ANG	MER	
507002	64368+71343+64406	BD	MER	ANG	MER	
507003	64369+71344+64407	BD	MER	ANG	MER	
507004	64388+71345+64408	BD	MER	ANG	MER	Bob Paisley
507005	64371+71346+64409	BD	MER	ANG	MER	
507006	64372+71347+64410	BD	MER	ANG	MER	
507007	64373+71348+64411	BD	MER	ANG	MER	
507008	64374+71349+64412	BD	MER	ANG	MER	
507009	64375+71350+64413	BD	MER	ANG	MER	Dixie Dean
507010	64376+71351+64414	BD	MER	ANG	MER	
507011	64377+71352+64415	BD	MER	ANG	MER	
507012	64378+71353+64416	BD	MER	ANG	MER	
507013	64379+71354+64417	BD	MER	ANG	MER	
507014	64380+71355+64418	BD	MER	ANG	MER	
507015	64381+71356+64419	BD	MER	ANG	MER	
507016	64382+71357+64420	BD	MER	ANG	MER	
507017	64383+71358+64421	BD	MER	ANG	MER	
507018	64384+71359+64422	BD	MER	ANG	MER	
507019	64385+71360+64423	BD	MER	ANG	MER	
507020	64386+71361+64424	BD	MER	ANG	MER	John Peel
507021	64387+71362+64425	BD	MER	ANG	MER	Red Rum
507023	64389+71364+64427	BD	MER	ANG	MER	
507024	64390+71365+64428	BD	MER	ANG	MER	
507025	64391+71366+64429	BD	MER	ANG	MER	
507026	64392+71367+64430	BD	MER	ANG	MER	
507027	64393+71368+64431	BD	MER	ANG	MER	
507028	64394+71369+64432	BD	MER	ANG	MER	
507029	64395+71370+64433	BD	MER	ANG	MER	
507030	64396+71371+64434	BD	MER	ANG	MER	
507031	64397+71372+64435	BD	MER	ANG	MER	
507032	64398+71373+64436	BD	MER	ANG	MER	
507033	64399+71374+64437	BD	MER	ANG	MER	Councillor Jack Spriggs

The Merseyrail network operates a fleet of 32 Class 507 third-rail sets, all painted in the silver and yellow house colours. Set No. 507001 leads set No. 507024 at Hillside on the line to Southport in the summer of 2011. John Binch

Merseyrail

Class 508/1

Passenger Train Operating Companies - Merseyrail

	Vehicle Length: (Driving) 64ft 11½in (19.80m)	Width: 9ft 3in (2.82m)
	(Inter) 65ft 4¼in (19.92m)	Horsepower: 880hp (656kW)
	Height: 11ft 6½in (3.58m)	Seats (total/car): 186S, 56S/74S/56S

Number	Formation DMSO+TSO+DMSO	Depot	Livery	Owner	Operator	Name
508103	64651+71485+64694	BD	MER	ANG	MER	
508104	64652+71486+64964	BD	MER	ANG	MER	
508108	64656+71490+64699	BD	MER	ANG	MER	
508110	64658+71492+64701	BD	MER	ANG	MER	
508111	64659+71493+64702	BD	SPL	ANG	MER	*The Beatles*
508112	64660+71494+64703	BD	MER	ANG	MER	
508114	64662+71496+64705	BD	MER	ANG	MER	
508115	64663+71497+64708	BD	MER	ANG	MER	
508117	64665+71499+64908	BD	MER	ANG	MER	
508120	64668+71502+64711	BD	MER	ANG	MER	
508122	64670+71504+64713	BD	MER	ANG	MER	
508123	64671+71505+64714	BD	MER	ANG	MER	
508124	64672+71506+64715	BD	MER	ANG	MER	
508125	64673+71507+64716	BD	MER	ANG	MER	
508126	64674+71508+64717	BD	MER	ANG	MER	
508127	64675+71509+64718	BD	MER	ANG	MER	
508128	64676+71510+64719	BD	MER	ANG	MER	
508130	64678+71512+64721	BD	MER	ANG	MER	
508131	64679+71513+64722	BD	MER	ANG	MER	
508134	64682+71516+64725	BD	MER	ANG	MER	
508136	64684+71518+64727	BD	MER	ANG	MER	
508137	64685+71519+64728	BD	MER	ANG	MER	
508138	64686+71520+64729	BD	MER	ANG	MER	
508139	64687+71521+64730	BD	MER	ANG	MER	
508140	64688+71522+64731	BD	MER	ANG	MER	
508141	64689+71523+64732	BD	MER	ANG	MER	
508143	64691+71525+64734	BD	MER	ANG	MER	

Above: *After initially working on the Southern Region, the Class 508 sets were transferred to the Merseyrail network to work alongside the Class 507s. Now all fully refurbished with revised front ends, Class 508/1 No. 508125 departs from Chester on 25 July 2011 with the 15.45 Chester to Chester via Liverpool service.* **Michael J. Collins**

Abellio
Greater Anglia

Address: ✉ Floor One, Oliver's Yard, 55 City Road, London, EC1V 1HQ
(subject to change)
✆ customerrelations@abellio.com *(subject to change)*
✆ 0845 600 7245 *(subject to change)*
ⓘ www.abellio.com *(subject to change)*

Managing Director: Dominic Booth
Franchise Dates: 1 February 2012 - 1 July 2014
Principal Routes: London Liverpool Street to Norwich, Cambridge, Enfield Town, Hertford East, Upminster, Southend Victoria, Southminster, Braintree, Sudbury, Clacton, Walton, Harwich Town, Felixstowe, Lowestoft, Great Yarmouth, Sheringham, Stansted Airport and Peterborough
Depots: Ilford (IL), Norwich (NC), Clacton (CC)
Parent Company: Abellio

Passenger Train Operating Companies - Greater Anglia

Class 90/0

Vehicle Length: 61ft 6in (18.74m) | Power Collection: 25kV ac overhead
Height: 13ft 0¼in (3.96m) | Horsepower: 7,860hp (5,860kW)
Width: 9ft 0in (2.74m) | Electrical Equipment: GEC

Number	Depot	Pool	Livery	Owner	Operator	Name
90001	NC	IANA	ORN	PTR	NXA	
90002	NC	IANA	ORN	PTR	NXA	
90003	NC	IANA	NXA	PTR	NXA	Raedwald of East Anglia
90004	NC	IANA	ORN	PTR	NXA	Eastern Daily Press 1870-2010 Serving Norfolk for 140 years
90005	NC	IANA	ORN	PTR	NXA	Vice-Admiral Lord Nelson
90006	NC	IANA	ORN	PTR	NXA	Roger Ford / Modern Railways Magazine
90007	NC	IANA	ORN	PTR	NXA	Sir John Betjeman
90008	NC	IANA	NXA	PTR	NXA	The East Anglian
90009	NC	IANA	ORN	PTR	NXA	
90010	NC	IANA	ORN	PTR	NXA	Bressingham Steam and Gardens
90011	NC	IANA	ORN	PTR	NXA	Let's Go - East of England
90012	NC	IANA	ORN	PTR	NXA	Royal Anglian Regiment
90013	NC	IANA	ORN	PTR	NXA	The Evening Star
90014	NC	IANA	ORN	PTR	NXA	Norfolk and Norwich Festival
90015	NC	IANA	NXA	PTR	NXA	Colchester Castle

Right: *The Greater Anglia franchise, now operated by Abellio, uses 15 Class 90/0 locomotives on its prime London Liverpool Street to Norwich route. The locos operate in full push-pull mode with Mk3 DVTs on the remote ends of trains. The Class 90s are usually coupled at the London end of formations. Painted in National Express silver and white livery, No. 90015 Colchester Castle is seen at Stratford.* **CJM**

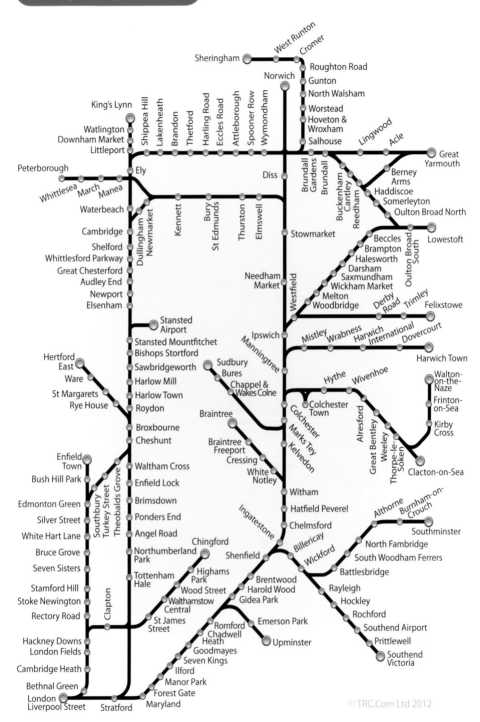

Passenger Train Operating Companies - Greater Anglia

© TRC.Com Ltd 2012

Mk 3 Hauled Stock

Vehicle Length: 75ft 0in (22.86m)		**Width:** 8ft 11in (2.71m)	
Height: 12ft 9in (3.88m)		**Bogie Type:** BT10	

AJ1G - RFM *Seating 24F*

Number	Depot	Livery	Owner
10200 (40519)	NC	ORN	PTR
10203 (40506)	NC	NXA	PTR
10206 (40507)	NC	ORN	PTR
10214 (11034)	NC	ORN	PTR
10216 (11041)	NC	ORN	PTR
10223 (11043)	NC	ORN	PTR
10228 (11035)	NC	NXA	PTR
10229 (11059)	NC	ORN	PTR
10247 (10011)	NC	ORN	PTR

AN2G - TSOB *Seating 52S*

10401 (12168)	NC	NXA	PTR
10402 (12010)	NC	ORN	PTR
10403 (12135)	NC	ORN	PTR
10404 (12068)	NC	ORN	PTR
10405 (12137)	NC	ORN	PTR
10406 (12020)	NC	ORN	PTR

AD1G - FO, *FOD *Seating 48F/34F**

11021 (S)	NC	VTS	PTR
11066	NC	ORN	PTR
11067	NC	ORN	PTR
11068	NC	NXA	PTR
11069	NC	ORN	PTR
11070	NC	ORN	PTR
11072*	NC	ORN	PTR
11073*	NC	NXA	PTR
11074 (S)	NC	VTS	PTR
11075	NC	ORN	PTR
11076	NC	ORN	PTR
11077	NC	ORN	PTR
11078*	NC	ORN	PTR
11080	NC	ORN	PTR
11081	NC	ORN	PTR
11082	NC	NXA	PTR
11085*	NC	ORN	PTR
11087*	NC	NXA	PTR
11088*	NC	NXA	PTR
11090*	NC	ORN	PTR
11091*	NC	NXA	PTR
11092	NC	ORN	PTR
11093*	NC	ORN	PTR
11094*	NC	ORN	PTR
11095*	NC	ORN	PTR
11096*	NC	ORN	PTR
11098*	NC	ORN	PTR
11099*	NC	ORN	PTR
11100*	NC	NXA	PTR
11101*	NC	ORN	PTR

AC2G - TSO *Seating 80S*

12005	NC	ORN	PTR
12009	NC	ORN	PTR
12012	NC	ORN	PTR
12013	NC	ORN	PTR
12015	NC	ORN	PTR
12016	NC	ORN	PTR
12019	NC	ORN	PTR
12021	NC	NXA	PTR
12024	NC	ORN	PTR
12026	NC	ORN	PTR
12027	NC	NXA	PTR
12030	NC	ORN	PTR
12031	NC	ORN	PTR
12032	NC	ORN	PTR
12034	NC	ORN	PTR
12035	NC	NXA	PTR
12037	NC	ORN	PTR
12040	NC	ORN	PTR
12041	NC	ORN	PTR
12042	NC	ORN	PTR
12046	NC	ORN	PTR
12049	NC	ORN	PTR
12051	NC	NXA	PTR
12056	NC	ORN	PTR
12057	NC	ORN	PTR
12060	NC	ORN	PTR
12061	NC	ORN	PTR
12062	NC	ORN	PTR
12064	NC	ORN	PTR
12066	NC	ORN	PTR
12067	NC	ORN	PTR
12073	NC	ORN	PTR
12079	NC	ORN	PTR
12081	NC	ORN	PTR
12082	NC	ORN	PTR
12084	NC	NXA	PTR
12089	NC	ORN	PTR
12090	NC	ORN	PTR
12091	NC	ORN	PTR
12093	NC	ORN	PTR
12097	NC	NXA	PTR
12098	NC	ORN	PTR
12099	NC	ORN	PTR
12103	NC	ORN	PTR
12105	NC	ORN	PTR
12107	NC	ORN	PTR
12108	NC	NXA	PTR
12109	NC	ORN	PTR
12110	NC	ORN	PTR
12111	NC	NXA	PTR
12114	NC	NXA	PTR
12115	NC	ORN	PTR
12116	NC	ORN	PTR
12118	NC	NXA	PTR
12120	NC	ORN	PTR
12125	NC	ORN	PTR
12126	NC	ORN	PTR
12129	NC	NXA	PTR
12130	NC	ORN	PTR
12132	NC	NXA	PTR
12137	NC	ORN	PTR
12139	NC	ORN	PTR
12141	NC	ORN	PTR
12143	NC	ORN	PTR
12146	NC	NXA	PTR
12147	NC	ORN	PTR
12148	NC	ORN	PTR
12150	NC	ORN	PTR
12151	NC	ORN	PTR
12153	NC	NXA	PTR
12154	NC	ORN	PTR
12159	NC	ORN	PTR
12164	NC	ORN	PTR
12166	NC	ORN	PTR
12167	NC	ORN	PTR
12170	NC	ORN	PTR
12171	NC	ORN	PTR

NZAH - DVT

82102	NC	ORN	PTR
82103§	NC	ORN	PTR
82104	NC	ORN	PTR
82105	NC	ORN	PTR
82107	NC	NXA	PTR
82112	NC	ORN	PTR
82114	NC	ORN	PTR
82118	NC	NXA	PTR
82121	NC	ORN	PTR
82127	NC	ORN	PTR
82132	NC	ORN	PTR
82133	NC	ORN	PTR
82136	NC	ORN	PTR
82139	NC	ORN	PTR
82143	NC	NXA	PTR
82152	NC	ORN	PTR

§ Fitted with de-icing equipment

Left: *Showing the older mid-blue livery, Greater Anglia loco-hauled First Open Disabled (FOD) No. 11096 is seen at Norwich depot.*
Antony Christie

Greater Anglia

Class 150/2

Vehicle Length: 64ft 9¾in (19.74m)
Height: 12ft 4½in (3.77m)
Width: 9ft 3⅛in (2.82m)

Engine: 1 x NT855R5 of 285hp per vehicle
Horsepower: 570hp (425kW)
Seats (total/car): 116S, 60S/56S

| 150280 | 52280+57280 | NR | ATW | PTR | NXA | On loan from Arriva Trains Wales |

Class 153

Vehicle Length: 76ft 5in (23.29m)
Height: 12ft 3⅛in (3.75m)
Width: 8ft 10in (2.70m)

Engine: 1 x NT855R5 of 285hp
Horsepower: 285hp (213kW)
Seats (total/car): 72S

Number	Formation DMSL	Depot	Livery	Owner	Operator	Name
153306	52306	NC	ORN	PTR	NXA	
153309	52309	NC	NXA	PTR	NXA	*Gerard Fiennes*
153314	52314	NC	ORN	PTR	NXA	
153322	52322	NC	ORN	PTR	NXA	*Benjamin Britten*
153335	52335	NC	NXA	PTR	NXA	*Michael Palin*

Left: *Five Class 153 'bubble' cars are allocated to Norwich Crown Point for local rural branch line use. Photographed from its small cab end, set No. 153306 is seen stabled between duties at Ipswich.* **Antony Christie**

Class 156

Vehicle Length: 75ft 6in (23.03m)
Height: 12ft 6in (3.81m)
Width: 8ft 11in (2.73m)

Engine: 1 x Cummins NT855R5 of 285hp
Horsepower: 570hp (425kW)
Seats (total/car): 146S, 70/76S

Number	Formation DMSL+DMS	Depot	Livery	Owner	Operator
156402	52402+57402	NC	ORN	PTR	NXA
156407	52407+57407	NC	ORN	PTR	NXA
156409	52409+57409	NC	ORN	PTR	NXA
156412	52412+57412	NC	ORN	PTR	NXA
156416	52416+57416	NC	ORN	PTR	NXA
156417¤	52417+57417	NC	ORN	PTR	NXA
156418	52418+57418	NC	ORN	PTR	NXA
156419	52419+57419	NC	NXA	PTR	NXA
156422	52422+57422	NC	ORN	PTR	NXA

¤ Stored due to collision damage

Name applied
156409 *Cromer Pier Seaside Special*

Right: *Looking rather tatty in terms of body condition, Class 156 No. 156422 is illustrated showing 'Travel the East Suffolk Lines' branding. Nine Class 156s are on the books of the Greater Anglia franchise, all being allocated to Norwich Crown Point depot.* **Antony Christie**

Passenger Train Operating Companies - Greater Anglia

Class 170/2
Turbostar

			Vehicle Length: 77ft 6in (23.62m)		Engine: 1 x MTU 6R 183TD13H 422hp per vehicle	
			Height: 12ft 4½in (3.77m)		Horsepower: 1,266hp (944kW)	
			Width: 8ft 10in (2.69m)		Seats (total/car): 7F-173S 7F-39S/68S/66S	

Number	Formation	Depot	Livery	Owner	Operator
	DMCL+MSL+DMSL				
170201	50201+56201+79201	NC	ORN	PTR	NXA
170202	50202+56202+79202	NC	ORN	PTR	NXA
170203	50203+56203+79203	NC	ORN	PTR	NXA
170204	50204+56204+79204	NC	ORN	PTR	NXA
170205	50205+56205+79205	NC	ORN	PTR	NXA
170206	50206+56206+79206	NC	ORN	PTR	NXA
170207	50207+56207+79207	NC	ORN	PTR	NXA
170208	50208+56208+79208	NC	ORN	PTR	NXA

		Vehicle Length: 77ft 6in (23.62m)		Engine: 1 x MTU 6R 183TD13H 422hp per vehicle
		Height: 12ft 4½in (3.77m)		Horsepower: 844hp (629kW)
		Width: 8ft 10in (2.69m)		Seats (total/car): 9F-110S 57S/9F-53S

Number	Formation	Depot	Livery	Owner	Operator		Number	Formation	Depot	Livery	Owner	Operator
	DMSL+DMCL						170271	50271+79271	NC	ORN	PTR	NXA
							170272	50272+79272	NC	ORN	PTR	NXA
170270	50270+79270	NC	ORN	PTR	NXA		170273	50273+79273	NC	ORN	PTR	NXA

Both two- and three-car versions of the Class 170/2 'Turbostar' operate for Greater Anglia, eight three-car and four two-car sets, all allocated to Norwich Crown Point. Painted in the older National Express blue colour scheme, three-car set No. 170206 is seen near March on 7 March 2011, forming an Ipswich to Peterborough service. **Michael J. Collins**

Class 315

			Vehicle Length: (Driving) 64ft 11½in (19.80m)		Width: 9ft 3in (2.82m)	
			(Inter) 65ft 4¾in (19.92m)		Horsepower: 880hp (656kW)	
			Height: 11ft 6½in (3.58m)		Seats (total/car): 318S, 74S/86S/84S/74S	

Number	Formation	Depot	Livery	Owner	Operator	Name
	DMSO(A)+TSO+PTSO+DMSO(B)					
315801	64461+71281+71389+64462	IL	ORN	EVL	NXA	
315802	64463+71282+71390+64464	IL	ORN	EVL	NXA	
315803	64465+71283+71391+64466	IL	ORN	EVL	NXA	
315804	64467+71284+71392+64468	IL	ORN	EVL	NXA	
315805	64469+71285+71393+64470	IL	ORN	EVL	NXA	
315806	64471+71286+71394+64472	IL	ORN	EVL	NXA	
315807	64473+71287+71395+64474	IL	ORN	EVL	NXA	
315808	64475+71288+71396+64476	IL	ORN	EVL	NXA	
315809	64477+71289+71397+64478	IL	ORN	EVL	NXA	
315810	64479+71290+71398+64480	IL	ORN	EVL	NXA	
315811	64481+71291+71399+64482	IL	ORN	EVL	NXA	
315812	64483+71292+71400+64484	IL	ORN	EVL	NXA	London Borough of Newham Host Borough 2012 Olympics Bid
315813	64485+71293+71401+64486	IL	ORN	EVL	NXA	
315814	64487+71294+71402+64488	IL	ORN	EVL	NXA	
315815	64489+71295+71403+64490	IL	ORN	EVL	NXA	
315816	64491+71296+71404+64492	IL	ORN	EVL	NXA	
315817	64493+71297+71405+64494	IL	ORN	EVL	NXA	Transport for London
315818	64495+71298+71406+64496	IL	ORN	EVL	NXA	

Greater Anglia

315819	64497+71299+71407+64498	IL	ORN	EVL	NXA	
315820	64499+71300+71408+64500	IL	ORN	EVL	NXA	
315821	64501+71301+71409+64502	IL	ORN	EVL	NXA	
315822	64503+71302+71410+64504	IL	ORN	EVL	NXA	
315823	64505+71303+71411+64506	IL	ORN	EVL	NXA	
315824	64507+71304+71412+64508	IL	ORN	EVL	NXA	
315825	64509+71305+71413+64510	IL	ORN	EVL	NXA	
315826	64511+71306+71414+64512	IL	ORN	EVL	NXA	
315827	64513+71307+71415+64514	IL	ORN	EVL	NXA	
315828	64515+71308+71416+64516	IL	ORN	EVL	NXA	
315829	64517+71309+71417+64518	IL	ORN	EVL	NXA	*London Borough of Havering Celebrating 40 years*
315830	64519+71310+71418+64520	IL	ORN	EVL	NXA	
315831	64521+71311+71419+64522	IL	ORN	EVL	NXA	
315832	64523+71312+71420+64524	IL	ORN	EVL	NXA	
315833	64525+71313+71421+64526	IL	ORN	EVL	NXA	
315834	64527+71314+71422+64528	IL	ORN	EVL	NXA	
315835	64529+71315+71423+64530	IL	ORN	EVL	NXA	
315836	64531+71316+71424+64532	IL	ORN	EVL	NXA	
315837	64533+71317+71425+64534	IL	ORN	EVL	NXA	
315838	64535+71318+71426+64536	IL	ORN	EVL	NXA	
315839	64537+71319+71427+64538	IL	ORN	EVL	NXA	
315840	64539+71320+71428+64540	IL	ORN	EVL	NXA	
315841	64541+71321+71429+64542	IL	ORN	EVL	NXA	
315842	64543+71322+71430+64544	IL	ORN	EVL	NXA	
315843	64545+71323+71431+64546	IL	ORN	EVL	NXA	
315844	64547+71324+71432+64548	IL	ORN	EVL	NXA	
315845	64549+71325+71433+64550	IL	ORN	EVL	NXA	*Herbie Woodward*
315846	64551+71326+71434+64552	IL	ORN	EVL	NXA	
315847	64553+71327+71435+64554	IL	ORN	EVL	NXA	
315848	64555+71328+71436+64556	IL	ORN	EVL	NXA	
315849	64557+71329+71437+64558	IL	ORN	EVL	NXA	
315850	64559+71330+71438+64560	IL	NXU	EVL	NXA	
315851	64561+71331+71439+64562	IL	ORN	EVL	NXA	
315852	64563+71332+71440+64564	IL	ORN	EVL	NXA	
315853	64565+71333+71441+64566	IL	ORN	EVL	NXA	
315854	64567+71334+71442+64568	IL	ORN	EVL	NXA	
315855	64569+71335+71443+64570	IL	ORN	EVL	NXA	
315856	64571+71336+71444+64572	IL	ORN	EVL	NXA	
315857	64573+71337+71445+64574	IL	ORN	EVL	NXA	
315858	64575+71338+71446+64576	IL	ORN	EVL	NXA	
315859	64577+71339+71447+64578	IL	ORN	EVL	NXA	
315860	64579+71340+71448+64580	IL	ORN	EVL	NXA	
315861	64581+71341+71449+64582	IL	ORN	EVL	NXA	

Left: *The Great Eastern suburban network radiating from London Liverpool Street is in the hands of a fleet of 61 four-car Class 315 units, a derivative of the 1972-design standard EMU developed from the PEP unit. All sets are allocated to Ilford depot. These are scheduled to continue operation until replaced by new stock ordered for the Crossrail project. Set No. 315817 Transport for London is illustrated.* **Antony Christie**

Class 317/5

Vehicle Length: (Driving) 65ft 0¾in (19.83m) Width: 9ft 3in (2.82m)
(Inter) 65ft 4¼in (19.92m) Horsepower: 1,000hp (746kW)
Height: 12ft 1½in (3.58m) Seats (total/car): 291S, 74S/79S/68S/70S

Number	Former Number	Formation DTSO(A)+MSO+TCO+DTSO(B)	Depot	Livery	Owner	Operator	Name
317501	(317301)	77024+62661+71577+77048	IL	NXA	ANG	NXA	
317502	(317302)	77001+62662+71578+77049	IL	NXA	ANG	NXA	
317503	(317303)	77002+62663+71579+77050	IL	NXA	ANG	NXA	
317504	(317304)	77003+62664+71580+77051	IL	NXA	ANG	NXA	
317505	(317305)	77004+62665+71581+77052	IL	NXA	ANG	NXA	
317506	(317306)	77005+62666+71582+77053	IL	NXA	ANG	NXA	
317507	(317307)	77006+62667+71583+77054	IL	NXA	ANG	NXA	University of Cambridge 800 years 1209-2009
317508	(317311)	77010+62697+71587+77058	IL	NXA	ANG	NXA	
317509	(317312)	77011+62672+71588+77059	IL	NXA	ANG	NXA	
317510	(317313)	77012+62673+71589+77060	IL	NXA	ANG	NXA	
317511	(317315)	77014+62675+71591+77062	IL	NXU	ANG	NXA	
317512	(317316)	77015+62676+71592+77063	IL	NXU	ANG	NXA	
317513	(317317)	77016+62677+71593+77064	IL	NXA	ANG	NXA	
317514	(317318)	77017+62678+71594+77065	IL	NXA	ANG	NXA	
317515	(317320)	77019+62680+71596+77067	IL	NXA	ANG	NXA	

Class 317/6

Vehicle Length: (Driving) 65ft 0¾in (19.83m) Width: 9ft 3in (2.82m)
(Inter) 65ft 4¼in (19.92m) Horsepower: 1,000hp (746kW)
Height: 12ft 1½in (3.58m) Seats (total/car): 24F/244S, 64S/70S/62S/24F-48S

Number	Former Number	Formation DTSO+MSO+TSO+DTCO	Depot	Livery	Owner	Operator	Name
317649	(317349)	77200+62846+71734+77220	IL	NXU	ANG	NXA	
317650	(317350)	77201+62847+71735+77221	IL	NXU	ANG	NXA	
317651	(317351)	77202+62848+71736+77222	IL	NXU	ANG	NXA	
317652	(317352)	77203+62849+71739+77223	IL	NXU	ANG	NXA	
317653	(317353)	77204+62850+71738+77224	IL	NXU	ANG	NXA	
317654	(317354)	77205+62851+71737+77225	IL	NXU	ANG	NXA	Richard Wells
317655	(317355)	77206+62852+71740+77226	IL	ORN	ANG	NXA	
317656	(317356)	77207+62853+71742+77227	IL	ORN	ANG	NXA	
317657	(317357)	77208+62854+71741+77228	IL	NXU	ANG	NXA	
317658	(317358)	77209+62855+71743+77229	IL	NXU	ANG	NXA	
317659	(317359)	77210+62856+71744+77230	IL	ORN	ANG	NXA	
317660	(317360)	77211+62857+71745+77231	IL	ORN	ANG	NXA	
317661	(317361)	77212+62858+71746+77232	IL	ORN	ANG	NXA	
317662	(317362)	77213+62859+71747+77233	IL	ORN	ANG	NXA	
317663	(317363)	77214+62860+71748+77234	IL	ORN	ANG	NXA	
317664	(317364)	77215+62861+71749+77235	IL	ORN	ANG	NXA	
317665	(317365)	77216+62862+71750+77236	IL	NXU	ANG	NXA	
317666	(317366)	77217+62863+71752+77237	IL	NXU	ANG	NXA	
317667	(317367)	77218+62864+71751+77238	IL	ORN	ANG	NXA	
317668	(317368)	77219+62865+71753+77239	IL	ORN	ANG	NXA	
317669	(317369)	77280+62886+71762+77284	IL	NXU	ANG	NXA	
317670	(317370)	77281+62887+71763+77285	IL	ORN	ANG	NXA	
317671	(317371)	77282+62888+71764+77286	IL	ORN	ANG	NXA	
317672	(317372)	77283+62889+71765+77287	IL	ORN	ANG	NXA	

Right: *Outer suburban Greater Anglia services are operated by Class 317s, with sets of both body style in operation. On 17 March 2011, set No. 317665 is seen in the sub-level station at Stansted Airport with a London Liverpool Street service.* **CJM**

Passenger Train Operating Companies - Greater Anglia

Greater Anglia

Passenger Train Operating Companies - Greater Anglia

Class 317/7

Vehicle Length: (Driving) 65ft 0¾in (19.83m) Width: 9ft 3in (2.82m)
(Inter) 65ft 4¼in (19.92m) Horsepower: 1,000hp (746kW)
Height: 12ft 1½in (3.58m) Seats (total/car): 22F/172S, 52S/62S/42S/22F-16S

Number	Former Number	Formation DTSO+MSO+TSO+DTCO	Depot	Livery	Owner	Operator	Name
317708	(317308)	77007+62668+71584+77055	IL	NXA	ANG	NXA	
317709	(317309)	77008+62669+71585+77056	IL	NXA	ANG	NXA	*Len Camp*
317710	(317310)	77009+62670+71586+77057	IL	NXA	ANG	NXA	
317714	(317314)	77013+62674+71590+77061	IL	NXA	ANG	NXA	
317719	(317319)	77018+62679+71595+77066	IL	NXA	ANG	NXA	
317722	(317322/392)	77021+62682+71598+77069	IL	NXA	ANG	NXA	
317723	(317323/393)	77022+62683+71599+77070	IL	NXA	ANG	NXA	*The Tottenham Flyer*
317729	(317329)	77028+62689+71605+77076	IL	NXA	ANG	NXA	
317732	(317332)	77031+62692+71608+77079	IL	NXA	ANG	NXA	

All nine Class 317/7s are scheduled to go 'off lease' in spring 2012 as part of the Anglia franchise change

Class 317/8

Vehicle Length: (Driving) 65ft 0¾in (19.83m) Width: 9ft 3in (2.82m)
(Inter) 65ft 4¼in (19.92m) Horsepower: 1,000hp (746kW)
Height: 12ft 1½in (3.58m) Seats (total/car): 20F/265S, 74S/79S/20F-42S/70S

Number	Former Number	Formation DTSO(A)+MSO+TCO+DTSO(B)	Depot	Livery	Owner	Operator	Name
317881	(317321)	77020+62681+71597+77068	IL	NXA	ANG	NXA	
317882	(317324)	77023+62684+71600+77071	IL	NXU	ANG	NXA	
317883	(317325)	77000+62685+71601+77072	IL	NXU	ANG	NXA	
317884	(317326)	77025+62686+71602+77073	IL	NXU	ANG	NXA	
317885	(317327)	77026+62687+71603+77074	IL	NXU	ANG	NXA	
317886	(317328)	77027+62688+71604+77075	IL	NXU	ANG	NXA	
317887	(317330)	77043+62704+71606+77077	IL	NXU	ANG	NXA	
317888	(317331)	77030+62691+71607+77078	IL	NXA	ANG	NXA	
317889	(317333)	77032+62693+71609+77080	IL	NXA	ANG	NXA	
317890	(317334)	77033+62694+71610+77081	IL	NXA	ANG	NXA	
317891	(317335)	77034+62695+71611+77082	IL	NXA	ANG	NXA	
317892	(317336)	77035+62696+71612+77083	IL	NXA	ANG	NXA	*Ilford Depot*

Left: *Twelve Class 317/8s are based at Ilford, for outer suburban use. Set No. 317888 was originally numbered 317331 and shows the original body profile. This set sports the now obsolete National Express grey and white livery. Car No. 77030 is nearest the camera, a DTSO(A) vehicle.*
Nathan Williamson

Class 321/3

Vehicle Length: (Driving) 65ft 0¾in (19.83m) Width: 9ft 3in (2.82m)
(Inter) 65ft 4¼in (19.92m) Horsepower: 1,328hp (996kW)
Height: 12ft 4¾in (3.78m) Seats (total/car): 16F/292S, 16F-57S/82S/75S/78S

Number	Formation DTCO+MSO+TSO+DTSO	Depot	Livery	Owner	Operator	Name
321301	78049+62975+71880+77853	IL	NXA	EVL	NXA	
321302	78050+62976+71881+77854	IL	NXA	EVL	NXA	
321303	78051+62977+71882+77855	IL	NXA	EVL	NXA	
321304	78052+62978+71883+77856	IL	NXA	EVL	NXA	
321305	78053+62979+71884+77857	IL	NXA	EVL	NXA	
321306	78054+62980+71885+77858	IL	NXA	EVL	NXA	
321307	78055+62981+71886+77859	IL	NXA	EVL	NXA	
321308	78056+62982+71887+77860	IL	NXA	EVL	NXA	
321309	78057+62983+71888+77861	IL	NXA	EVL	NXA	
321310	78058+62984+71889+77862	IL	NGE	EVL	NXA	

Number	Formation	Depot	Livery	Owner	Operator	Name
321311	78059+62985+71890+77863	IL	NXA	EVL	NXA	
321312	78060+62986+71891+77864	IL	NXA	EVL	NXA	Southend-on-Sea
321313	78061+62987+71892+77865	IL	NXA	EVL	NXA	University of Essex
321314	78062+62988+71893+77866	IL	NGE	EVL	NXA	
321315	78063+62989+71894+77867	IL	NXA	EVL	NXA	
321316	78064+62990+71895+77868	IL	NXA	EVL	NXA	
321317	78065+62991+71896+77869	IL	NXA	EVL	NXA	
321318	78066+62992+71897+77870	IL	NXA	EVL	NXA	
321319	78067+62993+71898+77871	IL	NXA	EVL	NXA	
321320	78068+62994+71899+77872	IL	NXA	EVL	NXA	
321321	78069+62995+71900+77873	IL	NXA	EVL	NXA	NSPCC Essex Full Stop
321322	78070+62996+71901+77874	IL	NXA	EVL	NXA	
321323	78071+62997+71902+77875	IL	NXA	EVL	NXA	
321324	78072+62998+71903+77876	IL	NXA	EVL	NXA	
321325	78073+62999+71904+77877	IL	NXA	EVL	NXA	
321326	78074+63000+71905+77878	IL	NXA	EVL	NXA	
321327	78075+63001+71906+77879	IL	NXU	EVL	NXA	
321328	78076+63002+71907+77880	IL	NXA	EVL	NXA	
321329	78077+63003+71908+77881	IL	NXA	EVL	NXA	
321330	78078+63004+71909+77882	IL	NXU	EVL	NXA	
321331	78079+63005+71910+77883	IL	NXU	EVL	NXA	
321332	78080+63006+71911+77884	IL	NXU	EVL	NXA	
321333	78081+63007+71912+77885	IL	NXU	EVL	NXA	Amsterdam
321334	78082+63008+71913+77886	IL	NXU	EVL	NXA	
321335	78083+63009+71914+77887	IL	NXU	EVL	NXA	Geoffrey Freeman Allen
321336	78084+63010+71915+77888	IL	NXU	EVL	NXA	
321337	78085+63011+71916+77889	IL	NXU	EVL	NXA	
321338	78086+63012+71917+77890	IL	NXU	EVL	NXA	
321339	78087+63013+71918+77891	IL	NXU	EVL	NXA	
321340	78088+63014+71919+77892	IL	NXU	EVL	NXA	
321341	78089+63015+71920+77893	IL	NXU	EVL	NXA	
321342	78090+63016+71921+77894	IL	NXU	EVL	NXA	R Barnes
321343	78091+63017+71922+77895	IL	NXU	EVL	NXA	
321344	78092+63018+71923+77896	IL	NXU	EVL	NXA	
321345	78093+63019+71924+77897	IL	NXU	EVL	NXA	
321346	78094+63020+71925+77898	IL	NGU	EVL	NXA	
321347	78131+63105+71991+78280	IL	NXU	EVL	NXA	
321348	78132+63106+71992+78281	IL	NXU	EVL	NXA	
321349	78133+63107+71993+78282	IL	NGE	EVL	NXA	
321350	78134+63108+71994+78283	IL	NXU	EVL	NXA	Gurkha
321351	78135+63109+71995+78284	IL	NXU	EVL	NXA	London Southend Airport
321352	78136+63110+71996+78285	IL	NXU	EVL	NXA	
321353	78137+63111+71997+78286	IL	NXU	EVL	NXA	
321354	78138+63112+71998+78287	IL	NXU	EVL	NXA	
321355	78139+63113+71999+78288	IL	NXU	EVL	NXA	
321356	78140+63114+72000+78289	IL	NGU	EVL	NXA	
321357	78141+63115+72001+78290	IL	NGE	EVL	NXA	
321358	78142+63116+72002+78291	IL	NGE	EVL	NXA	
321359	78143+63117+72003+78292	IL	NGE	EVL	NXA	
321360	78144+63118+72004+78293	IL	NXU	EVL	NXA	Phoenix
321361	78145+63119+72005+78294	IL	NGE	EVL	NXA	
321362	78146+63120+72006+78295	IL	NGE	EVL	NXA	
321363	78147+63121+72007+78296	IL	NGE	EVL	NXA	
321364	78148+63122+72008+78297	IL	NGE	EVL	NXA	
321365	78149+63123+72009+78298	IL	NGE	EVL	NXA	
321366	78150+63124+72010+78299	IL	NGE	EVL	NXA	

Class 321/4

Vehicle Length: (Driving) 65ft 0¾in (19.83m) Width: 9ft 3in (2.82m)
(Inter) 65ft 4¼in (19.92m) Horsepower: 1,328hp (996kW)
Height: 12ft 4¾in (3.78m) Seats (total/car): 16F/283S, 16F-52S/79S/74S/78S

Number	Formation DTCO+MSO+TSO+DTSO	Depot	Livery	Owner	Operator	Name
321421	78115+63083+71969+77963	IL	NXU	EVL	NXA	
321422	78116+63084+71970+77964	IL	NXU	EVL	NXA	
321423	78117+63085+71971+77965	IL	NXU	EVL	NXA	

Greater Anglia

321424	78118+63086+71972+77966	IL	NXA	EVL	NXA		
321425	78119+63087+71973+77967	IL	NXA	EVL	NXA		
321426	78120+63088+71974+77968	IL	NXA	EVL	NXA		
321427	78121+63089+71975+77969	IL	NXA	EVL	NXA		
321428	78122+63090+71976+77970	IL	NXA	EVL	NXA	*The Essex Commuter*	
321429	78123+69031+71977+77971	IL	NXA	EVL	NXA		
321430	78124+63092+71978+77972	IL	NXA	EVL	NXA		
321431	78151+63125+72011+78300	IL	NXA	EVL	NXA		
321432	78152+63126+72012+78301	IL	NXU	EVL	NXA		
321433	78153+63127+72013+78302	IL	NXU	EVL	NXA		
321434	78154+63128+72014+78303	IL	NXU	EVL	NXA		
321435	78155+63129+72015+78304	IL	NXU	EVL	NXA		
321436	78156+63130+72016+78305	IL	NXU	EVL	NXA		
321437	78157+63131+72017+78306	IL	NXU	EVL	NXA		
321438	78158+63132+72018+78307	IL	NGE	EVL	NXA		
321439	78159+63133+72019+78308	IL	NGE	EVL	NXA		
321440	78160+63134+72020+78309	IL	NGE	EVL	NXA		
321441	78161+63135+72021+78310	IL	NGE	EVL	NXA		
321442	78162+63136+72022+78311	IL	NGE	EVL	NXA		
321443	78125+63099+71985+78274	IL	NGE	EVL	NXA		
321444	78126+63100+71986+78275	IL	NGE	EVL	NXA	*Essex Lifeboats*	
321445	78127+63101+71987+78276	IL	NGE	EVL	NXA		
321446	78128+63102+71988+78277	IL	NGE	EVL	NXA	*George Mullings*	
321447	78129+63103+71989+78278	IL	NGE	EVL	NXA		
321448	78130+63104+71990+78279	IL	NGE	EVL	NXA		

Left & Below: *The main fleet for outer suburban Great Eastern line services are Class 321, with members of Class 321/3 and 321/4 in service from Ilford. In the view left we see set No. 321333 in all-white livery with National Express markings, while the view below shows set No. 321306 in full National Express East Anglia colours. The unit's DTCO vehicle is nearest the camera. Both views were recorded at Stratford. Both:* **CJM**

Class 360/1
Desiro

Vehicle Length: 66ft 9in (20.4m)	Horsepower: 1,341hp (1,000kW)
Height: 12ft 1½in (3.7m)	Seats (total/car): 16F/265S, 8F-59S/69S/78S/8F-59S
Width: 9ft 2in (2.79m)	

Number	Formation DMCO(A)+PTSO+TSO+DMCO(B)	Depot	Livery	Owner	Operator
360101	65551+72551+74551+68551	IL	FNA	ANG	NXA
360102	65552+72552+74552+68552	IL	FNA	ANG	NXA
360103	65553+72553+74553+68553	IL	FNA	ANG	NXA
360104	65554+72554+74554+68554	IL	FNA	ANG	NXA
360105	65555+72555+74555+68555	IL	FNA	ANG	NXA
360106	65556+72556+74556+68556	IL	FNA	ANG	NXA
360107	65557+72557+74557+68557	IL	FNA	ANG	NXA
360108	65558+72558+74558+68558	IL	FNA	ANG	NXA
360109	65559+72559+74559+68559	IL	FNA	ANG	NXA
360110	65560+72560+74560+68560	IL	FNA	ANG	NXA
360111	65561+72561+74561+68561	IL	FNA	ANG	NXA
360112	65562+72562+74562+68562	IL	FNA	ANG	NXA
360113	65563+72563+74563+68563	IL	FNA	ANG	NXA
360114	65564+72564+74564+68564	IL	FNA	ANG	NXA
360115	65565+72565+74565+68565	IL	NXA	ANG	NXA
360116	65566+72566+74566+68566	IL	FNA	ANG	NXA
360117	65567+72567+74567+68567	IL	FNA	ANG	NXA
360118	65568+72568+74568+68568	IL	FNA	ANG	NXA
360119	65569+72569+74569+68569	IL	FNA	ANG	NXA
360120	65570+72570+74570+68570	IL	FNA	ANG	NXA
360121	65571+72571+74571+68571	IL	FNA	ANG	NXA

Right: *The principal London area maintenance facility for the Greater Anglia franchise is Ilford, where the franchise holder and Bombardier have major repair and service facilities. In this view we see a Class 360/1, No. 360115, passing through the Ilford washing plant.* **CJM**

Below: *Still showing the blue livery from its First Group days, but now sporting National Express branding, set No. 360119 passes Stratford in mid-2011 bound for Liverpool Street. These are likely to be some of the first sets in new livery.* **CJM**

Greater Anglia

Class 379
Electrostat

Vehicle Length: (Driving) 66ft 9in (20.40m)	Width: 9ft 2in (2.80m)
(Inter) 65ft 6in (19.99m)	Horsepower: 2,010hp (1,500kW)
Height: 12ft 4in (3.77m)	Seats (total/car): 20F/189S, 60S/62S/43S/20F-24S

Number	Formation DMSO(A)+MSO+TSO+DMCO	Depot	Livery	Owner	Operator	Name
379001	61201+61701+61901+62101	IL	NXU	LTS	NXA	
379002	61202+61702+61902+62102	IL	NXU	LTS	NXA	
379003	61203+61703+61903+62103	IL	NXU	LTS	NXA	
379004	61204+61704+61904+62104	IL	NXU	LTS	NXA	
379005	61205+61705+61905+62105	IL	NXU	LTS	NXA	*Stansted Express*
379006	61206+61706+61906+62106	IL	NXU	LTS	NXA	
379007	61207+61707+61907+62107	IL	NXU	LTS	NXA	
379008	61208+61708+61908+62108	IL	NXU	LTS	NXA	
379009	61209+61709+61909+62109	IL	NXU	LTS	NXA	
379010	61210+61710+61910+62110	IL	NXU	LTS	NXA	
379011	61211+61711+61911+62111	IL	NXU	LTS	NXA	*Ely Cathedral*
379012	61212+61712+61912+62112	IL	NXU	LTS	NXA	*The West Anglian*
379013	61213+61713+61913+62113	IL	NXU	LTS	NXA	
379014	61214+61714+61914+62114	IL	NXU	LTS	NXA	
379015	61215+61715+61915+62115	IL	NXU	LTS	NXA	*City of Cambridge*
379016	61216+61716+61916+62116	IL	NXU	LTS	NXA	
379017	61217+61717+61917+62117	IL	NXU	LTS	NXA	
379018	61218+61718+61918+62118	IL	NXU	LTS	NXA	
379019	61219+61719+61919+62119	IL	NXU	LTS	NXA	
379020	61220+61720+61920+62120	IL	NXU	LTS	NXA	
379021	61221+61721+61921+62121	IL	NXU	LTS	NXA	
379022	61222+61722+61922+62122	IL	NXU	LTS	NXA	
379023	61223+61723+61923+62123	IL	NXU	LTS	NXA	
379024	61224+61724+61924+62124	IL	NXU	LTS	NXA	
379025	61225+61725+61925+62125	IL	NXU	LTS	NXA	*Go Discover*
379026	61226+61726+61926+62126	IL	NXU	LTS	NXA	
379027	61227+61727+61927+62127	IL	NXU	LTS	NXA	
379028	61228+61728+61928+62128	IL	NXU	LTS	NXA	
379029	61229+61729+61929+62129	IL	NXU	LTS	NXA	
379030	61230+61730+61930+62130	IL	NXU	LTS	NXA	

Below: *The latest trains to enter service on Greater Anglia routes are Bombardier Class 379 'Electrostar' sets, which entered traffic in 2011. The 30 units are based at Ilford and maintained under contract by Bombardier. They are used on the Liverpool Street to Stansted Airport and Cambridge routes. No. 379006 is seen at Cambridge alongside Class 317 No. 317886.* **CJM**

Passenger Train Operating Companies - Greater Anglia

Northern Rail

Address:	✉ Northern House, 9 Rougier Street, York, YO1 6HZ
	✆ customer.relations@northernrail.org
	✆ 0845 000125
	ⓘ www.northernrail.org
Managing Director:	Ian Bevan
Franchise Dates:	12 December 2004 - 1 April 2014
Principal Routes:	Regional services in Merseyside, Greater Manchester, South/ North Yorkshire, Lancashire, Cumbria and the North East
Depots:	Newton Heath (NH), Heaton (HT), Longsight (LG), Neville Hill (NL), Allerton (AN)
Parent Company:	Serco/Abellio

Class 142

Vehicle Length: 51ft 0½in (15.55m)
Height: 12ft 8in (3.86m)
Width: 9ft 2¼in (2.80m)

Engine: 1 x Cummins LTA10-R per vehicle
Horsepower: 460hp (343kW)
Seats (total/car): 106S, 56S/50S

Number	Formation DMS+DMSL	Depot	Livery	Owner	Operator
142001	55542+55592	NH	NOU	ANG	NOR
142003	55544+55594	NH	NOR	ANG	NOR
142004	55545+55595	NH	NOR	ANG	NOR
142005	55546+55596	NH	NOR	ANG	NOR
142007	55548+55598	NH	NOR	ANG	NOR
142009	55550+55600	NH	NOU	ANG	NOR
142011	55552+55602	NH	NOR	ANG	NOR
142012	55553+55603	NH	NOR	ANG	NOR
142013	55554+55604	NH	NOR	ANG	NOR
142014	55555+55605	NH	NOR	ANG	NOR
142015	55556+55606	HT	NOR	ANG	NOR
142016	55557+55607	HT	NOR	ANG	NOR
142017	55558+55608	HT	NOR	ANG	NOR
142018	55559+55609	HT	NOR	ANG	NOR
142019	55560+55610	HT	NOR	ANG	NOR
142020	55561+55611	HT	NOR	ANG	NOR
142021	55562+55612	HT	NOR	ANG	NOR
142022	55563+55613	HT	NOR	ANG	NOR
142023	55564+55614	NH	NOR	ANG	NOR
142024	55565+55615	NH	NOR	ANG	NOR
142025	55566+55616	HT	NOR	ANG	NOR
142026	55567+55617	HT	NOR	ANG	NOR
142027	55568+55618	NH	NOR	ANG	NOR
142028	55569+55619	NH	NOR	ANG	NOR
142029	55570+55620	NH	NOU	ANG	NOR
142030	55571+55621	NH	NOU	ANG	NOR
142031	55572+55622	NH	NOR	ANG	NOR
142032	55573+55623	NH	NOR	ANG	NOR
142033	55574+55624	NH	NOR	ANG	NOR
142034	55575+55625	HT	NOR	ANG	NOR
142035	55576+55626	NH	NOR	ANG	NOR
142036	55577+55627	NH	NOR	ANG	NOR
142037	55578+55628	NH	NOR	ANG	NOR
142038	55579+55629	NH	NOR	ANG	NOR
142039	55580+55630	NH	NOR	ANG	NOR
142040	55581+55631	NH	NOR	ANG	NOR
142041	55582+55632	NH	NOR	ANG	NOR
142042(S)	55583+55633	NH	NOR	ANG	NOR
142043	55584+55634	NH	NOR	ANG	NOR
142044	55585+55635	NH	NOR	ANG	NOR
142045	55586+55636	NH	NOR	ANG	NOR
142046	55587+55637	NH	NOR	ANG	NOR
142047	55588+55638	NH	NOR	ANG	NOR
142048	55589+55639	NH	NOR	ANG	NOR
142049	55590+55640	NH	NOR	ANG	NOR
142050	55591+55641	HT	NOR	ANG	NOR
142051	55701+55747	NH	NOR	ANG	NOR
142052	55702+55748	NH	NOR	ANG	NOR
142053	55703+55749	NH	NOR	ANG	NOR
142054	55704+55750	NH	NOR	ANG	NOR
142055	55705+55751	NH	NOR	ANG	NOR
142056	55706+55752	NH	NOR	ANG	NOR
142057	55707+55753	NH	NOR	ANG	NOR
142058	55708+55754	NH	NOR	ANG	NOR
142060	55710+55756	NH	NOR	ANG	NOR
142061	55711+55757	NH	NOR	ANG	NOR
142062	55712+55758	NH	NOR	ANG	NOR
142063	55713+55759	NH	NOU	ANG	NOR
142064	55714+55760	NH	NOU	ANG	NOR
142065	55715+55761	HT	NOR	ANG	NOR
142066	55716+55762	HT	NOR	ANG	NOR
142067	55717+55763	NH	NOR	ANG	NOR
142068	55718+55764	NH	NOU	ANG	NOR
142070	55720+55766	HT	NOR	ANG	NOR
142071	55721+55767	HT	NOR	ANG	NOR
142078	55728+55768	HT	NOR	ANG	NOR
142079	55729+55769	HT	NOR	ANG	NOR
142084	55764+55780	HT	NOR	ANG	NOR
142086	55736+55782	HT	NOR	ANG	NOR
142087	55737+55783	HT	NOR	ANG	NOR
142088	55738+55784	HT	NOR	ANG	NOR
142089	55739+55785	HT	NOR	ANG	NOR
142090	55740+55786	HT	NOR	ANG	NOR
142091	55741+55787	HT	NOR	ANG	NOR
142092	55742+55788	HT	NOR	ANG	NOR
142093	55743+55789	HT	NOR	ANG	NOR
142094	55744+55790	HT	NOR	ANG	NOR
142095	55745+55791	HT	NOR	ANG	NOR
142096	55746+55792	HT	NOR	ANG	NOR

Passenger Train Operating Companies - Northern Rail

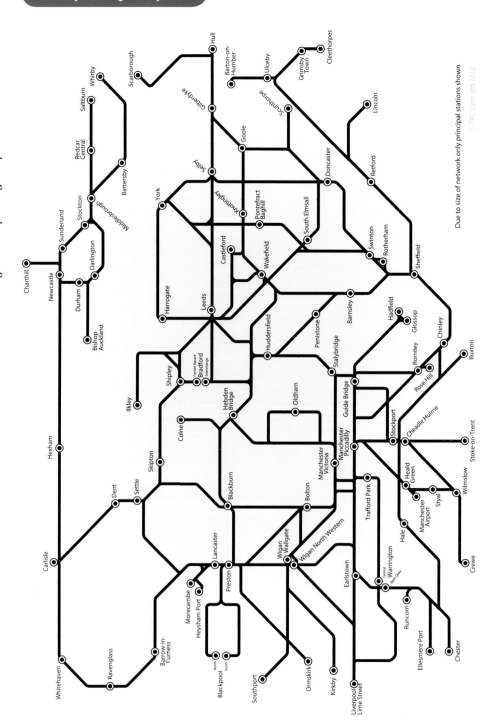

Due to size of network only principal stations shown

© TRC.Com Ltd 2012

Right: *The largest user of Class 142 'Pacer' stock in the UK is Northern, with sets based at Newton Heath (Manchester) and Heaton (Newcastle) depots. Today all sets are painted in a blue base colour onto which mauve and grey vinyl are applied together with the Northern branding. Set No. 142022 is seen at Doncaster in June 2011.*
Nathan Wiliamson

Class 144

	Vehicle Length: 50ft 2in (15.25m)	Engine: 1 x Cummins LTA10-R per vehicle
	Height: 12ft 2½in (3.73m)	Horsepower: 460hp (343kW)
	Width: 8ft 10½in (2.70m)	Seats (total/car): 87S, 45S/42S

Number	Formation DMS+DMSL	Depot	Livery	Owner	Operator
144001	55801+55824	NL	NOR	PTR	NOR
144002	55802+55825	NL	NOR	PTR	NOR
144003	55803+55826	NL	NOR	PTR	NOR
144004	55804+55827	NL	NOR	PTR	NOR
144005	55805+55828	NL	NOR	PTR	NOR
144006	55806+55829	NL	NOR	PTR	NOR
144007	55807+55830	NL	NOR	PTR	NOR
144008	55808+55831	NL	NOR	PTR	NOR
144009	55809+55832	NL	NOR	PTR	NOR
144010	55810+55833	NL	NOR	PTR	NOR
144011	55811+55834	NL	NOR	PTR	NOR
144012	55812+55835	NL	NOR	PTR	NOR
144013	55813+55836	NL	NOR	PTR	NOR

Name applied
144001   *The Penistone Line Partnership*

	Vehicle Length: 50ft 2in (15.25m)	Engine: 1 x Cummins LTA10-R per vehicle
	Height: 12ft 2½in (3.73m)	Horsepower: 690hp (515kW)
	Width: 8ft 10½in (2.70m)	Seats (total/car): 145S, 45S/58S/42S

Number	Formation DMS+MS+DMSL	Depot	Livery	Owner	Operator
144014	55814+55850+55837	NL	NOR	PTR	NOR
144015	55815+55851+55838	NL	NOR	PTR	NOR
144016	55816+55852+55839	NL	NOR	PTR	NOR
144017	55817+55853+55840	NL	NOR	PTR	NOR
144018	55818+55854+55841	NL	NOR	PTR	NOR
144019	55819+55855+55842	NL	NOR	PTR	NOR
144020	55820+55856+55843	NL	NOR	PTR	NOR
144021	55821+55857+55844	NL	NOR	PTR	NOR
144022	55822+55858+55845	NL	NOR	PTR	NOR
144023	55823+55859+55846	NL	NOR	PTR	NOR

Below: *The Walter Alexander-bodied Class 144s, assembled at BREL Derby, are operated in both two- and three-car formations. All sets are based at Leeds Neville Hill and now carry standard Northern livery. Two-car set No. 144005 is seen at Doncaster with its DMS vehicle nearest the camera.*
Nathan Williamson

Northern Rail

Class 150/1

Vehicle Length: 64ft 9¾in (19.74m)
Height: 12ft 4½in (3.77m)
Width: 9ft 3⅛in (2.82m)

Engine: 1 x NT855R5 of 285hp per vehicle
Horsepower: 570hp (425kW)
Seats (total/car): 124S, 59S/65S

Number	Formation DMSL+DMS	Depot	Livery	Owner	Operator
150103§	52103+57103	NH	WMD	ANG	NOR
150110	52110+57110	NH	WMD	ANG	NOR
150111	52111+57111	NH	CTL	ANG	NOR
150112	52112+57112	NH	CTL	ANG	NOR
150113	52113+57113	NH	CTL	ANG	NOR
150114	52114+57114	NH	CTL	ANG	NOR
150115	52115+57115	NH	CTL	ANG	NOR
150116	52116+57116	NH	CTL	ANG	NOR
150117§	52117+57117	NH	CTL	ANG	NOR
150118	52118+57118	NH	WMD	ANG	NOR
150119	52119+57119	NH	CTL	ANG	NOR
150132§	52132+57132	NH	WMD	ANG	NOR
150133	52133+57133	NH	NOR	ANG	NOR
150134	52134+57134	NH	NOR	ANG	NOR
150135	52135+57135	NH	NOR	ANG	NOR
150136	52136+57136	NH	NOR	ANG	NOR
150137	52137+57137	NH	NOR	ANG	NOR
150138	52138+57138	NH	NOR	ANG	NOR
150139	52139+57139	NH	NOR	ANG	NOR
150140	52140+57140	NH	NOR	ANG	NOR
150141	52141+57141	NH	NOR	ANG	NOR
150142	52142+57142	NH	NOR	ANG	NOR
150143	52143+57143	NH	NOR	ANG	NOR
150144	52144+57144	NH	NOR	ANG	NOR
150145	52145+57145	NH	NOR	ANG	NOR
150146	52146+57146	NH	NOR	ANG	NOR
150147	52147+57147	NH	NOR	ANG	NOR
150148	52148+57148	NH	NOR	ANG	NOR
150149	52149+57149	NH	NOR	ANG	NOR
150150	52150+57150	NH	NOR	ANG	NOR

§ Not part of core fleet

Left: *A fleet of 30 Class 150/1s are operated by Northern and allocated to Newton Heath depot in Manchester. These sets are usually used on North Western routes. Displaying standard Northern livery, set No. 150149 is seen at Manchester Piccadilly.*
Antony Christie

Class 150/2

Vehicle Length: 64ft 9¾in (19.74m)
Height: 12ft 4½in (3.77m)
Width: 9ft 3⅛in (2.82m)

Engine: 1 x NT855R5 of 285hp per vehicle
Horsepower: 570hp (425kW)
Seats (total/car): 132S, 62S/70S

Number	Formation DMSL+DMS	Depot	Livery	Owner	Operator
150201	52201+57201	NH	NOR	ANG	NOR
150203	52203+57203	NH	NOR ¤	ANG	NOR
150204	52204+57204	NH	CTL	ANG	NOR
150205	52205+57205	NH	NOR ¤	ANG	NOR
150206	52206+57206	NH	CTL	ANG	NOR
150207	52207+57207	NH	NOR ¤	ANG	NOR
150210	52210+57210	NH	CTL	ANG	NOR
150211	52211+57211	NH	NOR ¤	ANG	NOR
150214	52214+57214	NH	CTL	ANG	NOR
150215	52215+57215	NH	NOR ¤	ANG	NOR
150218	52218+57218	NH	NOR ¤	ANG	NOR
150220	52220+57220	NH	CTL	ANG	NOR
150222	52222+57222	NH	NOR ¤	ANG	NOR
150223	52223+57223	NH	NOR	ANG	NOR
150224	52224+57224	NH	NOR	ANG	NOR
150225	52225+57225	NH	NOR	ANG	NOR
150226	52226+57226	NH	NOR	ANG	NOR
150228	52228+57228	NH	NOR ¤	PTR	NOR
150268	52268+57268	NH	NOR ¤	PTR	NOR
150269	52269+57269	NH	NOR ¤	PTR	NOR
150270	52270+57270	NH	NOR ¤	PTR	NOR
150271	52271+57271	NH	NOR ¤	PTR	NOR
150272	52272+57272	NH	NOR ¤	PTR	NOR
150273	52273+57273	NH	NOR ¤	PTR	NOR
150274	52274+57274	NH	NOR ¤	PTR	NOR
150275	52275+57275	NH	NOR ¤	PTR	NOR
150276	52276+57276	NH	NOR ¤	PTR	NOR
150277	52277+57277	NH	NOR ¤	PTR	NOR
150285§	52285+57285	NH	ATW	PTR	NOR

§ On loan from Arriva Trains Wales

¤ Advertising liveries

150203 - Yorkshire	150276 - Sport
150205 - Yorkshire	150268 - Heritage
150207 - Yorkshire	150269 - Yorkshire
150211 - Yorkshire	150271 - Arts
150215 - Yorkshire	150272 - Colne Festival
150218 - Yorkshire	150273 - Yorkshire
150222 - Yorkshire	150274 - Events
150225 - Yorkshire	150275 - Yorkshire
150228 - Outdoors	150277 - Yorkshire
150270 - City Life	

Left: *Displaying Yorkshire livery, Class 150/2 No. 150269 is seen at Doncaster.* **Nathan Williamson**

Class 153

Vehicle Length: 76ft 5in (23.29m)
Height: 12ft 3½in (3.75m)
Width: 8ft 10in (2.70m)

Engine: 1 x NT855R5 of 285hp
Horsepower: 285hp (213kW)
Seats (total/car): 70S

Number	Formation DMSL	Depot	Livery	Owner	Operator
153301	52301	NL	NOR	ANG	NOR
153304	52304	NL	NOR	ANG	NOR
153307	52307	NL	NOR	ANG	NOR
153315	52315	NL	NOR	ANG	NOR
153316	52316	NL	NOR	PTR	NOR
153317	52317	NL	NOR	ANG	NOR
153324	52324	NL	NOR	PTR	NOR
153328	52328	NL	NOR	ANG	NOR
153330	52330	NL	NOR	PTR	NOR
153331	52331	NL	NOR	ANG	NOR
153332	52332	NL	NOR	ANG	NOR
153351	57351	NL	NOR	ANG	NOR
153352	57352	NL	NOR	ANG	NOR
153358	57358	NL	NOR	PTR	NOR
153359	57359	NL	NOR	PTR	NOR
153360	57360	NL	NOR	PTR	NOR
153363	57363	NL	NOR	PTR	NOR
153378	57378	NL	NOR	ANG	NOR

Right: *A total of 18 single-car Class 153s are operated by Northern. All are based at Leeds Neville Hill but can be found throughout the operating area, especially in the North West. In this view we see a pair of Class 153s, Nos. 153324 and 153331, departing north from Workington with a service bound for Carlisle.* **Nathan Williamson**

Class 155

Vehicle Length: 76ft 5in (23.29m)
Height: 12ft 3½in (3.75m)
Width: 8ft 10in (2.70m)

Engine: 1 x NT855R5 of 285hp
Horsepower: 570hp (425kW)
Seats (total/car): 156S, 76S/80S

Number	Formation DMSL+DMS	Depot	Livery	Owner	Operator
155341	52341+57341	NL	NOR	PTR	NOR
155342	52342+57342	NL	NOR	PTR	NOR
155343	52343+57343	NL	NOR	PTR	NOR
155344	52344+57344	NL	NOR	PTR	NOR
155345	52345+57345	NL	NOR	PTR	NOR
155346	52346+57346	NL	NOR	PTR	NOR
155347	52347+57347	NL	NOR	PTR	NOR

Right: *Only seven of the original Class 155 Leyland 'Super Sprinter' sets are still in traffic, owned by Porterbrook and operated by Northern. Until 2011 these were officially owned by West Yorkshire PTE but have now been sold to Porterbrook. Based at Leeds Neville Hill, these sets carry pictogram area advertising liveries. Set No. 155347 is illustrated.* **Ron Cover**

Class 156

Vehicle Length: 75ft 6in (23.03m)
Height: 12ft 6in (3.81m)
Width: 8ft 11in (2.73m)

Engine: 1 x Cummins NT855R5 of 285hp
Horsepower: 570hp (425kW)
Seats (total/car): 146S, 70/76S

Number	Formation DMSL+DMS	Depot	Livery	Owner	Operator
156420	52420+57420	AN	NOR	PTR	NOR
156421	52421+57421	AN	NOR	PTR	NOR
156423	52423+57423	AN	NOR	PTR	NOR
156424	52424+57424	AN	NOR	PTR	NOR
156425	52425+57425	AN	NOR	PTR	NOR
156426	52426+57426	AN	NOR	PTR	NOR
156427	52427+57427	AN	NOR	PTR	NOR
156428	52428+57428	AN	NOR	PTR	NOR
156429	52429+57429	AN	NOR	PTR	NOR
156438	52438+57438	HT	NOR	ANG	NOR

Northern Rail

156440	52440+57440	AN	NOR	PTR	NOR		156471	52471+57471	AN	NOR	ANG	NOR
156441	52441+57441	AN	NOR	PTR	NOR		156472	52472+57472	AN	NOR	ANG	NOR
156443	52443+57443	HT	NOR	ANG	NOR		156473*	52473+57473	AN	NOR	ANG	NOR
156444	52444+57444	HT	NOR	ANG	NOR		156475	52475+57475	HT	NOR	ANG	NOR
156448	52448+57448	HT	NOR	ANG	NOR		156479	52479+57479	AN	NOR	ANG	NOR
156451	52451+57451	HT	NOR	ANG	NOR		156480	52480+57480	HT	NOR	ANG	NOR
156452	52452+57452	AN	NOR	PTR	NOR		156481	52481+57481	AN	NOR	ANG	NOR
156454	52454+57454	HT	NOR	ANG	NOR		156482	52482+57482	AN	NOR	ANG	NOR
156455	52455+57455	AN	NOR	PTR	NOR		156483	52483+57483	AN	NOR	ANG	NOR
156459	52459+57459	AN	NOR	PTR	NOR		156484	52484+57484	HT	NOR	ANG	NOR
156460	52460+57460	AN	NOR	PTR	NOR		156486	52486+57486	AN	NOR	ANG	NOR
156461	52461+57461	AN	NOR	PTR	NOR		156487	52487+57487	AN	NOR	ANG	NOR
156463	52463+57463	HT	NOR	ANG	NOR		156488	52488+57488	AN	NOR	ANG	NOR
156464	52464+57464	AN	SPL	PTR	NOR		156489	52489+57489	AN	NOR	ANG	NOR
156466	52466+57466	AN	NOR	PTR	NOR		156490	52490+57490	HT	NOR	ANG	NOR
156468	52468+57468	AN	NOR	ANG	NOR		156491	52491+57491	AN	NOR	ANG	NOR
156469	52469+57469	HT	NOR	ANG	NOR		156497*	52497+57497	AN	NOR	ANG	NOR
156470*	52470+57470	AN	NOR	ANG	NOR		156498*	52498+57498	AN	NOR	ANG	NOR

Names applied
156441 *William Huskisson MP*
156444 *Councillor Bill Cameron*
156459 *Benny Rothman -*
        The Manchester Rambler
156460 *Driver John Axon GC*
156466 *Gracie Fields*
156464 *Lancashire DalesRail*

Left: *Both Allerton and Heaton depots have an allocation of Class 156s. Here set No. 156479 and a Class 153 arrive at Workington with a Barrow service.*
Antony Christie

Class 158/0

Vehicle Length: 76ft 1¾in (23.21m) Engine: 1 x Cummins NTA855R of 350hp per vehicle
Height: 12ft 6in (3.81m) Horsepower: 1,050hp (783kW)
Width: 9ft 3¼in (2.82m) Seats (total/car): 208S, 68S/70S/70S

Number	Formation	Depot	Livery	Owner	Operator
	DMSL+MSL+DMSL				
158752	52752+58716+57752	NL	NOR	PTR	NOR
158753	52753+58710+57753	NL	NOR	PTR	NOR
158754	52754+58708+57754	NL	NOR	PTR	NOR
158755	52755+58702+57755	NL	NOR	PTR	NOR
158756	52756+58712+57756	NL	NOR	PTR	NOR
158757	52757+58706+57757	NL	NOR	PTR	NOR
158758	52758+58714+57758	NL	NOR	PTR	NOR
158759	52759+58713+57759	NL	NOR	PTR	NOR

Vehicle Length: 76ft 1¾in (23.21m) Engine: 1 x Cummins NTA855R of 350hp per vehicle
Height: 12ft 6in (3.81m) Horsepower: 700hp (522kW)
Width: 9ft 3¼in (2.82m) Seats (total/car): 138S, 68S/70S

Number	Formation	Depot	Livery	Owner	Operator							
	DMSL+DMSL						158815	52815+57815	NL	NOR	ANG	NOR
							158816	52816+57816	NL	NOR	ANG	NOR
158784	52784+57784	NH	NOR	ANG	NOR		158817	52817+57817	NL	NOR	ANG	NOR
158787	52787+57787	NH	NOR	ANG	NOR		158843	52843+57843	NL	NOR	ANG	NOR
158790	52790+57790	NH	NOR	ANG	NOR		158844	52844+57844	NL	NOR	ANG	NOR
158791	52791+57791	NH	NOR	ANG	NOR		158845	52845+57845	NL	NOR	ANG	NOR
159792	52792+57792	NH	NOR	ANG	NOR		158848	52848+57848	NL	NOR	ANG	NOR
158793	52793+57793	NH	NOR	ANG	NOR		158849	52849+57849	NL	NOR	ANG	NOR
158794	52794+57794	NH	NOR	ANG	NOR		158850	52850+57850	NL	NOR	ANG	NOR
158795	52795+57795	NH	NOR	ANG	NOR		158851	52851+57851	NL	NOR	ANG	NOR
158796	52796+57796	NH	NOR	ANG	NOR		158853	52853+57853	NL	NOR	ANG	NOR
158797	52797+57797	NH	NOR	ANG	NOR		158855	52855+57855	NL	NOR	ANG	NOR

158859	52859+57859	NL	NOR	ANG	NOR	158872	52872+57872	NL	NOR ANG	NOR
158860	52860+57860	NL	NOR	ANG	NOR	§ Carries Welcome to Yorkshire livery				
158861	52861+57861	NL	SPL§	ANG	NOR					

Class 158/9

Vehicle Length: 76ft 1¾in (23.21m) *Engine: 1 x Cummins NTA855R of 350hp per vehicle*
Height: 12ft 6in (3.81m) *Horsepower: 700hp (522kW)*
Width: 9ft 3¼in (2.82m) *Seats (total/car): 142S, 70S/72S*

Number	Formation	Depot	Livery	Owner	Operator						
	DMSL+DMS					158905	52905+57905	NL	NOR	EVL	NOR
158901	52901+57901	NL	NOR	EVL	NOR	158906	52906+57906	NL	NOR	EVL	NOR
158902	52902+57902	NL	NOR	EVL	NOR	158907	52907+57907	NL	NOR	EVL	NOR
158903	52903+57903	NL	NOR	EVL	NOR	158908	52908+57908	NL	NOR	EVL	NOR
158904	52904+57904	NL	NOR	EVL	NOR	158909	52909+57909	NL	NOR	EVL	NOR
						158910	52910+57910	NL	NOR	EVL	NOR

Names applied
158784 *Barbara Castle*
158791 *County of Nottinghamshire*
158796 *Fred Trueman - Cricketing Legend*
158797 *Jane Tomlinson*
158860 *Ian Dewhirst*
158910 *William Wilberforce*

Right: *Displaying route-associated pictogram advertising livery, one of the original West Yorkshire '158s', No. 158908, now operated as part of the core Northern fleet passes Ais Gill on a S&C service to Carlisle.* **Jamie Squibbs**

Class 321/9

Vehicle Length: (Driving) 65ft 0¾in (19.83m) *Width: 9ft 3in (2.82m)*
(Inter) 65ft 4¼in (19.92m) *Horsepower: 1,328hp (996kW)*
Height: 12ft 4¾in (3.78m) *Seats (total/car): 293S, 70S/79S/74S/70S*

Number	Formation	Depot	Livery	Owner	Operator
	DTCO+MSO+TSO+DTSO				
321901	77990+63153+72128+77993	NL	NOM	EVL	NOR
321902	77991+63154+72129+77994	NL	NOM	EVL	NOR
321903	77992+63155+72130+77995	NL	NOM	EVL	NOR

Right: *For use on the Leeds to Doncaster WYPTE electrified route, three Class 321/9 four-car sets are allocated to Leeds Neville Hill. The sets rarely operate on the Wharfedale or Airedale routes. All are painted in revised Northern Rail livery incorporating Metro branding and lettering with red bodies and blue markings on driving cars. Set No. 321903 is seen at Doncaster.*
Nathan Williamson

Class 322

Vehicle Length: (Driving) 65ft 0¾in (19.83m) *Width: 9ft 3in (2.82m)*
(Inter) 65ft 4¼in (19.92m) *Horsepower: 1,328hp (996kW)*
Height: 12ft 4¾in (3.78m) *Seats (total/car): 291S, 74S/83S/76S/58S*

Number	Formation	Depot	Livery	Owner	Operator
	DTSO(A)+MSO+TSO+DTSO(B)				
322481	78163+62137+72023+77985	NL	NOR	EVL	NOR
322482	78164+62138+72024+77986	NL	NOR	EVL	NOR
322483	78165+62139+72025+77987	NL	NOR	EVL	NOR
322484	78166+63140+72026+77988	NL	NOR	EVL	NOR
322485	78167+63141+72027+77898	NL	NOR	EVL	NOR

Left: *In autumn 2011 the five former First ScotRail four-car Class 322s were transferred to Northern Rail at Leeds Neville Hill to supplement their fleet of Class 321/9s and 333 stock. Due to shortages of stock, some sets were introduced in October 2011 in unbranded ex-First Group blue, as shown on set No. 322483 at Doncaster on 29 October 2011 forming a service to Leeds.* **Derek Porter**

Class 323

Vehicle Length: (Driving) 76ft 8¼in (23.37m)
(Inter) 76ft 10¾in (23.44m)
Height: 12ft 4¾in (3.78m)
Width: 9ft 2¼in (2.80m)
Horsepower: 1,565hp (1,168kW)
Seats (total/car) 323223-225: 244S, 82S/80S/82S
323226-239: 284S, 98S/88S/98S

Number	Formation DMSO(A)+PTSO+DMSO(B)	Depot	Livery	Owner	Operator
323223	64023+72223+65023	LG	NOR	PTR	NOR
323224	64024+72224+65024	LG	NOR	PTR	NOR
323225	64025+72225+65025	LG	FSN	PTR	NOR
323226	64026+72226+65026	LG	FSN	PTR	NOR
323227	64027+72227+65027	LG	FSN	PTR	NOR
323228	64028+72228+65028	LG	NOR	PTR	NOR
323229	64029+72229+65029	LG	NOR	PTR	NOR
323230	64030+72230+65030	LG	FSN	PTR	NOR
323231	64031+72231+65031	LG	NOR	PTR	NOR
323232	64032+72232+65032	LG	NOR	PTR	NOR
323233	64033+72233+65033	LG	NOR	PTR	NOR
323234	64034+72234+65034	LG	NOR	PTR	NOR
323235	64035+72235+65035	LG	NOR	PTR	NOR
323236	64036+72236+65036	LG	NOR	PTR	NOR
323237	64037+72237+65037	LG	NOR	PTR	NOR
323238	64038+72238+65038	LG	FSN	PTR	NOR
323239	64039+72239+65039	LG	FSN	PTR	NOR

Above: *Northern operates a batch of 17 three-car Class 323 EMUs in the Manchester area. Two different seating configurations are to be found, with sets 323223-225 having reduced seating for Manchester Airport services. No 323225 approaches Longport with the 14.48 Manchester Piccadilly to Stoke-on-Trent on 7 March 2011. These units operate from Manchester Piccadilly to Crewe, Stoke and Hadfield, and are scheduled to undergo internal refurbishment.* **Cliff Beeton**

Class 333

Vehicle Length: (Driving) 77ft 10¾in (23.74m)
(Inter) 75ft 11in (23.14m)
Height: 12ft 1½in (3.79m)

Width: 9ft 0¼in (2.75m)
Horsepower: 1,877hp (1,400kW)
Seats (total/car): 353S, 90S/73S/100S/90S

Number	Formation DMSO(A)+PTSO+TSO+DMSO(B)	Depot	Livery	Owner	Operator	Name
333001	78451+74461+74477+78452	NL	NOM	ANG	NOR	
333002	78453+74462+74478+78454	NL	NOM	ANG	NOR	
333003	78455+74463+74479+78456	NL	NOM	ANG	NOR	
333004	78457+74464+74480+78458	NL	NOM	ANG	NOR	
333005	78459+74465+74481+78460	NL	NOM	ANG	NOR	
333006	78461+74466+74482+78462	NL	NOM	ANG	NOR	
333007	78463+74467+74483+78464	NL	NOM	ANG	NOR	Alderman J Arthur Godwin - First Lord Mayor of Bradford 1907
333008	78465+74468+74484+78466	NL	NOM	ANG	NOR	
333009	78467+74469+74485+78468	NL	NOM	ANG	NOR	
333010	78469+74470+74486+78470	NL	NOM	ANG	NOR	
333011	78471+74471+74487+78472	NL	NOM	ANG	NOR	
333012	78473+74472+74488+78474	NL	NOM	ANG	NOR	
333013	78475+74473+74489+78476	NL	NOM	ANG	NOR	
333014	78477+74474+74490+78478	NL	NOM	ANG	NOR	
333015	78479+74475+74491+78480	NL	NOM	ANG	NOR	
333016	78481+74476+74492+78482	NL	NOM	ANG	NOR	

Above and Right: *A fleet of Class 333 units were built by Siemens and CAF to operate on the electrified Aire Valley line radiating from Leeds to Bradford and Skipton. After introduction as three-car sets, an additional intermediate vehicle was added to strengthen the sets to four-car formation. All sets are based at Leeds Neville Hill and carry a version of Northern livery. In the above view, set No. 333013 is seen at Skipton, while the view right shows the 2+3 high-density interior.* **Ron Cover / Nathan Williamson**

South West Trains

Address: ✉ Friars Bridge Court, 41-45 Blackfriars Road, London, SE1 8NZ
✎ customerrelations@swtrains.co.uk
✆ 08700 00 5151
ⓘ www.southwesttrains.co.uk

Managing Director: Tim Shoveller
Franchise Dates: 4 December 1996 - February 2017
Principal Routes: London Waterloo - Weymouth, Exeter, Portsmouth and suburban services in Surrey, Berkshire, Hampshire
Depots: Wimbledon Park (WD), Bournemouth (BM), Clapham Junction (CJ)*, Salisbury (SA) * No stock allocated Northam (Siemens Transportation) (NT)
Parent Company: Stagecoach

Class 158

Vehicle Length: 76ft 1¾in (23.21m) Engine: 1 x Cummins NTA855R of 350hp per vehicle
Height: 12ft 6in (3.81m) Horsepower: 700hp (522kW)
Width: 9ft 3¼in (2.82m) Seats (total/car): 13F-114S, 13F-44S/70S

Number	Formation DMSL+DMSL	Depot	Livery	Owner	Operator
158880 (158737)	52737+57737	SA	SWM	PTR	SWT
158881 (158742)	52742+57742	SA	SWM	PTR	SWT
158882 (158743)	52743+57743	SA	SWM	PTR	SWT
158883 (158744)	52744+57744	SA	SWM	PTR	SWT
158884 (158772)	52772+57772	SA	SWM	PTR	SWT
158885 (158775)	52775+57775	SA	SWM	PTR	SWT
158886 (158779)	52779+57779	SA	SWM	PTR	SWT
158887 (158781)	52781+57781	SA	SWM	PTR	SWT
158888 (158802)	52802+57802	SA	SWM	PTR	SWT
158889 (158808)	52808+57808	SA	SWM	PTR	SWT
158890 (158814)	52814+57814	SA	SWM	PTR	SWT

Below: *Eleven Class 158 two-car sets are based at Salisbury and operated by South West Trains on local routes as well as supplementing 159 stock on the Yeovil/Salisbury to Waterloo route. All sets are refurbished and were renumbered into a new 158/8 series from their original numbers. Set No. 158880 is seen at Bristol Temple Meads.* **CJM**

South West Trains

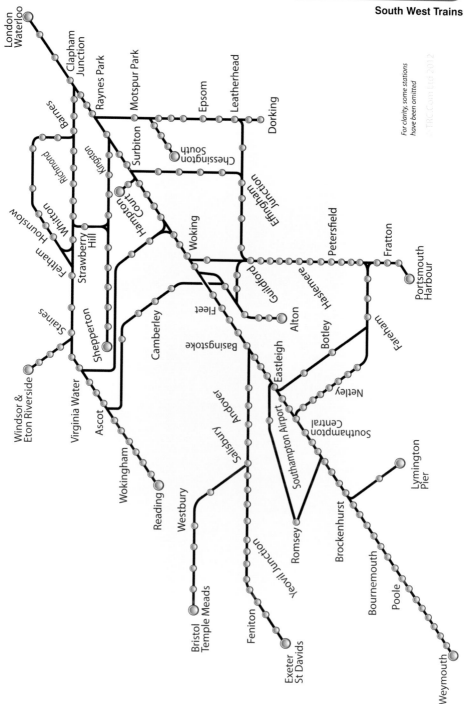

For clarity, some stations have been omitted

© TRC.Com Ltd 2012

Passenger Train Operating Companies - South West Trains

London Waterloo
Clapham Junction
Raynes Park
Barnes
Motspur Park
Epsom
Leatherhead
Dorking
Richmond
Kingston
Surbiton
Chessington South
Effingham Junction
Hounslow
Whitton
Feltham
Strawberry Hill
Hampton Court
Woking
Petersfield
Fratton
Staines
Shepperton
Camberley
Fleet
Guildford
Haslemere
Alton
Portsmouth Harbour
Windsor & Eton Riverside
Virginia Water
Ascot
Basingstoke
Eastleigh
Botley
Fareham
Wokingham
Andover
Southampton Airport
Netley
Lymington Pier
Salisbury
Southampton Central
Reading
Westbury
Romsey
Brockenhurst
Bristol Temple Meads
Yeovil Junction
Bournemouth
Poole
Feniton
Exeter St Davids
Weymouth

South West Trains

Class 159/0

Vehicle Length: 76ft 1¾in (23.21m) Engine: 1 x Cummins NTA855R of 400hp per vehicle
Height: 12ft 6in (3.81m)   Horsepower: 1,200hp (895kW)
Width: 9ft 3¼in (2.82m)   Seats (total/car): 24F-172S, 24F-28S/72S/72S

Number	Formation DMCL+MSL+DMSL	Depot	Livery	Owner	Operator	Name
159001	52873+58718+57873	SA	SWM	PTR	SWT	*City of Exeter*
159002	52874+58719+57874	SA	SWM	PTR	SWT	*City of Salisbury*
159003	52875+58720+57875	SA	SWM	PTR	SWT	*Templecombe*
159004	52876+58721+57876	SA	SWM	PTR	SWT	*Basingstoke and Deane*
159005	52877+58722+57877	SA	SWM	PTR	SWT	
159006	52878+58723+57878	SA	SWM	PTR	SWT	
159007	52879+58724+57879	SA	SWM	PTR	SWT	
159008	52880+58725+57880	SA	SWM	PTR	SWT	
159009	52881+58726+57881	SA	SWM	PTR	SWT	
159010	52882+58727+57882	SA	SWM	PTR	SWT	
159011	52883+58728+57883	SA	SWM	PTR	SWT	
159012	52884+58729+57884	SA	SWM	PTR	SWT	
159013	52885+58730+57885	SA	SWM	PTR	SWT	
159014	52886+58731+57886	SA	SWM	PTR	SWT	
159015	52887+58732+57887	SA	SWM	PTR	SWT	
159016	52888+58733+57888	SA	SWM	PTR	SWT	
159017	52889+58734+57889	SA	SWM	PTR	SWT	
159018	52890+58735+57890	SA	SWM	PTR	SWT	
159019	52891+58736+57891	SA	SWM	PTR	SWT	
159020	52892+58737+57892	SA	SWM	PTR	SWT	
159021	52893+58738+57893	SA	SWM	PTR	SWT	
159022	52894+58739+57894	SA	SWM	PTR	SWT	

Above: *The 30 Class 159 three-car main line sets operated by SWT are used on the Waterloo to Exeter route, frequently working in two- and three-set formations. All sets are refurbished and carry the Stagecoach main line white livery, off-set by red and orange swirl ends. A six-car formation is seen at Exeter, led by set No. 159009.* **Antony Christie**

Class 159/1

Vehicle Length: 76ft 1¾in (23.21m) Engine: 1 x Cummins NTA855R of 350hp per vehicle
Height: 12ft 6in (3.81m)   Horsepower: 1,050hp (782kW)
Width: 9ft 3¼in (2.82m)   Seats (total/car): 24F-170S, 24F-28S/70S/72S

Number	Formation DMCL+MSL+DMSL	Depot	Livery	Owner	Operator
159101 (158800)	52800+58717+57800	SA	SWM	PTR	SWT
159102 (158803)	52803+58703+57803	SA	SWM	PTR	SWT
159103 (158804)	52804+58704+57804	SA	SWM	PTR	SWT
159104 (158805)	52805+58705+57805	SA	SWM	PTR	SWT
159105 (158807)	52807+58707+57807	SA	SWM	PTR	SWT
159106 (158909)	52809+58709+57809	SA	SWM	PTR	SWT
159107 (158811)	52811+58711+57811	SA	SWM	PTR	SWT
159108 (158801)	52801+58701+57801	SA	SWM	PTR	SWT

Right: *In preparation for an expansion of SWT services, a further batch of Class 159 stock was modified from Class 158s by Wabtec Doncaster in 2006. These are classified as 159/1 and incorporate some minor differences from the original 22 Class 159/0s. The most noticeable from the outside is that only two opening quarter lights are provided on each side of each vehicle, whereas the 159/0s have four. Set No. 159106 is seen at Bristol Temple Meads in July 2011 forming a Waterloo via Salisbury service.* **CJM**

Class 444
Desiro

Vehicle Length: 77ft 3in (23.57m)	Horsepower: 2,682hp (2,000kW)		
Height: 12ft 1½in (3.7m)	Seats (total/car): 35F-299S, 35F-24S/47S/76S/76S/76S		
Width: 9ft 2in (2.7m)			

Number	Formation DMCO+TSO+TSO+TSRMB+DMSO	Depot	Livery	Owner	Operator	Name
444001	63801+67101+67151+67201+63851	NT	SWM	ANG	SWT	*Naomi House*
444002	63802+67102+67152+67202+63852	NT	SWM	ANG	SWT	
444003	63803+67103+67153+67203+63853	NT	SWM	ANG	SWT	
444004	63804+67104+67154+67204+63854	NT	SWM	ANG	SWT	
444005	63805+67105+67155+67205+63855	NT	SWM	ANG	SWT	
444006	63806+67106+67156+67206+63856	NT	SWM	ANG	SWT	
444007	63807+67107+67157+67207+63857	NT	SWM	ANG	SWT	
444008	63808+67108+67158+67208+63858	NT	SWM	ANG	SWT	
444009	63809+67109+67159+67209+63859	NT	SWM	ANG	SWT	
444010	63810+67110+67160+67210+63860	NT	SWM	ANG	SWT	
444011	63811+67111+67161+67211+63861	NT	SWM	ANG	SWT	
444012	63812+67112+67162+67212+63862	NT	SWM	ANG	SWT	*Destination Weymouth*
444013	63813+67113+67163+67213+63863	NT	SWM	ANG	SWT	
444014	63814+67114+67164+67214+63864	NT	SWM	ANG	SWT	
444015	63815+67115+67165+67215+63865	NT	SWM	ANG	SWT	
444016	63816+67116+67166+67216+63866	NT	SWM	ANG	SWT	
444017	63817+67117+67167+67217+63867	NT	SWM	ANG	SWT	
444018	63818+67118+67168+67218+63868	NT	SWM	ANG	SWT	*The FAB 444*
444019	63819+67119+67169+67219+63869	NT	SWM	ANG	SWT	
444020	63820+67120+67170+67220+63870	NT	SWM	ANG	SWT	
444021	63821+67121+67171+67221+63871	NT	SWM	ANG	SWT	
444022	63822+67122+67172+67222+63872	NT	SWM	ANG	SWT	
444023	63823+67123+67173+67223+63873	NT	SWM	ANG	SWT	
444024	63824+67124+67174+67224+63874	NT	SWM	ANG	SWT	
444025	63825+67125+67175+67225+63875	NT	SWM	ANG	SWT	
444026	63826+67126+67176+67226+63876	NT	SWM	ANG	SWT	
444027	63827+67127+67177+67227+63877	NT	SWM	ANG	SWT	
444028	63828+67128+67178+67228+63878	NT	SWM	ANG	SWT	
444029	63829+67129+67179+67229+63879	NT	SWM	ANG	SWT	
444030	63830+67130+67180+67230+63880	NT	SWM	ANG	SWT	
444031	63831+67131+67181+67231+63881	NT	SWM	ANG	SWT	
444032	63832+67132+67182+67232+63882	NT	SWM	ANG	SWT	
444033	63833+67133+67183+67233+63883	NT	SWM	ANG	SWT	
444034	63834+67134+67184+67234+63884	NT	SWM	ANG	SWT	
444035	63835+67135+67185+67235+63885	NT	SWM	ANG	SWT	
444036	63836+67136+67186+67236+63886	NT	SWM	ANG	SWT	
444037	63837+67137+67187+67237+63887	NT	SWM	ANG	SWT	
444038	63838+67138+67188+67238+63888	NT	SWM	ANG	SWT	
444039	63839+67139+67189+67239+63889	NT	SWM	ANG	SWT	
444040	63840+67140+67190+67240+63890	NT	SWM	ANG	SWT	

South West Trains

444041	63841+67141+67191+67241+63891	NT	SWM	ANG	SWT
444042	63842+67142+67192+67242+63892	NT	SWM	ANG	SWT
444043	63843+67143+67193+67243+63893	NT	SWM	ANG	SWT
444044	63844+67144+67194+67244+63894	NT	SWM	ANG	SWT
444045	63845+67145+67195+67245+63895	NT	SWM	ANG	SWT

Left: *As part of South West Trains' modernisation and replacement of slam door stock, a fleet of 45 five-car Class 444 'Desiro' sets were introduced to operate fast services on the Waterloo to Weymouth and Portsmouth lines. With its first class vehicle nearest the camera, set No. 444002 slows for a stop at Southampton with a Weymouth to Waterloo service.* **CJM**

Class 450/0
Desiro

Vehicle Length: 66ft 9in (20.4m)
Height: 12ft 1½in (3.7m)
Width: 9ft 2in (2.7m)

Horsepower: 2,682hp (2,000kW)
Seats (total/car): 24F-237S, 70S/24F-36S/61S/70S

Number	Formation	Depot	Livery	Owner	Operator	Name
	DMSO+TCO+TSO+DMSO					
450001	63201+64201+68101+63601	NT	SWO	ANG	SWT	
450002	63202+64202+68102+63602	NT	SWO	ANG	SWT	
450003	63203+64203+68103+63603	NT	SWO	ANG	SWT	
450004	63204+64204+68104+63604	NT	SWO	ANG	SWT	
450005	63205+64205+68205+63605	NT	SWO	ANG	SWT	
450006	63206+64206+68206+63606	NT	SWO	ANG	SWT	
450007	63207+64207+68207+63607	NT	SWO	ANG	SWT	
450008	63208+64208+68108+63608	NT	SWO	ANG	SWT	
450009	63209+64209+68109+63609	NT	SWO	ANG	SWT	
450010	63210+64210+68110+63610	NT	SWO	ANG	SWT	
450011	63211+64211+68111+63611	NT	SWO	ANG	SWT	
450012	63212+64212+68112+63612	NT	SWO	ANG	SWT	
450013	63213+64213+68113+63613	NT	SWO	ANG	SWT	
450014	63214+64214+68114+63614	NT	SWO	ANG	SWT	
450015	63215+64215+68115+63615	NT	SWO	ANG	SWT	Desiro
450016	63216+64216+68116+63616	NT	SWO	ANG	SWT	
450017	63217+64217+68117+63617	NT	SWO	ANG	SWT	
450018	63218+64218+68118+63618	NT	SWO	ANG	SWT	
450019	63219+64219+68119+63619	NT	SWO	ANG	SWT	
450020	63220+64220+68120+63620	NT	SWO	ANG	SWT	
450021	63221+64221+68121+63621	NT	SWO	ANG	SWT	
450022	63222+64222+68122+63622	NT	SWO	ANG	SWT	
450023	63223+64223+68123+63623	NT	SWO	ANG	SWT	
450024	63224+64224+68124+63624	NT	SWO	ANG	SWT	
450025	63225+64225+68125+63625	NT	SWO	ANG	SWT	
450026	63226+64226+68126+63626	NT	SWO	ANG	SWT	
450027	63227+64227+68127+63627	NT	SWO	ANG	SWT	
450028	63228+64228+68128+63628	NT	SWO	ANG	SWT	
450029	63229+64229+68129+63629	NT	SWO	ANG	SWT	
450030	63230+64230+68130+63630	NT	SWO	ANG	SWT	
450031	63231+64231+68131+63631	NT	SWO	ANG	SWT	
450032	63232+64232+68132+63632	NT	SWO	ANG	SWT	
450033	63233+64233+68133+63633	NT	SWO	ANG	SWT	
450034	63234+64234+68134+63634	NT	SWO	ANG	SWT	
450035	63235+64235+68135+63635	NT	SWO	ANG	SWT	
450036	63236+64236+68136+63636	NT	SWO	ANG	SWT	

450037	63237+64237+68137+63637	NT	SWO	ANG	SWT	
450038	63238+64238+68138+63638	NT	SWO	ANG	SWT	
450039	63239+64239+68139+63639	NT	SWO	ANG	SWT	
450040	63240+64240+68140+63640	NT	SWO	ANG	SWT	
450041	63241+64241+68141+63641	NT	SWO	ANG	SWT	
450042	63242+64242+68142+63642	NT	SWO	ANG	SWT	*Treloar College*
450071	63271+64271+68171+63671	NT	SWO	ANG	SWT	
450072	63272+64272+68172+63672	NT	SWO	ANG	SWT	
450073	63273+64273+68173+63673	NT	SWO	ANG	SWT	
450074	63274+64274+68174+63674	NT	SWO	ANG	SWT	
450075	63275+64275+68175+63675	NT	SWO	ANG	SWT	
450076	63276+64276+68176+63676	NT	SWO	ANG	SWT	
450077	63277+64277+68177+63677	NT	SWO	ANG	SWT	
450078	63278+64278+68178+63678	NT	SWO	ANG	SWT	
450079	63279+64279+68179+63679	NT	SWO	ANG	SWT	
450080	63280+64280+68180+63680	NT	SWO	ANG	SWT	
450081	63281+64281+68181+63681	NT	SWO	ANG	SWT	
450082	63282+64282+68182+63682	NT	SWO	ANG	SWT	
450083	63283+64283+68183+63683	NT	SWO	ANG	SWT	
450084	63284+64284+68184+63684	NT	SWO	ANG	SWT	
450085	63285+64285+68185+63685	NT	SWO	ANG	SWT	
450086	63286+64286+68186+63686	NT	SWO	ANG	SWT	
450087	63287+64287+68187+63687	NT	SWO	ANG	SWT	
450088	63288+64288+68188+63688	NT	SWO	ANG	SWT	
450089	63289+64289+68189+63689	NT	SWO	ANG	SWT	
450090	63290+64290+68190+63690	NT	SWO	ANG	SWT	
450091	63291+64291+68191+63691	NT	SWO	ANG	SWT	
450092	63292+64292+68192+63692	NT	SWO	ANG	SWT	
450093	63293+64293+68193+63693	NT	SWO	ANG	SWT	
450094	63294+64294+68194+63694	NT	SWO	ANG	SWT	
450095	63295+64295+68195+63695	NT	SWO	ANG	SWT	
450096	63296+64296+68196+63696	NT	SWO	ANG	SWT	
450097	63297+64297+68197+63697	NT	SWO	ANG	SWT	
450098	63298+64298+68198+63698	NT	SWO	ANG	SWT	
450099	63299+64299+68199+63699	NT	SWO	ANG	SWT	
450100	63300+64300+68200+63700	NT	SWO	ANG	SWT	
450101	63701+66851+66801+63751	NT	SWO	ANG	SWT	
450102	63702+66852+66802+63752	NT	SWO	ANG	SWT	
450103	63703+66853+66803+63753	NT	SWO	ANG	SWT	
450104	63704+66854+66804+63754	NT	SWO	ANG	SWT	
450105	63705+66855+66805+63755	NT	SWO	ANG	SWT	
450106	63706+66856+66806+63756	NT	SWO	ANG	SWT	
450107	63707+66857+66807+63757	NT	SWO	ANG	SWT	
450108	63708+66858+66808+63758	NT	SWO	ANG	SWT	
450109	63709+66859+66809+63759	NT	SWO	ANG	SWT	
450110	63710+66860+66810+63750	NT	SWO	ANG	SWT	
450111	63901+66921+66901+63921	NT	SWO	ANG	SWT	
450112	63902+66922+66902+63922	NT	SWO	ANG	SWT	
450113	63903+66923+66903+63923	NT	SWO	ANG	SWT	
450114	63904+66924+66904+63924	NT	SWO	ANG	SWT	*Fairbridge - investing in the Future*
450115	63905+66925+66905+63925	NT	SWO	ANG	SWT	
450116	63906+66926+66906+63926	NT	SWO	ANG	SWT	
450117	63907+66927+66907+63927	NT	SWO	ANG	SWT	
450118	63908+66928+66908+63928	NT	SWO	ANG	SWT	
450119	63909+66929+66909+63929	NT	SWO	ANG	SWT	
450120	63910+66930+66910+63930	NT	SWO	ANG	SWT	
450121	63911+66931+66911+63931	NT	SWO	ANG	SWT	
450122	63912+66932+66912+63932	NT	SWO	ANG	SWT	
450123	63913+66933+66913+63933	NT	SWO	ANG	SWT	
450124	63914+66934+66914+63934	NT	SWO	ANG	SWT	
450125	63915+66935+66915+63935	NT	SWO	ANG	SWT	
450126	63916+66936+66916+63936	NT	SWO	ANG	SWT	
450127	63917+66937+66917+63937	NT	SWO	ANG	SWT	

Above: *A total of 127 four-car Class 450 Desiro sets are in traffic with South West Trains, operating all outer suburban and some main line services. All sets are painted in the South West Trains/Stagecoach blue livery. Set No. 450087 is seen arriving at Clapham Junction Yard, empty from Waterloo.* **CJM**

Class 450/5
Desiro

Vehicle Length: 66ft 9in (20.4m)
Height: 12ft 1½in (3.7m)
Width: 9ft 2in (2.7m)
Horsepower: 2,682hp (2,000kW)
Seats (total/car): 240S, 64S/56S/56S/64S

Number	Formation DMSO+TSO+TSO+DMSO	Depot	Livery	Owner	Operator
450543 (450043)	63243+64243+68143+63643	NT	SWO	ANG	SWT
450544 (450044)	63244+64244+68144+63644	NT	SWO	ANG	SWT
450545 (450045)	63245+64245+68145+63645	NT	SWO	ANG	SWT
450546 (450046)	63246+64246+68146+63646	NT	SWO	ANG	SWT
450547 (450047)	63247+64247+68147+63647	NT	SWO	ANG	SWT
450548 (450048)	63248+64248+68148+63648	NT	SWO	ANG	SWT
450549 (450049)	63249+64249+68149+63649	NT	SWO	ANG	SWT
450550 (450050)	63250+64250+68150+63650	NT	SWO	ANG	SWT
450551 (450051)	63251+64251+68151+63651	NT	SWO	ANG	SWT
450552 (450052)	63252+64252+68152+63652	NT	SWO	ANG	SWT
450553 (450053)	63253+64253+68153+63653	NT	SWO	ANG	SWT
450554 (450054)	63254+64254+68154+63654	NT	SWO	ANG	SWT
450555 (450055)	63255+64255+68155+63655	NT	SWO	ANG	SWT
450556 (450056)	63256+64256+68156+63656	NT	SWO	ANG	SWT
450557 (450057)	63257+64257+68157+63657	NT	SWO	ANG	SWT
450558 (450058)	63258+64258+68158+63658	NT	SWO	ANG	SWT
450559 (450059)	63259+64259+68159+63659	NT	SWO	ANG	SWT
450560 (450060)	63260+64260+68160+63660	NT	SWO	ANG	SWT
450561 (450061)	63261+64261+68161+63661	NT	SWO	ANG	SWT
450562 (450062)	63262+64262+68162+63662	NT	SWO	ANG	SWT
450563 (450063)	63263+64263+68163+63663	NT	SWO	ANG	SWT
450564 (450064)	63264+64264+68164+63664	NT	SWO	ANG	SWT
450565 (450065)	63265+64265+68165+63665	NT	SWO	ANG	SWT
450566 (450066)	63266+64266+68166+63666	NT	SWO	ANG	SWT
450567 (450067)	63267+64267+68167+63667	NT	SWO	ANG	SWT
450568 (450068)	63268+64268+68168+63668	NT	SWO	ANG	SWT
450569 (450069)	63269+64269+68169+63669	NT	SWO	ANG	SWT
450570 (450070)	63270+64270+68170+63670	NT	SWO	ANG	SWT

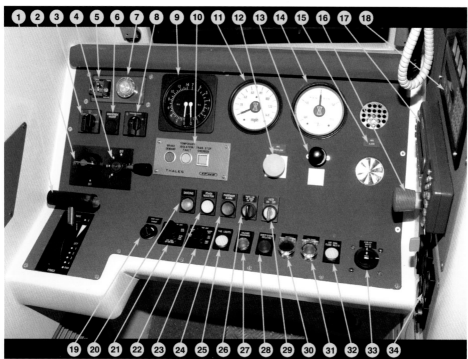

Above: *Desiro driving cab. 1 - Power/brake controller, 2 - Master key socket, 3 - Windscreen wiper switch, 4 - Master switch (off, for/net/rev), 5 - Driver's reminder appliance isolation switch, 6 - Windscreen washer button, 7 - Driver's reminder appliance, 8 - Windscreen heat switch, 9 - Main reservoir and brake pipe pressure gauge, 10 - TPWS control panel, 11 - Speedometer, 12 - AWS reset button, 13 - Horn valve, 14 - Traction/brake efficiency, 15 - AWS alarm and sunflower indicator, 16 - Emergency brake plunger, 17 - Cab-shore radio, 18 - Communications panel, 19 - Desk light dimmer switch, 20 - Sanding button, 21 - Cab light switch, 22 - Power reduction, 23 - Marker/head/tail light switch, 24 - Passenger alarm light, 25 - Tail light indicator, 26 - Pantograph VCB up/down, 27 - Hazard warning indicator, 28 - Safety system isolated warning light, 29 - HSCB on/off, 30 - Uncouple button, 31 - Low speed button, 32 - Air con close inlets, 33 - Door key switch on/off, 34 - Right side door controls.* **CJM**

Class 455/7

		Vehicle Length: (Driving) 65ft 0½in (19.83m)		Width: 9ft 3¼in (2.82m)
		(Inter) 65ft 4½in (19.92m)		Horsepower: 1,000hp (746kW)
		Height: 12ft 1½in (3.79m) [TSO- 11ft 6½in (3.58m)		Seats (total/car): 244S, 54S/68S/68S/54S

Number	Formation DMSO(A)+MSO+TSO+DTSO(B)	Depot	Livery	Owner	Operator
(45)5701	77727+62783+71545+77728	WD	SWS	PTR	SWT
(45)5702	77729+62784+71547+77730	WD	SWS	PTR	SWT
(45)5703	77731+62785+71540+77732	WD	SWS	PTR	SWT
(45)5704	77733+62786+71548+77734	WD	SWS	PTR	SWT
(45)5705	77735+62787+71565+77736	WD	SWS	PTR	SWT
(45)5706	77737+62788+71534+77738	WD	SWS	PTR	SWT
(45)5707	77739+62789+71536+77740	WD	SWS	PTR	SWT
(45)5708	77741+62790+71560+77742	WD	SWS	PTR	SWT
(45)5709	77743+62791+71532+77744	WD	SWS	PTR	SWT
(45)5710	77745+62792+71566+77746	WD	SWS	PTR	SWT
(45)5711	77747+62793+71542+77748	WD	SWS	PTR	SWT
(45)5712	77749+62794+71546+77750	WD	SWS	PTR	SWT
(45)5713	77751+62795+71567+77752	WD	SWS	PTR	SWT
(45)5714	77753+62796+71539+77754	WD	SWS	PTR	SWT
(45)5715	77755+62796+71535+77756	WD	SWS	PTR	SWT
(45)5716	77757+62798+71564+77758	WD	SWS	PTR	SWT
(45)5717	77759+62799+71528+77760	WD	SWS	PTR	SWT

South West Trains

(45)5718	77761+62800+71557+77762	WD	SWS	PTR	SWT
(45)5719	77763+62801+71558+77764	WD	SWS	PTR	SWT
(45)5720	77765+62802+71568+77766	WD	SWS	PTR	SWT
(45)5721	77767+62803+71553+77768	WD	SWS	PTR	SWT
(45)5722	77769+62804+71533+77770	WD	SWS	PTR	SWT
(45)5723	77771+62805+71526+77772	WD	SWS	PTR	SWT
(45)5724	77773+62806+71561+77774	WD	SWS	PTR	SWT
(45)5725	77775+62807+71541+77776	WD	SWS	PTR	SWT
(45)5726	77777+62608+71556+77778	WD	SWS	PTR	SWT
(45)5727	77779+62809+71562+77780	WD	SWS	PTR	SWT
(45)5728	77781+62810+71527+77782	WD	SWS	PTR	SWT
(45)5729	77783+62811+71550+77784	WD	SWS	PTR	SWT
(45)5730	77785+62812+71551+77786	WD	SWS	PTR	SWT
(45)5731	77787+62813+71555+77788	WD	SWS	PTR	SWT
(45)5732	77789+62814+71552+77790	WD	SWS	PTR	SWT
(45)5733	77791+62815+71549+77792	WD	SWS	PTR	SWT
(45)5734	77793+62816+71531+77794	WD	SWS	PTR	SWT
(45)5735	77795+62817+71563+77796	WD	SWS	PTR	SWT
(45)5736	77797+62818+71554+77798	WD	SWS	PTR	SWT
(45)5737	77799+62819+71544+77800	WD	SWS	PTR	SWT
(45)5738	77801+62820+71529+77802	WD	SWS	PTR	SWT
(45)5739	77803+62821+71537+77804	WD	SWS	PTR	SWT
(45)5740	77805+62822+71530+77806	WD	SWS	PTR	SWT
(45)5741	77807+62823+71559+77808	WD	SWS	PTR	SWT
(45)5742	77809+62824+71543+77810	WD	SWS	PTR	SWT
(45)5750*	77811+62825+71538+77812	WD	SWS	PTR	SWT	*Originally numbered (45)5743*

Above: *South West Trains suburban services are in the hands of three fleets of Class 455s, built in the 1980s at BREL York. The sets are now painted in the SWT local red livery. Class 455/7 No. 5728 and Class 455/8 No. 5866 pose side by side at Clapham Junction, showing the two different front end designs.* **Antony Christie**

Class 455/8

Vehicle Length: (Driving) 65ft 0½in (19.83m)
(Inter) 65ft 4½in (19.92m)
Height: 12ft 1½in (3.79m)

Width: 9ft 3¼in (2.82m)
Horsepower: 1,000hp (746kW)
Seats (total/car): 268S, 50S/84S/84S/50S

Number	Formation DMSO(A)+MSO+TSO+DTSO(B)	Depot	Livery	Owner	Operator
(45)5847	77671+62755+71683+77672	WD	SWS	PTR	SWT
(45)5848	77673+62756+71684+77674	WD	SWS	PTR	SWT
(45)5849	77675+62757+71685+77676	WD	SWS	PTR	SWT
(45)5850	77677+62758+71686+77678	WD	SWS	PTR	SWT
(45)5851	77679+62759+71687+77680	WD	SWS	PTR	SWT
(45)5852	77681+62760+71688+77682	WD	SWS	PTR	SWT

(45)5853	77683+62761+71689+77684	WD	SWS	PTR	SWT
(45)5854	77685+62762+71690+77686	WD	SWS	PTR	SWT
(45)5855	77687+62763+71691+77688	WD	SWS	PTR	SWT
(45)5856	77689+62764+71692+77690	WD	SWS	PTR	SWT
(45)5857	77691+62765+71693+77692	WD	SWS	PTR	SWT
(45)5858	77693+62766+71694+77694	WD	SWS	PTR	SWT
(45)5859	77695+62767+71695+77696	WD	SWS	PTR	SWT
(45)5860	77697+62768+71696+77698	WD	SWS	PTR	SWT
(45)5861	77699+62769+71697+77700	WD	SWS	PTR	SWT
(45)5862	77701+62770+71698+77702	WD	SWS	PTR	SWT
(45)5863	77703+62771+71699+77704	WD	SWS	PTR	SWT
(45)5864	77705+62772+71700+77706	WD	SWS	PTR	SWT
(45)5865	77707+62773+71701+77708	WD	SWS	PTR	SWT
(45)5866	77709+62774+71702+77710	WD	SWS	PTR	SWT
(45)5867	77711+62775+71703+77712	WD	SWS	PTR	SWT
(45)5868	77713+62776+71704+77714	WD	SWS	PTR	SWT
(45)5869	77715+62777+71705+77716	WD	SWS	PTR	SWT
(45)5870	77717+62778+71706+77718	WD	SWS	PTR	SWT
(45)5871	77719+62779+71707+77720	WD	SWS	PTR	SWT
(45)5872	77721+62780+71708+77722	WD	SWS	PTR	SWT
(45)5873	77723+62781+71709+77724	WD	SWS	PTR	SWT
(45)5874	77725+62782+71710+77726	WD	SWS	PTR	SWT

Class 455/9

Vehicle Length: (Driving) 65ft 0½in (19.83m)
(Inter) 65ft 4½in (19.92m)
Height: 12ft 1½in (3.79m)

Width: 9ft 3¼in (2.82m)
Horsepower: 1,000hp (746kW)
Seats (total/car): 236S, 50S/68S/68S/50S

Number	Formation	Depot	Livery	Owner	Operator
	DMSO(A)+MSO+TSO+DTSO(B)				
(45)5901	77813+62826+71714+77814	WD	SWS	PTR	SWT
(45)5902	77815+62827+71715+77816	WD	SWS	PTR	SWT
(45)5903	77817+62828+71716+77818	WD	SWS	PTR	SWT
(45)5904	77819+62829+71717+77820	WD	SWS	PTR	SWT
(45)5905	77821+62830+71725+77822	WD	SWS	PTR	SWT
(45)5906	77823+62831+71719+77824	WD	SWS	PTR	SWT
(45)5907	77825+62832+71720+77826	WD	SWS	PTR	SWT
(45)5908	77827+62833+71721+77828	WD	SWS	PTR	SWT
(45)5909	77829+62834+71722+77830	WD	SWS	PTR	SWT
(45)5910	77831+62835+71723+77832	WD	SWS	PTR	SWT
(45)5911	77833+62836+71724+77834	WD	SWS	PTR	SWT
(45)5912	77835+62837+67400+77836	WD	SWS	PTR	SWT
(45)5913	77837+62838+71726+77838	WD	SWS	PTR	SWT *(62838 stored, collision dam)*
(45)5914	77839+62839+71727+77840	WD	SWS	PTR	SWT
(45)5915	77841+62840+71728+77842	WD	SWS	PTR	SWT
(45)5916	77843+62841+71729+77844	WD	SWS	PTR	SWT
(45)5917	77845+62842+71730+77846	WD	SWS	PTR	SWT
(45)5918	77847+62843+71732+77848	WD	SWS	PTR	SWT
(45)5919	77849+62844+71718+77850	WD	SWS	PTR	SWT
(45)5920	77851+62845+71733+77852	WD	SWS	PTR	SWT

Right: *Class 455/9 No. 5915 poses for the camera at Vauxhall with a service to Waterloo. The 455/9s and 455/7s share the same front end body profile, but the sub-classes can be distinguished by the Class 455/7 fleet having one lower body profile vehicle which came from the original Class 508 stock built as four-car sets and later transferred to Merseyside as three-car units.* **Nathan Williamson**

Passenger Train Operating Companies - South West Trains

Class 458
Juniper

	Vehicle Length: (Driving) 69ft 6in (21.16m)	Width: 9ft 2in (2.79m)
	(Inter) 65ft 4in (19.91m)	Horsepower: 2,172hp (1,620kW)
	Height: 12ft 3in (3.73m)	Seats (total/car): 24F-250S, 12F-63S/49S/75S/12F-63S

Number	Formation DMCO(A)+TSO+MSO+DTCO(B)	Depot	Livery	Owner	Operator
(45)8001	67601+74001+74101+67701	WD	SWM	PTR	SWT
(45)8002	67602+74002+74102+67702	WD	SWM	PTR	SWT
(45)8003	67603+74003+74103+67703	WD	SWM	PTR	SWT
(45)8004	67604+74004+74104+67704	WD	SWM	PTR	SWT
(45)8005	67605+74005+74105+67705	WD	SWM	PTR	SWT
(45)8006	67606+74006+74106+67706	WD	SWM	PTR	SWT
(45)8007	67607+74007+74107+67707	WD	SWM	PTR	SWT
(45)8008	67608+74008+74108+67708	WD	SWM	PTR	SWT
(45)8009	67609+74009+74109+67709	WD	SWM	PTR	SWT
(45)8010	67610+74010+74110+67710	WD	SWM	PTR	SWT
(45)8011	67611+74011+74111+67711	WD	SWM	PTR	SWT
(45)8012	67612+74012+74112+67712	WD	SWM	PTR	SWT
(45)8013	67613+74013+74113+67713	WD	SWM	PTR	SWT
(45)8014	67614+74014+74114+67714	WD	SWM	PTR	SWT
(45)8015	67615+74015+74115+67715	WD	SWM	PTR	SWT
(45)8016	67616+74016+74116+67716	WD	SWM	PTR	SWT
(45)8017	67617+74017+74117+67717	WD	SWM	PTR	SWT
(45)8018	67618+74018+74118+67718	WD	SWM	PTR	SWT
(45)8019	67619+74019+74119+67719	WD	SWM	PTR	SWT
(45)8020	67620+74020+74120+67720	WD	SWM	PTR	SWT
(45)8021	67621+74021+74121+67721	WD	SWM	PTR	SWT
(45)8022	67622+74022+74122+67722	WD	SWM	PTR	SWT
(45)8023	67623+74023+74123+67723	WD	SWM	PTR	SWT
(45)8024	67624+74024+74124+67724	WD	SWM	PTR	SWT
(45)8025	67625+74025+74125+67725	WD	SWM	PTR	SWT
(45)8026	67626+74026+74126+67726	WD	SWM	PTR	SWT
(45)8027	67627+74027+74127+67727	WD	SWM	PTR	SWT
(45)8028	67628+74028+74128+67728	WD	SWM	PTR	SWT
(45)8029	67629+74029+74129+67729	WD	SWM	PTR	SWT
(45)8030	67630+74030+74130+67730	WD	SWM	PTR	SWT

■ It was announced in late 2011 that the eight Class 460 Gatwick Express units will transfer to South West Trains in 2013-14 and be refurbished and used to reform the 30 four-car Class 458/0 sets into 36 five-car Class 458/2 units to allow increased train lengths for Waterloo Windsor line operations. The conversion work will see four Class 460 vehicles become spare and used for component recovery. The rebuild contract has been let to Alstom, who are to sub-contract the physical rebuild work to Wabtec.

Above: *Soon after Stagecoach took over the South West Trains franchise, it was announced that a fleet of 30 Class 458 'Juniper' units were to be ordered. These were delivered between 1999-2002. The sets are now confined to the Waterloo to Reading route. A Waterloo-bound train departs from Reading with set No. (45)8006 nearest the camera.* **Antony Christie**

South Eastern

Address: ✉ Friars Bridge Court, 41-45 Blackfriars Road, London, SE1 8NZ
✆ info@southeasternrailway.co.uk
✆ 08700 000 2222
ⓘ www.southeasternrailway.co.uk

Managing Director: Charles Horton
Franchise Dates: 1 April 2006 - 31 March 2014
Principal Routes: London to Kent and parts of East Sussex, domestic services on HS1
Depots: Slade Green (SG), Ramsgate (RM), Ashford (AD*)
Parent Company: Govia
* Operated by Hitachi

Passenger Train Operating Companies - South Eastern

Class 375/3
Electrostar

Vehicle Length: (Driving) 66ft 9in (20.3m) / (Inter) 65ft 6in (19.96m)
Height: 12ft 4in (3.75m)
Width: 9ft 2in (2.79m)
Horsepower: 1,341hp (1,000kW)
Seats (total/car): 24F-152S, 12F-48S/56S/12F-48S

Number	Formation DMCO(A)+TSO+DMCO(B)	Depot	Livery	Owner	Operator	Name
375301	67921+74351+67931	RM	SET	EVL	SET	
375302	67922+74352+67932	RM	SET	EVL	SET	
375303	67923+74353+67933	RM	SET	EVL	SET	
375304	67924+74354+67934	RM	SET	EVL	SET	Medway Valley Line 1856-2006
375305	67925+74355+67935	RM	SET	EVL	SET	
375306	67926+74356+67936	RM	SET	EVL	SET	
375307	67927+74357+67937	RM	SET	EVL	SET	
375308	67928+74358+67938	RM	SET	EVL	SET	
375309	67929+74359+67939	RM	SET	EVL	SET	
375310	67930+74360+67940	RM	SET	EVL	SET	

Class 375/6
Electrostar

Vehicle Length: (Driving) 66ft 9in (20.3m) / (Inter) 65ft 6in (19.96m)
Height: 12ft 4in (3.75m)
Width: 9ft 2in (2.79m)
Horsepower: 2,012hp (1,500kW)
Seats (total/car): 24F-218S, 12F-48S/66S/56S/12F-48S

Number	Formation DMCO(A)+MSO+TSO+DMCO(B)	Depot	Livery	Owner	Operator	Name
375601	67801+74251+74201+67851	RM	SET	EVL	SET	
375602	67802+74252+74202+67852	RM	SET	EVL	SET	
375603	67803+74253+74203+67853	RM	SET	EVL	SET	
375604	67804+74254+74204+67854	RM	SET	EVL	SET	
375605	67805+74255+74205+67855	RM	SET	EVL	SET	
375606	67806+74256+74206+67856	RM	SET	EVL	SET	
375607	67807+74257+74207+67857	RM	SET	EVL	SET	
375608	67808+74258+74208+67858	RM	SET	EVL	SET	Bromley Travelwise
375609	67809+74259+74209+67859	RM	SET	EVL	SET	
375610	67810+74260+74210+67860	RM	SET	EVL	SET	Royal Tunbridge Wells
375611	67811+74261+74211+67861	RM	SET	EVL	SET	Dr William Harvey
375612	67812+74262+74212+67862	RM	SET	EVL	SET	
375613	67813+74263+74213+67863	RM	SET	EVL	SET	
375614	67814+74264+74214+67864	RM	SET	EVL	SET	
375615	67815+74265+74215+67865	RM	SET	EVL	SET	
375616	67816+74266+74216+67866	RM	SET	EVL	SET	
375617	67817+74267+74217+67867	RM	SET	EVL	SET	
375618	67818+74268+74218+67868	RM	SET	EVL	SET	
375619	67819+74269+74219+67869	RM	SET	EVL	SET	Driver John Neve

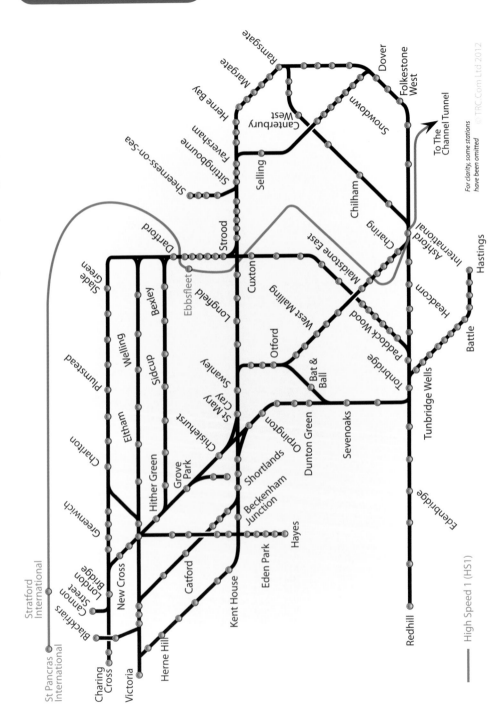

© TRC.Com Ltd 2012

To The
Channel Tunnel

*For clarity, some stations
have been omitted*

— High Speed 1 (HS1)

375620	67820+74270+74220+67870	RM	SET	EVL	SET	
375621	67821+74271+74221+67871	RM	SET	EVL	SET	
375622	67822+74272+74222+67872	RM	SET	EVL	SET	
375623	67823+74273+74223+67873	RM	SET	EVL	SET	*Hospice in the Weald*
375624	67824+74274+74224+67874	RM	SET	EVL	SET	
375625	67825+74275+74225+67875	RM	SET	EVL	SET	
375626	67826+74276+74226+67876	RM	SET	EVL	SET	
375627	67827+74277+74227+67877	RM	SET	EVL	SET	
375628	67828+74278+74228+67878	RM	SET	EVL	SET	
375629	67829+74279+74229+67879	RM	SET	EVL	SET	
375630	67830+74280+74230+67880	RM	SET	EVL	SET	

Class 375/7
Electrostar

Vehicle Length: (Driving) 66ft 9in (20.3m) (Inter) 65ft 6in (19.96m)
Height: 12ft 4in (3.75m)
Width: 9ft 2in (2.79m)
Horsepower: 2,012hp (1,500kW)
Seats (total/car): 24F-218S, 12F-48S/66S/56S/12F-48S

Number	Formation DMCO(A)+MSO+TSO+DMCO(B)	Depot	Livery	Owner	Operator	Name
375701	67831+74281+74231+67881	RM	SET	EVL	SET	*Kent Air Ambulance Explorer*
375702	67832+74282+74232+67882	RM	SET	EVL	SET	
375703	67833+74283+74233+67883	RM	SET	EVL	SET	
375704	67834+74284+74234+67884	RM	SET	EVL	SET	
375705	67835+74285+74235+67885	RM	SET	EVL	SET	
375706	67836+74286+74236+67886	RM	SET	EVL	SET	
375707	67837+74287+74237+67887	RM	SET	EVL	SET	
375708	67838+74288+74238+67888	RM	SET	EVL	SET	
375709	67839+74289+74239+67889	RM	SET	EVL	SET	
375710	67840+74290+74240+67890	RM	SET	EVL	SET	
375711	67841+74291+74241+67891	RM	SET	EVL	SET	
375712	67842+74292+74242+67892	RM	SET	EVL	SET	
375713	67843+74293+74243+67893	RM	SET	EVL	SET	
375714	67844+74294+74244+67894	RM	SET	EVL	SET	
375715	67845+74295+74245+67895	RM	SET	EVL	SET	

Class 375/8
Electrostar

Vehicle Length: (Driving) 66ft 9in (20.3m) (Inter) 65ft 6in (19.96m)
Height: 12ft 4in (3.75m)
Width: 9ft 2in (2.79m)
Horsepower: 2,012hp (1,500kW)
Seats (total/car): 24F-218S, 12F-48S/66S/56S/12F-48S

Number	Formation DMCO(A)+MSO+TSO+DMCO(B)	Depot	Livery	Owner	Operator	Name
375801	73301+79001+78201+73701	RM	SET	EVL	SET	
375802	73302+79002+78202+73702	RM	SET	EVL	SET	
375803	73303+79003+78203+73703	RM	SET	EVL	SET	
375804	73304+79004+78204+73704	RM	SET	EVL	SET	
375805	73305+79005+78205+73705	RM	SET	EVL	SET	
375806	73306+79006+78206+73706	RM	SET	EVL	SET	
375807	73307+79007+78207+73707	RM	SET	EVL	SET	
375808	73308+79008+78208+73708	RM	SET	EVL	SET	
375809	73309+79009+78209+73709	RM	SET	EVL	SET	
375810	73310+79010+78210+73710	RM	SET	EVL	SET	
375811	73311+79011+78211+73711	RM	SET	EVL	SET	
375812	73312+79012+78212+73712	RM	SET	EVL	SET	
375813	73313+79013+78213+73713	RM	SET	EVL	SET	
375814	73314+79014+78214+73714	RM	SET	EVL	SET	
375815	73315+79015+78215+73715	RM	SET	EVL	SET	
375816	73316+79016+78216+73716	RM	SET	EVL	SET	
375817	73317+79017+78217+73717	RM	SET	EVL	SET	
375818	73318+79018+78218+73718	RM	SET	EVL	SET	
375819	73319+79019+78219+73719	RM	SET	EVL	SET	
375820	73320+79020+78220+73720	RM	SET	EVL	SET	
375821	73321+79021+78221+73721	RM	SET	EVL	SET	
375822	73322+79022+78222+73722	RM	SET	EVL	SET	
375823	73323+79023+78223+73723	RM	SET	EVL	SET	
375824	73324+79024+78224+73724	RM	SET	EVL	SET	
375825	73325+79025+78225+73725	RM	SET	EVL	SET	

South Eastern

375826	73326+79026+78226+73726	RM	SET	EVL	SET	
375827	73327+79027+78227+73727	RM	SET	EVL	SET	
375828	73328+79028+78228+73728	RM	SET	EVL	SET	
375829	73329+79029+78229+73729	RM	SET	EVL	SET	
375830	73330+79030+78230+73730	RM	SET	EVL	SET	*City of London*

Set 375812 fitted with De-icing equipment

Class 375/9
Electrostar

Vehicle Length: (Driving) 66ft 9in (20.3m)	*Width: 9ft 2in (2.79m)*
(Inter) 65ft 6in (19.96m)	*Horsepower: 2,012hp (1,500kW)*
Height: 12ft 4in (3.75m)	*Seats (total/car): 24F-250S, 12F-59S/73S/59S/12F-59S*

Number	Formation DMCO(A)+MSO+TSO+DMCO(B)	Depot	Livery	Owner	Operator
375901	73331+79031+79061+73731	RM	SET	EVL	SET
375902	73332+79032+79062+73732	RM	SET	EVL	SET
375903	73333+79033+79063+73733	RM	SET	EVL	SET
375904	73334+79034+79064+73734	RM	SET	EVL	SET
375905	73335+79035+79065+73735	RM	SET	EVL	SET
375906	73336+79036+79066+73736	RM	SET	EVL	SET
375907	73337+79037+79067+73737	RM	SET	EVL	SET
375908	73338+79038+79068+73738	RM	SET	EVL	SET
375909	73339+79039+79069+73739	RM	SET	EVL	SET
375910	73340+79040+79070+73740	RM	SET	EVL	SET
375911	73341+79041+79071+73741	RM	SET	EVL	SET
375912	73342+79042+79072+73742	RM	SET	EVL	SET
375913	73343+79043+79073+73743	RM	SET	EVL	SET
375914	73344+79044+79074+73744	RM	SET	EVL	SET
375915	73345+79045+79075+73745	RM	SET	EVL	SET
375916	73346+79046+79076+73746	RM	SET	EVL	SET
375917	73347+79047+79077+73747	RM	SET	EVL	SET
375918	73348+79048+79078+73748	RM	SET	EVL	SET
375919	73349+79049+79079+73749	RM	SET	EVL	SET
375920	73350+79050+79080+73750	RM	SET	EVL	SET
375921	73351+79051+79081+73751	RM	SET	EVL	SET
375922	73352+79052+79082+73752	RM	SET	EVL	SET
375923	73353+79053+79083+73753	RM	SET	EVL	SET
375924	73354+79054+79084+73754	RM	SET	EVL	SET
375925	73355+79055+79085+73755	RM	SET	EVL	SET
375926	73356+79056+79086+73756	RM	SET	EVL	SET
375927	73357+79057+79087+73757	RM	SET	EVL	SET

Below: *Five different sub-classes of the 'Electrostar' product range are operated by South Eastern, used on outer suburban and main line services based at Ramsgate. Four-car Class 357/8 set No. 375808 is seen awaiting departure from London Charing Cross station with a Kent Coast train.* **Ron Cover**

Class 376
Electrostar

Vehicle Length: (Driving) 66ft 9in (20.3m)
(Inter) 65ft 6in (19.96m)
Height: 12ft 4in (3.75m)
Width: 9ft 2in (2.79m)
Horsepower: 2,682hp (2,000kW)
Seats (total/car): 216S, 36S/48S/48S/48S/36S + 116 perch

Number	Formation	Depot	Livery	Owner	Operator
	DMSO(A)+MSO+TSO+MSO+DMSO(B)				
376001	61101+63301+64301+63501+61601	SG	SET	EVL	SET
376002	61102+63302+64302+63502+61602	SG	SET	EVL	SET
376003	61103+63303+64303+63503+61603	SG	SET	EVL	SET
376004	61104+63304+64304+63504+61604	SG	SET	EVL	SET
376005	61105+63305+64305+63505+61605	SG	SET	EVL	SET
376006	61106+63306+64306+63506+61606	SG	SET	EVL	SET
376007	61107+63307+64307+63507+61607	SG	SET	EVL	SET
376008	61108+63308+64308+63508+61608	SG	SET	EVL	SET
376009	61109+63309+64309+63509+61609	SG	SET	EVL	SET
376010	61110+63310+64310+63510+61610	SG	SET	EVL	SET
376011	61111+63311+64311+63511+61611	SG	SET	EVL	SET
376012	61112+63312+64312+63512+61612	SG	SET	EVL	SET
376013	61113+63313+64313+63513+61613	SG	SET	EVL	SET
376014	61114+63314+64314+63514+61614	SG	SET	EVL	SET
376015	61115+63315+64315+63515+61615	SG	SET	EVL	SET
376016	61116+63316+64316+63516+61616	SG	SET	EVL	SET
376017	61117+63317+64317+63517+61617	SG	SET	EVL	SET
376018	61118+63318+64318+63518+61618	SG	SET	EVL	SET
376019	61119+63319+64319+63519+61619	SG	SET	EVL	SET
376020	61120+63320+64320+63520+61620	SG	SET	EVL	SET
376021	61121+63321+64321+63521+61621	SG	SET	EVL	SET
376022	61122+63322+64322+63522+61622	SG	SET	EVL	SET
376023	61123+63323+64323+63523+61623	SG	SET	EVL	SET
376024	61124+63324+64324+63524+61624	SG	SET	EVL	SET
376025	61125+63325+64325+63525+61625	SG	SET	EVL	SET
376026	61126+63326+64326+63526+61626	SG	SET	EVL	SET
376027	61127+63327+64327+63527+61627	SG	SET	EVL	SET
376028	61128+63328+64328+63528+61628	SG	SET	EVL	SET
376029	61129+63329+64329+63529+61629	SG	SET	EVL	SET
376030	61130+63330+64330+63530+61630	SG	SET	EVL	SET
376031	61131+63331+64331+63531+61631	SG	SET	EVL	SET
376032	61132+63332+64332+63532+61632	SG	SET	EVL	SET
376033	61133+63333+64333+63533+61633	SG	SET	EVL	SET
376034	61134+63334+64334+63534+61634	SG	SET	EVL	SET
376035	61135+63335+64335+63535+61635	SG	SET	EVL	SET
376036	61136+63336+64336+63536+61636	SG	SET	EVL	SET

Below: *To provide a high-capacity train for the inner suburban area of South Eastern, a version of the 'Electrostar' was introduced in 2005-06. These five-car trains had fewer seats than conventional sets with large standing and perching areas. Set No. 376001 arrives at Petts Wood on 19 August 2011 with the 14.20 Cannon Street to Orpington.* **Tim Easter**

South Eastern

Passenger Train Operating Companies - South Eastern

Class 395
Javelin

Vehicle Length: (Driving) 67ft 7in (20.6m)	Width: 9ft 2in (2.79m)
(Inter) 67ft 6in (20.5m)	Horsepower: 2,252hp (1,680kW)
Height: 12ft 6in (3.81m)	Seats (total/car): 340S, 28S/66S/66S/66S/66S/48S

Number	Formation DMSO(A)+MSO(A)+MSO(B)+ MSO(C)+MSO(D)+DMSO(B)	Depot	Livery	Owner	Operator	Name
395001	39011+39012+39013+39014+39015+39016	AD	HS1	EVL	SET	Dame Kelly Holmes
395002	39021+39022+39023+39024+39025+39026	AD	HS1	EVL	SET	Sebastian Coe
395003	39031+39032+39033+39034+39035+39036	AD	HS1	EVL	SET	Sir Steve Redgrave
395004	39041+39042+39043+39044+39045+39046	AD	HS1	EVL	SET	Sir Chris Hoy
395005	39051+39052+39053+39054+39055+39056	AD	HS1	EVL	SET	Dame Tanni Grey-Thompson
395006	39061+39062+39063+39064+39065+39066	AD	HS1	EVL	SET	Daley Thompson
395007	39071+39072+39073+39074+39075+39076	AD	HS1	EVL	SET	Steve Backley
395008	39081+39082+39083+39084+39085+39086	AD	HS1	EVL	SET	Ben Ainslie
395009	39091+39092+39093+39094+39095+39096	AD	HS1	EVL	SET	Rebecca Adlington
395010	39101+39102+39103+39104+39105+39106	AD	HS1	EVL	SET	
395011	39111+39112+39113+39114+39115+39116	AD	HS1	EVL	SET	
395012	39121+39122+39123+39124+39125+39126	AD	HS1	EVL	SET	
395013	39131+39132+39133+39134+39135+39136	AD	HS1	EVL	SET	
395014	39141+39142+39143+39144+39145+39146	AD	HS1	EVL	SET	
395015	39151+39152+39153+39154+39155+39156	AD	HS1	EVL	SET	
395016	39161+39162+39163+39164+39165+39166	AD	HS1	EVL	SET	Jamie Staff
395017	39171+39172+39173+39174+39175+39176	AD	HS1	EVL	SET	
395018	39181+39182+39183+39184+39185+39186	AD	HS1	EVL	SET	
395019	39191+39192+39193+39194+39195+39196	AD	HS1	EVL	SET	
395020	39201+39202+39203+39204+39205+39206	AD	HS1	EVL	SET	
395021	39211+39212+39213+39214+39215+39216	AD	HS1	EVL	SET	
395022	39221+39222+39223+39224+39225+39226	AD	HS1	EVL	SET	
395023	39231+39232+39233+39234+39235+39236	AD	HS1	EVL	SET	
395024	39241+39242+39243+39244+39245+39246	AD	HS1	EVL	SET	
395025	39251+39252+39253+39254+39255+39256	AD	HS1	EVL	SET	
395026	39261+39262+39263+39264+39265+39266	AD	HS1	EVL	SET	
395027	39271+39272+39273+39274+39275+39276	AD	HS1	EVL	SET	
395028	39281+39282+39283+39284+39285+39286	AD	HS1	EVL	SET	
395029	39291+39292+39293+39294+39295+39296	AD	HS1	EVL	SET	

Below: *The South Eastern-operated domestic services over High Speed 1 are worked by a fleet of 29 six-car Class 395 'Javelin' sets, built in Japan by Hitachi and now maintained at Ashford, Kent. The sets, with a top speed of 140mph (225km/h), are painted in South Eastern dark blue. They also operate over classic tracks in Kent providing through services off the high speed connection. Set No. 395001 is seen on HS1 near Rainham.* **Tim Easter**

Class 465/0
Networker

Vehicle Length: (Driving) 68ft 6½in (20.89m)	Width: 9ft 3in (2.81m)
(Inter) 65ft 9¾in (20.05m)	Horsepower: 2,252hp (1,680kW)
Height: 12ft 4½in (3.77m)	Seats (total/car): 348S, 86S/90S/86S/86S

Number	Formation DMSO(A)+TSO+TSO+DMSO(B)	Depot	Livery	Owner	Operator
465001	64759+72028+72029+64809	SG	SET	EVL	SET
465002	64760+72030+72031+64810	SG	SET	EVL	SET
465003	64761+72032+72033+64811	SG	SET	EVL	SET
465004	64762+72034+72035+64812	SG	SET	EVL	SET
465005	64763+72036+72037+64813	SG	SET	EVL	SET
465006	64764+72038+72039+64814	SG	SET	EVL	SET
465007	64765+72040+72041+64815	SG	SET	EVL	SET
465008	64766+72042+72043+64816	SG	SET	EVL	SET
465009	64767+72044+72045+64817	SG	SET	EVL	SET
465010	64768+72046+72047+64818	SG	SET	EVL	SET
465011	64769+72048+72049+64819	SG	SET	EVL	SET
465012	64770+72050+72051+64820	SG	SET	EVL	SET
465013	64771+72052+72053+64821	SG	SET	EVL	SET
465014	64772+72054+72055+64822	SG	SET	EVL	SET
465015	64773+72056+72057+64823	SG	SET	EVL	SET
465016	64774+72058+72059+64824	SG	SET	EVL	SET
465017	64775+72060+72061+64825	SG	SET	EVL	SET
465018	64776+72062+72063+64826	SG	SET	EVL	SET
465019	64777+72064+72065+64827	SG	SET	EVL	SET
465020	64778+72066+72067+64828	SG	SET	EVL	SET
465021	64779+72068+72069+64829	SG	SET	EVL	SET
465022	64780+72070+72071+64830	SG	SET	EVL	SET
465023	64781+72072+72073+64831	SG	SET	EVL	SET
465024	64782+72074+72075+64832	SG	SET	EVL	SET
465025	64783+72076+72077+64833	SG	SET	EVL	SET
465026	64784+72078+72079+64834	SG	SET	EVL	SET
465027	64785+72080+72081+64835	SG	SET	EVL	SET
465028	64786+72082+72083+64836	SG	SET	EVL	SET
465029	64787+72084+72085+64837	SG	SET	EVL	SET
465030	64788+72086+72087+64838	SG	SET	EVL	SET
465031	64789+72088+72089+64839	SG	SET	EVL	SET
465032	64790+72090+72091+64840	SG	SET	EVL	SET
465033	64791+72092+72093+64841	SG	SET	EVL	SET
465034	64792+72094+72095+64842	SG	SET	EVL	SET
465035	64793+72096+72097+64843	SG	SET	EVL	SET
465036	64794+72098+72099+64844	SG	SET	EVL	SET
465037	64795+72100+72101+64845	SG	SET	EVL	SET
465038	64796+72102+72103+64846	SG	SET	EVL	SET
465039	64797+72104+72105+64847	SG	SET	EVL	SET
465040	64798+72106+72107+64848	SG	SET	EVL	SET
465041	64799+72108+72109+64849	SG	SET	EVL	SET
465042	64800+72110+72111+64850	SG	SET	EVL	SET
465043	64801+72112+72113+64851	SG	SET	EVL	SET
465044	64802+72114+72115+64852	SG	SET	EVL	SET
465045	64803+72116+72117+64853	SG	SET	EVL	SET
465046	64804+72118+72119+64854	SG	SET	EVL	SET
465047	64805+72120+72121+64855	SG	SET	EVL	SET
465048	64806+72122+72123+64856	SG	SET	EVL	SET
465049	64807+72124+72125+64857	SG	SET	EVL	SET
465050	64808+72126+72127+64858	SG	SET	EVL	SET

Class 465/1
Networker

Vehicle Length: (Driving) 68ft 6½in (20.89m)	Width: 9ft 3in (2.81m)
(Inter) 65ft 9¾in (20.05m)	Horsepower: 2,252hp (1,680kW)
Height: 12ft 4½in (3.77m)	Seats (total/car): 348S, 86S/90S/86S/86S

Number	Formation DMSO(A)+TSO+TSO+DMSO(B)	Depot	Livery	Owner	Operator
465151	65800+72900+72901+65847	SG	SET	EVL	SET
465152	65801+72902+72903+65848	SG	SET	EVL	SET

Train Operating Companies

South Eastern

465153	65802+72904+72905+65849	SG	SET	EVL	SET
465154	65803+72906+72907+65850	SG	SET	EVL	SET
465155	65804+72908+72909+65851	SG	SET	EVL	SET
465156	65805+72910+72911+65852	SG	SET	EVL	SET
465157	65806+72912+72913+65853	SG	SET	EVL	SET
465158	65807+72914+72915+65854	SG	SET	EVL	SET
465159	65808+72916+72917+65855	SG	SET	EVL	SET
465160	65809+72918+72919+65856	SG	SET	EVL	SET
465161	65810+72920+72921+65857	SG	SET	EVL	SET
465162	65811+72922+72923+65858	SG	SET	EVL	SET
465163	65812+72924+72925+65859	SG	SET	EVL	SET
465164	65813+72926+72927+65860	SG	SET	EVL	SET
465165	65814+72928+72929+65861	SG	SET	EVL	SET
465166	65815+72930+72931+65862	SG	SET	EVL	SET
465167	65816+72932+72933+65863	SG	SET	EVL	SET
465168	65817+72934+72935+65864	SG	SET	EVL	SET
465169	65818+72936+72937+65865	SG	SET	EVL	SET
465170	65819+72938+72939+65866	SG	SET	EVL	SET
465171	65820+72940+72941+65867	SG	SET	EVL	SET
465172	65821+72942+72943+65868	SG	SET	EVL	SET
465173	65822+72944+72945+65869	SG	SET	EVL	SET
465174	65823+72946+72947+65870	SG	SET	EVL	SET
465175	65824+72948+72949+65871	SG	SET	EVL	SET
465176	65825+72950+72951+65872	SG	SET	EVL	SET
465177	65826+72952+72952+65873	SG	SET	EVL	SET
465178	65827+72954+72955+65874	SG	SET	EVL	SET
465179	65828+72956+72957+65875	SG	SET	EVL	SET
465180	65829+72958+72959+65876	SG	SET	EVL	SET
465181	65830+72960+72961+65877	SG	SET	EVL	SET
465182	65831+72962+72963+65878	SG	SET	EVL	SET
465183	65832+72964+72965+65879	SG	SET	EVL	SET
465184	65833+72966+72967+65880	SG	SET	EVL	SET
465185	65834+72968+72969+65881	SG	SET	EVL	SET
465186	65835+72970+72971+65882	SG	SET	EVL	SET
465187	65836+72972+72973+65883	SG	SET	EVL	SET
465188	65837+72974+72975+65884	SG	SET	EVL	SET
465189	65838+72976+72977+65885	SG	SET	EVL	SET
465190	65839+72978+72979+65886	SG	SET	EVL	SET
465191	65840+72980+72981+65887	SG	SET	EVL	SET
465192	65841+72982+72983+65888	SG	SET	EVL	SET
465193	65842+72984+72985+65889	SG	SET	EVL	SET
465194	65843+72986+72987+65890	SG	SET	EVL	SET
465195	65844+72988+72989+65891	SG	SET	EVL	SET
465196	65845+72990+72991+65892	SG	SET	EVL	SET
465197	65846+72992+72993+65893	SG	SET	EVL	SET

Class 465/2
Networker

Vehicle Length: (Driving) 68ft 6½in (20.89m) Width: 9ft 3in (2.81m)
(Inter) 65ft 9¾in (20.05m) Horsepower: 2,252hp (1,680kW)
Height: 12ft 4½in (3.77m) Seats (total/car): 348S, 86S/90S/86S/86S

Number	Formation DMSO(A)+TSO+TSO+DMSO(B)	Depot	Livery	Owner	Operator
465235	65734+72787+72788+65784	SG	SET	ANG	SET
465236	65735+72789+72790+65785	SG	SET	ANG	SET
465237	65736+72791+72792+65786	SG	SET	ANG	SET
465238	65737+72793+72794+65787	SG	SET	ANG	SET
465239	65738+72795+72796+65788	SG	SET	ANG	SET
465240	65739+72797+72798+65789	SG	SET	ANG	SET
465241	65740+72799+72800+65790	SG	SET	ANG	SET
465242	65741+72801+72802+65791	SG	SET	ANG	SET
465243	65742+72803+72804+65792	SG	SET	ANG	SET
465244	65743+72805+72806+65793	SG	SET	ANG	SET
465245	65744+72807+72808+65794	SG	SET	ANG	SET
465246	65745+72809+72810+65795	SG	SET	ANG	SET
465247	65746+72811+72812+65796	SG	SET	ANG	SET

465248	65747+72813+72814+65797	SG	SET	ANG	SET
465249	65748+72815+72816+65798	SG	SET	ANG	SET
465250	65749+72817+72818+65799	SG	SET	ANG	SET

Class 465/9
Networker

Vehicle Length: (Driving) 68ft 6½in (20.89m) Width: 9ft 3in (2.81m)
(Inter) 65ft 9¾in (20.05m) Horsepower: 2,252hp (1,680kW)
Height: 12ft 4½in (3.77m) Seats (total/car): 24F-302S, 12F-68S/76S/90S/12F-68S

Number	Formation	Depot	Livery	Owner	Operator	Name
	DMCO(A)+TSO+TSO+DMCO(B)					
465901 (465201)	65700+72719+72720+65750	SG	SET	ANG	SET	
465902 (465202)	65701+72721+72722+65751	SG	SET	ANG	SET	
465903 (465203)	65702+72723+72724+65752	SG	SET	ANG	SET	Remembrance
465904 (465204)	65703+72725+72726+65753	SG	SET	ANG	SET	
465905 (465205)	65704+72727+72728+65754	SG	SET	ANG	SET	
465906 (465206)	65705+72729+72730+65755	SG	SET	ANG	SET	
465907 (465207)	65706+72731+72732+65756	SG	SET	ANG	SET	
465908 (465208)	65707+72733+72734+65757	SG	SET	ANG	SET	
465909 (465209)	65708+72735+72736+65758	SG	SET	ANG	SET	
465910 (465210)	65709+72737+72738+65759	SG	SET	ANG	SET	
465911 (465211)	65710+72739+72740+65760	SG	SET	ANG	SET	
465912 (465212)	65711+72741+72742+65761	SG	SET	ANG	SET	
465913 (465213)	65712+72743+72744+65762	SG	SET	ANG	SET	
465914 (465214)	65713+72745+72746+65763	SG	SET	ANG	SET	
465915 (465215)	65714+72747+72748+65764	SG	SET	ANG	SET	
465916 (465216)	65715+72749+72750+65765	SG	SET	ANG	SET	
465917 (465217)	65716+72751+72752+65766	SG	SET	ANG	SET	
465918 (465218)	65717+72753+72754+65767	SG	SET	ANG	SET	
465919 (465219)	65718+72755+72756+65768	SG	SET	ANG	SET	
465920 (465220)	65719+72757+72758+65769	SG	SET	ANG	SET	
465921 (465221)	65720+72759+72760+65770	SG	SET	ANG	SET	
465922 (465222)	65721+72761+72762+65771	SG	SET	ANG	SET	
465923 (465223)	65722+72763+72764+65772	SG	SET	ANG	SET	
465924 (465224)	65723+72765+72766+65773	SG	SET	ANG	SET	
465925 (465225)	65724+72767+72768+65774	SG	SET	ANG	SET	
465926 (465226)	65725+72769+72770+65775	SG	SET	ANG	SET	
465927 (465227)	65726+72771+72772+65776	SG	SET	ANG	SET	
465928 (465228)	65727+72773+72774+65777	SG	SET	ANG	SET	
465929 (465229)	65728+72775+72776+65778	SG	SET	ANG	SET	
465930 (465230)	65729+72777+72778+65779	SG	SET	ANG	SET	
465931 (465231)	65730+72779+72780+65780	SG	SET	ANG	SET	
465932 (465232)	65731+72781+72782+65781	SG	SET	ANG	SET	
465933 (465233)	65732+72783+72784+65782	SG	SET	ANG	SET	
465934 (465234)	65733+72785+72786+65783	SG	SET	ANG	SET	

Right: *South Eastern operate a
sizeable fleet of BREL/ABB and Metro-
Cammell Class 465 'Networker' sets
on suburban services. All sets are based
at Slade Green. Class 465/0, 465/1
and 465/2 are all standard class units,
while the 34 members of Class 465/9,
converted from Class 465/2s, sport
limited first class seating in the two
driving cars. One of the second batch
of ABB-built sets, No. 465187, is seen
departing from Victoria.* **Ron Cover**

South Eastern

Passenger Train Operating Companies - South Eastern

Class 466
Networker

Vehicle Length: (Driving) 68ft 6½in (20.89m)   Horsepower: 1,126hp (840kW)
Height: 12ft 4½in (3.77m)   Seats (total/car): 168S, 86S/82S
Width: 9ft 3in (2.81m)

Number	Formation DMSO+DTSO	Depot	Livery	Owner	Operator
466001	64860+78312	SG	SET	ANG	SET
466002	64861+78313	SG	SET	ANG	SET
466003	64862+78314	SG	SET	ANG	SET
466004	64863+78315	SG	SET	ANG	SET
466005	64864+78316	SG	SET	ANG	SET
466006	64865+78317	SG	SET	ANG	SET
466007	64866+78318	SG	SET	ANG	SET
466008	64867+78319	SG	SET	ANG	SET
466009	64868+78320	SG	SET	ANG	SET
466010	64869+78321	SG	SET	ANG	SET
466011	64870+78322	SG	SET	ANG	SET
466012	64871+78323	SG	SET	ANG	SET
466013	64872+78324	SG	SET	ANG	SET
466014	64873+78325	SG	SET	ANG	SET
466015	64874+78326	SG	SET	ANG	SET
466016	64875+78327	SG	SET	ANG	SET
466017	64876+78328	SG	SET	ANG	SET
466018	64877+78329	SG	SET	ANG	SET
466019	64878+78330	SG	SET	ANG	SET
466020	64879+78331	SG	SET	ANG	SET
466021	64880+78332	SG	SET	ANG	SET
466022	64881+78333	SG	SET	ANG	SET
466023	64882+78334	SG	SET	ANG	SET
466024	64883+78335	SG	SET	ANG	SET
466025	64884+78336	SG	SET	ANG	SET
466026	64885+78337	SG	SET	ANG	SET
466027	64886+78338	SG	SET	ANG	SET
466028	64887+78339	SG	SET	ANG	SET
466029	64888+78340	SG	SET	ANG	SET
466030	64889+78341	SG	SET	ANG	SET
466031	64890+78342	SG	SET	ANG	SET
466032	64891+78343	SG	SET	ANG	SET
466033	64892+78344	SG	SET	ANG	SET
466034	64893+78345	SG	SET	ANG	SET
466035	64894+78346	SG	SET	ANG	SET
466036	64895+78347	SG	SET	ANG	SET
466037	64896+78348	SG	SET	ANG	SET
466038	64897+78349	SG	SET	ANG	SET
466039	64898+78350	SG	SET	ANG	SET
466040	64899+78351	SG	SET	ANG	SET
466041	64900+78352	SG	SET	ANG	SET
466042	64901+78353	SG	SET	ANG	SET
466043	64902+78354	SG	SET	ANG	SET

Above: *To permit the operation of short two-car trains on lightly used routes/services and give flexibility to operate six or 10-car trains' a batch of 43 two-car 'Networker' sets classified as 466 were introduced. Set No. 466030 is illustrated.*
Jamie Squibbs

Southern

Passenger Train Operating Companies - Southern

Address: ✉ Go-Ahead House, 26-28 Addiscombe Road, Croydon, CR9 5GA
✆ info@southernrailway.com
✆ 08451 272920
ⓘ www.southernrailway.com

Managing Director: Chris Burchell
Franchise Dates: 1 March 2003 - 25 July 2015
Principal Routes: London Victoria / London Bridge to Brighton, Coastway route, Uckfield / East Grinstead. Services to Surrey / Sussex, and Brighton to Ashford route
Depots: Brighton (BI), Selhurst (SU)
Parent Company: Govia

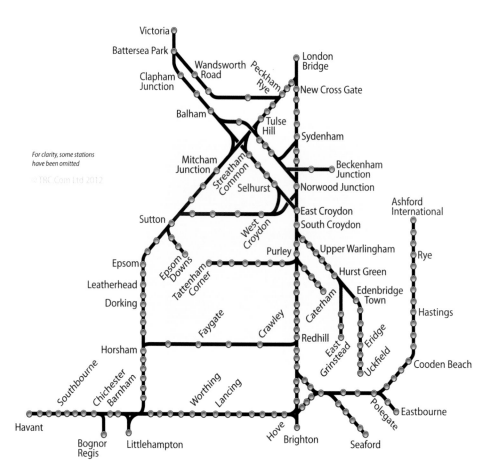

For clarity, some stations have been omitted

© TRC.Com Ltd 2012

Southern

Class 171/7
Turbostar

Vehicle Length: 77ft 6in (23.62m)
Height: 12ft 4½in (3.77m)
Width: 8ft 10in (2.69m)

Engine: 1 x MTU 6R 183TD13H 422hp per vehicle
Horsepower: 844hp (629kW)
Seats (total/car): 9F-107S 9F-43S/64S

Number	Formation DMCL+DMSL	Depot	Livery	Owner	Operator
171721	50721+79721	SU	SOU	PTR	SOU
171722	50722+79722	SU	SOU	PTR	SOU
171723	50723+79723	SU	SOU	PTR	SOU
171724	50724+79724	SU	SOU	PTR	SOU
171725	50725+79725	SU	SOU	PTR	SOU
171726	50726+79726	SU	SOU	PTR	SOU
171727	50727+79727	SU	SOU	PTR	SOU
171728	50728+79728	SU	SOU	PTR	SOU
171729	50729+79729	SU	SOU	PTR	SOU
171730	50392+79392	SU	SOU	PTR	SOU

171730 Previously numbered 170392

Class 171/8
Turbostar

Vehicle Length: 77ft 6in (23.62m)
Height: 12ft 4½in (3.77m)
Width: 8ft 10in (2.69m)

Engine: 1 x MTU 6R 183TD13H 422hp per vehicle
Horsepower: 1,688hp (1,259kW)
Seats (total/car): 18F-241S 9F-43S/74S/74S/9F-50SS

Number	Formation DMCL(A)+MS+MS+DMCL(B)	Depot	Livery	Owner	Operator
171801	50801+54801+56801+79801	SU	SOU	PTR	SOU
171802	50802+54802+56802+79802	SU	SOU	PTR	SOU
171803	50803+54803+56803+79803	SU	SOU	PTR	SOU
171804	50804+54804+56804+79804	SU	SOU	PTR	SOU
171805	50805+54805+56805+79805	SU	SOU	PTR	SOU
171806	50806+54806+56806+79806	SU	SOU	PTR	SOU

Left: Southern has a small fleet of two-and four-car Class 171 'Turbostar' diesel sets for non-electrified line use. Two-car set No. 171724 is illustrated from its DMSL vehicle at St Leonards, Hastings. **Jamie Squibbs**

Class 313/2

Vehicle Length: (Driving) 64ft 11½in (20.75m)
(Inter) 65ft 4¼in (19.92m)
Height: 11ft 9in (3.58m)
Width: 9ft 3in (2.82m)
Horsepower: 880hp (656kW)
Seats (total/car): 202S, 66S/70S/66S

Number	Formation DMSO+PTSO+BDMSO	Depot	Livery	Owner	Operator
313201 (313101)*	62529+71213+62593	BI	SOU	HSB	SOU
313202 (313102)	62530+71214+62594	BI	SOU	HSB	SOU
313203 (313103)	62531+71215+62595	BI	SOU	HSB	SOU
313204 (313104)	62532+71216+62596	BI	SOU	HSB	SOU
313205 (313105)	62533+71217+62597	BI	SOU	HSB	SOU
313206 (313106)	62534+71218+62598	BI	SOU	HSB	SOU
313207 (313107)	62535+71219+62599	BI	SOU	HSB	SOU
313208 (313108)	62536+71220+62600	BI	SOU	HSB	SOU
313209 (313109)	62537+71221+62601	BI	SOU	HSB	SOU
313210 (313110)	62538+71222+62602	BI	SOU	HSB	SOU
313211 (313111)	62539+71223+62603	BI	SOU	HSB	SOU
313212 (313112)	62540+71224+62604	BI	SOU	HSB	SOU
313213 (313113)	62541+71225+62605	BI	SOU	HSB	SOU
313214 (313114)	62542+71226+62606	BI	SOU	HSB	SOU
313215 (313115)	62543+71227+62607	BI	SOU	HSB	SOU
313216 (313116)	62544+71228+62608	BI	SOU	HSB	SOU
313217 (313117)	62545+71229+61609	BI	SOU	HSB	SOU
313219 (313119)	62547+71231+61611	BI	SOU	HSB	SOU
313220 (313120)	62548+71232+61612	BI	SOU	HSB	SOU

Passenger Train Operating Companies - Southern

Right: *19 former London Overground dual voltage Class 313s are now based at Brighton for operation on the Coastway route. The sets have been fully refurbished for their present role and all carry Southern livery, some with route-specific pictograms. Set No. 313217 is seen at Brighton Lovers Walk depot. Note the Coastway branding on the bodyside.*
Antony Christie

* DC only.

Class 377/1
Electrostar

Vehicle Length: (Driving) 66ft 9in (20.3m) Width: 9ft 2in (2.79m)
(Inter) 65ft 6in (19.96m) Horsepower: 2,012hp (1,500kW)
Height: 12ft 4in (3.75m) Seats (total/car): 24F-210S or 244S 12F-48S(56S)/62S(70S)/52S(62S)/12F-48S(56S)

Number	Formation DMCO(A)+MSO+TSO+DMCO(B)	Depot	Livery	Owner	Operator
377101	78501+77101+78901+78701	BI	SOU	PTR	SOU
377102	78502+77102+78902+78702	BI	SOU	PTR	SOU
377103	78503+77103+78903+78703	BI	SOU	PTR	SOU
377104	78504+77104+78904+78704	BI	SOU	PTR	SOU
377105	78505+77105+78905+78705	BI	SOU	PTR	SOU
377106	78506+77106+78906+78706	BI	SOU	PTR	SOU
377107	78507+77107+78907+78707	BI	SOU	PTR	SOU
377108	78508+77108+78908+78708	BI	SOU	PTR	SOU
377109	78509+77109+78909+78709	BI	SOU	PTR	SOU
377110	78510+77110+78910+78710	BI	SOU	PTR	SOU
377111	78511+77111+78911+78711	BI	SOU	PTR	SOU
377112	78512+77112+78912+78712	BI	SOU	PTR	SOU
377113	78513+77113+78913+78713	BI	SOU	PTR	SOU
377114	78514+77114+78914+78714	BI	SOU	PTR	SOU
377115	78515+77115+78915+78715	BI	SOU	PTR	SOU
377116	78516+77116+78916+78716	BI	SOU	PTR	SOU
377117	78517+77117+78917+78717	BI	SOU	PTR	SOU
377118	78518+77118+78918+78718	BI	SOU	PTR	SOU
377119	78519+77119+78919+78719	BI	SOU	PTR	SOU
377120	78520+77120+78920+78720	SU	SOU	PTR	SOU
377121	78521+77121+78921+78721	SU	SOU	PTR	SOU
377122	78522+77122+78922+78722	SU	SOU	PTR	SOU
377123	78523+77123+78923+78723	SU	SOU	PTR	SOU
377124	78524+77124+78924+78724	SU	SOU	PTR	SOU
377125	78525+77125+78925+78725	SU	SOU	PTR	SOU
377126	78526+77126+78926+78726	SU	SOU	PTR	SOU
377127	78527+77127+78927+78727	SU	SOU	PTR	SOU
377128	78528+77128+78928+78728	SU	SOU	PTR	SOU
377129	78529+77129+78929+78729	SU	SOU	PTR	SOU
377130	78530+77130+78930+78730	SU	SOU	PTR	SOU
377131	78531+77131+78931+78731	SU	SOU	PTR	SOU
377132	78532+77132+78932+78732	SU	SOU	PTR	SOU
377133	78533+77133+78933+78733	SU	SOU	PTR	SOU
377134	78534+77134+78934+78734	SU	SOU	PTR	SOU
377135	78535+77135+78935+78735	SU	SOU	PTR	SOU
377136	78536+77136+78936+78736	SU	SOU	PTR	SOU
377137	78537+77137+78937+78737	SU	SOU	PTR	SOU
377138	78538+77138+78938+78738	SU	SOU	PTR	SOU
377139	78539+77139+78939+78739	SU	SOU	PTR	SOU
377140	78540+77140+78940+78740	SU	SOU	PTR	SOU

Southern

377141	78541+77141+78941+78741	SU	SOU	PTR	SOU
377142	78542+77142+78942+78742	SU	SOU	PTR	SOU
377143	78543+77143+78943+78743	SU	SOU	PTR	SOU
377144	78544+77144+78944+78744	SU	SOU	PTR	SOU
377145	78545+77145+78945+78745	SU	SOU	PTR	SOU
377146	78546+77146+78946+78746	SU	SOU	PTR	SOU
377147	78547+77147+78947+78747	SU	SOU	PTR	SOU
377148	78548+77148+78948+78748	SU	SOU	PTR	SOU
377149	78549+77149+78949+78749	SU	SOU	PTR	SOU
377150	78550+77150+78950+78750	SU	SOU	PTR	SOU
377151	78551+77151+78951+78751	SU	SOU	PTR	SOU
377152	78552+77152+78952+78752	SU	SOU	PTR	SOU
377153	78553+77153+78953+78753	SU	SOU	PTR	SOU
377154	78554+77154+78954+78754	SU	SOU	PTR	SOU
377155	78555+77155+78955+78755	SU	SOU	PTR	SOU
377156	78556+77156+78956+78756	SU	SOU	PTR	SOU
377157	78557+77157+78957+78757	SU	SOU	PTR	SOU
377158	78558+77158+78958+78758	SU	SOU	PTR	SOU
377159	78559+77159+78959+78759	SU	SOU	PTR	SOU
377160	78560+77160+78960+78760	SU	SOU	PTR	SOU
377161	78561+77161+78961+78761	SU	SOU	PTR	SOU
377162	78562+77162+78962+78762	SU	SOU	PTR	SOU
377163	78563+77163+78963+78763	SU	SOU	PTR	SOU
377164	78564+77164+78964+78764	SU	SOU	PTR	SOU

Class 377/2
Electrostar

Vehicle Length: (Driving) 66ft 9in (20.3m)   *Width: 9ft 2in (2.79m)*
(Inter) 65ft 6in (19.96m)   *Horsepower: 2,012hp (1,500kW)*
Height: 12ft 4in (3.75m)   *Seats (total/car): 24F-222S, 12F-48S/69S/57S/12F-48S*

Number	Formation	Depot	Livery	Owner	Operator
	DMCO(A)+MSO+PTSO+DMCO(B)				
377201	78571+77171+78971+78771	BI	SOU	PTR	SOU
377202	78572+77172+78972+78772	BI	SOU	PTR	SOU
377203	78573+77173+78973+78773	BI	SOU	PTR	SOU
377204	78574+77174+78974+78774	BI	SOU	PTR	SOU
377205	78575+77175+78975+78775	SU	SOU	PTR	SOU
377206	78576+77176+78976+78776	SU	SOU	PTR	SOU
377207	78577+77177+78977+78777	BI	SOU	PTR	SOU
377208	78578+77178+78978+78778	BI	SOU	PTR	SOU
377209	78579+77179+78979+78779	BI	SOU	PTR	SOU
377210	78580+77180+78980+78780	SU	SOU	PTR	SOU
377211	78581+77181+78981+78781	SU	SOU	PTR	SOU
377212	78582+77182+78982+78782	SU	SOU	PTR	SOU
377213	78583+77183+78983+78783	BI	SOU	PTR	SOU
377214	78584+77184+78984+78784	SU	SOU	PTR	SOU
377215	78585+77185+78985+78785	BI	SOU	PTR	SOU

Class 377/3
Electrostar

Vehicle Length: (Driving) 66ft 9in (20.3m)   *Width: 9ft 2in (2.79m)*
(Inter) 65ft 6in (19.96m)   *Horsepower: 2,012hp (1,500kW)*
Height: 12ft 4in (3.75m)   *Seats (total/car): 24F-152S, 12F-48S/56S/12F-48S*

Number		Formation	Depot	Livery	Owner	Operator
		DMCO(A)+TSO+DMCO(B)				
377301	(375311)	68201+74801+68401	BI	SOU	PTR	SOU
377302	(375312)	68202+74802+68402	BI	SOU	PTR	SOU
377303	(375313)	68203+74803+68403	BI	SOU	PTR	SOU
377304	(375314)	68204+74804+68404	BI	SOU	PTR	SOU
377305	(375315)	68205+74805+68405	BI	SOU	PTR	SOU
377306	(375316)	68206+74806+68406	BI	SOU	PTR	SOU
377307	(375317)	68207+74807+68407	BI	SOU	PTR	SOU
377308	(375318)	68208+74808+68408	BI	SOU	PTR	SOU
377309	(375319)	68209+74809+68409	BI	SOU	PTR	SOU
377310	(375320)	68210+74810+68410	BI	SOU	PTR	SOU
377311	(375321)	68211+74811+68411	BI	SOU	PTR	SOU
377312	(375322)	68212+74812+68412	BI	SOU	PTR	SOU

377313	(375323)	68213+74813+68413	BI	SOU	PTR	SOU
377314	(375324)	68214+74814+68414	BI	SOU	PTR	SOU
377315	(375325)	68215+74815+68415	BI	SOU	PTR	SOU
377316	(375326)	68216+74816+68416	BI	SOU	PTR	SOU
377317	(375327)	68217+74817+68417	BI	SOU	PTR	SOU
377318	(375328)	68218+74818+68418	BI	SOU	PTR	SOU
377319	(375329)	68219+74819+68419	BI	SOU	PTR	SOU
377320	(375330)	68220+74820+68420	BI	SOU	PTR	SOU
377321	(375331)	68221+74821+68421	BI	SOU	PTR	SOU
377322	(375332)	68222+74822+68422	BI	SOU	PTR	SOU
377323	(375333)	68223+74823+68423	BI	SOU	PTR	SOU
377324	(375334)	68224+74824+68424	BI	SOU	PTR	SOU
377325	(375335)	68225+74825+68425	BI	SOU	PTR	SOU
377326	(375336)	68226+74826+68426	BI	SOU	PTR	SOU
377327	(375337)	68227+74827+68427	BI	SOU	PTR	SOU
377328	(375338)	68228+74828+68428	BI	SOU	PTR	SOU

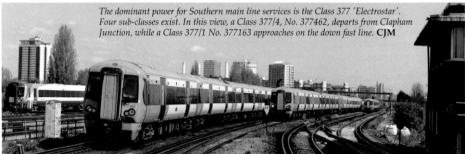

The dominant power for Southern main line services is the Class 377 'Electrostar'. Four sub-classes exist. In this view, a Class 377/4, No. 377462, departs from Clapham Junction, while a Class 377/1 No. 377163 approaches on the down fast line. **CJM**

Class 377/4
Electrostar

Vehicle Length: (Driving) 66ft 9in (20.3m)   Width: 9ft 2in (2.79m)
(Inter) 65ft 6in (19.96m)   Horsepower: 2,012hp (1,500kW)
Height: 12ft 4in (3.75m)   Seats (total/car): 20F-221S, 10F-48S/69S/56S/10F-48S

Number	Formation DMCO(A)+MSO+TSO+DMCO(B)	Depot	Livery	Owner	Operator
377401	73401+78801+78601+73801	BI	SOU	PTR	SOU
377402	73402+78802+78602+73802	BI	SOU	PTR	SOU
377403	73403+78803+78603+73803	BI	SOU	PTR	SOU
377404	73404+78804+78604+73804	BI	SOU	PTR	SOU
377405	73405+78805+78605+73805	BI	SOU	PTR	SOU
377406	73406+78806+78606+73806	BI	SOU	PTR	SOU
377407	73407+78807+78607+73807	BI	SOU	PTR	SOU
377408	73408+78808+78608+73808	BI	SOU	PTR	SOU
377409	73409+78809+78609+73809	BI	SOU	PTR	SOU
377410	73410+78810+78610+73810	BI	SOU	PTR	SOU
377411	73411+78811+78611+73811	BI	SOU	PTR	SOU
377412	73412+78812+78612+73812	BI	SOU	PTR	SOU
377413	73413+78813+78613+73813	BI	SOU	PTR	SOU
377414	73414+78814+78614+73814	BI	SOU	PTR	SOU
377415	73415+78815+78615+73815	BI	SOU	PTR	SOU
377416	73416+78816+78616+73816	SU	SOU	PTR	SOU
377417	73417+78817+78617+73817	BI	SOU	PTR	SOU
377418	73418+78818+78618+73818	BI	SOU	PTR	SOU
377419	73419+78819+78619+73819	BI	SOU	PTR	SOU
377420	73420+78820+78620+73820	BI	SOU	PTR	SOU
377421	73421+78821+78621+73821	BI	SOU	PTR	SOU
377422	73422+78822+78622+73822	BI	SOU	PTR	SOU
377423	73423+78823+78623+73823	BI	SOU	PTR	SOU
377424	73424+78824+78624+73824	BI	SOU	PTR	SOU
377425	73425+78825+78625+73825	BI	SOU	PTR	SOU
377426	73426+78826+78626+73826	BI	SOU	PTR	SOU
377427	73427+78827+78627+73827	BI	SOU	PTR	SOU

Southern

377428	73428+78828+78628+73828	BI	SOU	PTR	SOU	
377429	73429+78829+78629+73829	SU	SOU	PTR	SOU	
377430	73430+78830+78630+73830	BI	SOU	PTR	SOU	
377431	73431+78831+78631+73831	BI	SOU	PTR	SOU	
377432	73432+78832+78632+73832	BI	SOU	PTR	SOU	
377433	73433+78833+78633+73833	BI	SOU	PTR	SOU	
377434	73434+78834+78634+73834	BI	SOU	PTR	SOU	
377435	73435+78835+78635+73835	BI	SOU	PTR	SOU	
377436	73436+78836+78636+73836	BI	SOU	PTR	SOU	
377437	73437+78837+78637+73837	BI	SOU	PTR	SOU	
377438	73438+78838+78638+73838	BI	SOU	PTR	SOU	
377439	73439+78839+78639+73839	BI	SOU	PTR	SOU	
377440	73440+78840+78640+73840	BI	SOU	PTR	SOU	
377441	73441+78841+78641+73841	BI	SOU	PTR	SOU	
377442	73442+78842+78642+73842	BI	SOU	PTR	SOU	
377443	73443+78843+78643+73843	BI	SOU	PTR	SOU	
377444	73444+78844+78644+73844	BI	SOU	PTR	SOU	
377445	73445+78845+78645+73845	BI	SOU	PTR	SOU	
377446	73446+78846+78646+73846	BI	SOU	PTR	SOU	
377447	73447+78847+78647+73847	SU	SOU	PTR	SOU	
377448	73448+78848+78648+73848	BI	SOU	PTR	SOU	
377449	73449+78849+78649+73849	BI	SOU	PTR	SOU	
377450	73450+78850+78650+73850	BI	SOU	PTR	SOU	
377451	73451+78851+78651+73851	BI	SOU	PTR	SOU	
377452	73452+78852+78652+73852	SU	SOU	PTR	SOU	
377453	73453+78853+78653+73853	BI	SOU	PTR	SOU	
377454	73454+78854+78654+73854	BI	SOU	PTR	SOU	
377455	73455+78855+78655+73855	BI	SOU	PTR	SOU	
377456	73456+78856+78656+73856	BI	SOU	PTR	SOU	
377457	73457+78857+78657+73857	BI	SOU	PTR	SOU	
377458	73458+78858+78658+73858	BI	SOU	PTR	SOU	
377459	73459+78859+78659+73859	BI	SOU	PTR	SOU	
377460	73460+78860+78660+73860	SU	SOU	PTR	SOU	
377461	73461+78861+78661+73861	BI	SOU	PTR	SOU	
377462	73462+78862+78662+73862	BI	SOU	PTR	SOU	
377463	73463+78863+78663+73863	BI	SOU	PTR	SOU	
377464	73464+78864+78664+73864	BI	SOU	PTR	SOU	
377465	73465+78865+78665+73865	BI	SOU	PTR	SOU	
377466	73466+78866+78666+73866	BI	SOU	PTR	SOU	
377467	73467+78867+78667+73867	BI	SOU	PTR	SOU	
377468	73468+78868+78668+73868	BI	SOU	PTR	SOU	
377469	73469+78869+78669+73869	BI	SOU	PTR	SOU	
377470	73470+78870+78670+73870	BI	SOU	PTR	SOU	
377471	73471+78871+78671+73871	BI	SOU	PTR	SOU	
377472	73472+78872+78672+73872	BI	SOU	PTR	SOU	
377473	73473+78873+78673+73873	BI	SOU	PTR	SOU	
377474	73474+78874+78674+73874	BI	SOU	PTR	SOU	
377475	73475+78875+78675+73875	BI	SOU	PTR	SOU	

Left: *The 15 members of Class 377/2 are fitted for full dual voltage operation and used on the Croydon-Milton Keynes through service where a voltage change is carried out on the West London line between Kensington Olympia and North Pole Junction. Set No. 377207 is seen approaching Kensington Olympia running on dc power.* **CJM**

■ 130 additional Class 377 carriages for Southern have been ordered for delivery in 2013.

Class 442

Vehicle Length: (Driving) 75ft 11½in (23.15m)
(Inter) 75ft 5½in (22.99m)
Height: 12ft 4in (3.81m)
Width: 8ft 11½in (2.73m)
Horsepower: 1,608hp (1,200kW)
Seats (total/car): 24F-318S, 74S/76S/24F-28S/66S/74S

Number	Formation DTSO(A)+TSO+MBC+TSO+DTSO(B)	Depot	Livery	Owner	Operator
442401	77382+71818+62937+71841+77406	SL	SGX	ANG	SOU
442402	77383+71819+62938+71842+77407	SL	SGX	ANG	SOU
442403	77384+71820+62941+71843+77408	SL	SGX	ANG	SOU
442404	77385+71821+62939+71844+77409	SL	SGX	ANG	SOU
442405	77386+71822+62944+71845+77410	SL	SGX	ANG	SOU
442406	77389+71823+62942+71846+77411	SL	SGX	ANG	SOU
442407	77388+71824+62943+71847+77412	SL	SGX	ANG	SOU
442408	77387+71825+62945+71848+77413	SL	SGX	ANG	SOU
442409	77390+71826+62946+71849+77414	SL	SGX	ANG	SOU
442410	77391+71827+62948+71850+77415	SL	SGX	ANG	SOU
442411	77392+71828+62940+71851+77422	SL	SGX	ANG	SOU
442412	77393+71829+62947+71858+77417	SL	SGX	ANG	SOU
442413	77394+71830+62949+71853+77418	SL	SGX	ANG	SOU
442414	77395+71831+62950+71854+77419	SL	SGX	ANG	SOU
442415	77396+71832+62951+71855+77420	SL	SGX	ANG	SOU
442416	77397+71833+62952+71856+77421	SL	SGX	ANG	SOU
442417	77398+71834+62953+71857+77416	SL	SGX	ANG	SOU
442418	77399+71835+62954+71852+77423	SL	SGX	ANG	SOU
442419	77400+71836+62955+71859+77424	SL	SGX	ANG	SOU
442420	77401+71837+62956+71860+77425	SL	SGX	ANG	SOU
442421	77402+71838+62957+71861+77426	SL	SGX	ANG	SOU
442422	77403+71839+62958+71862+77427	SL	SGX	ANG	SOU
442423	77404+71840+62959+71863+77428	SL	SGX	ANG	SOU
442424	77405+71841+62960+71864+77429	SL	SGX	ANG	SOU

Right: With the merger of the Southern
and Gatwick Express franchise
operations, it was decided to take off
lease the Class 460 'Juniper' stock built
specifically for the route and replace
them with refurbished Class 442 sets
displaced by modernisation of the
Waterloo to Weymouth line. The 24
Class 442s have all been refurbished
and now have a middle Motor Brake
Composite vehicle. The sets are
painted in the distinctive Gatwick
Express livery. Set No 442411 is seen
approaching Clapham Junction. **CJM**

Class 455/8

Vehicle Length: (Driving) 65ft 0½in (19.83m)
(Inter) 65ft 4½in (19.92m)
Height: 12ft 1½in (3.79m)
Width: 9ft 3¼in (2.82m)
Horsepower: 1,000hp (746kW)
Seats (total/car): 310S, 74S/78S/84S/74S

Number	Formation DTSO(A)+MSO+TSO+DTSO(B)	Depot	Livery	Owner	Operator
455801	77627+62709+71657+77580	SU	SOU	EVL	SOU
455802	77581+62710+71664+77582	SU	SOU	EVL	SOU
455803	77583+62711+71639+77584	SU	SOU	EVL	SOU
455804	77585+62712+71640+77586	SU	SOU	EVL	SOU
455805	77587+62713+71641+77588	SU	SOU	EVL	SOU
455806	77589+62714+71642+77590	SU	SOU	EVL	SOU
455807	77591+62715+71643+77592	SU	SOU	EVL	SOU
455808	77637+62716+71644+77594	SU	SOU	EVL	SOU
455809	77623+62717+71648+77602	SU	SOU	EVL	SOU
455810	77597+62718+71646+77598	SU	SOU	EVL	SOU
455811	77599+62719+71647+77600	SU	SOU	EVL	SOU
455812	77595+62720+71645+77626	SU	SOU	EVL	SOU

Southern

455813	77603+62721+71649+77604	SU	SOU	EVL	SOU
455814	77605+62722+71650+77606	SU	SOU	EVL	SOU
455815	77607+62723+71651+77608	SU	SOU	EVL	SOU
455816	77609+62724+71652+77633	SU	SOU	EVL	SOU
455817	77611+62725+71653+77612	SU	SOU	EVL	SOU
455818	77613+62726+71654+77632	SU	SOU	EVL	SOU
455819	77615+62727+71637+77616	SU	SOU	EVL	SOU
455820	77617+62728+71656+77618	SU	SOU	EVL	SOU
455821	77619+62729+71655+77620	SU	SOU	EVL	SOU
455822	77621+62730+71658+77622	SU	SOU	EVL	SOU
455823	77601+62731+71659+77596	SU	SOU	EVL	SOU
455824	77593+62732+71660+77624	SU	SOU	EVL	SOU
455825	77579+62733+71661+77628	SU	SOU	EVL	SOU
455826	77630+62734+71662+77629	SU	SOU	EVL	SOU
455827	77610+62735+71663+77614	SU	SOU	EVL	SOU
455828	77631+62736+71638+77634	SU	SOU	EVL	SOU
455829	77635+62737+71665+77636	SU	SOU	EVL	SOU
455830	77625+62743+71666+77638	SU	SOU	EVL	SOU
455831	77639+62739+71667+77640	SU	SOU	EVL	SOU
455832	77641+62740+71668+77642	SU	SOU	EVL	SOU
455833	77643+62741+71669+77644	SU	SOU	EVL	SOU
455834	77645+62742+71670+77646	SU	SOU	EVL	SOU
455835	77647+62738+71671+77648	SU	SOU	EVL	SOU
455836	77649+62744+71672+77650	SU	SOU	EVL	SOU
455837	77651+62745+71673+77652	SU	SOU	EVL	SOU
455838	77653+62746+71674+77654	SU	SOU	EVL	SOU
455839	77655+62747+71675+77656	SU	SOU	EVL	SOU
455840	77657+62748+71676+77658	SU	SOU	EVL	SOU
455841	77659+62749+71677+77660	SU	SOU	EVL	SOU
455842	77661+62750+71678+77662	SU	SOU	EVL	SOU
455843	776636+2751+71679+77664	SU	SOU	EVL	SOU
455844	776656+2752+71680+77666	SU	SOU	EVL	SOU
455845	776676+2753+71681+77668	SU	SOU	EVL	SOU
455846	776696+2754+71682+77670	SU	SOU	EVL	SOU

Left: *The Southern-operated Class 455 stock has been largely altered from the similar sets operating on South West Trains. The front ends have lost their gangways and a cab air conditioning module is now fitted in the former central door. All 46 sets are allocated to Selhurst and are the backbone to Victoria area local suburban services. Set No. 455826 is illustrated at Clapham Junction.* **Antony Christie**

Class 456

Vehicle Length: (Driving) 65ft 3¼in (19.89m)
Height: 12ft 4½in (3.77m)
Width: 9ft 3in (2.81m)

Horsepower: 500hp (370kW)
Seats (total/car): 152S, 79S/73S

Number	Formation DMSO+DTSO	Depot	Livery	Owner	Operator
456001	64735+78250	SU	SOU	PTR	SOU
456002	64736+78251	SU	SOU	PTR	SOU
456003	64737+78252	SU	SOU	PTR	SOU
456004	64738+78253	SU	SOU	PTR	SOU
456005	64739+78254	SU	SOU	PTR	SOU
456006	64740+78255	SU	SOU	PTR	SOU
456007	64741+78256	SU	SOU	PTR	SOU
456008	64742+78257	SU	SOU	PTR	SOU
456009	64743+78258	SU	SOU	PTR	SOU
456010	64744+78259	SU	SOU	PTR	SOU
456011	64745+78260	SU	SOU	PTR	SOU
456012	64746+78261	SU	SOU	PTR	SOU
456013	64747+78262	SU	SOU	PTR	SOU
456014	64748+78263	SU	SOU	PTR	SOU
456015	64749+78264	SU	SOU	PTR	SOU
456016	64750+78265	SU	SOU	PTR	SOU
456017	64751+78266	SU	SOU	PTR	SOU
456018	64752+78267	SU	SOU	PTR	SOU
456019	64753+78268	SU	SOU	PTR	SOU
456020	64754+78269	SU	SOU	PTR	SOU
456021	64755+78270	SU	SOU	PTR	SOU
456022	64756+78271	SU	SOU	PTR	SOU
456023	64757+78272	SU	SOU	PTR	SOU
456024	64758+78273	SU	SOU	PTR	SOU

Name applied
456024   *Sir Cosmo Bonsor*

Right: *Soon after the Class 455 sets entered traffic on the Southern Region Central Division, a batch of 24 two-car Class 456s emerged from York Works, enabling two-, six- or ten-car formations to operate. Today all sets are allocated to Selhurst and operate for Southern. All are painted in Southern livery. Set No. 456022 is seen from its DMSO end near Norwood.*
Antony Christie

Class 460: In early 2012, two Class 460 sets Nos. 460001/002 were still in use on Gatwick Express duties, these were scheduled to be taken out of traffic by spring 2012 for conversion to Class 458 stock for South West Trains.

Class 09/0

Vehicle Length: 29ft 3in (8.91m)
Height: 12ft 8⅝in (3.87m)
Width: 8ft 6in (2.59m)
Engine: English Electric 6K
Horsepower: 400hp (298kW)
Electrical Equipment: English Electric

Number	Depot	Pool	Livery	Owner	Operator	Name
09026	BI	HWSU	GRN	SOU	SOU	*Cedric Wares*

Right: *Southern operate one shunting loco, Class 09/0 No. 09026 Cedric Wares. The loco is allocated to Brighton and performs shunting duties as required and also carries depot de-icing equipment to keep the tracks of Lovers Walk free from ice in the winter period. The loco is painted in mid green livery. The third rail de-icing equipment can be seen in this view behind the front foot step.*
Antony Christie

Class 73/2

Vehicle Length: 53ft 8in (16.35m)
Height: 12ft 5⅞in (3.79m)
Width: 8ft 8in (2.64m)
Power: 750V dc third rail or English Electric 6K
Horsepower: electric - 1,600hp (1,193kW)
Horsepower: diesel - 600hp (447kW)
Electrical Equipment: English Electric

Number	Depot	Pool	Livery	Owner	Operator	Name
73202 (73137)	SL	IVGA	GAT	PTR	SOU	*Dave Berry*

Right: *Class 73/2 No. 73202 Dave Berry is still on the books of Southern, based at Stewarts Lane, and is part of the Gatwick Express fleet. The loco was principally used as a rescue locomotive for the Gatwick Express Class 460 stock and in more recent years has been used as a route learner and pilot for hauling stock around the network.*
Antony Christie

Virgin Trains

Address: ✉ 85 Smallbrook Queensway, Birmingham, B5 4HA

✆ info@virgintrains.co.uk

© 0845 000 8000

ⓘ www.virgintrains.co.uk

Managing Director: Chris Gibb

Franchise Dates: 12 December 2006 - 8 December 2012

Principal Routes: London Euston - Birmingham, Holyhead, Manchester
Liverpool, Glasgow and Edinburgh

Depots: Edge Hill* (LL), Longsight** (MA), Oxley** (OY),
Wembley** (WB), Central Rivers (CZ)
** Operated by Alstom Transportation

Parent Company: Virgin Group

Class 57/3

Vehicle Length: 63ft 6in (19.38m)
Height: 12ft 10⅟₂in (3.91m)
Width: 9ft 2in (2.79m)
Engine: EMD 645-12F3B
Horsepower: 2,750hp (2,051kW)
Electrical Equipment: Brush

Number	Depot	Pool	Livery	Owner	Operator	Name/Notes
57302 (47827)	MA	IWCA	VWC	PBR	VWC	*Virgil Tracy*
57304 (47807)	MA	IWCA	VWC	PBR	VWC	*Gordon Tracy*
57307 (47225)	MA	IWCA	VWC	PBR	VWC	*Lady Penelope*
57308 (47846)	MA	IWCA	VWC	PBR	VWC	*Tin Tin*
57309 (47806)	MA	IWCA	VWC	PBR	VWC	*Brains*
57311 (47817)	MA	IWCA	VWC	PBR	VWC	*Parker*
57313 (47371)	MA	IWCA	BLU	PBR	ATW	*Used by Arriva Trains Wales*
57314 (47372)	MA	IWCA	ATE	PBR	ATW	*Used by Arriva Trains Wales*
57315 (47234)	MA	IWCA	ATE	PBR	ATW	*Used by Arriva Trains Wales*
57316 (47290)	MA	IWCA	BLU	PBR	ATW	*Used by Arriva Trains Wales*

■ 57313-57315 due to return to Virgin Trains use from January 2012.

Above: *From an original fleet of 16 Class 57/3s introduced for Virgin Trains, only six locos remain in daily Virgin traffic, six having been transferred to Network Rail and four used by Arriva Trains Wales. With its pink* Lady Penelope *nameplates, No. 57307 arrives at Llandudno Junction with a Virgin Pendolino service bound for Holyhead.* **Antony Christie**

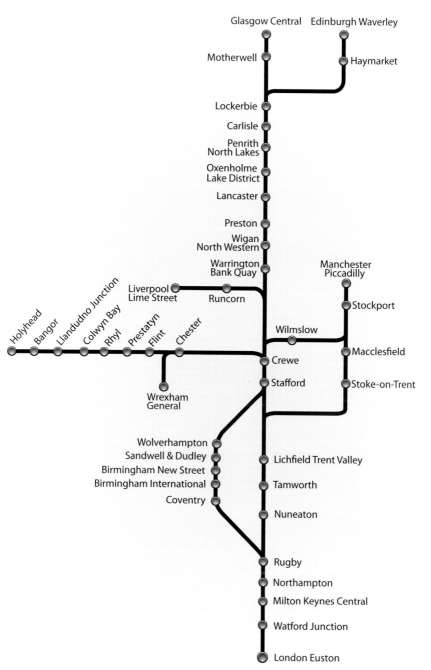

© TRC.Com Ltd 2012

Passenger Train Operating Companies – Virgin Trains

Virgin Trains

Class 221
Super Voyager

Vehicle Length: 77ft 6in (23.62m)	
Height: 12ft 4in (3.75m)	
Width: 8ft 11in (2.73m)	
Engine: 1 x Cummins 750hp per vehicle	
Horsepower: 5-car - 3,750hp (2,796kW). 4-car - 3,000hp (2,237kW)	
Seats (total/car): 26F/214S 42S/60S/60S/52S*/26F (*not in 4-car set)	

Number	Formation	Depot	Livery	Owner	Operator	Name
	221101 - 221118 - DMS+MS+MS+MSRMB+DMF					
221101	60351+60951+60851+60751+60451	CZ	VWC	HBS	VWC	*Louis Bleriot*
221102	60352+60952+60852+60752+60452	CZ	VWC	HBS	VWC	*John Cabot*
221103	60353+60953+60853+60753+60453	CZ	VWC	HBS	VWC	*Christopher Columbus*
221104	60354+60954+60854+60754+60454	CZ	VWC	HBS	VWC	*Sir John Franklin*
221105	60355+60955+60855+60755+60455	CZ	VWC	HBS	VWC	*William Baffin*
221106	60356+60956+60856+60756+60456	CZ	VWC	HBS	VWC	*William Barents*
221107	60357+60957+60857+60757+60457	CZ	VWC	HBS	VWC	*Sir Martin Frobisher*
221108	60358+60958+60858+60758+60458	CZ	VWC	HBS	VWC	*Sir Ernest Shackleton*
221109	60359+60959+60859+60759+60459	CZ	VWC	HBS	VWC	*Marco Polo*
221110	60360+60960+60860+60760+60460	CZ	VWC	HBS	VWC	*James Cook*
221111	60361+60961+60861+60761+60461	CZ	VWC	HBS	VWC	*Roald Amundsen*
221112	60362+60962+60862+60762+60462	CZ	VWC	HBS	VWC	*Ferdinand Magellan*
221113	60363+60963+60863+60763+60463	CZ	VWC	HBS	VWC	*Sir Walter Raleigh*
221114	60364+60964+60864+60764+60464	CZ	VWC	HBS	VWC	
221115	60365+60965+60865+60765+60465	CZ	VWC¤	HBS	VWC	*Polmadie Depot*
221116	60366+60966+60866+60766+60466	CZ	VWC	HBS	VWC	
221117	60367+60967+60867+60767+60467	CZ	VWC	HBS	VWC	
221118	60368+60968+60868+60768+60468	CZ	VWC	HBS	VWC	
221142	60392+60992+60994ø+60792+60492	CZ	VWC	HBS	VWC	*Bombardier Voyager*
221143	60393+60993+60794+60793+60493	CZ	VWC	HBS	VWC	*Auguste Picard*
221144	60394+-+-+-+60494	CZ	VWC	HBS	(Training)	

¤ One driving car carries Bombardier branding. ø MRSMB vehicle

Left Top: *Virgin Trains operate a fleet of 20 five-car 'Super Voyager' sets based at Central Rivers and used on West Coast services. In addition to operating over the North Wales coast, which is non-electrified, the Class 221 fleet also operate under the wires on main Anglo-Scottish services. Set No. 221116, now devoid of its original* David Livingstone *nameplates, arrives at Carlisle from Glasgow.*
Nathan Williamson

Left Bottom: *In 2011 it was decided to re-form the remaining Virgin Trains-operated four-car 'Super Voyager' sets into five-car formations, by disbanding set No. 221144, which donated its two intermediate vehicles to sets Nos. 221142/43. The two spare driving cars were then placed in warm store, being available if required. However, in summer 2011 both vehicles were coupled back to back and used for Virgin staff training, seen here in one of the bay platforms at Crewe.* **Alan Wright**

Class 390
Pendolino

Vehicle Length Driving: 75ft 6in (23.01m)
Height: 11ft 6in (3.50m)
Width: 9ft 11in (2.71m)

Horsepower: 6,840hp (5,100kW)
Seats (total/car): 147F/300S, 18F/39F/44F/46F/76S/66S/48S/64S/46S
31 sets are to be strengthened to eleven vehicles and four extra Class 390 sets are to be built by Virgin Rail Projects

Number	Formation DMRFO+MFO+PTFO+MFO+TSO+MSO+PTSRMB+MSO+DMSO	Depot	Livery	Owner	Operator	Name
390001	69101+69401+69501+69601+68801+69701+69801+69901+69201	MA	VWC	ANG	VWC	Virgin Pioneer
390002	69102+69402+69502+69602+68802+69702+69802+69902+69202	MA	VWC	ANG	VWC	Virgin Angel
390003	69103+69403+69503+69603+68803+69703+69803+69903+69203	MA	VWC	ANG	VWC	Virgin Hero
390004	69104+69404+69504+69604+68804+69704+69804+69904+69204	MA	VWC	ANG	VWC	Alstom Pendolino
390005	69105+69405+69505+69605+68805+69705+69805+69905+69205	MA	VWC	ANG	VWC	City of Wolverhampton
390006	69106+69406+69506+69606+68806+69706+69806+69906+69206	MA	VWC	ANG	VWC	Tate Liverpool
390007	69107+69407+69507+69607+68807+69707+69807+69907+69207	MA	VWC	ANG	VWC	Virgin Lady (branded Abigail Irozuru)
390008	69108+69408+69508+69608+68808+69708+69808+69908+69208	MA	VWC	ANG	VWC	Virgin King
390009	69109+69409+69509+69609+68809+69709+69809+69909+69209	MA	VWC	ANG	VWC	Treaty of Union
390010	69110+69410+69510+69610+68810+69710+69810+69910+69210	MA	VWC	ANG	VWC	A Decade of Progress
390011	69111+69411+69511+69611+68811+69711+69811+69911+69211	MA	VWC	ANG	VWC	City of Lichfield
390012	69112+69412+69512+69612+68812+69712+69812+69912+69212	MA	VWC	ANG	VWC	Virgin Star
390013	69113+69413+69513+69613+68813+69713+69813+69913+69213	MA	VWC	ANG	VWC	Virgin Spirit
390014	69114+69414+69514+69614+68814+69714+69814+69914+69214	MA	VWC	ANG	VWC	City of Manchester
390015	69115+69415+69515+69615+68815+69715+69815+69915+69215	MA	VWC	ANG	VWC	Virgin Crusader
390016	69116+69416+69516+69616+68816+69716+69816+69916+69216	MA	VWC	ANG	VWC	Virgin Champion
390017	69117+69417+69517+69617+68817+69717+69817+69917+69217	MA	VWC	ANG	VWC	Virgin Prince
390018	69118+69418+69518+69618+68818+69718+69818+69918+69218	MA	VWC	ANG	VWC	Virgin Princess
390019	69119+69419+69519+69619+68819+69719+69819+69919+69219	MA	VWC	ANG	VWC	Virgin Warrior
390020	69120+69420+69520+69620+68820+69720+69820+69920+69220	MA	VWC	ANG	VWC	Virgin Cavalier
390021	69121+69421+69521+69621+68821+69721+69821+69921+69221	MA	VWC	ANG	VWC	Virgin Dream
390022	69122+69422+69522+69622+68822+69722+69822+69922+69222	MA	VWC	ANG	VWC	Penny the Pendolino
390023	69123+69423+69523+69623+68823+69723+69823+69923+69223	MA	VWC	ANG	VWC	Virgin Glory
390024	69124+69424+69524+69624+68824+69724+69824+69924+69224	MA	VWC	ANG	VWC	Virgin Venturer
390025	69125+69425+69525+69625+68825+69725+69825+69925+69225	MA	VWC	ANG	VWC	Virgin Stagecoach
390026	69126+69426+69526+69626+68826+69726+69826+69926+69226	MA	VWC	ANG	VWC	Virgin Enterprise
390027	69127+69427+69527+69627+68827+69727+69827+69927+69227	MA	VWC	ANG	VWC	Virgin Buccaneer
390028	69128+69428+69528+69628+68828+69728+69828+69928+69228	MA	VWC	ANG	VWC	City of Preston
390029	69129+69429+69529+69629+68829+69729+69829+69929+69229	MA	VWC	ANG	VWC	City of Stoke-on-Trent
390030	69130+69430+69530+69630+68830+69730+69830+69930+69230	MA	VWC	ANG	VWC	City of Edinburgh
390031	69131+69431+69531+69631+68831+69731+69831+69931+69231	MA	VWC	ANG	VWC	City of Liverpool
390032	69132+69432+69532+69632+68832+69732+69832+69932+69232	MA	VWC	ANG	VWC	City of Birmingham
390033	69133+69433+69533+69633+68833+69733+69833+69933+69233	MA	VWC	ANG	VWC	City of Carlisle
390034	69134+69434+69534+69634+68834+69734+69834+69934+69234	MA	VWC	ANG	VWC	City of Lancaster
390035	69135+69435+69535+69635+68835+69735+69835+69935+69235	MA	VWC	ANG	VWC	City of Coventry
390036	69136+69436+69536+69636+68836+69736+69836+69936+69236	MA	VWC	ANG	VWC	Virgin Difference
390037	69137+69437+69537+69637+68837+69737+69837+69937+69237	MA	VWC	ANG	VWC	City of London
390038	69138+69438+69538+69638+68838+69738+69838+69938+69238	MA	VWC	ANG	VWC	Virgin Quest
390039	69139+69439+69539+69639+68839+69739+69839+69939+69239	MA	VWC	ANG	VWC	Virgin Pathfinder
390040	69140+69440+69540+69640+68840+69740+69840+69940+69240	MA	VWC	ANG	VWC	

Virgin Trains

390041	69141+69541+69641+68841+69741+69841+69241	MA	VWC	ANG	VWC
390042	69142+69442+69542+69842+68842+69742+69942+69242	MA	VWC	ANG	VWC
390043	69143+69443+69543+68843+69743+69843+69243	MA	VWC	ANG	VWC
390044	69144+69444+69544+68844+69744+69844+69244	MA	VWC	ANG	VWC
390045	69145+69445+69545+68845+69745+69845+69245	MA	VWC	ANG	VWC
390046	69146+69446+69546+68846+69746+69846+69246	MA	VWC	ANG	VWC
390047	69147+69447+69547+68847+69747+69847+69247	MA	VWC	ANG	VWC
390048	69148+69448+69548+68848+69748+69848+69248	MA	VWC	ANG	VWC
390049	69149+69449+69549+68849+69749+69849+69249	MA	VWC	ANG	VWC
390050	69150+69450+69550+68850+69750+69850+69250	MA	VWC	ANG	VWC
390051	69151+69451+69551+68851+69751+69851+69251	MA	VWC	ANG	VWC
390052	69152+69452+69552+68852+69752+69852+69252	MA	VWC	ANG	VWC
390053	69153+69453+69553+68853+69753+69853+69253	MA	VWC	ANG	VWC
390054	69154+69454+69554+68354+68954+69754+65854+69954+69254	MA	VWC	ANG	VWC §
390055	69155+69455+69555+68355+68955+69755+65855+69955+69255	MA	VWC	ANG	VWC §
390056	69156+69456+69556+68356+68956+69756+65856+69956+69256	MA	VWC	ANG	VWC *(Under construction due 2012)* §
390057	69157+69457+69557+68357+68957+69757+65857+69957+69257	MA	VWC	ANG	VWC *(Under construction due 2012)* §

■ The additional vehicles under construction for 31 sets will be an additional TSO 653xx series and an MSO 689xx series. These will be inserted after the 696xx MFO vehicle.

■ Pendolino set No. 390033 *City of Glasgow*, which was involved in the Grayrigg derailment on 23 February 2007, was withdrawn from service. After spending a period stored at Long Marston, some of the vehicles have now seen further use.

Cars 69133 and 69833 have been rebuilt as static training vehicles for use at the Virgin Trains training school in Crewe.

Nos. 69933 and 69733 are in use at the fire training school in Morton-in-Marsh, while Nos. 69533, 68833 and 69433 remain in store at Long Marston owned by Virgin Group.

Vehicle No. 69233 has been broken up.

Above: *Heading for London Euston, Pendolino set No. 390022 Penny the Pendolino passes South Kenton on the 'up' main line. The tilting Class 390 sets have revolutionised West Coast travel in recent years.* **CJM**

Mk3 Hauled Stock

Vehicle Length: 75ft 0in (22.86m)   Width: 8ft 11in (2.71m)
Height: 12ft 9in (3.88m)   Bogie Type: BT10

AJ1G - RFB *Seating 18F*

Number	Depot	Livery	Owner
10212	WB	VWC	PTR
10217	WB	VWC	PTE

AD1G - FO *Seating 48F*

Number	Depot	Livery	Owner
11007	WB	VWC	PTR
11018	WB	VWC	PTR

11048	WB	VWC	PTR

AC2G - TS0 (*TSOD) *Seating 76/70*S*

Number	Depot	Livery	Owner
12011	WB	VWC	PTR
12078	WB	VWC	PTR
12122*	WB	VWC	PTR
12133	WB	VWC	PTR
12138	WB	VWC	PTR

NL - DVT

Number	Depot	Livery	Owner
82101	WB	VWC	PTR§
82126	WB	VWC	PTR

§ Spare vehicle

■ The Virgin West Coast loco-hauled set is operated on an 'as required' basis to cover for a shortfall in Pendolino stock. Motive power is provided by DBS or Freightliner in the form of a Class 90/0 or a VWC Class 57/3.

Right Top: *The Virgin West Coast stand-in loco-hauled set, often referred to as the Pretendolino, is based at Wembley. The vehicles have all been upgraded to reflect as much as possible the service and interior style of the Class 390s and are painted in standard Virgin livery. TSO No. 12138 is shown at Euston.* **Stacey Thew**

Right Middle : *Three Mk3 FO vehicles operate in the stand-in set. Here No. 11007 is seen at Euston.* **Stacey Thew**

Right Bottom: *Two refreshment vehicles are available. Here RFB No. 10212 is illustrated.* **Stacey Thew**

The following vehicles are assigned as spare and could be used to form a second West Coast loco-hauled train if required in the future
TSOs 12017/054/059/ 094/124, FOs 11064/084/086, DVT 82101.

Colas Rail

Address: ✉ Dacre House, 19 Dacre Street, London, SW1H 0DJ
✍ enquiries@colasrail.co.uk
✆ 0207 593 5353
ⓘ www.colasrail.co.uk

Chairman: Charles-Albert Giral
Depots: Washwood Heath (AW), Rugby (RU), Eastleigh Works (ZG)

Class 47/7

Vehicle Length: 63ft 6in (19.35m)
Height: 12ft 10³⁄₈in (3.91m)
Width: 9ft 2in (2.79m)
Electric Train Heat fitted

Engine: Sulzer 12LDA28C
Horsepower: 2,580hp (1,922kW)
Electrical Equipment: Brush

Number		Depot	Pool	Livery	Owner	Operator	Name
47727	(47569)	AW	COLO	COL	COL	COL	*Rebecca*
47739	(47594)	AW	COLO	COL	COL	COL	*Robin of Templecombe*
47749	(47625)	AW	COLO	COL	COL	COL	*Demelza*

Left: *Colas Rail operates three Class 47/7s for general freight duties. The three were refurbished by Eastleigh and retain full train supply equipment No. 47749* Demelza *is illustrated passing Bristol Barton Hill hauling a preserved Class 37.* **Antony Christie**

Class 66/8

Vehicle Length: 70ft 0½in (21.34m)
Height: 12ft 10in (3.91m)
Width: 8ft 8¼in (2.65m)

Engine: EMD 12N-710G3B-EC
Horsepower: 3,300hp (2,462kW)
Electrical Equipment: EMD

Number		Depot	Pool	Livery	Owner	Operator	Name
66846	(66573)	RU	COLO	COL	COL	COL	
66847	(66574)	RU	COLO	COL	COL	COL	
66848	(66575)	RU	COLO	COL	COL	COL	
66849	(66576)	RU	COLO	COL	COL	COL	
66850	(66577)	RU	COLO	COL	COL	COL	*Wylam Dilly*

Left: *A major change-around of Class 66s took place in 2011, with the five locos used by Colas being sold to GBRf and five former Freightliner locos which were off lease passing to Colas Rail Freight. The five latest Colas locos were all overhauled at Eastleigh Works and repainted into the latest Colas Rail Freight colours and renumbered into the 66/8 number series. Soon after release from Eastleigh, No. 66849, the former 66576, is seen light loco at Newport.* **CJM**

DB Schenker - EWS

Address (UK): ✉ Lakeside Business Park, Caroline Way, Doncaster, DN4 5PN

📠 info@rail.dbschenker.co.uk

✆ 0870 140 5000

ⓘ www.rail.dbschenker.co.uk

Chief Executive: Alain Thauvette

Class 08

Vehicle Length: 29ft 3in (8.91m)
Height: 12ft 8⅝in (3.87m)
Width: 8ft 6in (2.59m)

Engine: English Electric 6K
Horsepower: 400hp (298kW)
Electrical Equipment: English Electric

Number	Depot	Pool	Livery	Owner	Operator
08405¤	DR	WNYX	EWS	DBS	DBS
08428	TO	WSSK	EWS	DBS	DBS
08442	EH	-	BRT	DBS	DBA
08480*	TO	WNYX	EWS	DBS	DBS
08495¤	EH	WSSK	EWS	DBS	DBS
08499(S)	WQ	WSXX	BLU	DBS	PUL
08500(S)	WQ	WNTS	EWS	DBS	-
08516	BK	-	LNW	DBS	*
08567	TO	WSSK	EWS	DBS	DBS
08578¤	TO	WNYX	EWS	DBS	DBS
08580(S)	WQ	WNTS	EWS	DBS	-
08593(S)	WQ	WNTS	EWS	DBS	-
08605¤(S)	TO	WNYX	EWS	DBS	-
08623	TO	WNYX	EWS	DBS	-
08630(S)	WQ	WNYX	EWS	DBS	-
08632	TO	WNYX	EWS	DBS	DBS
08633	WA	WFMU	EWS	DBS	-
08653	BS	WNYX	EWS	DBS	-
08676	TO	WSSI	EWS	DBS	DBS
08701¤	TO	WNTS	PCL	DBS	-
08703(S)	CE	WNYX	EWS	DBS	-
08706¤	TO	WSSI	EWS	DBS	DBS
08709	WQ	WNTS	EWS	DBS	-
08711	TO	WSSI	PCL	DBS	-
08714(S)	TO	WSXX	EWS	DBS	-
08735¤	EH	WSSK	EWS	DBS	DBS
08737(S)	TO	WNYX	EWS	DBS	-
08738(S)	TO	WNYX	ECR	DBS	-
08742¤(S)	TO	WNYX	PCL	DBS	-
08752(S)	TO	WNYX	EWS	DBS	-
08757¤	TO	WSSK	RES	DBS	DBS
08782	MG	WSSK	BLK	DBS	-
08784¤	TO	WNYX	EWS	DBS	-
08799	TO	WNYX	EWS	DBS	DBS
08802	TO	WSSI	EWS	DBS	DBS
08804¤	TO	WNYX	EWS	DBS	-
08824(S)	WQ	WSXX	BLK	DBS	-
08865	TO	WSSK	EWS	DBS	DBS
08877(S)	WQ	WSXX	BRD	DBS	-
08879¤	TO	WSSK	EWS	DBS	DBS
08886(S)	BS	WSSK	EWS	DBS	-
08888¤	TO	WSSI	EWS	DBS	-
08904(S)	TO	WNYX	EWS	DBS	-
08907	TO	WFMU	EWS	DBS	DBS
08922(S)	TO	WNYX	BRD	DBS	-
08939(S)	TO	WNYX	ECR	DBS	-
08993(S)+	TO	WNYX	EWS	DBS	-
08994(S)+	DR	WNYX	EWS	DBS	DBS
08995+	TO	WSSK	EWS	DBS	DBS

* DB/Arriva/LNWR
+ Numbered - Toton No. 1, 08993
was previously No. 08592, 08994 was
previously No. 08562, 08995 was
previously No. 08687.
¤ Remote Control fitted.

Above: *No. 08939 is operated by EWS (DBS) subsidiary Euro Cargo Rail and after a period of operating in France has now returned to the UK and is stored at Toton, where this image was recorded.* **Antony Christie**

Right: *The number of operational DBS Class 08s is reducing every month, with more and more shunting duties performed by train locomotives. No. 08711 painted in parcels red and grey livery is seen at Westbury.* **Antony Christie**

Names applied

08442	*Richard J Wenham*	08516	*Rory*
	Eastleigh Depot	08630	*Bob Brown*
	December 1989 - July 1999	08701	*Type 100*
08495	*Noel Kirton OBE*	08799	*Andy Bower / Fred*

Class 09/0

Vehicle Length: 29ft 3in (8.91m)
Height: 12ft 8⅝in (3.87m)
Width: 8ft 6in (2.59m)

Engine: English Electric 6K
Horsepower: 400hp (298kW)
Electrical Equipment: English Electric

Number	Depot	Pool	Livery	Owner	Operator
09006(S)	WQ	WNTS	EWS	DBS	-

Class 09/1

Vehicle Length: 29ft 3in (8.91m)
Height: 12ft 8⅝in (3.87m)
Width: 8ft 6in (2.59m)

Engine: English Electric 6K
Horsepower: 400hp (298kW)
Electrical Equipment: English Electric

Number		Depot	Pool	Livery	Owner	Operator
09106	(08759)	TO	WSSK	BRD	DBS	DBS

Class 09/2

Vehicle Length: 29ft 3in (8.91m)
Height: 12ft 8⅝in (3.87m)
Width: 8ft 6in (2.59m)

Engine: English Electric 6K
Horsepower: 400hp (298kW)
Electrical Equipment: English Electric

Number		Depot	Pool	Livery	Owner	Operator
09201	(08421)	CF	WSSI	BRD	DBS	DBS
09204	(08717)	TY	-	BRD	DBS	DBS

Class 37/7

Vehicle Length: 61ft 6in (18.74m)
Height: 13ft 0¼in (3.96m)
Width: 8ft 11⅝in (2.73m)

Engine: English Electric 12CSVT
Horsepower: 1,750hp (1,304kW)
Electrical Equipment: English Electric

Number		Hire No.	Depot	Pool	Livery	Owner	Operator
37703	(37067)	L25	CON/SS	WZKS	CON	DBS	CON
37714	(37024)	L26	CON/SS	WZKS	CON	DBS	CON
37716	(37094)	L23	CON/SS	WZKS	CON	DBS	CON
37718	(37084)	L22	CON/SS	WZKS	CON	DBS	CON
37800	(37143)	L33	CON/SS	WZKS	CON	DBS	CON
37884	(37183)	L34	CON/SS	WZKS	CON	DBS	CON

Below: *Although currently not working, DBS has a fleet of six Class 37/7s in Spain, which were used by Continental Rail on high speed line construction trains. In better days when it was still working, No. 37884 is seen at a rail loading plant.* **Gavin Lake**

■ These locos are scheduled to return to the UK in 2012 for component recovery and disposal

Class 58

				Vehicle Length: 62ft 9½in (19.13m)		Engine: Ruston Paxman 12RK3ACT		
				Height: 12ft 10in (3.91m)		Horsepower: 3,300hp (2,460kW)		
				Width: 9ft 1in (2.72m)		Electrical Equipment: Brush		

Number	Hire No.	Depot	Pool	Livery	Owner	Location	Operator	Name
58001	-		WNTS	ETF	DBS	France	ETF	
58004§	-		WNTS	TSO	DBS	France	TSO	
58005	-		WNTS	ETF	DBS	France	ETF	
58006§	-		WNTS	ETF	DBS	France	ETF	
58007	-		WNTS	TSO	DBS	France	TSO	
58008(S)	EH		WNTS	MLF	DBS	UK	-	
58009	-		WNTS	TSO	DBS	France	TSO	
58010	-		WNTS	FER	DBS	France	TSO	
58011§	-		WNTS	TSO	DBS	France	TSO	
58012(S)	TO		WNTS	MLG	DBS	UK	-	
58013	-		WNTS	ETF	DBS	France	ETF	
58015	L54	CON/SS	-	CON	DBS/T	Spain	TRN	
58017(S)	EH		WNTS	MLG	DBS	UK	-	
58018	EH		WNTS	TSO	DBS	France	TSO	
58020	L43	CON/SS	-	CON	DBS/T	Spain	TRN	
58021	-		WNTS	TSO	DBS	France	TSO	
58022(S)	CD		WNTS	MLG	DBS	UK	-	
58023(S)	TO		WNTS	MLF	DBS	UK	-	
58024	L42	CON/SS	-	CON	DBS/T	Spain	TRN	
58025	L41	CON/SS	-	CON	DBS	Spain	CON	
58026§	-		WNTS	TSO	DBS	France	TSO	
58027	L52	CON/SS	-	CON	DBS	Spain	CON	
58029	L44	CON/SS	-	CON	DBS/T	Spain	TRN	
58030	L46	CON/SS	-	CON	DBS/T	Spain	TRN	
58031	L45	CON/SS	-	CON	DBS/T	Spain	TRN	Cabellero Ferroviaro
58032	-		WNTS	ETF	DBS	France	ETF	
58033	-		WNTS	TSO	DBS	France	TSO	
58034	-		WNTS	TSO	DBS	France	TSO	
58035	-		WNTS	TSO	DBS	France	TSO	
58036	-		WNTS	ETF	DBS	France	ETF	
58037(S)	EH		WNTS	EWS	DBS	UK	-	
58038	58-038	-	WNTS	ETF	DBS	France	ETF	
58039	58-039	-	WNTS	ETF	DBS	France	ETF	
58040§	-		WNTS	TSO	DBS	France	TSO	
58041	L36	CON/SS	-	CON	DBS/T	Spain	TRN	
58042	-		WNTS	TSO	DBS	France	TSO	
58043	L37	CON/SS	-	CON	DBS/T	Spain	TRN	
58044	58-044	-	WZFF	ETF	DBS	France	ETF	
58046	-		WNTS	TSO	DBS	France	TSO	
58047	L51	CON/SS	-	CON	DBS/T	Spain	TRN	
58048(S)	CE		WNTS	EWS	DBS	UK	-	
58049§	-		WNTS	TSO	DBS	France	ETF	
58050	L53	CON/SS	-	CON	DBS	Spain	CON	

§ Stored at Alizay (Rouen)

Right: *Built between 1983-87, the BR Class 58 modular diesel-electric locos saw little use in the UK in real terms but have seen considerable use overseas, operating in Belgium, France and Spain. No. 58026, painted in TSO colours, is seen at Eastleigh depot after preparation for export to France. The 58s operated by Continental Rail in Spain have recently been transferred to Transfesa, a Spanish company partly owned by DB Schenker.* **Ron Cover**

DB Schenker

Class 59/2

	Vehicle Length: 70ft 0½in (21.34m)	Engine: EMD 16-645 E3C
	Height: 12ft 10in (3.91m)	Horsepower: 3,000hp (2,462kW)
	Width: 8ft 8¼in (2.65m)	Electrical Equipment: EMD

Number	Depot	Pool	Livery	Owner	Operator	Name
59201	TO	WDAK	EWS	DBS	DBS	Vale of York
59202	TO	WFMU	EWS	DBS	DBS	Vale of White Horse
59203	TO	WDAK	EWS	DBS	-	Vale of Pickering
59204	TO	WDAK	EWS	DBS	DBS	Vale of Glamorgan
59205	TO	WDAK	EWS	DBS	DBS	L Keith McNair
59206	TO	WDAK	DBS	DBS	DBS	John F. Yeoman Rail Pioneer

Above: *Cast nameplate* John F. Yeoman Rail Pioneer *as applied to No. 59206.* **CJM**

Left: *The six Class 59/2s originally owned by National Power and subsequently sold to EWS are maintained by Mendip Rail at Merehead, from where they operate aggregate trains from the Mendips. No. 59202 is seen at Merehead depot.* **Stacey Thew**

Class 60

	Vehicle Length: 70ft 0½in (21.34m)	Engine: Mirrlees MB275T
	Height: 12ft 10⅝in (3.92m)	Horsepower: 3,100hp (2,240kW)
	Width: 8ft 8in (2.64m)	Electrical Equipment: Brush

Number	Depot	Pool	Livery	Owner	Operator	Name
60002(S)	TO	WNTS	EWS	DBS	-	High Peak
60003(S)	TO	WNWX	EWS	DBS	-	Freight Transport Association
60004(S)	TO	WNTS	EWS	DBS	-	
60005(S)	TO	WNTS	EWS	DBS	-	
60007‡	TO	WCBK	DBS	DBS	DBS	The Spirit of Tom Kendell
60009(S)	TO	WNTS	EWS	DBS	-	
60010(S)	TO	WNWX	EWS	DBS	-	
60011	TO	WCAI	DBS	DBS	DBS	
60012(S)	TO	WNWX	EWS	DBS	-	
60013(S)	TO	WNTS	RFE	DBS	-	Robert Boyle
60015(S)	TO	WNWX	RFE	DBS	-	Bow Fell
60017(S)	TO	WNWX	EWS	DBS	-	Shotton Works Centenary Year 1996
60018(S)	TO	WNTS	EWS	DBS	-	
60019(S)	TO	WNWX	EWS	DBS	-	Pathfinder Tours 30 Years of Railtouring 1973-2003
60020(S)	TO	WNTS	EWS	DBS	-	
60021(S)	TO	WNWX	EWS	DBS	-	
60022(S)	TO	WNTS	EWS	DBS	-	
60024	TO	WCAK	EWS	DBS	DBS	
60025(S)	TO	WNTS	EWS	DBS	-	
60026(S)	TO	WNTS	EWS	DBS	-	
60027(S)	TO	WNTS	EWS	DBS	-	
60028(S)	TO	WNTS	RFE	DBS	-	John Flamsteed
60029(S)	TO	WNTS	EWS	DBS	-	Clitheroe Castle
60030(S)	TO	WNTS	EWS	DBS	-	
60032(S)	TO	WNWX	EWS	DBS	-	
60033(S)	TO	WNWX	COR	DBS	-	Tees Steel Express
60034(S)	TO	WNTS	RFE	DBS	-	Carnedd Llewelyn
60035(S)	TO	WNTS	EWS	DBS	-	
60036(S)	TO	WNTS	EWS	DBS	-	GEFCO
60037(S)	TO	WNWX	EWS	DBS	-	
60039(S)	TO	WNTS	EWS	DBS	-	

60040(S)	TO	WNWX	DBM	DBS	-	*The Territorial Army Centenary*
60041(S)	TO	WNTS	EWS	DBS	-	
60043(S)	TO	WNTS	EWS	DBS	-	
60044(S)	TO	WNTS	MLF	DBS	-	
60045	TO	WCAI	EWS	DBS	DBS	*The Permanent Way Institution*
60046(S)	TO	WNTS	RFE	DBS	-	*William Wilberforce*
60047(S)	TO	WNTS	EWS	DBS	-	
60048(S)	TO	WNTS	EWS	DBS	-	
60049	TO	WCAI	EWS	DBS	DBS	
60051(S)	TO	WNTS	EWS	DBS	-	
60052(S)	TO	WNTS	EWS	DBS	-	*Glofa Twr - The last deep mine in Wales - Tower Colliery*
60053(S)	TO	WNTS	EWS	DBS	-	
60054‡	TO	WCBI	DBS	DBS	DBS	
60056(S)	TO	WNTS	RFE	DBS	-	*William Beveridge*
60057(S)	TO	WNWX	RFE	DBS	-	*Adam Smith*
60059(S)	TO	WNWX	LHL	DBS	-	
60060(S)	TO	WNWX	RFE	DBS	-	
60061(S)	TO	WNTS	RFE	DBS	-	
60062(S)	TO	WNTS	EWS	DBS	-	
60063(S)	TO	WNWX	RFE	DBS	-	
60064(S)	TO	WNWX	RFE	DBS	-	*Back Tor*
60065	TO	WCAI	EWS	DBS	DBS	*Spirit of Jaguar*
60066(S)	TO	WNTS	RFE	DBS	-	*John Logie Baird*
60067(S)	TO	WNWX	RFE	DBS	-	
60069(S)	TO	WNWX	EWS	DBS	-	*Slioch*
60071	TO	WCBI	EWS	DBS	DBS	*Ribblehead Viaduct*
60072(S)	TO	WNWX	RFE	DBS	-	*Cairn Toul*
60073(S)	TO	WNTS	RFE	DBS	-	*Cairn Gorm*
60074 ‡	TO	WFMU	DBB	DBS	DBS	*Teenage Spirit*
60076(S)	TO	WNTR	RFE	DBS	-	
60077(S)	TO	WNWX	RFE	DBS	-	
60079(S)	TO	WNWX	RFE	DBS	-	
60083(S)	TO	WNTS	EWS	DBS	-	
60084(S)	TO	WNTS	RFE	DBS	-	*Cross Fell*
60085(S)	TO	WNWX	EWS	DBS	-	*Mini - Pride of Oxford*
60086(S)	TO	WNWX	RFE	DBS	-	
60087(S)	TO	WNWX	EWS	DBS	-	
60088(S)	TO	WNWX	MLG	DBS	-	
60090(S)	TO	WNTS	RFE	DBS	-	*Quinag*
60091‡	TO	WCBI	DBS	DBS	DBS	
60092(S)	CD	WNWX	RFE	DBS	-	*Reginald Munns*
60093(S)	TO	WNTS	EWS	DBS	-	
60094(S)	CD	WNTS	EWS	DBS	-	*Rugby Flyer*
60095(S)	TO	WNTS	RFE	DBS	-	
60096	TO	WNTS	EWS	DBS	DBS	
60097(S)	TO	WNTS	EWS	DBS	-	
60099	TO	WNTR	TAT	DBS	DBS	
60100(S)	TO	WNTS	EWS	DBS	-	
60500(S)*	TO	WNTS	EWS	DBS	-	

* Previously numbered 60016.   ‡ Refurbished (Super 60).

60010/015/019/040/059/063/079 - To undergo refurbishment.

Right: *Although at one time the Class 60s were considered to have fallen from favour and were to be eliminated, refurbishment and overhaul contracts in 2011 have seen a number programmed for overhaul and return to traffic. DBS need these locos to power some of their heaviest trains. Carrying the latest DB Schenker red and grey livery, No. 60011 is seen at Taunton on 12 April 2011.* **Nathan Williamson**

DB Schenker

Class 66

Vehicle Length: 70ft 0½in (21.34m)	Engine: EMD 12N-710G3B-EC
Height: 12ft 10in (3.91m)	Horsepower: 3,300hp (2,462kW)
Width: 8ft 8¼in (2.65m)	Electrical Equipment: EMD

Freight Operating Companies - DB Schenker

Number	Depot	Pool	Livery	Owner	Operator
66001‡	TO	WBAL	EWS	ANG	DBS
66002‡	TO	WAAN	EWS	ANG	DBS
66003	TO	WBAL	EWS	ANG	DBS
66004	TO	WFMU	EWS	ANG	DBS
66005	TO	WBSN	EWS	ANG	DBS
66006	TO	WBAL	EWS	ANG	DBS
66007	TO	WBAI	EWS	ANG	DBS
66008	TO	WBAI	EWS	ANG	DBS
66009	TO	WFMU	EWS	ANG	DBS
66010 ●	TO	WFMU	EWS	ANG	DBS
66011	TO	WBAI	EWS	ANG	DBS
66012	TO	WNTR	EWS	ANG	DBS
66013 ●	TO	WNTR	EWS	ANG	DBS
66014	TO	WBAK	EWS	ANG	DBS
66015	TO	WBAK	EWS	ANG	DBS
66016	TO	WBAK	EWS	ANG	DBS
66017	TO	WBSN	EWS	ANG	DBS
66018	TO	WBAI	EWS	ANG	DBS
66019	TO	WBAK	EWS	ANG	DBS
66020	TO	WBAI	EWS	ANG	DBS
66021	TO	WFMU	EWS	ANG	DBS
66022 ●	AZ	WBEN	EWS	ANG	DBS
66023	TO	WBAI	EWS	ANG	DBS
66024	TO	WBAL	EWS	ANG	DBS
66025	TO	WFMU	EWS	ANG	DBS
66026 ●	AZ	WBEN	EWS	ANG	ECR
66027	TO	WBAI	EWS	ANG	DBS
66028 ●	AZ	WBEN	EWS	ANG	ECR
66029 ●	AZ	WBEN	EWS	ANG	DBS
66030	TO	WNTR	EWS	ANG	DBS
66031 ●	TO	WFMU	EWS	ANG	DBS
66032 ●	TO	WBES	EWS	ANG	ECR
66033 ●	AZ	WBEN	EWS	ANG	DBS
66034	TO	WFMU	EWS	ANG	DBS
66035	TO	WBSN	EWS	ANG	DBS
66036 ●	AZ	WBEN	EWS	ANG	ECR
66037	TO	WBAI	EWS	ANG	DBS
66038 ●	AZ	WBEN	EWS	ANG	ECR
66039	TO	WSSK	EWS	ANG	DBS
66040	TO	WNTR	EWS	ANG	DBS
66041	TO	WBAI	EWS	ANG	DBS
66042 ●	AZ	WBEN	EWS	ANG	ECR
66043	TO	WBAL	EWS	ANG	DBS
66044	TO	WBSN	EWS	ANG	DBS
66045 ●	AZ	WBEN	EWS	ANG	ECR
66046	TO	WBAI	EWS	ANG	DBS
66047	TO	WBSN	EWS	ANG	DBS
66048(S)	TO	WNTS	STO	ANG	-
66049 ●	AZ	WBEN	EWS	ANG	ECR
66050	TO	WBAI	EWS	ANG	DBS
66051	TO	WBAK	EWS	ANG	DBS
66052 ●	AZ	WBEN	EWS	ANG	ECR
66053	TO	WBAK	EWS	ANG	DBS
66054	TO	WBAI	EWS	ANG	DBS
66055	TO	WNTR	EWS	ANG	DBS
66056	TO	WBLI	EWS	ANG	DBS
66057	TO	WBLI	EWS	ANG	DBS
66058	TO	WBAL	EWS	ANG	DBS
66059	TO	WBLI	EWS	ANG	DBS
66060	TO	WNTR	EWS	ANG	DBS
66061	TO	WBAI	EWS	ANG	DBS
66062 ●	AZ	WBEN	EWS	ANG	DBS
66063	TO	WBAL	EWS	ANG	DBS
66064 ●	AZ	WBEN	EWS	ANG	DBS
66065	TO	WBAI	EWS	ANG	DBS
66066	TO	WBAL	EWS	ANG	DBS
66067	TO	WBAI	EWS	ANG	DBS
66068	TO	WBAK	EWS	ANG	DBS
66069	TO	WBAI	EWS	ANG	DBS
66070	TO	WSSK	EWS	ANG	DBS
66071 ●	TO	WBES	EWS	ANG	DBS
66072 ●	AZ	WBEN	EWS	ANG	ECR
66073 ●	AZ	WBEN	EWS	ANG	ECR
66074	TO	WBAL	EWS	ANG	DBS
66075	TO	WBAI	EWS	ANG	DBS
66076	TO	WBAI	EWS	ANG	DBS
66077	TO	WBEN	EWS	ANG	DBS
66078	TO	WBAI	EWS	ANG	DBS
66079	TO	WBAK	EWS	ANG	DBS
66080	TO	WBAK	EWS	ANG	DBS
66081	TO	WBAK	EWS	ANG	DBS
66082	TO	WBAK	EWS	ANG	DBS
66083	TO	WNTR	EWS	ANG	DBS
66084	TO	WBAK	EWS	ANG	DBS
66085	TO	WBAI	EWS	ANG	DBS
66086	TO	WBAK	EWS	ANG	DBS
66087	TO	WBAI	EWS	ANG	DBS
66088	TO	WBAI	EWS	ANG	DBS
66089	TO	WBAI	EWS	ANG	DBS
66090	TO	WBAL	EWS	ANG	DBS
66091	TO	WBAI	EWS	ANG	DBS
66092	TO	WBAK	EWS	ANG	DBS
66093	TO	WBAI	EWS	ANG	DBS
66094	TO	WBAI	EWS	ANG	DBS
66095	TO	WBAK	EWS	ANG	DBS
66096 ●	AZ	WBAI	EWS	ANG	DBS
66097	TO	WNTR	DBS	ANG	DBS
66098	TO	WBAI	EWS	ANG	DBS
66099	TO	WBBK	EWS	ANG	DBS
66100	TO	WNTR	EWS	ANG	DBS
66101	TO	WNTR	DBS	ANG	DBS
66102	TO	WBBL	EWS	ANG	DBS
66103	TO	WBBL	EWS	ANG	DBS
66104	TO	WBBK	EWS	ANG	DBS
66105	TO	WBBK	EWS	ANG	DBS
66106	TO	WBBL	EWS	ANG	DBS
66107	TO	WBBL	EWS	ANG	DBS
66108	TO	WBBL	EWS	ANG	DBS
66109	TO	WBAK	EWS	ANG	DBS
66110	TO	WBBL	EWS	ANG	DBS
66111	TO	WFMU	EWS	ANG	DBS
66112	TO	WBBI	EWS	ANG	DBS
66113	TO	WBBI	EWS	ANG	DBS
66114	TO	WBBI	EWS	ANG	DBS
66115	TO	WBAI	EWS	ANG	DBS
66116 ●	AZ	WBAK	EWS	ANG	DBS
66117	TO	WBAL	EWS	ANG	DBS
66118	TO	WBAK	EWS	ANG	DBS
66119	TO	WBAI	EWS	ANG	DBS
66120	TO	WBAK	EWS	ANG	DBS
66121	TO	WBAI	EWS	ANG	DBS

66122	TO	WBAK	EWS	ANG	DBS
66123 ●	AZ	WBEN	EWS	ANG	DBS
66124	TO	WBSN	EWS	ANG	DBS
66125	TO	WBAI	EWS	ANG	DBS
66126	TO	WBAK	EWS	ANG	DBS
66127	TO	WBAI	EWS	ANG	DBS
66128	TO	WBAI	EWS	ANG	DBS
66129	TO	WBSN	EWS	ANG	DBS
66130	TO	WBAK	EWS	ANG	DBS
66131	TO	WBAI	EWS	ANG	DBS
66132	TO	WFMU	EWS	ANG	DBS
66133	TO	WBAI	EWS	ANG	DBS
66134	TO	WBSN	EWS	ANG	DBS
66135	TO	WBAK	EWS	ANG	DBS
66136	TO	WBAK	EWS	ANG	DBS
66137	TO	WBAI	EWS	ANG	DBS
66138	TO	WBAL	EWS	ANG	DBS
66139	TO	WBAI	EWS	ANG	DBS
66140	TO	WBAL	EWS	ANG	DBS
66141	TO	WBAK	EWS	ANG	DBS
66142	TO	WBAK	EWS	ANG	DBS
66143	TO	WBAI	EWS	ANG	DBS
66144	TO	WBAI	EWS	ANG	DBS
66145	TO	WSSK	EWS	ANG	DBS
66146 P	PN	WBEP	EWS	ANG	DBS
66147	TO	WNTR	EWS	ANG	DBS
66148	TO	WBAI	EWS	ANG	DBS
66149	TO	WBAL	EWS	ANG	DBS
66150	TO	WBAI	EWS	ANG	DBS
66151	TO	WBAI	EWS	ANG	DBS
66152	TO	WBAI	DBS	ANG	DBS
66153 P	PN	WBEP	EWS	ANG	DBS
66154	TO	WBAI	EWS	ANG	DBS
66155	TO	WBAI	EWS	ANG	DBS
66156	TO	WNTR	EWS	ANG	DBS
66157 P	PN	WBEP	EWS	ANG	DBS
66158	TO	WBAI	EWS	ANG	DBS
66159 P	PN	WBEP	EWS	ANG	DBS
66160	TO	WBAI	EWS	ANG	DBS
66161	TO	WBAI	EWS	ANG	DBS
66162	TO	WBAI	EWS	ANG	DBS
66163 P	PN	WBEP	DBS	ANG	DBS
66164	TO	WBAK	EWS	ANG	DBS
66165	TO	WBAI	EWS	ANG	DBS
66166 P	PN	WBEP	EWS	ANG	DBS
66167	TO	WBAK	EWS	ANG	DBS
66168	TO	WBAL	EWS	ANG	DBS
66169	TO	WBAK	EWS	ANG	DBS
66170	TO	WFMU	EWS	ANG	DBS
66171	TO	WBAK	EWS	ANG	DBS
66172	TO	WBAK	EWS	ANG	DBS
66173 P	PN	WBEP	EWS	ANG	DBS
66174	TO	WBAI	EWS	ANG	DBS
66175	TO	WNTR	EWS	ANG	DBS
66176	TO	WFMU	EWS	ANG	DBS
66177	TO	WBAI	EWS	ANG	DBS
66178 P	PN	WBEP	EWS	ANG	DBS
66179 ●	TO	WBAK	EWS	ANG	ECR
66180 P	PN	WBEP	EWS	ANG	DBS
66181	TO	WBAK	EWS	ANG	DBS
66182	TO	WBAK	EWS	ANG	DBS
66183	TO	WBAK	EWS	ANG	DBS
66184	TO	WBAL	EWS	ANG	DBS
66185	TO	WBAK	EWS	ANG	DBS
66186	TO	WBAI	EWS	ANG	DBS
66187	TO	WBAI	EWS	ANG	DBS
66188	TO	WBAK	EWS	ANG	DBS
66189 P	PN	WBEP	EWS	ANG	DBS
66190 ●	AZ	WBEN	EWS	ANG	ECR
66191 ●	AZ	WBEN	EWS	ANG	DBS
66192	TO	WBAI	EWS	ANG	DBS
66193	TO	WBAL	EWS	ANG	DBS
66194	TO	WBAI	EWS	ANG	DBS
66195 ●	AZ	WBEN	EWS	ANG	ECR
66196 P	PN	WBEP	EWS	ANG	DBS
66197	TO	WBAI	EWS	ANG	DBS
66198	TO	WBAK	EWS	ANG	DBS
66199	TO	WBAK	EWS	ANG	DBS
66200	TO	WBAI	EWS	ANG	DBS
66201	TO	WNTR	EWS	ANG	DBS
66202 ●	AZ	WBEN	EWS	ANG	ECR
66203 ●	AZ	WBEN	EWS	ANG	ECR
66204	TO	WBAI	EWS	ANG	DBS
66205 ●	AZ	WBEN	EWS	ANG	ECR
66206	TO	WFMU	EWS	ANG	DBS
66207	TO	WBAI	EWS	ANG	DBS
66208 ●	AZ	WBEN	EWS	ANG	ECR
66209 ●	AZ	WBEN	EWS	ANG	ECR
66210 ●	AZ	WBEN	EWS	ANG	ECR
66211 ●	AZ	WBEN	EWS	ANG	ECR
66212 ●	AZ	WBEN	EWS	ANG	ECR
66213	TO	WBAK	EWS	ANG	DBS
66214 ●	AZ	WBEN	EWS	ANG	ECR
66215 ●	AZ	WBEN	EWS	ANG	ECR
66216 ●	AZ	WBEN	EWS	ANG	ECR
66217 ●	AZ	WBEN	EWS	ANG	ECR
66218 ●	TO	WFMU	EWS	ANG	ECR
66219 ●	AZ	WBEN	EWS	ANG	ECR
66220 P	PN	WBEP	DBS	ANG	DBS
66221	TO	WBAI	EWS	ANG	DBS
66222 ●	AZ	WBEN	EWS	ANG	ECR
66223 ●	AZ	WBEN	EWS	ANG	ECR
66224 ●	AZ	WBEN	EWS	ANG	ECR
66225 ●	AZ	WBEN	EWS	ANG	ECR
66226 ●	AZ	WBEN	EWS	ANG	ECR
66227 P	PN	WBEP	EWS	ANG	DBS
66228 ●	AZ	WBEN	EWS	ANG	ECR
66229 ●	AZ	WBEN	EWS	ANG	ECR
66230	TO	WBAI	EWS	ANG	DBS
66231 ●	AZ	WBEN	EWS	ANG	ECR
66232	TO	WBAK	EWS	ANG	DBS
66233 ●	AZ	WBEN	EWS	ANG	ECR
66234 ●	AZ	WBEN	EWS	ANG	ECR
66235 ●	AZ	WBEN	EWS	ANG	ECR
66236 ●	AZ	WBEN	EWS	ANG	ECR
66237 P	PN	WBEP	EWS	ANG	DBS
66238	TO	WNTR	EWS	ANG	DBS
66239 ●	AZ	WBEN	EWS	ANG	ECR
66240 ●	AZ	WBEN	EWS	ANG	ECR
66241 ●	AZ	WBEN	EWS	ANG	ECR
66242 ●	AZ	WBEN	EWS	ANG	ECR
66243 ●	AZ	WBEN	EWS	ANG	ECR
66244 ●	AZ	WBEN	EWS	ANG	DBS
66245 ●	AZ	WBEN	EWS	ANG	DBS
66246 ●	AZ	WBEN	EWS	ANG	ECR
66247 ●	AZ	WBEN	EWS	ANG	ECR
66248 P	PN	WBEP	DBS	ANG	DBS
66249 ●	TO	WBES	EWS	ANG	DBS
66250	TO	WBAK	EWS	ANG	DBS

‡ Not fitted with combination couplers

DB Schenker

Names applied

66002	*Lafarge Quorn*
66048	*James the Engine*
66050	*EWS Energy*
66077	*Benjamin Gimbert GC*
66079	*James Nightall GC*
66152	*Derek Holmes Railway Operator*
66172	*Paul Melleney*
66200	*Railway Heritage Committee*
66250	*Robert K. Romak* (not standard nameplate)

● Class 66/0s marked with this symbol are modified and can operate with Euro Cargo Rail in France. Usually around 60 locos are in France at one time, but this figure is reduced in the autumn when a number return to the UK for RHTT operations. Locos working in France operate in the pool WBEN.

P Locomotives marked with a 'P' are operated by DB Schenker in Poland. Only locos from the series 66146-250 can be modified for this contract.

Above & Below: *The backbone of DB Schenker freight services are powered by the Class 66. Of the 250 originally introduced a significant number now operate in France and Poland. In the above view No. 66001, which does not have a combination coupler, is seen at Didcot. In the view below, we see No. 66097 displaying the latest DB Schenker red and grey livery passing near Cullompton with a scrap train in the summer of 2011.* **CJM/Antony Christie**

Class 67

Vehicle Length: 64ft 7in (19.68m)				Engine: EMD 12N-710G3B-EC		
Height: 12ft 9in (3.88m)				Horsepower: 2,980hp (2,223kW)		
Width: 8ft 9in (2.66m)				Electrical Equipment: EMD		

Number	Depot	Pool	Livery	Owner	Operator	Name
67001	CE	WAAN	ATW	ANG	DBS/ATW	
67002	CE	WAAN	ATW	ANG	DBS/ATW	
67003	CE	WAAN	ATW	ANG	DBS/ATW	
67004	CE	WABN	EWS	ANG	DBS	Post Haste
67005	CE	WAAN	ROY	ANG	DBS	Queen's Messenger
67006	CE	WAAN	ROY	ANG	DBS	Royal Sovereign
67007	CE	WABN	EWS	ANG	DBS	
67008	CE	WAAN	EWS	ANG	DBS	
67009	CE	WFMU	EWS	ANG	DBS	
67010	CE	WNTR	WSR	ANG	DBS/CRW	
67011	CE	WABN	EWS	ANG	DBS	
67012	CE	WAWN	WSR	ANG	DBS/CRW	A Shropshire Lad
67013	CE	WNTR	WSR	ANG	DBS/CRW	Dyfrbont Pontcysyllte
67014	CE	WAAN	WSR	ANG	DBS/CRW	Thomas Telford
67015	CE	WAWN	WSR	ANG	DBS/CRW	David J. Lloyd
67016	CE	WAFN	EWS	ANG	DBS	
67017	CE	WAFN	EWS	ANG	DBS	Arrow
67018	CE	WAFN	DBS	ANG	DBS	Keith Heller
67019	CE	WAAN	EWS	ANG	DBS	
67020	CE	WAAN	EWS	ANG	DBS	
67021	CE	WFMU	EWS	ANG	DBS	
67022	CE	WAAN	EWS	ANG	DBS	
67023	CE	WAAN	EWS	ANG	DBS	
67024	CE	WAAN	EWS	ANG	DBS	
67025	CE	WAAN	EWS	ANG	DBS	Western Star
67026	CE	WAAN	EWS	ANG	DBS	
67027	CE	WAAN	EWS	ANG	DBS	Rising Star
67028	CE	WAAN	EWS	ANG	DBS	
67029	CE	WAAN	EWE	ANG	DBS	Royal Diamond
67030	CE	WABN	EWS	ANG	DBS	

Below: *The 30 DBS-operated Class 67s can be found throughout the country, operating for their booked operator DBS, as well as Arriva Trains Wales, Chiltern Railways East Coast, First ScotRail and the charter sector. Two locos, Nos. 67005/006, are painted in Royal Train claret livery and made available for Royal Train use when needed. The full Royal is seen passing Teignmouth Docks on 3 June 2011 'top and tailed' by Royals Nos. 67005 and 67006.* **CJM**

DB Schenker

Class 90

	Vehicle Length: 61ft 6in (18.74m)				Power Collection: 25kV ac overhead	
	Height: 13ft 0¼in (3.96m)				Horsepower: 7,860hp (5,860kW)	
	Width: 9ft 0in (2.74m)				Electrical Equipment: GEC	

Number		Depot	Pool	Livery	Owner	Operator	Name
90017		CE	WNTS	EWS	DBS	-	
90018		CE	WEFE	EWS	DBS	DBS	
90019		CE	WEFE	FGS	DBS	DBS	
90020		CE	WEFE	EWS	DBS	DBS	Collingwood
90021(S)	(90221)	CE	WEFE	FGS	DBS	-	
90022	(90222)	CE	WNTS	RFE	DBS	-	Freightconnection
90023	(90223)	CE	WNTS	EWS	DBS	-	
90024	(90224)	CE	WEGE	FGS	DBS	DBS	
90025	(90225)	CE	WNTS	FGS	DBS	-	
90026(S)		CE	WNWX	EWS	DBS	-	
90027(S)	(90227)	CE	WNTS	RFD	DBS	-	Allerton T&RS Depot Quality Approved
90028		CE	WEFE	EWS	DBS	DBS	
90029(S)		CE	WNTR	EWS	DBS	-	The Institution of Civil Engineers
90030	(90130)	CE	WNTS	EWS	DBS	-	Crewe Locomotive Works
90031	(90131)	CE	WNTS	EWS	DBS	-	The Railway Children Partnership - Working for Street Children Worldwide
90032	(90132)	CE	WNTS	EWS	DBS	-	
90033	(90233)	CE	WNTS	RFI	DBS	-	
90034(S)	(90134)	CE	WNTS	EWS	DBS	-	
90035	(90135)	CE	WEFE	EWS	DBS	DBS	
90036	(90136)	CE	WEFE	RFE	DBS	DBS	
90037	(90137)	CE	WNTS	EWS	DBS	-	Spirit of Dagenham
90038	(90238)	CE	WNTS	RFI	DBS	-	
90039	(90239)	CE	WEFE	EWS	DBS	DBS	
90040	(90140)	CE	WNTS	EWS	DBS	-	The Railway Mission
90050	(90050)	CE	WNTS	FLG	DBS	-	

Left: *Although DBS operate a fleet of 25 Class 90s, that number of locos is never all to be found in traffic, with frequently up to 10-12 stored out of service at Crewe Electric Depot. Suggestions have been made that some will be sold in the future, possibly to an overseas operator. Painted in EWS maroon and gold livery, No. 90029 is seen at Carlisle.* **Nathan Williamson**

Class 92

	Vehicle Length: 70ft 1in (21.34m)				Power Collection: 25kV ac overhead / 750V dc third rail	
	Height: 13ft 0in (3.95m)				Horsepower: ac - 6,700hp (5,000kW) / dc 5,360hp (4,000kW)	
	Width: 8ft 8in (2.66m)				Electrical Equipment: Brush	

Number	Depot	Pool	Livery	Owner	Operator	Name
92001	CE	WTAE	EWS	HAL	DBS	Victor Hugo
92002(S)	CE	WNWX	RFE	HAL	-	H G Wells
92003(S)	CE	WFMU	RFE	HAL	-	Beethoven
92004(S)	CE	WNWX	RFE	HAL	-	Jane Austen
92005(S)	CE	WNTR	RFE	HAL	-	Mozart
92007	CE	WNTR	RFE	HAL	DBS	Schubert
92008(S)	CE	WNWX	RFE	HAL	-	Jules Verne
92009§	CE	WTHE	DBS	HAL	DBS	Marco Polo
92011(S)	CE	WNWX	RFE	HAL	-	Handel
92012(S)	CE	WNTR	RFE	HAL	DBS	Thomas Hardy
92013(S)	CE	WNWX	RFE	HAL	-	Puccini
92015§	CE	WNTR	DBS	HAL	DBS	D H Lawrence
92016§(S)	CE	WNTR	DBS	HAL	-	

92017	CE	WTAE	STO	HAL	DBS	*Bart the Engine*
92019	CE	WTAE	RFE	HAL	DBS	*Wagner*
92022(S)	CE	WNTR	RFE	HAL	-	*Charles Dickens*
92024(S)	CE	WNWX	RFE	HAL	-	*J S Bach*
92025(S)	CE	WNWX	RFE	HAL	-	*Oscar Wilde*
92026(S)	CE	WNTR	RFE	HAL	-	*Britten*
92027(S)	CE	WNWX	RFE	HAL	-	*George Eliot*
92029(S)	CE	WNWX	RFE	HAL	-	*Dante*
92030	CE	WNTR	RFE	HAL	DBS	*Ashford*
92031§	CE	WNTR	DBS	HAL	-	*The Institute of Logistics and Transport*
92034	CE	WTAE	RFE	HAL	DBS	*Kipling*
92035(S)	CE	WNWX	RFE	HAL	-	*Mendelssohn*
92036	CE	WTAE	RFE	HAL	DBS	*Bertolt Brecht*
92037(S)	CE	WNTR	RFE	HAL	-	*Sullivan*
92039(S)	CE	WNWX	RFE	HAL	-	*Johann Strauss*
92041	CE	WTAE	RFE	HAL	DBS	*Vaughan Williams*
92042§	CE	WTHE	DBS	HAL	DBS	

§ Fitted with equipment to allow operation over HS1

Right: *The Class 92 fleet are another of the DBS assets which are never all in traffic, with frequently more than half the fleet of 31 out of service. One loco which is usually kept in service is the Stobart-liveried No. 92017* Bart the Engine. *In this November 2010 view the loco is seen powering the Tesco train at Craigenhill on the West Coast Main Line.* **Robin Ralston**

Hauled Stock (Passenger)

AJ41 - RBR

Number	Depot	Livery	Owner
1658(S)	EH	MAR	DBR
1679	EH	LNE	DBR
1680	EH	LNE	DBR

AD1D - FO

Number	Depot	Livery	Owner
3186	DY	INT	DBR

AD1E - FOT

Number	Depot	Livery	Owner
3255 (3525)	EH	MAR	DBR

AD1F - FO

Number	Depot	Livery	Owner
3279	CE	MAR	DBR/FSR
3292	CE	MAR	DBR
3318	CE	MAR	DBR/FSR
3331	CE	MAR	DBR/FSR
3338(S)	EH	MAR	DBR
3358	CE	MAR	DBR/FSR
3368(S)	EH	MAR	DBR
3375(S)	EH	MAR	DBR
3388	EH	MAR	DBR

Mk1	Height: 12ft 9½in (3.89m)
Vehicle Length: 64ft 6in (19.65m)	Width: 9ft 3in (2.81m)

Mk2	Height: 12ft 9½in (3.89m)
Vehicle Length: 66ft 0in (20.11m)	Width: 9ft 3in (2.81m)

Mk 3	Height: 12ft 9in (3.88m)
Vehicle Length: 75ft 0in (22.86m)	Width: 8ft 11in (2.71m)

3399(S)	EH	MAR	DBR
3400	EH	MAR	DBR
3414	EH	MAR	DBR
3424	CE	MAR	DBR/FSR

AC21 - TSO

Number	Depot	Livery	Owner
4925(S)	EH	GRN	DBR *(for sale)*
4956(S)	EH	BLG	DBR *(for sale)*
5005(S)	EH	BLG	DBR *(for sale)*
5037(S)	EH	GRN	DBR *(for sale)*

AC2A - TSO

Number	Depot	Livery	Owner
5331	EH	MAR	DBR
5386(S)	EH	MAR	DBR

AC2B - TSO

Number	Depot	Livery	Owner
5482	TO	MAR	DBR

Freight Operating Companies

DB Schenker

AC2D - TSO

Number	Depot	Livery	Owner
5631	MH	MAR	DBR
5632	MH	MAR	DBR
5657	MH	MAR	DBR

AC2F - TSO

Number	Depot	Livery	Owner
5922	EH	MAR	DBR
5924	EH	MAR	DBR
5954	EH	MAR	DBR
5959	EH	MAR	DBR
6036	EH	MAR	DBR
6110	EH	MAR	DBR
6139	EH	MAR	DBR
6152	EH	MAR	DBR

AX51 - GEN

Number	Depot	Livery	Owner
6311 (92911)	TO	BLU	DBR (for sale)

AN1D - RMBF

Number	Depot	Livery	Owner
6720 (6602)	CE	MAR	DBR

AE2D - BSO

Number	Depot	Livery	Owner
9494	CE	MAR	DBR

AE2F - BSO

Number	Depot	Livery	Owner
9522	EH	MAR	DBR
9529	EH	MAR	DBR
9531	EH	MAR	DBR

AJ1G - RFM

Number		Depot	Livery	Owner
10205(S)	(40503)	AL	SPL	DBR
10211	(40510)	TO	EWE	DBS
10215	(11032)	CE	BLG	DBR
10226(S)	(11015)	LM	VIR	DBR
10233(S)	(10013)	LM	VIR	DBR
10235	(10015)	CE	BLG	DBR
10237	(10022)	BY	DRU	DBR
10250(S)	(10020)	ZW	VIR	DBR
10257	(10007)	BY	BLG	DBR

AU4G - SLEP

Number	Depot	Livery	Owner
10540	AL	-	DBR

10546	TO	EWE	DBS

AS4G - SLE

Number	Depot	Livery	Owner
10647(S)	LM	INT	DBR
10710(S)	LM	CWR	DBR
10731(S)	LM	INT	DBR

AD1G - FO

Number	Depot	Livery	Owner
11013	LM	DRU	DBR
11019	BY	DRU	DBR
11027	AL	BLU	DBR/DRS
11029	AL	BLG	DBR
11030	BY	DRU	DBR
11031	IL	BLG	DBR
11033	LM	DRU	DBR
11039	TO	EWE	DBS
11040	AL	BLG	DBR/CAG
11041(S)	LM	VIR	DBR
11044	BY	DRU	DBR
11046	BY	DRU	DBR
11052(S)	LM	VIR	DBR
11054	BY	DRU	DBR
11058(S)	LM	VIR	DBR
11097	CE	BLG	DBR

AC2G - TSO

Number	Depot	Livery	Owner
12053	AL	BLG	DBR/CAG

AB21 - BSK

Number	Depot	Livery	Owner
35290(S)	CP	CAR	DBR

GK2G - TRSB

Number		Depot	Livery	Owner
40402 (40002)		LM	VIR	DBR
40403 (40003)		LM	VIR	DBR
40416 (40016)		LM	VIR	DBR
40419 (40019)		LM	VIR	DBR
40434 (40234)		LM	VIR	DBR

Saloon

Number	Depot	Livery	Owner
45029(S)	ML	EWS	DBR

Hauled Stock (NPCCS)

Mk 3 (DVT)	Height: 12ft 9in (3.88m)
Vehicle Length: 61ft 9in (18.83m)	Width: 8ft 11in (2.71m)

NZAG - DVT

Number	Depot	Livery	Owner
82106(S)	LM	VIR	DBR
82108(S)	LB	VIR	DBR
82110(S)	LM	VIR	DBR
82113(S)	LM	VIR	DBR
82116(S)	LM	VIR	DBR
82120(S)	LM	VIR	DBR
82122(S)	LM	VIR	DBR
82131(S)	LB	VIR	DBR
82137(S)	LM	VIR	DBR
82138(S)	LM	VIR	DBR

82141(S)	LM	VIR	DBR
82144(S)	LB	VIR	DBR
82146	TO	DBE	DBS
82148(S)	LM	VIR	DBR
82150(S)	LM	VIR	DBR
82301 (82117)	CE	WSR	DBR
82302 (82151)	CE	WSR	DBR
82303 (82135)	CE	WSR	DBR
82304 (82130)	CE	WSR	DBR
82305 (82134)	CE	WSR	DBR

NKA1 - H-GUV

Number	Depot	Livery	Owner
92203 (S)	CP	RES	DBS
94103 (W) (95103)	CX	RES	DBS
94104 (S) (95104)	TO	RES	DBS
94106 (S) (95106)	MH	RES	DBS
94113 (S) (95113)	OM	RES	DBS
94116 (S) (95116)	TY	RES	DBS
94121 (S) (95121)	TO	RES	DBS
94137 (S) (95137)	ML	RES	DBS
94147 (S) (95147)	ML	RES	DBS
94150 (S) (95150)	SP	RES	DBS
94153 (S) (95153)	WE	RES	DBS
94160 (S) (95160)	MH	RES	DBS
94166 (S) (95166)	BS	RES	DBS
94170 (S) (95170)	MH	RES	DBS
94176 (S) (95176)	ML	RES	DBS
94177 (S) (95177)	TO	RES	DBS

NAA1 - PCV

Number	Depot	Livery	Owner
94302 (S) (75124)	TY	RES	DBS
94303 (S) (75131)	TY	RES	DBS
94304 (S) (75107)	MH	RES	DBS
94306 (S) (75112)	TY	RES	DBS
94307 (S) (75127)	CX	RES	DBS
94308 (S) (75125)	MH	RES	DBS
94310 (S) (75119)	WE	RES	DBS
94311 (S) (75105)	WE	RES	DBS
94313 (S) (75129)	WE	RES	DBS
94316 (S) (75108)	TO	RES	DBS
94317 (S) (75117)	TO	RES	DBS
94318 (S) (75115)	CX	RES	DBS

NBA1, NOA1, NQA, NRA1 - BVHS

Number	Depot	Livery	Owner
94400 (92524)	CX	RES	DBS
94406 (92956)	MH	RES	DBS
94408 (92981)	TY	RES	DBS
94410 (92941)	WE	RES	DBS
94411 (92945)	CX	RES	DBS
94412 (92945)	ML	RES	DBS
94413 (92236)	ML	RES	DBS
94416 (92746)	MY	RES	DBS
94420 (92263)	MH	RES	DBS
94422 (92651)	TO	RES	DBS
94423 (92914)	BS	RES	DBS
94427 (92754)	WE	RES	DBS
94428 (92166)	MY	RES	DBS
94429 (92232)	TE	RES	DBS
94431 (92604)	MH	RES	DBS
94432 (92999)	MY	RES	DBS
94433 (92643)	MH	RES	DBS
94434 (92584)	TY	RES	DBS
94435 (92134)	TO	RES	DBS
94438 (92251)	TO	RES	DBS
94440 (92645)	MY	RES	DBS
94445 (92615)	WE	RES	DBS
94451 (92257)	WE	RES	DBS
94458 (92974)	CX	RES	DBS
94462 (92270)	CD	RES	DBS
94463 (92995)	TY	RES	DBS
94470 (92113)	TO	RES	DBS
94479 (92132)	TO	RES	DBS

Number	Depot	Livery	Owner
94191 (S) (95351)	SP	RES	DBS
94192 (S) (95352)	MY	RES	DBS
94195 (S) (95355)	BS	RES	DBS
94197 (S) (95357)	BS	RES	DBS
94207 (S) (95367)	TO	RES	DBS
94208 (S) (95368)	TO	RES	DBS
94209 (W) (95369)	CX	RES	DBS
94213 (S) (95373)	MY	RES	DBS
94214 (S) (95374)	MH	RES	DBS
94217 (S) (93131)	MH	RES	DBS
94221 (S) (93905)	MH	RES	DBS
94222 (S) (93474)	MH	RES	DBS
94225 (S) (93849)	MH	RES	DBS
94227 (S) (93585)	TE	RES	DBS
94229 (S) (93720)	MH	RES	DBS

Number	Depot	Livery	Owner
94322 (S) (75111)	MH	RES	DBS
94323 (S) (75110)	TY	RES	DBS
94326 (S) (75123)	TY	RES	DBS
94331 (S) (75022)	CX	RES	DBS
94332 (S) (75011)	TY	RES	DBS
94333 (S) (75016)	TY	RES	DBS
94334 (S) (75017)	CD	RES	DBS
94335 (S) (75032)	TY	RES	DBS
94336 (S) (75031)	TY	RES	DBS
94338 (S) (75008)	WE	RES	DBS
94340 (S) (75012)	CD	RES	DBS
94343 (S) (75027)	MH	RES	DBS
94344 (S) (75014)	TO	RES	DBS

Number	Depot	Livery	Owner
94481 (92641)	CX	RES	DBS
94482 (92639)	MH	RES	DBS
94488 (92105)	CD	RES	DBS
94490 (92230)	MH	RES	DBS
94492 (92721)	WE	RES	DBS
94495 (92755)	TY	RES	DBS
94497 (92717)	ML	RES	DBS
94498 (92555)	MH	RES	DBS
94499 (92577)	CD	BLG	DBS
94501 (92725)	TO	RES	DBS
94504 (92748)	TY	RES	DBS
94512 (92582)	TY	RES	DBS
94514 (92122)	MY	RES	DBS
94515 (92513)	EH	DBS	DBS
94518 (92258)	MY	RES	DBS
94519 (92916)	ML	RES	DBS
94520 (92917)	TY	RES	DBS
94521 (92917)	CD	RES	DBS
94522 (92907)	TY	RES	DBS
94525 (92229)	TY	RES	DBS
94526 (92518)	TY	RES	DBS
94527 (92728)	TY	RES	DBS
94528 (92252)	ML	RES	DBS
94529 (92267)	CD	RES	DBS
94530 (92409)	MY	RES	DBS
94531 (94456)	TY	RES	DBS
94532 (94489)	LM	RES	DBS
94534 (94430)	MY	RES	DBS
94536 (94491)	MY	RES	DBS
94538 (94426)	EH	RES	DBS

Freight Operating Companies

DB Schenker

94539 (92302)	MH	RES	DBS
94540 (92860)	TJ	RES	DBS
94541 (92316)	ML	RES	DBS
94542 (92330)	TY	RES	DBS
94543 (92389)	MY	RES	DBS

94544 (92345)	MH	RES	DBS
94545 (92329)	TE	RES	DBS
94546 (92804)	TY	RES	DBS
94547 (92392)	MH	RES	DBS
94548 (92344)	TY	RES	DBS

NAA1 - PCV
Number	Depot	Livery	Owner
95300 (94300)	MH	RES	DBS
95301 (94301)	MH	RES	DBS

NRA1 - BAA
Number	Depot	Livery	Owner
95400 (95203)	MH	EWS	DBS
95410 (95213)	MH	EWS	DBS

NOA1 - H-GUV
Number	Depot	Livery	Owner
95727 (95127)	WE	RES	DBS
95754 (95154)	TY	RES	DBS
95761 (95161)	WE	RES	DBS
95763 (95163)	BS	RES	DBS

NX5G - NGV
Number	Depot	Livery	Owner
96371(S) (10545)	WB	EPS	DBS
96372(S) (10564)	LM	EPS	DBS
96373(S) (10568)	LM	EPS	DBS
96374(S) (10585)	LM	EPS	DBS
96375(S) (10587)	LM	EPS	DBS

Below: *The DBS Management Train, kept at Toton, is used by the senior management team of DB Schenker to visit operational locations in the UK or take potential customers to inspect facilities. The train is formed of a Mk3 DVT (82146), a FO (11039), RFM 10211 and sleeping car No. 10546. The train is usually power by silver-liveried Class 67 No. 67029 Royal Diamond. In this view the train led by the DVT heads along the Lostwithiel to Fowey line.* **Antony Christie**

Euro Cargo Rail A part of DB Schenker

Address: ✉ Immeuble la Palacio, 25-29 Place de la Madeleine, Paris, 75008
📠 info@eurocargorail.com
☎ +33 977 400000
ⓘ www.eurocargorail.com

Class 21

Vehicle Length: (21/5) 48ft 2in (14.70m), (21/6) 46ft 3in (14.13m)
Height: (21/5) 13ft 8in (4.16m), (21/6) 13ft 9in (4.19m)
Width: 8ft 8¼in (2.65m)
Engine: (21/5) Caterpillar 3512B DITA of 2,011hp
Engine: (21/6) MTU 8V 4000 R41L of 1,475hp
Hydraulic Equipment: Voith

Number	Depot	Pool	Livery	Owner	Operator		Number	Depot	Pool	Livery	Owner	Operator
21544	DM	WLAN	MAR	ANG	ECR		21547	DM	WLAN	MAR	ANG	ECR
21545	DM	WLAN	MAR	ANG	ECR		21610	DM	WLAN	MAR	ANG	ECR
21546	DM	WLAN	MAR	ANG	ECR		21611	DM	WLAN	MAR	ANG	ECR

Class 77
(JT42CWRM)

Vehicle Length: 70ft 0½in (21.34m)
Height: 12ft 10in (3.91m)
Width: 8ft 8¼in (2.65m)
Engine: EMD 12N-710G3B-EC
Horsepower: 3,300hp (2,462kW)
Electrical Equipment: EMD

Number	Depot	Livery	Owner	Opt'r
77001	ND	ELR	DBS	ECR
77002	ND	ELR	DBS	ECR
77003	ND	ELR	DBS	ECR
77004	ND	ELR	DBS	ECR
77005	ND	ELR	DBS	ECR
77006	ND	ELR	DBS	ECR
77007‡	ND	ELR	DBS	ECR
77008	ND	ELR	DBS	ECR
77009	ND	ELR	DBS	ECR
77010	ND	ELR	DBS	ECR
77011	ND	ELR	DBS	ECR
77012	ND	ELR	DBS	ECR
77013	ND	ELR	DBS	ECR
77014	ND	ELR	DBS	ECR
77015	ND	ELR	DBS	ECR
77016	ND	ELR	DBS	ECR
77017	ND	ELR	DBS	ECR
77018	ND	ELR	DBS	ECR
77019	ND	ELR	DBS	ECR
77020‡	ND	ELR	DBS	ECR
77021	ND	ELR	DBS	ECR
77022	ND	ELR	DBS	ECR
77023	ND	ELR	DBS	ECR
77024	ND	ELR	DBS	ECR
77025	ND	ELR	DBS	ECR
77026‡	ND	ELR	DBS	ECR
77027	ND	ELR	DBS	ECR
77028	ND	ELR	DBS	ECR
77029‡	ND	ELR	DBS	ECR
77030	ND	ELR	DBS	ECR
77031‡	ND	ELR	DBS	ECR
77032	ND	ELR	DBS	ECR
77033	ND	ELR	DBS	ECR
77034‡	ND	ELR	DBS	ECR
77035	ND	ELR	DBS	ECR
77036	ND	ELR	DBS	ECR
77037†	ND	ELR	DBS	ECR
77038‡	ND	ELR	DBS	ECR
77039‡	ND	ELR	DBS	ECR
77040	ND	ELR	DBS	ECR
77041‡	ND	ELR	DBS	ECR
77042‡	ND	ELR	DBS	ECR
77043‡	ND	ELR	DBS	ECR
77044‡	ND	ELR	DBS	ECR
77045	ND	ELR	DBS	ECR
77046‡	ND	ELR	DBS	ECR
77047	ND	ELR	DBS	ECR
77048	ND	ELR	DBS	ECR
77049‡	ND	ELR	DBS	ECR
77050‡	ND	ELR	DBS	ECR
77051‡	ND	ELR	DBS	ECR
77052‡	ND	ELR	DBS	ECR
77053‡	ND	ELR	DBS	ECR
77054‡	ND	ELR	DBS	ECR
77055‡	ND	ELR	DBS	ECR
77056‡	ND	ELR	DBS	ECR
77057‡	ND	ELR	DBS	ECR
77058	ND	ELR	DBS	ECR
77059	ND	ELR	DBS	ECR
77060	ND	ELR	DBS	ECR

‡ Working for DBS in Germany, re-classified as Class 247 and running in number range 247 007 onwards; final three digits remain the same.

† Working for MEG in Germany as 247-037.

Right: *The 60 Euro Cargo Rail Class 66s, numbered in the 77xxx series for Mainland Europe were built at the London (Ontario) plant of Electro-Motive in 2008-10 and shipped from Halifax (Nova Scotia) to Rotterdam for commissioning. By the time the locos arrived a downturn in work saw a number laid up. Several have now entered traffic with ECR and others with parent company DB Schenker. No. 77044 is seen passing St Marys in Canada, during shipping to Rotterdam.* **CJM**

Direct Rail Services

Address (UK): ✉ Kingmoor Depot, Etterby Road, Carlisle, Cumbria, CA3 9NZ

✎ info@directrailservices.com

✆ 01228 406600

ⓘ www.directrailservices.com

| **Managing Director:** | Neil McNicholas |
| **Depots:** | Carlisle Kingmoor (KM), Crewe Gresty Bridge (CG) |

Class 20/3

Vehicle Length: 46ft 9¼in (14.26m)
Height: 12ft 7⅝in (3.84m)
Width: 8ft 9in (2.66m)

Engine: English Electric 8SVT Mk2
Horsepower: 1,000hp (745kW)
Electrical Equipment: English Electric

Number		Depot	Pool	Livery	Owner	Operator	Name
20301	(20047)	KM	GBEE	DRU	DRS	GBR	*Max Joule 1958 - 1999*
20302	(20084)	KM	GBEE	DRU	DRS	GBR	
20303	**(20127)**	**KM**	**XHNC**	**DRC**	**DRS**	**DRS**	
20304	(20120)	KM	GBEE	DRU	DRS	GBR	
20305	(20095)	KM	GBEE	DRU	DRS	GBR	*Gresty Bridge*
20306(S)	**(20131)**	**KM**	**XHNC**	**DRS**	**DRS**	**-**	
20307(S)	**(20128)**	**KM/CS**	**XHSS**	**DRS**	**DRS**	**-**	
20308	**(20187)**	**KM**	**XHNC**	**DRC**	**DRS**	**DRS/GBR**	
20309	**(20075)**	**KM**	**XHNC**	**DRC**	**DRS**	**DRS**	
20310(S)	**(20190)**	**KM/CS**	**XHSS**	**DRS**	**DRS**	**-**	
20312(S)	**(20042)**	**KM/CS**	**XHSS**	**DRC**	**DRS**	**-**	
20313(S)	**(20194)**	**KM/CS**	**XHSS**	**DRS**	**DRS**	**-**	
20315(S)	**(20104)**	**KM/CS**	**XHSS**	**DRS**	**DRS**	**-**	

■ *Nos. 20301/302/304/305 fitted with trip cock equipment to allow operation over LUL tracks. 20308 is a reserve for this contract.*

Left: *The once 15 strong DRS Class 20 fleet is down to just a handful of operational locos. Four of the fleet are now operated by GBRf as part of a contract to deliver new London Transport surface line stock from Derby via Old Dalby to the LUL network. No 20303 in DRS Compass livery and 20303 in earlier DRS colours are seen on a flask train.* **Antony Christie**

Class 37/0

Vehicle Length: 61ft 6in (18.74m)
Height: 13ft 0¼in (3.96m)
Width: 8ft 11⅝in (2.73m)

Engine: English Electric 12CSVT
Horsepower: 1,750hp (1,304kW)
Electrical Equipment: English Electric

Number	Depot	Pool	Livery	Owner	Operator	Name
37038	KM	XHSS	DRS	DRS	DRS	
37059	KM	XHNC	DRC	DRS	DRS	
37069	KM	XHNC	DRC	DRS	DRS	
37087	KM	XHNC	DRS	DRS	DRS	*Keighley & Worth Valley Railway*
37194	KM	XHNC	DRC	DRS	DRS	
37197(S)	BH	XHNC	BLU	DRS	-	
37218	KM	XHNC	DRC	DRS	DRS	
37229	KM	XHNC	DRC	DRS	DRS	*Jonty Jarvis*
37259(S)	BH	XHSS	DRU	DRS	-	
37261	KM	XHNC	DRC	DRS	DRS	

Class 37/4

Vehicle Length: 61ft 6in (18.74m)			Engine: English Electric 12CSVT		
Height: 13ft 0¼in (3.96m)			Horsepower: 1,750hp (1,304kW)		
Width: 8ft 11⅝in (2.73m)			Electrical Equipment: English Electric		
Electric Train Heat fitted					

Number		Depot	Pool	Livery	Owner	Operator	Name
37401(S)	(37268)	KM	XHHP	EWS	DRS	-	
37402(S)	(37274)	TO	XHSS	TLF	DBS	- (Spares)	
37405(S)	(37282)	TO	XHSS	EWS	DRS	- (Spares)	Strathclyde Region
37406(S)	(37295)	KM	XHHP	EWS	DRS	-	The Saltire Society
37409	(37270)	KM	XHNC	DRC	DRS	DRS	Lord Hinton
37410(S)	(37273)	KM	XHHP	EWS	DRS	-	
37411(S)	(37290)*	KM	XHHP	GRN	DRS	-	
37416(S)	(37302)	KM	XHHP	GSW	DRS	-	
37417(S)	(37269)	KM	XHHP	EWS	DRS	-	
37419(S)	(37291)	BH	XHSS	DRC	DRS	-	
37422(S)	(37266)	KM	XHHP	EWS	DRS	-	
37423	(37296)	KM	XHNC	DRC	DRS	DRS	Spirit of the Lakes
37425(S)	(37292)	BH	XHHP	BLL	DRS	-	
37426(S)	(37299)	KM	XHHP	EWS	DRS	-	
37427(S)	(37288)	KM	XHHP	EWS	DRS	-	

Class 37/5

Vehicle Length: 61ft 6in (18.74m)			Engine: English Electric 12CSVT		
Height: 13ft 0¼in (3.96m)			Horsepower: 1,750hp (1,304kW)		
Width: 8ft 11⅝in (2.73m)			Electrical Equipment: English Electric		

Number		Depot	Pool	Livery	Owner	Operator	Name/Notes
37510		KM	XHNC	DRC	DRS	DRS	
37667	(37151)	KM	XHNC	DRC	DRS	DRS	
37682(S)	(37236)	KM	XHHP	DRC	DRS	-	
37683(S)	(37187)	CG	XHSS	DRS	DRS	-	(At Waterman Railways Crewe - training loco)
37688	(37205)	KM	XHNC	DRC	DRS	DRS	Kingmoor TMD

Class 37/6

Vehicle Length: 61ft 6in (18.74m)			Engine: English Electric 12CSVT		
Height: 13ft 0¼in (3.96m)			Horsepower: 1,750hp (1,304kW)		
Width: 8ft 11⅝in (2.73m)			Electrical Equipment: English Electric		

Number		Depot	Pool	Livery	Owner	Operator	Name
37601	(37501)	KM	XHNC	DRC	DRS	DRS	Class 37 – 'Fifty'
37602	(37502)	KM	XHNC	DRS	DRS	-	
37603	(37504)	KM	XHNC	DRC	DRS	DRS	
37604	(37506)	KM	XHNC	DRC	DRS	DRS	
37605(S)	(37507)	KM/CS	XHXX	DRS	DRS	-	
37606(S)	(37508)	KM	XHSS	DRS	DRS	-	
37607	(37511)	KM	XHNC	DRS	DRS	DRS	
37608	(37512)	KM	XHNC	DRC	DRS	-	
37609(S)	(37514)	KM	XHSS	DRS	DRS	-	
37610	(37687)	KM	XHNC	DRC	DRS	DRS	T. S. (Ted) Cassady 14.5.61-6.4.08
37611	(37690)	KM	XHNC	DRC	DRS	DRS	
37612	(37691)	KM	XHSS	DRS	DRS	DRS	

Below: *Direct Rail Services hold the contract to provide traction for a number of the UK Network Rail test trains, usually operating in 'top and tail' mode. Here Nos. 37069 and 37059 pass Worcester on 11 April 2011 with a Derby to Tyseley via Gloucester train.* **CJM**

Direct Rail Services

Class 47/4 & 47/7

Vehicle Length: 63ft 6in (19.35m)
Height: 12ft 10⅜in (3.91m)
Width: 9ft 2in (2.79m)
Electric Train Heat fitted

Engine: Sulzer 12LDA28C
Horsepower: 2,580hp (1,922kW)
Electrical Equipment: Brush

Number		Depot	Pool	Livery	Owner	Operator	Name
47703(S)	(47514)	KM	XHSS	FRB	DRS	-	
47709(S)	(47499)	KM/ZG	XHHP	DRC	DRS	-	
47712(S)	(47505)	KM	XHAC	DRC	DRS	(at LNWR Crewe)	Pride of Carlisle
47747(S)	(47615)	KM	XHSS	EWS	DRS	-	
47790	(47673)	KM	XHAC	NBP	DRS	DRS	Galloway Princess
47791(S)	(47675)	KM	XHSS	RES	DRS	-	
47501		KM	XHAC	DRC	DRS	DRS	Craftsman
47802	(47552)	KM	XHAC	DRC	DRS	DRS	Pride of Cumbria
47805	(47650)	KM	XHAC	DRC	DRS	DRS	
47810	(47247/655)	BH	XHAC	DRC	DRS	DRS	Peter Bath MBE 1927-2006
47813	(47129/658)	KM	XHSS	DRC	DRS	DRS	
47818	(47240/663)	BH	XHHP	DRC	DRS	DRS	
47828	(47266/629)	BH	XHAC	DRC	DRS	DRS	
47832	(47560)	KM	XHAC	NBP	DRS	DRS	Solway Princess
47839	(47621)	KM	XHAC	RIV	DRS	DRS	
47841	(47622)	KM	XHNC	DRC	DRS	DRS	
47853	(47614)	KM	XHNC	DRC	DRS	DRS	

Left: *A fleet of 17 Class 47s are on the books of Direct Rail Services, but not all are in traffic, some being stored and under long term repair. DRS hold the contract with National Express East Anglia (Greater Anglia) to provide 'thunderbird' duties for their Norwich - Liverpool Street route. No. 47712* Pride of Carlisle *is seen stabled at Colchester.* **Stacey Thew**

Class 57/0

Vehicle Length: 63ft 6in (19.38m)
Height: 12ft 10⅛in (3.91m)
Width: 9ft 2in (2.79m)

Engine: EMD 645-12E3
Horsepower: 2,500hp (1,864kW)
Electrical Equipment: Brush

Number		Depot	Pool	Livery	Owner	Operator	Name/Notes
57002	(47322)	KM	XHCK	DRC*	PTR	DRS	* with Colas branding
57003	(47317)	KM	XHCK	DRC	PTR	DRS	
57004	(47347)	KM	XHCK	DRC	PTR	DRS	
57007	(47332)	KM	XHCK	DRC	PTR	DRS	
57008	(47060)	KM	XHCK	DRC	PTR	DRS	Telford International Railfreight Park June - 2009
57009	(47079)	KM	XHCK	DRC	PTR	DRS	
57010(S)	(47231)	KM	XHSS	DRC	PTR	-	
57011	(47329)	KM	XHCK	DRC	PTR	DRS	
57012(S)	(47204)	KM	XHSS	DRC	PTR	-	

Left: *Nine Class 57s are operated by Direct Rail Services, all painted in full DRS Compass livery. The locos operate alongside the Class 47 fleet and are scheduled to be equipped with electric train supply in 2012. No. 57009 is seen stabled at Plymouth North Road station after arriving with a pair of flask escort vehicles en route to Devonport Dockyard to collect a flask wagon for return to Sellafield.* **Nathan Williamson**

Class 66/3, 66/4

Vehicle Length: 70ft 0½in (21.34m)
Height: 12ft 10in (3.91m)
Width: 8ft 8¼in (2.65m)

Engine: EMD 12N-710G3B-EC
Horsepower: 3,300hp (2,462kW)
Electrical Equipment: EMD

Number	Depot	Pool	Livery	Owner	Operator
66301	KM	XHIM	DRC	BEA	DRS
66302	KM	XHHP	DRC	BEA	DRS
66303	KM	XHIM	DRC	BEA	DRS
66304	KM	XHIM	DRC	BEA	DRS
66305	KM	XHHP	DRC	BEA	DRS
66421§	KM	XHIM	DRC	HAL	DRS
66422§	KM	XHIM	DRC	HAL	DRS
66423	KM	XHIM	DRC	HAL	DRS
66424	KM	XHIM	DRC	HAL	DRS
66425	KM	XHIM	DRC	HAL	DRS
66426	KM	XHIM	DRC	HAL	DRS
66427	KM	XHIM	DRC	HAL	DRS
66428	KM	XHIM	DRC	HAL	DRS
66429	KM	XHIM	DRC	HAL	DRS
66430	KM	XHIM	DRC	HAL	DRS
66431	KM	XHIM	DRC	HAL	DRS
66432	KM	XHIM	DRC	HAL	DRS
66433	KM	XHIM	DRC	HAL	DRS
66434	KM	XHIM	DRC	HAL	DRS

§ For Freightliner

Above: *The Class 66 fleet operated by DRS is in rapid decline, with at the end of 2011 the first 13 locos already taken off lease and placed with new owners, and locos up to No. 66422 are scheduled to return to their lease owner by early 2012. Nos. 66420 and 66430 are seen heading west at Aller Junction, Newton Abbot.* **Antony Christie**

■ As this edition of *Rail Guide 2012* closed for press, it was confirmed that Direct Rail Services had ordered a fleet of 15 Vossloh 'Eurolight 4000' locomotives for delivery to the UK in 2013-14. The locos will be built in Spain. An option in the contract exists for a further 10. No official UK numbering was issued in January 2012.

Direct Rail Services

Coaching Stock

Mk2	Height: 12ft 9½in (3.89m)
Vehicle Length: 66ft 0in (20.11m)	Width: 9ft 3in (2.81m)

AC2 - BSO

Number	Depot	Livery	Owner
9419	KM	DRC	DRS
9428	KM	DRC	DRS

AB1D - BFK

Number	Depot	Livery	Owner
17159	ZG	DRO	DRS

Left: *Direct Rail Services operate just three passenger vehicles, mainly as support coaches for loaded flask trains. Mk2c BSO No. 9428 is shown carrying the latest DRS Compass livery. Note the window in the former end gangway connection.* **Antony Christie**

Royal Mail (operations contracted to DBS)

Address: ✉ 148 Old Street, London, EC1V 9HQ

✍ press.office@royalmail.com ☎ 0207 250 2468 ⓘ www.royalmailgroup.com

Class 325

Vehicle Length: (Driving) 65ft 0¾in (19.82m)	Width: 9ft 2in (2.82m)
(Inter) 65ft 4¼in (19.92m)	Horsepower: 1,278hp (990kW)
Height: 12ft 4¾in (3.76m)	Seats (total/car): None - luggage space

Number	Formation DTPMV+MPMV+TPMV+DTPMV	Depot	Livery	Owner	Operator	Name
325001	68300+68340+68360+68301	CE	RML	RML	DBS	
325002	68302+68341+68361+68303	CE	RML	RML	DBS	*Royal Mail North Wales & North West*
325003	68304+68342+68362+68305	CE	RML	RML	DBS	
325004	68306+68343+68363+68307	CE	RML	RML	DBS	
325005	68308+68344+68364+68309	CE	RML	RML	DBS	*John Grierson*
325006	68310+68345+68365+68311	CE	RML	RML	DBS	
325007	68312+68346+68366+68313	CE	RML	RML	DBS	*Peter Howarth C.B.E*
325008	68314+68347+68367+68315	CE	RML	RML	DBS	
325009	68316+68348+68368+68317	CE	RML	RML	DBS	
325010(S)	68318+68349+68369+68319	CE/IL	RML	RML	DBS	
325011	68320+68350+68370+68321	CE	RML	RML	DBS	
325012	68322+68351+68371+68323	CE	RML	RML	DBS	
325013	68324+68352+68372+68325	CE	RML	RML	DBS	
325014	68326+68353+68373+68327	CE	RML	RML	DBS	
325015	68328+68354+68374+68329	CE	RML	RML	DBS	
325016	68330+68355+68375+68331	CE	RML	RML	DBS	

Left: *The 16 Royal Mail-owned four-car EMU Mail units of Class 323 are operated by DB Schenker and work only a limited service over the West Coast Main Line, where they use their overhead power equipment. These sets were built as dual ac/dc voltage sets, but the dc third rail equipment is now isolated. At least one unit, No. 325010, is long term stored and the limited operation worked sees only a handful of units operational. Set No. 325011 brings up the rear of a southbound WCML working.* **Antony Christie**

Europorte – GB Railfreight (GBRf)

Address: ✉ 15-25 Artillery Lane, London, E1 7HA
✆ gbrfinfo@gbrailfreight.com
☎ 0207 983 5177
ⓘ www.gbrailfreight.com

Managing Director: John Smith

Depots: Peterborough (PT), Wembley (SV), St Leonards (SE)
Coquelles (CQ), Ashford Hitachi (AD)

Class 08/0, 09

Vehicle Length: 29ft 3in (8.91m)			Engine: English Electric 6K		
Height: 12ft 8⅝in (3.87m)			Horsepower: 400hp (298kW)		
Width: 8ft 6in (2.59m)			Electrical Equipment: English Electric		

Number	Depot	Pool	Livery	Owner	Operator
08401	CF	GBWM	GRN	HEC	GBF
08925	CF	GBWM	BLU	GBF	GBF
08934	MR	GBWM	BLK	GBF	GBF
09002	§	GBWM	GRN	GBF	GBF
09009	§	GBWM	GRN	GBF	GBF

§ Working at Barton Dock, Trafford Park

Right: *Five shunters are operated by GBRf; No. 09002 is seen at Trafford Park. Note its revised front end marker/tail lights.*
Tim Blazey

Class 20/3

Vehicle Length: 46ft 9¼in (14.26m)				Engine: English Electric 8SVT Mk2		
Height: 12ft 7⅝in (3.84m)				Horsepower: 1,000hp (745kW)		
Width: 8ft 9in (2.66m)				Electrical Equipment: English Electric		

DRS traction operated under contract by GBRf

Number		Depot	Pool	Livery	Owner	Operator	Name
20301	(20047)	KM	GBEE	DRU	DRS	GBR	*Max Joule 1958 – 1999*
20302	(20084)	KM	GBEE	DRU	DRS	GBR	
20304	(20120)	KM	GBEE	DRU	DRS	GBR	
20305	(20095)	KM	GBEE	DRU	DRS	GBR	*Gresty Bridge*
20308	(20187)	KM	GBEE	DRC	DRS	GBR	

Class 66/7

Vehicle Length: 70ft 0½in (21.34m)		Engine: EMD 12N-710G3B-EC	
Height: 12ft 10in (3.91m)		Horsepower: 3,300hp (2,462kW)	
Width: 8ft 8¼in (2.65m)		Electrical Equipment: EMD	

Number	Depot	Pool	Livery	Owner	Operator	Name
66701	PT	GBRT	GBR	EVL	GBR	
66702	PT	GBRT	GBR	EVL	GBR	*Blue Lightning*
66703	PT	GBCM	GBR	EVL	GBR	*Doncaster PSB 1981 - 2002*
66704	PT	GBCM	GBR	EVL	GBR	*Colchester Power Signalbox*
66705	PT	GBCM	GBR	EVL	GBR	*Golden Jubilee*
66706	PT	GBCM	GBR	EVL	GBR	*Nene Valley*
66707	PT	GBCM	GBR	EVL	GBR	*Sir Sam Fay / Great Central Railway*
66708	PT	GBRT	GBR	EVL	GBR	*Jayne*
66709	PT	GBRT	MED	EVL	GBR	*Joseph Arnold Davies*
66710	PT	GBCM	GBR	EVL	GBR	*Phil Packer*
66711	PT	GBCM	GBR	EVL	GBR	
66712	PT	GBCM	GBR	EVL	GBR	*Peterborough Power Signalbox*
66713	PT	GBCM	GBR	EVL	GBR	*Forest City*
66714	PT	GBCM	GBR	EVL	GBR	*Cromer Lifeboat*
66715	PT	GBCM	GBR	EVL	GBR	*Valour*
66716	PT	GBCM	GBR	EVL	GBR	*Locomotive & Carriage Institution Centenary 1911-2011*
66717	PT	GBCM	GBR	EVL	GBR	*Good Old Boy*
66718	PT	GBCM	GBM	EVL	GBR	*Gwyneth Dunwoody*
66719	PT	GBCM	GBM	EVL	GBR	*Metro-Land*
66720	PT	GBCM	SPL	EVL	GBR	
66721	PT	GBCM	GBM	EVL	GBR	*Harry Beck*

Europorte – GBRf

66722		PT	GBCM	GBM	EVL	GBR	*Sir Edward Watkin*
66723		PT	GBSD	GBF	EVL	GBR	*Chinook*
66724		PT	GBSD	GBF	EVL	GBR	*Drax Power Station*
66725		PT	GBSD	GBF	EVL	GBR	*Sunderland*
66726		PT	GBCM	GBF	EVL	GBR	*Sheffield Wednesday*
66727		PT	GBSD	GBF	EVL	GBR	*Andrew Scott CBE*
66728		PT	GBMU	GBN	PTR	GBR	*Institution of Railway Operators*
66729		PT	GBMU	GBN	PTR	GBR	*Derby County*
66730		PT	GBMU	GBF	PTR	GBR	*Whitemoor*
66731		PT	GBMU	GBN	PTR	GBR	*interhubGB*
66732		PT	GBMU	GBN	PTR	GBR	*GBRf The First Decade 1999-2009 John Smith - MD*
66733‡	(66401)	PT	GBFM	BLU	PTR	GBR	
66734‡	(66402)	PT	GBFM	GBN	PTR	GBR	*The Eco Express*
66735‡	(66403)	PT	GBFM	GBN	PTR	GBR	
66736‡	(66404)	PT	GBFM	GBN	PTR	GBR	*Wolverhampton Wanderers*
66737‡	(66405)	PT	GBFM	GBN	PTR	GBR	*Lesia*
66738	(66578)	PT	GBRT	FLU	GBR	GBR	
66739	(66579)	PT	GBRT	FLU	GBR	GBR	
66740	(66580)	PT	GBRT	FLU	GBR	GBR	
66741	(66581)	PT	GBRT	FLU	GBR	GBR	
66742	(66406, 66841)	PT	GBHL	COL	PTR	GBR	
66743	(66407, 66842)	PT	GBHL	COL	PTR	GBR	
66744	(66408, 66843)	PT	GBRT	COL	PTR	GBR	
66745	(66409, 66844)	PT	GBHL	COL	PTR	GBR	
66746	(66410, 66845)	PT	GBHL	COL	PTR	GBR	

‡ Fitted with RETB equipment

Left: *The main motive power operated by GBRf for freight flows are Class 66s, a total of 46 being in traffic at the end of 2011. The most 'impressive' is No. 66720 painted in a special 'night and day' colour scheme, devised by a young schoolgirl in a staff competition. The loco is seen on the Nene Valley Railway.* **GBRf**

Class 73

Vehicle Length: 53ft 8in (16.35m)	*Power: 750V dc third rail or English Electric 6K*	
Height: 12ft 5⁹⁄₁₆in (3.79m)	*Horsepower: electric - 1,600hp (1,193kW)*	
Width: 8ft 8in (2.64m)	*Horsepower: diesel - 600hp (447kW)*	
	Electrical Equipment: English Electric	

Number		Depot	Pool	Livery	Owner	Operator	Name
73119		SE	GBED	BLU	GBR	GBR	
73141		SE	GBED	FGF	GBR	GBR	*Charlotte*
73204	(73125)	SE	GBED	GBR	GBR	GBR	*Janice*
73205	(73124)	SE	GBED	INT	GBR	GBR	*Jeanette*
73206	(73123)	SE	GBED	GBR	GBR	GBR	*Lisa*
73207	(73122)	SE	GBED	BLL	GBR	GBR	
73208	(73121)	SE	GBED	BLU	GBR	GBR	*Kirsten*
73209§	(73120)	SE	GBZZ	GBR	GBR	GBR	*Alison*
73212	(73102)	SE	GBED	GBU	GBR	GBR	
73213	(73112)	SE	GBED	FGU	GBR	GBR	

Freight Operating Companies - Europorte GBRf

§ To be trial fitted with new design MTU power unit and replacement electronics as development loco for all GBRf Class 73**s**.

Right: *GBRf operate a fleet of 10 Class 73s which are normally used in the former Southern Region area working under third rail conditions. No. 73205 in InterCity colours is illustrated.* **Antony Christie**

Class 92

Vehicle Length: 70ft 1in (21.34m)			Power Collection: 25kV ac overhead / 750V dc third rail			
Height: 13ft 0in (3.95m)			Horsepower: ac - 6,700hp (5,000kW) / dc 5,360hp (4,000kW)			
Width: 8ft 8in (2.66m)			Electrical Equipment: Brush			

Number	Depot	Pool	Livery	Owner	Operator	Name
92006(S)	DM	PTXX	SNF	GBR	-	Louis Armand
92010(S)	CO	PTXX	EU2	GBR	-	Moliere
92014(S)	CE	PTXX	SNF	GBR	-	Emile Zola
92018(S)	DM	PTXX	SNF	GBR	-	Stendhal
92020(S)	DM	PTXX	EU2	GBR	-	Milton
92021(S)	CO	PTXX	EU2	GBR	-	Purcell
92023(S)	CE	PTXX	EU2	GBR	-	Ravel
92028	CO	GBET	EU2	GBR	GBR	Saint Saens
92032	CO	GBET	GBN	GBR	GBR	
92033(S)	DM	PTXX	SNF	GBR	-	Berlioz
92038(S)	CE	GBET	EU2	GBR	-	Voltaire
92040(S)	CO	PTXX	EU2	GBR	-	Goethe
92043	CO	GBET	EU2	GBR	GBR	Debussy
92044	CO	GBET	EU2	GBR	GBR	Couperin
92045(S)	Brush	PTXX	EU2	GBR	-	Chaucer
92046(S)	Brush	PTXX	EU2	GBR	-	Sweelinck

Right: *Following the takeover of GBRf by Europorte, the company took on the Europorte Class 92s. Since then further '92s' have been added to the fleet with the purchase of other off-lease examples. It is planned to return a number but not all of these modern locos to full operation. It is also suggested that a possible rebuilding of a small number with dual power capabilities could be on the cards. No. 92032 carrying the latest GBRf livery is illustrated.* **Ron Cover**

■ GBRf also operates Class 08 No. 08934 at either Peterborough or Whitemoor. The loco is owned by Alstom and is listed in that section of *Rail Guide 2012*.

Coaching Stock

Barrier Vans

Mk1		Height: 12ft 9½in (3.89m)	
Vehicle Length: 64ft 6in (19.65m)		Width: 9ft 3in (2.81m)	

AW51

Number	Depot	Livery	Owner
6376 (ADB975973, 1021)	PG	BLU	PTR
6377 (ADB975975, 1042)	PG	BLU	PTR
6378 (ADB975971, 1054)	PG	BLU	PTR
6379 (ADB975972, 1039)	PG	BLU	PTR

Class Di 8

In late 2011, GBRf purchased 10 former Cargo-Net, Norway Class Di 8 locos for use within the SSI Lackenby Steelworks in Redcar. The 2,100hp (1,566kW) locos were built in 1996-97 by Mak in Kiel, Germany as an order for 20 locos. In the UK the fleet classified by the UIC as 308 will be painted in a joint GBRf/SSI livery. The locos in the UK are: 8701, 8703, 8704, 8711, 8712, 8716, 8717, 8718, 8719, 8720.

Freightliner

Address: ✉ 3rd Floor, The Podium, 1 Eversholt Street, London, NW1 2FL
⌨ pressoffice@freightliner.co.uk
✆ 0207 200 3900
ⓘ www.freightliner.com

Chief Executive:	Peter Maybury
Managing Director Intermodal:	Adam Cunliffe
Managing Director Heavy Haul:	Paul Smart
Depots:	Freightliner Diesels (FD), Freightliner Electrics (FE), Freightliner Shunters (FS), Ipswich* (IP), Leeds Midland Road (LD), Southampton Maritime (SZ)
	* Stabling point
Parent Company:	Arcapita

Class 08/0

Vehicle Length: 29ft 3in (8.91m)
Height: 12ft 8⅝in (3.87m)
Width: 8ft 6in (2.59m)
Engine: English Electric 6K
Horsepower: 400hp (298kW)
Electrical Equipment: English Electric

Number	Depot	Pool	Livery	Owner	Operator
08077(S)	FS/LH	DHLT	FLR	FLR	FLR
08530(S)	LH	DFLS	FLR	PTR	FLR
08531	FS	DFLS	FLR	PTR	FLR
08575	SZ	DHLT	FLR	PTR	FLR
08585	SZ¤	DFLS	FLR	PTR	FLR
08624	SZ*	DFLS	BLU	PTR	FLR
08691	SZ	DHLT	FLR	FLR	FLR
08785	FD	DFLS	FLR	PTR	FLR
08891	FD	DFLS	FLR	PTR	FLR

* 08624 Working at Tilbury
¤ 08585 At L H GroupServices

08393 also at L H Group Services

Names applied
08585 *Vicky*
08691 *Terri*

Left: *Painted in full Freightliner green and yellow livery, No. 08691 Terri is seen at Freightliner's Leeds Midland Road depot.* **Bill Wilson**

Class 47/4

Vehicle Length: 63ft 6in (19.35m)
Height: 12ft 10⅜in (3.91m)
Width: 9ft 2in (2.79m)
Electric Train Heat fitted
Engine: Sulzer 12LDA28C
Horsepower: 2,580hp (1,922kW)
Electrical Equipment: Brush

Number		Depot	Pool	Livery	Owner	Operator
47811	(47656)	FD	DFLH	GRN	FLR	FLR (pilot)
47816(S)	(47661)	FD	DFLH	GRN	FLR	-
47830(S)	(47649)	BH	DFLH	GRN	FLR	-

Class 66/4

Vehicle Length: 70ft 0½in (21.34m)
Height: 12ft 10in (3.91m)
Width: 8ft 8¼in (2.65m)
Engine: EMD 12N-710G3B-EC
Horsepower: 3,300hp (2,462kW)
Electrical Equipment: EMD

Number	Depot	Pool	Livery	Owner	Operator	Name/Note
66411	*Exported, working in Poland for Freightliner Poland*					
66412	*Exported, working in Poland for Freightliner Poland*					
66413	LD	DFHG	DRC	CBR	FLT	

66414	LD	DFHG	TES	HAL	FLT
66415	LD	DFHG	DRC	HAL	FLT
66416	LD	DFHG	DRC	HAL	FLT

66417 *Exported, working in Poland for Freightliner Poland*

66418	LD	DFHG	DRC	HAL	FLT
66419	LD	DFHG	DRC	HAL	FLT
66420	LD	DFHG	DRC	HAL	FLT

Class 66/5

Vehicle Length: 70ft 0½in (21.34m)
Height: 12ft 10in (3.91m)
Width: 8ft 8¼in (2.65m)

Engine: EMD 12N-710G3B-EC
Horsepower: 3,300hp (2,462kW)
Electrical Equipment: EMD

Number	Depot	Pool	Livery	Owner	Operator	Name
66501	LD	DFGM	FLR	PTR	FLR	*Japan 2001*
66502	LD	DFGM	FLR	PTR	FLR	*Basford Hall Centenary 2001*
66503	LD	DFGM	FLR	PTR	FLR	*The Railway Magazine*
66504	LD	DFGM	FLR	PTR	FLR	
66505	LD	DFRT	FLR	PTR	FLR	
66506	LD	DFHH	FLR	EVL	FLR	*Crewe Regeneration*
66507(S)	LD	DFRT	FLR	EVL	-	
66508	LD	DFRT	FLR	EVL	FLR	
66509	LD	DFHH	FLR	EVL	FLR	
66510	LD	DFRT	FLR	EVL	FLR	
66511	LD	DFRT	FLR	EVL	FLR	
66512	LD	DFHH	FLR	EVL	FLR	
66513	LD	DFHH	FLR	EVL	FLR	
66514	LD	DFRT	FLR	EVL	FLR	
66515	LD	DFGM	FLR	EVL	FLR	
66516	LD	DFGM	FLR	EVL	FLR	
66517	LD	DFGM	FLR	EVL	FLR	
66518	LD	DFRT	FLR	EVL	FLR	
66519	LD	DFHH	FLR	EVL	FLR	
66520	LD	DFRT	FLR	EVL	FLR	
66522	LD	DFRT	FLR	EVL	FLR	*east london express*
66523	LD	DFRT	FLR	EVL	FLR	
66524	LD	DFHH	FLR	EVL	FLR	
66525	LD	DFHH	FLR	EVL	FLR	
66526	LD	DFHH	FLR	PTR	FLR	*Driver Steve Dunn (George)*
66527	LD	DFHH	FLR	EVL	FLR	*Don Raider*
66528	LD	DFHH	FLR	PTR	FLR	
66529	LD	DFHH	FLR	PTR	FLR	
66530	LD	DFGM	FLR	PTR	FLR	
66531	LD	DFHH	FLR	PTR	FLR	
66532	LD	DFGM	FLR	PTR	FLR	*P&O Nedlloyd Atlas*
66533	LD	DFGM	FLR	PTR	FLR	*Hanjin Express / Senator Express*
66534	LD	DFGM	FLR	PTR	FLR	*OOCL Express*
66535	LD	DFGM	FLR	PTR	FLR	
66536	LD	DFGM	FLR	PTR	FLR	
66537	LD	DFGM	FLR	PTR	FLR	
66538	LD	DFIM	FLR	EVL	FLR	
66539	LD	DFIM	FLR	EVL	FLR	
66540	LD	DFIM	FLR	EVL	FLR	*Ruby*
66541	LD	DFIM	FLR	EVL	FLR	
66542	LD	DFIM	FLR	EVL	FLR	
66543	LD	DFIM	FLR	EVL	FLR	
66544	LD	DFHG	FLR	PTR	FLR	
66545	LD	DFHG	FLR	PTR	FLR	
66546	LD	DFHG	FLR	PTR	FLR	
66547	LD	DFHG	FLR	PTR	FLR	
66548	LD	DFHG	FLR	PTR	FLR	
66549	LD	DFHG	FLR	PTR	FLR	
66550	LD	DFHG	FLR	PTR	FLR	
66551	LD	DFHG	FLR	PTR	FLR	
66552	LD	DFHG	FLR	PTR	FLR	*Maltby Raider*
66553	LD	DFHG	FLR	PTR	FLR	

Freight Operating Companies - Freightliner

Freightliner

66554	LD	DFHG	FLR	EVL	FLR	
66555	LD	DFHG	FLR	EVL	FLR	
66556	LD	DFHG	FLR	EVL	FLR	
66557	LD	DFHG	FLR	EVL	FLR	
66558	LD	DFIM	FLR	EVL	FLR	
66559	LD	DFIM	FLR	EVL	FLR	
66560	LD	DFHG	FLR	EVL	FLR	
66561	LD	DFHG	FLR	EVL	FLR	
66562	LD	DFIM	FLR	EVL	FLR	
66563	LD	DFIM	FLR	EVL	FLR	
66564	LD	DFIM	FLR	EVL	FLR	
66565	LD	DFIM	FLR	EVL	FLR	
66566	LD	DFIM	FLR	EVL	FLR	
66567	LD	DFIM	FLR	EVL	FLR	
66568	LD	DFIM	FLR	EVL	FLR	
66569	LD	DFIM	FLR	EVL	FLR	
66570	LD	DFIM	FLR	EVL	FLR	
66571	LD	DFIM	FLR	EVL	FLR	
66572	LD	DFIM	FLR	EVL	FLR	
66582	*Exported, working in Poland for Freightliner Poland as 66009FPL*					
66583	*Exported, working in Poland for Freightliner Poland as 66010FPL*					
66584	*Exported, working in Poland for Freightliner Poland as 66011FPL*					
66585	LD	DFHG	FLR	HAL	FLR	*The Drax Flyer*
66586	*Exported, working in Poland for Freightliner Poland as 66008FPL*					
66587	LD	DFFT	FLR	HAL	FLR	
66588	LD	DFIN	FLR	HAL	FLR	
66589	LD	DFIN	FLR	HAL	FLR	
66590	LD	DFIN	FLR	HAL	FLR	
66591	LD	DFIN	FLR	LTS	FLR	
66592	LD	DFIN	FLR	LTS	FLR	*Johnson Stevens Agencies*
66593	LD	DFIN	FLR	LTS	FLR	*3MG Mersey Multimodal Gateway*
66594	LD	DFIN	FLR	LTS	FLR	*NYK Spirit of Kyoto*
66595	LD	DFHG	FLR	BEA	FLR	
66596	LD	DFHG	FLR	BEA	FLR	
66597	LD	DFHG	FLR	BEA	FLR	*Viridor*
66598	LD	DFHG	FLR	BEA	FLR	
66599	LD	DFHG	FLR	BEA	FLR	

Above: *Freightliner operates locomotives of Class 66/5, 66/6 and 66/9. Several slightly different front end designs can be found within the fleet, with some four and some five-door body configurations. Class 66/9 No. 66955 is illustrated pulling off the North London line at Stratford with a container train bound for Felixstowe. This example has the five-door bodywork, with its three-door side nearest the camera.* **CJM**

Class 66/6

Some stored members of Class 66/6 have operated after being placed in stored status.

Number	Depot	Pool	Livery	Owner	Operator	Name
66601	LD	DFHH	FLR	PTR	FLR	The Hope Valley
66602	LD	DFHH	FLR	PTR	FLR	
66603	LD	DFHH	FLR	PTR	FLR	
66604	LD	DFHH	FLR	PTR	FLR	
66605	LD	DFHH	FLR	PTR	FLR	
66606	LD	DFHH	FLR	PTR	FLR	
66607	LD	DFHG	FLR	PTR	FLR	
66608 *Exported, working in Poland for Freightliner Poland as 92 70 0066 608-5*						
66609 *Exported, working in Poland for Freightliner Poland as 66603FPL*						
66610	LD	DFHG	FLR	PTR	FLR	
66611 *Exported, working in Poland for Freightliner Poland as 66604FPL*						
66612 *Exported, working in Poland for Freightliner Poland as 92 70 0066 612-7*						
66613	LD	DFTZ	FLR	PTR	-	
66614	LD	DFHG	FLR	PTR	FLR	
66615	LD	DFHG	FLR	PTR	FLR	
66616	LD	DFHG	FLR	PTR	FLR	
66617	LD	DFHG	FLR	PTR	FLR	
66618	LD	DFHG	FLR	PTR	FLR	Railways Illustrated Annual Photographic Awards - Alan Barnes
66619	LD	DFHG	FLR	PTR	FLR	Derek W. Johnson MBE
66620	LD	DFHG	FLR	PTR	FLR	
66621	LD	DFHG	FLR	PTR	FLR	
66622	LD	DFHG	FLR	PTR	FLR	
66623	LD	DFHG	AIN	EVL	FLR	Bill Bolsover
66624 *Exported, working in Poland for Freightliner Poland as 66602FPL*						
66625 *Exported, working in Poland for Freightliner Poland as 66601FPL*						

The Class 66/9 locomotives have improved gearing, a lower maximum speed but greater pulling power and are thus deployed on Freightliner's heaviest trains, such as the High Output Ballast Cleaning rain and Track Renewal Train. No. 66619 Derek W. Johnson MBE *is illustrated at Westbury.* **Antony Christie**

Class 66/9

Number	Depot	Pool	Livery	Owner	Operator	Name
66951	LD	DFHG	FLR	EVL	FLR	
66952	LD	DFHG	FLR	EVL	FLR	
66953	LD	DFHG	FLR	BEA	FLR	
66954	LD	DFIN	FLR	BEA	FLR	
66955	LD	DFIN	FLR	BEA	FLR	
66956	LD	DFIN	FLR	BEA	FLR	
66957	LD	DFIN	FLR	BEA	FLR	Stephenson Locomotive Society 1909-2009

Freightliner

Class 70 - PH37ACmi

Vehicle Length: 71ft 2½in (21.71m)
Height: 12ft 10in (3.91m)
Width: 8ft 8in (2.64m)

Engine: GE V16-cyliner PowerHaul 616
Horsepower: 3,700hp (2,750kW)
Electrical Equipment: General Electric

Number	Depot	Pool	Livery	Owner	Operator	Name/Notes
70001	FD	DFGI	FLP	LTS	FLR	*PowerHaul*
70002	FD	DFGH	FLP	LTS	FLR	
70003	FD	DFGH	FLP	LTS	FLR	
70004	FD	DFGH	FLP	LTS	FLR	*The Coal Industry Society*
70005	FD	DFGH	FLP	LTS	FLR	
70006	FD	DFGH	FLP	LTS	FLR	
70007	FD	DFGI	FLP	LTS	FLR	
70008	FD	DFGI	FLP	LTS	FLR	
70009	FD	DFGI	FLP	LTS	FLR	
70010	FD	DFGH	FLP	LTS	FLR	
70011	FD	DFGH	FLP	LTS	FLR	
(70012	-	-	-	GE	-)	*Returned to General Electric, Erie, PA, USA*
70013	FD	DFGH	FLP	LTS	FLR	
70014	FD	DFGH	FLP	LTS	FLR	
70015	FD	DFGH	FLP	LTS	FLR	
70016	FD	DFGH	FLP	LTS	FLR	
70017	FD	DFGI	FLP	LTS	FLR	
70018	FD	DHLT	FLP	LTS	FLR	
70019	FD	DHLT	FLP	LTS	FLR	*Due for delivery Autumn 2012*
70020	FD	DHLT	FLP	LTS	FLR	*Due for delivery Autumn 2012*

Above: *The latest locos to be delivered to Freightliner are the Class 70s, built by General Electric in the United States. Delivery has been protracted and by the end of 2011 only 11 locos were in traffic in the UK. The locos are used on a mix of Heavy Haul and Intermodal duties but performance has not been as good as expected. No. 70006 is illustrated.* **Antony Christie**

■ *Originally 30 locomotives were ordered in 2007 for delivery in 2009-10. Eighteen locos were delivered by February 2012; a further batch are due in winter 2012.*

Class 86/5 & 86/6

Vehicle Length: 58ft 6in (17.83m)
Height: 13ft 0⅝in (3.97m)
Width: 8ft 8¼in (2.64m)

Power Collection: 25kV ac overhead
Horsepower: 5,900hp (4,400kW)
Electrical Equipment: GEC

Number		Depot	Pool	Livery	Owner	Operator
86501	(86608/86408)	FE	DFGC	FLR	FLR	FLR
86604	(86404)	FE	DFNC	FLR	FLR	FLR
86605	(86405)	FE	DFNC	FLR	FLR	FLR
86607	(86407)	FE	DFNC	FLR	FLR	FLR
86609	(86409)	FE	DFNC	FLR	PTR	FLR

86610	(86410)	FE	DFNC	FLR	PTR	FLR
86612	(86412)	FE	DFNC	FLR	PTR	FLR
86613	(86413)	FE	DFNC	FLR	PTR	FLR
86614(S)	(86414)	CP	DHLT	FLR	PTR	FLR
86621(S)	(86421)	FE	DHLT	FLR	PTR	FLR
86622	(86422)	FE	DFNC	FLP	PTR	FLR
86627	(86427)	FE	DFNC	FLR	PTR	FLR
86628	(86428)	FE	DFNC	FLR	PTR	FLR
86632	(86432)	FE	DFNC	FLR	PTR	FLR
86637	(86437)	FE	DFNC	FLP	PTR	FLR
86638	(86438)	FE	DFNC	FLR	PTR	FLR
86639	(86439)	FE	DFNC	FLR	PTR	FLR

Below: *A total of 17 Class 86s are operated by Freightliner, including the unique Class 86/5. Here No. 86501 is seen double-heading Class 90 No. 90045 south of Rugby. The Class 90 sports the latest PowerHaul livery derived from the Class 70 colour scheme.* **Darren Wetherall**

Class 90

Vehicle Length: 61ft 6in (18.74m)	Power Collection: 25kV ac overhead
Height: 13ft 0¼in (3.96m)	Horsepower: 7,860hp (5,860kW)
Width: 9ft 0in (2.74m)	Electrical Equipment: GEC

Number	Depot	Pool	Livery	Owner	Operator
90016	CP	DFLC	FLR	PTR	FLR
90041	CP	DFLC	FLR	PTR	FLR
90042(S)	CP	DFLC	FLY	PTR	-
90043	CP	DFLC	FLY	PTR	FLR
90044	CP	DFLC	FLY	PTR	FLR
90045	CP	DFLC	FLP	PTR	FLR
90046	CP	DFLC	FLR	PTR	FLR
90047	CP	DFLC	FLY	PTR	FLR
90048	CP	DFLC	FLR	PTR	FLR
90049	CP	DFLC	FLP	PTR	FLR

Name applied

90043 *Freightliner Coatbridge*

Above: *Ten Class 90s owned by Porterbrook are operated by Freightliner and are used alongside the Class 86s on North West to Felixstowe workings via the North London line. Freightliner grey-liveried No. 90047 is seen heading towards the North London line at Stratford with a train from Felixstowe.* **CJM**

Mendip Rail

Address:	✉ Torr Works, East Cranmore, Shepton Mallet, Somerset, BA4 5SQ
	📧 info@mendip-rail.co.uk
	☎ 01749 880672
	ⓘ www.mendip-rail.co.uk
Managing Director:	Alan Taylor
Depots:	Merehead (MD), Whatley (WH)
Parent Company:	Aggregate Industries and Hanson

Class 08

Vehicle Length: 29ft 3in (8.91m)
Height: 12ft 8⅝in (3.87m)
Width: 8ft 6in (2.59m)
Engine: English Electric 6K
Horsepower: 400hp (298kW)
Electrical Equipment: English Electric

Number	Depot	Pool	Livery	Owner	Operator						
08643	MD	MBDL	GRN	FOS	MRL	08652	WH	MBDL	HAN	HAN	MRL
08650	MD	MBDL	FOS	FOS	MRL	08731	MD	MBDL	BLU	FOS	MRL
						08947	WH	MBDL	BLU	FOS	MRL

Class 59/0

Vehicle Length: 70ft 0½in (21.34m)
Height: 12ft 10in (3.91m)
Width: 8ft 8¼in (2.65m)
Engine: EMD 16-645 E3C
Horsepower: 3,000hp (2,462kW)
Electrical Equipment: EMD

Number	Depot	Pool	Livery	Owner	Operator	Name	
59001	MD	XYPO	AGI	FOS	MRL	*Yeoman Endeavour*	■ Loco No. 59003 Yeoman
59002	MD	XYPO	FOS	FOS	MRL	*Alan J Day*	Highlander, *originally used by Foster*
59003	-	-	HHP	HHP	HHP	*Yeoman Highlander*	*Yeoman in the UK, is now owned*
59004	MD	XYPO	FOS	FOS	MRL	*Paul A Hammond*	*and operated by Heavy Haul Power*
59005	MD	XYPO	AGI	FOS	MRL	*Kenneth J Painter*	*International and based in Germany.*

Above: *Mendip Rail are the umbrella organisation responsible for operating the eight Class 59s owned by Aggregate Industries (Yeoman) and Hanson. Maintained at Merehead, the locos are the backbone of the Mendip aggregate traffic. Foster Yeoman No. 59002 is seen on the turntable at Minehead during the 2011 celebrations to mark 25 years of '59' operation in the UK.* **CJM**

Class 59/1

Number	Depot	Pool	Livery	Owner	Operator	Name
59101	MD	XYPA	HAN	HAN	MRL	*Village of Whatley*
59102	MD	XYPA	HAN	HAN	MRL	*Village of Chantry*
59103	MD	XYPA	HAN	HAN	MRL	*Village of Mells*
59104	MD	XYPA	HAN	HAN	MRL	*Village of Great Elm*

Below: *Class 59/1 No. 59102 is seen at the head of a rake of high-capacity aggregate hoppers. The loco is painted in Hanson livery.* **Chris Perkins**

SW1001 'Switcher'

Vehicle Length: 40ft 6in (12.34m)	Engine: GM 8-645E
Height: 14ft 3in (4.34m)	Horsepower: 1,000hp (746kW)
Width: 10ft 0in (3.04m)	Electrical Equipment: EMD

Number	Depot	Pool	Livery	Owner	Operator	Name
44	MD	-	FOS	FOS	MRL	*Western Yeoman II*
120	WH	-	HAN	HAN	MRL	

Right: *Long before the Class 59s were ordered by Foster Yeoman, the company invested in a US yard switcher for use at Merehead. It was a modified version of a production SW1001 switcher built by General Motors. The loco is still in traffic at Merehead and carries the running number 44 and the name Western Yeoman II. Mendip Rail later purchased another switcher which is numbered 120 and used at Whatley.* **Brian Garrett**

Freight Operating Companies - Mendip Rail

Eurotunnel

Address (UK): ✉ The Channel Tunnel Group Ltd, UK Terminal,
                Ashford Road, Folkestone, CT18 8XX

        ✍ info@eurotunnel.com

        ✆ 01303 282222

        ⓘ www.eurotunnel.com

Chairman & CEO: Jacques Gounon
Depot: Coquelles, France (CO)

Shuttle

All locomotives are allocated to the Eurotunnel Maintenance Facility in Coquelles, France, but can be stabled and receive light repair at Cheriton terminal in the UK.

Class 9/0

Vehicle Length: 72ft 2in (22m)	Power Collection: 25kV ac overhead
Height: 13ft 9in (4.20m)	Horsepower: 7,720hp (5,760kW)
Width: 9ft 9in (3.01m)	Electrical Equipment: Brush

Original loco order, many now rebuilt and upgraded to Class 9/8.

9005	*Jessye Norman*	9018	*Wilhelmena Fernandez*	9033	*Montserrat Caballé*
9007	*Dame Joan Sutherland*	9022	*Dame Janet Baker*	9036	*Alain Fondary*
9011	*José Van Dam*	9024	*Gotthard 1882*	9037	*Gabriel Bacquier*
9013	*Maria Callas*	9026	*Furkatunnel 1982*		
9015	*Lötschberg 1913*	9029	*Thomas Allen*		

Left: *Unrefurbished Class 9/0 'shuttle' No. 9011* José Van Dam *is seen arriving at Cheriton, the UK Euro Tunnel terminal, on the rear of a shuttle service from France.*
Alisdair Anderson

Class 9/1

Class 9/1 locos presently under refurbishment and upgrade, being renumbered in 9711-9723 series.

Vehicle Length: 72ft 2in (22m)	Power Collection: 25kV ac overhead
Height: 13ft 9in (4.20m)	Horsepower: 7,720hp (5,760kW)
Width: 9ft 9in (3.01m)	Electrical Equipment: Brush

9105	9106	9108	9109	9110	9112

Class 9/7

Vehicle Length: 72ft 2in (22m)	Power Collection: 25kV ac overhead
Height: 13ft 9in (4.20m)	Horsepower: 9,387hp (7,000kW)
Width: 9ft 9in (3.01m)	Electrical Equipment: Brush

9701	9704	9707	9713 (9103)	9717 (9107)	9723 (9113)
9702	9705	9711 (9101)	9714 (9104)	9721 (9111)	
9703	9706	9712 (9102)	9716 (9106)	9722 (9112)	

Class 9/8

Rebuilt from Class 9/0 locos, 800 added to original running number on conversion.

Vehicle Length: 72ft 2in (22m)	Power Collection: 25kV ac overhead
Height: 13ft 9in (4.20m)	Horsepower: 9,387hp (7,000kW)
Width: 9ft 9in (3.01m)	Electrical Equipment: Brush

9801	*Lesley Garrett*	9808	*Elisabeth Soderstrom*	9816	*Willard White*
9802	*Stuart Burrows*	9809	*François Pollet*	9817	*José Carreras*
9803	*Benjamin Luxon*	9810	*Jean-Philippe Courtis*	9819	*Maria Ewing*
9804	*Victoria de Los Angeles*	9812	*Luciano Pavarotti*	9820	*Nicolai Ghiaurov*
9806	*Régine Crespin*	9814(S)	*Lucia Popp*	9821	*Teresa Berganza*

9823	Dame Elisabeth Legge-Schwarzkopf	9828	Dame Kiri Te Kanawa	9835	Nicolai Gedda
9825		9831		9838	Hildegard Behrens
9827	Barbara Hendricks	9832	Renata Tebaldi	9840	
		9834	Mirella Freni		

Right: *Class 9/8 'shuttle' No. 9812 Luciano Pavarotti arrives at the UK Euro Tunnel terminal at Cheriton with a car shuttle from France.* **Alisdair Anderson**

MaK DE1004

Vehicle Length: 54ft 2in (16.50m) Diesel Engine: MTU 12V396tc Horsepower: 1,260hp (939.5kW) Electrical Equipment: BBC

0001 (21901)	0003 (21903)	0005 (21905)	0007 (21907) [6457]
0002 (21902)	0004 (21904)	0006 (21906) [6456]	

Hunslet/Schöma

Diesel Engine: Deutz Horsepower: 200hp (270kW) Mechanical Equipment: Hunslet

0031	Frances	0034	Amanda	0037	Lydie	0040	Jill
0032	Elisabeth	0035	Mary	0038	Jenny	0041	Kim
0033	Silke	0036	Lawrence	0039	Pacita	0042	Nicole

Above: *Originally built by Hunslet and rebuilt by Schöma in 1994 for use with Eurotunnel as engineering traction for terminal and tunnel use, No. 0041, at one time named* Kim, *is seen at Cheriton, Folkestone in early 2011.* **Bob Darvill**

Network Rail

Intrastructure Companies - Network Rail

Address: ✉ Kings Place, 90 York Way, London, N1 9AG

✎ enquiries@networkrail.co.uk

✆ Helpline: 08457 114141, Switchboard: 0203 356 9595

ⓘ www.networkrail.co.uk

Chief Executive: David Higgins **Director Operations:** Robin Gisby

Depots: Heaton (HT), Barrow Hill (BH), Derby (DF), Rugby (RU), Eastleigh (ZG)

Class 08

Vehicle Length: 29ft 3in (8.91m)	Engine: English Electric 6K	
Height: 12ft 8⅝sin (3.87m)	Horsepower: 400hp (298kW)	
Width: 8ft 6in (2.59m)	Electrical Equipment: English Electric	

Number	Depot	Pool	Livery	Owner	Operator						
08417	DF	QADD	NRL	NRL	NRL	08956	DF	QADD	BLU	NRL	NRL

Left: Network Rail own just two Class 08s. No. 08417 (illustrated) was in late 2011 based at the Railway Technical Centre (RTC), Derby where it was used to form and remarshal test train stock. The loco is painted in all-over Network Rail yellow and has wasp ends. **Antony Christie**

Class 31/1 & 31/4

Vehicle Length: 56ft 9in (17.29m)	Engine: English Electric 12SVT	
Height: 12ft 7in (3.91m)	Horsepower: 1,470hp (1,097kW)	
Width: 8ft 9in (2.65m)	Electrical Equipment: Brush	
31/4 Fitted with Electric Train Heat		

Number	Depot	Pool	Livery	Owner	Operator						
31105	DF	QADD	NRL	NRL	NRL	31285	DF	QADD	NRL	NRL	NRL
31233	DF	QADD	NRL	NRL	NRL	31465*	DF	QADD	NRL	NRL	NRL
						* Previously numbered 31565, 31213					

Left: Network Rail own and operate a fleet of four Class 31s for powering test train formations. All are based at the RTC, Derby. The locos have received some modifications from their normal traffic days; this mainly involves front lights and mounting brackets for extra lights or camera equipment. With No. 31233 propelling from the rear, Network Rail's DBSO No. 9703 heads the 4Z08 22.49 Bristol Barton Hill to Derby RTC working past Northway, to the south of Worcester. **John Stretton**

Class 43

Vehicle Length: 58ft 5in (18.80m)			Engine: MTU 16V4000 R31R			
Height: 12ft 10in (3.90m)			Horsepower: 2,250hp (1,680kW)			
Width: 8ft 11in (2.73m)			Electrical Equipment: Brush			

Number	Depot	Pool	Livery	Owner	Operator	Name
43013	HT	QCAR	NRL	PTR	NRL	
43014	HT	QCAR	NRL	PTR	NRL	
43062	HT	QCAR	NRL	PTR	NRL	John Armitt

Right: *Three HST power cars are owned by Porterbrook Leasing and used by Network Rail to operate the New Measurement Train, which, formed of Mk3 stock, operates over most main lines in the UK on a timetabled basis to review track condition. Depending on the tests being conducted, the train's formation can be varied. Showing its recently acquired roof line headlight, No. 43013 passes Totnes on 25 May 2011 while in charge of a Plymouth to Paddington test run.* **Nathan Williamson**

Class 57/3

Vehicle Length: 63ft 6in (19.38m)			Engine: EMD 645-12F3B
Height: 12ft 10½in (3.91m)			Horsepower: 2,750hp (2,051kW)
Width: 9ft 2in (2.79m)			Electrical Equipment: Brush

Number	Depot	Pool	Livery	Owner	Operator
57301 (47845)	ZG	QADD	NRL	PBR	NRL
57303 (47705)	ZG	QADD	NRL	PBR	NRL
57305 (47822)	ZG	QADD	NRL	PBR	NRL
57306 (47814)	ZG	QADD	NRL	PBR	NRL
57310 (47831)	ZG	QADD	NRL	PBR	NRL
57312 (47330)	ZG	QADD	NRL	PBR	NRL

Right: *The first of the Network Rail modified Class 57/3s emerged from Knights Rail Services, Eastleigh in October 2011 ready for the winter period when the '57s' were deployed on snow and ice prevention and 'Thunderbird' duties. No. 57312 is seen at Knights Rail, Eastleigh.* **Carl Watson**

Class 73/1

Vehicle Length: 53ft 8in (16.35m)		Power: 750V dc third rail or English Electric 6K
Height: 12ft 5⅜in (3.79m)		Horsepower: electric - 1,600hp (1,193kW)
Width: 8ft 8in (2.64m)		Horsepower: diesel - 600hp (447kW)
		Electrical Equipment: English Electric

Number	Depot	Pool	Livery	Owner	Operator
73138	DF	QADD	NRL	NRL	NRL

Right: *One Class 73/1 is currently on the books of Network Rail, and is usually deployed powering test trains involving operation over third rail electrified areas. The loco's 600hp diesel engine is used to power the train away from the juice between Derby and test sites. In this view the loco is seen on the Midland Main Line at East Hyde, showing its revised front end equipment.* **Tim Easter**

Infrastructure Companies

Network Rail

Class 86/9

Vehicle Length: 58ft 6in (17.83m) — Power Collection: 25kV ac overhead
Height: 13ft 0⅝in (3.97m) — Horsepower: 2,950hp (2,200kW)
Width: 8ft 8¼in (2.64m) — Electrical Equipment: GEC

Number		Depot	Pool	Livery	Owner	Operator	Name
86901	(86253)	ZA	QACL	NRL	NRL	NRL	*Chief Engineer*
86902	(86210)	ZA	QACL	NRL	NRL	NRL	*Rail Vehicle Engineering*

Class 97/3 & 37

Vehicle Length: 61ft 6in (18.74m) — Engine: English Electric 12CSVT
Height: 13ft 0¼in (3.96m) — Horsepower: 1,750hp (1,304kW)
Width: 8ft 11⅝in (2.73m) — Electrical Equipment: English Electric

Number		Depot	Pool	Livery	Owner	Operator	Name
37198		BH	MBDL	NRL	NRL	NRL	
97301	(37100)	ZA	QETS	NRL	NRL	NRL	
97302	(37170)	ZA	QETS	NRL	NRL	NRL	
97303	(37178)	ZA	QETS	NRL	NRL	NRL	
97304	(37217)	ZA	QETS	NRL	NRL	NRL	*John Tiley*

Left: *Five Class 37s are used by Network Rail, four of these being classified as Class 97/3 and have been used in the development of ERTMS cab signalling on the Cambrian Line. When not required for this work the locos can be seen powering any other Network Rail service, including autumn Rail Head Treatment Trains, track test trains or route training. No. 97301 is seen at Exeter.*
Nathan Williamson

Class 313/2

Vehicle Length: (Driving) 64ft 11½in (20.75m) — Width: 9ft 3in (2.82m)
(Inter) 65ft 4¼in (19.92m) — Horsepower: 880hp (656kW)
Height: 11ft 9in (3.58m) — Seats (total/car): 202S, 66S/70S/66S

Great Northern Route - ERTMS development unit

Number	Formation DMSO+PTSO+BDMSO	Depot	Livery	Owner	Operator
313220 (313120)	62548+71232+61612	-	-	NRL	NRL

Class 950

Vehicle Length: 64ft 9¾in (19.74m) — Engine: 1 x NT855R5 of 285hp per vehicle
Height: 12ft 4½in (3.77m) — Horsepower: 570hp (425kW)
Width: 9ft 3⅛in (2.82m) — Seats (total/car): 124S, 59S/65S

Number	Formation	Depot	Livery	Owner	Operator	Note
950001	999600+999601	ZA	NRL	NRL	NRL	Track assessment train (Class 150 outline)

Left: *The Class 150 outline track test train is frequently seen throughout the Network Rail system, visiting most parts of the country and branch lines at least once a year. All test equipment is housed on one coach (leading in illustration) and the other vehicle is basically a DMS. Note the two large forward-facing lights aimed towards the track in this view of the set near Dainton.* **Antony Christie**

De-Icing Cars

Vehicle Length: 66ft 4in (20.22m)
Height: 12ft 4in (3.75m)
Width: 9ft 2in (2.82m)

Horsepower: 500hp (370kW)
Seats (total/car): None

Number	Vehicle	Depot	Livery	Owner	Operator	Notes
489102	68501 (977975)	TN	NRL	NRL	NRL	De-icing vehicle modified from Class 489 DMBS
489105	68504	TN	NRL	NRL	GBR	De-icing vehicle modified from Class 489 DMBS
489106	68505	TN	NRL	NRL	GBR	De-icing vehicle modified from Class 489 DMBS
489109	68508 (977976)	TN	NRL	NRL	NRL	De-icing vehicle modified from Class 489 DMBS

Right: *Four former Gatwick Express GLV vehicles, originally modified from HAP power cars, are operated by Network Rail for third rail de-icing duties. Normally based at Tonbridge, the vehicles are operated by GBRf and are generally marshalled either end of a Class 73. In this view at Folkestone, de-icing cars 68505, 68504 and 68508 sandwich ED No. 73204.*
Brian Stephenson

Hauled Stock

Royal Train

Mk2
Vehicle Length: 66ft 0in (20.11m)

Height: 12ft 9½in (3.89m)
Width: 9ft 3in (2.81m)

Mk 3
Vehicle Length: 75ft 0in (22.86m)

Height: 12ft 9in (3.88m)
Width: 8ft 11in (2.71m)

Number		Type	Depot	Livery	Operator	Use
2903	(11001)	AT5G	ZN	ROY	NRL/DBS	HM The Queen's Saloon
2904	(12001)	AT5G	ZN	ROY	NRL/DBS	HRH The Duke of Edinburgh's Saloon
2915	(10735)	AT5G	ZN	ROY	NRL/DBS	Royal Household Sleeping Coach
2916	(40512)	AT5G	ZN	ROY	NRL/DBS	HRH The Prince of Wales's Dining Coach
2917	(40514)	AT5G	ZN	ROY	NRL/DBS	Kitchen Car and Royal Household Dining Coach
2918	(40515)	AT5G	ZN	ROY	NRL/DBS	Royal Household Coach
2919	(40518)	AT5G	ZN	ROY	NRL/DBS	Royal Household Coach
2920	(17109)	AT5B	ZN	ROY	NRL/DBS	Generator Coach and Household Sleeping Coach
2921	(17107)	AT5B	ZN	ROY	NRL/DBS	Brake, Coffin Carrier and Household Accommodation
2922		AT5G	ZN	ROY	NRL/DBS	HRH The Prince of Wales's Sleeping Coach
2923		AT5G	ZN	ROY	NRL/DBS	Royal Passenger Saloon

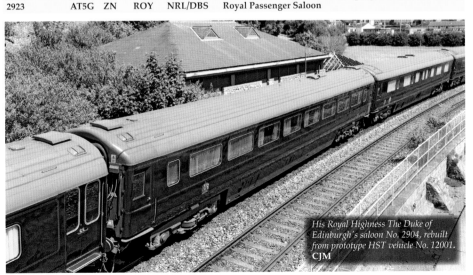

His Royal Highness The Duke of Edinburgh's saloon No. 2904, rebuilt from prototype HST vehicle No. 12001.
CJM

Network Rail

Hauled Stock

Number		Type	Depot	Livery	Operator	Use
1205	(6348)	AJIF/RFO	ZA	VIR	NRL	Out of use
1256	(3296)	AJIF/RFO	ZA	NRL	NRL	Special vehicle
5981		AC2F/TSO	ZA	NRL	NRL	Special vehicle
6260	(92116)	AX51/GEN	ZA	RTK	NRL/LUL	Generator
6261	(92988)	AX51/GEN	ZA	NRL	NRL	Generator
6262	(92928)	AX51/GEN	ZA(S)	NRL	NRL	Generator
6263	(92961)	AX51/GEN	ZA	NRL	NRL	Generator
6264	(92923)	AX51/GEN	ZA	NRL	NRL	Generator
9481		AE2D/BSO	ZA	NRL	NRL	Radio Survey coach
9701	(9528)	AF2F/DBSO	ZA	NRL	NRL	Remote driving car (Mentor train)
9702	(9510)	AF2F/DBSO	ZA	NRL	NRL	Remote driving car
9703	(9517)	AF2F/DBSO	ZA	NRL	NRL	Remote driving car
9708	(9530)	AF2F/DBSO	ZA	NRL	NRL	Remote driving car (Structure Gauging)
9714	(9536)	AF2F/DBSO	ZA	NRL	NRL	Remote driving car
62384		MBS	ZA	NRL	NRL	Ultrasonic test car (under conversion)
72612	(6156)	Mk2f/TSO	ZA	NRL	NRL	Brake force runner
72616	(6007)	Mk2f/TSO	ZA	NRL	NRL	Brake force runner
72630	(6094)	Mk2f/TSO	ZA	NRL	NRL	Brake force runner
72631	(6096)	Mk2f/TSO	ZA	NRL	NRL	Brake force runner
72639	(6070)	Mk2f/TSO	ZA	NRL	NRL	Brake force runner
82115		MK3/DVT	ZA	VIR	NRL	Driving Van Trailer
92114	(81443)	Mk1/BG	ZA	NRL	NRL	Special vehicle
92939	(92039)	Mk1/BG	ZA	INT	NRL	Special vehicle
99666	(3250)	Mk2e/FO	ZA	NRL	NRL	Ultrasonic Test Train
971001	(94150)	Mk1/NKA	BS	NRL	NRL	Tool Van
971002	(94190)	Mk1/NKA	WT	NRL	NRL	Tool Van
971003	(94191)	Mk1/NKA	BS	NRL	NRL	Tool Van
971004	(94168)	Mk1/NKA	KY	NRL	NRL	Tool Van
975025	(60755)	6B Buffet	ZA	GRN	NRL	Control Inspection Saloon *Caroline*
975081	(35313)	Mk1/BSK	ZA	NRL	NRL	Structure Gauging Train
975091	(34615)	Mk1/BSK	ZA	NRL	NRL	Overhead line test coach - *Mentor*
975280	(21263)	Mk1/BCK	ZA	NRL	NRL	Staff coach
975464	(35171)	Mk1/BSK	IS	NRL	NRL	Snowblower coach *Ptarmigan*
975486	(34100)	Mk1/BSK	IS	NRL	NRL	Snowblower coach *Polar Bear*
975814	(41000)	HST/TF	EC	NRL	NRL	NMT Conference coach
975984	(40000)	HST/TRUB	EC	NRL	NRL	NMT Lecture coach
977337	(9395)	Mk2/BSO	ZA	NRL	NRL	Track recording - Staff coach
977868	(5846)	Mk2e/TSO	ZA	NRL	NRL	Radio Survey coach
977869	(5858)	Mk2e/TSO	ZA	NRL	NRL	Radio Survey coach
977969	(14112)	Mk2/BFK	ZA	NRL	NRL	Staff coach (Former Royal Saloon 2906)
977974	(5854)	Mk2e/TSO	ZA	NRL	NRL	Laboratory coach (Owned by Delta Rail)
977983	(3407)	Mk2f/FO	ZA	NRL	NRL	Hot Box Detection coach
977984	(40501)	HST/TRFK	EC	NRL	NRL	NMT Staff coach
977985	(6019)	Mk2f/TSO	ZA	NRL	NRL	Structure Gauging Train
977986	(3189)	Mk2d/FO	ZA	NRL	NRL	Track Recording coach
977993	(44053)	HST/TGS	EC	NRL	NRL	NMT Overhead Line Test coach
977994	(44087)	HST/TGS	EC	NRL	NRL	NMT Recording coach

Left: *Originally Mk1 BSK No. 35313, this vehicle has been in departmental use for many years and has seen many roles, including at one time a driving control car. In recent years the vehicle has been used in the structure gauging train, coupled to the optical vehicle. One end of this vehicle is painted matt black to avoid 'flash' from the optical vehicle. No. 975081 is seen at Totnes.* **Nathan Williamson**

977995 (40719)	HST/TRFM	EC	NRL	NRL	NMT Generator coach
977996 (44062)	HST/TGS	EC	NRL	NRL	NMT Battery coach
977997 (72613)	Mk2f/TSO	ZA	NRL	NRL	Radio Survey Test Vehicle (originally TSO 6126)
999508	Saloon	ZA	NRL	NRL	Track Recording coach - UTU3
999550	Mk2	ZA	NRL	NRL	Track Recording coach (Purpose built)
999602 (62483)	Mk1/REP	ZA	NRL	SEC	Ultrasonic Test coach - UTU3
999605 (62482)	Mk1/REP	ZA	NRL	NRL	Ultrasonic Test coach - UTU2
999606 (62356)	Mk1/REP	ZA	NRL	NRL	Ultrasonic Test coach - UTU4

Right: In recent years several former Mk2 DBSOs have been taken over by Network Rail to operate at the remote end of test trains. Some have had specific modifications made to operate with selected trains. In this view, vehicle No. 9701 leads former inspection saloon No. 999508 and a Class 97/3 through Totnes.
Nathan Williamson

Snowploughs
Independent Drift Ploughs – ZZA

Number	Allocation
ADB965203	Tees
ADB965206	Doncaster
ADB965208	Inverness
ADB965209	Bristol Barton H
ADB965210	Tonbridge
ADB965211	Wigan
ADB965217	Mossend
ADB965219	Mossend
ADB965223	Margam
ADB965224	Carlisle
ADB965230	Carlisle
ADB965231	Bristol Barton H
ADB965232	Peterborough
ADB965233	Peterborough
ADB965234	Carlisle
ADB965235	Margam
ADB965236	Tonbridge

ADB965237	Wigan
ADB965240	Inverness
ADB965241	Doncaster
ADB965242	Tees
ADB965243	Mossend

Right: Twenty-two large independent drift ploughs are registered with Network Rail, stationed strategically around the country. No. ADB965242 is illustrated.
Antony Christie

Beilhack Patrol Ploughs (ex-Class 40 bogies) – ZZA

Number	Allocation
ADB965576	Mossend
ADB965577	Mossend
ADB965578	Carlisle
ADB965579	Carlisle
ADB965580	Wigan
ADB965581	Wigan
ADB966096	Doncaster
ADB866097	Doncaster
ADB966098	Peterborough
ADB966099	Peterborough

Above: *Five pairs of ex-Class 40 bogie snowploughs are also available to Network Rail. No. ADB965577 allocated to Mossend is illustrated.* **Antony Christie**

Beilhack Snow Blowers – ZWA

Number	Allocation		
ADB968500	Rutherglen	ADB968501	Rutherglen

Network Rail   ø Vehicles owned by Fastline are in the process of sale to new operators

Track Machines (On-Track Plant)

Plasser & Theurer DTS-62-N – Dynamic Track Stabiliser – ZWA

DR72201	Fastline ø	DR72208	Fastline ø	DR72213	Balfour Beatty
DR72203	Fastline ø	DR72211	Balfour Beatty		

Plasser & Theurer 09-16-CSM – Tamper/Liner – ZWA

DR73103	Colas	DR73105(S)	Colas

Plasser & Theurer 09-32-CSM – Tamper/Liner – ZWA

DR73106(S)	Fastline ø

Plasser & Theurer 09-32-RT – Tamper/Liner – ZWA

DR73108	*Tiger*	Amey

Plasser & Theurer 09-3X – Tamper/Liner – ZWA

DR73109		SB Rail	DR73110	*Peter White*	SB Rail

Plasser & Theurer 09-3X-D-RT – Tamper/Liner ZWA

DR73111	*Reading Panel 1965 - 2005*	Network Rail	DR73116	Network Rail
DR73113		Network Rail	DR73117	Network Rail
DR73114	*Ron Henderson*	Network Rail	DR73118	Network Rail
DR73115		Network Rail		

Above: *Plasser & Theurer 09-3X-D-RT tamper/liner No. DR73115 at Taunton.* **Nathan Williamson**

Plasser & Theurer 07-275 – Switch/Crossing Tamper – ZWA

DR73311	*Cyril Dryland*	Balfour Beatty	DR73314(S)	VolkerRail

Plasser & Theurer 07-32 – Duomatic Tamper/Liner – ZWA

DR73404(S)	Fastline ø	DR73424	Balfour Beatty	DR73434	Balfour Beatty
DR73413(S)	Fastline ø	DR73428	J H Russell	DR73435(S)	Fastline ø
DR73423(S)	Fastline ø	DR73431(S)	Fastline ø		

Plasser & Theurer 08-16/90 – Tamper/Liner – ZWA

DR73502	Balfour Beatty	DR73503 (S)	Balfour Beatty

Plasser & Theurer 08-32U RT – Plain Line Tamper – ZWA

DR73803 *Alexander Graham Bell*   SBRail

Plasser & Theurer 08-16U RT – Plain Line Tamper – ZWA

DR73804 *James Watt* SBRail

Plasser & Theurer 08-16(32)U RT – Plain Line Tamper – ZWA

DR73805	Colas	DR73806 *Karine* Colas

Plasser & Theurer 08-275 – Switch/Crossing Tamper – ZWA

DR73902(S)		Fastline ø
DR73903(S)	*George Mullineux*	Fastline ø

Plasser & Theurer 08-4x4/4S - RT – Switch/Crossing Tamper – ZWA

DR73904	*Thomas Telford*	SBRail	DR73908		Colas
DR73905	*Eddie King*	Amey	DR73909	*Saturn*	Colas
DR73906	*Panther*	Amey	DR73910	*Jupiter*	Colas
DR73907		Colas			

Right: *Plasser & Theurer 08-4x4/4S - RT Switch and Crossing tamper No. DR73909 at Bristol. This image was recorded when the vehicle was operated by Carillion.* **Lee Martin**

Plasser & Theurer 08-16/4x4C - RT – Switch/Crossing Tamper – ZWA

DR73911 (S)	*Puma*	Amey	DR73913		Colas
DR73912 (S)	*Lynx*	Amey			

Right: *Plasser & Theurer 08-16/4x 44C-RT Switch and Crossing tamper No. DR73912 is seen at Totnes. This machine is currently stored.* **Nathan Williamson**

Plasser & Theurer 08-4x4S - RT – Switch/Crossing Tamper – ZWA

DR73914   *Robert McAlpine*   SBRail

Plasser & Theurer 08-16/4x4C - RT – Switch/Crossing Tamper – ZWA

DR73915	*William Arrol*	SBRail	DR73916	*First Engineering*	SBRail

Plasser & Theurer 08-4x4S - RT – Switch/Crossing Tamper – ZWA

DR73917	Balfour Beatty	DR93918	Balfour Beatty

Plasser & Theurer 08-16/4x4 C100 - RT – Tamper – ZWA

DR73919	Colas

Plasser & Theurer 08-16/4x4C80 - RT – Tamper – ZWA

DR73920	Amey	DR73922	*John Snowdon*	Amey
DR73921	Amey			

Left: *Plasser & Theurer 08-16/4x4C80-RT tamper operated by Amey, working over the West Coast Main Line.* **Antony Christie**

Plasser & Theurer 08-4x4S - RT – Switch/Crossing Tamper – ZWA

DR73923	*Mercury*	Colas

Plasser & Theurer 08-16/4x4C100 - RT – Tamper – ZWA

DR73924	*Atlas*	Colas	DR73927		Balfour Beatty
DR73925	*Europa*	Colas	DR73928		Balfour Beatty
DR73926	*Stephen Keith Blanchard*	Balfour Beatty			

Plasser & Theurer 08-4x4S - RT – Switch/Crossing Tamper – ZWA

DR73929	Colas	DR73930	Colas

Plasser & Theurer 08-16/4x4C100 - RT – Tamper – ZWA

DR73931	Colas

Left: *Colas Rail-operated Plasser & Theurer 08-16/4x4C100-RT tamper No. DR73931 passing Newport.* **CJM**

Plasser & Theurer 08-4x4/4S - RT – Switch/Crossing Tamper

DR73932	SBRail

Plasser & Theurer 08-16/4x4C100 - RT – Tamper – ZWA

DR73933	SBRail	DR73934	SB Rail

Right: *Displaying SB Rail white livery, Plasser & Theurer 08-16/4x4C100-RT tamper No. DR73933 is seen at Craigentinny.*
Jack Boskett

Plasser & Theurer 08-4x4/4S - RT – Switch/Crossing Tamper – ZWA

DR73935	Colas	DR73936	Colas

Plasser & Theurer 08-16/4x4C100 - RT – Tamper – ZWA

DR73937	Balfour Beatty	DR73938	Balfour Beatty	DR73939	Balfour Beatty

Plasser & Theurer 08-4x4/4S - RT – Switch/Crossing Tamper – ZWA

DR73940	SBRail	DR73941	SBRail	DR73942	Colas

Plasser & Theurer 08-16/4x4C100 - RT – Tamper – ZWA

DR73943	Balfour Beatty	DR73944	Balfour Beatty	DR73945	Balfour Beatty

Plasser & Theurer Euromat 08-4x4/4S – ZWA

DR73946	VolkerRail

Plasser & Theurer 08-4x4/4S - RT – Switch/Crossing Tamper ZWA

DR73947	Colas	DR73948	Colas

Plasser & Theurer 08-16/90 275 – Switch/Crossing Tamper – ZWA

DR75201	Balfour Beatty	DR75202	Balfour Beatty

Plasser & Theurer 08-16/90 SP-T – Switch/Crossing Tamper – ZWA

DR75203	MLP Maintenance

Plasser & Theurer 08-275ZW – Switch/Crossing Tamper – ZWY

DR75204	Trackwork

Right: *The unique Plasser & Theurer 08-275ZW switch and crossing tamper operated by Trackwork.*
Nathan Williamson

Matisa B45 Tamper – ZWA

DR75301	VolkerRail	DR75302	VolkerRail	DR75303	VolkerRail

Matisa B41UE Tamper – ZWA

DR75401	VolkerRail	DR75405	VolkerRail	DR75409	Balfour Beatty
DR75402	VolkerRail	DR75406	Colas	DR75410	Balfour Beatty
DR75403	VolkerRail	DR75407	Colas	DR75411	Balfour Beatty
DR75404	VolkerRail	DR75408	Balfour Beatty		

Infrastructure Companies - Network Rail

Left: Matisa B41UE tamper No. DR75405 is seen at Banbury painted in VolkerRail Plant blue, black and grey livery. **Antony Christie**

Matisa B66UC Tamper – ZWA

DR75501	Balfour Beatty	DR75502	Balfour Beatty

Plasser & Theurer RM74 – Ballast Cleaner – ZWB

DR76304(S)	Plasser	DR76318(S)	Plasser

Plasser & Theurer RM95RT – Ballast Cleaner – ZWA

DR76323	Network Rail	DR76324	Network Rail

Plasser & Theurer RM900RT Ballast Cleaner – ZWA / ZWQ

DR76501 (HOBC-1)	Network Rail	DR76503 (HOBC-3)	Network Rail
DR76502 (HOBC-2)	Network Rail		

Plasser & Theurer RM90 NR Ballast Cleaner – ZWA

DR76601	*Olwen*		Colas

Plasser & Theurer VM80 NR – ZWA

DR76701	Network Rail	DR76703	Network Rail	DR76711	Network Rail
DR76702	Network Rail	DR76710	Network Rail		

Matisa D75 Undercutter – ZWA

DR76750	Network Rail

Plasser & Theurer 09-16 CM NR – ZWA

DR76801	Network Rail

Plasser & Theurer AFM 2000 RT – Rail Finishing Machine – ZWA

DR77001	SBRail	DR77002	SBRail

Plasser & Theurer USP 5000C – Ballast Regulator – ZWA

DR77315(S)	Balfour Beatty	DR77322	Balfour Beatty	DR77336	Balfour Beatty
DR77316(S)	Balfour Beatty	DR77327	Colas		
DR77319	Colas	DR77335	Colas		

Matisa R24S – Ballast Regulator – ZWA

DR77801	VolkerRail	DR77802	VolkerRail

Left: Now operated by VolkerRail, but seen here in Grant Plant orange and blue livery, Matisa R24S ballast regulator No. DR77802 is pictured at Doncaster. **Lee Martin**

Infrastructure Companies – Network Rail

Plasser & Theurer USP 5000RT – Ballast Regulator – ZWA

DR77901		Colas	DR77906		Network Rail
DR77903	*Frank Jones*	Network Rail	DR77907		Network Rail
DR77904		Network Rail	DR77908*		SBRail
DR77905		Network Rail	* Previously DR77902		

Above: *Showing Colas Rail orange and yellow livery, Plasser & Theurer USP 5000RT ballast regulator No. DR77901 is viewed at Exeter St Davids Yard.* **CJM**

Plasser & Theurer Self-Propelled Heavy Duty Twin Jib Crane – YJB

DR78211	Network Rail	DR78216	Balfour Beatty	DR78221	Balfour Beatty
DR78212	Network Rail	DR78217	SB Rail	DR78222	Balfour Beatty
DR78213	VolkaRail	DR78218	Balfour Beatty	DR78223	Balfour Beatty
DR78215	SB Rail	DR78219	SB Rail	DR78224	Balfour Beatty

Right: *The major Balfour Beatty base for track machines is Ashford (Kent). Here Plasser & Theurer self-propelled heavy duty twin jib crane No. DR78222 is seen at work with its jibs raised.* **Antony Christie**

Cowens Sheldon Self-Propelled Heavy Duty Twin Jib Crane – YJB

DR78226	Colas	DR78231	(stored)	DR78235	Colas
DR78229	Network Rail	DR78234	(stored)	DR78237	(stored)

Donelli PD350 Single Line Track Relayer

DR78416	Balfour Beatty	GR5092	VolkerRail	DR78491	VolkerRail
DR78417	Balfour Beatty	DR78490	VolkerRail		

Harsco Track Technologies NTC Power Wagon – YJA

DR78701	Balfour Beatty	DR78702	Balfour Beatty

Infrastructure Companies

Network Rail

Matisa P95 Track Renewal Train – YJA

DR78801	Network Rail	DR78812	Network Rail	DR78831	Network Rail
DR78802	Network Rail	DR78821	Network Rail	DR78832	Network Rail
DR78811	Network Rail	DR78822	Network Rail		

Schweebau SPML15 – Rail Grinder – ZWA

DR79200	Loram

Loram/Barclay SPML17 – Rail Grinder – ZWA

DR79201	Loram

Left: *Built by Loram and re-engineered by Hunslet Barclay, rail grinder type SPML17 No. DR79201 is seen stabled at Eastleigh.* **Antony Christie**

Speno RPS 32-2 – Rail Grinder – ZWA

DR79221	Speno	DR79223	Speno	DR79225	Speno
DR79222	Speno	DR79224	Speno	DR79226	Speno

Loram C21 – Rail Grinder – ZWA

Set 01		Set 02		Set 03	
DR79231	Loram	DR79241	Loram	DR79251	Loram
DR79232	Loram	DR79242	Loram	DR79252	Loram
DR79233	Loram	DR79243	Loram	DR79253	Loram
DR79234	Loram	DR79244	Loram	DR79254	Loram
DR79235	Loram	DR79245	Loram	DR79255	Loram
DR79236	Loram	DR79246	Loram	DR79256	Loram
DR79237	Loram	DR79247 *Roger Smith*	Loram	DR79257	Loram

Harsco Track Technologies RGH-20C Switch/Crossing Rail Grinder – ZWA

DR79261 + DR79271	Network Rail	DR79264 + DR79274	Network Rail
DR79262 + DR79272	Network Rail	DR79265 + DR79275	Network Rail
DR79263 + DR79273	Network Rail	DR79266 + DR79276	Network Rail

State of the art Harsco Track Technologies RGH-20C rail grinder set Nos. DR79624 +DR79274 is shown while operating in the First Great Western area. **Antony Christie**

Pandrol Jackson – Stoneblower – YZA

DR80200	Network Rail	DR80205	Network Rail	DR80210(S)	Network Rail
DR80201(S)	Network Rail	DR80206	Network Rail	DR80211	Network Rail
DR80202(S)	Network Rail	DR80207	Network Rail	DR80212	Network Rail
DR80203(S)	Network Rail	DR80208	Network Rail		
DR80204	Network Rail	DR80209	Network Rail		

Harsco Track Technologies – Stoneblower – YZA

DR80213	Network Rail	DR80215	Network Rail	DR80217	Network Rail
DR80214	Network Rail	DR80216	Network Rail		

Harsco Track Technologies – Switch/Crossing Stoneblower – YZA

DR80301	*Stephen Cornish*	Network Rail	DR80303	Network Rail
DR80302		Network Rail		

Above: *Harsco Track Technologies general-purpose stoneblower No. DR80303 is seen at Westbury.* **Antony Christie**

Plasser & Theurer Heavy Duty Diesel Hydraulic Crane – YOB

DR81505	Balfour Beatty	DR81513	Balfour Beatty	DR81525	Balfour Beatty
DR81507	Balfour Beatty	DR51517	Balfour Beatty	DR81532	Balfour Beatty
DR81508	Balfour Beatty	DR81519	Balfour Beatty		
DR81511	Balfour Beatty	DR81522	Balfour Beatty		

Cowans Sheldon Heavy Duty Diesel Hydraulic Crane

DR81541	Corus	DR81545	Corus

Kirow KRC810UK 100 tonne Diesel Hydraulic Crane – ZOA

DR81601	*Nigel Chester*	VolkerRail	DR81602	Balfour Beatty

Kirow KRC1200UK 125 tonne Diesel Hydraulic Crane – ZOA

DR81611	*Malcolm L Pearce*	Balfour Beatty	DR81613	VolkerRail
DR81612		Colas		

Kirow KRC250UK Heavy Duty Diesel Hydraulic Crane – ZOA

DR81621	VolkerRail	DR81623	SBRail	DR81625	SBRail
DR81622	VolkerRail	DR81624	SBRail		

Infrastructure Companies - Network Rail

Network Rail

Plasser & Theurer 08-16 Universal Tamper/Liner

DR86101(S)	Balfour Beatty

Plasser & Theurer Loading Station

DR88101	Network Rail

Starfer Single Line Spoil Handling System Train

DR92201	Network Rail	DR92205	Network Rail	DR92209	Network Rail
DR92202	Network Rail	DR92206	Network Rail	DR92210	Network Rail
DR92203	Network Rail	DR92207	Network Rail	DR92211	Network Rail
DR92204	Network Rail	DR92208	Network Rail	DR92212	Network Rail

Skako Ballast Distribution Train – YDA 'Octopus'

DR92213	Network Rail	DR92217	Network Rail	DR92221	Network Rail
DR92214	Network Rail	DR92218	Network Rail	DR92222	Network Rail
DR92215	Network Rail	DR92219	Network Rail		
DR92216	Network Rail	DR92220	Network Rail		

Plasser & Theurer NFS-D Ballast Distribution Train Hopper – YDA

DR92223	Network Rail	DR92229	Network Rail	DR92235	Network Rail
DR92224	Network Rail	DR92230	Network Rail	DR92236	Network Rail
DR92225	Network Rail	DR92231	Network Rail	DR92237	Network Rail
DR92226	Network Rail	DR92232	Network Rail	DR92238	Network Rail
DR92227	Network Rail	DR92233	Network Rail	DR92239	Network Rail
DR92228	Network Rail	DR92234	Network Rail	DR92240	Network Rail

Plasser & Theurer MFS-D Ballast Distribution Train Hopper – YDA

DR92241	Network Rail	DR92246	Network Rail	DR92251	Network Rail
DR92242	Network Rail	DR92247	Network Rail	DR92252	Network Rail
DR92243	Network Rail	DR92248	Network Rail	DR92253	Network Rail
DR92244	Network Rail	DR92249	Network Rail	DR92254	Network Rail
DR92245	Network Rail	DR92250	Network Rail		

Plasser & Theurer MFS-SB Swivel Conveyer Wagon – YDA

DR92259	Network Rail	DR92261	Network Rail
DR92260	Network Rail	DR92262	Network Rail

Plasser & Theurer MFS-PW Single Line Handling Train Power Wagon – YOA

DR92263	Network Rail

Plasser & Theurer NB-PW Ballast Distribution Train Power Wagon – YOA

DR92264	Network Rail

Plasser & Theurer MFS-D Ballast Distribution Train Hopper – YDA

DR92265	Network Rail	DR92270	Network Rail	DR92275	Network Rail
DR92266	Network Rail	DR92271	Network Rail	DR92276	Network Rail
DR92267	Network Rail	DR92272	Network Rail	DR92277	Network Rail
DR92268	Network Rail	DR92273	Network Rail	DR92278	Network Rail
DR92269	Network Rail	DR92274	Network Rail	DR92279	Network Rail

Plasser & Theurer MFS-SB Swivel Conveyer Wagon – YDA

DR92280	Network Rail	DR92281	Network Rail

Plasser & Theurer MFS-A Materials Handling Train Interface Wagon – YDA

DR92282	Network Rail	DR92283	Network Rail

Plasser & Theurer PW-RT Materials Handling Train Power Wagon – YOA

DR92285	Network Rail

Plasser & Theurer NPW-RT Materials Handling Train Power Wagon – YOA

DR92286	Network Rail

Right: Plasser & Theurer NPW-RT materials handling train power wagon No. DR92286, working as part of the Taunton track renewals train, is seen at Westbury. **Antony Christie**

Plasser & Theurer MFS-SB Swivel Conveyer Wagon – YDA

DR92287	Network Rail	DR92290	Network Rail	DR92293	Network Rail
DR92288	Network Rail	DR92291	Network Rail	DR92294	Network Rail
DR92289	Network Rail	DR92292	Network Rail		

Plasser & Theurer MFS-D Ballast Distribution Train Hopper – YDA

DR92295	Network Rail	DR92307	Network Rail	DR92319	Network Rail
DR92296	Network Rail	DR92308	Network Rail	DR92320	Network Rail
DR92297	Network Rail	DR92309	Network Rail	DR92321	Network Rail
DR92298	Network Rail	DR92310	Network Rail	DR92322	Network Rail
DR92299	Network Rail	DR92311	Network Rail	DR92323	Network Rail
DR92300	Network Rail	DR92312	Network Rail	DR92324	Network Rail
DR92301	Network Rail	DR92313	Network Rail	DR92325	Network Rail
DR92302	Network Rail	DR92314	Network Rail	DR92326	Network Rail
DR92303	Network Rail	DR92315	Network Rail	DR92327	Network Rail
DR92304	Network Rail	DR92316	Network Rail	DR92328	Network Rail
DR92305	Network Rail	DR92317	Network Rail	DR92329	Network Rail
DR92306	Network Rail	DR92318	Network Rail	DR92330	Network Rail

Right: Plasser & Theurer MFS-D ballast distribution train hopper No. DR92308, working as part of the Taunton track renewals train, is seen at Westbury. **Antony Christie**

Plasser & Theurer PW-RT Materials Handling Train Power Wagon – YOA

DR92331	Network Rail

Plasser & Theurer NPW-RT Materials Handling Train Power Wagon – YOA

DR92332	Network Rail

Plasser & Theurer MFS-SB Swivel Conveyer Wagon – YDA

DR92333	Network Rail	DR92336	Network Rail	DR92339	Network Rail
DR92334	Network Rail	DR92337	Network Rail	DR92340	Network Rail
DR92335	Network Rail	DR92338	Network Rail		

Infrastructure Companies - Network Rail

Network Rail

Plasser & Theurer MFS-D Ballast Distribution Train Hopper – YDA

DR92341	Network Rail	DR92354	Network Rail	DR92367	Network Rail
DR92342	Network Rail	DR92355	Network Rail	DR92368	Network Rail
DR92343	Network Rail	DR92356	Network Rail	DR92369	Network Rail
DR92344	Network Rail	DR92357	Network Rail	DR92370	Network Rail
DR92345	Network Rail	DR92358	Network Rail	DR92371	Network Rail
DR92346	Network Rail	DR92359	Network Rail	DR92372	Network Rail
DR92347	Network Rail	DR92360	Network Rail	DR92373	Network Rail
DR92348	Network Rail	DR92361	Network Rail	DR92374	Network Rail
DR92349	Network Rail	DR92362	Network Rail	DR92375	Network Rail
DR92350	Network Rail	DR92363	Network Rail	DR92376	Network Rail
DR92351	Network Rail	DR92364	Network Rail	DR92377	Colas
DR92352	Network Rail	DR92365	Network Rail		
DR92353	Network Rail	DR92366	Network Rail		

Plasser & Theurer MFS-A Materials Handling Train Interface Wagon – YDA

DR92400	Colas

Plasser & Theurer PW-RT Materials Handling Train Power Wagon

DR92431	Network Rail

Plasser & Theurer NPW-RT Materials Handling Train Power Wagon

DR92432	Network Rail

Plasser & Theurer MFS-SB Swivel Conveyer Wagon

DR92433	Network Rail	DR92436	Network Rail	DR92439	Network Rail
DR92434	Network Rail	DR92437	Network Rail	DR92440	Network Rail
DR92435	Network Rail	DR92438	Network Rail		

Plasser & Theurer MFS-D Ballast Distribution Train Hopper – YDA

DR92441	Network Rail	DR92453	Network Rail	DR92465	Network Rail
DR92442	Network Rail	DR92454	Network Rail	DR92466	Network Rail
DR92443	Network Rail	DR92455	Network Rail	DR92467	Network Rail
DR92444	Network Rail	DR92456	Network Rail	DR92468	Network Rail
DR92445	Network Rail	DR92457	Network Rail	DR92469	Network Rail
DR92446	Network Rail	DR92458	Network Rail	DR92470	Network Rail
DR92447	Network Rail	DR92459	Network Rail	DR92471	Network Rail
DR92448	Network Rail	DR92460	Network Rail	DR92472	Network Rail
DR92449	Network Rail	DR92461	Network Rail	DR92473	Network Rail
DR92450	Network Rail	DR92462	Network Rail	DR92474	Network Rail
DR92451	Network Rail	DR92463	Network Rail	DR92475	Network Rail
DR92452	Network Rail	DR92464	Network Rail	DR92476	Network Rail

Sleeper Delivery Train – Generator Wagon – YFA

DR92501	Fastline ø	DR92502	Fastline ø	DR92503	Fastline ø

Twin Jib Rail Recovery Train 'Slinger' – YFA

DR92504	Fastline ø	DR92507	Fastline ø	DR92510	Fastline ø
DR92505	Fastline ø	DR92508	Fastline ø	DR92511	Fastline ø
DR92506	Fastline ø	DR92509	Fastline ø	DR92512	Fastline ø

Single Jib Rail Recovery Train 'Slinger' – YFA

DR92513	Fastline ø	DR92515	Fastline ø	DR92517	Fastline ø
DR92514	Fastline ø	DR92516	Fastline ø	DR92518	Fastline ø

Sleeper Delivery Train – Twin Crane 'Slinger' – YFA

DR92519	Fastline

Sleeper Delivery Train – Generator Wagon 'Slinger' – YFA

DR92520	Fastline ø	DR92522	Fastline ø	DR92524	Fastline ø
DR92521	Fastline ø	DR92523	Fastline ø	DR92525	Fastline ø

Sleeper Delivery Train – Twin Crane 'Slinger' – YFA

DR92526	Fastline ø	DR92529	Fastline ø	DR92532	Fastline ø
DR92527	Fastline ø	DR92530	Fastline ø		
DR92528	Fastline ø	DR92531	Fastline ø		

Sleeper Delivery Train – Generator Wagon 'Slinger' – YFA

DR92533	Fastline ø	DR92534	Fastline ø

Sleeper Delivery Train – Twin Crane 'Slinger' – YFA

DR92535	Fastline ø	DR92539	Fastline ø	DR92543	Fastline ø
DR92536	Fastline ø	DR92540	Fastline ø	DR92544	Fastline ø
DR92537	Fastline ø	DR92541	Fastline ø	DR92545	Fastline ø
DR92538	Fastline ø	DR92542	Fastline ø	DR92546	Fastline ø

Sleeper Delivery Train – Generator Wagon 'Slinger' – YFA

DR92547	Fastline ø	DR92548	Fastline ø	DR92549	Fastline ø

Sleeper Delivery Train – Twin Crane 'Slinger' – YFA

DR92550	Fastline ø	DR92558	Fastline ø	DR92566	Fastline ø
DR92551	Fastline ø	DR92559	Fastline ø	DR92567	Fastline ø
DR92552	Fastline ø	DR92560	Fastline ø	DR92568	Fastline ø
DR92553	Fastline ø	DR92561	Fastline ø	DR92569	Fastline ø
DR92554	Fastline ø	DR92562	Fastline ø	DR92570	Fastline ø
DR92555	Fastline ø	DR92563	Fastline ø	DR92571	Fastline ø
DR92556	Fastline ø	DR92564	Fastline ø		
DR92557	Fastline ø	DR92565	Fastline ø		

W H Davis Sleeper Wagons – YXA

DR92601	Network Rail	DR92623	Network Rail	DR92645	Network Rail
DR92602	Network Rail	DR92624	Network Rail	DR92646	Network Rail
DR92603	Network Rail	DR92625	Network Rail	DR92647	Network Rail
DR92604	Network Rail	DR92626	Network Rail	DR92648	Network Rail
DR92605	Network Rail	DR92627	Network Rail	DR92649	Network Rail
DR92606	Network Rail	DR92628	Network Rail	DR92650	Network Rail
DR92607	Network Rail	DR92629	Network Rail	DR92651	Network Rail
DR92608	Network Rail	DR92630	Network Rail	DR92652	Network Rail
DR92609	Network Rail	DR92631	Network Rail	DR92653	Network Rail
DR92610	Network Rail	DR92632	Network Rail	DR92654	Network Rail
DR92611	Network Rail	DR92633	Network Rail	DR92655	Network Rail
DR92612	Network Rail	DR92634	Network Rail	DR92656	Network Rail
DR92613	Network Rail	DR92635	Network Rail	DR92657	Network Rail
DR92614	Network Rail	DR92636	Network Rail	DR92658	Network Rail
DR92615	Network Rail	DR92637	Network Rail	DR92659	Network Rail
DR92616	Network Rail	DR92638	Network Rail	DR92660	Network Rail
DR92617	Network Rail	DR92639	Network Rail	DR92661	Network Rail
DR92618	Network Rail	DR92640	Network Rail	DR92662	Network Rail
DR92619	Network Rail	DR92641	Network Rail	DR92663	Network Rail
DR92620	Network Rail	DR92642	Network Rail	DR92664	Network Rail
DR92621	Network Rail	DR92643	Network Rail	DR92665	Network Rail
DR92622	Network Rail	DR92644	Network Rail		

Infrastructure Companies - Network Rail

Right: *YEA 'Perch' rail wagon DR979039 with rail loading brackets is seen at the rail disposal siding at Hackney Yard, Newton Abbot.*
Nathan Williamson

Network Rail

W H Davis Flat/Workshop/Barrier Wagons – YSA

DR92701	Network Rail	DR92703	Network Rail	DR92705	Network Rail
DR92702	Network Rail	DR92704	Network Rail	DR92706	Network Rail

Cowans Sheldon 75 tonne Diesel Hydraulic Recovery Crane – ZIA* ZIB¤

ARDC96710¤ Network Rail (BS)   ARDC96714* Network Rail (MG)
ARDC96713¤ Network Rail (SP)   ARDC96715¤ Network Rail (TO)

Network Rail 75 tonne recovery crane No. ARDC96714. This vehicle is classified as ZIA, while other cranes of the same type are classified as ZIB. **Antony Christie**

Eiv de Brieve DU94BA – TRAMM – ZWA

DR97001   High Speed 1 (HS1)

Windhoff Overhead Line – MPV – YXA

DR97011	High Speed 1 (HS1)	DR97013	High Speed 1 (HS1)
DR97012	High Speed 1 (HS1)	DR97014	High Speed 1 (HS1)

Windhoff Overhead Line – MPV – YXA

DR98001	Network Rail	DR98005	Network Rail	DR98009	Network Rail	DR98013	Network Rail
DR98002	Network Rail	DR98006	Network Rail	DR98010	Network Rail	DR98014	Network Rail
DR98003	Network Rail	DR98007	Network Rail	DR98011	Network Rail		
DR98004	Network Rail	DR98008	Network Rail	DR98012	Network Rail		

Above: *Four Windhoff MPVs are seen powering a Network Rail overhead cabling train near Atherstone, Warwickshire on 1 June 2011.* **Phil Grain**

Plasser & Theurer General Purpose Machine (GP-TRAMM) – ZWA

DR98210	Amey	DR98216	Balfour Beatty	DR98218	Balfour Beatty	DR98220	Balfour Beatty
DR98215	Balfour Beatty	DR98217	Balfour Beatty	DR98219	Balfour Beatty		

Above: *Plasser & Theurer GP-TRAMM with vehicle DR98218 nearest the camera is seen on the connection track between Yeovil Pen Mill and Yeovil Junction with the Balfour Beatty drain cleaning train.* **Antony Christie**

Geismar General Purpose Machine (GP-TRAMM)

DR98303	BAR

Geismar VMT860 PL/UM – ZWA

DR98305	Network Rail	DR98307	Colas
DR98306	Network Rail	DR98308	Colas

Windhoff Multi Purpose Vehicle (MPV) – YXA

Above: *A fleet of 32 Windhoff two-carriage Multi Purpose Vehicles (MPVs) are operated nationwide by Network Rail. The vehicles can carry various pods for different types of equipment, including rail head treatment and de-icing fluid. DR98911 and DR98961 are seen at Par.* **Stacey Thew**

Network Rail

DR98901 + DR98951	Network Rail	DR98912 + DR98962	Network Rail	DR98923 + DR98973	Network Rail
DR98902 + DR98952	Network Rail	DR98913 + DR98963	Network Rail	DR98924 + DR98974	Network Rail
DR98903 + DR98953	Network Rail	DR98914 + DR98964	Network Rail	DR98925 + DR98975	Network Rail
DR98904 + DR98954	Network Rail	DR98915 + DR98965	Network Rail	DR98926 + DR98976	Network Rail
DR98905 + DR98955	Network Rail	DR98916 + DR98966	Network Rail	DR98927 + DR98977	Network Rail
DR98906 + DR98956	Network Rail	DR98917 + DR98967	Network Rail	DR98928 + DR98978	Network Rail
DR98907 + DR98957	Network Rail	DR98918 + DR98968	Network Rail	DR98929 + DR98979	Network Rail
DR98908 + DR98958	Network Rail	DR98919 + DR98969	Network Rail	DR98930 + DR98980	Network Rail
DR98909 + DR98959	Network Rail	DR98920 + DR98970	Network Rail	DR98931 + DR98981	Network Rail
DR98910 + DR98960	Network Rail	DR98921 + DR98971	Network Rail	DR98932 + DR98982	Network Rail
DR98911 + DR98961	Network Rail	DR98922 + DR98972	Network Rail		

Rail Wagon – YEA 'Perch'

DR979001	Network Rail	DR979035	Network Rail	DR979069	Network Rail	DR979103	Network Rail
DR979002	Network Rail	DR979036	Network Rail	DR979070	Network Rail	DR979104	Network Rail
DR979003	Network Rail	DR979037	Network Rail	DR979071	Network Rail	DR979105	Network Rail
DR979004	Network Rail	DR979038	Network Rail	DR979072	Network Rail	DR979106	Network Rail
DR979005	Network Rail	DR979039	Network Rail	DR979073	Network Rail	DR979107	Network Rail
DR979006	Network Rail	DR979040	Network Rail	DR979074	Network Rail	DR979108	Network Rail
DR979007	Network Rail	DR979041	Network Rail	DR979075	Network Rail	DR979109	Network Rail
DR979008	Network Rail	DR979042	Network Rail	DR979076	Network Rail	DR979110	Network Rail
DR979009	Network Rail	DR979043	Network Rail	DR979077	Network Rail	DR979111	Network Rail
DR979010	Network Rail	DR979044	Network Rail	DR979078	Network Rail	DR979112	Network Rail
DR979011	Network Rail	DR979045	Network Rail	DR979079	Network Rail	DR979113	Network Rail
DR979012	Network Rail	DR979046	Network Rail	DR979080	Network Rail	DR979114	Network Rail
DR979013	Network Rail	DR979047	Network Rail	DR979081	Network Rail	DR979115	Network Rail
DR979014	Network Rail	DR979048	Network Rail	DR979082	Network Rail	DR979116	Network Rail
DR979015	Network Rail	DR979049	Network Rail	DR979083	Network Rail	DR979117	Network Rail
DR979016	Network Rail	DR979050	Network Rail	DR979084	Network Rail	DR979118	Network Rail
DR979017	Network Rail	DR979051	Network Rail	DR979085	Network Rail	DR979119	Network Rail
DR979018	Network Rail	DR979052	Network Rail	DR979086	Network Rail	DR979120	Network Rail
DR979019	Network Rail	DR979053	Network Rail	DR979087	Network Rail	DR979121	Network Rail
DR979020	Network Rail	DR979054	Network Rail	DR979088	Network Rail	DR979122	Network Rail
DR979021	Network Rail	DR979055	Network Rail	DR979089	Network Rail	DR979123	Network Rail
DR979022	Network Rail	DR979056	Network Rail	DR979090	Network Rail	DR979124	Network Rail
DR979023	Network Rail	DR979057	Network Rail	DR979091	Network Rail	DR979125	Network Rail
DR979024	Network Rail	DR979058	Network Rail	DR979092	Network Rail	DR979126	Network Rail
DR979025	Network Rail	DR979059	Network Rail	DR979093	Network Rail	DR979127	Network Rail
DR979026	Network Rail	DR979060	Network Rail	DR979094	Network Rail	DR979128	Network Rail
DR979027	Network Rail	DR979061	Network Rail	DR979095	Network Rail	DR979129	Network Rail
DR979028	Network Rail	DR979062	Network Rail	DR979096	Network Rail	DR979130	Network Rail
DR979029	Network Rail	DR979063	Network Rail	DR979097	Network Rail	DR979131	Network Rail
DR979030	Network Rail	DR979064	Network Rail	DR979098	Network Rail	DR979132	Network Rail
DR979031	Network Rail	DR979065	Network Rail	DR979099	Network Rail	DR979133	Network Rail
DR979032	Network Rail	DR979066	Network Rail	DR979100	Network Rail	DR979134	Network Rail
DR979033	Network Rail	DR979067	Network Rail	DR979101	Network Rail		
DR979034	Network Rail	DR979068	Network Rail	DR979102	Network Rail		

Continuous Welded Rail Clamping Wagon – YEA 'Perch'

DR979409	Network Rail	DR979412	Network Rail	DR979415	Network Rail

Continuous Welded Rail End of Train Wagon – YEA 'Porpoise'

DR979505	Network Rail	DR979509	Network Rail	DR979513	Network Rail	DR979515	Network Rail
DR979506	Network Rail	DR979511	Network Rail	DR979514	Network Rail		

Continuous Welded Rail 'Chute' Wagon – YEA 'Porpoise'

DR979500	Network Rail	DR979502	Network Rail	DR979507	Network Rail	DR979510	Network Rail
DR979501	Network Rail	DR979503	Network Rail	DR979508	Network Rail	DR979512	Network Rail

Continuous Welded Rail Gantry Wagon – YEA 'Perch'

DR979604	Network Rail	DR979611	Network Rail	DR979614	Network Rail
DR979607	Network Rail	DR979612	Network Rail		
DR979609	Network Rail	DR979613	Network Rail		

Right: *Continuous welded rail end of train wagon No. DR979515 is seen in a rail formation passing Langstone Rock.* **Antony Christie**

Below: *'Perch' rail wagon DR979112 formed in the point and crossing train at Westbury.* **Antony Christie**

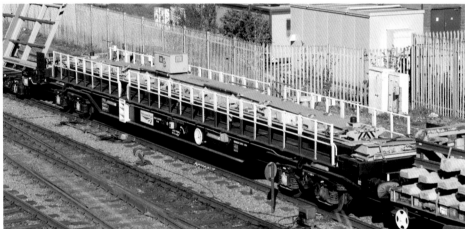

Plasser & Theurer EM-SAT RT900 Survey Vehicle

DR999800	*Richard Spoors*	Network Rail
DR999801		Network Rail

Swedish Rail Vacuum

99709	Railcare, Sweden*	*operated in the UK

Balfour Beatty Rail Services

Address: ✉ 130 Wilton Road, London, SW1V 4LQ
📠 info@bbrail.com
☎ 0207 216 6800
ⓘ www.bbrail.com

Managing Director: Peter Anderson   **Depot:** Ashford (AD)

Hauled Stock

Mk1 Vehicle Length: 64ft 6in (19.65m)   Height: 12ft 9½in (3.89m)   Width: 9ft 3in (2.81m)

Number		Type	Depot	Livery	Operator	Use
977163	(35487)	Mk1/BSK	AD	BBR	BBR	Staff & Generator coach
977165	(35408)	Mk1/BSK	AD	BBR	BBR	Staff & Generator coach
977166	(35419)	Mk1/BSK	AD	BBR	BBR	Staff & Generator coach
977167	(35400)	Mk1/BSK	AD	BBR	BBR	Staff & Generator coach
977168	(35289)	Mk1/BSK	AD	BBR	BBR	Staff & Generator coach

Infrastructure Companies - Network Rail, Balfour Beatty

Alstom Transport

Address: ✉ PO Box 70, Newbold Road, Rugby, Warwickshire, CV21 2WR

📠 info@transport.alstom.com ✆ 01788 577111, ⓘ www.transport.alstom.com

Managing Director: Paul Robinson

Facilities: Following the assembly of the Virgin Trains Class 390 Pendolino stock, Alstom closed down its UK production facility at Washwood Heath, Birmingham. However, the company still operates from many specialist sites in mainland Europe and if Alstom win further new-build contracts in the UK, these will be assembled in Europe.

Depots: Chester (CH), Liverpool - Edge Hill (LL), Manchester - Longsight (MA), Wolverhampton - Oxley (OY), Wembley (WB)

Class 08

			Vehicle Length: 29ft 3in (8.91m)		Engine: English Electric 6K	
			Height: 12ft 8⅝in (3.87m)		Horsepower: 400hp (298kW)	
			Width: 8ft 6in (2.59m)		Electrical Equipment: English Electric	

Number	Depot	Pool	Livery	Owner	Operator
08451(S)	AT	ATZZ	GBF	ALS	-
08454	WB	ATLO	BLK	ALS	ALS
08611	MA	ATLO	VT1	ALS	ALS
08617	WB	ATLO	BLK	ALS	ALS
08696	AT	ATLO	GRN	ALS	ALS
08721	AT	ATLO	BLU	ALS	ALS
08790	AT	ATLO	BLU	ALS	ALS
08887(S)	AT	ATZZ	BLK	ALS	-

Names applied
08696 *Longsight TMD*
08611 *M A Smith*
08790 *Starlet*
08721 *Downside CS*

Right: *Painted in Alstom black livery, No. 08454 is seen at Wembley carriage sidings.* CJM

Bombardier Transportation

Address: ✉ Litchurch Lane, Derby, DE24 8AD

📠 info@bombardier.com ✆ 01332 344666, ⓘ www.bombardier.com

Chief Country Representative: Paul Roberts

Works: Derby (ZD), Crewe (ZC)

Facilities: Bombardier Transportation is one of the largest transport builders in the world, with offices and building facilities in many countries. Its product range extends well beyond rail vehicles and includes aircraft, boats and leisure equipment.

In terms of the UK, two main sites are located in Derby (Litchurch Lane) and Crewe. New-build work is undertaken at the Derby site, which mainly concentrates on electric and diesel multiple-unit designs.

Class 08

				Vehicle Length: 29ft 3in (8.91m)		Engine: English Electric 6K	
				Height: 12ft 8⅝in (3.87m)		Horsepower: 400hp (298kW)	
				Width: 8ft 6in (2.59m)		Electrical Equipment: English Electric	

Number	Depot	Pool	Livery	Owner	Operator	Name
08682 (D3849)	ZD	INDL	GRN	BOM	BOM	Lionheart
08846 (No. 3)	ZD	INDL	BOM	BOM	BOM	

Class 423 (4VEP)

		Vehicle Length: 64ft 6in (19.65m)		Horsepower: 1,000hp (745.7kW)	
		Height: 12ft 11in (3.93m)		Seats (total/car): Nil	
		Width: 9ft 0in (2.74m)		Tractor unit for internal use	

Number	Formation DTC+TSO+MBS+DTC	Depot	Livery	Owner	Operator
(42)3905	76397+70904+62266+76398	AF	COX	BOM	BOM (Chart Leacon depot pilot) Out of use
(42)3918	76527+70950+62321+76528	AF	COX	BOM	BOM (Chart Leacon depot pilot) Out of use

Class 424
Classic

Vehicle Length: 64ft 6in (19.65m)			Horsepower: Unpowered			
Height: 12ft 11in (3.93m)			Seats (total/car): 64S			
Width: 9ft 0in (2.74m)			**Demonstrator vehicle**			

Number	Formation	Depot	Livery	Owner	Operator	Use
424001(S)	76112	ZB	SIL	BOM	-	**Networker Classic demonstrator**

Electro-Motive

Address: ✉ Electro-Motive Diesels Inc, 9301 West 55th Street, LaGrange, Illinois, USA, 60525

Electro-Motive Diesels Inc, Oxford Street, London, Ontario, Canada

⌨ info@emdiesels.com ✆ +1 (800) 255 5355, ⓘ www.emdiesels.com

Facilities: Formerly part of General Motors, Electro-Motive is one of the two largest loco builders in the world. Its main production facility is in London, Ontario, Canada. Production from this site sees locos transported throughout the world, including the UK and mainland Europe. In terms of the UK, the JT42CWRM or Class 66 has been built in copious numbers for many different users. The design has also been built for mainland European operators including DBS subsidiary Euro Cargo Rail. Most recently the JT42CWRM design has been built for use in Gabon. EMD is now owned by Progress Rail, a part of the Caterpillar Group.

Right: *The Electro-Motive plant in London, Ontario, Canada is likely to see a reduced new-build operation, following the take-over of operations by Progress Rail, a part of the Caterpillar Group and the opening of major new facilities in Muncie, Indiana. This company seems to favour production facilities in the US. In happier days at the EMD plant, we see EWS Class 66/0 No. 66050 in the 'de-snag' area before final testing and packing for dispatch to the UK.*
CJM

General Electric

Address: ✉ GE Transportation Rail, 2901 East Lake Road, Erie, Pennsylvania, USA, 16531

UK office: Inspira House, Martinfield, Welwyn Garden City, Herts, AL7 1GW

⌨ info@getransportation.com ✆ 01707 383700 ⓘ www.getransportation.com

Chief Executive Officer: Lorenzo Simonelli

Facilities: General Electric have only recently entered the UK loco arena, and are currently fulfilling an order for 'PowerHaul' locomotives for Freightliner. The company operates a huge construction facility in Erie, Pennsylvania, USA where the UK locos are being built.

Hitachi Europe Ltd

Address: ✉ 16 Upper Woburn Place, London, WC1H 0AF

⌨ hirofumi.ojima@hitachi-eu.com ✆ 0207 970 2700, ⓘ www.hitachi-rail.com

Facilities: Hitachi Rail, one of the newer names to the UK rail scene, won the contract to design, build, test and manage the fleet of Class 395 EMUs used for domestic services on HS1. In 2009 the company formed the construction arm of the consortium awarded the IEP project to design, build and introduce the next generation of high speed passenger trains in the UK.

Hitachi are now building construction facilities in the UK at Newton Aycliffe, County Durham. The first 60 vehicles of the IEP will be constructed in Japan and shipped to the UK.

Knights Rail Services

Address: ✉ Shoeburyness: Building D23, MoD Shoeburyness, Blackgate Road,
Shoeburyness, Essex, SS3 9SR
Eastleigh: Eastleigh Rail Works, Campbell Road, Eastleigh, Hampshire,
SO50 5AD
✆ gosborne@knightsrail.co.uk ✆ 01702 299631, ⓘ www.rail-services.net

Managing Director: Bruce Knights

Facilities: Knights Rail Services offer high quality rail engineering services to all vehicle owners.
They are based in the former loco/carriage works at Eastleigh.

Depots: Eastleigh (ZG), Shoeburyness (SN)

Class 07

Vehicle Length: 26ft 9½in (8.16m)			Engine: Paxman 6RPHL MkIII	
Height: 12ft 10in (3.91m)			Horsepower: 275hp (205kW)	
Width: 8ft 6in (2.59m)			Electrical Equipment: AEI	

Number	Depot	Pool	Livery	Owner	Operator
07007 (D2991)	ZG	MBDL	BLU	KRS	KRS

Left: *Knights Rail Services, based at the former Eastleigh Works, operates former BR Class 07 No. 07007 as its workshop pilot. The loco is painted in BR rail blue and sports its TOPS five-digit number.* **Antony Christie**

Ex DB (Germany) Class 323

Former German shunting locos, built by Gmeinder and now owned by Northumbria Rail and used at Eastleigh
Works by Knights Rail Services and Arlington Fleet Services for pilotage.

Number	Depot	Pool	Livery	Owner	Operator
323-539-7	ZG	-	-	NHR	KRS
323-674-2	ZG	-	-	NHR	KRS

Pullman Group

Address: ✉ Train Maintenance Depot, Leckwith Road, Cardiff, CF11 8HP
✆ sales@pullmans.net ✆ 029 2036 8850, ⓘ www.pullmans.net

Managing Director: Colin Robinson

Facilities: Pullman Rail operates from part of the former Canton depot in Cardiff and provides a
quality engineering service mainly to DMU and coaching stock vehicles.

Depot: Cardiff Canton (CF)

Class 08

Vehicle Length: 29ft 3in (8.91m)			Engine: English Electric 6K	
Height: 12ft 8⅝in (3.87m)			Horsepower: 400hp (298kW)	
Width: 8ft 6in (2.59m)			Electrical Equipment: English Electric	

Number	Depot	Pool	Livery	Owner	Operator
08499	CF	WSXX	BLU	DBS	PUL

Train Engineering Companies – Knights Rail, Pullman

Railcare Ltd

Address: ✉ Wolverton Works, Stratford Road, Wolverton, Milton Keynes, MK12 5NT
🖎 info@railcare.com ✆ 08000 741122, ⓘ www.railcare.com

Managing Director: Colin Love
Depots: Glasgow (ZH), Wolverton (ZN)

Class 08

		Vehicle Length: 29ft 3in (8.91m)		Engine: English Electric 6K
		Height: 12ft 8⅝in (3.87m)		Horsepower: 400hp (298kW)
		Width: 8ft 6in (2.59m)		Electrical Equipment: English Electric

Number	Depot	Pool	Livery	Owner	Operator	Name
08568	ZH	RCZH	ALS	RCL	RCL	*St Rollox*
08629	ZN	RCZN	ROY	RCL	RCL	
08649	ZN	RCZN	WEX	RCL	RCL	
08730	ZH	RCZH	ALS	RCL	RCL	*The Caley*

Rail Vehicle Engineering Ltd

Address: ✉ Vehicles Workshop, RTC Business Park, London Road, Derby, DE24 8UP
🖎 enquiries@rvel.co.uk ✆ 01332 331210, ⓘ www.rvel.co.uk

Managing Director: Andy Lynch
Depot: Derby (DF)

Class 08

		Vehicle Length: 29ft 3in (8.91m)		Engine: English Electric 6K
		Height: 12ft 8⅝in (3.87m)		Horsepower: 400hp (298kW)
		Width: 8ft 6in (2.59m)		Electrical Equipment: English Electric

Number	Depot	Pool	Livery	Owner	Operator
08536	DF	HISE	EMT	EMT	RVE
08697	DF	EMSL	EMT	EMT	RVE

Class 31/1, 31/4

		Vehicle Length: 56ft 9in (17.29m)	Engine: English Electric 12SVT
		Height: 12ft 7in (3.91m)	Horsepower: 1,470hp (1,097kW)
		Width: 8ft 9in (2.65m)	Electrical Equipment: Brush
		Class 31/4 - Fitted with Electric Erain Heat. Class 31/6 - Fitted with through wiring	

Number		Depot	Pool	Livery	Owner	Operator	Name
31106		DF	RVLO	BLU	HJA	RVE	
31422	(31310)	DF	RVLS	INT	RVE	RVE	*Cerberus*
31459	(31256)	DF	RVLO	BLK	RVE	RVE	*Hydra*
31468(S)	(31568, 31321)	DF	RVLS	BLK	RVE	RVE	

Right: *Rail Vehicle Engineering Ltd Class 31/1 No. 31106 painted in rail blue and owned by Howard Johnson is seen with a Network Rail test train at Exeter.* **Antony Christie**

Class 73/1

		Vehicle Length: 53ft 8in (16.35m)	Power: 750V dc third rail or English Electric 6K
		Height: 12ft 5¹¹⁄₁₆in (3.79m)	Horsepower: electric - 1,600hp (1,193kW)
		Width: 8ft 8in (2.64m)	Horsepower: diesel - 600hp (447kW)
			Electrical Equipment: English Electric

Number	Depot	Pool	Livery	Owner	Operator	Notes
73104	DF	RVLO	GRN	RVE	RVE	
73139	DF	RVLO	PUL	RVE	RVE	
73211	DF	-	-	RVE	-	Spares for 73104 project

73104 to be rebuilt with 2 x Cummins CSK19 power units to provide Type 3 output electri-diesel loco, due to emerge in 2012.

Siemens Transportation

Address: ✉ Kings Heath Traincare Facility, Heathfield Way, Kings Heath,
Northampton, NN5 7QP
📠 enquiries@siemenstransportation.co.uk ✆ 01604 594500
ⓘ www.siemenstransportation.co.uk

Managing Director UK: Steve Scrimshaw

Depots: Ardwick, Manchester (AK), Kings Heath, Northampton (NN),
Northam, Southampton (NT)

Class 01.5

Number	Depot	Pool	Livery	Owner	Operator	Name
01551 (H016)	AK	MBDL	WAB	WAB	SIE	*Lancelot*

Barrier Wagons

Number	Depot	Pool	Livery	Owner	Operator	Notes
6321 (96385, 86515)	NN	SIEM	BLU	SIE	-	Desiro stock barrier wagon
6322 (93686, 86859)	NN	SIEM	BLU	SIE	-	Desiro stock barrier wagon
6323 (96387, 86973)	NN	SIEM	BLU	SIE	-	Desiro stock barrier wagon
6324 (96388, 86562)	CP	SIEM	BLU	SIE	-	Desiro stock barrier wagon
6325 (96389, 86135)	NN	SIEM	BLU	SIE	-	Desiro stock barrier wagon

Wabtec

Brush Traction,
Loughborough

Address: ✉ PO Box 17, Loughborough, Leicestershire, LE11 1HS
📠 sales@brushtraction.com ✆ 01509 617000, ⓘ www.brushtraction.com

Managing Director: John Bidewell

Facilities: The world famous name of Brush Traction, based in Loughborough, is now part of the Wabtec Group. In recent years the site has been responsible for the majority of UK loco building. The company has been synonymous with loco building for the UK and overseas markets for many years. Although recent main line loco builds have been awarded overseas, the facilities at the Loughborough plant where the Class 31, 47, 60, Eurotunnel Shuttle locos and the Class 57s emerged are still available for new-build work. Recently the site has concentrated on re-build operations including the highly successful re-engining of the HST fleet with MTU power units for First Group,

East Coast, Grand Central and Network Rail. In 2011-12 the works was overhauling GBRf traction, including the re-engineering of a Class 73 with an MTU power unit.
The site is fully rail connected.

Left: First Great Westen No. 57604 in mock Great Western green and Freightliner Class 66 No. 66504 stand inside the main erecting shop at Brush Loughborough. **Darren Ford**

Doncaster

Address: ✉ PO Box 400, Doncaster Works, Hexthorpe Road, Doncaster, DN1 1SL
 ✎ wabtecrail@wabtec.com ✆ 01302 340700, ⓘ www.wabtecrail.co.uk

Managing Director: John Meehan
Depot: Doncaster (ZB)

Class 08

	Vehicle Length: 29ft 3in (8.91m)	Engine: English Electric 6K
	Height: 12ft 8⅝in (3.87m)	Horsepower: 400hp (298kW)
	Width: 8ft 6in (2.59m)	Electrical Equipment: English Electric

Number	Depot	Pool	Livery	Owner	Operator	Name
08472	EC	RFSH	BLK	WAB	ICE	
08571	ZB	RFSH	WAB	WAB	ICE	
08596(S)	ZB	RFSH	WAB	WAB	NXE	
08615	ZB	RFSH	WAB	WAB	NXE	
08669	ZB	RFSH	WAB	WAB	WAB	Bob Machin
08724	ZB	RFSH	WAB	WAB	WAB	
08764	ZB	MBDL	BLU	WAB	TRN	Old Tom
08853	ZB	RFSH	BLU	WAB	WAB	
08871	ZB	RFSH	COT	WAB	WAB	
08927(S)	ZB	TTLS	EWS	WAB	DBS	

Right: *Painted in Wabtec black livery, complete with wasp warning end and a knuckle coupling, No. 08669* Bob Machin *is seen shunting at Wabtec Doncaster.* **Nathan Williamson**

Coaching Stock

| | Vehicle Length: 75ft 0in (22.86m) | Width: 8ft 11in (2.71m) |
| | Height: 12ft 9in (3.88m) | Bogie Type: BT10 |

NX5G - NGV

Number	Depot	Livery	Owner
96374(S) (10585)	ZB	EPS	WAB

Used for train supply testing of overhauled passenger stock

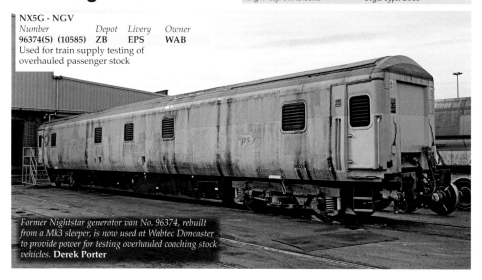

Former Nightstar generator van No. 96374, rebuilt from a Mk3 sleeper, is now used at Wabtec Doncaster to provide power for testing overhauled coaching stock vehicles. **Derek Porter**

Wabtec

Scotland (Previously Brush Barclay)

Address: ⊠ Caledonia Works, West Langlands Street, Kilmarnock, Ayrshire,
Scotland, KA1 2QD
✎ sales@brushtraction.com ✆ 01563 523573, ⓘ www.brushtraction.com

Managing Director: John Bidewell

Facilities: The Wabtec site in Scotland concentrates on vehicle overhaul and refurbishment, including EMU, DMU and loco hauled vehicles as well as HST stock

Train Builders

Siemens Transportation Ltd

Address: ⊠ Ashby Park, Ashby de la Zouch, Leicestershire, LE65 1JD
✎ uk.mobility@siemens.com ✆ 01530 258000
ⓘ www.siemens.co.uk/mobility

Managing Director UK: Steve Scrimshaw

Facilities: Siemens is now an established provider of UK EMU and DMU rolling stock with various derivatives of its 'Desiro' product line. Siemens, while having maintenance facilities in the UK, performs all new-build work in mainland Europe at its Krefeld/Uerdingen factory in Germany. Testing of vehicles is performed in Germany before delivery at the world famous test track at Wildenrath.

Below: *Siemens operates one of the most advanced test tracks in the world at Wildenrath in Germany, where 90 per cent of the company products are tested up to line speed before delivery to customers. The site has both overhead and third rail electrification and operates full facilities to test diesel traction as well. In this view we see one of the First ScotRail Class 380 sets, No. 380002, next to a Belgian 1800 class and a 'Dispolok' electric loco.* **CJM**

Train Engineering Companies – Wabtec, Siemens

Europhoenix Ltd

Address: ✉ 58A High Street, Stony Stratford, Milton Keynes, MK11 1AX

✐ info@europhoenix.eu ✆ 01467 624366, ⓘ www.europhoenix.eu

Facilities: Europhoenix have purchased redundant Class 56, 86 and 87 locos; these are offered to Continental European operators fully refurbished and modified to suit customer needs.

Class 56

Vehicle Length: 63ft 6in (19.35m)	Engine: Ruston Paxman 16RK3CT
Height: 13ft 0in (3.96m)	Horsepower: 3,250hp (2,420kW)
Width: 9ft 2in (2.79m)	Electrical Equipment: Brush

Locomotives Nos. 56018, 56101, 56115 and 56117 purchased in December 2011, for export to Floyd, Hungary.

Class 86

Vehicle Length: 58ft 6in (17.83m)	Power Collection: 25kV ac overhead
Height: 13ft 0⅝in (3.97m)	Horsepower: 5,900hp (4,400kW)
Width: 8ft 8¼in (2.64m)	Electrical Equipment: GEC

Number	Location	Hire to	Number	Location	Hire to	Number	Location	Hire to
86215	XX	Floyd (Hungary)	86231	LM	-	86247	LM	-
86217	LM	-	86232	LM	-	86248	XX	Floyd (Hungary)
86218	XX	Floyd (Hungary)	86233	XX	Floyd (Hungary)	86250	XX	Floyd (Hungary)
86226	LM	-	86234	LM	-	86251	LM	-
86228	LM	-	86235	LM	-	86424 (Now with AC Loco Group)		
86229	LM	-	86242	LM	-	■ A further six Class 86s are		
			86246	LM	-	expected to operate for Floyd		

Class 87

Vehicle Length: 58ft 6in (17.83m)	Power Collection: 25kV ac overhead
Height: 13ft 1¼in (3.99m)	Horsepower: 7,860hp (5,680kW)
Width: 8ft 8¼in (2.64m)	Electrical Equipment: GEC

Number	Owner	Location		Number	Owner	Location
87009	EPX	LM		87023	EPX	LM
87017	EPX	LM		(Hire locomotives)		

Names applied	
87017	Iron Duke
87023	Velocity

Right: *Europhoenix have been responsible for the restoration of a number of ac electric locos for further use in both the UK and mainland Europe. After supplying several Class 86s to Hungary, in 2011 the company restored a pair of Class 87s to front line use, Nos. 87017 and 87023. The pair are seen posed outside the company's workshops at Long Marston.*
Antony Christie

Porterbrook

Address: ✉ Burdett House, Becket Street, Derby, DE1 1JP

✐ enquiries@porterbrook.co.uk ✆ 01332 262405, ⓘ www.porterbrook.co.uk

Managing Director: Paul Francis

Facilities: Porterbrook Leasing have made available the off-lease Class 87s to mainland European operators, with a significant number being exported to operate in Bulgaria.

Stored in the UK

Number	Owner	Location
87025	PTR	LM

Exported

Number	Present operator	Number	Present operator	Number	Present operator	Number	Present operator
87003	BZK Bulgaria	87008	BZK Bulgaria	87019	BZK Bulgaria	87029	BZK Bulgaria
87004	BZK Bulgaria	87010	BZK Bulgaria	87020	BZK Bulgaria	87033	BZK Bulgaria
87006	BZK Bulgaria	87012	BZK Bulgaria	87022	BZK Bulgaria	87034	BZK Bulgaria
87007	BZK Bulgaria	87013	BZK Bulgaria	87026	BZK Bulgaria		
		87014	BZK Bulgaria	87028	BZK Bulgaria		

Angel Trains

Address: ✉ Portland House, Bressenden Place, London, SW1E 5BH
📠 reception@angeltrains.co.uk 📞 0207 592 0500, ⓘ www.angeltrains.co.uk

Chief Executive: Malcolm Brown
Owned by: Babcock Brown, AMP Capital & Deutsche Bank

British American Railway Services

Incorporating: RMS Locotec, RT Rail, Dartmoor Railway, Devon & Cornwall Railways, Weardale Railway, Ealing Community Transport and Hanson Rail

Address: ✉ London Riverside, London, SE1 2AQ
President: Ed Ellis
Depots: RMS Wakefield (ZS), Washwood Heath (WH)

UK operation is part of Iowa Pacific Holdings. BARS is also a Train Operating Company.

Class 08

Vehicle Length: 29ft 3in (8.91m)			Engine: English Electric 6K		
Height: 12ft 8⅝in (3.87m)			Horsepower: 400hp (298kW)		
Width: 8ft 6in (2.59m)			Electrical Equipment: English Electric		

Number	Depot	Pool	Livery	Owner	Operator	Number					
08308	IS	MRSO	FSR	ECT	FSR	08750	ZB	MRSO	BLK	ECT	IND
08423	ZS	INDL	RMS	RMS	IND	08754	ZB	MRSO	BLU	ECT	IND
08573	ZB	MRSO	BLK	ECT	BOM	08756	MR	MRSO	GRY	ECT	GBR
08588	ZB	MRSO	BLK	ECT	IND	08762	ZB	MRSO	BLK	ECT	CEM
08613	§	MOLO	BLU	RMS	IND	08870	ZS	MBDL	BLG	RMS	IND
08622	ZS	INDL	BLU	RMS	IND	08873	ZB	MRSO	HUN	ECT	FLR
08648	ZB	INDL	YEL	BAR	IND	08885	ZS	INDL	GBR	RMS	GBR
						08936	ZS	MBDL	BLU	RMS	IND

§ at Onllwyn

Left: *British American Railway-owned Class 08 No. 08308 painted in a mauve and grey livery with yellow warning ends is seen at Inverness while on hire to First ScotRail.* **Antony Christie**

Class 20

Vehicle Length: 46ft 9¼in (14.26m)			Engine: English Electric 8SVT Mk2		
Height: 12ft 7⅝in (3.84m)			Horsepower: 1,000hp (745kW)		
Width: 8ft 9in (2.66m)			Electrical Equipment: English Electric		

Number		Depot	Pool	Livery	Owner	Operator
20189		BH	MOLO	GRN	C20	BAR
20227		LUL	MOLO	RFG	C20	BAR
20901	(20101)	DR	MOLO	TLG	BAR	BAR
20905	(20225)	DR	MOLO	TLG	BAR	BAR

Class 31/1, 31/4 & 31/6

						Vehicle Length: 56ft 9in (17.29m)	*Engine: English Electric 12SVT*
						Height: 12ft 7in (3.91m)	*Horsepower: 1,470hp (1,097kW)*
						Width: 8ft 9in (2.65m)	*Electrical Equipment: Brush*
						31/4 Fitted with Electric Train Heat, 31/6 through wired	

Number		Depot	Pool	Livery	Owner	Operator	Name
31190		WH	HTLX	GRN	BAR	- (Spot hire)	
31452	(31552/279)	WH	HTLX	DCG	ECT	ECT	
31454	(31554, 31228)	WH	HTLX	ICS	BAR	RVE	
31601	(31186)	WH	HTLX	DCG	BAR	RVE	
31602	(31191)	WH	HTLX	NRL	BAR	RVE	Driver Dave Green 19B

Right: *The two Class 31/6 locos, fitted with through ETH wiring, but unable to provide train heat from their own equipment, are operated by BAR. No. 31601 is painted in green livery and carries Devon & Cornwall Railway branding. The loco is seen at Paignton while on hire to Network Rail to power a test train.*
Alex Martin Brown

Class 56

					Vehicle Length: 63ft 6in (19.35m)	*Engine: Ruston Paxman 16RK3CT*
					Height: 13ft 0in (3.96m)	*Horsepower: 3,250hp (2,420kW)*
					Width: 9ft 2in (2.79m)	*Electrical Equipment: Brush*

Number		Depot	Pool	Livery	Owner	Operator	
56303	(56125)	WH	HTLX	GRN	BAR	BAR	
56311	(56057)	WH	HTLX	GRY	BAR	BAR	
56312	(56003)	WH	HTLX	GRY	BAR	BAR	*Advertising livery for York Rail Fest*
(56313) (S)	56128	WH	HTLX	FRB	BAR	-	
(56314) (S)	56114	WF	HTLX	-	BAR	-	

In December 2011, BAR purchased Nos. 56091 and 56103 from DBS.

Right: *After Hanson Rail merged with British American Railway, the two Class 56s operated by Hanson commenced operation with BAR, joining forces with No. 56303 acquired from RVEL. Here ex-RVEL No. 56303 in green livery and BAR No. 56311 in grey livery, both with Devon & Cornwall Railway branding, are illustrated.* **Ryan Tranmer**

Class 73

					Vehicle Length: 53ft 8in (16.35m)	*Power: 750V dc third rail or English Electric 6K*
					Height: 12ft 5⅝in (3.79m)	*Horsepower: electric - 1,600hp (1,193kW)*
					Width: 8ft 8in (2.64m)	*Horsepower: diesel - 600hp (447kW)*
						Electrical Equipment: English Electric

Number	Depot	Pool	Livery	Owner	Operator	Name
73107	SE	MBED	GRY	RTR	ECT	*Redhill 1844 - 1994*
73201 (73142)	SE	MBED	BLU	PTR	ECT	*Broadlands*

Coaching Stock

Mk2	*Height: 12ft 9½in (3.89m)*	
Vehicle Length: 66ft 0in (20.11m)	*Width: 9ft 3in (2.81m)*	

AF2F - DBSO

Number	Depot	Livery	Owner			Depot	Livery	Owner
9704	LM	-	BAR		9707	LM	-	BAR
9705	LM	-	BAR		9709	LM	-	BAR
					9710	LM	-	BAR

Cargo-D

Rolling stock owned by this operator is currently stored following the businesses Cargo-D and Rail Blue Charters entering administration in October 2011. The administrator is RSM Tenon.

Hauled stock

Mk2 Vehicle Length: 66ft 0in (20.11m)		Height: 12ft 9½in (3.89m) Width: 9ft 3in (2.81m)			Mk 3 Vehicle Length: 75ft 0in (22.86m)		Height: 12ft 9in (3.88m) Width: 8ft 11in (2.71m)		
Number	Type	Depot	Livery	Operator	6173	AC2F/TSO	TO	BLG	WCR
1252 (3280)	AJ1F/RFO	LM	VIR	CAD	9497	AC2E/BSO	WN	BLG	CAD
1254 (3391)	AJ1F/RFO	BH	BLG	WCR	9506	AE2E/BSO	BH	BLG	CAD/FSR
1657	AJ41/RBR	BH	DRS	CAD	9508	AE2E/BSO	TO	BLG	FSR
3241*	AD1F/FO	BH	BLG	CAD	9525	AE2E/BSO	BH	BLG	CAS
3366	AD1F/FO	BH	BLG	CAD	10202 (40504)	AJ1G/RFM	BH	BLG	CAD
3374	AD1F/FO	BH	BLG	WCR	10242 (10002)	AJ1G/RFM	CE	BLG	CRW
5787	AD2E/TSO	BH	BLG	CAD	10245 (10019)	AJ1G/RFM	AL	BLG	CAD
5797	AD2E/TSO	BH	BLG	CAD	10246 (10014)	AJ1G/RFM	WN	BLG	CRW
5810	AC2E/TSO	TO	BLG	CAD	10249 (10012)	AJ1G/RFM	CF	ATW	ATW
5866	AC2E/TSO	WN	BLG	CAD	10588	AU4G/SLEP	WN	BLG	CAD
5876	AC2E/TSO	BH	BLG	CAD	11064	AD1H/FO	BH	BLG	CAD
5901	AC2F/TSO	BH	BLG	CAD	11065	AD1H/FO	BH	BLG	CAD
5906	AC2F/TSO	BH	BLG	CAD	11071	AD1H/FO	BH	BLG	CRW
5919	AC2F/TSO	BH	BLG	CAD	11079	AD1H/FO	CE	VIR	CAD
5925*	AC2F/TSO	BH	BLG	CAD	11083	AD1H/FOD	BH	BLG	CRW
5941	AC2F/TSO	BH	BLG	CAD	11084	AD1H/FO	BH	BLG	CAD/VWC
5958	AC2F/TSO	BH	BLG	CAD	11086	AD1H/FO	BH	BLG	CAD
5971	AC2F/TSO	TO	BLG	WCR	11089	AD1H/FO	WN	BLG	CAD
5995	AC25/TSO	TO	BLG	CAD	12014	AC2G/TSO	AL	BLG	CRW
6001	AC2F/TSO	TO	BLG	CAD	12017	AC2G/TSO	WB	VIR	CRW/VWC
6008	AC2F/TSO	BH	BLG	CAD	12038	AC2G/TSO	AL	BLG	CRW
6045	AC2F/TSO	BH	VIR	CAD	12043	AC2G/TSO	AL	BLG	CRW
6046	AC2F/TSO	BH	BLG	CAD	12059	AC2G/TSO	WB	VIR	CRW/VWC
6064	AC2F/TSO	BH	BLG	CAD	12094	AC2G/TSO	AL	VIR	CRW/VWC
6117	AC2F/TSO	BH	BLG	FSR	12119	AC2G/TSO	IL	BLG	CRW
6122	AC2F/TSO	BH	BLG	CAD	96603(S)	Motorail	LM	GRN	-
6134	AC2F/TSO	KT	ICS	CAD	96604(S)	Motorail	LM	GRN	-
6151	AC2F/TSO	BH	BLG	CAD	* Owned by Eversholt				
6168	AC2F/TSO	WN	BLG	CAD					

Below: *Now looking for a new home is blue and grey-liveried kitchen car No. 80042, previously numbered 1646. The vehicle is fitted with central door locking and would be an excellent addition to any charter train fleet.* **Nathan Williamson**

Electric Traction Limited

Address: ✉ Woodlands, Manse Road, Inverurie, Scotland, AB51 3UJ
Depot: Long Marston (LM)
Electric Traction Ltd provide spot hire of Class 86 and 87 traction, as well as providing engineering and graphic design services to the rail industry.

Class 86

Vehicle Length: 58ft 6in (17.83m)					*Power Collection: 25kV ac overhead*	
Height: 13ft 0⅝in (3.97m)					*Horsepower: 5,900hp (4,400kW)*	
Width: 8ft 8¼in (2.64m)					*Electrical Equipment: GEC*	

Number		Depot	Pool	Livery	Owner	Operator	Name
86101		WA	ACAC	BLU	ETL	ETL	
86213		WA	ETLO	INS	ETL	ETL	*Lancashire Witch*
86401		CP	ETLO	NSE	ETL	ETL	*Northampton Town*
86701	(86205)	CP	ETLO	ETL	ETL	ETL	*Orion*
86702	(86260)	IL	ETLO	ETL	ETL	ETL	*Cassiopeia*

Right: *Electric Traction Ltd operate two fully restored Class 86s, Nos. 86701/702, rebuilt from Class 86/2s Nos. 86205/260. The locos are usually kept at Willesden and available for spot hire as required. No. 86702* Cassiopeia *is seen at Carlisle.*
Jamie Squibbs

Class 87

Vehicle Length: 58ft 6in (17.83m)					*Power Collection: 25kV ac overhead*	
Height: 13ft 1¼in (3.99m)					*Horsepower: 7,860hp (5,680kW)*	
Width: 8ft 8¼in (2.64m)					*Electrical Equipment: GEC*	

Number	Depot	Pool	Livery	Owner	Operator	Name
87002	CP	ETLO	BLU	ETL	ETL	*Royal Sovereign*

Right: *In 1970s rail blue with TOPS number and cast* Royal Sovereign *nameplate, No. 87002 has been fully restored to main line standard and is available to either the spot hire or charter market. With First Capital Connect Class 313/0 No. 313060 restarting from its Harringay stop, No. 87002 passes at speed with a charter from Doncaster to Brighton, which the ac electric operated to Willesden.* **Brian Morrison**

Eversholt Rail Group (Previously HSBC Rail)

Address: ✉ PO Box 29499, 1 Eversholt Street, London, NW1 2ZF
          ✉ info@eversholtrail.co.uk ℂ 0207 380 5040, ⓘ www.eversholtrail.co.uk
Chief Operating Officer: Mary Kenny

Rolling Stock Hire Companies – Electric Traction, Eversholt

Harry Needle Railroad Company

Address: ✉ Harry Needle Railway Shed, Barrow Hill Roundhouse, Campbell Drive, Chesterfield, Derbyshire, S43 2PR

Managing Director: Harry Needle

Depot: Barrow Hill (BH)

Harry Needle Railroad Company also operates as a scrap dealer in dismantling locomotives and rolling stock. ø Reported for sale

Class 01.5

Number		Depot	Pool	Livery	Owner	Operator	
01552	(TH167V)	BH	HNRL	IND	HNR	IND	
01564	(12088)	BH	HNRL	BLK	HNR	IND	At Butterwell

Class 07

Vehicle Length: 26ft 9½in (8.16m)
Height: 12ft 10in (3.91m)
Width: 8ft 6in (2.59m)
Engine: Paxman 6RPHL MkIII
Horsepower: 275hp (205kW)
Electrical Equipment: AEI

Number	Depot	Pool	Livery	Owner	Operator
07001	BH	HNRS	HNR	HNR	IND
07013	BH	HNRS	BLU	HNR	HNR

Class 08 & 09

Vehicle Length: 29ft 3in (8.91m)
Height: 12ft 8⅝in (3.87m)
Width: 8ft 6in (2.59m)
Engine: English Electric 6K
Horsepower: 400hp (298kW)
Electrical Equipment: English Electric

Number	Depot	Pool	Livery	Owner	Operator
08389	BH	HNRL	EWS	HNR	BUR
08492‡	BH	HNRL	BLU	HNR	HNR
08502	BH	HNRL	NOR	HNR	NOR
08507	BH	HNRL	HNR	HNR	POB
08527(S)	BH	HNRL	JAR	HNR	IND
08685	BH	HNRL	EWS	HNR	HNR
08704	BH	HNRL	BLU	HNR	HNR
08765	BU	HNRL	EWS	HNR	HNR
08786	BH	HNRL	BRD	HNR	HNR
08818	BH	HNRL	HNR	HNR	IND
08834	BH	HNRL	DRS	HNR	OLD
08868	CP	HNRL	LNW	HNR	LNW
08892	BU	HNRL	DRS	HNR	HNR

Number	Depot	Pool	Livery	Owner	Operator
08905	BH	HNRL	EWS	HNR	IND
08918	BH	HNRL	EWS	HNR	BUR
08924	BH	HNRL	EWS	HNR	HNR
08929(S)	LM	HNRS	BLK	HNR	-
08943	CZ	MBDL	HNR	HNR	NRM
08954	BU	HNRS	TGG	HNR	BUR
09012‡	BH	HNRS	EWS	HNT	-
09014	WH	HNRS	EWS	HNR	-
09018(S)	BU	HNRS	HNR	HNR	BUR
09019	BH	HNRS	EWS	HNR	-

08507 also carries international No. 98 70 0008507-4
09012 also carries international No. 98 70 0009012-4

Left: *Painted in Harry Needle Railroad Company yellow and grey livery complete with HNRC branding, No. 08943 is seen at Waterloo International involved in 'The Railway Children' play. This air braked loco is normally used at Central Rivers depot near Burton.* **Antony Christie**

Class 20

	Vehicle Length: 46ft 9¼in (14.26m)	Engine: English Electric 8SVT Mk2
	Height: 12ft 7⅝in (3.84m)	Horsepower: 1,000hp (745kW)
	Width: 8ft 9in (2.66m)	Electrical Equipment: English Electric

Number		Depot	Pool	Livery	Owner	Operator
20016(S)	ø	BH	HNRS	BLU	HNR	-
20056		BH	HNRL	COR	HNR	TAT
20057(S)	ø	LM	HNRS	BLU	HNR	-
20066		BH	HNRL	TAT	HNR	TAT
20081(S)	ø	LM	HNRS	BLU	HNR	-
20088(S)	ø	LM	HNRS	RFG	HNR	-
20092(S)		BH	HNRS	LAF	HNR	-
20096		BH	HNRS	BLU	HNR	HNR

Number	Depot	Pool	Livery	Owner	Operator
20107‡	BH	HNRS	BLU	HNR	HNR
20118	BH	HNRS	GRY	HNR	LAF
20121	WEN	HNRS	BLU	HNR	HNR
20132	BH	HNRS	GRN	HNR	HNR
20138(S)	LM	HNRS	RFT	HNR	-
20166	WEN	HNRS	GRN	HNR	HNR
20168	EA	HNRL	LAF	HNR	LAF

‡ Main line certified

Number		Depot	Pool	Livery	Owner	Operator
20311	(20102)	BH	HNRL	DRS	HNR	-
20314	(20117)	BH	HNRL	DRC	HNR	
20903(S)	(20083)	LM	HNRS	DRS	HNR	-
20904(S)	(20041)	LM	HNRS	DRS	HNR	-
20906	(20219)	BH	HNRL	DRS	HNR	HNR

Right: *Two Harry Needle-owned Class 20s Nos. 20056 and 20066 are modified for use at Tata Steel, Scunthorpe. The locos sport blue and yellow livery, are fitted with roof warning lights and carry steel works numbering of 81 and 82. No. 82 is seen in the steel works yard in spring 2011.*
Nathan Williamson

Name applied
20168 *Sir George Earle*

20056 carries Tata Steel No. 81.
20066 carries Tata Steel No. 82.

Class 37/0

	Vehicle Length: 61ft 6in (18.74m)	Engine: English Electric 12CSVT
	Height: 13ft 0¼in (3.96m)	Horsepower: 1,750hp (1,304kW)
	Width: 8ft 11⅝in (2.73m)	Electrical Equipment: English Electric

Number		Depot	Pool	Livery	Owner	Operator/Notes
37029		BH	HNRS	GRN	HNR	HNR *(At Epping & Ongar Railway)*
37057(S)		BH	HNRS	BLU	HNR	- (spares)
37165(S)	(37374)	CS	HNRS	CIV	HNR	

Class 37/4

	Vehicle Length: 61ft 6in (18.74m)	Engine: English Electric 12CSVT
	Height: 13ft 0¼in (3.96m)	Horsepower: 1,750hp (1,304kW)
	Width: 8ft 11⅝in (2.73m)	Electrical Equipment: English Electric
	Electric Train Heat fitted	

Number		Depot	Pool	Livery	Owner	Operator
37415(S)	(37277)	LM	HNRS	EWS	HNR	-
37428	ø (37281)	LM	HNRS	MAR	HNR	-

Class 37/5

	Vehicle Length: 61ft 6in (18.74m)	Engine: English Electric 12CSVT
	Height: 13ft 0¼in (3.96m)	Horsepower: 1,750hp (1,304kW)
	Width: 8ft 11⅝in (2.73m)	Electrical Equipment: English Electric

Number		Depot	Pool	Livery	Owner	Operator
37503	(37017)	BH	HNRL	EWS	HNR	HNR
37521(S)	(37117)	BH	HNRL	EWS	HNR	-
37670(S)	(37182)	BH	HNRS	DBS	HNR	-
37696(S)	(37228) ø	BH	HNRS	TGG	HNR	-

HNRC

Class 47

Vehicle Length: 63ft 6in (19.35m)				Engine: Sulzer 12LDA28C	
Height: 12ft 10⅜in (3.91m)				Horsepower: 2,580hp (1,922kW)	
Width: 9ft 2in (2.79m)				Electrical Equipment: Brush	
Electric Train Heat fitted to Class 47/4 and 47/7					

Number	Depot	Pool	Livery	Owner	Opertor
47714 (47511)	OD	HNRL	ANG	HNR	SEC*
47761 (47038/564)	BH	HNRL	RES	HNR	-
47829(S) (47264/619) ø	LM	HNRL	POL	HNR	-

* Operating at Old Dalby

Nemesis Rail

Address: ⊠ Nemesis Rail Ltd, Burton Depot

✎ enquiries@ nemesisrail.com ℰ 01246 472331, ⓘ www.nemesisrail.com

Formed from the demise of FM Rail

Depot: Burton (BU)

Class 31/1

Vehicle Length: 56ft 9in (17.29m)		Engine: English Electric 12SVT	
Height: 12ft 7in (3.91m)		Horsepower: 1,470hp (1,097kW)	
Width: 8ft 9in (2.65m)		Electrical Equipment: Brush	

Number	Depot	Pool	Livery	Owner	Operator	Name
31128	NY	NRLO	BLU	NEM	NYM	*Charybdis*

Class 33/1

Vehicle Length: 50ft 9in (15.47m)		Engine: Sulzer 8LDA28A	
Height: 12ft 8in (3.86m)		Horsepower: 1,550hp (1,156kW)	
Width: 9ft 3in (2.81m)		Electrical Equipment: Crompton Parkinson	

Number	Depot	Pool	Livery	Owner	Operator	Name
33103	BU	MBDL	BLU	NEM	NEM	*Swordfish*

On loan to Swanage Railway

Left: *Painted in rail blue livery and sporting two sections of its miniature snowplough, No. 33103 is seen from its No. 1 or cooler group end.*
Bill Wilson

Class 37/5

Vehicle Length: 61ft 6in (18.74m)		Engine: English Electric 12CSVT	
Height: 13ft 0¼in (3.96m)		Horsepower: 1,750hp (1,304kW)	
Width: 8ft 11⅝in (2.73m)		Electrical Equipment: English Electric	

Number	Depot	Pool	Livery	Owner	Operator
37679(S) (37123)	BU	MBDL	TGG	NEM	-

Class 45/1

Vehicle Length: 67ft 11in (20.70m)		Engine: Sulzer 12LDA28B	
Height: 12ft 11in (3.91m)		Horsepower: 2,500hp (1,862kW)	
Width: 9ft 1½in (2.78m)		Electrical Equipment: Crompton Parkinson	

Number	Depot	Pool	Livery	Owner	Operator	Name
45112	BH	MBDL	BLU	NEM	NEM	*Royal Army Ordnance Corps*

Class 47

Vehicle Length: 63ft 6in (19.35m)			Engine: Sulzer 12LDA28C			
Height: 12ft 10⅜in (3.91m)			Horsepower: 2,580hp (1,922kW)			
Width: 9ft 2in (2.79m)			Electrical Equipment: Brush			
Electric Train Heat fitted to Class 47/4 and 47/7						

Number	Depot	Pool	Livery	Owner	Opertor		Number	Depot	Pool	Livery	Owner	Operator
47375	BH	MBDL	BLU	NEM	NEM		47716	BH	MBDL	RES	NEM	NEM
47488	BH	MBDL	GRN	NEM	NEM		47744	BH	MBDL	EWS	NEM	NEM

Porterbrook

Address: ✉ Ivatt House, The Point, Pinnacle Way, Pride Park, Derby, DE24 8ZS
📠 enquiries@porterbrook.co.uk ✆ 01332 285050, ⓘ www.porterbrook.co.uk

Managing Director: Paul Francis

Owned by: Antin Infrastructure Partners, Deutsche Bank & OP Trust

Transmart Trains

Address: ✉ Green Farm House, Falfield, Wootton-under-Edge, Gloucestershire, GL12 8DL

Managing Director: Oliver Buxton

Depots: Selhurst (SU), Stewarts Lane (SL)

Part of Cambrian Transport

Class 73

Vehicle Length: 53ft 8in (16.35m)			Power: 750V dc third rail or English Electric 6K	
Height: 12ft 5¹⁶⁄₁₆in (3.79m)			Horsepower: electric - 1,600hp (1,193kW)	
Width: 8ft 8in (2.64m)			Horsepower: diesel - 600hp (447kW)	
			Electrical Equipment: English Electric	

‡ At Barry Railway
• Not main line certified

Number	Depot	Pool	Livery	Owner	Operator	Name	
73109	SU	MBED	SWT	TTS	TTS		■ Former Gatwick Express Class
73118	‡	-	GRY	TTS	TTS		488 vehicles Nos. 72505, 72620,
73133•	‡	-	GRN	TTS	TTS		72621, 72629, 72710 from sets
73136	SU	MBED	GRN	TTS	TTS	*Perseverance*	488206 and 488311 are also owned by Transmart Trains.

Above: *Former Eurostar Class 73/1 No. 73118 is now on the books of Transmart Trains, outbased at Blaenavon in Wales. This loco retains its drop-head Scharfenberg couplers and is painted in Eurostar grey colours.* **Jamie Squibbs**

Listings provide details of locomotives and stock authorised for operation on the UK National Rail network and that can be seen operating special and charter services.
Preserved locomotives authorised for main line operation are found in the preserved section.

Bo'ness and Kinneil Railway

Number	Type	Depot	Livery	Operator	Use
464	AO3/BCK	BT	CAL	BOK	Charter train use
1375 (99803)	AO2/TK	BT	CAL	BOK	Charter train use
3096 (99827)	AD11/FO	BT	MAR	BOK	Charter train use
3115	AD11/FO	BT	MAR	BOK	Charter train use
3150	AD11/FO	BT	MAR	BOK	Charter train use
4831 (99824)	AC21/TSO	BT	MAR	BOK	Charter train use
4832 (99823)	AC21/TSO	BT	CHC	BOK	Charter train use
4836 (99831)	AC21/TSO	BT	MAR	BOK	Charter train use
4856 (99829)	AC21/TSO	BT	MAR	BOK	Charter train use
5028 (99830)	AC21/TSO	BT	CAR	BOK	Charter train use
5412	AC2A/TSO	BT	MAR	BOK	Charter train use
13229 (99826)	AA11/FK	BT	MAR	BOK	Charter train use
13230 (99828)	AA11/FK	BT	MAR	BOK	Charter train use

Flying Scotsman Railway Ltd

Number	Type	Depot	Livery	Operator	Notes/Name
316 (S) (975608)	AO11/PFK	CS	PUL	FSL	Pullman *Magpie*
321 (S)	AO11/PFK	CS	PUL	FSL	Pullman *Swift*
337 (S)	AO11/PSK	CS	PUL	FSL	Pullman Car No. 337

Great Scottish & Western Railway Co

Number	Type	Depot	Livery	Operator	Notes/Name
313 (S) (99964)	AO11/PFK	CS	MAR	GSW	Royal Scotsman - *Finch*
317 (99967)	AO11/PFK	CS	MAR	GSW	Royal Scotsman - *Raven*
319 (99965)	AO11/PFK	CS	MAR	GSW	Royal Scotsman - *Snipe*
324 (99961)	AO11/PFP	CS	MAR	GSW	Royal Scotsman - *Amber*
329 (99962)	AO11/PFP	CS	MAR	GSW	Royal Scotsman - *Pearl*
331 (99963)	AO11/PFP	CS	MAR	GSW	Royal Scotsman - *Topaz*
1999 (99131)	AO10/SAL	CS	MAR	GSW	Royal Scotsman - *Lochaber*

Hastings Diesels Limited

The following vehicles are owned by Hastings Diesels Ltd and kept at St Leonards. Usually a six-car train is formed which is fitted with central door locking and is main line certified (original class numbers shown in brackets).
60000 (201), 60019 (202), 60116 (202), 60018 (202), 60501 (201), 60528 (202), 60529 (202), 69337 (422 EMU), 70262 (411 EMU).
In Autumn 2011 the set **1001** was formed **60116+60529+70262+69337+60501+60118**

Left: *A true credit to the preservation movement is the restored Hastings DEMU stock, which is authorised to operate over Network Rail. The vehicles are now fitted with central door locking and are allocated to St Leonards depot. Carrying set No. 1001, the six-car mixed DEMU and EMU formation is seen traversing the West Somerset Railway.*
Michael J. Collins

Mid-Hants Railway

Number	Type	Depot	Livery	Operator
1105 (99531/302)	AJ41/RG	RL	GRN	MHR
21252	AB31/BCK	RL	GRN	MHR

North Yorkshire Moors Railway

Class 08

Vehicle Length: 29ft 3in (8.91m)
Height: 12ft 8⅝in (3.87m)
Width: 8ft 6in (2.59m)

Engine: English Electric 6K
Horsepower: 400hp (298kW)
Electrical Equipment: English Electric

Number	Depot	Pool	Livery	Owner	Operator	Notes
08850	NY	MBDL	BLU	NYM	NYM	*Restricted main line use*

Class 25

Vehicle Length: 50ft 6in (15.39m)
Height: 12ft 8in (3.86m)
Width: 9ft 1in (2.76m)

Engine: Sulzer 6LDA28B
Horsepower: 1,250hp (932kW)
Electrical Equipment: Brush

Number	Depot	Pool	Livery	Owner	Operator	Name	Notes
25278	NY	MBDL	GRN	NYM	NYM	*Sybilia*	*Restricted main line use*

Coaching Stock

Number	Type	Depot	Livery	Operator	
1823	AN21/RMB	NY	MAR	NYM	
3860	AC21/TSO	NY	MAR	NYM	
3872	AC21/TSO	NY	CAR	NYM	
3948	AC2I/TSO	NY	CAR	NYM	Spare vehicle
4198	AC21/TSO	NY	CAR	NYM	
4252	AC21/TSO	NY	CAR	NYM	
4290	AC21/TSO	NY	MAR	NYM	
4455	AC21/TSO	NY	CAR	NYM	
4786	AC21/TSO	NY	MAR	NYM	
4817	AC21/TSO	NY	CHC	NYM	
5000	AC21/TSO	NY	MAR	NYM	
5029	AC21/TSO	NY	CHC	NYM	
9267	AE21/BSO	NY	CHC	NYM	
9274	AE21/BSO	NY	CHC	NYM	
21100	AB31/BCK	NY	CHC	NYM	
16156 (7156)	AA31/CK	NY	MAR	NYM	
35089	AB2I/BSK	NY	MAR	NYM	

Railfilms Limited

Number	Type	Depot	Livery	Operator	Notes/Name
84 (99884)		EH	PUL	RAF	
310 (99107)	AO11/PFL	EH	PUL	RAF	*Pegasus*
1659 (16509)	AJ41/RBR	EH	PUL	RAF	
3188	AD1D/FO	EH	PUL	RAF	*Sovereign*
3231	AD1E/FO	EH	PUL	RAF	*Apollo*
5067 (99993)	AC21/TSO	CP	MAR	RAF	
9004	GWR	EH	GWR	RAF	
13508 (S)	AA1B/FK	CS	MAR	RAF	
17080	AO3/BCK	EH	PUL	RAF	

Ridings Railtours

Number	Type	Depot	Livery	Operator
5520 (S)	AC2C/TSO	SV	PUL	RRS
13581 (S)	AA1D/FK	SV	ICS	RRS
13583 (S)	AA1D/FK	SV	ICS	RRS

Riviera Trains

Class 47

	Vehicle Length: 63ft 6in (19.35m)		Engine: Sulzer 12LDA28C			
	Height: 12ft 10⅜in (3.91m)		Horsepower: 2,580hp (1,922kW)			
	Width: 9ft 2in (2.79m)		Electrical Equipment: Brush			
	Electric Train Heat fitted					

Number	Depot	Pool	Livery	Owner	Operator	Name
47769 (47491)	CP	RTLO	VIR	RIV	RIV	
47812 D1916 (47657)	CP	RTLO	GRN	RIV	RIV	
47815 D1748 (47660)	CP	RTLO	GRN	RIV	RIV	*Great Western*
47843 (47623)	CP	RTLO	RIV	RIV	RIV	*Vulcan*
47847 (47577)	CP	RTLO	RIV	RIV	RIV	
47848 (47632)	CP	RTLO	RIV	RIV	RIV	*Titan Star*

Left: *One of the largest private train operators in the UK is Crewe-based Riviera Trains, which supplies coaching stock for charter operations, as well as traction. Locos are also supplied on a spot hire basis if needed. Green-liveried Class 47 No. 47815 is seen at Kingswear on the Torbay & Dartmouth Railway after working, with a steam loco, one of the 2011 season Torbay Express services. This loco is ETH fitted and also has green spot multiple control.* **Nathan Williamson**

Coaching Stock

Number	Type	Depot	Livery	Operator	Notes/Name
1200 (6459)	AJ1F/RFO	EH	RIV	RIV	Set 04 - The Great Briton - *Amber*
1203 (3291)	AJ1F/RFO	EH	RIV	RIV	
1212 (6453)	AJ1F/RFO	EH	VIR	RIV	Set 05 - The Norfolkman
1250 (3372)	AJ1F/RFO	EH	VIR	RIV	Set 07 - The West Coast Set
1651	AJ41/RBR	EH	MAR	RIV	Set 02 - The Royal Scot Set
1657	AJ41/RBR	EH	BLG	RIV	
1671	AJ41/RBR	EH	CHC	RIV	
1683	AJ41/RBR	BH	BLU	RIV	Set 04 - The Great Briton - *Carol*
1691	AJ41/RBR	CP	CCM	RIV	Set 02 - The Royal Scot Set
1692	AJ41/RBR	CP	CHC	RIV	Set 01 - The British Classic Set
1699	AJ41/RBR	CP	BLU	RIV	Set 04 - The Great Briton
1813	AN21/RMB	CP	MAR	RIV	Set 03
1832	AN21/RMB	EH	CCM	RIV	
1842	AN21/RMB	EH	CCM	RIV	Set 02 - The Royal Scot Set
1863	AN21/RMB	EH	CHC	RIV	Set 01 - The British Classic Set
2834 (21267)	AU51/SLSC	EH	LNR	RIV	
3066 (99566)	AD11/FO	EH	CCM	RIV	Set 02 - The Royal Scot Set
3068 (99568)	AD11/FO	EH	CCM	RIV	Set 02 - The Royal Scot Set
3069 (99540)	AD11/FO	EH	CCM	RIV	Set 02 - The Royal Scot Set
3097	AD11/FO	EH	CCM	RIV	Set 02 - The Royal Scot Set
3098	AD11/FO	EH	CHC	RIV	Set 01 - The British Classic Set
3100	AD11/FO	EH	CHC	RIV	
3107	AD11/FO	EH	CHC	RIV	Set 01 - The British Classic Set
3110 (99124)	AD11/FO	EH	CHC	RIV	Set 01 - The British Classic Set
3112 (99357)	AD11/FO	EH	CHC	RIV	Set 01 - The British Classic Set
3114 (S)	AD11/FO	EH	GRN	RIV	
3119	AD11/FO	EH	CCM	RIV	Set 02 - The Royal Scot Set

3120	AD11/FO	EH	CCM	RIV	Set 03
3121	AD11/FO	EH	LNE	RIV	Set 02 - The Royal Scot Set
3122	AD11/FO	EH	CHC	RIV	Set 01 - The British Classic Set
3123	AD11/FO	EH	CHC	RIV	Set 03
3124 (S)	AD11/FO	EH	GRN	RIV	
3127 (S)	AD11/FO	EH	GRN	RIV	
3131 (S) (99190)	AD11/FO	EH	MAR	RIV	
3132 (S) (99191)	AD11/FO	EH	MAR	RIV	
3133 (S) (99192)	AD11/FO	EH	MAR	RIV	
3140	AD11/FO	EH	CHC	RIV	Set 01 - The British Classic Set
3141 (3608)	AD11/FO	EH	MRN	RIV	Set 03
3144 (3602)	AD11/FO	EH	MRN	RIV	Set 03
3146	AD11/FO	EH	MRN	RIV	Set 03
3147 (3604)	AD11/FO	EH	LNE	RIV	Set 03
3149	AD11/FO	EH	CCM	RIV	Set 02 - The Royal Scot Set
3181 (S)	AD1D/FO	EH	RIV	RIV	*Topaz*
3223 (S)	AD1E/FO	BU	RIV	RIV	*Diamond*
3227	AD1E/FO	EH	RIV	RIV	
3240 (S)	AD1E/FO	BU	RIV	RIV	*Sapphire*
3277	AD1F/FO	EH	ANG	RIV	Set 05 - The Norfolkman
3279	AD1F/FO	EH	MAR	RIV	Set 05 - The Norfolkman
3295	AD1F/FO	EH	ANG	RIV	Set 05 - The Norfolkman
3304	AD1F/FO	EH	VIR	RIV	Set 07 - The West Coast Set
3314	AD1F/FO	EH	VIR	RIV	Set 07 - The West Coast Set
3325	AD1F/FO	EH	VIR	RIV	Set 07 - The West Coast Set
3330	AD1F/FO	EH	RIV	RIV	Set 04 - The Great Briton - *Brunel*
3333	AD1F/FO	EH	VIR	RIV	Set 07 - The West Coast Set
3334	AD1F/FO	EH	ANG	RIV	Set 05 - The Norfolkman
3336	AD1F/FO	CD	ANG	RIV	Set 05 - The Norfolkman
3340	AD1F/FO	EH	VIR	RIV	Set 07 - The West Coast Set
3344	AD1F/FO	EH	RIV	RIV	Set 07 - The West Coast Set
3345	ADIF/FO	EH	VIR	RIV	Set 07 - The West Coast Set
3348	AD1F/FO	EH	RIV	RIV	Set 04 - The Great Briton - *Gainsborough*
3356	AD1F/FO	EH	RIV	RIV	Set 04 - The Great Briton - *Tennyson*
3364	AD1F/FO	EH	RIV	RIV	Set 04 - The Great Briton - *Shakespeare*
3379	AD1F/FO	EH	ANG	RIV	
3384	AD1F/FO	EH	RIV	RIV	Set 04 - The Great Briton - *Dickens*
3386	AD1F/FO	EH	VIR	RIV	Set 07 - The West Coast Set
3390	AD1F/FO	EH	RIV	RIV	Set 04 - The Great Briton - *Constable*
3397	AD1F/FO	EH	RIV	RIV	Set 04 - The Great Briton - *Wordsworth*
3417	AD1F/FO	EH	ANG	RIV	
3426	AD1F/FO	EH	RIV	RIV	Set 04 - The Great Briton - *Elgar*
4902	AC21/TSO	EH	CHC	RIV	Set 01 - The British Classic Set
4927	AC21/TSO	EH	CHC	RIV	Set 01 - The British Classic Set
4946 (S) (99000)	AC21/TSO	EH	MAR	RIV	
4949	AC21/TSO	EH	CHC	RIV	Set 03
4959	AC21/TSO	ZA	CHC	RIV	
4986	AC21/TSO	EH	GRN	RIV	Set 03
4991	AC21/TSO	EH	CHC	RIV	
4996 (99001)	AC21/TSO	CD	MAR	RIV	
4998	AC21/TSO	ZA	MAR	RIV	Set 03
5007 (S)	AC21/TSO	EH	GRN	RIV	
5008 (99002)	AC21/TSO	CD	MAN	RIV	
5009	AC21/TSO	EH	CHC	RIV	Set 01 - The British Classic Set
5023	AC21/TSO	EH	RIV	RIV	Set 03
5027 (S)	AC21/TSO	EH	GRN	RIV	
5040	AC21/TSO	EH	CHC	RIV	Set 01 - The British Classic Set
5276	AC2A/TSO	EH	RIV	RIV	Set 02 - The Royal Scot Set
5292	AC2A/TSO	EH	CHC	RIV	Set 02 - The Royal Scot Set
5309 (S)	AC2A/TSO	EH	CHC	RIV	
5322	AC2A/TSO	EH	RIV	RIV	Set 02 - The Royal Scot Set
5341	AC2A/TSO	EH	CCM	RIV	Set 02 - The Royal Scot Set
5350	AC2A/TSO	EH	CHC	RIV	Set 01 - The British Classic Set - *Dawn*
5366	AC2A/TSO	EH	CHC	RIV	Set 02 - The Royal Scot Set
5494 (S)	AC2B/TSO	SV	NSE	RIV	
5647 (S)	AC2D/TSO	EH	RIV	RIV	
5739 (S)	AC2D/TSO	SV	NWM	RIV	

Riviera

5748	AC2E/TSO	EH	INT	RIV	
5769	AC2E/TSO	EH	INT	RIV	
5792	AC2E/TSO	EH	VIR	RIV	
5910	AC2F/TSO	EH	VIR	RIV	Set 07 - The West Coast Set
5921	AC2F/TSO	EH	RIV	RIV	Set 05 - The Norfolkman
5929	AC2F/TSO	EH	ANG	RIV	Set 05 - The Norfolkman
5937	AC2F/TSO	EH	VIR	RIV	
5945	AC2F/TSO	EH	VIR	RIV	Set 07 - The West Coast Set
5946	AC2F/TSO	EH	VIR	RIV	Set 07 - The West Coast Set
5950	AC2F/TSO	EH	RIV	RIV	
5952 (S)	AC2F/TSO	EH	VIR	RIV	
5955 (S)	AC2F/TSO	EH	VIR	RIV	
5961	AC2F/TSO	EH	VIR	RIV	Set 07 - The West Coast Set
5964	AC2F/TSO	EH	ANG	RIV	
5985	AC2F/TSO	EH	ANG	RIV	Set 05 - The Norfolkman
5987	AC2F/TSO	EH	VIR	RIV	Set 07 - The West Coast Set
5997	AC2F/TSO	EH	VIR	RIV	Set 07 - The West Coast Set
5998	AC2F/TSO	EH	ANG	RIV	Set 05 - The Norfolkman
6006	AC2F/TSO	CF	ANG	RIV	Set 05 - The Norfolkman
6024 (S)	AC2F/TSO	EH	VIR	RIV	
6027	AC2F/TSO	EH	RIV	RIV	Set 07 - The West Coast Set
6042	AC2F/TSO	EH	ANG	RIV	Set 05 - The Norfolkman
6051	AC2F/TSO	EH	VIR	RIV	Set 07 - The West Coast Set
6054	AC2F/TSO	EH	VIR	RIV	Set 07 - The West Coast Set
6067 (S)	AC2F/TSO	EH	VIR	RIV	
6107	AC2F/TSO	EH	RIV	RIV	
6141	AC2F/TSO	EH	RIV	RIV	Set 07 - The West Coast Set
6158	AC2F/TSO	EH	VIR	RIV	Set 07 - The West Coast Set
6176 (S)	AC2F/TSO	EH	VIR	RIV	
6177	AC2F/TSO	EH	RIV	RIV	
6310 (81448)	AX51/GEN	EH	CHC	RIV	
6320	AZ5Z/SAL	SK	MRN	RIV	
6720 (6602)	AN1D/RMBF	EH	MRN	RIV	
9504	AC2E/BSO	EH	VIR	RIV	Set 07 - The West Coast Set
9507	AC2E/BSO	EH	VIR	RIV	
9520	AE2F/BSO	EH	RIV	RIV	Set 07 - The West Coast Set
9526	AC2F/BSO	EH	INT	RIV	
9527	AC2F/BSO	EH	ANG	RIV	
9537	AE2F/BSO	EH	ADV	RIV	Boat Train saver
6722 (6611)	AN1D/RMBF	LM	FSW	RIV	
17015 (14015)	AB11/BFK	EH	CHC	RIV	Set 02 - The Royal Scot
17056 (S) (14056)	AB1A/BFK	EH	MAR	RIV	
17077 (14077)	AB1A/BFK	EH	RIV	RIV	Set 04 - The Great Briton - *Catherine*
17105 (2905)	AX5B/BFK	EH	RIV	RIV	Set 02 - Staff Couchette
21224	AB31/BCK	EH	MAR	RIV	Directors saloon
21245 (99356)	AB31/BCK	EH	MAR	RIV	Set 03
21269	AB31/BCK	EH	LNE	RIV	
21272 (99129)	AB31/BCK	EH	CHC	RIV	Set 01 - The British Classic Set
35469 (99763)	AB21/BSK	EH	CCM	RIV	Set 03
80041 (1690)	AK51/RK	EH	MAR	RIV	Set 03 - Pride of the Nation
80042 (1646)	AJ41/RK	EH	BLG	RIV	

Left: *Riviera Trains operates a sizeable fleet of Mk1 and Mk2 coaching stock which is deployed on many of the steam and diesel charters seen around the UK. The vehicles are in the main well restored and in good condition. Here we see Mk1 RBR No. 1671 painted in Great Western-style chocolate and cream colours.* **Nathan Williamson**

Right: *The 2011-introduced 'Cruise Saver Travel Express' used Riviera-owned stock. Vehicle No. 9537, a Mk2F BSO is painted in Cruise Saver livery, as seen at Eastleigh.*
Nathan Williamson

Scottish Railway Preservation Society

Number	Type	Depot	Livery	Operator
1859 (99822)	AN21/RMB	BT	MAR	SRP
21241	AB31/BCK	BT	CHC	SRP
35185	AB21/BSK	BT	MAR	SRP

Stratford Class 47 Group

Vehicle Length: 63ft 6in (19.35m)	Engine: Sulzer 12LDA28C
Height: 12ft 10⅝in (3.91m)	Horsepower: 2,580hp (1,922kW)
Width: 9ft 2in (2.79m)	Electrical Equipment: Brush
Electric Train Heat fitted	

Number	Depot	Pool	Livery	Owner	Operator	Name
47580 (47732)	MNR	MBDL	LLB	S4G	S4G	County of Essex

Right: *Stratford Class 47 Group Class 47/4 No. 47580 County of Essex is restored to large logo blue livery or 'Stratford livery' and is usually kept on the Mid-Norfolk Railway. The loco has a full main line certificate and is frequently found operating charter services.* **Antony Christie**

Venice Simplon Orient Express (VSOE)

Number	Name	Type	Depot	Livery	Operator	Notes
213 (99535)	Minerva	AO40/PFP	SL	PUL	VSO	
239 (S)	Agatha	AO40/PFP	SL	PUL	VSO	
243 (99541)	Lucille	AO40/PFP	SL	PUL	VSO	
245 (99534)	Ibis	AO40/PFK	SL	PUL	VSO	
254 (99536)	Zena	AO40/PFP	SL	PUL	VSO	
255 (99539)	Ione	AO40/PFK	SL	PUL	VSO	
261 (S)	Car No. 83	AO40/PTP	SL	PUL	VSO	
264 (S)	Ruth	AO40/PCK	SL	PUL	VSO	

Private Train Operators – Riviera, SRPS, Stratford 47 Group, VSOE

VSOE

280 (99537)	Audrey	AO40/PFK	SL	PUL	VSO
281 (99546)	Gwen	AO40/PFK	SL	PUL	VSO
283 (S)	Mona	AO40/PFK	SL	PUL	VSO
284 (99543)	Vera	AO40/PFK	SL	PUL	VSO
285 (S)	Car No. 85	AO40/PTP	SL	PUL	VSO
286 (S)	Car No. 86	AO40/PTP	SL	PUL	VSO
288 (S)	Car No. 88	AO40/PTB	SL	PUL	VSO
292 (S)	Car No. 92	AO40/PTB	SL	PUL	VSO
293 (S)	Car No. 93	AO40/PTB	SL	PUL	VSO
301 (99530)	Perseus	AO41/PFP	SL	PUL	VSO
302 (99531)	Phoenix	AO41/PFP	SL	PUL	VSO
307 (S)	Carina	AO41/PFK	SL	PUL	VSO
308 (99532)	Cygnus	AO41/PFP	SL	PUL	VSO
325 (2907)		AJ11/RFO	CP	PUL	VSO
1207 (6422)		AJ11/RFO	CP	-	VSO
1221 (3371)		AJ11/RFO	CP	-	VSO
1566		AK51/RKB	CP	VSN	VSO
1953		AJ41/RBR	CP	VSN	VSO
3174	Glamis	AD1D/FO	CP	VSN	VSO
3182	Warwick	AD1D/FO	CP	VSN	VSO
3232		AD1E/FO	BH	BLG	CAD
3247	Chatsworth	AD1E/FO	CP	VSN	VSO
3267	Belvoir	AD1E/FO	CP	VSN	VSO
3273	Alnwick	AD1E/FO	CP	VSN	VSO
3275	Harlech	AD1E/FO	CP	VSN	VSO
6313 (92167)		AX51/GEN	SL	PUL	VSO
9502		AE2E/BSO	SL	PUL	VSO
10541 (99968)		AO4G/SSV	CS	MRN	VSO	Royal Scotsman - State Car 5
10556 (99969)		AO4G/SSV	CS	MRN	VSO	Royal Scotsman - Service Car
10569 (S)	Leviathan	AU4G/SLEP	CP	PUL	VSO
10729	Crewe	AS4G/SLE	CP	VSN	VSO
10734 (2914)	Balmoral	AS4G/SLE	CP	VSN	VSO
17167 (14167)		AB1D/BFK	CP	VSN	VSO
35466 (99545)		AB21/BSK	SL	PUL	VSO
92904		NBA	CP	PUL	VSO

Left: The VSOE 'British Pullman' is one of the most elegant trains in the world, formed of historic Pullman cars from a bygone era, superbly restored to modern day standards. The train is maintained at Stewarts Lane in south London. Here we see car 301 Perseus and Pullman First Parlour, marshalled in the train passing Ashford, Kent. **Antony Christie**

Left: In addition to the luxury Pullman vehicles of the British Pullman train, VSOE operate a small number of support carriages for staff and stores. One is No. 99545, a Mk1 BSK which was previously numbered 35466. The vehicle is seen at the rear of a VSOE Pullman train at Totnes. **Nathan Williamson**

Vintage Trains

Class 47

Vehicle Length: 63ft 6in (19.35m)
Height: 12ft 10⅜in (3.91m)
Width: 9ft 2in (2.79m)
Electric Train Heat fitted

Engine: Sulzer 12LDA28C
Horsepower: 2,580hp (1,922kW)
Electrical Equipment: Brush

Number	Depot	Pool	Livery	Owner	Operator
47773 (47541)	TM	MBDL	GRN	VTN	VTN

Coaching Stock

Number	Type	Depot	Livery	Owner	Operator
335 (99361)	AO11/PSK	TM	PUL	VTN	VTN
349 (99349)	AO11/PSP	TM	PUL	VTN	VTN
353 (99353)	AO11/PSP	TM	PUL	VTN	VTN
1201 (6445)	AJ1F/RFO	TM	CHC	VTN	VTN
3309	AD1F/FO	CS	ICS	VTN	-
3351	AD1F/FO	TM	CHC	VTN	VTN
3416	AD1F/FO	CS	ICS	VTN	-
5148(S)	AC2Z/TSO	TM	REG	VTN	-
5157	AC2Z/TSO	TM	CHC	VTN	VTN
5177	AC2Z/TSO	TM	CHC	VTN	VTN
5179(S)	AC2Z/TSO	TM	REG	VTN	-
5183(S)	AC2Z/TSO	TM	REG	VTN	-
5186(S)	AC2Z/TSO	TM	REG	VTN	-
5191	AC2Z/TSO	TM	CHC	VTN	VTN
5193(S)	AC2Z/TSO	TM	LNE	VTN	-
5194(S)	AC2Z/TSO	TM	REG	VTN	-
5198	AC2Z/TSO	TM	CHC	VTN	VTN
5212(S)	AC2Z/TSO	TM	LNE	VTN	-
5221(S)	AC2Z/TSO	TM	REG	VTN	-
5928	AC2F/TSO	TM	CHC	VTN	VTN
9101 (9398)	AH2Z/BSOT	TM	CHC	VTN	VTN
9496	AE2E/BSO	TM	CHC	VTN	VTN
9711	AF2F/DBSO	TM	?	VTN	VTN
17018 (99108)	AB11/BFK	TM	CHC	VTN	VTN
17090	AB1A/BFK	TM	CHC	VTN	VTN

West Coast Railway Company

Class 03

Vehicle Length: 26ft 3in (7.92m)
Height: 12ft 7⁷⁄₁₆in (3.72m)
Width: 8ft 6in (2.59m)

Engine: Gardner 8L3
Horsepower: 204hp (149kW)
Mechanical Equipment: Wilson-Drewry

Number	Depot	Pool	Livery	Owner	Operator	Name
03196(S)	CS	MBDL	GRN	WCR	WCR	Joyce
D2381(S)	CS	MBDL	BLK	WCR	WCR	

Class 08

Vehicle Length: 29ft 3in (8.91m)
Height: 12ft 8⅝in (3.87m)
Width: 8ft 6in (2.59m)

Engine: English Electric 6K
Horsepower: 400hp (298kW)
Electrical Equipment: English Electric

Number	Depot	Pool	Livery	Owner	Operator	Name
08418	CS	MBDL	EWS	WCR	WCR	
08485	CS	MBDL	BLU	WCR	WCR	
08678	CS	MBDL	GLX	WCR	WCR	Artila

Class 33

Vehicle Length: 50ft 9in (15.47m)
Height: 12ft 8in (3.86m)
Width: 33/0, 33/1 9ft 3in (2.81m), 33/2 8ft 8in (2.64m)

Engine: Sulzer 8LDA28A
Horsepower: 1,550hp (1,156kW)
Electrical Equipment: Crompton P'n

Number	Depot	Pool	Livery	Owner	Operator	Name
33025	CS	MBDL	WCR	WCR	WCR	Glen Falloch
33029	CS	MBDL	WCR	WCR	WCR	Glen Roy
33030 (S)	CS	MBDL	DRS	WCR	-	
33207	CS	MBDL	WCR	WCR	WCR	Jim Martin

WCRC

Class 37

	Vehicle Length: 61ft 6in (18.74m)	Engine: English Electric 12CSVT
	Height: 13ft 0¼in (3.96m)	Horsepower: 1,750hp (1,304kW)
	Width: 8ft 11⅝in (2.73m)	Electrical Equipment: English Electric

Number	Depot	Pool	Livery	Owner	Operator	Name
37214	CS	MBDL	WCR	WCR	WCR	Loch Laidon
37248 (S)	CS	MBDL	WCR	TTT	WCR	
37516 (S) (37086)	CS	MBDL	WCR	WCR	-	
37517 (S) (37018)	CS	MBDL	LHL	WCR	-	
37668 (S) (37257)	CS	MBDL	EWS	WCR	-	
37669 (S) (37129)	CS	MBDL	EWS	WCR	-	
37676 (37126)	CS	MBDL	WCR	WCR	WCR	Loch Rannoch
37685 (37234)	CS	MBDL	WCR	WCR	WCR	Loch Arkaig
37706 (37016)	CS	MBDL	WCR	WCR	WCR	
37710 (S) (37044)	CS	MBDL	LHL	WCR	-	
37712 (37102)	CS	MBDL	WCR	WCR	WCR	

Above: *Another of the large operators of privately owned locomotives and coaching stock is the West Coast Railway Co, based at Carnforth and Southall. The company maroon livery is applied to most locos and coaches. Class 37/5 No. 37676* Loch Rannoch *is seen heading south at Crewe with a rake of WCRC stock.* **John Stretton**

Class 47

	Vehicle Length: 63ft 6in (19.35m)	Engine: Sulzer 12LDA28C
	Height: 12ft 10⅜in (3.91m)	Horsepower: 2,580hp (1,922kW)
	Width: 9ft 2in (2.79m)	Electrical Equipment: Brush
	Electric Train Heat fitted to Class 47/4, 47/7 and 47/8	

Number	Depot	Pool	Livery	Owner	Operator	Name
47194 (S)	CS	MBDL	TLF	WCR	-	
47237	CS	MBDL	WCR	WCR	WCR	
47245	CS	MBDL	WCR	WCR	WCR	
47270	CS	MBDL	BLU	WCR	WCR	Swift
47355 (S)	CS	MBDL	WCR	WCR	-	
47492	CS	MBDL	RES	WCR	WCR	
47500 (47770)	CS	MBDL	WCR	WCR	WCR	
47526 (S)	CS	MBDL	BLU	WCR	-	
47746 (S) (47605)	CS	MBDL	WCR	WCR	-	
47760 (47562)	CS	MBDL	WCR	WCR	WCR	
47768 (47490)	CS	MBDL	EWS	WCR	WCR	
47772 (S) (47537)	CS	MBDL	RES	WCR	-	
47776 (S) (47578)	CS	MBDL	RES	WCR	-	
47786 (47821)	CS	MBDL	WCR	WCR	WCR	Roy Castle OBE
47787 (47823)	CS	MBDL	WCR	WCR	WCR	Windsor Castle
47804 (47792)	CS	MBDL	WCR	WCR	WCR	
47826 (47637)	CS	MBDL	WCR	WCR	WCR	
47851/D1648 (47639)	CS	MBDL	WCR	WCR	WCR	
47854 (47674)	CS	MBDL	WCR	WCR	WCR	

Class 57/0

Vehicle Length: 63ft 6in (19.38m)			Engine: EMD 645-12E3		
Height: 12ft 10⅛in (3.91m)			Horsepower: 2,500hp (1,860kW)		
Width: 9ft 2in (2.79m)			Electrical Equipment: Brush		

Number	Depot	Pool	Livery	Owner	Operator
57001 (47356)	CS	MBDL	WCR	WCR	WCR
57005 (47350)	CS	MBDL	ADV	WCR	WCR
57006 (47187)	CS	MBDL	ADV	WCR	WCR

Class 57/6

Vehicle Length: 63ft 6in (19.38m)			Engine: EMD 645-12E3		
Height: 12ft 10⅛in (3.91m)			Horsepower: 2,500hp (1,860kW)		
Width: 9ft 2in (2.79m)			Electrical Equipment: Brush		

Number	Depot	Pool	Livery	Owner	Operator
57601 (47825)	CS	MBDL	WCR	WCR	WCR

Class 57/6 No. 57601 is the sole loco operated by West Coast which is in the original modern traction WCRC colour scheme of maroon with a grey between-cab bodyside band. This loco was the original Porterbrook prototype for the Electric Train Supply Class 57, which after a period of use with First Great Western was sold to West Coast. The loco is seen piloting a steam special on Dainton bank. **Antony Christie**

Coaching Stock

Number	Name	Type	Depot	Livery	Operator	Notes
159 (99980)		AO10/SAL	CS	SPL	WCR*	LNWR saloon (ex-Q of Scots)
326 (S) (99402)	Emerald	AO11/PFP	CS	PUL	WCR	
347 (99347)	Car No. 347	AO11/PSO	CS	WCR	WCR	
348 (99348)	Car No. 348	AO11/PSP	CS	WCR	WCR	
350 (99350)	Car No. 350	AO11/PSP	CS	GRN	WCR	
352 (99352)	Car No. 352	AO11/PSP	CS	PUL	WCR	
354 (99354)	The Hadrian Bar	AO11/PSP	CS	PUL	WCR	
504 (99678)	Ullswater	AP1Z/PFK	CS	PUL	WCR	
506 (99679)	Windermere	AP1Z/PFK	CS	PUL	WCR	
546 (S) (99670)	City of Manchester	AQ1Z/PFP	CS	PUL	WCR	
548 (99671)	Grasmere	AQ1Z/PFP	CS	PUL	WCR	
549 (99672)	Bassenthwaite	AQ1Z/PFP	CS	PUL	WCR	
550 (99673)	Rydal Water	AQ1Z/PFP	CS	PUL	WCR	
551 (99674)	Buttermere	AQ1Z/PFP	CS	PUL	WCR	
552 (99675)	Ennerdale Water	AQ1Z/PFP	CS	PUL	WCR	
553 (99676)	Crummock Water	AQ1Z/PFP	CS	PUL	WCR	
586 (99677)	Derwent Water	AR1Z/PFB	CS	PUL	WCR	
807 (99881)		AO10/SAL	CS	SPL	WCR*	GNR Saloon (ex-Q of Scots)
1644 (S)		AJ41/RBR	CS	ICS	WCR	
1650 (S)		AJ41/RBR	CS	ICS	WCR	
1652 (S)		AJ41/RBR	CS	ICS	WCR	
1655 (S)		AJ41/RBR	CS	ICS	WCR	
1663 (S)		AJ41/RBR	CS	ICS	WCR	
1670 (S)		AJ41/RBR	CS	ICS	WCR	
1730		AJ41/RBR	CS	WCR	WCR	
1800 (5970)	Tintagel	AN2F/RSS	CS	CHC	WCR	
1840		AN21/RMB	CS	GRN	WCR	Set - The Green Train
1860		AN21/RMB	CS	WCR	WCR	
1861 (99132)		AN21/RMB	CS	WCR	WCR	
1882 (99311)		AN21/RMB	CS	WCR	WCR	

WCRC

Number	Name	Type		Livery	Operator	Notes
1961		AJ41/RBR	CS	GRN	WCR	Set - The Green Train
2127 (S)		AO11/SLF	CS	MAR	WCR	
2833 (21270)		AU51/SLSC	CS	BLU	WCR	
3058	*Florence*	AD11/FO	CS	WCR	WCR	
3093 (977594)	*Paula*	AD11/FO	CS	WCR	WCR	
3105 (99121)	*Julia*	AD11/FO	CS	WCR	WCR	
3106 (99122)	*Alexandra*	AD11/FO	CS	WCR	WCR	
3113 (99125)	*Jessica*	AD11/FO	CS	WCR	WCR	
3117 (99127)	*Christina*	AD11/FO	CS	WCR	WCR	
3128 (99371)	*Victoria*	AD11/FO	CS	WCR	WCR	
3130 (99128)	*Pamela*	AD11/FO	CS	WCR	WCR	
3136 (3605)	*Diana*	AD11/FO	CS	WCR	WCR	
3143 (3609)	*Patricia*	AD11/FO	CS	WCR	WCR	
3313		AD1F/FO	CS	WCR	WCR	
3326		AD1F/FO	CS	WCR	WCR	
3350		AD1F/FO	CS	WCR	WCR	
3352		AD1F/FO	CS	WCR	WCR	
3359		AD1F/FO	CS	WCR	WCR	
3360		AD1F/FO	CS	ICS	WCR	
3362		AD1F/FO	CS	ICS	WCR	
3392 (S)		AD1F/FO	CS	BPM	WCR	Blue Pullman vehicle
3395		AD1F/FO	CS	WCR	WCR	
3408		AD1F/FO	CS	WCR	WCR	
3431		AD1F/FO	CS	WCR	WCR	
3766 (99317)		AC21/SO	CS	WCR	WCR	
4860 (S) (99193)		AC21/TSO	CS	MAR	WCR	
4905		AC21/TSO	CS	WCR	WCR	
4912 (99318)		AC21/TSO	CS	WCR	WCR	
4931 (99329)		AC21/TSO	CS	WCR	WCR	
4932 (S)		AC21/TSO	CS	BLG	WCR	
4940		AC21/TSO	CS	WCR	WCR	
4951		AC21/TSO	CS	WCR	WCR	
4954 (99326)		AC21/TSO	CS	WCR	WCR	
4958		AC21/TSO	CS	WCR	WCR	
4960		AC21/TSO	CS	WCR	WCR	
4973		AC21/TSO	CS	WCR	WCR	
4984		AC21/TSO	CS	WCR	WCR	
4994		AC21/TSO	CS	WCR	WCR	
4997 (S)		AC21/TSO	CS	BLG	WCR	
5032 (99194)		AC21/TSO	CS	WCR	WCR	
5033 (99328)		AC21/TSO	CS	WCR	WCR	
5035 (99195)		AC21/TSO	CS	WCR	WCR	
5044 (99327)		AC21/TSO	CS	WCR	WCR	
5125 (S)		AC2Z/TSO	BH	GRN	WCR	
5171		AC2Z/TSO	CS	GRN	WCR	
5200		AC2Z/TSO	CS	GRN	WCR	
5216		AC2Z/TSO	CS	GRN	WCR	
5222		AC2Z/TSO	CS	MAR	WCR	
5229	*The Green Knight*	AC2Z/SO	CS	MAR	WTN	
5236		AC2Z/SO	CS	GRN	WCR	
5237		AD2Z/SO	CS	GRN	WCR	
5239	*The Red Knight*	AD2Z/SO	CS	MAR	WTN	
5249		AD2Z/SO	CS	GRN	WCR	
5278	*Melisande*	AC2A/TSO	CS	CHC	WTN	
5419		AC2A/TSO	CS	WCR	WTN	
5453		AC2B/TSO	CS	WCR	WCR	
5463 (S)		AC2B/TSO	CS	WCR	WCR	
5478		AC2B/TSO	CS	WCR	WCR	
5487		AC2B/TSO	CS	WCR	WCR	
5491		AC2B/TSO	CS	WCR	WCR	
5569		AC2C/TSO	CS	WCR	WCR	
5669 (S)		AC2D/TSO	CS	BPM	WCR	
5756 (S)		AC2E/TSO	CS	WCR	WCR	
6000		AC2F/TSO	CS	WCR	WCR	
6014 (S)		AC2F/TSO	CS	ICS	WCR	At Hellifield
6022		AC2F/TSO	CS	WCR	WCR	
6041		AC2F/TSO	CS	WCR	WCR	
6103		AC2F/TSO	CS	WCR	WCR	
6115 (S)		AC2F/TSO	CS	WCR	WCR	

Private Train Operators – WCRC

Number	Name	Type	Depot	Livery	Owner	Notes
6135 (S)		AC2F/TSO	CS	ICS	WCR	At Hellifield
6312 (92925)		AX51/GEN	CS	WCR	WCR	
6528 (5592)		AG2C/TSOT	CS	WCR	WCR	
6723		AN1D/RMBF	CS	WCR	WCR	
6724		AN1D/RMBF	CS	WCR	WCR	
9104 (S) (9401)		AH2Z/BSOT	CS	WCR	WCR	
9391	Pendragon	AE2Z/BSO	CS	PUL	WTN	
9392		AE2Z/BSO	CS	WCR	WCR	Set - The Green Train
9440		AE2C/BSO	CS	WCR	WCR	
9448 (S)		AE2C/BSO	CS	WCR	WCR	
9493 (S)		AE2D/BSO	EM	BPM	CWR	Blue Pullman vehicle
13227		AA11/FK	CS	WCR	WCR	
13306 (S)		AA11/FK	CS	WCR	WCR	
13320 (S)		AA11/FK	CS	WCR	WCR	
13321 (99316)		AA11/FK/RBR	CS	WCR	WCR	
13440 (S)		AA1A/FK	CS	GRN	WCR	Set - The Green Train
17102 (99680)		AB1A/BFK	CS	MAB	WCR	
17168 (S) (99319)		AB1D/BFK	CS	WCR	WCR	
18756 (99721)		AA21/SK	CS	WCR	WCR	
18767 (99710)		AA21/SK	CS	WCR	WCR	
18806 (99722)		AA21/SK	CS	WCR	WCR	
18808 (99706)		AA21/SK	CS	WCR	WCR	
18862 (99718)		AA21/SK	CS	WCR	WCR	
18893 (99712)		Kitchen	CS	WCR	WCR	
19208 (99884)	Car No. 84	AA21/SK	CS	WCR	WCR	
21256 (99304)		AB31/BCK	CS	WCR	WCR	
21266		AB31/BCK	CS	WCR	WCR	
34525 (S) (99966)		AR51/GEN	CS	WCR	WCR	
35407 (99886)		AB21/BSK	CS	SPL	WCR	LNWR livery (Q of Scots)
45018 (99052)		AO10/SAL	CS	QOS	WCR	
45026 (S)		SAL	CS	MAR	WCR	LMS Inspection Saloon
96175		GUV	CS	MAR	WCR	Water carrier
99723 (35459)		AB21/BSK	CS	WCR	WCR	

WCR* - Owned by Scottish Highland Railway Co

Above: *A large number of Mk1, Mk2 and Pullman passenger carriages are operated by West Coast; these are used for charter work or are available for hire. The vehicles are maintained in a first class condition and the majority sport WCRC livery. A number of modifications have been made to vehicles to reflect their charter role. In this view we see vehicle 99347, which was previously Pullman 347.*
Nathan Williamson

Right: *Mk2C TSOT No. 6528, modified from TSO No. 5592 in BR days' is seen carrying West Coast maroon livery, lines in black and yellow.* **Antony Christie**

Loco Support Coaches

Most preserved locomotives authorised for main line operation, either steam or diesel, operate with a support coach conveying owners' representatives, engineering staff and light maintenance equipment. Support coaches can be allocated to a specific locomotive or operate with a pool of locos.

Number	Type	Depot	Livery	Support Coach for
14007 (99782) *Mercator*	AB11/BSK	BH	MAR	61264 or 60163
14064	AB11/BSK	CS	MAR	30777, 45305, 70013
14099 (17099)	AB11/BSK	BQ	MAR	44871, 45305 or 70013
17013 (14013) *Botaurus*	AB11/BFK	SH	PUL	60019
17019 (99792)	AB11/BFK	CS	MAR	30777 or 70013
17025 (14025)	AB11/BFK	CS	MAR	45690
17041 (99141)	AB1Z/BFK	BQ	MAR	71000
17096	AB1B/BFK	SL	CHC	35028
21096 (99080)	AB31/BCK	NY	MAR	60007
21232 (99040)	AB31/BCK	CQ	MAR	6201
21236 (99120)	AB31/BCK	ZG	GRN	30828
21249 (S)	AB21/BCK	-	MAR	60163
21268	AB31/BCK	YK	MAR	60163
35317	AD21/BSK	BQ	GRN	30850
35322 (99035)	AB21/BSK	CS	MAR	70000 and WCRC traction
35329	AB21/BSK	RL	GRN	Mid Hants fleet
35333 (99180)	AB21/BSK	DI	CHC	6024
35449 (99241)	AB21/BSK	BQ	MAR	45231
35457 (99995)	AB21/BSK	NY	MAR	60532
35461 (99720)	AB21/BSK	TM	CHC	5029
35463 (99312)	AB21/BSK	CS	WCR	WCR fleet
35464	AB21/BSK	PR	MAR	Swanage Railway
35465 (99991)	AB21/BSK	BQ	CCM	Jeremy Hosking / 70000
35468 (99953)	AB21/BSK	NY	MAR	NYMR fleet
35470	AB21/BSK	TM	CHC	Vintage Trains fleet
35476 (99041)	AB21/BSK	SK	MAR	46233
35486 (99405)	AB21/BSK	--	MAR	60009 or 61994
35508	AB1C/BSK	BQ	MAR	East Lancs fleet
35517 (17088)	AB1K/BSKk	BQ	MAR	East Lancs fleet
35518 (17097)	AB11/BFK	SH	GRN	34067
80204 (35297)	NNX	CS	MAR	WCRC fleet
80217 (35299)	NNX	CS	MAR	WCRC fleet
80220 (35276)	NNX	NY	MAR	62005

Below: *Support carriages for main line steam or diesel locos are very important to transport staff and carry a limited supply of spare parts. Painted in all-over green livery is Mk2 BFK No. 35518, originally No. 17097. It is currently used as the support coach to Bulleid No. 34067* Tangmere, *and in this illustration is seen at Taunton.* **Antony Christie**

Locomotives

Number	Class	Owner	Location

No locos were off lease at the time of going to press

Diesel Multiple Units

Number	Class	Owner	Location

No DMUs were off lease at the time of going to press

Electric Multiple Units

Number	Class	Owner	Location
365526	365	EVL	ZC*
460001	460	PTR (for SWT)	
460002	460	PTR (for SWT)	
460003	460	PTR (for SWT)	
460004	460	PTR (for SWT)	
460005	460	PTR (for SWT)	
460006	460	PTR (for SWT)	

Number	Class	Owner	Location
460007	460	PTR (for SWT)	
460008	460	PTR (for SWT)	
508201	508	ANG	ZG
508202	508	ANG	ZG
508203	508	ANG	ZG
508204	508	ANG	ZG
508205	508	ANG	ZG
508206	508	ANG	ZG
508207	508	ANG	ZG

Number	Class	Owner	Location
508208	508	ANG	ZG
508209	508	ANG	ZG
508210	508	ANG	ZG
508211	508	ANG	ZG
508212	508	ANG	ZG
508301	508	ANG	ZG
508302	508	ANG	ZG
508303	508	ANG	ZG

* Collision damage

Right: *At the end of 2011 only a handful of electric multiple-units were off lease, and moves were ongoing to return these to service. A total of 15 Class 508s are currently off lease at Eastleigh; these were previously used by London Overground and South Eastern. Set No. 508301 is illustrated.* **Antony Christie**

Coaching Stock - Passenger

Number	Type	Owner	Location
1209 (6457)	RFO	EVL	ZH
1211 (3305)	RFO	EVL	BU
1219 (3418)	RFO	EVL	KT
1253 (3432)	RFO	EVL	LM
1258 (3322)	RFO	EVL	CS§
3229	FO	EVL	KT
3434	FO	EVL	OY
3438	FO	EVL	LM
5636	TSO	EVL	PM
5679	TSO	EVL	KT
5737	TSO	EVL	CS§
5740	TSO	EVL	CS§
5745	TSO	EVL	CS§
5750	TSO	EVL	KT
5754	TSO	EVL	KT
5788	TSO	EVL	KT
5793	TSO	EVL	KT
5821	TSO	EVL	KT
5881	TSO	EVL	KT
5886	TSO	EVL	KT
5888	TSO	EVL	CS§
5899	TSO	EVL	KT

Number	Type	Owner	Location
5900	TSO	EVL	CS§
5903	TSO	EVL	CS§
5905	TSO	EVL	KT
5912	TSO	EVL	KT
5930	TSO	EVL	KT
5936	TSO	EVL	LM
5947	TSO	EVL	ZG¤
5948	TSO	EVL	CS§
5962	TSO	EVL	KT
5981	TSO	EVL	ZA
5983	TSO	EVL	CS§
5991	TSO	EVL	KT
6049	TSO	EVL	KT
6052	TSO	EVL	KT
6059	TSO	EVL	KT
6061	TSO	EVL	ZG¤
6073	TSO	EVL	KT
6120	TSO	EVL	KT
6121	TSO	EVL	KT
6151	TSO	EVL	ZG
6160	TSO	EVL	LM
6164	TSO	EVL	KT

¤ For export to New Zealand
§ Transferred to West Coast Railway at end of 2011.

Number	Type	Owner	Location
9480	BSO	EVL	KT
9490	BSO	EVL	KT
9498	BSO	EVL	KT
9500	BSO	EVL	LM
9505	BSO	EVL	LM
9516	BSO	EVL	KT
9522	BSO	EVL	CE
9523	BSO	EVL	KT
10204 (40502)	RFM	PTR	3M
10231 (10016)	RFM	PTR	LM
10240 (10003)	RFM	PTR	LM
10241 (10009)	RFM	PTR	IL
10253 (10026)	RFM	PTR	LM
10256 (10028)	RFM	PTR	YO¶
10260 (10001)	RFM	PTR	YO¶

¶ Instruction vehicle - Yoker

Number	Type	Owner	Location
10547	SLE	PTR	IS
10596	SLE	PTR	LM
10661	Concept vehicle at Wolverton		
10667	SLE	-	LM
10682	SLE	PTR	TO
10698	SLE	-	LM
10733	SLE	-	MM

Off-lease Rolling Stock

11006	FO	PTR	LM	12047	TSO	PTR	LM	12134	TSO	PTR	LM
11011	FO	PTR	LM	12063	TSO	PTR	LM	12142	TSO	PTR	LM
11026	FO	PTR	LM	12065	TSO	PTR	LM	12144	TSO	PTR	LM
				12083	TSO	PTR	LM	12156	TSO	PTR	LM
12008	TSO	PTR	ZB	12087	TSO	PTR	LM	12158	TSO	PTR	BN
12022	TSO	PTR	ZB	12092	TSO	PTR	LM	12160	TSO	PTR	LM
12029	TSO	PTR	LM	12095	TSO	PTR	LM	12163	TSO	PTR	BN
12036	TSO	PTR	LM	12101	TSO	PTR	LM				

Coaching Stock - HST

Number	Type	Owner	Location								
40208 (40008)	TRSB	ANG	ZG	40434 (40034)	TRSB	PTR	LM	40745 (40345)	TRSB	ANG	ZG
40209 (40009)	TRSB	ANG	ZG	40709 (40309)	TRSB	ANG	ZG	40747 (40347)	TRSB	ANG	ZG
40228 (40028)	TRSB	ANG	ZG	40712 (40312)	TRSB	ANG	LM				
40402 (40002)	TRSB	PTR	LM	40714 (40314)	TRSB	ANG	LM	42324 owned by East Midlands			
40403 (40003)	TRSB	PTR	LM	40717 (40317)	TRSB	ANG	ZG	Trains now at Birkenshaw Fire			
40416 (40016)	TRSB	PTR	LM	40724 (40324)	TRSN	ANG	LB	Training School			
40417 (40017)	TRSB	PTR	ZK	40725 (40325)	TRSB	ANG	ZG				
40419 (40019)	TRSB	PTR	LM	40726 (40326)	TRSB	ANG	ZG				
40425 (40025)	TRSB	PTR	ZK	40731 (40331)	TRSB	ANG	ZG				
				40736 (40336)	TRSB	ANG	ZG				
				40738 (40338)	TRSB	ANG	ZG				
				40744 (40344)	TRSB	ANG	ZG				

Coaching Stock - NPCCS

Number	Type	Owner	Location								
82109	DVT	PTR	ZB	82141	DVT	PTR	LM	96602 (96150)	NV	EVL	RU
82110	DVT	PTR	LM	82145	DVT	PTR	LM	96603 (96155)	NV	EVL	ZG
82111	DVT	PTR	LM	82149	DVT	PTR	FC	96604 (96156)	NV	EVL	ZG
82124	DVT	PTR	Brush					96605 (96157)	NV	EVL	ZG
82125	DVT	PTR	LM	92159 (81534)	BG	EVL	KT	96606 (96213)	NV	EVL	RU
82128	DVT	PTR	LM	92901 (92001)	BG	EVL	WB	96607 (96215)	NV	EVL	ZG
82129	DVT	PTR	LM	92931 (92031)	BG	EVL	PY	96608 (96216)	NV	EVL	RU
82140	DVT	PTR	LM					96609 (96217)	NV	EVL	RU
				96100 (93734)	GUV	EVL	TM				
				96139 (93751)	GUV	EVL	WB				
				96181 (93875)	GUV	EVL	LM				

Above: *A sizeable number of carriages both passenger and non-passenger are stored off lease. Many of these are stored in the safe surroundings of Long Marston, a rail-connected site with many miles of sidings suitable for the stabling of vehicles. In this view we see an off-lease HST Mk3 buffet car, No. 40723, which is reported to have collision damage. The vehicle still sports the older Midland Main Line livery.* **Antony Christie**

Preserved motive power is listed in this section. Those in a red typeface are authorised for main line operation. For information on preserved steam traction and railway centres, please refer to our sister publication *Railways Restored*, edited by Alan Butcher and published by Ian Allan Publishing.

Locomotives

Main line certified shown in red

Number	Operator/Base	Status

Prototype Locomotives

LMS7050	NRM	STC
LMS7051	MID	OPR
LMS7069	GWR	RES
D0226	KWV	OPR
18000	DID	STC
DELTIC	NRM	STC

Non Classified

D2511	KWV	OPR
D2767	BKR	OPR
D2774	STR	RES
DS75	NRS	STC

Class 01

D2953	PRL	OPR
D2956	ELR	OPR

Class 02

D2854	PRL	OPR
D2858	MRC	RES
D2860	NRM	OPR
D2866	PRL	RES
D2867	BAT	OPR
D2868	MSM	OPR

Class 03

03018	MFM	RES
03020	LDL	STO
03022	SWI	OPR
D2023	KES	OPR
D2024	KES	STO
03027	PRL	RES
03037	-	OPR
D2041	COL	OPR
D2046	PVR	RES
D2051	NNR	STO
03059	IOW	OPR
03062	ELR	OPR
03063	NNR	OPR
03066	BHR	OPR
03069	GWR	OPR
03072	LHR	OPR
03073	RAC	OPR
03078	TYN	OPR
03079	DER	OPR
03081	MFM	RES
03084	ECC	OPR
03089	MFM	OPR
03090	NRS	OPR
03094	CRT	OPR
03099	PRL	OPR
D2112	KES	OPR
03113	PRL	RES
D2117	LHR	OPR
D2118	PRL	RES
03119	EPO	OPR
03120	FHL	OPR

03128	APF	STO
D2133	WSR	OPR
03134	DEE	OPR
D2138	MRC	OPR
D2139	PRL	RES
03141	PRB	RES
03144	WEN	OPR
03145	MOL	OPR
D2148	RIB	OPR
03152	SWI	OPR
03158	LWR	OPR
03162	LAN	OPR
03170	BAT	OPR
D2178	GWI	OPR
03180	PRL	OPR
D2182	GWR	OPR
D2184	COL	OPR
03189	RIB	RES
D2192	PDR	OPR
03197	LDL	RES
D2199	PRL	OPR
03371	ROW	OPR
03399	MFM	OPR

Class 04

D2203	EMB	OPR
D2205	WSR	STO
D2207	NYM	OPR
D2229	PRL	RES
D2245	BAT	STO
D2246	SDR	OPR
D2271	WSR	STO
D2272	PRL	RES
D2279	EAR	OPR
D2280	NNR	RES
D2284	PRL	OPR
D2298	BRC	OPR
D2302	BHR	OPR
D2310	BAT	OPR
D2324	PRL	STO
D2325	MFM	OPR
D2334	CVR	OPR
D2337	PRL	RES

Class 05

05001	IOW	OPR
D2578	BHR	OPR
D2587	PRL	RES
D2595	RIB	OPR

Class 06

06003	MSM	OPR

Class 07

07005	GCR	RES
07010	AVR	OPR
07011	SEL	OPR
07012	APF	RES
07013	BHR	RES

Class 08

D3000	PRL	RES
D3002	PVR	OPR

D3014	PDR	OPR
08011	CPR	OPR
08012	CRT	OPR
08015	SVR	OPR
08016	PRL	OPR
08021	BRM	OPR
08022	CWR	OPR
08032	MHR	OPR
08046	CRB	OPR
08054	EMB	OPR
08060	CWR	OPR
08064	NRS	OPR
D3101	GCR	OPR
08102	LWR	OPR
08108	KES	OPR
08114	GCR	OPR
08123	CWR	OPR
08133	SVR	OPR
D3255	CVR	STO
08164	ELR	OPR
08168	BAT	OPR
D3261	SWI	RES
08195	LAN	OPR
08220	NHC	STO
08238	DFR	OPR
08266	KWV	OPR
08288	MHR	OPR
08359	TSR	OPR
08377	WSR	OPR
08388	NHD	STO
08436	SWN	OPR
08443	BKR	RES
08444	BWR	OPR
08471	SVR	OPR
08473	DFR	STO
08476	SWN	OPR
08479	ELR	OPR
08490	STR	OPR
08528	BAT	OPR
08556	NYM	OPR
08590	MRC	OPR
08598	IND	OPR
08604	DID	OPR
08628	RIB	OPR
08631	MNR	OPR
08635	SVR	RES
08683	GWR	RES
08694	GCR	RES
08700	ELR	OPR
08767	NNR	OPR
08769	SVR	OPR
08772	NNR	OPR
08773	EMB	OPR
08780	SOU	OPR
08830	RAC	OPR
08850	NYM	OPR§
08891	SVR	RES
08896	SVR	OPR
08911	NRM	OPR
08937	DAR	OPR
08944	ELR	OPR

§ Battersby-Whitby only

Class 09

09001		
09004	SPV	OPR
09010	SDR	RES
09017	NRM	OPR
09024	PRI	RES
09025	SWI	OPR

Class 10

D3452	BWR	OPR
D3489	SPV	OPR
D4067	GCR	OPR
D4092	BHR	RES

Class 11

12052	CRB	STO
12061	PRL	RES
12077	MRC	OPR
12082	MHR	OPR
(Runs as 12049)		
12093	CRB	OPR
12099	SVR	OPR
12131	NNR	OPR

Class 12

15224	SPV	OPR

Class 14

D9500	PRL	RES
D9502	PRL	STO
D9504	NVR	OPR
D9513	EMB	OPR
D9516	WEN	OPR
D9518	WSR	OPR
D9520	NVR	OPR
D9521	DFR	OPR
D9523	DVR	OPR
D9524	EHC	RES
D9525	PRL	OPR
D9526	WSR	OPR
D9529	NVR	OPR
D9531	ELR	RES
D9537	RIP	RES
D9539	RIB	OPR
D9551	DEE	OPR
D9553	GWR	STO
D9555	DFR	OPR

Class 15

D8233	ELR	RES

Class 17

D8568	CPR	RES

Class 20

D8000	NRM	OPR
20001	ECC	OPR
20007	GCR	OPR
20020	BKR	RES
20031	KWV	OPR
20035	CVR	STO
20048	MRC	RES
20059	BRM	RES
20063	GWR	STO
20069	MNR	OPR
20087	ELR	OPR
20098	GCR	RES
20110	SDR	OPR
20137	GWR	OPR
20142	BAR	OPR
20154	GCR	OPR
20169	SRC	RES
20177	SVR	STO
20188	SVR	OPR
20189	MRC	OPR
20205	MRC	RES
20214	LHR	OPR
20227	MRC	OPR
20228	BIR	OPR

Class 24

24032	NYM	RES
24054	ELR	OPR
24061	NYM	RES
24082	GWR	OPR

Class 25

25035	GCR	OPR
25057	NNR	OPR
25059	KWV	OPR
25067	BAT	OPR
25072	CRB	RES
25083	CRB	RES
25173	EPO	OPR
25185	PDR	OPR
25191	SDR	STO
25235	BKR	RES
25244	EKR	STO
25262	SDR	OPR
25265	GCR	RES
25278	NYM	OPR
25279	GCR	OPR
25283	DFR	RES
25309	WCR	RES
25313	WEN	RES
25321	MRC	OPR
25322	CVR	RES

Class 26

26001	CRB	OPR
26002	STR	RES
26004	BKR	STO
26007	GCR	OPR
26010	LAN	OPR
26011	BHR	RES
26014	CRB	OPR
26024	BKR	OPR
26025	STR	RES
26035	CRB	RES
26038	CAN	RES
26040	MET	RES
26043	GWR	RES

Class 27

27001	BKR	OPR
27005	BKR	STO
27007	MHR	RES
27024	LHR	OPR
27050	STR	RES
27056	GCR	OPR
27059	SVR	RES
27066	DFR	OPR

Class 28

D5705	ELR	RES

Class 31

D5500	NRM	OPR
31101	BAT	RES
31108	MRC	OPR
31119	EMB	OPR
31130	BAT	OPR
31162	EHC	OPR
31163	CPR	OPR
31203	PBR	OPR
31206	RST	OPR
31207	NNR	OPR
31210	DFR	RES
31235	MNR	OPR
31255	COL	OPR
31270	PRL	OPR
31271	NVR	OPR
31289	NLR	OPR
31327	STR	OPR
31410	SRC	RES
31414	ECC	OPR
31415	BHR	RES
31418	MRC	RES
31435	EMB	OPR
31438	EPO	OPR
31461	BAT	STO
31463	GCR	OPR
31466	DFR	OPR
31530	MNR	RES

Class 33

33002	SDR	OPR
33008	BAT	RES
33012	SWN	OPR
33019	BAT	OPR
33021	BRM	RES
33034	SWN	RES
33035	ECC	OPR
33046	MRC	STO
33048	WSR	OPR
33052	KES	OPR
33053	MHR	OPR
33057	WSR	RES
33063	SPV	OPR
33065	SPV	RES
33102	CVR	RES
33108	BHR	RES
33109	ELR	OPR
33110	BWR	RES
33111	SWN	OPR
33116	GCR	OPR
33117	ELR	RES
33201	MRC	OPR
33202	MFM	OPR
33208	MHR	OPR

Class 35

D7017	WSR	OPR
D7018	WSR	RES
D7029	SVR	RES
D7076	ELR	OPR

Class 37

D6700	NRM	OPR

37003	MNR	OPR
37009	GCR	RES
37023	ALY	RES
37025	BKR	RES
37032	NNR	RES
37037	MNR	OPR
37042	EVR	OPR
37075	CVR	OPR
37097	CRB	OPR
37108	RAC	OPR
37109	ELR	OPR
37116	CPR	OPR
37142	BWR	OPR
37146	SRC	RES
37152	PRL	RES
37175	BKR	RES
37188	PRL	RES
37207	PVR	RES
37215	GWR	OPR
37216	PBR	OPR
37219	PBR	OPR
37227	BAT	OPR
37240	LAN	OPR
37250	WED	RES
37254	SPV	OPR
37255	GCR	OPR
37263	DFR	RES
37264	BRM	RES
37275	BHR	OPR
37294	EMB	RES
37308	EHD	RES
37314	MRC	OPR
37324	GWR	OPR
37372	BHR	RES
37403	BKR	RES
37407	CVR	STO
37413	NEM	RES
37418	ELR	RES
37421	PBR	RES
37424	CVR	STO
37518	ELR	OPR
37674	SRC	RES
37679	NLR	RES
37901	ELR	OPR
37905	BAT	OPR
37906	SVR	OPR

Class 40
D200	NRM	RES
40012	MRC	OPR
40013	BHR	OPR
40106	WAS	OPR
40118	BRM	RES
40135	ELR	OPR
40145	ELR	OPR

Class 41
41001	NRM	STC

Class 42
D821	SVR	OPR
D832	WSR	OPR

Class 44
D4	MRC	RES
44008	PRL	OPR

Class 45
45014	BAT	STO
45041	MRC	OPR
45060	BHR	OPR
45105	BHR	RES
45108	MRC	RES
45118	NLR	RES
45125	GCR	OPR
45132	MHR	RES
45133	MRC	RES
45135	ELR	RES
45149	GWR	RES

Class 46
46010	GCN	OPR
46035	RAC	STO
46045	MRC	OPR

Class 47
47004	EMB	OPR
47105	GWR	OPR
47117	GCR	OPR
47192	DAR	OPR
47205	NLR	OPR
47292	GCR	OPR
47306	BWR	OPR
47367	NNR	OPR
47376	GWR	RES
47401	MRC	OPR
47402	ELR	OPR
47417	MRC	RES
47449	LAN	OPR
47484	BHR	RES
47524	CVR	RES
47540	WEN	STO
47596	MNR	RES
47635	BAT	OPR
47640	BAT	OPR
47643	BKR	OPR
47701	DAR	OPR
47703	WEN	OPR
47715	WEN	OPR
47765	GCR	RES
47771	COL	RES
47773	BRM	OPR
47785	ECC	RES
47793	MFM	OPR
47798	NRM	OPR
47799	SRC	RES
47840	WST	OPR

Class 50
50002	SDR	RES
50007	MRC	OPR
50008	ELR	OPR
50015	ELR	OPR
50017	PVR	RES
50019	MNR	OPR
50021	BRM	RES
50026	EHD	RES
50027	NYM	OPR
50029	PRL	STO
50030	PRL	RES
50031	SVR	RES
50033	BRM	STO
50135	EHD	OPR
50042	BWR	OPR

50044	MRC	OPR
50049	SVR (CF)	OPR
50050	YEO	RES

Class 52
D1010	WSR	OPR
D1013	SVR	OPR
D1015	BRM	OPR
D1023	NRM	OPR
D1041	ELR	STO
D1048	MRC	RES
D1062●	SVR	OPR

Class 55
55002	NRM	RES
55009	BHR	OPR
55015	BHR	RES
55016	BHR	OPR
55019	BHR	OPR
55022	ELR	OPR

Class 56
56006	BHR	OPR
56007	---	RES
56086	BAT	RES
56097	GCR	OPR
56098	BAT	RES
56301	BHR	OPR
56302	BHR	OPR

Class 58
58016	BHR	RES

Class 97
97650	LWR	OPR
97651	STR	OPR
97654	PRL	OPR

Class 71
71001	NRS	STO

Class 73
73001	DFR	OPR
73003	SWI	OPR
73005	SVR(EH)	RES
73006	RAC	OPR
73101	AVR	OPR
73103	THK	STO
73110	GCR	OPR
73114	BAT	OPR
73117	BHR	OPR
73128	PBR	OPR
73129	GWR	OPR
73130	FIN	OPR
73134	BHR	OPR
73140	SPV	OPR
73210	MNR	OPR

Class 76
E26020	NRM	STC

Class 77
E27000	MRC	STC
E27001	MSM	STC

Class 81
81002	BHR	STC

Class 82		
82008	BHR	STC

Class 83		
83012	BHR	STC

Class 84		
84001	BHR	STC

Class 85		
85101	BHR	STC

Class 86		
86101	BHR	OPR
86233	MLM	STC
86259	BRM	OPR

Class 87		
87001	NRM	STC
87002	MLM	OPR
87035	RAC	RES

Class 89		
89001	BHR	STC

London Transport		
12	LUL	OPR

● Scheduled to go main line

Below: *Class 52 'Western' No. D1010 Western Campaigner masquerading as No. D1035 Western Yeoman stands at Minehead on the West Somerset Railway.* **CJM**

Diesel Units

Number	Base
Unclassified	
APT-E	NRS
LEV1	NNR
RB004	TEL
79018	MRC
79612	MRC
79900	ECC
79960	NNR
79962	KWV
79963	NNR
79964	KWV
79976	GCR
79978	COL

Class 100	
56301	MNR

Class 101	
50222	BIR
50256	EKR
50338	BIR
51505	ECC
51187	CRT
51188	ECC
51189	KWV
51192	ELR
51205	CRT
51210	WEN
51226	MNR
51228	NNR
51247	WEN

51427	GCR
51434	MNR
51499	MNR
51503	MNR
51505	EAR
51511	NYM
51512	CRT
51213	EAR
51803	KWV
53160	MRC
53164	CHS
53170	ECC
53193	GCR
53203	GCR
53204	NYM
53253	MRC
53266	GCR
53321	GCR
53746	WEN
54055	CRT
54062	NNR
54365	EAR
54408	SPV
56343	EKR
56352	ELR
56358	EAR
59117	MNR
59539	NYM

Class 104	
50447	LAN
50454	LAN

50455	TEL
50479	TEL
50494	CVR
50517	CVR
50528	LAN
50531	TEL
50547	CVR
50556	TEL
56182	CVR
59137	CVR
59228	TEL

Class 105	
51485	ELR
56121	ELR
56456	LAN

Class 107	
51990	STR
52005	NVR
52006	AVR
52008	STR
52025	AVR
52030	STR
59791	NVR

Class 108	
50599	EAR
50619	DFR
50632	PBR
50929	KWV
50980	BWR

51562	ELR
51565	KWV
51566	DFR
51567	MRC
51568	KEI
51571	KES
51572	WEN
51907	LAN
51909	MSR
51914	DFR
51919	BVR
51922	ELR
51933	DFR
51941	SVR
51942	PBR
51947	BWR
51950	GWR
51973	MRC
52044	PBR
52048	BVR
52053	KEI
52054	BWR
52062	GWR
52064	SVR
53628	KEI
53645	GCR
53926	GCR
53971	KES
54223	EAR
54270	PBR
54279	LDL
54490	LAN

54504	SWN	59761	BRC	59510	GWR	55966	MRC
56208	SVR			59513	PDR	55976	MRC
56224	ECC	**Class 116**		59514	SWI	59609	MRC
56271	MSR	51131	BAT	59516	SWN		
56484	MRC	51138	GCR	59517	PDR	**Class 140**	
56491	KEI	51151	GCR	59520	PBR	140001 - 55500/01	KEI
56492	DFR	51321	BAT	59521	MRC		
56495	KLR	59003	PDR	59522	CHS	**Class 141**	
59245	APF	59004	PDR	59603	CHS	141103	WED
59250	SVR	59444	CHS			141108	COL
59387	DFR			**Class 119**		141110	WED
59389	GCR	**Class 117**		51073	ECC	141113	MRC
		51339	GWR	51074	SWI		
Class 109		51341	MRC	51104	SWI	**Class 201, 202 & 203**	
50416	LAN	51342	EPO			60116	HAD
56171	LAN	51346	SWN	**Class 120**		60118	HAD
		51347	GWI	59276	GCR	60501	HAD
Class 110		51351	PBR			60529	HAD
51813	WEN	51353	MRC	**Class 121**		60750	WPH
51842	WEN	51356	SWN	55019	BRM	201001	HAD
52071	LHR	51359	NLR	55023	CPR		
52077	LHR	51360	ECC	55024	BRM	**Class 205**	
59701	CVR	51363	GWR	55028	SWN	60117	PBR
		51365	GWR	55029	RST	60822	LDL
Class 111		51367	STR	55033	COL	60828	PBR
59575	MRC	51372	TIT	54289	ECC	60154 X 1101 EKR	
		51381	MFM	56287	COL	60800 X 1101 EKR	
Class 114		51382	GWR			70549	ELR
50015	MRC	51384	EPO	**Class 122**		Set 205009	EDR
50019	MRC	51388	SWN	55000	SDR	Set 205025	MHR
54057	STR	51392	SWN	55001	ELR	Set 205028	DAR
56006	MRC	51395	MRC	55003	GWR	Set 205032	DAR
56015	MRC	51397	PBR	55005	BAT	Set 205033	LDL
		51398	MRC	55006	ECC	Set 205205	EPO
Class 115		51400	WEN	55009	MNR		
51655	(BIR)¤	51401	GWI	55012	SHI	**Class 207**	
51663	WSR	51402	STR			60127	SWI
51669	SPV	51405	GWR	**Class 126**		60130 X 207202 ELR	
51677	(BIR)¤	51407	GWR	51017	BKR	60138	WPH
51859	WSR	59486	SWN	51043	BKR	60142	SPV
51880	WSR	59488	PDR	59404	BKR	60145	SEL
51886	BRC	59492	SWN	79443	BKR	60149	SEL
51887	WSR	59494	PDR			60616	SPV
51899	BRC	59500	WEN	**Class 127**		60901	SWI
59659	SDR	59503	PDR	51592	SDR	60904 X 207202 ELR	
59664	(BIR)¤	59506	WSR	51604	SDR	60916	SPV
59678	-	59507	PDR	51616	GCR		
59719	SDR	59508	GWI	51618	LAN	901001	CVR
59740	SDR	59509	WEN	51622	GCR		

Right: *On the Great Central Railway, Metropolitan Cammell 'power twin' Nos. 50321 + 51427 have been preserved. The pair are restored to early 1960s 'whisker' livery and are seen on 24 July 2011 providing a Loughborough to Quorn service at Woodthorpe.* **Michael J. Collins**

Preserved Motive Power

Electric Units

Unclassified
28249	NRM
29666	MRC
29670	MRC
79998	DEE
79999	DEE

BEL
85	SOU
87	KEI
91	RAM

BIL
10656 (2090)	NRS
12123 (2090)	NRS

COR
10096	EKR
11161	EKR
11179	NRM
11201	BLU
11825	EKR

DD
13004	NIR

Class 302
75033	MFM
75250	MFM

Class 303
303032	SHP

Class 306
306017	EAR

Class 307
75023	ERM

Class 308
75881	ERM

Class 309
309616	COV
309624	COV

Class 405 (SUB)
S8143S	NRM
4732	COV

Class 411/412 (CEP)
61742	DAR
61743	DAR
61798	EVR
61799	EVR
61804	EVR
61805	EVR
70229	EVR
70257	GCR
70273	DFR
70284	NIR
70292	SMP
70296	NIR
70354	EVR
70527	WRN
70531	SMP
70539	EVR
70576	SNI
70607	EVR
Set 1198	PBR
Set 7105	EKR

Class 414 (HAP)
61275	NRM
61287 (4311)	COV
75395	NRM
75407 (4311)	COV

Class 415 (EPB)
14351 (5176)	NIR
14352 (5176)	NIR
15345	COV
15396 (5176)	NIR

Class 416 (EPB)
65302	FIN
65304	FIN
65373 (5759)	EKR
77558 (5759)	EKR
14573 (6307)	COV
16117 (6307)	COV
65321 (5791)	COV
77112 (5793)	COV

Class 419 (MLV)
68001	EKR
68002	EKR
68003	EVR
68004	MNR
68005	EVR
68008	EKR
68009	EKR

Class 421 (CIG)
62364	DFR
62378	DFR
62887	LWR
69339	GCR
76726	DFR
76740	DFR
76797	DFR
76811	DFR
76812	DAR
Set 1496	DAR
Set 1497	MNR
Set 1498	EPO
Set 1399	PBR
Set 1881	BEL

Class 422 (BEP)
69304	NIR
69310	DAR
69318	COL
69332	DAR
69333	LDL

69337	HAD

Class 423 (VEP)
(42)3417	BLU
76875	NRM

Class 457
67300	COV

Class 488
72501	ECC
72617	ECC

Class 489
68500	ECC
68506	ECC

Class 501
61183	COV
75186	COV

Class 502
28361	TEB
29896	TEB

Class 503
28690	COV
29298	COV
29720	COV

Class 504
65451	ELR
77172	ELR

Left: *Now preserved on the Epping and Onger Railway, former Southern Region CIG No. 1498 is seen on the Swanage Railway powered by a push-pull Class 33/1. This unit was one of the last CIGs in traffic, operating the Brockenhurst to Lymington Pier service until 2010.* **Mark V. Pike**

Over the years a number of former BR locomotives have, after withdrawal from normal duties, taken up use for industrial operators. The list below represents those which are understood to still be in existence in late 2011. Some locos operated at preservation sites are deemed to be 'industrial' but these are grouped in the preserved section.

Class 03

03179 *Clive*	First Capital Connect, Hornsey Depot

Class 08

08202	Celsa Steel, Cardiff
08331 (H001)	Cemex, Washwood Heath
08375	P D Ports, Teesport No. 21
08398 (402D) *Annabel*	Imerys Clay Company, Bugle
08411	LH Group, Burton - owned by Classic Traction
08441	Colne Valley Railway
08445	Daventry International Railfreight Terminal (DIRFT) - at LH Group, Burton
08447	John G. Russell Transit, Hillington, Glasgow
08460	Colne Valley Railway
08484 *Captain Nathaniel Darell*	Felixstowe Dock & Railway
08503	Rye Farm, Wishaw
08511	Felixstowe Dock & Railway
08523	Weardale Railway
08535	Corus, Shotton Works
08598	The Potter Group, Ely
08600	LH Group Services, Barton-under-Needwood
08613	Hanson Traction, Washwood Heath
08622 (H028) (7)	Weardale Railway
08643	Aggregate Industries, Whatley
08648	P D Ports, Teesport No. 20
08650 *Isle of Grain*	Aggregate Industries, Isle of Grain
08652	Hanson Aggregates, Whatley Quarry
08670	Colne Valley Railway
08699	Corus, Shotton Works
08728	St. Modwen Storage, Long Marston
08731	Aggregate Industries, Merehead
08743 *Bryan Turner*	LH Group Services, Barton under Needwood
08774 *Arthur Vernon Dawson*	AV Dawson, Middlesbrough
08787	Hanson Aggregates, Machen
08807	AV Dawson, Middlesbrough
08809	Corus, Shotton (at Washwood Heath 12/10)
08818 *Molly*	Faber Prest Ports, Flixborough Wharf
08823 (D3991)	Thames Steel, Isle of Sheppey
08847	Stored at Norwich Crown Point (Cotswold Rail - for sale)
08870 (H024)	Castle Cement, Ketton
08872	European Metal Reprocessing, Attercliffe
08873	Freightliner Terminal, Southampton
08881 (D4095)	Lafarge Aggregates, Mountsorrel
08903 *John W. Antill*	SembCorp Utilities Teesside, Wilton
08912	AV Dawson, Middlesbrough
08913	Daventry International Freight Terminal (Owned by Hunslet)
08915	Stephenson Railway Museum
08933	Aggregate Industries, Merehead
08936	Corus, Shotton Works
08937 *Bluebell Mel*	Aggregate Industries, Meldon Quarry
08947	Aggregate Industries, Merehead
09022	Boston Docks Co

Class 11

12088	Butterwell

Class 14

D9529 (14029)	Aggregate Industries, Bardon Quarry

Class 56

56009 (56201)	Brush Traction, Loughborough

Industrial

These lists give details of former UK diesel and electric locos exported for further use overseas and understood to still be operational.

Class 03
D2013   Italy
D2032   Italy
D2033   Italy
D2036   Italy

Class 04
D2216   Italy
D2232   Italy
D2289   Italy
D2295   Italy

Class 08
D3047   Lamco Liberia
D3092   Lamco Liberia
D3094   Lamco Liberia
D3098   Lamco Liberia
D3100   Lamco Liberia

Class 10
D3639   Conakry (Guinea)
D3649   Conakry (Guinea)

Class 14
D9534   Bruges

Class 37
37714   Continental Rail, Spain
37716   Continental Rail, Spain
37718   Continental Rail, Spain
37800   Continental Rail, Spain
37884   Continental Rail, Spain

Class 58
58001   ETF France
58004§   TSO France
58005   ETF France
58006§   ETF France
58007   TSO France
58009   TSO France
58010   TSO France
58011§   TSO France
58013   ETF France
58015   Transfesa, Spain
58018   TSO France
58020   Transfesa, Spain
58021   TSO France
58024   Transfesa, Spain
58025   Continental Rail, Spain
58026§   TSO France
58027   Continental Rail, Spain
58029   Transfesa, Spain
58030   Transfesa Spain
58031   Transfesa, Spain
58032   ETF France
58033   TSO France
58034   TSO France
58035   TSO France
58036   ETF France
58038   ETF France
58039   ETF France
58040§   TSO France
58041   Transfesa, Spain
58042   TSO France
58043   Transfesa, Spain

58044   ETF France
58046   TSO France
58047   Transfesa, Spain
58049§   ETF France
58050   Continental Rail, Spain
§ Stored at Alizay (Rouen)

Class 59
59003   HHPI, Germany

Class 66
66010   ECR, France
66022   ECR, France
66026   ECR, France
66032   ECR, France
66036   ECR, France
66038   ECR, France
66042   ECR, France
66045   ECR, France
66049   ECR, France
66052   ECR, France
66064   ECR, France
66072   ECR, France
66073   ECR, France
66123   ECR, France
66146   ECR, Poland
66153   ECR, Poland
66157   ECR, Poland
66159   ECR, Poland
66163   ECR, Poland
66166   ECR, Poland
66173   ECR, Poland

Below: *A sizeable number of former UK-based EWS (DBS) Class 66/0s are now working in France and Poland. In this view we see Euro Cargo Rail-branded No. 66240 powering an empty wood train passing Châlons-en-Champagne near Reims.* **Michael J. Collins**

66178	ECR, Poland	66233	ECR, France	86218	Floyd, Hungary	
66179	ECR, France	66234	ECR, France		As 0450-004-1	
66180	ECR, Poland	66235	ECR, France	86232	Floyd, Hungary	
66189	ECR, Poland	66236	ECR, France		As 0450-003-3	
66190	ECR, France	66237	ECR, Poland	86248	Floyd, Hungary	
66195	ECR, France	66240	ECR, France		As 0450-001-7	
66196	ECR, Poland	66241	ECR, France	86250	Floyd, Hungary	
66202	ECR, France	66242	ECR, France		As 0450-002-5	
66203	ECR, France	66244	ECR, France			
66205	ECR, France	66246	ECR, France	Class 87		
66208	ECR, France	66247	ECR, France	87003	BZK Bulgaria	
66209	ECR, France	66248	ECR, Poland	87004	BZK Bulgaria	
66210	ECR, France			87006	BZK Bulgaria	
66211	ECR, France	66411	Freightliner, Poland	87007	BZK Bulgaria	
66212	ECR, France	66412	Freightliner, Poland	87008	BZK Bulgaria	
66214	ECR, France	66417	Freightliner, Poland	87010	BZK Bulgaria	
66215	ECR, France	66582	Freightliner, Poland	87012	BZK Bulgaria	
66216	ECR, France	66583	Freightliner, Poland	87013	BZK Bulgaria	
66217	ECR, France	66584	Freightliner, Poland	87014	BZK Bulgaria (spares)	
66218	ECR, France	66586	Freightliner, Poland	87019	BZK Bulgaria	
66219	ECR, France	66608	Freightliner, Poland	87020	BZK Bulgaria	
66220	ECR, Poland	66609	Freightliner, Poland	87022	BZK Bulgaria	
66222	ECR, France	66611	Freightliner, Poland	87026	BZK Bulgaria	
66223	ECR, France	66612	Freightliner, Poland	87028	BZK Bulgaria	
66224	ECR, France	66624	Freightliner, Poland	87029	BZK Bulgaria	
66225	ECR, France	66625	Freightliner, Poland	87033	BZK Bulgaria	
66226	ECR, France			87034	BZK Bulgaria	
66228	ECR, France	Class 86				
66229	ECR, France	86215	Floyd, Hungary			
66231	ECR, France		As 0450-005-x			

Below: *When introduced in 1973 for 'Electric Scot' services between Euston and Glasgow, no one would have ever imagined that one day these locos would be working in Bulgaria. However, times change and in 2012, 17 Class 87/0s are working in Eastern Europe. No. 87003-0 is illustrated.* **Philip Wormald**

A number of preserved modern traction locomotives have been allocated five-digit Class 89 TOPS numbers to allow their operation either under power or dead over the National Network. The numbers allocated are shown below; not all locos may currently be authorised for use on Network Rail metals.

The first two digits are the class, the third is the power type, while the final two digits are the final two of the original running number. If two locos clash with the same number, the second to be registered will have 1 added to the number.

Class 89 TOPS No.	BR No.	Type	Name
89100	20050	Class 20	-
89101	20001	Class 20	-
89110	20110	Class 20	-
89127	20227	Class 20	-
89166	20166	Class 20	-
89188	20188	Class 20	-
89200	31018	Class 31	-
89204	26004	Class 26	-
89210	27059	Class 27	-
89212	LT 12	Met Loco	Sarah Siddons
89223	25173	Class 25	-
89233	25283	Class 25	-
89247	27001	Class 27	-
89254	24054	Class 24	-
89259	25309	Class 25	-
89261	24061	Class 24	-
89262	25262	Class 25	-
89280	31162	Class 31	-
89317	D7017	Class 35	-
89376	D7076	Class 35	-
89400	E27000	Class 77	Electra
89401	47401	Class 47	North Eastern
89402	50002	Class 50	Superb
89403	71001	Class 71	-
89404	44004	Class 44	Great Gable

89405	47105	Class 47	-
89407	50007	Class 50	Sir Edward Elgar
89408	50008	Class 50	Thunderer
89412	40012	Class 40	Aureol
89413	D1013	Class 52	Western Ranger
89415	50015	Class 50	Valiant
89416	D1015	Class 52	Western Champion
89417	50017	Class 50	Royal Oak
89420	45108	Class 45	-
89421:1	D821	Class 42	Greyhound
89421:2	50021	Class 50	Rodney
89423	45125	Class 45	-
89424	D1023	Class 52	Western Fusilier
89427	50027	Class 50	Lion
89431	50031	Class 50	Hood
89432	D832	Class 42	Onslaught
89435	40135	Class 40	-
89440	45133	Class 45	-
89441	D1041	Class 52	Western Prince
89442	47192	Class 47	-
89443	50042	Class 50	Triumph
89444	50044	Class 50	Exeter
89445	40145	Class 40	-
89448	D1048	Class 52	Western Lady
89449	50049	Class 50	Defiance
89453	45041	Class 45	Royal Tank Regiment
89460	45060	Class 45	Sherwood Forester
89462	D1062	Class 52	Western Courier
89466	47449	Class 47	-
89472	46035	Class 46	Ixion
89500	55022	Class 55	Royal Scots Grey
89502	55002	Class 55	The King's Own Yorkshire Light Infantry
89503	81002	Class 81	-
89509	55009	Class 55	Alycidon
89515	55015	Class 55	Tulyar
89516	55016	Class 55	Gordon Highlander
89519	55019	Class 55	Royal Highland Fusilier
89523	DP1	Proto	Deltic
89535	83012	Class 83	-
89561	85101	Class 85	-

Left: E3061, later 85006, then 85101 is now preserved by the AC Locomotive Group and kept at Barrow Hill. Under the requirements of TOPS, when this loco has been hauled over the National Network it has been allocated a unique identity as 89561. The loco is seen at Exeter on display at an open weekend. CJM

Several preserved steam locomotives have been allocated five-digit TOPS numbers to allow their operation over the National Network. The numbers allocated are shown below; not all locos may currently be authorised for use on Network Rail metals.

TOPS No.	Railway No.	Type	Name
98150	1450	GWR 14xx	
98166	1466	GWR 14xx	
98186	686	0-6-0T	Lady Armaghdale
98212	41312	LMS 2MT	
98219	55189	CR 0-4-4T	
98221	46521	LMS 2MT	
98238	1638	GWR 16xx	
98240	3440	GWR 34xx	City of Truro
98241	46441	LMS 2MT	
98243	46443	LMS 2MT	
98253	30053	SR M7	
98254	58926	LNWR 2F	
98273	65243	NBR J36	Maude
98315	7715	GWR 57xx	
98321	69621	GER N7	A. J. Hill
98372	30072	SR USA	
98400	41000	LMS 4P	
98406	43106	LMS 4MT	
98414	75014	BR 4MT	
98425	7325	GWR 7321	
98426	31625	SR U	
98427	44027	LMS 4F	
98435	80135	BR 4MT	
98455	4555	GWR 45xx	
98457	9600	GWR 8750	
98460	7760	GWR 57xx	
98466	9466	GWR 94xx	
98469	75069	BR 4MT	
98472	5572	GWR 4575	
98476	76079	BR 4MT	
98478	68078	WD 4F	
98479	80079	BR 4MT	
98480	80080	BR 4MT	
98482	3882	0-6-0ST	Barbara
98488	4588	GWR 4575	
98494	65894	LNER J27	
98498	80098	BR 4MT	
98500	45000	LMS 5MT	
98502	7802	GWR 78xx	Bradley Manor
98505	45305	LMS 5MT	Alderman A E Draper
98507	45407	LMS 5MT	Lancashire Fusilier
98510	45110	LMS 5MT	
98512	7812	GWR 78xx	Erlestoke Manor
98519	7819	GWR 78xx	Hinton Manor
98525	45025	LMS 5MT	
98526	30925	SR V	Cheltenham
98529	73129	BR 5MT	
98530	4930	GWR 49xx	Hagley Hall
98531	45231	LMS 5MT	Sherwood Forester
98532	44932	LMS 5MT	
98536	4936	GWR 49xx	Kinlet Hall
98549	4965	GWR 49xx	Rood Ashton Hall
98553	4953	GWR 49xx	Pitchford Hall
98560	6960	GWR 6959	Raveningham Hall
98564	61264	LNER B1	
98565	42765	LMS 6P5F	
98567	44767	LMS 5MT	George Stephenson
98568	42968	LMS 5MT	
98571	44871	LMS 5MT	
98572	5972	GWR 49xx	Olton Hall
98577	30777	SR N15	Sir Lamiel
98596	73096	BR 5MT	
98598	6998	GWR 6959	Burton Agnes Hall
98605	62005	LNER K1	
98628	30828	SR S15	
98641	30841	SR S15	
98642	61994	LNER K4	The Great Marquess
98690	45690	LMS 6P5F	Leander
98693	45593	LMS 6P5F	Kolhapur
98696	45596	LMS 6P5F	Bahamas
98700	70000	BR 7P	Britannia
98701	34101	SR WC	Hartland
98709	53809	SDJR 7F	
98713	70013	BR 7P	Oliver Cromwell
98715	46115	LMS 7P	Scots Guardsman
98716	34016	SR WC	Bodmin
98727	34027	SR WC	Taw Valley
98728	5029	GWR 4073	Nunney Castle
98729	7029	GWR 4073	Clun Castle
98750	30850	SR LN	Lord Nelson
98751	5051	GWR 4073	Earl Bathurst
98767	34067	SR BB	Tangmere
98771	60800	LNER V2	Green Arrow
98772	34072	SR BB	257 Squadron
98780	5080	GWR 4073	Defiant
98792	34092	SR WC	City of Wells
98800	6000	GWR 60xx	King George V
98801	46201	LMS 8P	Princess Elizabeth
98802	71000	BR 8P	Duke of Gloucester
98803	46203	LMS 8P	Princess Margaret Rose
98805	35005	SR MN	Canadian Pacific
98809	60009	LNER A4	Union of South Africa
98824	6024	GWR 60xx	King Edward I
98828	35028	SR MN	Clan Line
98829	46229	LMS 8P	Duchess of Hamilton
98832	60532	LNER A2	Blue Peter
98834	46233	LMS 8P	Duchess of Sutherland
98851	48151	LMS 8F	
98857	2857	GWR 28xx	
98863	60163	LNER A1	Tornado
98868	60022	LNER A4	Mallard
98872	60103	LNER A3	Flying Scotsman
98873	48773	LMS 8F	
98898	60007	LNER A4	Sir Nigel Gresley
98920	92220	BR 9F	Evening Star

Above: *Although carrying its correct 'Black Five' number 45407, this loco on TOPS is officially No. 98507. The loco is seen at York.* **Ron Cover**

Coupling Codes & Couplings

With the introduction of modern traction from the 1950s a number of different methods of multiple operation were introduced, covering the different control principle of locomotives, for example those using electro-pneumatic or electro-magnetic systems.

Six main systems are in operation today:

Blue Star ★ using the electro-pneumatic system and fitted to Classes 20, 25, 31, 33, 37, 40 and 73.

Green Spot ● a unique system installed on some Class 47s operated by the freight sector.

Orange Square ■ an English Electric system used only on the Class 50s.

Red Diamond ◆ a 1970s system developed for the modern freight locos of Classes 56 and 58.

In addition to the above coded systems, the American-developed main line locos of Classes 59, 66, 67 and 70 use the US standard AAR (Association of American Railroads) system. Direct Rail Services (DRS) have also developed a unique system which is installed on some of the company's Class 20, 37, 47 and 57 locos.

A number of locomotives have either been built with or modified to incorporate Time Division Multiplex (TDM) remote operation equipment, which uses coach lighting type Railway Clearing House (RCH) nose end jumper cables.

Some of the surviving first generation DMMU sets carry a **Blue Square** ■ multiple operation system.

Details of the main coupling systems in operation in the UK are included in the accompanying illustrations.

Standard Coupling

Above: Class 59 and 66 front end layout (non-DBS operated). 1-Coupling hook, 2-Coupling shackle, 3-Air brake pipe (red), 4-Main reservoir pipe (yellow), 5-Buffer, 6-Association of American Railroads (AAR) jumper socket. No. 66726 illustrated. **CJM**

Standard Coupling

Above: Standard coupling arrangement to be found on many classes of UK loco. 1-Electric Train Supply (ETS) jumper socket, 2-Main reservoir air pipe (yellow), 3-Vacuum brake pipe, 4-Coupling hook and shackle, 5-Air brake pipe (red), 6-Electric Train Supply (ETS) jumper cable. Loco No. 47580 illustrated. **CJM**

Drop Head Buck-Eye with TDM Coupling

Above: The unique front end layout of the Royal Mail Class 325. 1-Brake pipe (red), 2-Main reservoir pipe (yellow), 3-Electric Train Supply (ETS) socket, 4-Time Division Multiplex (TDM) jumper socket, 5-Drop-head buck-eye coupling, 6-Electric Train Supply (ETS) cable. **CJM**

Couplings

Drop Head Dellner Coupling

Above: *Following the introduction of Virgin Trains 'Voyager' and 'Pendolino' stock, a fleet of 16 Class 57/3s were introduced with drop head Dellner couplers and cabling to provide 'hotel power'. The coupling is seen in this illustration in the raised position. 1-Electric Train Supply (ETS) jumper socket, 2-Main reservoir pipe (yellow), 3-Air brake pipe (red), 4-Coupling hook, 5-Dellner coupling face, 6-Electric Train Supply (ETS) jumper cable.* **CJM**

BSI Coupling

Above: *With the birth of modern multiple-unit trains came the Bergische Stahl Industrie (BSI) automatic coupling, first seen in the UK on the Tyne & Wear Metro vehicles in 1978. The modern generation of UK DMUs now concentrate on the Compact BSI coupler with a CK2 coupling interface. The couplers are engaged by the compression of the two coupling faces which completes a physical connection and also opens a watertight cover to an electrical connection box. The full train air connection is made during the coupling compression process. The coupling is complete by the driver pressing a 'couple' button in the driving cab. 1-Emergency air connection, 2-Coupling face, 3-Electric connection (behind plate), 4-Air connection. The coupling shown is on a Class 166.* **CJM**

Tightlock with Drum Connection

Above: *The Tightlock coupler is a derivative of the Association of American Railroads (AAR) Type H coupler, later under the control of American Public Transportation Association (APTA). A modified Type H coupler was introduced in the UK from the early 1970s and has become a standard fitting on many of the later BR and several post-privatisation EMUs. The UK Tightlock design can be supplied with or without an electrical connection box and with or without a pneumatic connection. This view shows a fully automated version as fitted to the 'Networker' fleet. Attachment is achieved by driving the two vehicles together which physically connects the vehicles, while a 'roll-cover' box opens to connect electric and pneumatic services. 1-Emergency air connector, 2-Manual release handle, 3-Semi-rotary electric/pneumatic cover, 4-Physical coupler.* **CJM**

Tightlock with Nose End Connections

Above: *The BR Southern Region-designed Class 455 and 456 units have a semi-automatic Tightlock used for physical connections, while air and electrical connections are made by waist height flexible pipes. 1-Main reservoir pipe (yellow), 2-Control jumper, 3-Tightlock coupler, 4-Couple/Uncouple drum switch, 5-Manual release handle, 6-Control jumper receptacle.* **CJM**

Dellner Coupling with Drum Connector

Above: *Dellner couplers have become the standard in the UK and much of Europe; these are fully automatic and come in various forms. 1-Emergency air supply, 2-Dellner coupling plate, 3-Pneumatic connection, 4-Roll-cover to electrical connections, 5-Air supply. Coupling of Class 360 illustrated.* **CJM**

Couplings

Dellner Coupling

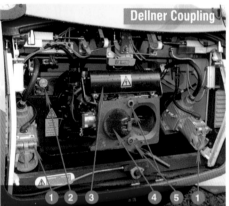

Dellner Coupling

Above: *A large number of different design of Dellner couplers exist on UK rolling stock. Some feature full automatic operation including pneumatic and electrical connections, while others only provide physical coupling. This view shows a pair of Voyager units coupled together with Dellner couplers. The electrical connection box is above the physical coupler. After trains are 'pushed' together the driver operates a 'couple' button in the cab to complete the attachment. Uncoupling is achieved by the driver pressing an 'uncouple' button and driving the trains apart.* **CJM**

Left: *The Virgin Trains 'Pendolino' stock use Dellner couplers with a rotary covered electrical connector plate above. These couplers are supplemented by electric train supply connections either side to provide 'hotel power' to Class 390 sets from attached Class 57 locos. 1-Electric Train Supply (ETS) socket, 2-Emergency air connector, 3-Electrical connector plate under semi-rotary cover, 4-Dellner physical coupler, 5-Pneumatic connections. In normal use the Dellner coupler on 'Pendolino' stock is covered by a front fairing.* **CJM**

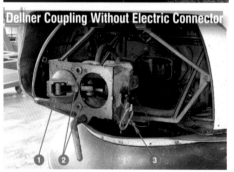

Dellner Coupling Without Electric Connector

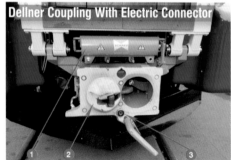

Dellner Coupling With Electric Connector

Above: *Under the front end fairing of the Eurostar Class 373 stock a standard Scharfenberg is located for assistance purposes and shunting. No electrical provision is made and the couplers are seldom used. 1-Scharfenberg coupling face, 2 Pneumatic connections, 3-Manual uncoupling handle.* **CJM**

Above: *In as-installed condition and having never been coupled to another set, a Class 380 Scharfenberg coupler is viewed, showing the auto opening electrical connection box above. 1-Electrical connection box, 2-Coupling face plate, 3-Pneumatic connection.* **CJM**

Couplings

Emergency HST Bar Coupling

Above: *If High Speed Trains are required to be coupled to conventional hook couplings an adaptor coupling is carried on the HST for this purpose. It has to be first attached to the front of the HST by opening the front panel and attaching the aluminium bar to a coupling lug. The other end is then at the right level and length to attach to a standard loco hook coupling without the loco's buffers touching the HST's bodywork. Standard air connection is provided. Locos fitted with swing head or combination couplers cannot be used to assist HST stock. A Class 59/1 is seen attached to HST power car No. 43150 in this view at Westbury.* **Greg Welsh**

Right: *All DBS Class 66s (except 66001/002) and all Class 67s are fitted with swing-head combination couplers allowing attachment to other like fitted locos or rolling stock using a knuckle coupling. Two Class 66s are seen here attached using the swing-head coupler. Note that the buffers do not touch and that all traction and breaking forces are transmitted through the coupler. Standard buffer beam air connections are provided on one main reservoir and one brake pipe. The auto coupler can be disconnected by using the white uncoupling handle seen on the left.* **Antony Christie**

DBS Combination Coupler

Couplings

Transport for London
London Underground

Address: ✉ Floor 11, Windsor House, 50 Victoria Street, London SW1H 0TL

📠 pressoffice@tfl.gov.uk

☎ 0845 604 4141

ⓘ www.tfl.gov.uk

Managing Director:　Mike Brown

Operations: The London Underground system, now operated by Transport for London (TfL), operates services on 10 lines in and around the capital and uses a mix of surface and tunnel stock.

Bakerloo Line　Tube Line. Operates services between Elephant & Castle and Harrow & Wealdstone.
Rolling Stock: 1972 Mk2, livery - red, white and blue, allocated to Stonebridge Park. Scheduled for replacement in 2018.

Central Line　Tube Line. Operates services between West Ruislip/Ealing and Epping
Rolling Stock: 1992, livery - red, white and blue, allocated to Hainault.

Circle Line　Sub-Surface Line. Operates circle network in Central London and the branch from Edgware Road to Hammersmith.
Rolling Stock: 'C' stock, introduced 1969-78, livery - red, white and blue, allocated to Hammersmith.

District Line　Sub-Surface Line. Operates services between Wimbledon, Richmond, Ealing, Edgware Road, Kensington Olympia and Upminster.
Rolling Stock: 'C' and 'D' stock, livery - red, white and blue, allocated to Ealing Common and Upminster.

Jubilee Line　Tube Line. Operates services between Stanmore and Stratford.
Rolling Stock: 1996, livery - red, white and blue, allocated to Wembley Park.

Metropolitan Line　Sub-Surface Line. Operates services from Amersham, Chesham, Watford and Uxbridge to Aldgate.
Rolling Stock: 'A' stock and 'S' stock, livery - red, white and blue, allocated to Wembley Park.

Northern Line　Tube Line. Operates services between Morden and Edgware, Mill Hill East and High Barnet.
Rolling Stock: 1995 Stock, livery - red, white and blue, allocated to Morden.

Piccadilly Line　Tube Line. Operates services between Heathrow Airport / Uxbridge and Cockfosters.
Rolling Stock: 1973 Stock, livery - red, white and blue, allocated to Northfields and Cockfosters. Stock due for replacement in 2014.

Victoria Line　Tube Line. Operates services between Brixton and Walthamstow Central
Rolling Stock: 2009 Stock, livery - red, white and blue, allocated to Northumberland Park.

Waterloo & City Line　Tube Line. Operates services between Waterloo and Bank
Rolling Stock: 1992 Stock, livery - red, white and blue, allocated to Waterloo.

Above: *The Transport for London District Line currently uses D78 stock introduced between 1980-83. A total of 78 sets were built by Metro-Cammell to replace CO/CP and R stock. On 27 July 2011 a rake of D78 stock arrives at Upminster.* **Antony Christie**

Below: *The much needed modernisation of the Transport for London Metropolitan Line commenced in 2010 with new S stock entering service, built by Bombardier of Derby. A total of 191 trains will be introduced by 2014, with operations extending to the Circle, District and Hammersmith & City lines. Led by vehicle 21004, a rake of new S stock is seen at Croxley on the Metropolitan Line in October 2010.* **John Binch**

For space reasons, we are unable in this publication to provide vehicle numbers for London Underground stock.

Transport for London
Docklands Light Railway

Contact details as London Underground.

Operations: The Docklands Light Railway operates between Bank and Tower Gateway and Woolwich Arsenal, Beckton and Stratford, as well as a Lewisham to Stratford service.

Class B90 (twin)

Train Length: 94ft 5in (28.80m)
Width: 8ft 7in (2.65m)
Power Supply: 750V dc third rail
Seating: 52 + 4 tip-up
Horsepower: 375hp (280kW)
Electrical Equipment: Brush

22	25	28	31	34	37	40	43
23	26	29	32	35	38	41	44
24	27	30	33	36	39	42	

Class B92 (twin)

Train Length: 94ft 5in (28.80m)
Width: 8ft 7in (2.65m)
Power Supply: 750V dc third rail
Seating: 54 + 4 tip-up
Horsepower: 375hp (280kW)
Electrical Equipment: Brush

45	51	57	63	69	75	81	87
46	52	58	64	70	76	82	88
47	53	59	65	71	77	83	89
48	54	60	66	72	78	84	90
49	55	61	67	73	79	85	91
50	56	62	68	74	80	86	

Class B2K (twin)

Train Length: 94ft 5in (28.80m)
Width: 8ft 7in (2.65m)
Power Supply: 750V dc third rail
Seating: 52 + 4 tip-up
Horsepower: 375hp (280kW)
Electrical Equipment: Brush

01	04	07	10	13	16	94	97
02	05	08	11	14	92	95	98
03	06	09	12	15	93	96	99

Class B07 (twin)

Train Length: 94ft 5in (28.80m)
Width: 8ft 7in (2.65m)
Power Supply: 750V dc third rail
To be extended to three-car sets in time for 2012 Olympic Games
Seating: 52 + 4 tip-up
Horsepower: 375hp (280kW)
Electrical Equipment: Bombardier

101	108	115	122	129	136	143	150
102	109	116	123	130	137	144	151
103	110	117	124	131	138	145	152
104	111	118	125	132	139	146	153
105	112	119	126	133	140	147	154
106	113	120	127	134	141	148	155
107	114	121	128	135	142	149	

Left: *Class B90 set No. 43 is seen on the Docklands Light Railway at Lewisham.* **Antony Christie**

Transport for London
Croydon Tramlink

Contact details as London Underground.
Operations: The Croydon Tramlink operates between Croydon and Wimbledon, New Addington, Beckenham, and Elmers End.

Six-axle stock

Train Length: 98ft 9in (30.1m)			Seating: 70		
Width: 8ft 7in (2.65m)			Horsepower: 643hp (480kW)		
Power Supply: 750V dc overhead			Electrical Equipment: Bombardier		

2530	2533	2536	2539	2542	2545	2548	2551
2531	2534	2537	2540	2543	2546	2549	2552
2532	2535	2538	2541	2544	2547	2550	2553

Name applied
2535   ***Stephen Parascandolo***
        1980-2007

Right: *Transport for London Croydon Tramlink set No. 2533 is seen at Arena.*
Murdoch Currie

Manchester Metrolink

Address: ✉ Greater Manchester PTE, 2 Piccadilly Gardens, Manchester, M1 3BG
             RATP Metrolink, Metrolink House, Queens Road, Manchester, M8 0RY
         ✎ customerservices@metrolink.co.uk
         ✆ 0161 205 2000   ⓘ www.metrolink.co.uk

Metrolink is operated for GMPTE by Metrolink RATP Dev UK Ltd.
Operations: Manchester Metrolink operates a street and dedicated track tram system around Manchester. Services operate from the city centre to Bury, Altrincham, Eccles via MediaCity UK and St Werbergh's Road.

T-68 Six-axle stock

Train Length: 95ft 1in (29m)		Seating: 82 + 4 tip-up
Width: 8ft 7in (2.65m)		Horsepower: 697hp (520kW)
Power Supply: 750V dc overhead		Electrical Equipment: Firema

1001		1010		1019	
1002		1011	*VANS . The original since 1966*	1020	*Lancashire Fusilier*
1003		1012		1021	
1004	*VANS . The original since 1966*	1013		1022	*Poppy Appeal*
1005		1014		1023	
1006	*VANS . The original since 1966*	1015		1024	
1007	*East Lancashire Railway*	1016		1025	
1008		1017	*Bury Hospice*	1026	
1009		1018		1001-1026 to be phased out	

Light Rail

Above: *It was announced in late 2011 that 12 of the original 28 T-68 Manchester Metrolink cars will be withdrawn following delivery of further M5000 stock. Set No. 1019 is seen at Manchester Victoria on a Bury line service.* **Ron Cover**

T-68 Six-axle stock

Train Length: 95ft 1in (29m)	Seating: 82 + 4 tip-up	
Width: 8ft 7in (2.65m)	Horsepower: 697hp (520kW)	
Power Supply: 750V dc overhead	Electrical Equipment: Ansaldo	

2001	2002	2003	2004	2005	2006

M5000 stock

Train Length: 93ft 1in (28.4m)	Seating: 52 + 8 tip-up	
Width: 8ft 7in (2.65m)	Horsepower: 643hp (480kW)	
Power Supply: 750V dc overhead	Electrical Equipment: Bombardier	

3001	3012	3023	3034	3045	3056	3067
3002	3013	3024	3035	3046	3057	3068
3003	3014	3025	3036	3047	3058	3069
3004	3015	3026	3037	3048	3059	3070
3005	3016	3027	3038	3049	3060	3071
3006	3017	3028	3039	3050	3061	3072
3007	3018	3029	3040	3051	3062	3073
3008	3019	3030	3041	3052	3063	3074
3009	3020	3031	3042	3053	3064	
3010	3021	3032	3043	3054	3064	
3011	3022	3033	3044	3055	3066	

Name carried

3009	50th Avviversary Coronation Street 1960-2010

At the start of 2012, vehicles up to 3047 had been delivered and sets 3001-3017 were in daily use.

Left: *One of the new M5000 Manchester Trams, No. 3010, is seen departing from the 2011, opened St. Werburgh's Road station on 21 October 2011.* **John Binch**

Nottingham Express Transit

Address: ✉ Transdev Tram UK Ltd, Garrick House, 74 Chiswick High Road, London, W4 1SY
Nottingham City Transport Ltd, Lower Parliament Street, Nottingham, NG1 1GG
🖥 info@thetram.net © 0115 942 7777, ⓘ www.thetram.net

Operations: Nottingham Express Transit (NET) operate trams between Hucknall and Nottingham.

Incentro AT6/5

Train Length: 108ft 3in (29m)	Seating: 54 + 4 tip-up
Width: 7ft 9in (2.4m)	Horsepower: 697hp (520kW)
Power Supply: 750V dc overhead	Electrical Equipment: Bombardier

201
202 *DH Lawrence*
203 *Bendigo Thompson*
204 *Erica Beardsmore*
205 *Lord Byron*
206 *Angela Alcock*
207 *Mavis Worthington*
208 *Dinah Minton*
209 *Sid Standard*
210 *Sir Jesse Boot*
211 *Robin Hood*
212 *William Booth*
213 *Mary Potter*
214 *Dennis McCarthy*
215 *Brian Clough*

Right: *NET tram No. 207 is seen at Station Street station.* **Murdoch Currie**

Midland Metro

Address: ✉ Travel West Midlands, PO Box 3565, Birmingham, B1 3JR
🖥 info@travelmetro.co.uk © 0121 254 7272, ⓘ www.travelmetro.co.uk

Operations: Midland Metro operates trams between Birmingham Snow Hill and Wolverhampton.

T-69 Six-axle stock

Train Length: 108ft 3in (29m)	Seating: 54 + 4 tip-up
Width: 7ft 9in (2.4m)	Horsepower: 697hp (520kW)
Power Supply: 750V dc overhead	Electrical Equipment: Bombardier

01(S)	*Sir Frank Whittle*	07	*Billy Wright*	13	*Anthony Nolan*
02		08	*Joseph Chamberlain*	14	*Jim Eames*
03	*Ray Lewis*	09	*Jeff Astle*	15	*Agenoria*
04		10	*John Stanley Webb*	16	*Gerwyn John*
05	*Sister Dora*	11	*Theresa Stewart*		
06	*Alan Garner*	12			

Right: *T-69 six-axle tram No. 08 stands at Black Lake station on the Midland Metro network.* **John Binch**

Light Rail

Sheffield Super Tram

Address: ✉ Stagecoach Supertram, Nunnery Depot, Woodburn Road, Sheffield, S9 3LS
🖥 enquiries@supertram.com
✆ 0114 272 8282
ⓘ www.supertram.com

Operations: Sheffield Super Tram operates services within Sheffield city centre and to Herdings Park, Halfway, Meadowhall Interchange, Middlewood and Malin Bridge.

Six-axle stock

Train Length: 113ft 6in (34.75m)				Seating: 80 + 6 tip-up			
Width: 8ft 7in (2.65m)				Horsepower: 800hp (596kW)			
Power Supply: 750V dc overhead				Electrical Equipment: Siemens			

101	105	109	113	117	121	125
102	106	110	114	118	122	
103	107	111	115	119	123	
104	108	112	116	120	124	

Left: *Sheffield Supertram Duewag eight-axle-articulated vehicle No. 120 has received a representation of the 1950s Sheffield Corporation blue/cream livery to commemorate the end of the original trams in the city centre on 8 October 1960. No. 120 heads away from the Park Square triangle with a Malin Bridge to Halfway service. The tram has been adorned with the Sheffield Corporation crest on the front end but when photographed was not numbered.*
John Binch

Tyne & Wear Metro

Address: ✉ Tyne & Wear Passenger Transport Executive (NEXUS), Nexus House,
33 St James Boulevard, Newcastle upon Tyne, NE1 4AX
🖥 enquiries@nexus.co.uk
✆ 0191 203 3333
ⓘ www.nexus.org.uk

Operations: Tyne & Wear Metro operates tram services within Newcastle city centre and to Whitley Bay, Newcastle Airport, South Shields, Sunderland and South Hylton.

Six-axle stock

Train Length: 91ft 3in (27.80m)				Seating: 68 tip-up			
Width: 8ft 7in (2.65m)				Horsepower: 500hp (374kW)			
Power Supply: 1500V dc overhead				Electrical Equipment: Siemens			

4001	4011	4021	4031	4041	4051	4061	
4002	4012	4022	4032	4042	4052	4062	
4003	4013	4023	4033	4043	4053	4063	
4004	4014	4024	4034	4044	4054	4064	
4005	4015	4025	4035	4045	4055	4065	
4006	4016	4026	4036	4046	4056	4066	
4007	4017	4027	4037	4047	4057	4067	
4008	4018	4028	4038	4048	4058	4068	
4009	4019	4029	4039	4049	4059	4069	
4010	4020	4030	4040	4050	4060	4070	

4071	4074	4077	4080	4083	4086	4089
4072	4075	4078	4081	4084	4087	4090
4073	4076	4079	4082	4085	4088	

Names applied
4026 *George Stephenson*
4041 *Harry Cowans*
4060 *Thomas Bewick*
4064 *Michael Campbell*
4065 *Dame Catherine Cookson*
4073 *Danny Marshall*
4077 *Robert Stephenson*
4078 *Ellen Wilkinson*

Right: *Newcastle Metro vehicle No. 4047, painted in blue and yellow livery, is seen on Ouseburn Viaduct. These sets are currently in the process of a major refurbishment at Wabtec, Doncaster.* **John Binch**

Glasgow Subway

Address: ✉ SPT, Consort House, 12 West George Street, Glasgow, G2 1HN

    ✈ enquiry@spt.co.uk

    ✆ 0141 332 6811

    ⓘ www.spt.co.uk

Glasgow Subway is operated by Strathclyde Partnership for Transport (SPT).
Operations: Circular network around Glasgow city centre.

Single Power Cars

Length: 42ft 2in (12.81m)   *Seating: 36S*
Width: 7ft 7in (2.34m)   *Horsepower: 190hp (142.4kW)*
Power Supply: 600V dc third rail   *Electrical Equipment: GEC*

101	105	109	113	117	121	125	129	133
102	106	110	114	118	122	126	130	
103	107	111	115	119	123	127	131	
104	108	112	116	120	124	128	132	

Trailer Cars

Length: 41ft 6in (12.70m)   *Seating: 40S*
Width: 7ft 7in (2.34m)

| 201 | 202 | 203 | 204 | 205 | 206 | 207 | 208 |

Right: *A three-car set of Glasgow Underground stock is seen at Govan forming an Outer Circle train. Car No. 132 is leading.* **Murdoch Currie**

Light Rail

Rail Data Tables

Livery Codes

ABL	Arriva Trains Blue
ADV	Advenza Freight, blue with yellow branding
AGI	Aggregate Industries green, silver and green
AIN	Aggregate Industries - blue
ALS	Alstom Transportation
ANG	Anglia - mid blue
ANN	Anglia - turquoise/white with National Express East Anglia branding
ATE	Arriva Trains Executive - turquoise/cream with branding
ATT	Arriva Trains Wales - two-tone turquoise
ATW	Arriva Trains Wales - turquoise/cream
AXC	Arriva Cross Country - brown, silver, pink
BBR	Balfour Beatty Rail blue/white
BLG	Blue and Grey
BLK	Black
BLL	BR rail blue with large logo
BLU	Blue
BLW	Carillion Rail blue/white
BOM	Bombardier Transportation
BPM	Blue Pullman - Nankin blue and white
BRD	BR Departmental mid grey
BRT	BR Trainload two-tone grey
C2C	c2c - blue/pink
CAL	Caledonian Railway
CAR	Carmine & Cream
CEN	Central Trains blue and two-tone green
CHC	Chocolate & Cream
CIV	BR Civil Engineers - grey and yellow
COL	Colas - Orange, lime green and black
CON	Continental Rail - light/mid blue
COR	Corus Steel - light blue or yellow
COX	Connex white and yellow
CRG	Chilton Railways - grey
CRW	Chilton Railways - white/blue
CTL	Central Trains blue, green with yellow doors
CWR	Cotswold Rail - silver with branding
DBB	DB Schenker - light blue
DBM	DB Schenker - maroon
DBS	DB Schenker - red
DCG	Devon & Cornwall Railway - green
DRC	Direct Rail Services - blue Compass branding
DRO	Direct Rail Services - Ocean Liner blue
DRS	Direct Rail Services - blue
DRU	Direct Rail Services - unbranded blue
ECG	East Coast - grey
ECR	European Cargo Rail - grey
ECS	East Coast - silver
ECW	East Coast - white
ECT	East Coast branded National Express livery
EMT	East Midlands Trains, white, blue, swirl cab ends
EPS	European Passenger Services
EPX	Europhoenix red/silver
ETF	ETF Rail - yellow with green band
EU2	Eurotunnel - Europorte2
EUS	Eurostar - white, yellow and blue
EWE	English Welsh Scottish Executive
EWS	English Welsh Scottish - red with gold band
FCC	First Capital Connect, First Group Urban Lights - mauve/blue with pink, blue and white lower branding
FER	Fertis - grey with branding
FGB	First Great Western blue
FGF	First Group - GBRf (Barbie)
FGL	First Great Western local lines
FGN	First Great Western branded Northern blue
FGS	First Group ScotRail with EWS branding
FGT	First Great Western, Thames/London area branding
FGW	First Great Western, as FST with FGW branding
FHT	First Hull Trains, as FST with Hull Trains branding
FLF	Fastline Freight - grey with yellow/white chevrons
FLG	Freightliner green unbranded
FLP	Freightliner - green/yellow - PowerHaul
FLR	Freightliner - green/yellow - original
FLU	Freightliner - green/yellow - unbranded
FLY	Freightliner grey
FNA	First livery with National Express East Anglia branding
FOS	Foster Yeoman
FRB	Fragonset black
FSN	Northern branded First Group
FSP	First Scotrail Strathclyde carmine and cream (some with turquoise band)
FSR	First ScotRail, as FST with FSR branding
FSS	First ScotRail, blue with white Saltire branding
FST	First Group - dark blue, pink and white swirl
FSW	First Group - green and white with gold branding
FTP	First TransPennine, as FST with FTP branding
GAT	Gatwick Express, white, mid-grey and red with red doors
GBE	GB Railfreight - Europorte branding
GBF	GB Railfreight - swirl
GBM	GB Railfreight Metronet
GBN	GB Railfreight/Eurotunnel new livery
GBR	GB Railfreight - blue
GBU	GB Railfreight swirl (no First branding)
GLX	Glaxochem - grey, blue and black
GNE	Great North Eastern Railway - blue
GRN	Green
GRY	Grey
GSW	Great Scottish & Western Railway - maroon
GTL	Grand Central Railway - black
GTO	Grand Central Railway - black with orange
GWG	First Great Western - green
GWR	Great Western Railway - green
HAN	Hanson
HEC	Heathrow Connect - grey, orange
HEL	Heathrow Connect - Terminal 4 'Link'
HEX	Heathrow Express - silver, grey
HNR	Harry Needle Railroad - yellow/grey

Data Tables

HS1	High Speed 1 - blue with powder blue doors		RIV	Riviera Trains - maroon
HUN	Hunslet		RML	Royal Mail Limited - red
ICS	InterCity Swallow - two-tone grey off-set with red and white body band		ROY	Royal Train - claret
IND	Industrial colours of operator		RTB	Railtrack - blue
INT	InterCity two-tone grey off-set with red and white body band		RTK	Railtrack - grey/brown
JAR	Jarvis maroon		SCE	Stagecoach - white with East Midlands branding
LAF	Lafarge Aggregates - green/white		SCT	ScotRail Caledonian Sleeper - mauve/ white
LHL	Loadhaul Freight - black and orange		SEC	Serco
LLB	Large Logo Blue		SET	South Eastern Trains - white with branding
LMI	London Midland grey, green and black		SGK	Southern Gatwick Express - blue, white and red with swirl ends
LNE	LNER tourist green/cream		SIL	Silver
LOG	London Overground, white and blue with orange doors		SKL	Silverlink London Overground, SLK with London Overground branding
LUL	London Underground red		SLF	Silverlink, with First Great Western branding
MAB	Statesman Pullman - maroon/beige		SLK	Silverlink, mauve, green and white
MAI	MainTrain - blue with branding		SNF	Railfreight grey with SNCF branding
MAL	Malcolm Rail		SNT	SNCF domestic on Eurostar, silver, while and yellow
MAR	Maroon		SOU	Southern - white, black and green
MED	Medite - black		SPL	Special livery
MER	Merseyrail - silver and yellow		STN	Stansted Express
MLF	Mainline Freight - aircraft blue		STO	Stobart Rail
MLG	Mainline Freight - branded double grey		SWM	South West Trains main line white and blue
MML	Midland Main Line - turquoise/white		SWO	South West Trains outer suburban blue
NBP	Northern Belle Pullman cream/umber		SWS	South West Trains suburban red
NE2	National Express with c2c branding		SWT	South West Trains blue, red, grey
NGE	First Great Eastern grey/blue with cab end swirl, branded National Express		TAT	Tata Steel - blue
NOM	Northern Rail - blue Metro branded		TES	Tesco
NOR	Northern - blue, purple, grey		TEX	TransPennine Express - As FST with TPE brand
NOU	Northern unbranded		TGG	Transrail Grey with 'T' branding
NRL	Network Rail - yellow with branding		THM	Thameslink - blue, white, yellow
NSE	Network SouthEast - red, white and blue		TLF	Trainload Freight - grey
NUB	Northern Rail blue - unbranded ScotRail		TLL	Trainload grey with Loadhaul branding
NWT	North West Trains - dark blue		TLP	Thameslink promotional multi-coloured stripes
NXA	National Express East Anglia (Now Abellio)		TPD	Trans Pennine/Central Trains logo
NXE	National Express East Coast		TSO	Travaux du Sud Ouest - yellow
NXG	National Express East Coast branding on GNER blue livery		TTG	Two-tone grey
NXS	National Express brand on Silverlink		VIR	Virgin - red/grey
NXU	National Express unbranded white/grey		VSN	VSOE Northern
ONE	One Anglia mid blue (Now Abellio)		VT1	Virgin - red/grey unbranded
ORN	One Railway with National Express branding (Now Abellio)		VWC	Virgin West Coast, silver, red, white and black
PCL	BR Parcels red/grey		WAB	Wabtec Rail - black
POL	Police livery		WAG	West Anglia Great Northern - purple
PTR	Porterbrook		WAL	Wales & Borders 'Alphaline' silver/grey
PUL	Pullman - umber/cream		WCR	West Coast Railway - maroon
PUR	Artemis purple		WES	Wessex Trains - maroon
QOS	Queen of Scots Pullman		WET	Wessex Trains - silver, maroon/pink doors
REG	Regional Railways blue, white		WEX	Wessex Rail Engineering
RES	Rail express systems - red and graphite		WHT	White
RFD	Railfreight Distribution		WMD	West Midlands Network, light blue and green
RFE	Railfreight grey with EWS branding		WSR	Wrexham & Shropshire two-tone grey
RFG	Railfreight grey		YEL	Yellow
RFI	Railfreight International			
RFP	Railfreight with Petroleum branding			
RFT	BR Railfreight - grey, red and yellow, with large logo and numbers			

Data Tables

Rail Data Tables

Operational Pool Codes

ADFL	Advenza Freight - Freight locos
ATLO	West Coast Traincare - Locomotives
ATTB	West Coast Traincare - Class 57/3 with Dellner
ATZZ	West Coast Traincare - Locos for disposal
CDJD	Serco Railtest - Shunting locos
COLO	Colas Rail - Operational locomotives
CREL	Cotswold Rail - Locomotives
DFFT	Freightliner - Restricted duties
DFGC	Freightliner Class 86/5 trials locomotive
DFGH	Freightliner - Heavy Haul Class 70
DFGI	Freightliner - Intermodal Class 70
DFGM	Freightliner - Intermodal Class 66/5
DFHG	Freightliner - Heavy Haul Class 66/5 & 66/6
DFHH	Freightliner - Heavy Haul Class 66/5 & 66/6
DFIM	Freightliner - Intermodal Class 66/5
DFIN	Freightliner - Intermodal - low emission
DFLC	Freightliner - Class 90
DFLS	Freightliner - Class 08
DFNC	Freightliner - Class 86/6
DFRT	Freightliner - Class 66 Infrastructure contracts
DFTZ	Freightliner - Stored Class 66
DHLT	Freightliner - Awaiting repairs
EFOO	First Great Western - Class 57
EFPC	First Great Western - HST power cars
EFSH	First Great Western - Class 08
EJLO	London Midland - Class 08
EMPC	East Midlands Trains - HST power cars
EMSL	East Midlands Trains - Class 08
EPXX	Europhoenix Class 86
GBCM	Europorte/GBRf - Class 66 commercial contracts
GBED	Europorte/GBRf- Class 73
GBET	Europorte/GBRf - Class 57
GBFM	Europorte/GBRf - Class 66 modified with RETB
GBMU	Europorte/GBRf - Class 66 modified for MU
GBRT	Europorte/GBRf - Class 66 Infrastructure
GBSD	Europorte/GBRf - Class 66 RETB
GBWM	Europorte/GBRf - Class 08
GBZZ	Europorte/GBRf - Stored locomotives
GCHP	Grand Central - HST power cars
GPSS	Eurostar UK - Class 08
HNRL	Harry Needle Railroad - Class 08, 20 hire locos
HNRS	Harry Needle Railroad - Stored locomotives
HTCX	Hanson Traction - Class 56
HYWD	South West Trains - Class 73
IANA	National Express East Anglia - Class 90
IECA	National Express East Coast - Class 91
IECP	National Express East Coast - HST power cars
INDL	Industrial (unofficial code)
IVGA	Gatwick Express - Class 73/2
IWCA	Virgin West Coast - Class 57/3
MBDL	Private operators - Diesel traction
MBED	Private operators - Class 73
MRSO	Mainline Rail - Class 08
PTXX	Eurotunnel - Europort2 Class 92
QACL	Network Rail - Class 86 load banks
QADD	Network Rail - Class 31
QCAR	Network Rail - HST power cars
QETS	Network Rail - Class 97/3
RCZH	Railcare Springburn - Class 08
RCZN	Railcare Wolverton - Class 08
RFSH	Wabtec Rail Doncaster - Class 08
RVLO	Rail Vehicle Engineering Derby - Locos
RVLS	Rail Vehicle Engineering Derby - Stored locos
SIEM	Siemens Transportation - Barriers
TTLS	Traditional Traction - Locomotives
WAAN	DB Schenker - Class 67
WABN	DB Schenker - Class 67 RETB fitted
WATN	DB Schenker - Class 67 hire to Arriva T W
WBAI	DB Schenker - Class 66 Industrial
WBAK	DB Schenker - Class 66 Construction
WBAM	DB Schenker - Class 66 Energy
WBAN	DB Schenker - Class 66 Network
WBBI	DB Schenker - Class 66 Industrial RETB fitted
WBBM	DB Schenker - Class 66 Energy RETB fitted
WBBN	DB Schenker - Class 66 Network RETB fitted
WBEI	DB Schenker - Class 66 Euro in the UK
WBEN	DB Schenker - Class 66 Euro Cargo Rail
WBEP	DB Schenker - Class 66 Poland
WBES	DB Schenker - Class 66 ECR RHTT
WBLI	DB Schenker - Class 66 Industrial Auto coupler
WCAI	DB Schenker - Class 60 Industrial 990 gal fuel
WCAK	DB Schenker - Class 60 Construction 990 gal fuel
WCAM	DB Schenker - Class 60 Energy 990 gal fuel
WCBI	DB Schenker - Class 60 Industrial 1150 gal fuel
WCBK	DB Schenker - Class 60 Construct'n 1150 gal fuel
WDAI	DB Schenker - Class 59/2 Industrial
WDAK	DB Schenker - Class 59/2 Construction
WDAM	DB Schenker - Class 59/2 Liverpool Bulk
WEFE	DB Schenker - Class 90
WEGE	DB Schenker - Class 90 Hire to anglia
WFMS	DB Schenker - Class 60 Fleet Management
WFMU	DB Schenker - Fleet Management
WKBN	DB Schenker - Class 37 Network RETB fitted
WLAN	DB Schenker - Euro Cargo Rail Class 21
WNTR	DB Schenker - Stored locos - reserve
WNTS	DB Schenker - Stored locos - serviceable
WNXX	DB Schenker - Stored locos - unserviceable
WNYX	DB Schenker - Stored locos - parts recovery
WNZX	DB Schenker - Awaiting disposal
WRLN	DB Schenker - Class 08, 09 - North London
WSEN	DB Schenker - Euro Cargo Rail - Class 08
WSSA	DB Schenker - Class 08, 09 - Axiom Rail
WSSI	DB Schenker - Class 08, 09 Industrial
WSSM	DB Schenker - Class 08, 09 Energy
WSSK	DB Schenker - Class 08, 09 Network/Const'n
WSXX	DB Schenker - Class 08, 09 Stored
WTAE	DB Schenker - Class 92 Network
WTHE	DB Schenker - Class 92 HS1 authorised
WZFF	DB Schenker - Class 58 France
WZGF	DB Schenker - Class 56, 92 France
WZTS	DB Schenker - Class 08, 56, 58 Stored (hire pool)
XHAC	Direct Rail Services - Class 47
XHCK	Direct Rail Services - Class 57
XHHP	Direct Rail Services - Holding Pool
XHIM	Direct Rail Services - Class 66 - Intermodal
XHNC	Direct Rail Services - Nuclear Traffic
XHSS	Direct Rail Services - Stored
XYPA	Mendip Rail - Hanson Group
XYPO	Mendip Rail - Foster Yeoman (Aggregate Inds)

■ Pools are given only for locomotive groups which are included in this book. Pool codes for multiple-units are not included.

Data Tables

Preserved site codes

		MID	Middleton Railway
		MLM	Motorail - Long Marston
		MNF	Mid-Norfolk Railway
		MOR	Moreton-on-Lugg
ACL	AC Locomotive Group	MRC	Middleton Railway Centre
ALY	Allelys, Studley	MSM	Museum of Science & Industry, Manchester
APF	Appleby-Frodingham RPS	MSR	Midsomer Norton
AVR	Avon Valley Railway	NHD	Newton Heath Depot
BAT	Battlefield Line	NIR	Northamptonshire Ironstone Railway
BEL	5Bel Trust Barrow Hill	NLR	Northampton & Lamport Railway
BHR	Barrow Hill Roundhouse	NNR	North Norfolk Railway
BIR	Barry Island Railway	NRM	National Railway Museum, York
BKR	Bo'ness & Kinneil Railway	NRS	National Railway Museum, Shildon
BLU	Bluebell Railway	NYM	North Yorkshire Moors Railway
BRC	Buckinghamshire Railway Centre	PBR	Pontypool & Blaenavon Railway
BRM	Birmingham Railway Museum, Tyseley	PDR	Paignton & Dartmouth Railway
BVR	Bridgend Valleys Railway	PRL	Peak Rail
BWR	Bodmin & Wenford Railway	PVR	Plym Valley Railway
CAN	Canton (Pullman Rail)	RAC	Railway Age, Crewe
CHS	Chasewater Railway	RAM	Rampart, Derby
COL	Colne Valley Railway	RIB	Ribble Steam Railway
COV	Coventry Electric Railway Museum	RIP	Rippingdale Station
CPR	Chinnor & Princes Risborough Railway	ROW	Rowley Mill
CRB	Caledonian Railway, Brechin	RST	Rushden Station Transport Museum
CRT	Cambrian Railway Trust	SEL	St Leonards Railway Engineering
CVR	Churnet Valley Railway	SHP	Summerlee Heritage Park
CWR	Cholsey & Wallingford Railway	SLN	Stewarts Lane Depot
DAR	Dartmoor Railway	SNI	Snibston Railway
DEE	Royal Deeside Railway	SPV	Spa Valley Railway
DER	Derwent Valley Railway	SRC	Stainmore Railway Co
DFR	Dean Forest Railway	STR	Strathspey Railway
DID	Didcot Railway Centre	SVR	Severn Valley Railway
EAR	East Anglian Railway Museum	SWI	Swindon & Cricklade Railway
ECC	Ecclesbourne Valley Railway	SWN	Swanage Railway
EDR	Eden Valley Railway	TEB	Friends of 502 Group, Tebay
EHC	Elsecar Heritage Centre	TEL	Telford Horsehay Steam Trust
EHD	Eastleigh DBS Depot	THK	Throckmorton Airfield
EKR	East Kent Railway	TIT	Titley Junction
ELR	East Lancashire Railway	TSR	Telford Steam Railway
EMB	Embsay Steam Railway	TYN	North Tyneside Railway
EPO	Epping - Ongar Railway	VOG	Vale of Glamorgan Railway
FHL	Fawley Hall (Private)	WAS	Washwood Heath
FIN	Finmere Station, Oxfordshire	WCR	West Coast Railway Co
GCN	Great Central Railway (North)	WED	Weardale Railway
GCR	Great Central Railway	WEN	Wensleydale Railway
GKR	Graham Kirk Rail	WPH	Walthamstow Pump House
GWI	Gwili Railway	WSR	West Somerset Railway
GWR	Gloucestershire & Warwickshire Railway	XXX	Private unspecified site
HAD	Hastings Diesels	YEO	Yeovil Railway Centre
IOW	Isle of Wight Railway		
KEI	Keith & Dufftown Railway		
KES	Kent & East Sussex Railway	Status	
KIN	MoD Kineton	OPR	Operational
KWV	Keighley & Worth Valley Railway	OPR	Operational Main Line certified
LAN	Llangollen Railway	RES	Under restoration
LDL	Lavender Line	STC	Static exhibit
LHG	L H Group Services, Burton	STO	Stored
LHR	Lakeside & Haverthwaite Railway		
LNW	London North Western, Crewe		
LWR	Lincolnshire Wolds Railway		
MET	Methill (Private)		
MFM	Mangapps Farm Railway Museum		
MHR	Mid Hants Railway		

Data Tables

Rail Data Tables

Depot Codes

Code	Facility	Name	Operator
AB	SD	Aberdeen Guild Street	DBS
AC	CSD	Aberdeen Clayhills	ICE
AD	EMUD	Ashford Hitachi	HIT/SET
AF	T&RSMD	Ashford Chart Leacon	BOM
AH	MoD	Ashchurch	MoD
AK	DMUD	Ardwick	SIE/FTP
AL	DMUD	Aylesbury	CRW
AN	TMD/WRD	Allerton, Liverpool	DBS/NOR
AP	TMD	Ashford Rail Plant	BBR
AS	Store	Allelys	ALL
AT	TMD	Various sites	ALS
AW	SD	Washwood Heath	Hanson
AY	SD	Ayr	DBS
AZ	TMD	Ashford	BBR
AZ	TMD	Alizay (France)	ECR (DBS)
BA	TMD	Crewe Basford Hall	FLR, DBS
BC	MoD	Bicester	MoD
BD	T&RSMD	Birkenhead North	MER
BF	EMUD	Bedford Cauldwell Walk	FCC
BG	SD	Hull Botanic Gardens	NOR
BH	Eng	Barrow Hill Roundhouse	BHE
BI	EMUD	Brighton	SOU
BK	T&RSMD	Barton Hill	LNWR
BM	T&RSMD	Bournemouth	SWT
BN	T&RSMD	Bounds Green	ICE
BO	T&RSMD	Burton	Nemesis
BP	SD	Blackpool CS	NOR
BQ	TMD	Bury	ELR
BR	SD	Bristol Kingsland Road	NRL, FLR
BS	TMD	Bescot	DBS
BT	TMD	Bo'ness	BOK
BW	SD	Barrow-in-Furness	NOR
BZ	T&RSMD	St Blazey	DBS
CA	SD	Cambridge Coldhams Ln	AXI
CB	STORE	Crewe Brook Sidings	DBS
CC	T&RSMD	Clacton	NXA
CD	SD	Crewe Diesel	RIV, DBS
CE	IEMD	Crewe Electric	DBS
CF	DMUD	Cardiff Canton	PUL, ATW
CG	TMD	Crewe Gresty Bridge	DRS
CH	DMUD	Chester	ALS, ATW
CJ	SD	Clapham Junction	SWT
CK	DMUD	Corkerhill	FSR
CL	Store	Carlisle Upperby	DBS
CM	SD	Camden	LMI
CO	IEMD	Coquelles (France)	EUR
CP	CARMD	Crewe Carriage Shed	LNW
CQ	T&RSMD	Crewe Railway Age	CHC
CR	SD	Colchester	NXA
CS	T&RSMD	Carnforth	WCR
CT	SD	Cleethorpes	FTP
CW	MoD	Caerwent	MoD
CX	Store	Cardiff Tidal	DBS
CY	Store	Crewe Coal/South Yards	DRS
CZ	TMD	Central Rivers	BOM
DD	SD	Doncaster Wood Yard	DBS
DF	T&RSMD	Rail Vehicle Engineering	RVE
DI	Pres	Didcot Railway Centre	GWS
DM	TMD	Dollands Moor	DBS
DO	Store	Donnington Railfreight	-
DR	TMD	Doncaster Carr	DBS
DT	SD	Didcot Triangle	DBS
DV	SD	Dover	SET
DW	SD	Doncaster West Yard	NRL, WAB
DY	T&RSMD	Derby Etches Park	EMT
EA	SD	Earles Sidings	DBS
EC	T&RSMD	Craigentinny (Edinburgh)	ICE
ED	DMUD	Eastfield	FSR
EF	MPVD	Effingham Junction	AMS
EH	SD	Eastleigh	DBS
EM	EMUD	East Ham	c2c
EN	CARMD	Euston Downside	NRL
EU	SD	Euston Station Sidings	VWC
EZ	DMUD	Exeter	FGW
FB	Store	Ferrybridge	DBS
FC*		Fire College (Moreton-on-Lugg)	
FD	Mobile	Diesel loco	FLR
FE	Mobile	Electric loco	FLR
FF	TRSMD	Forest - Brussels	SNCB, NMBS, EUS
FH	TRACK	Frodingham	GRP
FN	Hire	France	ECR
FP	CSD	Ferme Park	ICE
FR	EMUD	Fratton	SWT
FS	Mobile	Diesel Shunter	FLR
FW	SD	Fort William	DBS
FX	TMD	Felixstowe	FDH
GI	EMUD	Gillingham	SET
GL	TMD	Gloucester	CWR, ADV
GP	SD	Grove Park	SET
GW	EMUD	Glasgow Shields	FSR
HA	TMD	Haymarket	FSR
HD	SD	Holyhead	ATW
HE	EMUD	Hornsey	FCC
HF	SD	Hereford	DBS
HG	Store	Hither Green	DBS
HI	TM	Hitchin	BBR
HJ	SD	Hoo Junction	DBS
HM	SD/WRD	Healey Mills	DBS
HT	T&RSMD	Heaton	NOR, GTL
HY	SD	Oxford Hinksey Yard	NRL
IL	T&RSMD	Ilford	NXA
IM	SD	Immingham	DBS
IP	SD	Ipswich	FLR
IS	TMD	Inverness	FSR
KC	Store	Carlisle Currock WRD	DBS
KD	SD	Kingmoor Yard	DRS
KK	EMUD	Kirkdale	MER
KM	TMD	Carlisle Kingmoor	DRS
KR	T&RSMD	Kidderminster	SVR
KT	Store	Kineton	MoD
KY	SD/WRD	Knottingley	DBS
LA	T&RSMD	Laira	FGW
LB	Eng	Loughborough	BTL
LD	TMD	Leeds Midland Road	FLR
LE	T&RSMD	Landore	FGW
LG	T&RSMD	Longsight Electric	ALT
LH	Eng	LH Group	LHG
LL	CSD	Liverpool Edge Hill	ALS
LM	Store	Long Marston	MLS
LO	T&RSMD	Longsight Diesel	NOR

Code	Type	Name	Operator
LP*	Eng	EMD Longport	EMD
LR	SD	Leicester	DBS
LT	MoD	Longtown	MoD
LU	MoD	Ludgershall	MoD
LY	T&RSMD	Le Landy - Paris	SNCF, EUS
MA	CARMD	Manchester International	ALS
MD	TMD	Merehead	MRL
MG	TMD	Margam	DBS
MH	SD	Millerhill	DBS
ML	SD	Motherwell	DRS
MM	Store	Moreton in Marsh	-
MN	DMUD	Machynlleth	ATW
MQ	Store	Meldon Quarry	BAR
MR	SD	March	GBR
MW	MoD	Marchwood Military Port	MoD
MY	SD/Store	Mossend Yard	DBS, FLR
NB	SD	New Brighton	MER
NC	T&RSMD	Norwich Crown Point	NXA
ND	Works	NedTrans, Tilburg	NDZ
NG	T&RSMD	New Cross Gate	LOL
NH	DMUD	Newton Heath	NOR
NL	T&RSMD	Neville Hill (Leeds)	EMT, ICE
NM	SD	Nottingham Eastcroft	EMT
NN	EMUD	Northampton, Kings Heath	SIE, LMI
NT	EMUD	Northam	SIE, SWT
NY	T&RSMD	Grosmont	NYM
OD	Eng	Old Dalby	ALS
OH	EMUD	Old Oak Common Electric	SIE
ON	SD	Orpington	SET
OO	HSTMD	Old Oak Common HST	FGW
OX	CSD	Oxford Carriage Sidings	FGW
OY	CARMD	Oxley	ALS
PB	SD	Peterborough	DBS
PC	TRSMD	Polmadie	ALS
PE	SD	Peterborough Nene	FCC
PF	SD	Peak Forest	DBS
PG	TRSMD	Peterborough	GBR
PH	SD	Perth	FSR
PM	TRSMD	St Philip's Marsh (Bristol)	FGW
PN	SD	Preston Station	NOR
PN	TMD	Poznan (Poland)	ECR (DBS)
PQ	SD	Harwich Parkeston Quay	DBS
PT	SD	Peterborough	GBR
PY	MoD	Shoeburyness (Pigs Bay)	MoD, KRS
PZ	TRSMD	Penzance (Long Rock)	FGW
RE	EMUD	Ramsgate	SET
RG	DMUD	Reading	FGW
RH	SD	Redhill	DBS
RL	TRSMD	Ropley	MHR
RO	SD	Rotherham Steel	DBS
RU	TMD	Rugby Rail Plant	GRP
RY	EMUD	Ryde	SWT
SA	DMUD	Salisbury	SWT
SB	TMD	Shrewsbury	NOR
SE	TRSMD	St Leonards	SLR
SG	EMUD	Slade Green	SET
SH	CARMD	Southall Railway Centre	WCR
SI	EMUD	Soho	LMI
SJ	TRSMD	Stourbridge Junction	LMI
SK	TRSMD	Swanwick	MRC
SL	TRSMD	Stewarts Lane	DBS, VSO, SOU
SM	SD	Sheffield Station	NOR
SN	SD	Shoeburyness	c2c
SO*		Southend	
SP	CRDC	Springs Branch	DBS
SQ	SD	Stockport	NOR
ST	SD	Southport	MER
SU	TRSMD	Selhurst	SOU
SX	SD	Shrewsbury	ATW
SZ	TMD	Southampton Maritime	FLR
TB	SD	Three Bridges	DBS
TE	TMD	Thornaby/Tees Yard	DBS
TF	SD	Orient Way	NXA
TG	SD	Tonbridge	GBR
TI	TRSMD	Temple Mills	EUS
TJ	TMD	Tavistock Junction	COL
TM	SD	Tyseley Loco Works	BRM
TN	SD	Taunton Fairwater	NRL, FLR
TO	TMD	Toton	DBS
TS	DMUD	Tyseley	LMI
TT	Store	Toton Training Compound	DBS
TY	Store	Tyne Yard	DBS
VI	SD	Victoria	SET
VR	SD	Aberystwyth	ATW
VZ	EMUD	Strawberry Hill	SIE, SWT
WA	SD	Warrington Arpley	DBS
WB	TRSMD	Wembley	ALS
WD	EMUD	East Wimbledon	SWT
WE	SD	Willesden Brent	DBS
WF	SD	Wansford	NVR
WH	Eng	Whatley	MRL
WH*	TMD	Washwood Heath	HAN
WK	SD	West Kirby	MER
WN	EMUD	Willesden	LOG
WO	TMD	Wolsingham	WER
WP	SD	Worksop	DBS
WS	SD	Worcester	LMI
WW	SD	West Worthing	SOU
WY	SD/CSD	Westbury Yard	DBS
WZ*	TRSMD	Washwood Heath	HAN
XW	TMD	Crofton	BOM
XX	-	Exported	-
YK	DMUD	Siemens York	SIE, FTP
YL	TMD	York Leeman Road	JAR, FLF
YM	Store	National Railway Museum	NRM
YN	SD	York North Yard	DBS
YO	SD	Yoker	FSR
ZA	Eng	RTC Derby	SER, NRL, AEA
ZB	Eng	Doncaster	WAB
ZC	Eng	Crewe	BOM
ZD	Eng	Derby Litchurch Lane	BOM
ZG	Eng	Eastleigh Works	KRS
ZH	Eng	Glasgow	RCL
ZI	Eng	Ilford	BOM
ZK	Eng	Kilmarnock	BTL
ZL	Eng	Cardiff Canton	PUL
ZN	Eng	Wolverton	RCL
ZS	Eng	Locotech Wakefield	BAR
ZW	Eng	Stoke-on-Trent (Marcroft)	AXI
WZ	Eng	Warsaw (Poland)	DBS
3M*		3M Industries, Bracknell	

* Unofficial code

Rail Data Tables

Operator Codes

ADV	Advenza Freight	LMI	London Midland
ALL	Allelys Heavy Haul	LNW	L&WR Railway Co
ALS	Alstom	LOG	London Overground
AMS	Amec Spie Rail	LUL	London Underground Ltd
ATW	Arriva Trains Wales	MER	Merseyrail
AXC	Arriva Cross Country	MHR	Mid Hants Railway
AXI	Axiom Rail	MoD	Ministry of Defence
BAR	British American Railway Services	MRC	Midland Railway Centre
BBR	Balfour Beatty	MRL	Mendip Rail Ltd
BHE	Barrow Hill Roundhouse	MRS	Motorail Logistics
BOK	Bo'ness and Kinneil	NDZ	NedTrains
BOM	Bombardier	NOR	Northern Rail
BRM	Birmingham Railway Museum	NRL	Network Rail
BTL	Brush Traction Limited	NRM	National Railway Museum
C2C	c2c Rail	NVR	Nene Valley Railway
CAD	Cargo-D	NXA	National Express East Anglia
CAR	Carillion	NYM	North Yorkshire Moors Railway
CHS	Crewe Heritage Centre	OLD	Old Dalby Test Track
COL	Colas Rail	POB	Port of Boston
CON	Continental Rail (Spain)	PUL	Pullman Group
COR	Corus Steel	RAF	Railfilms Ltd
CRW	Chiltern Railways	RCL	Railcare Ltd
CWR	Cotswold Rail	RIV	Riviera Trains
DBA	DB Arriva	RRS	Ridings Railtours
DBS	DB Schenker West	RVE	Rail Vehicle Engineering
DRS	Direct Rail Services	S4G	Stratford 47 Group
ECR	Euro Cargo Rail (DBS)	SET	Southeastern Trains
ELR	East Lancashire Railway	SIE	Siemens
EMT	East Midlands Trains	SIL	Stagecoach Island Line
ETF	ETF Freight (France)	SLR	St Leonards Rail Engineering
ETL	Electric Traction Ltd	SNB	Société Nationale des Chemins de fer Belges
EU2	Eurotunnel Europorte2	SNF	Société Nationale des Chemins de fer Français
EUR	Eurotunnel	SOU	Southern
EUS	Eurostar	SRP	Scottish Railway Preservation Society
FCC	First Capital Connect	SVR	Severn Valley Railway
FDH	Felixstowe Dock & Harbour	SWT	South West Trains
FGW	First Great Western	TRN	Transfesa
FHT	First Hull Trains	TSO	Travaux du Sud Ouest (France)
FLF	Fastline Freight	TTS	Transmart Trains
FLR	Freightliner	VSO	Venice Simplon Orient Express
FMR	FM Rail	VTN	Vintage Trains
FSL	Flying Scotsman Railway Ltd	VWC	Virgin West Coast
FSR	First ScotRail	WAB	Wabtec
FTP	First TransPennine	WCR	West Coast Railway Co
GBR	GB Railfreight	WSR	Wrexham & Shropshire Railway
GRP	Grant Rail Plant	WTN	Wessex Trains
GTL	Grand Central Railway		
GWS	Great Western Society		
HEC	Heathrow Connect		
HEX	Heathrow Express		
HIT	Hitachi		
HNR	Harry Needle Railroad		
ICE	Inter City East Coast		
IND	Industrial operator		
IRY	Ian Riley		
JAR	Jarvis		
JHS	Jeremy Hoskins		
KRS	Knights Rail Services		
LAF	Lafarge Aggregates		

COLAS RAIL

Data Tables

ABC Rail Guide 2012

Owner Codes

AEA	AEA Rail Technology
ALS	Alstom
ANG	Angel Trains
ATW	Arriva Trains Wales
BAA	British Airports Authority
BCC	Bridgend County Council
BEA	Beacon Rail
BOM	Bombardier
BOT	Bank of Tokyo (Mitsubishi)
BTM	BTMU Capital Corporation
C20	Class 20 Locomotive Ltd
CAD	Cargo-D
CBR	CB Rail
CCC	Cardiff County Council
COL	Colas Rail
CRW	Chiltern Railways
CWR	Cotswold Rail
DBR	DB Regio
DBS	DB Schenker West
DBS/T	DB Schenker/Transfesa
DRS	Direct Rail Services
ECR	Euro Cargo Rail (DBS)
ECT	ECT Main Line Rail
EMT	East Midlands Trains
ETL	Electric Traction Ltd
EU2	Eurotunnel Europorte2
EUR	Eurotunnel
EUS	Eurostar
EVL	Eversholt Leasing
FGP	First Group
FLF	Fastline Freight
FLR	Freightliner

FOS	Foster Yeoman
GBR	GB Railfreight
GTL	Grand Central Railway Ltd
HAL	Halifax Assets Finance Ltd
HAN	Hanson Traction
HEC	Hunslet Engine Co
HBS	Halifax-Bank of Scotland
HJA	Howard Johnson Associates
HNR	Harry Needle Railroad
IRY	Ian Riley
JAR	Jarvis
KRS	Knights Rail Services
LTS	Lloyds TSB Finance
NRL	Network Rail
NYM	North Yorkshire Moors Railway
PTR	Porterbrook
QWR	QW Rail Leasing
RCL	Railcare Limited
RIV	Riviera Trains
RML	Royal Mail
RMS	RMS Locotech
RTR	RT Rail
RVE	Rail Vehicle Engineering
S4G	Stratford Class 47 Group
SEC	Serco
SIE	Siemens
SNB	Société Nationale des Chemins de fer Belges
SNF	Société Nationale des Chemins de fer Français
SOU	Southern (Govia)
SWT	South West Trains (Stagecoach)
TTS	Transmart Trains
VTN	Vintage Trains
WAB	Wabtec
WCR	West Coast Railway Co
WYP	West Yorkshire PTE

Below: *To replace the Class 142s in Devon, which were on sub-lease from Northern, a fleet of Class 150/1s from London Midland and London Overground have been transferred to Exeter. Painted in all-over First Great Western blue, set No. 150129 departs from Dawlish on 3 July 2011, forming the 10.21 Exmouth to Paignton service.* **CJM**

Data Tables

Station three-letter Codes

Abbey Wood	ABW	Appley Bridge	APB	Banstead	BAD	Bere Alston	BAS
Aber	ABE	Apsley	APS	Barassie	BSS	Bere Ferrers	BFE
Abercynon	ACY	Arbroath	ARB	Barbican	ZBB	Berkhamsted	BKM
Aberdare	ABA	Ardgay	ARD	Bardon Mill	BLL	Berkswell	BKW
Aberdeen	ABD	Ardlui	AUI	Bare Lane	BAR	Berney Arms	BYA
Aberdour	AUR	Ardrossan Harbour	ADS	Bargeddie	BGI	Berry Brow	BBW
Aberdovey	AVY	Ardrossan South Beach	ASB	Bargoed	BGD	Berrylands	BRS
Abererch	ABH	Ardrossan Town	ADN	Barking	BKG	Berwick	BRK
Abergavenny	AGV	Ardwick	ADK	Barking Underground	ZBK	Berwick-upon-Tweed	BWK
Abergele & Pensarn	AGL	Argyle Street	AGS	Barlaston	BRT	Bescar Lane	BES
Aberystwyth	AYW	Arisaig	ARG	Barming	BMG	Bescot Stadium	BSC
Accrington	ACR	Arlesey	ARL	Barmouth	BRM	Betchworth	BTO
Achanalt	AAT	Armathwaite	AWT	Barnehurst	BNH	Bethnal Green	BET
Achnasheen	ACN	Arnside	ARN	Barnes	BNS	Betws-y-Coed	BYC
Achnashellach	ACH	Arram	ARR	Barnes Bridge	BNI	Beverley	BEV
Acklington	ACK	Arrochar & Tarbet	ART	Barnetby	BTB	Bexhill	BEX
Acle	ACL	Arundel	ARU	Barnham	BAA	Bexley	BXY
Acocks Green	ACG	Ascot	ACT	Barnhill	BNL	Bexleyheath	BXH
Acton Bridge	ACB	Ascott-u-Wychwood	AUW	Barnsley	BNY	Bicester North	BCS
Acton Central	ACC	Ash	ASH	Barnstaple	BNP	Bicester Town	BIT
Acton Main Line	AML	Ash Vale	AHV	Barnt Green	BTG	Bickley	BKL
Adderley Park	ADD	Ashburys	ABY	Barrhead	BRR	Bidston	BID
Addiewell	ADW	Ashchurch	ASC	Barrhill	BRL	Biggleswade	BIW
Addlestone	ASN	Ashfield	ASF	Barrow Haven	BAV	Bilbrook	BBK
Adisham	ADM	Ashford International	AFK	Barrow upon Soar	BWS	Billericay	BIC
Adlington (Cheshire)	ADC	Ashford (Eurostar)	ASI	Barrow-in-Furness	BIF	Billingham	BIL
Adlington (Lancs)	ADL	Ashford (Surrey)	AFS	Barry	BRY	Billingshurst	BIG
Adwick	AWK	Ashley	ASY	Barry Docks	BYD	Bingham	BIN
Aigburth	AIG	Ashtead	AHD	Barry Island	BYI	Bingley	BIY
Ainsdale	ANS	Ashton-under-Lyne	AHN	Barry Links	BYL	Birchgrove	BCG
Aintree	AIN	Ashurst	AHS	Barton-on-Humber	BAU	Birchington-on-Sea	BCH
Airbles	AIR	Ashurst New Forest	ANF	Basildon	BSO	Birchwood	BWD
Airdrie	ADR	Ashwell & Morden	AWM	Basingstoke	BSK	Birkbeck	BIK
Albany Park	AYP	Askam	ASK	Bat & Ball	BBL	Birkdale	BDL
Albrighton	ALB	Aslockton	ALK	Bath Spa	BTH	Birkenhead Central	BKC
Alderley Edge	ALD	Aspatria	ASP	Bathgate	BHG	Birkenhead North	BKN
Aldermaston	AMT	Aspley Guise	APG	Batley	BTL	Birkenhead Park	BKP
Aldershot	AHT	Aston	AST	Battersby	BTT	Birmingham Int	BHI
Aldrington	AGT	Atherstone	ATH	Battersea Park	BAK	Birmingham Moor St	BMO
Alexandra Palace	AAP	Atherton	ATN	Battle	BAT	Birmingham New St	BHM
Alexandra Parade	AXP	Attadale	ATT	Battlesbridge	BLB	Birmingham Snow Hill	BSW
Alexandria	ALX	Attenborough	ATB	Bayford	BAY	Bishop Auckland	BIA
Alfreton	ALF	Attleborough	ATL	Beaconsfield	BCF	Bishopbriggs	BBG
Allens West	ALW	Auchinleck	AUK	Bearley	BER	Bishops Stortford	BIS
Alloa	ALO	Audley End	AUD	Bearsden	BRN	Bishopstone	BIP
Alness	ASS	Aughton Park	AUG	Bearsted	BSD	Bishopton	BPT
Alnmouth	ALM	Aviemore	AVM	Beasdale	BSL	Bitterne	BTE
Alresford	ALR	Avoncliff	AVF	Beaulieu Road	BEU	Blackburn	BBN
Alsager	ASG	Avonmouth	AVN	Beauly	BEL	Blackheath	BKH
Althorne	ALN	Axminster	AXM	Bebington	BEB	Blackhorse Road	BHO
Althorpe	ALP	Aylesbury	AYS	Beccles	BCC	Blackpool North	BPN
Altnabreac	ABC	Aylesbury Parkway	AVP	Beckenham Hill	BEC	Blackpool P Beach	BPB
Alton	AON	Aylesford	AYL	Beckenham Junction	BKJ	Blackpool South	BPS
Altrincham	ALT	Aylesham	AYH	Bedford	BDM	Blackrod	BLK
Alvechurch	ALV	Ayr	AYR	Bedford St Johns	BSJ	Blackwater	BAW
Ambergate	AMB	Bache	BAC	Bedhampton	BDH	Blaenau Ffestiniog	BFF
Amberley	AMY	Baglan	BAJ	Bedminster	BMT	Blair Atholl	BLA
Amersham	AMR	Bagshot	BAG	Bedworth	BEH	Blairhill	BAI
Ammanford	AMF	Baildon	BLD	Bedwyn	BDW	Blake Street	BKT
Ancaster	ANC	Baillieston	BIO	Beeston	BEE	Blakedown	BKD
Anderston	AND	Balcombe	BAB	Bekesbourne	BKS	Blantyre	BLT
Andover	ADV	Baldock	BDK	Belle Vue	BLV	Blaydon	BLO
Anerley	ANZ	Balham	BAL	Bellgrove	BLG	Bleasby	BSB
Angel Road	AGR	Balloch	BHC	Bellingham	BGM	Bletchley	BLY
Angmering	ANG	Balmossie	BSI	Bellshill	BLH	Bloxwich	BLX
Annan	ANN	Bamber Bridge	BMB	Belmont	BLM	Bloxwich North	BWN
Anniesland	ANL	Bamford	BAM	Belper	BLP	Blundellsands & Crosby	BLN
Ansdell & Fairhaven	AFV	Banavie	BNV	Beltring	BEG	Blythe Bridge	BYB
Appleby	APP	Banbury	BAN	Belvedere	BVD	Bodmin Parkway	BOD
Appledore (Kent)	APD	Bangor (Gwynedd)	BNG	Bempton	BEM	Bodorgan	BOR
Appleford	APF	Bank Hall	BAH	Ben Rhydding	BEY	Bognor Regis	BOG
				Benfleet	BEF	Bogston	BGS
				Bentham	BEN	Bolton	BON
				Bentley	BTY	Bolton-on-Dearne	BTD
				Bentley (South Yorks)	BYK	Bookham	BKA

Data Tables

Bootle	BOC	Brough	BUH	Carlton	CTO	Chorleywood	CLW
Bootle New Strand	BNW	Broughty Ferry	BYF	Carluke	CLU	Christchurch	CHR
Bootle Oriel Road	BOT	Broxbourne	BXB	Carmarthen	CMN	Christs Hospital	CHH
Bordesley	BBS	Bruce Grove	BCV	Carmyle	CML	Church & Oswaldtwistle	CTW
Borough Green	BRG	Brundall	BDA	Carnforth	CNF	Church Fenton	CHF
Borth	BRH	Brundall Gardens	BGA	Carnoustie	CAN	Church Stretton	CTT
Bosham	BOH	Brunstane	BSU	Carntyne	CAY	Cilmeri	CIM
Boston	BSN	Brunswick	BRW	Carpenders Park	CPK	City Thameslink	CTK
Botley	BOE	Bruton	BRU	Carrbridge	CAG	Clacton on Sea	CLT
Bottesford	BTF	Bryn	BYN	Carshalton	CSH	Clandon	CLA
Bourne End	BNE	Buckenham	BUC	Carshalton Beeches	CSB	Clapham High Street	CLP
Bournemouth	BMH	Buckley	BCK	Carstairs	CRS	Clapham Junction	CLJ
Bournville	BRV	Bucknell	BUK	Cartsdyke	CDY	Clapham (Yorkshire)	CPY
Bow Brickhill	BWB	Bugle	BGL	Castle Bar Park	CBP	Clapton	CPT
Bowes Park	BOP	Builth Road	BHR	Castle Cary	CLC	Clarbeston Road	CLR
Bowling	BWG	Bulwell	BLW	Castleford	CFD	Clarkston	CKS
Boxhill & Westhumble	BXW	Bures	BUE	Castleton	CAS	Claverdon	CLV
Bracknell	BCE	Burgess Hill	BUG	Castleton Moor	CSM	Claygate	CLG
Bradford Forster Sq	BDQ	Burley Park	BUY	Caterham	CAT	Cleethorpes	CLE
Bradford Interchange	BDI	Burley-in-Wharfedale	BUW	Catford	CTF	Cleland	CEA
Bradford-on-Avon	BOA	Burnage	BNA	Catford Bridge	CFB	Clifton	CLI
Brading	BDN	Burneside	BUD	Cathays	CYS	Clifton Down	CFN
Braintree	BTR	Burnham	BNM	Cathcart	CCT	Clitheroe	CLH
Braintree Freeport	BTP	Burnham-on-Crouch	BUU	Cattal	CTL	Clock House	CLK
Bramhall	BML	Burnley Barracks	BUB	Causeland	CAU	Clunderwen	CUW
Bramley	BLE	Burnley Central	BNC	Cefn-y-Bedd	CYB	Clydebank	CYK
Bramley (Hants)	BMY	Burnley Manchester Rd	BYM	Chadwell Heath	CTH	Coatbridge Central	CBC
Brampton (Cumbria)	BMP	Burnside	BUI	Chafford Hundred	CFH	Coatbridge Sunnyside	CBS
Brampton (Suffolk)	BRP	Burntisland	BTS	Chalfont & Latimer	CFO	Coatdyke	COA
Branchton	BCN	Burscough Bridge	BCB	Chalkwell	CHW	Cobham & Stoke d'An	CSD
Brandon	BND	Burscough Junction	BCJ	Chandlers Ford	CFR	Codsall	CSL
Branksome	BSM	Bursledon	BUO	Chapel-en-le-Frith	CEF	Cogan	CGN
Braystones	BYS	Burton Joyce	BUJ	Chapelton	CPN	Colchester	COL
Bredbury	BDY	Burton-on-Trent	BUT	Chapeltown	CLN	Colchester Town	CET
Breich	BRC	Bury St Edmunds	BSE	Chappel & Wakes Colne	CWC	Coleshill Parkway	CEH
Brentford	BFD	Busby	BUS	Charing	CHG	Collingham	CLM
Brentwood	BRE	Bush Hill Park	BHK	Charing Cross (FSR)	CHC	Collington	CLL
Bricket Wood	BWO	Bushey	BSH	Charlbury	CBY	Colne	CNE
Bridge of Allan	BEA	Butlers Lane	BUL	Charlton	CTN	Colwall	CWL
Bridge of Orchy	BRO	Buxted	BXD	Chartham	CRT	Colwyn Bay	CWB
Bridgend	BGN	Buxton	BUX	Chassen Road	CSR	Combe	CME
Bridgeton	BDG	Byfleet & New Haw	BFN	Chatelherault	CTE	Commondale	COM
Bridgwater	BWT	Bynea	BYE	Chatham	CTM	Congleton	CNG
Bridlington	BDT	Cadoxton	CAD	Chathill	CHT	Conisbrough	CNS
Brierfield	BRF	Caergwrle	CGW	Cheadle Hulme	CHU	Connel Ferry	CON
Brigg	BGG	Caerphilly	CPH	Cheam	CHE	Cononley	CEY
Brighouse	BGH	Caersws	CWS	Cheddington	CED	Conway Park	CNP
Brighton	BTN	Caldicot	CDT	Chelford	CEL	Conwy	CNW
Brimsdown	BMD	Caledonian Rd & Bby	CIR	Chelmsford	CHM	Cooden Beach	COB
Brinnington	BNT	Calstock	CSK	Chelsfield	CLD	Cookham	COO
Bristol Parkway	BPW	Cam & Dursley	CDU	Cheltenham Spa	CNM	Cooksbridge	CBR
Bristol Temple Meads	BRI	Camberley	CAM	Chepstow	CPW	Coombe Halt	COE
Brithdir	BHD	Camborne	CBN	Cherry Tree	CYT	Copplestone	COP
British Steel Redcar	RBS	Cambridge	CBG	Chertsey	CHY	Corbridge	CRB
Briton Ferry	BNF	Cambridge Heath	CBH	Cheshunt	CHN	Corby	COR
Brixton	BRX	Cambuslang	CBL	Chessington North	CSN	Corkerhill	CKH
Broad Green	BGE	Camden Road	CMD	Chessington South	CSS	Corkickle	CKL
Broadbottom	BDB	Camelon	CMO	Chester	CTR	Corpach	CPA
Broadstairs	BSR	Canley	CNL	Chester Road	CRD	Corrour	CRR
Brockenhurst	BCU	Cannock	CAO	Chesterfield	CHD	Coryton	COY
Brockholes	BHS	Canonbury	CNN	Chester-le-Street	CLS	Coseley	CSY
Brockley	BCY	Canterbury East	CBE	Chestfield & Swalecliffe	CSW	Cosford	COS
Bromborough	BOM	Canterbury West	CBW	Chetnole	CNO	Cosham	CSA
Bromborough Rake	BMR	Cantley	CNY	Chichester	CCH	Cottingham	CGM
Bromley Cross	BMC	Capenhurst	CPU	Chilham	CIL	Cottingley	COT
Bromley North	BMN	Carbis Bay	CBB	Chilworth	CHL	Coulsdon South	CDS
Bromley South	BMS	Cardenden	CDD	Chingford	CHI	Coventry	COV
Bromsgrove	BMV	Cardiff Bay	CDB	Chinley	CLY	Cowden	CWN
Brondesbury	BSY	Cardiff Central	CDF	Chippenham	CPM	Cowdenbeath	COW
Brondesbury Park	BSP	Cardiff Queen Street	CDQ	Chipstead	CHP	Cradley Heath	CRA
Brookmans Park	BPK	Cardonald	CDO	Chirk	CRK	Craigendoran	CGD
Brookwood	BKO	Cardross	CDR	Chislehurst	CIT	Cramlington	CRM
Broome	BME	Carfin	CRF	Chiswick	CHK	Craven Arms	CRV
Broomfleet	BMF	Cark	CAK	Cholsey	CHO	Crawley	CRW
Brora	BRA	Carlisle	CAR	Chorley	CRL	Crayford	CRY

Data Tables

Crediton	CDI	Dent	DNT	Dyce	DYC	Exmouth	EXM
Cressing	CES	Denton	DTN	Dyffryn Ardudwy	DYF	Exton	EXN
Cressington	CSG	Deptford	DEP	Eaglescliffe	EAG	Eynsford	EYN
Creswell	CWD	Derby	DBY	Ealing Broadway	EAL	Failsworth	FLS
Crewe	CRE	Derby Road	DBR	Earlestown	ERL	Fairbourne	FRB
Crewkerne	CKN	Derker	DKR	Earley	EAR	Fairfield	FRF
Crews Hill	CWH	Devonport	DPT	Earlsfield	EAD	Fairlie	FRL
Crianlarich	CNR	Dewsbury	DEW	Earlswood (Surrey)	ELD	Fairwater	FRW
Criccieth	CCC	Didcot Parkway	DID	Earlswood (Midlands)	EWD	Falconwood	FCN
Cricklewood	CRI	Digby & Sowton	DIG	East Croydon	ECR	Falkirk Grahamston	FKG
Croftfoot	CFF	Dilton Marsh	DMH	East Didsbury	EDY	Falkirk High	FKK
Crofton Park	CFT	Dinas Powys	DNS	East Dulwich	EDW	Falls of Cruachan	FOC
Cromer	CMR	Dinas Rhondda	DMG	East Farleigh	EFL	Falmer	FMR
Cromford	CMF	Dingle Road	DGL	East Garforth	EGF	Falmouth Docks	FAL
Crookston	CKT	Dingwall	DIN	East Grinstead	EGR	Falmouth Town	FMT
Cross Gates	CRG	Dinsdale	DND	East Kilbride	EKL	Fareham	FRM
Crossflatts	CFL	Dinting	DTG	East Malling	EML	Farnborough (Main)	FNB
Crosshill	COI	Disley	DSL	East Midlands Parkway	EMD	Farnborough North	FNN
Crosskeys	CKY	Diss	DIS	East Tilbury	ETL	Farncombe	FNC
Crossmyloof	CMY	Dockyard	DOC	East Worthing	EWR	Farnham	FNH
Croston	CSO	Dodworth	DOD	Eastbourne	EBN	Farningham Road	FNR
Crouch Hill	CRH	Dolau	DOL	Eastbrook	EBK	Farnworth	FNW
Crowborough	COH	Doleham	DLH	Easterhouse	EST	Farringdon	ZFD
Crowhurst	CWU	Dolgarrog	DLG	Eastham Rake	ERA	Fauldhouse	FLD
Crowle	CWE	Dolwyddelan	DWD	Eastleigh	ESL	Faversham	FAV
Crowthorne	CRN	Doncaster	DON	Eastrington	EGN	Faygate	FGT
Croy	CRO	Dorchester South	DCH	Ebbw Vale Parkway	EBV	Fazakerley	FAZ
Crystal Palace	CYP	Dorchester West	DCW	Eccles	ECC	Fearn	FRN
Cuddington	CUD	Dore	DOR	Eccles Road	ECS	Featherstone	FEA
Cuffley	CUF	Dorking	DKG	Eccleston Park	ECL	Felixstowe	FLX
Culham	CUM	Dorking Deepdene	DPD	Edale	EDL	Feltham	FEL
Culrain	CUA	Dorking West	DKT	Eden Park	EDN	Feniton	FNT
Cumbernauld	CUB	Dormans	DMS	Edenbridge	EBR	Fenny Stratford	FEN
Cupar	CUP	Dorridge	DDG	Edenbridge Town	EBT	Fernhill	FER
Curriehill	CUH	Dove Holes	DVH	Edge Hill	EDG	Ferriby	FRY
Cuxton	CUX	Dover Priory	DVP	Edinburgh Park	EDP	Ferryside	FYS
Cwmbach	CMH	Dovercourt	DVC	Edinburgh Waverley	EDB	Ffairfach	FFA
Cwmbran	CWM	Dovey Junction	DVY	Edmonton Green	EDR	Filey	FIL
Cynghordy	CYN	Downham Market	DOW	Effingham Junction	EFF	Filton Abbey Wood	FIT
Dagenham Dock	DDK	Drayton Green	DRG	Eggesford	EGG	Finchley Rd & Frognal	FNY
Daisy Hill	DSY	Drayton Park	DYP	Egham	EGH	Finsbury Park	FPK
Dalgety Bay	DAG	Drem	DRM	Egton	EGT	Finstock	FIN
Dalmally	DAL	Driffield	DRF	Elephant & Castle	EPH	Fishbourne (Sussex)	FSB
Dalmarnock	DAK	Drigg	DRI	Elgin	ELG	Fishersgate	FSG
Dalmeny	DAM	Droitwich Spa	DTW	Ellesmere Port	ELP	Fishguard Harbour	FGH
Dalmuir	DMR	Dronfield	DRO	Elmers End	ELE	Fiskerton	FSK
Dalreoch	DLR	Drumchapel	DMC	Elmstead Woods	ESD	Fitzwilliam	FZW
Dalry	DLY	Drumfrochar	DFR	Elmswell	ESW	Five Ways	FWY
Dalston	DLS	Drumgelloch	DRU	Elsecar	ELR	Fleet	FLE
Dalston Kingsland	DLK	Drumry	DMY	Elsenham	ESM	Flimby	FLM
Dalton	DLT	Dublin Ferryport	DFP	Elstree & Borehamwood	ELS	Flint	FLN
Dalwhinnie	DLW	Dublin Port - Stena	DPS	Eltham	ELW	Flitwick	FLT
Danby	DNY	Duddeston	DUD	Elton & Orston	ELO	Flixton	FLI
Danescourt	DCT	Dudley Port	DDP	Ely	ELY	Flowery Field	FLF
Danzey	DZY	Duffield	DFI	Emerson Park	EMP	Folkestone Central	FKC
Darlington	DAR	Duirinish	DRN	Emsworth	EMS	Folkestone West	FKW
Darnall	DAN	Duke Street	DST	Enfield Chase	ENC	Ford	FOD
Darsham	DSM	Dullingham	DUL	Enfield Lock	ENL	Forest Gate	FOG
Dartford	DFD	Dumbarton Central	DBC	Enfield Town	ENF	Forest Hill	FOH
Darton	DRT	Dumbarton East	DBE	Entwistle	ENT	Formby	FBY
Darwen	DWN	Dumbreck	DUM	Epsom	EPS	Forres	FOR
Datchet	DAT	Dumfries	DMF	Epsom Downs	EPD	Forsinard	FRS
Davenport	DVN	Dumpton Park	DMP	Erdington	ERD	Fort Matilda	FTM
Dawlish	DWL	Dunbar	DUN	Eridge	ERI	Fort William	FTW
Dawlish Warren	DWW	Dunblane	DBL	Erith	ERH	Four Oaks	FOK
Deal	DEA	Duncraig	DCG	Esher	ESH	Foxfield	FOX
Dean	DEN	Dundee	DEE	Essex Road	EXR	Foxton	FXN
Dean Lane	DNN	Dunfermline Q'n Margaret	DFL	Etchingham	ETC	Frant	FRT
Deansgate	DGT	Dunfermline Town	DFE	Euxton Balshaw Lane	EBA	Fratton	FTN
Deganwy	DGY	Dunkeld & Birnam	DKD	Evesham	EVE	Freshfield	FRE
Deighton	DHN	Dunlop	DNL	Ewell East	EWE	Freshford	FFD
Delamere	DLM	Dunrobin Castle	DNO	Ewell West	EWW	Frimley	FML
Denby Dale	DBD	Dunston	DOT	Exeter Central	EXC	Frinton on Sea	FRI
Denham	DNM	Dunton Green	DNG	Exeter St Davids	EXD	Frizinghall	FZH
Denham Golf Club	DGC	Durham	DHM	Exeter St Thomas	EXT	Frodsham	FRD
Denmark Hill	DMK	Durrington-on-Sea	DUR	Exhibition Centre	EXG	Frome	FRO

Fulwell	FLW
Furness Vale	FNV
Furze Platt	FZP
Gainsborough Central	GNB
Gainsborough Lea Rd	GBL
Garelochhead	GCH
Garforth	GRF
Gargrave	GGV
Garrowhill	GAR
Garscadden	GRS
Garsdale	GSD
Garston (Hertfordshire)	GSN
Garswood	GSW
Gartcosh	GRH
Garth (Bridgend)	GMG
Garth (Powys)	GTH
Garve	GVE
Gathurst	GST
Gatley	GTY
Gatwick Airport	GTW
Georgemas Junction	GGJ
Gerrards Cross	GER
Gidea Park	GDP
Giffnock	GFN
Giggleswick	GIG
Gilberdyke	GBD
Gilfach Fargoed	GFF
Gillingham (Dorset)	GIL
Gillingham (Kent)	GLM
Gilshochill	GSC
Gipsy Hill	GIP
Girvan	GIR
Glaisdale	GLS
Glan Conwy	GCW
Glasgow Central	GLC
Glasgow Queen Street	GLQ
Glasshoughton	GLH
Glazebrook	GLZ
Gleneagles	GLE
Glenfinnan	GLF
Glengarnock	GLG
Glenrothes with Thornton	GLT
Glossop	GLO
Gloucester	GCR
Glynde	GLY
Gobowen	GOB
Godalming	GOD
Godley	GDL
Godstone	GDN
Goldthorpe	GOE
Golf Street	GOF
Golspie	GOL
Gomshall	GOM
Goodmayes	GMY
Goole	GOO
Goostrey	GTR
Gordon Hill	GDH
Goring & Streatley	GOR
Goring-by-Sea	GBS
Gorton	GTO
Gospel Oak	GPO
Gourock	GRK
Gowerton	GWN
Goxhill	GOX
Grange Park	GPK
Grange-Over-Sands	GOS
Grangetown	GTN
Grantham	GRA
Grateley	GRT
Gravelly Hill	GVH
Gravesend	GRV
Grays	GRY
Great Ayton	GTA
Great Bentley	GRB
Great Chesterford	GRC
Great Coates	GCT
Great Malvern	GMV
Great Missenden	GMN
Great Yarmouth	GYM
Green Lane	GNL
Green Road	GNR
Greenbank	GBK
Greenfaulds	GRL
Greenfield	GNF
Greenford	GFD
Greenhithe for Bluewater	GNH
Greenock Central	GKC
Greenock West	GKW
Greenwich	GNW
Gretna Green	GEA
Grimsby Docks	GMD
Grimsby Town	GMB
Grindleford	GRN
Grosmont	GMT
Grove Park	GRP
Guide Bridge	GUI
Guildford	GLD
Guiseley	GSY
Gunnersbury	GUN
Gunnislake	GSL
Gunton	GNT
Gwersyllt	GWE
Gypsy Lane	GYP
Habrough	HAB
Hackbridge	HCB
Hackney Central	HKC
Hackney Downs	HAC
Hackney Wick	HKW
Haddenham & T Parkway	HDM
Haddiscoe	HAD
Hadfield	HDF
Hadley Wood	HDW
Hag Fold	HGF
Hagley	HAG
Hairmyres	HMY
Hale	HAL
Halesworth	HAS
Halewood	HED
Halifax	HFX
Hall Green	HLG
Hall I 'Th' Wood	HID
Hall Road	HLR
Halling	HAI
Haltwhistle	HWH
Ham Street	HMT
Hamble	HME
Hamilton Central	HNC
Hamilton Square	BKQ
Hamilton West	HNW
Hammerton	HMM
Hampden Park	HMD
Hampstead Heath	HDH
Hampton	HMP
Hampton Court	HMC
Hampton Wick	HMW
Hampton-in-Arden	HIA
Hamstead	HSD
Hamworthy	HAM
Hanborough	HND
Handforth	HTH
Hanwell	HAN
Hapton	HPN
Harlech	HRL
Harlesden	HDN
Harling Road	HRD
Harlington	HLN
Harlow Mill	HWM
Harlow Town	HWN
Harold Wood	HRO
Harpenden	HPD
Harrietsham	HRM
Harringay	HGY
Harringay Green Lanes	HRY
Harrington	HRR
Harrogate	HGT
Harrow & Wealdstone	HRW
Harrow-on-the-Hill	HOH
Hartford	HTF
Hartlebury	HBY
Hartlepool	HPL
Hartwood	HTW
Harwich International	HPQ
Harwich Town	HWC
Haslemere	HSL
Hassocks	HSK
Hastings	HGS
Hatch End	HTE
Hatfield	HAT
Hatfield & Stainforth	HFS
Hatfield Peverel	HAP
Hathersage	HSG
Hattersley	HTY
Hatton	HTN
Havant	HAV
Havenhouse	HVN
Haverfordwest	HVF
Hawarden	HWD
Hawarden Bridge	HWB
Hawkhead	HKH
Haydon Bridge	HDB
Haydons Road	HYR
Hayes & Harlington	HAY
Hayes (Kent)	HYS
Hayle	HYL
Haymarket	HYM
Haywards Heath	HHE
Hazel Grove	HAZ
Headcorn	HCN
Headingley	HDY
Headstone Lane	HDL
Heald Green	HDG
Healing	HLI
Heath High Level	HHL
Heath Low Level	HLL
Heathrow Airport T123	HXX
Heathrow Airport T4	HAF
Heathrow Terminal 5	HWV
Heaton Chapel	HTC
Hebden Bridge	HBD
Heckington	HEC
Hedge End	HDE
Hednesford	HNF
Heighington	HEI
Helensburgh Central	HLC
Helensburgh Upper	HLU
Hellifield	HLD
Helmsdale	HMS
Helsby	HSB
Hemel Hempstead	HML
Hendon	HEN
Hengoed	HNG
Henley-in-Arden	HNL
Henley-on-Thames	HOT
Hensall	HEL
Hereford	HFD
Herne Bay	HNB
Herne Hill	HNH
Hersham	HER
Hertford East	HFE
Hertford North	HFN
Hessle	HES
Heswall	HSW
Hever	HEV
Heworth	HEW
Hexham	HEX
Heyford	HYD
Heysham Port	HHB
High Brooms	HIB
High St (Glasgow)	HST
High Street Kensington	ZHS
High Wycombe	HWY
Higham	HGM
Highams Park	HIP
Highbridge & Burnham	HIG
Highbury & Islington	HHY
Hightown	HTO
Hildenborough	HLB
Hillfoot	HLF
Hillington East	HLE
Hillington West	HLW
Hillside	HIL
Hilsea	HLS
Hinchley Wood	HYW
Hinckley	HNK
Hindley	HIN
Hinton Admiral	HNA
Hitchin	HIT
Hither Green	HGR
Hockley	HOC
Hollingbourne	HBN
Hollinwood	HOD
Holmes Chapel	HCH
Holmwood	HLM
Holton Heath	HOL
Holyhead	HHD
Holytown	HLY
Homerton	HMN
Honeybourne	HYB
Honiton	HON
Honley	HOY
Honor Oak Park	HPA
Hook	HOK
Hooton	HOO
Hope (Derbyshire)	HOP
Hope (Flintshire)	HPE
Hopton Heath	HPT
Horley	HOR
Hornbeam Park	HBP
Hornsey	HRN
Horsforth	HRS
Horsham	HRH
Horsley	HSY
Horton-in-Ribblesdale	HIR
Horwich Parkway	HWI
Hoscar	HSC
Hough Green	HGN
Hounslow	HOU
Hove	HOV
Hoveton & Wroxham	HXM
How Wood	HWW
Howden	HOW
Howwood (Renfrew)	HOZ
Hoylake	HYK
Hubberts Bridge	HBB
Hucknall	HKN
Huddersfield	HUD
Hull Paragon	HUL
Humphrey Park	HUP
Huncoat	HCT
Hungerford	HGD
Hunmanby	HUB
Huntingdon	HUN
Huntly	HNT
Hunts Cross	HNX
Hurst Green	HUR
Hutton Cranswick	HUT
Huyton	HUY
Hyde Central	HYC
Hyde North	HYT
Hykeham	HKM
Hyndland	HYN
Hythe	HYH
IBM	IBM
Ifield	IFI

Data Tables

Ilford	IFD	Kingston	KNG	Leuchars (St Andrews)	LEU	London Fenchurch St	FST
Ilkley	ILK	Kingswood	KND	Levenshulme	LVM	London Fields	LOF
Imperial Wharf	IMW	Kingussie	KIN	Lewes	LWS	London King's Cross	KGX
Ince	INC	Kintbury	KIT	Lewisham	LEW	London Liverpool St	LST
Ince & Elton	INE	Kirby Cross	KBX	Leyland	LEY	London Marylebone	MYB
Ingatestone	INT	Kirk Sandall	KKS	Leyton Midland Road	LEM	London Paddington	PAD
Insch	INS	Kirkby	KIR	Leytonstone High Road	LER	London Road (Brighton)	LRB
Invergordon	IGD	Kirkby in Ashfield	KKB	Lichfield City	LIC	London Road (Guildford)	LRD
Invergowrie	ING	Kirkby Stephen	KSW	Lichfield Trent Valley	LTV	London St Pancras	STP
Inverkeithing	INK	Kirkby-in-Furness	KBF	Lidlington	LID	London Victoria	VIC
Inverkip	INP	Kirkcaldy	KDY	Limehouse	LHS	London Waterloo	WAT
Inverness	INV	Kirkconnel	KRK	Lincoln Central	LCN	London Waterloo East	WAE
Invershin	INH	Kirkdale	KKD	Lingfield	LFD	Long Buckby	LBK
Inverurie	INR	Kirkham & Wesham	KKM	Lingwood	LGD	Long Eaton	LGE
Ipswich	IPS	Kirkhill	KKH	Linlithgow	LIN	Long Preston	LPR
Irlam	IRL	Kirknewton	KKN	Liphook	LIP	Longbeck	LGK
Irvine	IRV	Kirkwood	KWD	Liskeard	LSK	Longbridge	LOB
Isleworth	ISL	Kirton Lindsey	KTL	Liss	LIS	Longcross	LNG
Islip	ISP	Kiveton Bridge	KIV	Lisvane & Thornhill	LVT	Longfield	LGF
Iver	IVR	Kiveton Park	KVP	Little Kimble	LTK	Longniddry	LND
Ivybridge	IVY	Knaresborough	KNA	Little Sutton	LTT	Longport	LPT
Jewellery Quarter	JEQ	Knebworth	KBW	Littleborough	LTL	Longton	LGN
Johnston	JOH	Knighton	KNI	Littlehampton	LIT	Looe	LOO
Johnstone	JHN	Knockholt	KCK	Littlehaven	LVN	Lostock	LOT
Jordanhill	JOR	Knottingley	KNO	Littleport	LTP	Lostock Gralam	LTG
Kearsley	KSL	Knucklas	KNU	Liverpool Central	LVC	Lostock Hall	LOH
Kearsney	KSN	Knutsford	KNF	Liverpool James Street	LVJ	Lostwithiel	LOS
Keighley	KEI	Kyle of Lochalsh	KYL	Liverpool Lime Street	LIV	Loughborough	LBO
Keith	KEH	Ladybank	LDY	Liverpool South Parkway	LPY	Loughborough Junction	LGJ
Kelvedon	KEL	Ladywell	LAD	Livingston North	LSN	Lowdham	LOW
Kelvindale	KVD	Laindon	LAI	Livingston South	LVG	Lower Sydenham	LSY
Kemble	KEM	Lairg	LRG	Llanaber	LLA	Lowestoft	LWT
Kempston Hardwick	KMH	Lake	LKE	Llanbedr	LBR	Ludlow	LUD
Kempton Park	KMP	Lakenheath	LAK	Llanbister Road	LLT	Luton	LUT
Kemsing	KMS	Lamphey	LAM	Llanbradach	LNB	Luton Airport Parkway	LTN
Kemsley	KML	Lanark	LNK	Llandaf	LLN	Luxulyan	LUX
Kendal	KEN	Lancaster	LAN	Llandanwg	LDN	Lydney	LYD
Kenley	KLY	Lancing	LAC	Llandecwyn	LLC	Lye	LYE
Kennett	KNE	Landywood	LAW	Llandeilo	LLL	Lymington Pier	LYP
Kennishead	KNS	Langbank	LGB	Llandovery	LLV	Lymington Town	LYT
Kensal Green	KNL	Langho	LHO	Llandrindod	LLO	Lympstone Commando	LYC
Kensal Rise	KNR	Langley	LNY	Llandudno	LLD	Lympstone Village	LYM
Kensington Olympia	KPA	Langley Green	LGG	Llandudno Junction	LLJ	Lytham	LTM
Kent House	KTH	Langley Mill	LGM	Llandybie	LLI	Macclesfield	MAC
Kentish Town	KTN	Langside	LGS	Llanelli	LLE	Machynlleth	MCN
Kentish Town West	KTW	Langwathby	LGW	Llanfairfechan	LLF	Maesteg	MST
Kenton	KNT	Langwith-Whaley Thorns	LAG	Llanfairpwll	LPG	Maesteg (Ewenny Rd)	MEW
Kents Bank	KBK	Lapford	LAP	Llangadog	LLG	Maghull	MAG
Kettering	KET	Lapworth	LPW	Llangammarch	LLM	Maiden Newton	MDN
Kew Bridge	KWB	Larbert	LBT	Llangennech	LLH	Maidenhead	MAI
Kew Gardens	KWG	Largs	LAR	Llangynllo	LGO	Maidstone Barracks	MDB
Keyham	KEY	Larkhall	LRH	Llanharan	LLR	Maidstone East	MDE
Keynsham	KYN	Lawrence Hill	LWH	Llanhilleth	LTH	Maidstone West	MDW
Kidbrooke	KDB	Layton	LAY	Llanishen	LLS	Malden Manor	MAL
Kidderminster	KID	Lazonby & Kirkoswald	LZB	Llanrwst	LWR	Mallaig	MLG
Kidsgrove	KDG	Lea Green	LEG	Llansamlet	LAS	Malton	MLT
Kidwelly	KWL	Lea Hall	LEH	Llantwit Major	LWM	Malvern Link	MVL
Kilburn High Road	KBN	Leagrave	LEA	Llanwrda	LNR	Manchester Airport	MIA
Kildale	KLD	Lealholm	LHM	Llanwrtyd	LNW	Manchester Oxford Rd	MCO
Kildonan	KIL	Leamington Spa	LMS	Llwyngwril	LLW	Manchester Piccadilly	MAN
Kilgetty	KGT	Leasowe	LSW	Llwynypia	LLY	Manchester United FC	MUF
Kilmarnock	KMK	Leatherhead	LHD	Loch Awe	LHA	Manchester Victoria	MCV
Kilmaurs	KLM	Ledbury	LED	Loch Eil Outward Bound	LHE	Manea	MNE
Kilpatrick	KPT	Lee	LEE	Lochailort	LCL	Manningtree	MNG
Kilwinning	KWN	Leeds	LDS	Locheilside	LCS	Manor Park	MNP
Kinbrace	KBC	Leicester	LEI	Lochgelly	LCG	Manor Road	MNR
Kingham	KGM	Leigh (Kent)	LIH	Lochluichart	LCC	Manorbier	MRB
Kinghorn	KGH	Leigh-on-Sea	LES	Lochwinnoch	LHW	Manors	MAS
Kings Langley	KGL	Leighton Buzzard	LBZ	Lockerbie	LOC	Mansfield	MFT
King's Lynn	KLN	Lelant	LEL	Lockwood	LCK	Mansfield Woodhouse	MSW
Kings Norton	KNN	Lelant Saltings	LTS	London Blackfriars	BFR	March	MCH
Kings Nympton	KGN	Lenham	LEN	London Bridge	LBG	Marden	MRN
Kings Park	KGP	Lenzie	LNZ	London Cannon Street	CST	Margate	MAR
Kings Sutton	KGS	Leominster	LEO	London Charing Cross	CHX	Market Harborough	MHR
Kingsknowe	KGE	Letchworth Garden City	LET	London Euston	EUS	Market Rasen	MKR

Data Tables

Markinch	MNC	Morfa Mawddach	MFA	Newton (Lanarks)	NTN	Pantyffynnon	PTF
Marks Tey	MKT	Morley	MLY	Newton St Cyres	NTC	Par	PAR
Marlow	MLW	Morpeth	MPT	Newton-le-Willows	NLW	Parbold	PBL
Marple	MPL	Mortimer	MOR	Newtonmore	NWR	Park Street	PKT
Marsden	MSN	Mortlake	MTL	Newton-on-Ayr	NOA	Parkstone (Dorset)	PKS
Marske	MSK	Moses Gate	MSS	Newtown (Powys)	NWT	Parson Street	PSN
Marston Green	MGN	Moss Side	MOS	Ninian Park	NNP	Partick	PTK
Martin Mill	MTM	Mossley	MSL	Nitshill	NIT	Parton	PRN
Martins Heron	MAO	Mossley Hill	MSH	Norbiton	NBT	Patchway	PWY
Marton	MTO	Mosspark	MPK	Norbury	NRB	Patricroft	PAT
Maryhill	MYH	Moston	MSO	Normans Bay	NSB	Patterton	PTT
Maryland	MYL	Motherwell	MTH	Normanton	NOR	Peartree	PEA
Maryport	MRY	Motspur Park	MOT	North Berwick	NBW	Peckham Rye	PMR
Matlock	MAT	Mottingham	MTG	North Camp	NCM	Pegswood	PEG
Matlock Bath	MTB	Mottisfont & Dunbridge	DBG	North Dulwich	NDL	Pemberton	PEM
Mauldeth Road	MAU	Mouldsworth	MLD	North Fambridge	NFA	Pembrey & Burry Port	PBY
Maxwell Park	MAX	Moulsecoomb	MCB	North Llanrwst	NLR	Pembroke	PMB
Maybole	MAY	Mount Florida	MFL	North Queensferry	NQU	Pembroke Dock	PMD
Maze Hill	MZH	Mount Vernon	MTV	North Road	NRD	Penally	PNA
Meadowhall	MHS	Mountain Ash	MTA	North Sheen	NSH	Penarth	PEN
Meldreth	MEL	Muir of Ord	MOO	North Walsham	NWA	Pencoed	PCD
Melksham	MKM	Muirend	MUI	North Wembley	NWB	Pengam	PGM
Melton	MES	Musselburgh	MUB	Northallerton	NTR	Penge East	PNE
Melton Mowbray	MMO	Mytholmroyd	MYT	Northampton	NMP	Penge West	PNW
Menheniot	MEN	Nafferton	NFN	Northfield	NFD	Penhelig	PHG
Menston	MNN	Nailsea & Backwell	NLS	Northfleet	NFL	Penistone	PNS
Meols	MEO	Nairn	NRN	Northolt Park	NLT	Penkridge	PKG
Meols Cop	MEC	Nantwich	NAN	Northumberland Park	NUM	Penmaenmawr	PMW
Meopham	MEP	Narberth	NAR	Northwich	NWI	Penmere	PNM
Merrytown	MEY	Narborough	NBR	Norton Bridge	NTB	Penrhiwceiber	PER
Merstham	MHM	Navigation Road	NVR	Norwich	NRW	Penrhyndeudraeth	PRH
Merthyr Tydfil	MER	Neath	NTH	Norwood Junction	NWD	Penrith	PNR
Merthyr Vale	MEV	Needham Market	NMT	Nottingham	NOT	Penryn	PYN
Metheringham	MGM	Neilston	NEI	Nuneaton	NUN	Pensarn (Gwynedd)	PES
MetroCentre	MCE	Nelson	NEL	Nunhead	NHD	Penshurst	PHR
Mexborough	MEX	Neston	NES	Nunthorpe	NNT	Pentre-Bach	PTB
Micheldever	MIC	Netherfield	NET	Nutbourne	NUT	Pen-y-Bont	PNY
Micklefield	MIK	Nethertown	NRT	Nutfield	NUF	Penychain	BPC
Middlesbrough	MBR	Netley	NTL	Oakengates	OKN	Penyffordd	PNF
Middlewood	MDL	New Barnet	NBA	Oakham	OKM	Penzance	PNZ
Midgham	MDG	New Beckenham	NBC	Oakleigh Park	OKL	Perranwell	PRW
Milford Haven	MFH	New Brighton	NBN	Oban	OBN	Perry Barr	PRY
Milford (Surrey)	MLF	New Clee	NCE	Ockendon	OCK	Pershore	PSH
Mill Hill Broadway	MIL	New Cross	NWX	Ockley	OLY	Perth	PTH
Mill Hill (Lancashire)	MLH	New Cross Gate	NXG	Old Hill	OHL	Peterborough	PBO
Millbrook (Bedfordshire)	MLB	New Cumnock	NCK	Old Roan	ORN	Petersfield	PTR
Millbrook (Hants)	MBK	New Eltham	NEH	Old Street	OLD	Petts Wood	PET
Milliken Park	MIN	New Hey	NHY	Oldfield Park	OLF	Pevensey & Westham	PEV
Millom	MLM	New Holland	NHL	Oldham Mumps	OLM	Pevensey Bay	PEB
Mills Hill	MIH	New Hythe	NHE	Oldham Werneth	OLW	Pewsey	PEW
Milngavie	MLN	New Lane	NLN	Olton	OLT	Pilning	PIL
Milnrow	MLR	New Malden	NEM	Ore	ORE	Pinhoe	PIN
Milton Keynes Central	MKC	New Mills Central	NMC	Ormskirk	OMS	Pitlochry	PIT
Minffordd	MFF	New Mills Newtown	NMN	Orpington	ORP	Pitsea	PSE
Minster	MSR	New Milton	NWM	Orrell	ORR	Pleasington	PLS
Mirfield	MIR	New Pudsey	NPD	Orrell Park	OPK	Plockton	PLK
Mistley	MIS	New Southgate	NSG	Otford	OTF	Pluckley	PLC
Mitcham Eastfields	MTC	Newark Castle	NCT	Oulton Broad North	OUN	Plumley	PLM
Mitcham Junction	MIJ	Newark North Gate	NNG	Oulton Broad South	OUS	Plumpton	PMP
Mobberley	MOB	Newbridge	NBE	Outwood	OUT	Plumstead	PLU
Monifieth	MON	Newbury	NBY	Overpool	OVE	Plymouth	PLY
Monks Risborough	MRS	Newbury Racecourse	NRC	Overton	OVR	Pokesdown	POK
Montpelier	MTP	Newcastle	NCL	Oxenholme Lake District	OXN	Polegate	PLG
Montrose	MTS	Newcraighall	NEW	Oxford	OXF	Polesworth	PSW
Moorfields	MRF	Newhaven Harbour	NVH	Oxshott	OXS	Pollokshaws East	PWE
Moorgate	ZMG	Newhaven Town	NVN	Oxted	OXT	Pollokshaws West	PWW
Moorside	MSD	Newington	NGT	Paddock Wood	PDW	Pollokshields East	PLE
Moorthorpe	MRP	Newmarket	NMK	Padgate	PDG	Pollokshields West	PLW
Morar	MRR	Newport (Essex)	NWE	Paignton	PGN	Polmont	PMT
Morchard Road	MRD	Newport (S. Wales)	NWP	Paisley Canal	PCN	Polsloe Bridge	POL
Morden South	MDS	Newquay	NQY	Paisley Gilmour Street	PYG	Ponders End	PON
Morecambe	MCM	Newstead	NSD	Paisley St James	PYJ	Pontarddulais	PTD
Moreton (Dorset)	MTN	Newton Abbot	NTA	Palmers Green	PAL	Pontefract Baghill	PFR
Moreton (Merseyside)	MRT	Newton Aycliffe	NAY	Pangbourne	PAN	Pontefract Monkhill	PFM
Moreton-in-Marsh	MIM	Newton for Hyde	NWN	Pannal	PNL	Pontefract Tanshelf	POT

Data Tables

Rail Data Tables

Pontlottyn	PLT	Redhill	RDH	Sanderstead	SNR	Shotts	SHS
Pontyclun	PYC	Redland	RDA	Sandhills	SDL	Shrewsbury	SHR
Pont-y-Pant	PYP	Redruth	RED	Sandhurst	SND	Sidcup	SID
Pontypool & New Inn	PPL	Reedham (Norfolk)	REE	Sandling	SDG	Sileby	SIL
Pontypridd	PPD	Reedham (Surrey)	RHM	Sandown	SAN	Silecroft	SIC
Poole	POO	Reigate	REI	Sandplace	SDP	Silkstone Common	SLK
Poppleton	POP	Renton	RTN	Sandwell & Dudley	SAD	Silver Street	SLV
Port Glasgow	PTG	Retford	RET	Sandwich	SDW	Silverdale	SVR
Port Sunlight	PSL	Rhiwbina	RHI	Sandy	SDY	Singer	SIN
Port Talbot Parkway	PTA	Rhoose Cardiff Int Airport	RIA	Sankey for Penketh	SNK	Sittingbourne	SIT
Portchester	PTC	Rhosneigr	RHO	Sanquhar	SQH	Skegness	SKG
Porth	POR	Rhyl	RHL	Sarn	SRR	Skewen	SKE
Porthmadog	PTM	Rhymney	RHY	Saundersfoot	SDF	Skipton	SKI
Portlethen	PLN	Ribblehead	RHD	Saunderton	SDR	Slade Green	SGR
Portslade	PLD	Rice Lane	RIL	Sawbridgeworth	SAW	Slaithwaite	SWT
Portsmouth & Southsea	PMS	Richmond	RMD	Saxilby	SXY	Slateford	SLA
Portsmouth Arms	PMA	Rickmansworth	RIC	Saxmundham	SAX	Sleaford	SLR
Portsmouth Harbour	PMH	Riddlesdown	RDD	Scarborough	SCA	Sleights	SLH
Possilpark & Parkhouse	PPK	Ridgmont	RID	Scotscalder	SCT	Slough	SLO
Potters Bar	PBR	Riding Mill	RDM	Scotstounhill	SCH	Small Heath	SMA
Poulton-le-Fylde	PFY	Risca & Pontymister	RCA	Scunthorpe	SCU	Smallbrook Junction	SAB
Poynton	PYT	Rishton	RIS	Sea Mills	SML	Smethwick Galton Bridge	SGB
Prees	PRS	Robertsbridge	RBR	Seaford	SEF	Smethwick Rolfe Street	SMR
Prescot	PSC	Roby	ROB	Seaforth & Litherland	SFL	Smitham	SMI
Prestatyn	PRT	Rochdale	RCD	Seaham	SEA	Smithy Bridge	SMB
Prestbury	PRB	Roche	ROC	Seamer	SEM	Snaith	SNI
Preston	PRE	Rochester	RTR	Seascale	SSC	Snodland	SDA
Preston Park	PRP	Rochford	RFD	Seaton Carew	SEC	Snowdown	SWO
Prestonpans	PST	Rock Ferry	RFY	Seer Green & Jordans	SRG	Sole Street	SOR
Prestwick Int Airport	PRA	Rogart	ROG	Selby	SBY	Solihull	SOL
Prestwick Town	PTW	Rogerstone	ROR	Selhurst	SRS	Somerleyton	SYT
Priesthill & Darnley	PTL	Rolleston	ROL	Sellafield	SEL	South Acton	SAT
Princes Risborough	PRR	Roman Bridge	RMB	Selling	SEG	South Bank	SBK
Prittlewell	PRL	Romford	RMF	Selly Oak	SLY	South Bermondsey	SBM
Prudhoe	PRU	Romiley	RML	Settle	SET	South Croydon	SCY
Pulborough	PUL	Romsey	ROM	Seven Kings	SVK	South Elmsall	SES
Purfleet	PFL	Roose	ROO	Seven Sisters	SVS	South Greenford	SGN
Purley	PUR	Rose Grove	RSG	Sevenoaks	SEV	South Gyle	SGL
Purley Oaks	PUO	Rose Hill Marple	RSH	Severn Beach	SVB	South Hampstead	SOH
Putney	PUT	Rosyth	ROS	Severn Tunnel Junction	STJ	South Kenton	SOK
Pwllheli	PWL	Rotherham Central	RMC	Shalford	SFR	South Merton	SMO
Pyle	PYL	Roughton Road	RNR	Shanklin	SHN	South Milford	SOM
Quakers Yard	QYD	Rowlands Castle	RLN	Shaw & Crompton	SHA	South Ruislip	SRU
Queenborough	QBR	Rowley Regis	ROW	Shawford	SHW	South Tottenham	STO
Queens Park (Glasgow)	QPK	Roy Bridge	RYB	Shawlands	SHL	South Wigston	SWS
Queens Park (London)	QPW	Roydon	RYN	Sheerness-on-Sea	SSS	South Woodham Ferrers	SOF
Queens Road, Peckham	QRP	Royston	RYS	Sheffield	SHF	Southall	STL
Queenstown Road	QRB	Ruabon	RUA	Shelford	SED	Southampton Airport	SOA
Quintrell Downs	QUI	Rufford	RUF	Shenfield	SNF	Southampton Central	SOU
Radcliffe (Notts)	RDF	Rugby	RUG	Shenstone	SEN	Southbourne	SOB
Radlett	RDT	Rugeley Town	RGT	Shepherd's Bush	SPB	Southbury	SBU
Radley	RAD	Rugeley Trent Valley	RGL	Shepherds Well	SPH	Southease	SEE
Radyr	RDR	Runcorn	RUN	Shepley	SPY	Southend Central	SOC
Rainford	RNF	Runcorn East	RUE	Shepperton	SHP	Southend East	SOE
Rainham (Essex)	RNM	Ruskington	RKT	Shepreth	STH	Southend Victoria	SOV
Rainham (Kent)	RAI	Ruswarp	RUS	Sherborne	SHE	Southminster	SMN
Rainhill	RNH	Rutherglen	RUT	Sherburn-in-Elmet	SIE	Southport	SOP
Ramsgate	RAM	Ryde St Johns Road	RYR	Sheringham	SHM	Southwick	SWK
Ramsgreave & Wilpshire	RGW	Ryde Esplanade	RYD	Shettleston	SLS	Sowerby Bridge	SOW
Rannoch	RAN	Ryde Pier Head	RYP	Shieldmuir	SDM	Spalding	SPA
Rauceby	RAU	Ryder Brow	RRB	Shifnal	SFN	Spean Bridge	SBR
Ravenglass for Eskdale	RAV	Rye	RYE	Shildon	SHD	Spital	SPI
Ravensbourne	RVB	Rye House	RYH	Shiplake	SHI	Spondon	SPO
Ravensthorpe	RVN	Salford Central	SFD	Shipley	SHY	Spooner Row	SPN
Rawcliffe	RWC	Salford Crescent	SLD	Shippea Hill	SPP	Spring Road	SRI
Rayleigh	RLG	Salfords	SAF	Shipton	SIP	Springburn	SPR
Raynes Park	RAY	Salhouse	SAH	Shirebrook	SHB	Springfield	SPF
Reading	RDG	Salisbury	SAL	Shirehampton	SHH	Squires Gate	SQU
Reading West	RDW	Saltaire	SAE	Shireoaks	SRO	St Albans	SAC
Rectory Road	REC	Saltash	STS	Shirley	SRL	St Albans Abbey	SAA
Redbridge	RDB	Saltburn	SLB	Shoeburyness	SRY	St Andrews Road	SAR
Redcar Central	RCC	Saltcoats	SLT	Sholing	SHO	St Austell	SAU
Redcar East	RCE	Saltmarshe	SAM	Shoreham (Kent)	SEH	St Bees	SBS
Reddish North	RDN	Salwick	SLW	Shoreham-by-Sea	SSE	St Budeaux Ferry Road	SBF
Reddish South	RDS	Sandal & Agbrigg	SNA	Shortlands	SRT	St Budeaux Victoria Rd	SBV
Redditch	RDC	Sandbach	SDB	Shotton	SHT		

Data Tables

St Columb Road	SCR	Sudbury Hill Harrow	SDH	Tile Hill	THL	Wallyford	WAF
St Denys	SDN	Sugar Loaf	SUG	Tilehurst	TLH	Walmer	WAM
St Erth	SER	Summerston	SUM	Tipton	TIP	Walsall	WSL
St Germans	SGM	Sunbury	SUU	Tir-Phil	TIR	Walsden	WDN
St Helens Central	SNH	Sunderland	SUN	Tisbury	TIS	Waltham Cross	WLC
St Helens Junction	SHJ	Sundridge Park	SUP	Tiverton Parkway	TVP	Walthamstow Central	WHC
St Helier	SIH	Sunningdale	SNG	Todmorden	TOD	Walthamstow Queen's Rd	WMW
St Ives (Cornwall)	SIV	Sunnymeads	SNY	Tolworth	TOL	Walton (Merseyside)	WAO
St James Park	SJP	Surbiton	SUR	Ton Pentre	TPN	Walton on the Naze	WON
St James Street	SJS	Sutton Coldfield	SUT	Tonbridge	TON	Walton-on-Thames	WAL
St Johns	SAJ	Sutton Common	SUC	Tondu	TDU	Wanborough	WAN
St Keyne	SKN	Sutton Parkway	SPK	Tonfanau	TNF	Wandsworth Common	WSW
St Leonards Warrior Sq	SLQ	Sutton (Surrey)	SUO	Tonypandy	TNP	Wandsworth Road	WWR
St Margarets (London)	SMG	Swale	SWL	Tooting	TOO	Wandsworth Town	WNT
St Margarets (Herts)	SMT	Swanley	SAY	Topsham	TOP	Wanstead Park	WNP
St Mary Cray	SMY	Swanscombe	SWM	Torquay	TQY	Warblington	WBL
St Michaels	STM	Swansea	SWA	Torre	TRR	Ware	WAR
St Neots	SNO	Swanwick	SNW	Totnes	TOT	Wareham	WRM
St Pancras International	SPX	Sway	SWY	Tottenham Hale	TOM	Wargrave	WGV
Stafford	STA	Swaythling	SWG	Totton	TTN	Warminster	WMN
Staines	SNS	Swinderby	SWD	Town Green	TWN	Warnham	WNH
Stallingborough	SLL	Swindon	SWI	Trafford Park	TRA	Warrington Bank Quay	WBQ
Stalybridge	SYB	Swineshead	SWE	Trefforest	TRF	Warrington Central	WAC
Stamford	SMD	Swinton (Gr Manchester)	SNN	Trefforest Estate	TRE	Warwick	WRW
Stamford Hill	SMH	Swinton (Yorks)	SWN	Trehafod	TRH	Warwick Parkway	WRP
Stanford-le-Hope	SFO	Sydenham	SYD	Treherbert	TRB	Water Orton	WTO
Stanlow & Thornton	SNT	Sydenham Hill	SYH	Treorchy	TRY	Waterbeach	WBC
Stansted Airport	SSD	Syon Lane	SYL	Trimley	TRM	Wateringbury	WTR
Stansted Mountfitchet	SST	Syston	SYS	Tring	TRI	Waterloo (Merseyside)	WLO
Staplehurst	SPU	Tackley	TAC	Troed-y-rhiw	TRD	Watford High Street	WFH
Stapleton Road	SRD	Tadworth	TAD	Troon	TRN	Watford Junction	WFJ
Starbeck	SBE	Taffs Well	TAF	Trowbridge	TRO	Watford North	WFN
Starcross	SCS	Tain	TAI	Truro	TRU	Watlington	WTG
Staveley (Cumbria)	SVL	Talsarnau	TAL	Tulloch	TUL	Watton-at-Stone	WAS
Stechford	SCF	Talybont	TLB	Tulse Hill	TUH	Waun-Gron Park	WNG
Steeton & Silsden	SON	Tal-y-Cafn	TLC	Tunbridge Wells	TBW	Wavertree Tech Park	WAV
Stepps	SPS	Tame Bridge Parkway	TAB	Turkey Street	TUR	Wedgwood	WED
Stevenage	SVG	Tamworth	TAM	Tutbury & Hatton	TUT	Weeley	WEE
Stevenston	STV	Taplow	TAP	Twickenham	TWI	Weeton	WET
Stewartby	SWR	Tattenham Corner	TAT	Twyford	TWY	Welham Green	WMG
Stewarton	STT	Taunton	TAU	Ty Croes	TYC	Welling	WLI
Stirling	STG	Taynuilt	TAY	Ty Glas	TGS	Wellingborough	WEL
Stockport	SPT	Teddington	TED	Tygwyn	TYG	Wellington (Shropshire)	WLN
Stocksfield	SKS	Teesside Airport	TEA	Tyndrum Lower	TYL	Welshpool	WLP
Stocksmoor	SSM	Teignmouth	TGM	Tyseley	TYS	Welwyn Garden City	WGC
Stockton	STK	Telford Central	TFC	Tywyn	TYW	Welwyn North	WLW
Stoke Mandeville	SKM	Templecombe	TMC	Uckfield	UCK	Wem	WEM
Stoke Newington	SKW	Tenby	TEN	Uddingston	UDD	Wembley Central	WMB
Stoke-on-Trent	SOT	Teynham	TEY	Ulceby	ULC	Wembley Stadium	WCX
Stone	SNE	Thames Ditton	THD	Ulleskelf	ULL	Wemyss Bay	WMS
Stone Crossing	SCG	Thatcham	THA	Ulverston	ULV	Wendover	WND
Stonebridge Park	SBP	Thatto Heath	THH	Umberleigh	UMB	Wennington	WNN
Stonegate	SOG	The Hawthorns	THW	University	UNI	West Allerton	WSA
Stonehaven	STN	The Lakes	TLK	Uphall	UHA	West Brompton	WBP
Stonehouse	SHU	Theale	THE	Upholland	UPL	West Byfleet	WBY
Stoneleigh	SNL	Theobalds Grove	TEO	Upminster	UPM	West Calder	WCL
Stourbridge Junction	SBJ	Thetford	TTF	Upper Halliford	UPH	West Croydon	WCY
Stourbridge Town	SBT	Thirsk	THI	Upper Holloway	UHL	West Drayton	WDT
Stowmarket	SMK	Thornaby	TBY	Upper Tyndrum	UTY	West Dulwich	WDU
Stranraer	STR	Thorne North	TNN	Upper Warlingham	UWL	West Ealing	WEA
Stratford (London)	SRA	Thorne South	TNS	Upton	UPT	West Ham	WEH
Stratford-upon-Avon	SAV	Thornford	THO	Upwey	UPW	West Hampstead	WHD
Strathcarron	STC	Thornliebank	THB	Urmston	URM	West Hampstead T'link	WHP
Strawberry Hill	STW	Thornton Abbey	TNA	Uttoxeter	UTT	West Horndon	WHR
Streatham	STE	Thornton Heath	TTH	Valley	VAL	West Kilbride	WKB
Streatham Common	SRC	Thorntonhall	THT	Vauxhall	VXH	West Kirby	WKI
Streatham Hill	SRH	Thorpe Bay	TPB	Virginia Water	VIR	West Malling	WMA
Streethouse	SHC	Thorpe Culvert	TPC	Waddon	WDO	West Norwood	WNW
Strines	SRN	Thorpe-le-Soken	TLS	Wadhurst	WAD	West Ruislip	WRU
Stromeferry	STF	Three Bridges	TBD	Wainfleet	WFL	West Runton	WRN
Strood	SOO	Three Oaks	TOK	Wakefield Kirkgate	WKK	West St Leonards	WLD
Stroud	STD	Thurgarton	THU	Wakefield Westgate	WKF	West Sutton	WSU
Sturry	STU	Thurnscoe	THC	Walkden	WKD	West Wickham	WWI
Styal	SYA	Thurso	THS	Wallasey Grove Road	WLG	West Worthing	WWO
Sudbury	SUY	Thurston	TRS	Wallasey Village	WLV	Westbury (Wilts)	WSB
Sudbury & Harrow Road	SUD	Tilbury Town	TIL	Wallington	WLT	Westcliff	WCF

Data Tables

Westcombe Park	WCB	Whittlesford Parkway	WLF	Winsford	WSF	Workington	WKG
Westenhanger	WHA	Whitton	WTN	Wishaw	WSH	Worksop	WRK
Wester Hailes	WTA	Whitwell	WWL	Witham	WTM	Worle	WOR
Westerfield	WFI	Whyteleafe	WHY	Witley	WTY	Worplesdon	WPL
Westerton	WES	Whyteleafe South	WHS	Witton	WTT	Worstead	WRT
Westgate-on-Sea	WGA	Wick	WCK	Wivelsfield	WVF	Worthing	WRH
Westhoughton	WHG	Wickford	WIC	Wivenhoe	WIV	Wrabness	WRB
Weston Milton	WNM	Wickham Market	WCM	Woburn Sands	WOB	Wraysbury	WRY
Weston-super-Mare	WSM	Widdrington	WDD	Woking	WOK	Wrenbury	WRE
Wetheral	WRL	Widnes	WID	Wokingham	WKM	Wressle	WRS
Weybridge	WYB	Widney Manor	WMR	Woldingham	WOH	Wrexham Central	WXC
Weymouth	WEY	Wigan North Western	WGN	Wolverhampton	WVH	Wrexham General	WRX
Whaley Bridge	WBR	Wigan Wallgate	WGW	Wolverton	WOL	Wye	WYE
Whalley	WHE	Wigton	WGT	Wombwell	WOM	Wylam	WYM
Whatstandwell	WTS	Wildmill	WMI	Wood End	WDE	Wylde Green	WYL
Whifflet	WFF	Willesden Junction	WIJ	Wood Street	WST	Wymondham	WMD
Whimple	WHM	Williamwood	WLM	Woodbridge	WDB	Wythall	WYT
Whinhill	WNL	Willington	WIL	Woodgrange Park	WGR	Yalding	YAL
Whiston	WHN	Wilmcote	WMC	Woodhall	WDL	Yardley Wood	YRD
Whitby	WTB	Wilmslow	WML	Woodhouse	WDH	Yarm	YRM
Whitchurch (Cardiff)	WHT	Wilnecote	WNE	Woodlesford	WDS	Yate	YAE
Whitchurch (Hants)	WCH	Wimbledon	WIM	Woodley	WLY	Yatton	YAT
Whitchurch (Shropshire)	WTC	Wimbledon Chase	WBO	Woodmansterne	WME	Yeoford	YEO
White Hart Lane	WHL	Winchelsea	WSE	Woodsmoor	WSR	Yeovil Junction	YVJ
White Notley	WNY	Winchester	WIN	Wool	WOO	Yeovil Pen Mill	YVP
Whitecraigs	WCR	Winchfield	WNF	Woolston	WLS	Yetminster	YET
Whitehaven	WTH	Winchmore Hill	WIH	Woolwich Arsenal	WWA	Ynyswen	YNW
Whitland	WTL	Windermere	WDM	Woolwich Dockyard	WWD	Yoker	YOK
Whitley Bridge	WBD	Windsor & Eton Central	WNC	Wootton Wawen	WWW	York	YRK
Whitlocks End	WTE	Windsor & Eton Riverside	WNR	Worcester Foregate St	WOF	Yorton	YRT
Whitstable	WHI	Winnersh	WNS	Worcester Park	WCP	Ystrad Mynach	YSM
Whittlesea	WLE	Winnersh Triangle	WTI	Worcester Shrub Hill	WOS	Ystrad Rhondda	YSR

Left: *Motor Standard Open No. 38225 from Class 378 'Capitalstar' set No. 378228, one of the dual voltage sets able to operate on both 25kV ac overhead and 750V dc third rail.* **CJM**

BDMSO	Battery Driving Motor Standard Open
DM	Driving Motor
DMBS	Driving Motor Brake Standard
DMCL	Driving Motor Composite Lavatory
DMCO	Driving Motor Composite Open
DMF	Driving Motor First
DMFO	Driving Motor Brake Open
DMFLO	Driving Motor First Luggage Open
DMRFO	Driving Motor Restaurant First Open
DMS	Driving Motor Standard
DMSL	Driving Motor Standard Lavatory
DMSO	Driving Motor Standard Open
DTCO	Driving Trailer Composite Open
DTPMV	Driving Trailer Parcels Mail Van
DTSO	Driving Trailer Standard Open
MBC	Motor Brake Composite
MBSO	Motor Brake Standard Open
MC	Motor Composite

MFL	Motor First Lavatory
MPMV	Motor Parcels Mail Van
MS	Motor Standard
MSL	Motor Standard Lavatory
MSLRB	Motor Standard Lavatory Restaurant Buffet
MSO	Motor Standard Open
MSRMB	Motor Standard Restaurant Micro Buffet
PTSO	Pantograph Trailer Standard Open
RB	Restaurant Buffet
TBFO	Trailer Brake First Open
TCO	Trailer Composite Open
TFO	Trailer First Open
TPMV	Trailer Parcels Mail Van
TSO	Trailer Standard Open
TSRMB	Trailer Standard Restaurant Micro Buffet
(A) - A Car	
(B) - B Car	

Data Tables

This cross number checklist indicates in which section of the ABC Rail Guide 2012 full details of rolling stock can be found.

Number Cross-Link Codes

Code	Name	Code	Name	Code	Name
3MP	3M Productions	FLF	Fastline Freight	PRE	Preserved
AEA	Abellio East Anglia	FLR	Freightliner	PUL	Pullman Rail
ALS	Alstom	FMR	FM Rail	RAF	Railfilms
ATW	Arriva Trains Wales	FSL	Flying Scotsman Railway Ltd	RCL	Railcare
AXC	Arriva CrossCountry	FSR	First ScotRail	RIV	Riviera
BAR	British American Railway	FTP	First TransPennine	RRS	Ridings Railtours
BOK	Bo'ness & Kinneil Railway	GBR	GB Railfreight	RVE	Rail Vehicle Engineering
BOM	Bombardier Transportation	GSW	Great Scottish & Western Rly	S47	Stratford Class 47 Group
C2C	c2c Railway	GTL	Grand Central Railway	SEC	Serco Railtest
CAD	Cargo-D	HAN	Hanson Traction	SET	Southeastern Trains
COL	Colas	HEC	Heathrow Connect	SIE	Siemens
CRW	Chiltern Railways	HEX	Heathrow Express	SIL	Stagecoach Island Line
CWR	Cotswold Rail	HNR	Harry Needle Railroad Co	SNF	SNCF (French Railways)
DBS	DB Schenker	IND	Industrial	SOU	Southern
DRS	Direct Rail Services	JAR	Jarvis	SRP	Scottish Railway Preservation Soc
ECR	Euro Cargo Rail	JHS	Jeremy Hoskins	SUP	Support Coaches
EMT	East Midlands Trains	KRS	Knights Rail Services	SWT	South West Trains
EPX	Europhoenix Ltd	LMI	London Midland	TTS	Transmart Trains
ETL	Electric Traction Ltd	LOG	London Overground	VSO	Venice Simplon Orient Express
EUR	Eurotunnel	MER	Merseyrail	VTN	Vintage Trains
EUR	Europorte2	MHR	Mid Hants Railway	VWC	Virgin West Coast
EUS	Eurostar UK	MRL	Mendip Rail Ltd	WAB	Wabtec
EXP	Exported	NEM	Nemesis Rail	WCR	West Coast Railway
FCC	First Capital Connect	NOR	Northern	WSR	Wrexham & Shropshire Railway
FGW	First Great Western	NRL	Network Rail Limited	WTN	Wessex Trains
FHT	First Hull Trains	NXE	National Express East Coast		
		NYM	North Yorkshire Moors Railway		
		OLS	Off Lease		

Locomotives - Diesel & Electric

No.		No.		No.		No.		No.	
D0226	PRE	D2178	PRE	D2774	PRE	D7076	PRE	LMS7050	PRE
		D2182	PRE	D2854	PRE			LMS7051	PRE
D4	PRE	D2184	PRE	D2858	PRE	D8000	PRE	LMS7069	PRE
		D2192	PRE	D2860	PRE				
D200	PRE	D2199	PRE	D2866	PRE	D8233	PRE	E26020	PRE
				D2867	PRE			E27000	PRE
		D2203	PRE	D2868	PRE	D8568	PRE	E27001	PRE
		D2205	PRE	D2953	PRE				
D821	PRE	D2207	PRE	D2956	PRE	D9500	PRE	9005	EUR
D832	PRE	D2229	PRE			D9502	PRE	9006	EUR
		D2245	PRE	D3000	PRE	D9504	PRE	9007	EUR
D1010	PRE	D2246	PRE	D3002	PRE	D9513	PRE	9011	EUR
D1013	PRE	D2271	PRE	D3014	PRE	D9516	PRE	9013	EUR
D1015	PRE	D2272	PRE	D3101	PRE	D9518	PRE	9015	EUR
D1023	PRE	D2279	PRE	D3255	PRE	D9520	PRE	9018	EUR
D1041	PRE	D2280	PRE	D3261	PRE	D9521	PRE	9022	EUR
D1048	PRE	D2284	PRE	D3452	PRE	D9523	PRE	9023	EUR
D1062	PRE	D2298	PRE	D3489	PRE	D9524	PRE	9024	EUR
		D2302	PRE	D4067	PRE	D9525	PRE	9026	EUR
D2023	PRE	D2310	PRE	D4092	PRE	D9526	PRE	9027	EUR
D2024	PRE	D2324	PRE			D9529	IND	9029	EUR
D2041	PRE	D2325	PRE	D5500	PRE	D9531	PRE	9031	EUR
D2046	PRE	D2334	PRE			D9537	PRE	9033	EUR
D2051	PRE	D2337	PRE	D5705	PRE	D9539	PRE	9036	EUR
D2117	PRE					D9551	PRE	9037	EUR
D2118	PRE	D2511	PRE	D6700	PRE	D9553	PRE	9101	EUR
D2133	PRE	D2578	PRE			D9555	PRE	9103	EUR
D2138	PRE	D2587	PRE	D7017	PRE			9105	EUR
D2139	PRE	D2595	PRE	D7018	PRE	DELTIC	PRE	9106	EUR
D2148	PRE	D2767	PRE	D7029	PRE	DS75	PRE	9107	EUR

Data Tables

No.	Code	No.	Code	No.	Code	No.	Code	No.	Code
9108	EUR	03119	PRE	08401	GBR	08613	BAR	08769	PRE
9109	EUR	03120	PRE	08405	DBS	08615	WAB	08772	PRE
9110	EUR	03128	PRE	08410	FGW	08616	LMI	08773	PRE
9111	EUR	03134	PRE	08411	IND	08617	ALS	08774	IND
9112	EUR	03141	PRE	08417	NRL	08622	BAR	08780	PRE
9701	EUR	03144	PRE	08418	WCR	08623	DBS	08782	DBS
9702	EUR	03145	PRE	08423	BAR	08624	FLR	08784	DBS
9703	EUR	03152	PRE	08428	DBS	08629	RCL	08785	FLR
9704	EUR	03158	PRE	08436	PRE	08628	PRE	08786	HNR
9705	EUR	03162	PRE	08441	IND	08630	DBS	08787	IND
9706	EUR	03170	PRE	08442	DBS	08631	PRE	08790	ALS
9707	EUR	03179	IND	08443	PRE	08632	DBS	08795	FGW
9712	EUR	03189	PRE	08444	PRE	08633	DBS	08799	DBS
9714	EUR	03196	WCR	08445	IND	08635	PRE	08802	DBS
9723	EUR	03371	PRE	08447	IND	08641	FGW	08804	DBS
9801	EUR	03381	WCR	08451	ALS	08643	MRL	08805	LMI
9802	EUR	03399	PRE	08454	ALS	08644	FGW	08807	IND
9803	EUR			08460	IND	08645	FGW	08809	IND
9804	EUR	05001	PRE	08471	PRE	08648	BAR	08818	HNR
9808	EUR			08472	WAB	08649	RCL	08822	FGW
9809	EUR	06003	PRE	08473	PRE	08650	MRL	08823	IND
9810	EUR			08476	PRE	08652	MRL	08824	DBS
9812	EUR	07001	HNR	08479	PRE	08653	DBS	08830	PRE
9814	EUR	07005	PRE	08480	DBS	08663	FGW	08834	HNR
9816	EUR	07007	KRS	08483	FGW	08669	WAB	08836	FGW
9817	EUR	07010	PRE	08484	IND	08670	IND	08846	BOM
9819	EUR	07011	PRE	08485	WCR	08676	DBS	08847	IND
9820	EUR	07012	PRE	08490	PRE	08678	WCR	08850	PRE
9821	EUR	07013	PRE	08492	HNR	08682	BOM	08853	WAB
9825	EUR			08495	DBS	08683	PRE	08865	DBS
9828	EUR	08011	PRE	08499	PUL	08685	HNR	08868	HNR
9832	EUR	08012	PRE	08500	DBS	08690	EMT	08870	BAR
9834	EUR	08015	PRE	08502	HNR	08691	FLR	08871	WAB
9835	EUR	08016	PRE	08503	IND	08694	PRE	08872	IND
9838	EUR	08021	PRE	08507	HNR	08696	ALS	08873	BAR
9840	EUR	08022	PRE	08511	IND	08697	RVE	08877	DBS
		08032	PRE	08516	DBS	08699	IND	08879	DBS
01509	CRW	08046	PRE	08523	IND	08700	PRE	08881	IND
01551	SIE	08054	PRE	08525	EMT	08701	DBS	08885	BAR
01552	HNR	08060	PRE	08527	HNR	08703	DBS	08887	ALS
01564	HNR	08064	PRE	08528	PRE	08706	DBS	08886	DBS
		08077	FLR	08530	FLR	08709	DBS	08888	DBS
03018	PRE	08102	PRE	08531	FLR	08711	DBS	08891	FLR
03020	PRE	08108	PRE	08535	IND	08714	DBS	08892	HNR
03022	PRE	08114	PRE	08536	RVE	08721	ALS	08896	PRE
03027	PRE	08123	PRE	08556	PRE	08724	WAB	08899	EMT
03037	PRE	08133	PRE	08567	DBS	08728	IND	08903	IND
03059	PRE	08164	PRE	08568	RCL	08730	RCL	08904	DBS
03062	PRE	08168	PRE	08571	WAB	08731	MRL	08905	HNR
03066	PRE	08195	PRE	08573	BAR	08735	DBS	08907	DBS
03069	PRE	08220	PRE	08575	FLR	08737	DBS	08908	EMT
03072	PRE	08238	PRE	08578	DBS	08738	DBS	08911	PRE
03073	PRE	08266	PRE	08580	DBS	08742	IND	08912	IND
03078	PRE	08266	PRE	08585	FLR	08743	IND	08913	IND
03079	PRE	08308	BAR	08588	BAR	08750	BAR	08915	IND
03081	PRE	08331	IND	08590	PRE	08752	DBS	08918	HNR
03084	PRE	08359	PRE	08593	DBS	08754	BAR	08922	DBS
03089	PRE	08375	IND	08596	WAB	08756	BAR	08924	HNR
03090	PRE	08377	PRE	08598	IND	08757	DBS	08927	WAB
03094	PRE	08388	PRE	08600	IND	08762	BAR	08929	HNR
03099	PRE	08389	HNR	08604	PRE	08764	WAB	08933	IND
03112	HNR	08393	LHG	08605	DBS	08765	HNR	08934	ALS
03113	PRE	08398	IND	08611	ALS	08767	PRE	08936	BAR

Data Tables

No.	Code	No.	Code	No.	Code	No.	Code	No.	Code
08937	PRE	20154	PRE	25279	PRE	31465	NRL	37207	PRE
08939	DBS	20166	PRE	25283	PRE	31466	PRE	37214	WCR
08943	HNR	20168	HNR	25309	PRE	31468	RVE	37215	PRE
08944	PRE	20169	PRE	25311	PRE	31530	PRE	37216	PRE
08947	MRL	20177	PRE	25321	PRE	31601	BAR	37218	DRS
08948	EUS	20188	PRE	25322	PRE	31602	RVE	37219	PRE
08950	EMT	20189	BAR					37227	PRE
08956	NRL	20205	PRE	26001	PRE	33002	PRE	37229	DRS
08993	DBS	20214	PRE	26002	PRE	33008	PRE	37240	PRE
08994	DBS	20227	BAR	26004	PRE	33012	PRE	37248	WCR
08995	DBS	20301	GBR	26007	PRE	33018	PRE	37250	PRE
09002	GBR	20302	GBR	26010	PRE	33019	PRE	37254	PRE
09004	PRE	20303	DRS	26011	PRE	33021	PRE	37255	PRE
09006	DBS	20304	GBR	26014	PRE	33025	WCR	37259	DRS
09007	LOG	20305	GBR	26024	PRE	33029	WCR	37261	DRS
09009	GBR	20306	DRS	26025	PRE	33030	WCR	37263	PRE
09010	PRE	20307	DRS	26035	PRE	33035	PRE	37264	PRE
09012	HNR	20308	GBR	26038	PRE	33046	PRE	37275	PRE
09015	PRE	20309	DRS	26040	PRE	33048	PRE	37294	PRE
09018	HNR	20310	DRS	26043	PRE	33052	PRE	37308	PRE
09024	PRE	20311	HNR			33053	PRE	37314	PRE
09106	DBS	20312	DRS	27001	PRE	33057	PRE	37324	PRE
09201	DBS	20313	DRS	27005	PRE	33063	PRE	37372	PRE
09204	DBS	20314	HNR	27007	PRE	33065	PRE	37401	DRS
		20315	DRS	27024	PRE	33102	PRE	37402	DRS
12052	PRE	20901	HNR	27050	PRE	33103	NEM	37403	PRE
12061	PRE	20903	HNR	27056	PRE	33108	PRE	37405	DRS
12077	PRE	20904	HNR	27059	PRE	33109	PRE	37406	DRS
12082	PRE	20905	HNR	27066	PRE	33110	PRE	37407	PRE
12088	IND	20906	HNR			33111	PRE	37409	DRS
12093	PRE			31101	PRE	33116	PRE	37410	DRS
12099	PRE	21544	ECR	31105	NRL	33117	PRE	37411	DRS
12131	PRE	21545	ECR	31106	RVE	33201	PRE	37413	NEM
		21546	ECR	31108	PRE	33202	PRE	37415	HNR
15224	PRE	21547	ECR	31119	PRE	33207	WCR	37416	DRS
				31128	NEM	33208	PRE	37417	DRS
18000	PRE	21610	ECR	31130	PRE			37418	PRE
		21611	ECR	31162	PRE	37003	PRE	37419	DRS
20001	PRE	21901	EUR	31163	PRE	37009	PRE	37421	PRE
20007	PRE	21902	EUR	31190	BAR	37023	PRE	37422	DRS
20016	HNR	21903	EUR	31203	PRE	37025	PRE	37423	DRS
20020	PRE	21904	EUR	31206	PRE	37029	HNR	37424	PRE
20031	PRE	21905	EUR	31207	PRE	37032	PRE	37425	DRS
20048	PRE			31210	PRE	37037	PRE	37427	DRS
20056	HNR	24032	PRE	31233	NRL	37038	DRS	37428	HNR
20057	HNR	24054	PRE	31235	PRE	37042	DRS	37502	FLR
20059	PRE	24061	PRE	31270	PRE	37059	DRS	37503	HNR
20066	HNR	24082	PRE	31271	PRE	37069	DRS	37510	DRS
20069	PRE			31285	NRL	37075	PRE	37516	WCR
20081	HNR	25035	PRE	31289	PRE	37087	DRS	37517	WCR
20087	PRE	25057	PRE	31327	PRE	37097	PRE	37518	PRE
20088	HNR	25059	PRE	31410	PRE	37108	PRE	37521	HNR
20092	HNR	25067	PRE	31414	PRE	37109	PRE	37601	DRS
20096	HNR	25072	PRE	31415	PRE	37116	PRE	37602	DRS
20098	PRE	25083	PRE	31418	PRE	37142	PRE	37603	DRS
20107	HNR	25173	PRE	31422	RVE	37146	PRE	37604	DRS
20110	PRE	25185	PRE	31435	PRE	37152	PRE	37605	DRS
20118	HNR	25191	PRE	31438	PRE	37165	HNR	37606	DRS
20121	HNR	25235	PRE	31452	BAR	37175	PRE	37607	DRS
20132	HNR	25244	PRE	31454	BAR	37188	PRE	37608	DRS
20137	PRE	25262	PRE	31459	RVE	37194	DRS	37609	DRS
20138	HNR	26265	PRE	31461	PRE	37197	DRS	37610	DRS
20142	PRE	25278	NYM	31463	PRE	37198	NRL	37611	DRS

Data Tables

Data Tables

No.	Code	No.	Code	No.	Code	No.	Code	No.	Code
37612	DRS	43036	FGW	43139	FGW	43274	ICE	47192	PRE
37667	DRS	43037	FGW	43140	FGW	43277	ICE	47194	WCR
37668	WCR	43040	FGW	43141	FGW	43285	AXC	47205	PRE
37669	WCR	43041	FGW	43142	FGW	43290	ICE	47237	WCR
37674	PRE	43042	FGW	43143	FGW	43295	ICE	47245	WCR
37676	WCR	43043	EMT	43144	FGW	43296	ICE	47270	WCR
37679	PRE	43044	EMT	43145	FGW	43299	ICE	47292	PRE
37682	DRS	43045	EMT	43146	FGW	43300	ICE	47306	PRE
37683	DRS	43046	EMT	43147	FGW	43301	AXC	47355	WCR
37685	WCR	43047	EMT	43148	FGW	43302	ICE	47367	PRE
37688	DRS	43048	EMT	43149	FGW	43303	AXC	47375	NEM
37696	HNR	43049	EMT	43150	FGW	43304	AXC	47376	PRE
37703	DBS	43050	EMT	43151	FGW	43305	ICE	47401	PRE
37706	WCR	43052	EMT	43152	FGW	43306	ICE	47402	PRE
37710	WCR	43053	FGW	43153	FGW	43307	ICE	47417	PRE
37712	WCR	43054	EMT	43154	FGW	43308	ICE	47449	PRE
37714	DBS	43055	EMT	43155	FGW	43309	ICE	47484	PRE
37716	DBS	43056	FGW	43156	FGW	43310	ICE	47488	NEM
37718	DBS	43058	EMT	43158	FGW	43311	ICE	47492	WCR
37800	DBS	43059	EMT	43159	FGW	43312	ICE	47500	WCR
37884	DBS	43060	EMT	43160	FGW	43313	ICE	47501	DRS
37901	PRE	43061	EMT	43161	FGW	43314	ICE	47524	PRE
37905	PRE	43062	NRL	43162	FGW	43315	ICE	47526	WCR
37906	PRE	43063	FGW	43163	FGW	43316	ICE	47580	S47
		43064	EMT	43164	FGW	43317	ICE	47596	PRE
40012	PRE	43066	EMT	43165	FGW	43318	ICE	47635	PRE
40013	PRE	43069	FGW	43168	FGW	43319	ICE	47640	PRE
40106	PRE	43070	FGW	43169	FGW	43320	ICE	47643	PRE
40118	PRE	43071	FGW	43170	FGW	43321	AXC	47701	PRE
40135	PRE	43073	EMT	43171	FGW	43357	AXC	47703	DRS
40145	PRE	43075	EMT	43172	FGW	43366	AXC	47709	DRS
		43076	EMT	43174	FGW	43367	ICE	47712	DRS
41001	PRE	43078	FGW	43175	FGW	43378	AXC	47714	HNR
		43079	FGW	43176	FGW	43384	AXC	47715	PRE
43002	FGW	43081	EMT	43177	FGW	43423	GTL	47716	NEM
43003	FGW	43082	EMT	43179	FGW	43465	GTL	47727	COL
43004	FGW	43083	EMT	43180	FGW	43467	GTL	47739	COL
43005	FGW	43086	FGW	43181	FGW	43468	GTL	47744	NEM
43009	FGW	43087	FGW	43182	FGW	43480	GTL	47746	WCR
43010	FGW	43088	FGW	43183	FGW	43484	GTL	47747	DRS
43012	FGW	43089	EMT	43185	FGW			47749	COL
43013	NRL	43091	FGW	43186	FGW	44008	PRE	47760	WCR
43014	NRL	43092	FGW	43187	FGW			47761	HNR
43015	FGW	43093	FGW	43188	FGW	45014	PRE	47763	PRE
43016	FGW	43094	FGW	43189	FGW	45041	PRE	47765	PRE
43017	FGW	43097	FGW	43190	FGW	45060	PRE	47768	WCR
43018	FGW	43098	FGW	43191	FGW	45105	PRE	47769	RIV
43020	FGW	43122	FGW	43192	FGW	45108	PRE	47771	PRE
43021	FGW	43124	FGW	43193	FGW	45112	NEM	47772	WCR
43022	FGW	43125	FGW	43194	FGW	45118	PRE	47773	VTN
43023	FGW	43126	FGW	43195	FGW	45125	PRE	47776	WCR
43024	FGW	43127	FGW	43196	FGW	45132	PRE	47785	PRE
43025	FGW	43128	FGW	43197	FGW	45133	PRE	47786	WCR
43026	FGW	43129	FGW	43198	FGW	45135	PRE	47787	WCR
43027	FGW	43130	FGW			45149	PRE	47790	DRS
43028	FGW	43131	FGW	43206	ICE			47791	DRS
43029	FGW	43132	FGW	43207	AXC	46010	PRE	47793	PRE
43030	FGW	43133	FGW	43208	ICE	46035	PRE	47798	PRE
43031	FGW	43134	FGW	43238	ICE	46045	PRE	47799	PRE
43032	FGW	43135	FGW	43239	ICE			47802	DRS
43033	FGW	43136	FGW	43251	ICE	47004	PRE	47804	WCR
43034	FGW	43137	FGW	43257	ICE	47105	PRE	47805	DRS
43035	FGW	43138	FGW	43272	ICE	47117	PRE	47810	DRS

No.	Op.	No.	Op.	No.	Op.	No.	Op.	No.	Op.
47811	DRS	56313	BAR	58032	DBS	60036	DBS	66011	DBS
47812	RIV	56314	BAR	58033	DBS	60037	DBS	66012	DBS
47813	DRS			58034	DBS	60039	DBS	66013	DBS
47815	RIV	57001	WCR	58035	DBS	60040	DBS	66014	DBS
47816	FLR	57002	DRS	58036	DBS	60041	DBS	66015	DBS
47818	DRS	57003	DRS	58037	DBS	60043	DBS	66016	DBS
47826	WCR	57004	DRS	58038	DBS	60044	DBS	66017	DBS
47828	DRS	57005	WCR	58039	DBS	60045	DBS	66018	DBS
47829	HNR	57006	WCR	58040	DBS	60046	DBS	66019	DBS
47830	FLR	57007	DRS	58041	DBS	60047	DBS	66020	DBS
47832	DRS	57008	DRS	58042	DBS	60048	DBS	66021	DBS
47839	DRS	57009	DRS	58043	DBS	60049	DBS	66022	DBS
47840	PRE	57010	DRS	58044	DBS	60051	DBS	66023	DBS
47841	DRS	57011	DRS	58046	DBS	60052	DBS	66024	DBS
47843	RIV	57012	DRS	58047	DBS	60053	DBS	66025	DBS
47847	RIV	57301	NRL	58048	DBS	60054	DBS	66026	DBS
47848	RIV	57302	VWC	58049	DBS	60056	DBS	66027	DBS
47851	WCR	57303	NRL	58050	DBS	60057	DBS	66028	DBS
47853	DRS	57304	VWC			60059	DBS	66029	DBS
47854	WCR	57305	NRL	59001	MRL	60060	DBS	66030	DBS
		57306	NRL	59002	MRL	60061	DBS	66031	DBS
50002	PRE	57307	VWC	59003	EXP	60062	DBS	66032	DBS
50007	PRE	57308	VWC	59004	MRL	60063	DBS	66033	DBS
50008	PRE	57309	VWC	59005	MRL	60064	DBS	66034	DBS
50015	PRE	57310	NRL	59101	MRL	60065	DBS	66035	DBS
50017	PRE	57311	VWC	59102	MRL	60066	DBS	66036	DBS
50019	PRE	57312	NRL	59103	MRL	60067	DBS	66037	DBS
50021	PRE	57313	ATW	59104	MRL	60069	DBS	66038	DBS
50026	PRE	57314	ATW	59201	DBS	60071	DBS	66039	DBS
50027	PRE	57315	ATW	59202	DBS	60072	DBS	66040	DBS
50029	PRE	57316	ATW	59203	DBS	60073	DBS	66041	DBS
50030	PRE	57601	WCR	59204	DBS	60074	DBS	66042	DBS
50031	PRE	57602	FGW	59205	DBS	60076	DBS	66043	DBS
50033	PRE	57603	FGW	59206	DBS	60077	DBS	66044	DBS
50135	PRE	57604	FGW			60079	DBS	66045	DBS
50042	PRE	57605	FGW	60002	DBS	60083	DBS	66046	DBS
50044	PRE			60003	DBS	60084	DBS	66047	DBS
50049	PRE	58001	DBS	60004	DBS	60085	DBS	66048	DBS
50050	PRE	58004	DBS	60005	DBS	60086	DBS	66049	DBS
		58005	DBS	60007	DBS	60087	DBS	66050	DBS
55002	PRE	58006	DBS	60009	DBS	60088	DBS	66051	DBS
55009	PRE	58007	DBS	60010	DBS	60090	DBS	66052	DBS
55015	PRE	58008	DBS	60011	DBS	60091	DBS	66053	DBS
55016	PRE	58009	DBS	60012	DBS	60092	DBS	66054	DBS
55019	PRE	58010	DBS	60013	DBS	60093	DBS	66055	DBS
55022	PRE	58011	DBS	60015	DBS	60094	DBS	66056	DBS
		58012	DBS	60017	DBS	60095	DBS	66057	DBS
56007	PRE	58013	DBS	60018	DBS	60096	DBS	66058	DBS
56018	EPX	58015	DBS	60019	DBS	60097	DBS	66059	DBS
56009	IND	58016	PRE	60020	DBS	60099	DBS	66060	DBS
56086	PRE	58017	DBS	60021	DBS	60100	DBS	66061	DBS
56091	BAR	58018	DBS	60022	DBS	60500	DBS	66062	DBS
56097	PRE	58020	DBS	60024	DBS			66063	DBS
56098	PRE	58021	DBS	60025	DBS	66001	DBS	66064	DBS
56101	EPX	58022	DBS	60026	DBS	66002	DBS	66065	DBS
56103	BAR	58023	DBS	60027	DBS	66003	DBS	66066	DBS
56115	EPX	58024	DBS	60028	DBS	66004	DBS	66067	DBS
56117	EPX	58025	DBS	60029	DBS	66005	DBS	66068	DBS
56301	PRE	58026	DBS	60030	DBS	66006	DBS	66069	DBS
56302	PRE	58027	DBS	60032	DBS	66007	DBS	66070	DBS
56303	BAR	58029	DBS	60033	DBS	66008	DBS	66071	DBS
56311	BAR	58030	DBS	60034	DBS	66009	DBS	66072	DBS
56312	BAR	58031	DBS	60035	DBS	66010	DBS	66073	DBS

Data Tables

Number	Code	Number	Code	Number	Code	Number	Code	Number	Code
66074	DBS	66137	DBS	66200	DBS	66416	FLT	66545	FLR
66075	DBS	66138	DBS	66201	DBS	66417	FLT	66546	OLS
66076	DBS	66139	DBS	66202	DBS	66418	FLT	66547	OLS
66077	DBS	66140	DBS	66203	DBS	66419	FLT	66548	FLR
66078	DBS	66141	DBS	66204	DBS	66420	FLT	66549	FLR
66079	DBS	66142	DBS	66205	DBS	66421	DRS	66550	FLR
66080	DBS	66143	DBS	66206	DBS	66422	DRS	66551	OLS
66081	DBS	66144	DBS	66207	DBS	66423	DRS	66552	OLS
66082	DBS	66145	DBS	66208	DBS	66424	DRS	66553	FLR
66083	DBS	66146	DBS	66209	DBS	66425	DRS	66554	FLR
66084	DBS	66147	DBS	66210	DBS	66426	DRS	66555	FLR
66085	DBS	66148	DBS	66211	DBS	66427	DRS	66556	FLR
66086	DBS	66149	DBS	66212	DBS	66428	DRS	66557	FLR
66087	DBS	66150	DBS	66213	DBS	66429	DRS	66558	FLR
66088	DBS	66151	DBS	66214	DBS	66430	DRS	66559	FLR
66089	DBS	66152	DBS	66215	DBS	66431	DRS	66560	FLR
66090	DBS	66153	DBS	66216	DBS	66432	DRS	66561	FLR
66091	DBS	66154	DBS	66217	DBS	66433	DRS	66562	FLR
66092	DBS	66155	DBS	66218	DBS	66434	DRS	66563	FLR
66093	DBS	66156	DBS	66219	DBS			66564	FLR
66094	DBS	66157	DBS	66220	DBS	66501	FLR	66565	FLR
66095	DBS	66158	DBS	66221	DBS	66502	FLR	66566	FLR
66096	DBS	66159	DBS	66222	DBS	66503	FLR	66567	FLR
66097	DBS	66160	DBS	66223	DBS	66504	FLR	66568	FLR
66098	DBS	66161	DBS	66224	DBS	66505	FLR	66569	FLR
66099	DBS	66162	DBS	66225	DBS	66506	FLR	66570	FLR
66100	DBS	66163	DBS	66226	DBS	66507	OLS	66571	FLR
66101	DBS	66164	DBS	66227	DBS	66508	FLR	66572	FLR
66102	DBS	66165	DBS	66228	DBS	66509	FLR	66582	EXP
66103	DBS	66166	DBS	66229	DBS	66510	FLR	66583	EXP
66104	DBS	66167	DBS	66230	DBS	66511	FLR	66584	EXP
66105	DBS	66168	DBS	66231	DBS	66512	FLR	66585	FLR
66106	DBS	66169	DBS	66232	DBS	66513	FLR	66586	EXP
66107	DBS	66170	DBS	66233	DBS	66514	FLR	66587	FLR
66108	DBS	66171	DBS	66234	DBS	66515	FLR	66588	FLR
66109	DBS	66172	DBS	66235	DBS	66516	FLR	66589	FLR
66110	DBS	66173	DBS	66236	DBS	66517	FLR	66590	FLR
66111	DBS	66174	DBS	66237	DBS	66518	FLR	66591	FLR
66112	DBS	66175	DBS	66238	DBS	66519	FLR	66592	FLR
66113	DBS	66176	DBS	66239	DBS	66520	FLR	66593	FLR
66114	DBS	66177	DBS	66240	DBS	66522	FLR	66594	FLR
66115	DBS	66178	DBS	66241	DBS	66523	FLR	66595	FLR
66116	DBS	66179	DBS	66242	DBS	66524	FLR	66596	FLR
66117	DBS	66180	DBS	66243	DBS	66525	FLR	66597	FLR
66118	DBS	66181	DBS	66244	DBS	66526	FLR	66598	FLR
66119	DBS	66182	DBS	66245	DBS	66527	FLR	66599	FLR
66120	DBS	66183	DBS	66246	DBS	66528	FLR		
66121	DBS	66184	DBS	66247	DBS	66529	FLR	66601	FLR
66122	DBS	66185	DBS	66248	DBS	66530	FLR	66602	FLR
66123	DBS	66186	DBS	66249	DBS	66531	FLR	66603	FLR
66124	DBS	66187	DBS	66250	DBS	66532	FLR	66604	FLR
66125	DBS	66188	DBS			66533	FLR	66605	FLR
66126	DBS	66189	DBS	66301	DRS	66534	FLR	66606	FLR
66127	DBS	66190	DBS	66302	DRS	66535	FLR	66607	FLR
66128	DBS	66191	DBS	66303	DRS	66536	FLR	66608	FLR
66129	DBS	66192	DBS	66304	DRS	66537	FLR	66609	FLR
66130	DBS	66193	DBS	66305	DRS	66538	FLR	66610	FLR
66131	DBS	66194	DBS			66539	FLR	66611	FLR
66132	DBS	66195	DBS	66411	FLT	66540	FLR	66612	FLR
66133	DBS	66196	DBS	66412	FLT	66541	FLR	66613	OLS
66134	DBS	66197	DBS	66413	FLT	66542	FLR	66614	FLR
66135	DBS	66198	DBS	66414	FLT	66543	FLR	66615	FLR
66136	DBS	66199	DBS	66415	FLT	66544	OLS	66616	FLR

66617	FLR	66952	FLR	73006	PRE	77030	ECR	86424	ETL
66618	FLR	66953	FLR	73101	PRE	77031	ECR	86501	FLR
66619	FLR	66954	FLR	73103	PRE	77032	ECR	86602	FLR
66620	FLR	66955	FLR	73104	RVE	77033	ECR	86604	FLR
66621	FLR	66956	FLR	73107	BAR	77034	ECR	86605	FLR
66622	FLR	66957	FLR	73109	TTS	77035	ECR	86607	FLR
66623	FLR			73110	PRE	77036	ECR	86609	FLR
66624	EXP	67001	DBS	73114	PRE	77037	ECR	86610	FLR
66625	EXP	67002	DBS	73117	PRE	77038	ECR	86612	FLR
		67003	DBS	73118	TTS	77039	ECR	86613	FLR
66701	GBR	67004	DBS	73119	GBR	77040	ECR	86614	FLR
66702	GBR	67005	DBS	73128	PRE	77041	ECR	86621	FLR
66703	GBR	67006	DBS	73129	PRE	77042	ECR	86622	FLR
66704	GBR	67007	DBS	73130	PRE	77043	ECR	86623	FLR
66705	GBR	67008	DBS	73133	TTS	77044	ECR	86627	FLR
66706	GBR	67009	DBS	73134	PRE	77045	ECR	86628	FLR
66707	GBR	67010	CRW	73136	TTS	77046	ECR	86632	FLR
66708	GBR	67011	DBS	73138	NRL	77047	ECR	86633	FLR
66709	GBR	67012	CRW	73139	RVE	77048	ECR	86637	FLR
66710	GBR	67013	CRW	73140	PRE	77049	ECR	86638	FLR
66711	GBR	67014	CRW	73141	GBR	77050	ECR	86639	FLR
66712	GBR	67015	CRW	73201	BAR	77051	ECR	86701	ETL
66713	GBR	67016	DBS	73202	SOU	77052	ECR	86702	ETL
66714	GBR	67017	DBS	73204	GBR	77053	ECR	86901	NRL
66715	GBR	67018	DBS	73205	GBR	77054	ECR	86902	NRL
66716	GBR	67019	DBS	73206	GBR	77055	ECR		
66717	GBR	67020	DBS	73207	GBR	77056	ECR	87001	PRE
66718	GBR	67021	DBS	73208	GBR	77057	ECR	87002	ETL
66719	GBR	67022	DBS	73209	GBR	77058	ECR	87003	EXP
66720	GBR	67023	DBS	73210	PRE	77059	ECR	87004	EXP
66721	GBR	67024	DBS	73211	RVL	77060	ECR	87006	EXP
66722	GBR	67025	DBS	73212	GBR			87007	EXP
66723	GBR	67026	DBS	73213	GBR	81002	PRE	87008	EXP
66724	GBR	67027	DBS					87009	EPX
66725	GBR	67028	DBS	77001	ECR	82008	PRE	87010	EXP
66726	GBR	67029	DBS	77002	ECR			87012	EXP
66727	GBR	67030	DBS	77003	ECR	83012	PRE	87013	EXP
66728	GBR			77004	ECR			87014	EXP
66729	GBR	70001	FLR	77005	ECR	84001	PRE	87017	EPX
66730	GBR	70002	FLR	77006	ECR			87019	EXP
66731	GBR	70003	FLR	77007	ECR	85101	PRE	87020	EXP
66732	GBR	70004	FLR	77008	ECR			87022	EXP
66733	GBR	70005	FLR	77009	ECR	86101	ETL	87023	EPX
66734	GBR	70006	FLR	77010	ECR	86213	ETL	87025	OLS
66735	GBR	70007	FLR	77011	ECR	86215	EPX	87026	EXP
66736	GBR	70008	FLR	77012	ECR	86217	EPX	87028	EXP
66737	GBR	70009	FLR	77013	ECR	86218	EPX	87029	EXP
66738	GBR	70010	FLR	77014	ECR	86226	EPX	87033	EXP
66738	GBR	70011	FLR	77015	ECR	86228	EPX	87034	EXP
66740	GBR	70013	FLR	77016	ECR	86229	EPX	87035	PRE
66741	GBR	70014	FLR	77017	ECR	86231	EPX		
66742	GBR	70015	FLR	77018	ECR	86232	EPX	89001	PRE
66743	GBR	70016	FLR	77019	ECR	86233	PRE		
66744	GBR	70017	FLR	77020	ECR	86234	EPX	90001	AEA
66745	GBR	70018	FLR	77021	ECR	86235	EPX	90002	AEA
66746	GBR	70019	FLR	77022	ECR	86242	EPX	90003	AEA
		70020	FLR	77023	ECR	86246	EPX	90004	AEA
66846	COL			77024	ECR	86247	EPX	90005	AEA
66847	COL	71001	PRE	77025	ECR	86248	EPX	90006	AEA
66848	COL			77026	ECR	86250	EXP	90007	AEA
66849	COL	73001	PRE	77027	ECR	86251	EPX	90008	AEA
66850	COL	73003	PRE	77028	ECR	86259	PRE	90009	AEA
66951	FLR	73005	PRE	77029	ECR	86401	ETL	90010	AEA

No.	Code	No.	Code	No.	Code	No.	Code	No.	Code
90011	AEA	91124	ICE	97651	PRE	51392	PRE	52062	PRE
90012	AEA	91125	ICE	97654	PRE	51395	PRE	52064	PRE
90013	AEA	91126	ICE			51397	PRE	52071	PRE
90014	AEA	91127	ICE	**Diesel Multiple**		51398	PRE	52077	PRE
90015	AEA	91128	ICE	**Units**		51400	PRE		
90016	FLR	91129	ICE	APT-E	PRE	51401	PRE	53160	PRE
90017	DBS	91130	ICE	LEV1	PRE	51402	PRE	53164	PRE
90018	DBS	91131	ICE	RB004	PRE	51405	PRE	53170	PRE
90019	DBS	91132	ICE			51407	PRE	53193	PRE
90020	DBS			50015	PRE	51434	PRE	53203	PRE
90021	DBS	92001	DBS	50019	PRE	51485	PRE	53204	PRE
90022	DBS	92002	DBS	50222	PRE	51499	PRE	53253	PRE
90023	DBS	92003	DBS	50256	PRE	51503	PRE	53266	PRE
90024	DBS	92004	DBS	50338	PRE	51505	PRE	53321	PRE
90025	DBS	92005	DBS	50416	PRE	51511	PRE	53628	PRE
90026	DBS	92006	GBR	50447	PRE	51512	PRE	53645	PRE
90027	DBS	92007	DBS	50454	PRE	51513	PRE	53746	PRE
90028	DBS	92008	DBS	50479	PRE	51562	PRE	53926	PRE
90029	DBS	92009	DBS	50528	PRE	51565	PRE	53971	PRE
90030	DBS	92010	GRB	50531	PRE	51566	PRE		
90031	DBS	92011	DBS	50556	PRE	51567	PRE	54055	PRE
90032	DBS	92012	DBS	50599	PRE	51568	PRE	54057	PRE
90033	DBS	92013	DBS	50619	PRE	51571	PRE	54062	PRE
90034	DBS	92014	GBR	50632	PRE	51572	PRE	54207	PRE
90035	DBS	92015	DBS	50929	PRE	51592	PRE	54223	PRE
90036	DBS	92016	DBS	50980	PRE	51604	PRE	54270	PRE
90037	DBS	92017	DBS			51616	PRE	54279	PRE
90038	DBS	92018	GBR	51017	PRE	51618	PRE	54289	PRE
90039	DBS	92019	DBS	51043	PRE	51622	PRE	54365	PRE
90040	DBS	92020	GBR	51073	PRE	51655	PRE	54408	PRE
90041	FLR	92021	GBR	51074	PRE	51663	PRE	54490	PRE
90042	FLR	92022	DBS	51104	PRE	51669	PRE	54504	PRE
90043	FLR	92023	GBR	51131	PRE	51677	PRE		
90044	FLR	92024	DBS	51138	PRE	51803	PRE	55000	PRE
90045	FLR	92025	DBS	51151	PRE	51813	PRE	55001	PRE
90046	FLR	92026	DBS	51187	PRE	51842	PRE	55003	PRE
90047	FLR	92027	DBS	51188	PRE	51859	PRE	55005	PRE
90048	FLR	92028	GBR	51189	PRE	51880	PRE	55006	PRE
90049	FLR	92029	DBS	51192	PRE	51886	PRE	55009	PRE
90050	FLR	92030	DBS	51205	PRE	51887	PRE	55012	PRE
		92031	DBS	51210	PRE	51899	PRE	55023	PRE
91101	ICE	92032	GBR	51226	PRE	51907	PRE	55028	PRE
91102	ICE	92033	GBR	51228	PRE	51909	PRE	55029	PRE
91103	ICE	92034	DBS	51247	PRE	51914	PRE	55032	ATW
91104	ICE	92035	DBS	51321	PRE	51919	PRE	55033	PRE
91105	ICE	92036	DBS	51339	PRE	51922	PRE	55966	PRE
91106	ICE	92037	DBS	51341	PRE	51933	PRE	55976	PRE
91107	ICE	92038	GBR	51342	PRE	51941	PRE		
91108	ICE	92039	DBS	51346	PRE	51942	PRE	56006	PRE
91109	ICE	92040	GBR	51347	PRE	51947	PRE	56015	PRE
91110	ICE	92041	DBS	51351	PRE	51950	PRE	56121	PRE
91111	ICE	92042	DBS	51353	PRE	51973	PRE	56171	PRE
91112	ICE	92043	EUR	51356	PRE	51990	PRE	56208	PRE
91113	ICE	92044	EUR	51359	PRE			56224	PRE
91114	ICE	92045	EUR	51360	PRE	52005	PRE	56271	PRE
91115	ICE	92046	EUR	51363	PRE	52006	PRE	56287	PRE
91116	ICE			51365	PRE	52008	PRE	56301	PRE
91117	ICE	97301	NRL	51367	PRE	52025	PRE	56343	PRE
91118	ICE	97302	NRL	51372	PRE	52030	PRE	56352	PRE
91119	ICE	97303	NRL	51381	PRE	52044	PRE	56358	PRE
91120	ICE	97304	NRL	51382	PRE	52048	PRE	56456	PRE
91121	ICE			51384	PRE	52053	PRE	56484	PRE
91122	ICE	97650	PRE	51388	PRE	52054	PRE	56491	PRE

No.	Code	No.	Code	No.	Code	No.	Code	No.	Code
56492	PRE	79963	PRE	142049	NOR	143618	FGW	150129	FGW
56495	PRE	79964	PRE	142050	NOR	143619	FGW	150130	FGW
		79976	PRE	142051	NOR	143620	FGW	150131	FGW
59003	PRE	79978	PRE	142052	NOR	143621	FGW	150132	NOR
59004	PRE			142053	NOR	143622	ATW	150133	NOR
59117	PRE	121019	PRE	142054	NOR	143623	ATW	150134	NOR
59228	PRE	121020	CRW	142055	NOR	143624	ATW	150135	NOR
59245	PRE	121024	PRE	142056	NOR	143625	ATW	150136	NOR
59250	PRE	121032	ATW	142057	NOR			150137	NOR
59276	PRE	121034	CRW	142058	NOR	144001	NOR	150138	NOR
59387	PRE			142060	NOR	144002	NOR	150139	NOR
59389	PRE	139001	LMI	142061	NOR	144003	NOR	150140	NOR
59404	PRE	139002	LMI	142062	NOR	144004	NOR	150141	NOR
59444	PRE			142063	NOR	144005	NOR	150142	NOR
59486	PRE	140001	PRE	142064	NOR	144006	NOR	150143	NOR
59488	PRE			142065	NOR	144007	NOR	150144	NOR
59492	PRE	142001	NOR	142066	NOR	144008	NOR	150145	NOR
59494	PRE	142002	ATW	142067	NOR	144009	NOR	150146	NOR
59500	PRE	142003	NOR	142068	NOR	144010	NOR	150147	NOR
59503	PRE	142004	NOR	142069	ATW	144011	NOR	150148	NOR
59506	PRE	142005	NOR	142070	NOR	144012	NOR	150149	NOR
59507	PRE	142006	ATW	142071	NOR	144013	NOR	150150	NOR
59508	PRE	142007	NOR	142072	ATW	144014	NOR	150201	NOR
59509	PRE	142009	NOR	142073	ATW	144015	NOR	150202	FGW
59510	PRE	142010	ATW	142074	ATW	144016	NOR	150203	NOR
59513	PRE	142011	NOR	142075	ATW	144017	NOR	150205	NOR
59514	PRE	142012	NOR	142076	NOR	144018	NOR	150207	NOR
59516	PRE	142013	NOR	142077	ATW	144019	NOR	150208	ATW
59517	PRE	142014	NOR	142078	NOR	144020	NOR	150209	FGW
59520	PRE	142015	NOR	142079	NOR	144021	NOR	150211	NOR
59521	PRE	142016	NOR	142080	ATW	144022	NOR	150214	LMI
59522	PRE	142017	NOR	142081	ATW	144023	NOR	150215	NOR
59539	PRE	142018	NOR	142082	ATW			150216	LMI
59575	PRE	142019	NOR	142083	ATW	150001	FGW	150218	NOR
59603	PRE	142020	NOR	142084	NOR	150002	FGW	150219	FGW
59609	PRE	142021	NOR	142085	ATW	150101	FGW	150221	FGW
59659	PRE	142022	NOR	142086	NOR	150102	FGW	150222	NOR
59664	PRE	142023	NOR	142087	NOR	150103	NOR	150223	NOR
59678	PRE	142024	NOR	142088	NOR	150104	FGW	150224	NOR
59701	PRE	142025	NOR	142089	NOR	150105	LMI	150225	NOR
59719	PRE	142026	NOR	142090	NOR	150106	FGW	150228	NOR
59740	PRE	142027	NOR	142091	NOR	150107	LMI	150232	FGW
59761	PRE	142028	NOR	142092	NOR	150108	FGW	150233	FGW
59791	PRE	142029	NOR	142093	NOR	150109	LMI	150234	FGW
		142030	NOR	142094	NOR	150110	NOR	150236	ATW
60117	PRE	142031	NOR	142095	NOR	150111	NOR	150238	FGW
60127	PRE	142032	NOR	142096	NOR	150112	NOR	150239	FGW
60142	PRE	142033	NOR			150113	NOR	150240	ATW
60145	PRE	142034	NOR	143601	ATW	150114	NOR	150241	ATW
60149	PRE	142035	NOR	143602	ATW	150115	NOR	150242	ATW
60616	PRE	142036	NOR	143603	FGW	150116	NOR	150243	FGW
60822	PRE	142037	NOR	143604	ATW	150117	NOR	150244	FGW
60828	PRE	142038	NOR	143605	ATW	150118	NOR	150245	ATW
60901	PRE	142039	NOR	143606	ATW	150119	NOR	150246	FGW
60904	PRE	142040	NOR	143607	ATW	150120	FGW	150247	FGW
60916	PRE	142041	NOR	143608	ATW	150121	FGW	150248	FGW
		142042	NOR	143609	ATW	150122	FGW	150249	FGW
70549	PRE	142043	NOR	143610	ATW	150123	FGW	150250	ATW
79018	PRE	142044	NOR	143611	FGW	150124	FGW	150251	ATW
79612	PRE	142045	NOR	143612	FGW	150125	FGW	150252	ATW
79900	PRE	142046	NOR	143614	ATW	150126	FGW	150253	ATW
79960	PRE	142047	NOR	143615	ATW	150127	FGW	150254	ATW
79962	PRE	142048	NOR	143617	FGW	150128	FGW	150256	ATW

Data Tables

No.	Code	No.	Code	No.	Code	No.	Code	No.	Code
150258	ATW	153335	AEA	156419	AEA	156482	NOR	158730	FSR
150259	ATW	153351	NOR	156420	NOR	156483	NOR	158731	FSR
150260	ATW	153352	NOR	156421	NOR	156484	NOR	158732	FSR
150261	FGW	153353	ATW	156422	AEA	156485	FSR	158733	FSR
150262	ATW	153354	LMI	156423	NOR	156486	NOR	158734	FSR
150263	FGW	153355	EMT	156424	NOR	156487	NOR	158735	FSR
150264	ATW	153356	LMI	156425	NOR	156488	NOR	158736	FSR
150265	FGW	153357	EMT	156426	NOR	156489	NOR	158737	FSR
150266	FGW	153358	NOR	156427	NOR	156490	NOR	158738	FSR
150267	ATW	153359	NOR	156428	NOR	156491	NOR	158739	FSR
150268	NOR	153360	NOR	156429	NOR	156492	FSR	158740	FSR
150269	NOR	153361	FGW	156430	FSR	156493	FSR	158741	FSR
150270	NOR	153362	ATW	156431	FSR	156494	FSR	158749	FGW
150271	NOR	153363	NOR	156432	FSR	156495	FSR	158752	NOR
150272	NOR	153364	LMI	156433	FSR	156496	FSR	158753	NOR
150273	NOR	153365	LMI	156434	FSR	156497	NOR	158754	NOR
150274	NOR	153366	LMI	156435	FSR	156498	NOR	158755	NOR
150275	NOR	153367	ATW	156436	FSR	156499	FSR	158756	NOR
150276	NOR	153368	FGW	156437	FSR	156500	FSR	158757	NOR
150277	NOR	153369	FGW	156438	NOR	156501	FSR	158758	NOR
150278	ATW	153370	FGW	156439	FSR	156502	FSR	158759	NOR
150279	ATW	153371	LMI	156440	NOR	156503	FSR	158763	FGW
150280	AEA	153372	FGW	156441	NOR	156504	FSR	158766	FGW
150281	ATW	153373	FGW	156442	FSR	156505	FSR	158767	FGW
150282	ATW	153374	EMT	156443	NOR	156506	FSR	158769	FGW
150283	ATW	153375	LMI	156444	NOR	156507	FSR	158770	EMT
150284	ATW	153376	EMT	156445	FSR	156508	FSR	158773	EMT
150285	NOR	153377	FGW	156446	FSR	156509	FSR	158774	EMT
		153378	NOR	156447	FSR	156510	FSR	158777	EMT
153301	NOR	153379	EMT	156448	NOR	156511	FSR	158780	EMT
153302	EMT	153380	FGW	156449	FSR	156512	FSR	158782	FSR
153303	ATW	153381	EMT	156450	FSR	156513	FSR	158783	EMT
153304	NOR	153382	FGW	156451	NOR	156514	FSR	158784	NOR
153305	FGW	153383	EMT	156452	NOR			158785	EMT
153306	AEA	153384	EMT	156453	FSR	158701	FSR	158786	FSR
153307	NOR	153385	EMT	156454	NOR	158702	FSR	158787	NOR
153308	EMT			156455	NOR	158703	NOR	158788	EMT
153309	AEA	155341	NOR	156456	FSR	158704	FSR	158789	FSR
153310	EMT	155342	NOR	156457	FSR	158705	FSR	158790	NOR
153311	EMT	155343	NOR	156458	FSR	158706	FSR	158791	NOR
153312	ATW	155344	NOR	156459	NOR	158707	FSR	158792	NOR
153313	EMT	155345	NOR	156460	NOR	158708	FSR	158793	NOR
153314	AEA	155346	NOR	156461	NOR	158709	FSR	158794	NOR
153315	NOR	155347	NOR	156462	FSR	158710	FSR	158795	NOR
153316	NOR			156463	NOR	158711	FSR	158796	NOR
153317	NOR	156401	EMT	156464	NOR	158712	FSR	158797	NOR
153318	FGW	156402	AEA	156465	FSR	158713	FSR	158798	FGW
153319	EMT	156403	EMT	156466	NOR	158714	FSR	158799	EMT
153320	ATW	156404	EMT	156467	FSR	158715	FSR	158806	EMT
153321	EMT	156405	EMT	156468	NOR	158716	FSR	158810	EMT
153322	AEA	156406	EMT	156469	NOR	158717	FSR	158812	EMT
153323	ATW	156407	AEA	156470	NOR	158718	FSR	158813	EMT
153324	NOR	156408	EMT	156471	NOR	158719	FSR	158815	NOR
153325	FGW	156409	AEA	156472	NOR	158720	FSR	158816	NOR
153326	EMT	156410	EMT	156473	NOR	158721	FSR	158817	NOR
153327	ATW	156411	EMT	156474	FSR	158722	FSR	158818	ATW
153328	NOR	156412	AEA	156475	NOR	158723	FSR	158819	ATW
153329	FGW	156413	EMT	156476	FSR	158724	FSR	158820	ATW
153330	NOR	156414	EMT	156477	FSR	158725	FSR	158821	ATW
153331	NOR	156415	EMT	156478	FSR	158726	FSR	158822	ATW
153332	NOR	156416	AEA	156479	NOR	158727	FSR	158823	ATW
153333	FGW	156417	AEA	156480	NOR	158728	FSR	158824	ATW
153334	LMI	156418	AEA	156481	NOR	158729	FSR	158825	ATW

Data Tables

No.	Code	No.	Code	No.	Code	No.	Code	No.	Code
158826	ATW	158907	NOR	165018	CRW	166215	FGW	170308	FTP
158827	ATW	158908	NOR	165019	CRW	166216	FGW	170309	FTP
158828	ATW	158909	NOR	165020	CRW	166217	FGW	170393	FSR
158829	ATW	158910	NOR	165021	CRW	166218	FGW	170394	FSR
158830	ATW	158950	FGW	165022	CRW	166219	FGW	170395	FSR
158831	ATW	158951	FGW	165023	CRW	166220	FGW	170396	FSR
158832	ATW	158952	FGW	165024	CRW	166221	FGW	170397	AXC
158833	ATW	158953	FGW	165025	CRW			170398	AXC
158834	ATW	158954	FGW	165026	CRW	168001	CRW	170401	FSR
158835	ATW	158955	FGW	165027	CRW	168002	CRW	170402	FSR
158836	ATW	158956	FGW	165028	CRW	168003	CRW	170403	FSR
158837	ATW	158957	FGW	165029	CRW	168004	CRW	170404	FSR
158838	ATW	158958	FGW	165030	CRW	168005	CRW	170405	FSR
158839	ATW	158959	FGW	165031	CRW	168106	CRW	170406	FSR
158840	ATW			165032	CRW	168107	CRW	170407	FSR
158841	ATW	159001	SWT	165033	CRW	168108	CRW	170408	FSR
158843	NOR	159002	SWT	165034	CRW	168109	CRW	170409	FSR
158844	NOR	159003	SWT	165035	CRW	168110	CRW	170410	FSR
158845	NOR	159004	SWT	165036	CRW	168112	CRW	170411	FSR
158846	EMT	159005	SWT	165037	CRW	168113	CRW	170412	FSR
158847	EMT	159006	SWT	165038	CRW	168214	CRW	170413	FSR
158848	NOR	159007	SWT	165039	CRW	168215	CRW	170414	FSR
158849	NOR	159008	SWT	165101	FGW	168216	CRW	170415	FSR
158850	NOR	159009	SWT	165102	FGW	168217	CRW	170416	FSR
158851	NOR	159010	SWT	165103	FGW	168218	CRW	170417	FSR
158852	EMT	159011	SWT	165104	FGW	168219	CRW	170418	FSR
158853	NOR	159012	SWT	165105	FGW			170419	FSR
158854	EMT	159013	SWT	165106	FGW	170101	AXC	170420	FSR
158855	NOR	159014	SWT	165107	FGW	170102	AXC	170421	FSR
158856	EMT	159015	SWT	165108	FGW	170103	AXC	170422	FSR
158857	EMT	159016	SWT	165109	FGW	170104	AXC	170423	FSR
158858	EMT	159017	SWT	165110	FGW	170105	AXC	170424	FSR
158859	NOR	159018	SWT	165111	FGW	170106	AXC	170425	FSR
158860	NOR	159019	SWT	165112	FGW	170107	AXC	170426	FSR
158861	NOR	159020	SWT	165113	FGW	170108	AXC	170427	FSR
158862	EMT	159021	SWT	165114	FGW	170109	AXC	170428	FSR
158863	EMT	159022	SWT	165115	FGW	170110	AXC	170429	FSR
158864	EMT	159101	SWT	165116	FGW	170111	AXC	170430	FSR
158865	EMT	159102	SWT	165117	FGW	170112	AXC	170431	FSR
158866	EMT	159103	SWT	165118	FGW	170113	AXC	170432	FSR
158867	FSR	159104	SWT	165119	FGW	170114	AXC	170433	FSR
158868	FSR	159105	SWT	165120	FGW	170115	AXC	170434	FSR
158869	FSR	159106	SWT	165121	FGW	170116	AXC	170450	FSR
158870	FSR	159107	SWT	165122	FGW	170117	AXC	170451	FSR
158871	FSR	159108	SWT	165123	FGW	170201	AEA	170452	FSR
158872	NOR			165124	FGW	170202	AEA	170453	FSR
158880	SWT	165001	CRW	165125	FGW	170203	AEA	170454	FSR
158881	SWT	165002	CRW	165126	FGW	170204	AEA	170455	FSR
158882	SWT	165003	CRW			170205	AEA	170456	FSR
158883	SWT	165004	CRW	166201	FGW	170206	AEA	170457	FSR
158884	SWT	165005	CRW	166202	FGW	170207	AEA	170458	FSR
158885	SWT	165006	CRW	166203	FGW	170208	AEA	170459	FTP
158886	SWT	165007	CRW	166204	FGW	170270	AEA	170460	FTP
158887	SWT	165008	CRW	166205	FGW	170271	AEA	170461	FSR
158888	SWT	165009	CRW	166206	FGW	170272	AEA	170470	FSR
158889	SWT	165010	CRW	166207	FGW	170273	AEA	170471	FSR
158890	SWT	165011	CRW	166208	FGW	170301	FTP	170472	FSR
158901	NOR	165012	CRW	166209	FGW	170302	FTP	170473	FSR
158902	NOR	165013	CRW	166210	FGW	170303	FTP	170474	FSR
158903	NOR	165014	CRW	166211	FGW	170304	FTP	170475	FSR
158904	NOR	165015	CRW	166212	FGW	170305	FTP	170476	FSR
158905	NOR	165016	CRW	166213	FGW	170306	FTP	170477	FSR
158906	NOR	165017	CRW	166214	FGW	170307	FTP	170478	FSR

Data Tables

Number Cross-Link

Number	Code	Number	Code	Number	Code	Number	Code	Number	Code
170501	LMI	172211	LMI	180108	FGW	205009	PRE	221121	AXC
170502	LMI	172212	LMI	180109	FHT	205025	PRE	221122	AXC
170503	LMI	172213	LMI	180110	FHT	205028	PRE	221123	AXC
170504	LMI	172214	LMI	180111	FHT	205032	PRE	221124	AXC
170505	LMI	172215	LMI	180112	GTL	205033	PRE	221125	AXC
170506	LMI	172216	LMI	180113	FHT	205101	PRE	221126	AXC
170507	LMI	172217	LMI	180114	GTL	205205	PRE	221127	AXC
170508	LMI	172218	LMI					221128	AXC
170509	LMI	172219	LMI	185101	FTP	220001	AXC	221129	AXC
170510	LMI	172220	LMI	185102	FTP	220002	AXC	221130	AXC
170511	LMI	172221	LMI	185103	FTP	220003	AXC	221131	AXC
170512	LMI	172222	LMI	185104	FTP	220004	AXC	221132	AXC
170513	LMI	172331	LMI	185105	FTP	220005	AXC	221133	AXC
170514	LMI	172332	LMI	185106	FTP	220006	AXC	221134	AXC
170515	LMI	172333	LMI	185107	FTP	220007	AXC	221135	AXC
170516	LMI	172334	LMI	185108	FTP	220008	AXC	221136	AXC
170517	LMI	172335	LMI	185109	FTP	220009	AXC	221137	AXC
170518	AXC	172336	LMI	185110	FTP	220010	AXC	221138	AXC
170519	AXC	172337	LMI	185111	FTP	220011	AXC	221139	AXC
170520	AXC	172338	LMI	185112	FTP	220012	AXC	221140	AXC
170521	AXC	172339	LMI	185113	FTP	220013	AXC	221141	AXC
170522	AXC	172340	LMI	185114	FTP	220014	AXC	221142	VWC
170523	AXC	172341	LMI	185115	FTP	220015	AXC	221143	VWC
170630	LMI	172342	LMI	185116	FTP	220016	AXC		
170631	LMI	172343	LMI	185117	FTP	220017	AXC	222001	EMT
170632	LMI	172344	LMI	185118	FTP	220018	AXC	222002	EMT
170633	LMI	172345	LMI	185119	FTP	220019	AXC	222003	EMT
170634	LMI			185120	FTP	220020	AXC	222004	EMT
170635	LMI	175001	ATW	185121	FTP	220021	AXC	222005	EMT
170636	AXC	175002	ATW	185122	FTP	220022	AXC	222006	EMT
170637	AXC	175003	ATW	185123	FTP	220023	AXC	222007	EMT
170638	AXC	175004	ATW	185124	FTP	220024	AXC	222008	EMT
170639	AXC	175005	ATW	185125	FTP	220025	AXC	222009	EMT
		175006	ATW	185126	FTP	220026	AXC	222010	EMT
171721	SOU	175007	ATW	185127	FTP	220027	AXC	222011	EMT
171722	SOU	175008	ATW	185128	FTP	220028	AXC	222012	EMT
171723	SOU	175009	ATW	185129	FTP	220029	AXC	222013	EMT
171724	SOU	175010	ATW	185130	FTP	220030	AXC	222014	EMT
171725	SOU	175011	ATW	185131	FTP	220031	AXC	222015	EMT
171726	SOU	175101	ATW	185132	FTP	220032	AXC	222016	EMT
171727	SOU	175102	ATW	185133	FTP	220033	AXC	222017	EMT
171728	SOU	175103	ATW	185134	FTP	220034	AXC	222018	EMT
171729	SOU	175104	ATW	185135	FTP			222019	EMT
171730	SOU	175105	ATW	185136	FTP	221101	VWC	222020	EMT
171801	SOU	175106	ATW	185137	FTP	221102	VWC	222021	EMT
171802	SOU	175107	ATW	185138	FTP	221103	VWC	222022	EMT
171803	SOU	175108	ATW	185139	FTP	221104	VWC	222023	EMT
171804	SOU	175109	ATW	185140	FTP	221105	VWC	222101	EMT
171805	SOU	175110	ATW	185141	FTP	221106	VWC	222102	EMT
171806	SOU	175111	ATW	185142	FTP	221107	VWC	222103	EMT
		175112	ATW	185143	FTP	221108	VWC	222104	EMT
172001	LOG	175113	ATW	185144	FTP	221109	VWC		
172002	LOG	175114	ATW	185145	FTP	221110	VWC		
172003	LOG	175115	ATW	185146	FTP	221111	VWC		
172004	LOG	175116	ATW	185147	FTP	221112	VWC		
172005	LOG			185148	FTP	221113	VWC		
172006	LOG	180101	GTL	185149	FTP	221114	VWC		
172007	LOG	180102	FGW	185150	FTP	221115	VWC		
172008	LOG	180103	FGW	185151	FTP	221116	VWC		
172101	CRW	180104	FGW			221117	VWC		
172102	CRW	180105	GTL	201001	PRE	221118	VWC		
172103	CRW	180106	FGW			221119	AXC		
172104	CRW	180107	GTL	202202	PRE	221120	AXC		

Electric Multiple Units

Number	Code
85	PRE
87	PRE
91	PRE
2090	PRE
4732	PRE
5176	PRE
5759	PRE
5791	PRE
5793	PRE

No.		No.		No.		No.		No.	
6307	PRE	70257	PRE	313040	FCC	314215	FSR	315861	AEA
7105	PRE	70273	PRE	313041	FCC	314216	FSR		
8143	PRE	70284	PRE	313042	FCC			317337	FCC
		70292	PRE	313043	FCC	315801	AEA	317338	FCC
10096	PRE	70296	PRE	313044	FCC	315802	AEA	317339	FCC
11161	PRE	70354	PRE	313045	FCC	315803	AEA	317340	FCC
11179	PRE	70527	PRE	313046	FCC	315804	AEA	317341	FCC
11201	PRE	70531	PRE	313047	FCC	315805	AEA	317342	FCC
11825	PRE	70539	PRE	313048	FCC	315806	AEA	317343	FCC
		70576	PRE	313049	FCC	315807	AEA	317344	FCC
13004	PRE	70607	PRE	313050	FCC	315808	AEA	317345	FCC
15345	PRE			313051	FCC	315809	AEA	317346	FCC
		71032	PRE	313052	FCC	315810	AEA	317347	FCC
28249	PRE			313053	FCC	315811	AEA	317348	FCC
28361	PRE	72501	PRE	313054	FCC	315812	AEA	317501	AEA
28690	PRE	72617	PRE	313055	FCC	315813	AEA	317502	AEA
29298	PRE			313056	FCC	315814	AEA	317503	AEA
29666	PRE	75033	PRE	313057	FCC	315815	AEA	317504	AEA
29670	PRE	75186	PRE	313058	FCC	315816	AEA	317505	AEA
29720	PRE			313059	FCC	315817	AEA	317506	AEA
29896	PRE	75250	PRE	313060	FCC	315818	AEA	317507	AEA
		75395	PRE	313061	FCC	315819	AEA	317508	AEA
61183	PRE	75407	PRE	313062	FCC	315820	AEA	317509	AEA
61275	PRE			313063	FCC	315821	AEA	317510	AEA
61287	PRE	76529	PRE	313064	FCC	315822	AEA	317511	AEA
61742	PRE	76712	PRE	313121	NRL	315823	AEA	317512	AEA
61743	PRE	76726	PRE	313122	FCC	315824	AEA	317513	AEA
61798	PRE	76740	PRE	313123	FCC	315825	AEA	317514	AEA
61799	PRE	76746	PRE	313134	FCC	315826	AEA	317515	AEA
61804	PRE	76797	PRE	313201	SOU	315827	AEA	317649	AEA
61805	PRE	76811	PRE	313202	SOU	315828	AEA	317650	AEA
		76812	PRE	313203	SOU	315829	AEA	317651	AEA
62351	PRE	76817	PRE	313204	SOU	315830	AEA	317652	AEA
62364	PRE	76875	PRE	313205	SOU	315831	AEA	317653	AEA
62384	NRL			313206	SOU	315832	AEA	317654	AEA
62378	PRE	77172	PRE	313207	SOU	315833	AEA	317655	AEA
62887	PRE			313208	SOU	315834	AEA	317656	AEA
		79998	PRE	313209	SOU	315835	AEA	317657	AEA
65451	PRE	79999	PRE	313210	SOU	315836	AEA	317658	AEA
65302	PRE			313211	SOU	315837	AEA	317659	AEA
65304	PRE	303032	PRE	313212	SOU	315838	AEA	317660	AEA
				313213	SOU	315839	AEA	317661	AEA
67300	PRE	306017	PRE	313214	SOU	315840	AEA	317662	AEA
				313215	SOU	315841	AEA	317663	AEA
68001	PRE	309616	PRE	313216	SOU	315842	AEA	317664	AEA
68002	PRE	309624	PRE	313217	SOU	315843	AEA	317665	AEA
68003	PRE			313219	SOU	315844	AEA	317666	AEA
68004	PRE	313018	FCC	313220	SOU	315845	AEA	317667	AEA
68005	PRE	313024	FCC			315846	AEA	317668	AEA
68008	PRE	313025	FCC	314201	FSR	315847	AEA	317669	AEA
68009	PRE	313026	FCC	314202	FSR	315848	AEA	317670	AEA
68500	PRE	313027	FCC	314203	FSR	315849	AEA	317671	AEA
68506	PRE	313028	FCC	314204	FSR	315850	AEA	317672	AEA
		313029	FCC	314205	FSR	315851	AEA	317708	AEA
69304	PRE	313030	FCC	314206	FSR	315852	AEA	317709	AEA
69310	PRE	313031	FCC	314207	FSR	315853	AEA	317710	AEA
69318	PRE	313032	FCC	314208	FSR	315854	AEA	317714	AEA
69332	PRE	313033	FCC	314209	FSR	315855	AEA	317719	AEA
69333	PRE	313035	FCC	314210	FSR	315856	AEA	317722	AEA
69337	PRE	313036	FCC	314211	FSR	315857	AEA	317723	AEA
69339	PRE	313037	FCC	314212	FSR	315858	AEA	317729	AEA
		313038	FCC	314213	FSR	315859	AEA	317732	AEA
70229	PRE	313039	FCC	314214	FSR	315860	AEA	317881	AEA

Data Tables

317882	AEA	319368	FCC	320303	FSR	321343	AEA	321439	AEA
317883	AEA	319369	FCC	320304	FSR	321344	AEA	321440	AEA
317884	AEA	319370	FCC	320305	FSR	321345	AEA	321441	AEA
317885	AEA	319371	FCC	320306	FSR	321346	AEA	321442	AEA
317886	AEA	319372	FCC	320307	FSR	321347	AEA	321443	AEA
317887	AEA	319373	FCC	320308	FSR	321348	AEA	321444	AEA
317888	AEA	319374	FCC	320309	FSR	321349	AEA	321445	AEA
317889	AEA	319375	FCC	320310	FSR	321350	AEA	321446	AEA
317890	AEA	319376	FCC	320311	FSR	321351	AEA	321447	AEA
317891	AEA	319377	FCC	320312	FSR	321352	AEA	321448	AEA
317892	AEA	319378	FCC	320313	FSR	321353	AEA		
		319379	FCC	320314	FSR	321354	AEA	321901	NOR
318250	FSR	319380	FCC	320315	FSR	321355	AEA	321902	NOR
318251	FSR	319381	FCC	320316	FSR	321356	AEA	321903	NOR
318252	FSR	319382	FCC	320317	FSR	321357	AEA		
318253	FSR	319383	FCC	320318	FSR	321358	AEA	322481	NOR
318254	FSR	319384	FCC	320319	FSR	321359	AEA	322482	NOR
318255	FSR	319385	FCC	320320	FSR	321360	AEA	322483	NOR
318256	FSR	319386	FCC	320321	FSR	321361	AEA	322484	NOR
318257	FSR			320322	FSR	321362	AEA	322485	NOR
318258	FSR	319421	FCC			321363	AEA		
318259	FSR	319422	FCC	321301	AEA	321364	AEA	323201	LMI
318260	FSR	319423	FCC	321302	AEA	321365	AEA	323202	LMI
318261	FSR	319424	FCC	321303	AEA	321366	AEA	323203	LMI
318262	FSR	319425	FCC	321304	AEA			323204	LMI
318263	FSR	319426	FCC	321305	AEA	321401	FCC	323205	LMI
318264	FSR	319427	FCC	321306	AEA	321402	FCC	323206	LMI
318265	FSR	319428	FCC	321307	AEA	321403	FCC	323207	LMI
318266	FSR	319429	FCC	321308	AEA	321404	FCC	323208	LMI
318267	FSR	319430	FCC	321309	AEA	321405	FCC	323209	LMI
318268	FSR	319431	FCC	321310	AEA	321406	FCC	323210	LMI
318269	FSR	319432	FCC	321311	AEA	321407	FCC	323211	LMI
318270	FSR	319433	FCC	321312	AEA	321408	FCC	323212	LMI
		319434	FCC	321313	AEA	321409	FCC	323213	LMI
319001	FCC	319435	FCC	321314	AEA	321410	FCC	323214	LMI
319002	FCC	319436	FCC	321315	AEA	321411	LMI	323215	LMI
319003	FCC	319437	FCC	321316	AEA	321412	LMI	323216	LMI
319004	FCC	319438	FCC	321317	AEA	321413	LMI	323217	LMI
319005	FCC	319439	FCC	321318	AEA	321414	LMI	323218	LMI
319006	FCC	319440	FCC	321319	AEA	321415	LMI	323219	LMI
319007	FCC	319441	FCC	321320	AEA	321416	LMI	323220	LMI
319008	FCC	319442	FCC	321321	AEA	321417	LMI	323221	LMI
319009	FCC	319443	FCC	321322	AEA	321418	FCC	323222	LMI
319010	FCC	319444	FCC	321323	AEA	321419	FCC	323223	NOR
319011	FCC	319445	FCC	321324	AEA	321420	FCC	323224	NOR
319012	FCC	319446	FCC	321325	AEA	321421	AEA	323225	NOR
319013	FCC	319447	FCC	321326	AEA	321422	AEA	323226	NOR
		319448	FCC	321327	AEA	321423	AEA	323227	NOR
319214	FCC	319449	FCC	321328	AEA	321424	AEA	323228	NOR
319215	FCC	319450	FCC	321329	AEA	321425	AEA	323229	NOR
319216	FCC	319451	FCC	321330	AEA	321426	AEA	323230	NOR
319217	FCC	319452	FCC	321331	AEA	321427	AEA	323231	NOR
319218	FCC	319453	FCC	321332	AEA	321428	AEA	323232	NOR
319219	FCC	319454	FCC	321333	AEA	321429	AEA	323233	NOR
319220	FCC	319455	FCC	321334	AEA	321430	AEA	323234	NOR
		319456	FCC	321335	AEA	321431	AEA	323235	NOR
319361	FCC	319457	FCC	321336	AEA	321432	AEA	323236	NOR
319362	FCC	319458	FCC	321337	AEA	321433	AEA	323237	NOR
319363	FCC	319459	FCC	321338	AEA	321434	AEA	323238	NOR
319364	FCC	319460	FCC	321339	AEA	321435	AEA	323239	NOR
319365	FCC			321340	AEA	321436	AEA	323240	LMI
319366	FCC	320301	FSR	321341	AEA	321437	AEA	323241	LMI
319367	FCC	320302	FSR	321342	AEA	321438	AEA	323242	LMI

❏ 323243	LMI	❏ 334013	FSR	❏ 350235	LMI	❏ 357030	C2C	❏ 360118	AEA
		❏ 334014	FSR	❏ 350236	LMI	❏ 357031	C2C	❏ 360119	AEA
❏ 325001	DBS	❏ 334015	FSR	❏ 350237	LMI	❏ 357032	C2C	❏ 360120	AEA
❏ 325002	DBS	❏ 334016	FSR	❏ 350238	LMI	❏ 357033	C2C	❏ 360121	AEA
❏ 325003	DBS	❏ 334017	FSR	❏ 350239	LMI	❏ 357034	C2C		
❏ 325004	DBS	❏ 334018	FSR	❏ 350240	LMI	❏ 357035	C2C	❏ 360201	HEC
❏ 325005	DBS	❏ 334019	FSR	❏ 350241	LMI	❏ 357036	C2C	❏ 360202	HEC
❏ 325006	DBS	❏ 334020	FSR	❏ 350242	LMI	❏ 357037	C2C	❏ 360203	HEC
❏ 325007	DBS	❏ 334021	FSR	❏ 350243	LMI	❏ 357038	C2C	❏ 360204	HEC
❏ 325008	DBS	❏ 334022	FSR	❏ 350244	LMI	❏ 357039	C2C	❏ 360205	HEC
❏ 325009	DBS	❏ 334023	FSR	❏ 350245	LMI	❏ 357040	C2C		
❏ 325010	DBS	❏ 334024	FSR	❏ 350246	LMI	❏ 357041	C2C	❏ 365501	FCC
❏ 325011	DBS	❏ 334025	FSR	❏ 350247	LMI	❏ 357042	C2C	❏ 365502	FCC
❏ 325012	DBS	❏ 334026	FSR	❏ 350248	LMI	❏ 357043	C2C	❏ 365503	FCC
❏ 325013	DBS	❏ 334027	FSR	❏ 350249	LMI	❏ 357044	C2C	❏ 365504	FCC
❏ 325014	DBS	❏ 334028	FSR	❏ 350250	LMI	❏ 357045	C2C	❏ 365505	FCC
❏ 325015	DBS	❏ 334029	FSR	❏ 350251	LMI	❏ 357046	C2C	❏ 365506	FCC
❏ 325016	DBS	❏ 334030	FSR	❏ 350252	LMI	❏ 357201	C2C	❏ 365507	FCC
		❏ 334031	FSR	❏ 350253	LMI	❏ 357202	C2C	❏ 365508	FCC
❏ 332001	HEX	❏ 334032	FSR	❏ 350254	LMI	❏ 357203	C2C	❏ 365509	FCC
❏ 332002	HEX	❏ 334033	FSR	❏ 350255	LMI	❏ 357204	C2C	❏ 365510	FCC
❏ 332003	HEX	❏ 334034	FSR	❏ 350256	LMI	❏ 357205	C2C	❏ 365511	FCC
❏ 332004	HEX	❏ 334035	FSR	❏ 350257	LMI	❏ 357206	C2C	❏ 365512	FCC
❏ 332005	HEX	❏ 334036	FSR	❏ 350258	LMI	❏ 357207	C2C	❏ 365513	FCC
❏ 332006	HEX	❏ 334037	FSR	❏ 350259	LMI	❏ 357208	C2C	❏ 365514	FCC
❏ 332007	HEX	❏ 334038	FSR	❏ 350260	LMI	❏ 357209	C2C	❏ 365515	FCC
❏ 332008	HEX	❏ 334039	FSR	❏ 350261	LMI	❏ 357210	C2C	❏ 365516	FCC
❏ 332009	HEX	❏ 334040	FSR	❏ 350262	LMI	❏ 357211	C2C	❏ 365517	FCC
❏ 332010	HEX			❏ 350263	LMI	❏ 357212	C2C	❏ 365518	FCC
❏ 332011	HEX	❏ 350101	LMI	❏ 350264	LMI	❏ 357213	C2C	❏ 365519	FCC
❏ 332012	HEX	❏ 350102	LMI	❏ 350265	LMI	❏ 357214	C2C	❏ 365520	FCC
❏ 332013	HEX	❏ 350103	LMI	❏ 350266	LMI	❏ 357215	C2C	❏ 365521	FCC
❏ 332014	HEX	❏ 350104	LMI	❏ 350267	LMI	❏ 357216	C2C	❏ 365522	FCC
		❏ 350105	LMI			❏ 357217	C2C	❏ 365523	FCC
❏ 333001	NOR	❏ 350106	LMI	❏ 357001	C2C	❏ 357218	C2C	❏ 365524	FCC
❏ 333002	NOR	❏ 350107	LMI	❏ 357002	C2C	❏ 357219	C2C	❏ 365525	FCC
❏ 333003	NOR	❏ 350108	LMI	❏ 357003	C2C	❏ 357220	C2C	❏ 365526	OLS
❏ 333004	NOR	❏ 350109	LMI	❏ 357004	C2C	❏ 357221	C2C	❏ 365527	FCC
❏ 333005	NOR	❏ 350110	LMI	❏ 357005	C2C	❏ 357222	C2C	❏ 365528	FCC
❏ 333006	NOR	❏ 350111	LMI	❏ 357006	C2C	❏ 357223	C2C	❏ 365529	FCC
❏ 333007	NOR	❏ 350112	LMI	❏ 357007	C2C	❏ 357224	C2C	❏ 365530	FCC
❏ 333008	NOR	❏ 350113	LMI	❏ 357008	C2C	❏ 357225	C2C	❏ 365531	FCC
❏ 333009	NOR	❏ 350114	LMI	❏ 357009	C2C	❏ 357226	C2C	❏ 365532	FCC
❏ 333010	NOR	❏ 350115	LMI	❏ 357010	C2C	❏ 357227	C2C	❏ 365533	FCC
❏ 333011	NOR	❏ 350116	LMI	❏ 357011	C2C	❏ 357228	C2C	❏ 365534	FCC
❏ 333012	NOR	❏ 350117	LMI	❏ 357012	C2C			❏ 365535	FCC
❏ 333013	NOR	❏ 350118	LMI	❏ 357013	C2C	❏ 360101	AEA	❏ 365536	FCC
❏ 333014	NOR	❏ 350119	LMI	❏ 357014	C2C	❏ 360102	AEA	❏ 365537	FCC
❏ 333015	NOR	❏ 350120	LMI	❏ 357015	C2C	❏ 360103	AEA	❏ 365538	FCC
❏ 333016	NOR	❏ 350121	LMI	❏ 357016	C2C	❏ 360104	AEA	❏ 365539	FCC
		❏ 350122	LMI	❏ 357017	C2C	❏ 360105	AEA	❏ 365540	FCC
❏ 334001	FSR	❏ 350123	LMI	❏ 357018	C2C	❏ 360106	AEA	❏ 365541	FCC
❏ 334002	FSR	❏ 350124	LMI	❏ 357019	C2C	❏ 360107	AEA		
❏ 334003	FSR	❏ 350125	LMI	❏ 357020	C2C	❏ 360108	AEA	❏ 373001	EUS
❏ 334004	FSR	❏ 350126	LMI	❏ 357021	C2C	❏ 360109	AEA	❏ 373002	EUS
❏ 334005	FSR	❏ 350127	LMI	❏ 357022	C2C	❏ 360110	AEA	❏ 373003	EUS
❏ 334006	FSR	❏ 350128	LMI	❏ 357023	C2C	❏ 360111	AEA	❏ 373004	EUS
❏ 334007	FSR	❏ 350129	LMI	❏ 357024	C2C	❏ 360112	AEA	❏ 373005	EUS
❏ 334008	FSR	❏ 350130	LMI	❏ 357025	C2C	❏ 360113	AEA	❏ 373006	EUS
❏ 334009	FSR	❏ 350231	LMI	❏ 357026	C2C	❏ 360114	AEA	❏ 373007	EUS
❏ 334010	FSR	❏ 350232	LMI	❏ 357027	C2C	❏ 360115	AEA	❏ 373008	EUS
❏ 334011	FSR	❏ 350233	LMI	❏ 357028	C2C	❏ 360116	AEA	❏ 373009	EUS
❏ 334012	FSR	❏ 350234	LMI	❏ 357029	C2C	❏ 360117	AEA	❏ 373010	EUS

Data Tables

373011	EUS	373312	EUS	375805	SET	376010	SET	377136	SOU
373012	EUS	373313	EUS	375806	SET	376011	SET	377137	SOU
373013	EUS	373314	EUS	375807	SET	376012	SET	377138	SOU
373014	EUS			375808	SET	376013	SET	377139	SOU
373015	EUS	375301	SET	375809	SET	376014	SET	377140	SOU
373016	EUS	375302	SET	375810	SET	376015	SET	377141	SOU
373017	EUS	375303	SET	375811	SET	376016	SET	377142	SOU
373018	EUS	375304	SET	375812	SET	376017	SET	377143	SOU
373019	EUS	375305	SET	375813	SET	376018	SET	377144	SOU
373020	EUS	375306	SET	375814	SET	376019	SET	377145	SOU
373021	EUS	375307	SET	375815	SET	376020	SET	377146	SOU
373022	EUS	375308	SET	375816	SET	376021	SET	377147	SOU
373101	EUS	375309	SET	375817	SET	376022	SET	377148	SOU
373102	EUS	375310	SET	375818	SET	376023	SET	377149	SOU
373103	EUS	375601	SET	375819	SET	376024	SET	377150	SOU
373104	EUS	375602	SET	375820	SET	376025	SET	377151	SOU
373105	EUS	375603	SET	375821	SET	376026	SET	377152	SOU
373106	EUS	375604	SET	375822	SET	376027	SET	377153	SOU
373107	EUS	375605	SET	375823	SET	376028	SET	377154	SOU
373108	EUS	375606	SET	375824	SET	376029	SET	377155	SOU
373201	EUS	375607	SET	375825	SET	376030	SET	377156	SOU
373202	EUS	375608	SET	375826	SET	376031	SET	377157	SOU
373203	EUS	375609	SET	375827	SET	376032	SET	377158	SOU
373204	EUS	375610	SET	375828	SET	376033	SET	377159	SOU
373205	EUS	375611	SET	375829	SET	376034	SET	377160	SOU
373206	EUS	375612	SET	375830	SET	376035	SET	377161	SOU
373207	EUS	375613	SET	375901	SET	376036	SET	377162	SOU
373208	EUS	375614	SET	375902	SET			377163	SOU
373209	EUS	375615	SET	375903	SET	377101	SOU	377164	SOU
373210	EUS	375616	SET	375904	SET	377102	SOU	377201	SOU
373211	EUS	375617	SET	375905	SET	377103	SOU	377202	SOU
373212	EUS	375618	SET	375906	SET	377104	SOU	377203	SOU
373213	EUS	375619	SET	375907	SET	377105	SOU	377204	SOU
373214	EUS	375620	SET	375908	SET	377106	SOU	377205	SOU
373215	EUS	375621	SET	375909	SET	377107	SOU	377206	SOU
373216	EUS	375622	SET	375910	SET	377108	SOU	377207	SOU
373217	EUS	375623	SET	375911	SET	377109	SOU	377208	SOU
373218	EUS	375624	SET	375912	SET	377110	SOU	377209	SOU
373219	EUS	375625	SET	375913	SET	377111	SOU	377210	SOU
373220	EUS	375626	SET	375914	SET	377112	SOU	377211	SOU
373221	EUS	375627	SET	375915	SET	377113	SOU	377212	SOU
373222	EUS	375628	SET	375916	SET	377114	SOU	377213	SOU
373223	EUS	375629	SET	375917	SET	377115	SOU	377214	SOU
373224	EUS	375630	SET	375918	SET	377116	SOU	377215	SOU
373225	EUS	375701	SET	375919	SET	377117	SOU	377301	SOU
373226	EUS	375702	SET	375920	SET	377118	SOU	377302	SOU
373227	EUS	375703	SET	375921	SET	377119	SOU	377303	SOU
373228	EUS	375704	SET	375922	SET	377120	SOU	377304	SOU
373229	EUS	375705	SET	375923	SET	377121	SOU	377305	SOU
373230	EUS	375706	SET	375924	SET	377122	SOU	377306	SOU
373231	EUS	375707	SET	375925	SET	377123	SOU	377307	SOU
373232	EUS	375708	SET	375926	SET	377124	SOU	377308	SOU
373301	EUS	375709	SET	375927	SET	377125	SOU	377309	SOU
373302	EUS	375710	SET			377126	SOU	377310	SOU
373303	EUS	375711	SET	376001	SET	377127	SOU	377311	SOU
373304	EUS	375712	SET	376002	SET	377128	SOU	377312	SOU
373305	EUS	375713	SET	376003	SET	377129	SOU	377313	SOU
373306	EUS	375714	SET	376004	SET	377130	SOU	377314	SOU
373307	EUS	375715	SET	376005	SET	377131	SOU	377315	SOU
373308	EUS	375801	SET	376006	SET	377132	SOU	377316	SOU
373309	EUS	375802	SET	376007	SET	377133	SOU	377317	SOU
373310	EUS	375803	SET	376008	SET	377134	SOU	377318	SOU
373311	EUS	375804	SET	376009	SET	377135	SOU	377319	SOU

❏ 377320	SOU	❏ 377455	SOU	❏ 378152	LOG	❏ 379021	AEA	❏ 390014	VWC
❏ 377321	SOU	❏ 377456	SOU	❏ 378153	LOG	❏ 379022	AEA	❏ 390015	VWC
❏ 377322	SOU	❏ 377457	SOU	❏ 378154	LOG	❏ 379023	AEA	❏ 390016	VWC
❏ 377323	SOU	❏ 377458	SOU	❏ 378201	LOG	❏ 379024	AEA	❏ 390017	VWC
❏ 377324	SOU	❏ 377459	SOU	❏ 378202	LOG	❏ 379025	AEA	❏ 390018	VWC
❏ 377325	SOU	❏ 377460	SOU	❏ 378203	LOG	❏ 379026	AEA	❏ 390019	VWC
❏ 377326	SOU	❏ 377461	SOU	❏ 378204	LOG	❏ 379027	AEA	❏ 390020	VWC
❏ 377327	SOU	❏ 377462	SOU	❏ 378205	LOG	❏ 379028	AEA	❏ 390021	VWC
❏ 377328	SOU	❏ 377463	SOU	❏ 378206	LOG	❏ 379029	AEA	❏ 390022	VWC
❏ 377401	SOU	❏ 377464	SOU	❏ 378207	LOG	❏ 379030	AEA	❏ 390023	VWC
❏ 377402	SOU	❏ 377465	SOU	❏ 378208	LOG			❏ 390024	VWC
❏ 377403	SOU	❏ 377466	SOU	❏ 378209	LOG	❏ 380001	FSR	❏ 390025	VWC
❏ 377404	SOU	❏ 377467	SOU	❏ 378210	LOG	❏ 380002	FSR	❏ 390026	VWC
❏ 377405	SOU	❏ 377468	SOU	❏ 378211	LOG	❏ 380003	FSR	❏ 390027	VWC
❏ 377406	SOU	❏ 377469	SOU	❏ 378212	LOG	❏ 380004	FSR	❏ 390028	VWC
❏ 377407	SOU	❏ 377470	SOU	❏ 378213	LOG	❏ 380005	FSR	❏ 390029	VWC
❏ 377408	SOU	❏ 377471	SOU	❏ 378214	LOG	❏ 380006	FSR	❏ 390030	VWC
❏ 377409	SOU	❏ 377472	SOU	❏ 378215	LOG	❏ 380007	FSR	❏ 390031	VWC
❏ 377410	SOU	❏ 377473	SOU	❏ 378216	LOG	❏ 380008	FSR	❏ 390032	VWC
❏ 377411	SOU	❏ 377474	SOU	❏ 378217	LOG	❏ 380009	FSR	❏ 390033	OLS
❏ 377412	SOU	❏ 377475	SOU	❏ 378218	LOG	❏ 380010	FSR	❏ 390034	VWC
❏ 377413	SOU	❏ 377501	FCC	❏ 378219	LOG	❏ 380011	FSR	❏ 390035	VWC
❏ 377414	SOU	❏ 377502	FCC	❏ 378220	LOG	❏ 380012	FSR	❏ 390036	VWC
❏ 377415	SOU	❏ 377503	FCC	❏ 378221	LOG	❏ 380013	FSR	❏ 390037	VWC
❏ 377416	SOU	❏ 377504	FCC	❏ 378222	LOG	❏ 380014	FSR	❏ 390038	VWC
❏ 377417	SOU	❏ 377505	FCC	❏ 378223	LOG	❏ 380015	FSR	❏ 390039	VWC
❏ 377418	SOU	❏ 377506	FCC	❏ 378224	LOG	❏ 380016	FSR	❏ 390040	VWC
❏ 377419	SOU	❏ 377507	FCC	❏ 378225	LOG	❏ 380017	FSR	❏ 390041	VWC
❏ 377420	SOU	❏ 377508	FCC	❏ 378226	LOG	❏ 380018	FSR	❏ 390042	VWC
❏ 377421	SOU	❏ 377509	FCC	❏ 378227	LOG	❏ 380019	FSR	❏ 390043	VWC
❏ 377422	SOU	❏ 377510	FCC	❏ 378228	LOG	❏ 380020	FSR	❏ 390044	VWC
❏ 377423	SOU	❏ 377511	FCC	❏ 378229	LOG	❏ 380021	FSR	❏ 390045	VWC
❏ 377424	SOU	❏ 377512	FCC	❏ 378230	LOG	❏ 380022	FSR	❏ 390046	VWC
❏ 377425	SOU	❏ 377513	FCC	❏ 378231	LOG	❏ 380101	FSR	❏ 390047	VWC
❏ 377426	SOU	❏ 377514	FCC	❏ 378232	LOG	❏ 380102	FSR	❏ 390048	VWC
❏ 377427	SOU	❏ 377515	FCC	❏ 378233	LOG	❏ 380103	FSR	❏ 390049	VWC
❏ 377428	SOU	❏ 377516	FCC	❏ 378234	LOG	❏ 380104	FSR	❏ 390050	VWC
❏ 377429	SOU	❏ 377517	FCC	❏ 378235	LOG	❏ 380105	FSR	❏ 390051	VWC
❏ 377430	SOU	❏ 377518	FCC	❏ 378236	LOG	❏ 380106	FSR	❏ 390052	VWC
❏ 377431	SOU	❏ 377519	FCC	❏ 378255	LOG	❏ 380107	FSR	❏ 390053	VWC
❏ 377432	SOU	❏ 377520	FCC	❏ 378256	LOG	❏ 380108	FSR	❏ 390054	VWC
❏ 377433	SOU	❏ 377521	FCC	❏ 378257	LOG	❏ 380109	FSR	❏ 390055	VWC
❏ 377434	SOU	❏ 377522	FCC			❏ 380110	FSR	❏ 390056	VWC
❏ 377435	SOU	❏ 377523	FCC	❏ 379001	AEA	❏ 380111	FSR	❏ 390057	VWC
❏ 377436	SOU			❏ 379002	AEA	❏ 380112	FSR		
❏ 377437	SOU	❏ 378135	LOG	❏ 379003	AEA	❏ 380113	FSR	❏ 395001	SET
❏ 377438	SOU	❏ 378135	LOG	❏ 379004	AEA	❏ 380114	FSR	❏ 395002	SET
❏ 377439	SOU	❏ 378136	LOG	❏ 379005	AEA	❏ 380115	FSR	❏ 395003	SET
❏ 377440	SOU	❏ 378137	LOG	❏ 379006	AEA	❏ 380116	FSR	❏ 395004	SET
❏ 377441	SOU	❏ 378138	LOG	❏ 379007	AEA			❏ 395005	SET
❏ 377442	SOU	❏ 378139	LOG	❏ 379008	AEA	❏ 390001	VWC	❏ 395006	SET
❏ 377443	SOU	❏ 378140	LOG	❏ 379009	AEA	❏ 390002	VWC	❏ 395007	SET
❏ 377444	SOU	❏ 378141	LOG	❏ 379010	AEA	❏ 390003	VWC	❏ 395008	SET
❏ 377445	SOU	❏ 378142	LOG	❏ 379011	AEA	❏ 390004	VWC	❏ 395009	SET
❏ 377446	SOU	❏ 378143	LOG	❏ 379012	AEA	❏ 390005	VWC	❏ 395010	SET
❏ 377447	SOU	❏ 378144	LOG	❏ 379013	AEA	❏ 390006	VWC	❏ 395011	SET
❏ 377448	SOU	❏ 378145	LOG	❏ 379014	AEA	❏ 390007	VWC	❏ 395012	SET
❏ 377449	SOU	❏ 378146	LOG	❏ 379015	AEA	❏ 390008	VWC	❏ 395013	SET
❏ 377450	SOU	❏ 378147	LOG	❏ 379016	AEA	❏ 390009	VWC	❏ 395014	SET
❏ 377451	SOU	❏ 378148	LOG	❏ 379017	AEA	❏ 390010	VWC	❏ 395015	SET
❏ 377452	SOU	❏ 378149	LOG	❏ 379018	AEA	❏ 390011	VWC	❏ 395016	SET
❏ 377453	SOU	❏ 378150	LOG	❏ 379019	AEA	❏ 390012	VWC	❏ 395017	SET
❏ 377454	SOU	❏ 378151	LOG	❏ 379020	AEA	❏ 390013	VWC	❏ 395018	SET

Data Tables

395019 SET	444015 SWT	450032 SWT	450123 SWT	455730 SWT
395020 SET	444016 SWT	450033 SWT	450124 SWT	455731 SWT
395021 SET	444017 SWT	450034 SWT	450125 SWT	455732 SWT
395022 SET	444018 SWT	450035 SWT	450126 SWT	455733 SWT
395023 SET	444019 SWT	450036 SWT	450127 SWT	455734 SWT
395024 SET	444020 SWT	450037 SWT	450543 SWT	455735 SWT
395025 SET	444021 SWT	450038 SWT	450544 SWT	455736 SWT
395026 SET	444022 SWT	450039 SWT	450545 SWT	455737 SWT
395027 SET	444023 SWT	450040 SWT	450546 SWT	455738 SWT
395028 SET	444024 SWT	450041 SWT	450547 SWT	455739 SWT
395029 SET	444025 SWT	450042 SWT	450548 SWT	455740 SWT
	444026 SWT	450071 SWT	450549 SWT	455741 SWT
411198 PRE	444027 SWT	450072 SWT	450550 SWT	455742 SWT
	444028 SWT	450073 SWT	450551 SWT	455750 SWT
421304 PRE	444029 SWT	450074 SWT	450552 SWT	455801 SOU
421399 PRE	444030 SWT	450075 SWT	450553 SWT	455802 SOU
421497 PRE	444031 SWT	450076 SWT	450554 SWT	455803 SOU
421498 PRE	444032 SWT	450077 SWT	450555 SWT	455804 SOU
423576 KRS	444033 SWT	450078 SWT	450556 SWT	455805 SOU
423905 BOM	444034 SWT	450079 SWT	450557 SWT	455806 SOU
423918 BOM	444035 SWT	450080 SWT	450558 SWT	455807 SOU
	444036 SWT	450081 SWT	450559 SWT	455808 SOU
424001 BOM	444037 SWT	450082 SWT	450560 SWT	455809 SOU
	444038 SWT	450083 SWT	450561 SWT	455810 SOU
442401 SOU	444039 SWT	450084 SWT	450562 SWT	455811 SOU
442402 SOU	444040 SWT	450085 SWT	450563 SWT	455812 SOU
442403 SOU	444041 SWT	450086 SWT	450564 SWT	455813 SOU
442404 SOU	444042 SWT	450087 SWT	450565 SWT	455814 SOU
442405 SOU	444043 SWT	450088 SWT	450566 SWT	455815 SOU
442406 SOU	444044 SWT	450089 SWT	450567 SWT	455816 SOU
442407 SOU	444045 SWT	450090 SWT	450568 SWT	455817 SOU
442408 SOU		450091 SWT	450569 SWT	455818 SOU
442409 SOU		450092 SWT	450570 SWT	455819 SOU
442410 SOU	450001 SWT	450093 SWT		455820 SOU
442411 SOU	450002 SWT	450094 SWT	455701 SWT	455821 SOU
442412 SOU	450003 SWT	450095 SWT	455702 SWT	455822 SOU
442413 SOU	450004 SWT	450096 SWT	455703 SWT	455823 SOU
442414 SOU	450005 SWT	450097 SWT	455704 SWT	455824 SOU
442415 SOU	450006 SWT	450098 SWT	455705 SWT	455825 SOU
442416 SOU	450007 SWT	450099 SWT	455706 SWT	455826 SOU
442417 SOU	450008 SWT	450100 SWT	455707 SWT	455827 SOU
442418 SOU	450009 SWT	450101 SWT	455708 SWT	455828 SOU
442419 SOU	450010 SWT	450102 SWT	455709 SWT	455829 SOU
442420 SOU	450011 SWT	450103 SWT	455710 SWT	455830 SOU
442421 SOU	450012 SWT	450104 SWT	455711 SWT	455831 SOU
442422 SOU	450013 SWT	450105 SWT	455712 SWT	455832 SOU
442423 SOU	450014 SWT	450106 SWT	455713 SWT	455833 SOU
442424 SOU	450015 SWT	450107 SWT	455714 SWT	455834 SOU
	450016 SWT	450108 SWT	455715 SWT	455835 SOU
	450017 SWT	450109 SWT	455716 SWT	455836 SOU
444001 SWT	450018 SWT	450110 SWT	455717 SWT	455837 SOU
444002 SWT	450019 SWT	450111 SWT	455718 SWT	455838 SOU
444003 SWT	450020 SWT	450112 SWT	455719 SWT	455839 SOU
444004 SWT	450021 SWT	450113 SWT	455720 SWT	455840 SOU
444005 SWT	450022 SWT	450114 SWT	455721 SWT	455841 SOU
444006 SWT	450023 SWT	450115 SWT	455722 SWT	455842 SOU
444007 SWT	450024 SWT	450116 SWT	455723 SWT	455843 SOU
444008 SWT	450025 SWT	450117 SWT	455724 SWT	455844 SOU
444009 SWT	450026 SWT	450118 SWT	455725 SWT	455845 SOU
444010 SWT	450027 SWT	450119 SWT	455726 SWT	455846 SOU
444011 SWT	450028 SWT	450120 SWT	455727 SWT	455847 SWT
444012 SWT	450029 SWT	450121 SWT	455728 SWT	455848 SWT
444013 SWT	450030 SWT	450122 SWT	455729 SWT	455849 SWT
444014 SWT	450031 SWT			

Data Tables

455850	SWT	456018	SOU	465016	SET	465178	SET	465926	SET
455851	SWT	456019	SOU	465017	SET	465179	SET	465927	SET
455852	SWT	456020	SOU	465018	SET	465180	SET	465928	SET
455853	SWT	456021	SOU	465019	SET	465181	SET	465929	SET
455854	SWT	456022	SOU	465020	SET	465182	SET	465930	SET
455855	SWT	456023	SOU	465021	SET	465183	SET	465931	SET
455856	SWT	456024	SOU	465022	SET	465184	SET	465932	SET
455857	SWT			465023	SET	465185	SET	465933	SET
455858	SWT	458001	SWT	465024	SET	465186	SET	465934	SET
455859	SWT	458002	SWT	465025	SET	465187	SET		
455860	SWT	458003	SWT	465026	SET	465188	SET	466001	SET
455861	SWT	458004	SWT	465027	SET	465189	SET	466002	SET
455862	SWT	458005	SWT	465028	SET	465190	SET	466003	SET
455863	SWT	458006	SWT	465029	SET	465191	SET	466004	SET
455864	SWT	458007	SWT	465030	SET	465192	SET	466005	SET
455865	SWT	458008	SWT	465031	SET	465193	SET	466006	SET
455866	SWT	458009	SWT	465032	SET	465194	SET	466007	SET
455867	SWT	458010	SWT	465033	SET	465195	SET	466008	SET
455868	SWT	458011	SWT	465034	SET	465196	SET	466009	SET
455869	SWT	458012	SWT	465035	SET	465197	SET	466010	SET
455870	SWT	458013	SWT	465036	SET			466011	SET
455871	SWT	458014	SWT	465037	SET	465235	SET	466012	SET
455872	SWT	458015	SWT	465038	SET	465236	SET	466013	SET
455873	SWT	458016	SWT	465039	SET	465237	SET	466014	SET
455874	SWT	458017	SWT	465040	SET	465238	SET	466015	SET
455901	SWT	458018	SWT	465041	SET	465239	SET	466016	SET
455902	SWT	458019	SWT	465042	SET	465240	SET	466017	SET
455903	SWT	458020	SWT	465043	SET	465241	SET	466018	SET
455904	SWT	458021	SWT	465044	SET	465242	SET	466019	SET
455905	SWT	458022	SWT	465045	SET	465243	SET	466020	SET
455906	SWT	458023	SWT	465046	SET	465244	SET	466021	SET
455907	SWT	458024	SWT	465047	SET	465245	SET	466022	SET
455908	SWT	458025	SWT	465048	SET	465246	SET	466023	SET
455909	SWT	458026	SWT	465049	SET	465247	SET	466024	SET
455910	SWT	458027	SWT	465050	SET	465248	SET	466025	SET
455911	SWT	458028	SWT			465249	SET	466026	SET
455912	SWT	458029	SWT	465151	SET	465250	SET	466027	SET
455913	SWT	458030	SWT	465152	SET			466028	SET
455914	SWT			465153	SET	465901	SET	466029	SET
455915	SWT	460001	(SWT)	465154	SET	465902	SET	466030	SET
455916	SWT	460002	(SWT)	465155	SET	465903	SET	466031	SET
455917	SWT	460003	(SWT)	465156	SET	465904	SET	466032	SET
455918	SWT	460004	(SWT)	465157	SET	465905	SET	466033	SET
455919	SWT	460005	(SWT)	465158	SET	465906	SET	466034	SET
455920	SWT	460006	(SWT)	465159	SET	465907	SET	466035	SET
		460007	(SWT)	465160	SET	465908	SET	466036	SET
456001	SOU	460008	(SWT)	465161	SET	465909	SET	466037	SET
456002	SOU			465162	SET	465910	SET	466038	SET
456003	SOU	465001	SET	465163	SET	465911	SET	466039	SET
456004	SOU	465002	SET	465164	SET	465912	SET	466040	SET
456005	SOU	465003	SET	465165	SET	465913	SET	466041	SET
456006	SOU	465004	SET	465166	SET	465914	SET	466042	SET
456007	SOU	465005	SET	465167	SET	465915	SET	466043	SET
456008	SOU	465006	SET	465168	SET	465916	SET		
456009	SOU	465007	SET	465169	SET	465917	SET	483002	SIL
456010	SOU	465008	SET	465170	SET	465918	SET	483004	SIL
456011	SOU	465009	SET	465171	SET	465919	SET	483006	SIL
456012	SOU	465010	SET	465172	SET	465920	SET	483007	SIL
456013	SOU	465011	SWT	465173	SET	465921	SET	483008	SIL
456014	SOU	465012	SET	465174	SET	465922	SET	483009	SIL
456015	SOU	465013	SET	465175	SET	465923	SET		
456016	SOU	465014	SET	465176	SET	465924	SET	489102	NRL
456017	SOU	465015	SET	465177	SET	465925	SET	489105	NRL

Data Tables

489106	NRL	508201	OLS	506	WCR	1999	GSW	3231	RAF
489109	NRL	508202	OLS	546	WCR			3232	VSO
		508203	OLS	548	WCR	2127	WCR	3240	RIV
507001	MER	508204	OLS	549	WCR	2833	WCR	3241	CAD
507002	MER	508205	OLS	550	WCR	2834	RIV	3247	VSO
507003	MER	508206	OLS	551	WCR	2903	NRL	3255	DBS
507004	MER	508207	OLS	552	WCR	2904	NRL	3267	VSO
507005	MER	508208	OLS	553	WCR	2915	NRL	3269	DBS
507006	MER	508209	OLS	586	WCR	2916	NRL	3273	VSO
507007	MER	508210	OLS	807	WCR	2917	NRL	3275	VSO
507008	MER	508211	OLS			2918	NRL	3277	RIV
507009	MER	508212	OLS	1105	MHR	2919	NRL	3279	RIV
507010	MER	508301	OLS	1200	RIV	2920	NRL	3292	DBS
507011	MER	508302	OLS	1201	VTN	2921	NRL	3295	RIV
507012	MER	508303	OLS	1203	RIV	2922	NRL	3303	OLS
507013	MER			1204	OLS	2923	NRL	3304	RIV
507014	MER	901001	PRE	1205	NRL			3309	VTN
507015	MER			1207	VSO	3066	RIV	3313	WCR
507016	MER	**Coaching Stock**		1209	OLS	3068	RIV	3314	RIV
507017	MER	84	RAF	1211	OLS	3069	RIV	3318	DBS
507018	MER	159	WCR	1212	RIV	3093	WCR	3325	RIV
507019	MER	213	VSO	1219	OLS	3096	BOK	3326	WCR
507020	MER	239	VSO	1221	VSO	3097	RIV	3330	RIV
507021	MER	243	VSO	1250	RIV	3098	RIV	3331	DBS
507023	MER	245	VSO	1252	CAD	3105	WCR	3333	RIV
507024	MER	254	VSO	1253	OLS	3106	WCR	3334	RIV
507025	MER	255	VSO	1254	CAD	3107	RIV	3336	RIV
507026	MER	261	VSO	1256	NRL	3110	RIV	3338	DBS
507027	MER	264	VSO	1258	OLS	3112	RIV	3340	RIV
507028	MER	280	VSO	1375	BOK	3113	WCR	3344	RIV
507029	MER	281	VSO	1566	VSO	3114	RIV	3345	RIV
507030	MER	283	VSO	1644	WCR	3115	BOK	3348	RIV
507031	MER	284	VSO	1650	WCR	3117	WCR	3350	WCR
507032	MER	285	VSO	1651	RIV	3119	RIV	3351	VTN
507033	MER	286	VSO	1652	WCR	3120	RIV	3352	WCR
		288	VSO	1655	WCR	3121	RIV	3356	RIV
508103	MER	292	VSO	1657	RIV	3122	RIV	3358	DBS
508104	MER	293	VSO	1658	DBS	3123	RIV	3359	WCR
508108	MER	301	VSO	1659	RAF	3124	RIV	3360	WCR
508110	MER	302	VSO	1663	WCR	3125	JHS	3362	WCR
508111	MER	307	VSO	1670	WCR	3127	RIV	3364	RIV
508112	MER	308	VSO	1671	RIV	3128	WCR	3366	CAD
508114	MER	310	RAF	1679	DBS	3130	WCR	3368	DBS
508115	MER	313	GSW	1680	DBS	3131	RIV	3374	CAD
508117	MER	316	FSL	1683	RIV	3132	RIV	3375	DBS
508120	MER	317	GSW	1691	RIV	3133	RIV	3379	RIV
508122	MER	319	GSW	1692	RIV	3136	WCR	3384	RIV
508123	MER	321	FSL	1699	RIV	3140	RIV	3386	RIV
508124	MER	324	GSW	1730	WCR	3141	RIV	3388	DBS
508125	MER	325	VSO	1800	WCR	3143	WCR	3390	RIV
508126	MER	326	WCR	1813	RIV	3144	RIV	3392	WCR
508127	MER	329	GSW	1823	NYM	3146	RIV	3395	WCR
508128	MER	331	GSW	1832	RIV	3147	RIV	3397	RIV
508130	MER	335	VTN	1840	WCR	3148	JHS	3399	DBS
508131	MER	337	FSL	1842	RIV	3149	RIV	3400	DBS
508134	MER	348	WCR	1859	SRP	3150	BOK	3408	WCR
508136	MER	349	VTN	1860	WCR	3174	VSO	3414	DBS
508137	MER	350	WCR	1861	WCR	3181	RIV	3416	VTN
508138	MER	352	WCR	1862	WCR	3182	VSO	3417	RIV
508139	MER	353	VTN	1863	RIV	3186	DBS	3424	DBS
508140	MER	354	WCR	1882	WCR	3188	RAF	3426	RIV
508141	MER	464	BOK	1953	VSO	3223	RIV	3431	WCR
508143	MER	504	WCR	1961	WCR	3229	OLS	3434	OLS

Data Tables

No.	Code	No.	Code	No.	Code	No.	Code	No.	Code
3438	OLS	5179	VTN	5853	ATW	6022	WCR	6720	RIV
3766	WCR	5183	VTN	5866	CAD	6024	RIV	6722	OLS
3860	NYM	5186	VTN	5876	CAD	6027	RIV	6723	CWR
3872	NYM	5191	VTN	5869	ATW	6029	WCR	6724	CWR
3948	NYM	5193	VTN	5881	OLS	6035	ATW		
		5194	VTN	5886	OLS	6036	DBS	9004	RAF
4198	NYM	5198	VTN	5888	OLS	6041	WCR	9101	VTN
4252	NYM	5200	WCR	5899	OLS	6042	RIV	9104	WCR
4290	NYM	5212	VTN	5900	OLS	6045	CAD	9267	NYM
4455	NYM	5216	WCR	5901	CAD	6046	CAD	9274	NYM
4786	NYM	5221	VTN	5903	OLS	6049	OLS	9391	WCR
4817	NYM	5222	WCR	5905	OLS	6050	WCR	9392	WCR
4831	BOK	5229	WCR	5906	CAD	6051	RIV	9419	DRS
4832	BOK	5236	WCR	5910	RIV	6052	OLS	9428	DRS
4836	BOK	5237	WCR	5912	OLS	6054	RIV	9440	WCR
4856	BOK	5239	WCR	5913	ATW	6055	OLS	9448	WCR
4860	WCR	5249	WCR	5919	CAD	6059	OLS	9480	OLS
4902	RIV	5276	RIV	5921	RIV	6061	OLS	9481	NRL
4905	WCR	5278	WCR	5922	DBS	6064	CAD	9488	GCR
4912	WCR	5292	RIV	5924	DBS	6067	RIV	9490	OLS
4925	DBS	5309	RIV	5925	CAD	6073	OLS	9493	WCR
4927	RIV	5322	RIV	5928	VTN	6103	WCR	9494	DBS
4931	WCR	5331	DBS	5929	RIV	6107	RIV	9496	VTN
4932	WCR	5341	RIV	5930	OLS	6110	DBS	9497	CAD
4940	WCR	5350	RIV	5936	OLS	6115	WCR	9498	OLS
4946	RIV	5365	RIV	5937	RIV	6117	CAD	9500	OLS
4949	RIV	5366	RIV	5941	CAD	6119	ATW	9502	VSO
4951	WCR	5376	RIV	5943	WCR	6120	OLS	9503	ATW
4954	WCR	5386	DBS	5945	RIV	6121	OLS	9504	RIV
4956	DBS	5419	WCR	5946	RIV	6122	CAD	9505	OLS
4958	WCR	5453	WCR	5947	OLS	6134	CAD	9506	CAD
4959	RIV	5463	WCR	5948	OLS	6135	WCR	9507	RIV
4960	WCR	5478	WCR	5950	RIV	6137	ATW	9508	CAD
4973	WCR	5482	DBS	5952	RIV	6139	DBS	9509	ATW
4984	WCR	5487	WCR	5954	DBS	6141	RIV	9516	OLS
4986	RIV	5491	WCR	5955	RIV	6151	CAD	9520	RIV
4991	RIV	5494	RIV	5958	CAD	6152	DBS	9521	ATW
4994	WCR	5520	RRS	5959	DBS	6158	RIV	9522	DBS
4996	RIV	5569	WCR	5961	RIV	6160	OLS	9523	OLS
4997	WCR	5631	DBS	5962	OLS	6162	ATW	9524	ATW
4998	RIV	5632	DBS	5964	RIV	6164	OLS	9525	CAD
		5636	OLS	5965	ATW	6168	CAD	9526	RIV
5000	NYM	5647	RIV	5971	CAD	6170	ATW	9527	RIV
5005	DBS	5657	DBS	5976	ATW	6173	CAD	9529	DBS
5007	RIV	5669	WCR	5978	WCR	6175	WCR	9531	DBS
5008	RIV	5679	OLS	5981	NRL	6176	RIV	9537	RIV
5009	RIV	5737	OLS	5985	RIV	6177	RIV	9539	ATW
5023	RIV	5739	RIV	5983	OLS	6179	WCR	9701	NRL
5027	RIV	5740	OLS	5987	RIV	6183	ATW	9702	NRL
5028	BOK	5745	OLS	5991	OLS	6310	RIV	9703	NRL
5029	NYM	5748	RIV	5995	CAD	6311	DBS	9704	OLS
5032	WCR	5750	OLS	5997	RIV	6312	WCR	9705	OLS
5033	WCR	5754	OLS	5998	RIV	6313	VSO	9707	OLS
5035	WCR	5756	WCR			6320	RIV	9708	NRL
5037	DBS	5769	RIV	6000	WCR	6700	FSR	9709	OLS
5040	RIV	5787	CAD	6001	CAD	6701	FSR	9710	OLS
5044	WCR	5788	OLS	6006	RIV	6702	FSR	9711	VTN
5067	RAF	5789	DRS	6008	CAD	6703	FSR	9714	NRL
5125	WCR	5792	RIV	6009	WCR	6704	FSR	9801	FSR
5148	VTN	5793	OLS	6012	WCR	6705	FSR	9802	FSR
5157	VTN	5797	CAD	6013	ATW	6706	FSR	9803	FSR
5171	WCR	5810	CAD	6014	WCR	6707	FSR	9804	FSR
5177	VTN	5821	OLS	6021	WCR	6708	FSR	9805	FSR

Data Tables

9806	FSR	10318	ICE	10600	FSR	11067	AEA	11301	ICE		
9807	FSR	10319	ICE	10601	FGW	11068	AEA	11302	ICE		
9808	FSR	10320	ICE	10605	FSR	11069	AEA	11303	ICE		
9809	FSR	10321	ICE	10607	FSR	11070	AEA	11304	ICE		
9810	FSR	10323	ICE	10610	FSR	11071	CAD	11305	ICE		
		10324	ICE	10612	FGW	11072	AEA	11306	ICE		
10200	AEA	10325	ICE	10613	FSR	11073	AEA	11307	ICE		
10202	CAD	10326	ICE	10614	FSR	11074	AEA	11308	ICE		
10203	AEA	10328	ICE	10616	FGW	11075	AEA	11309	ICE		
10204	3MP	10329	ICE	10617	FSR	11076	AEA	11310	ICE		
10205	DBS	10330	ICE	10647	DBS	11077	AEA	11311	ICE		
10206	AEA	10331	ICE	10648	FSR	11078	AEA	11312	ICE		
10208	CRW	10332	ICE	10650	FSR	11079	CAD	11313	ICE		
10211	DBS	10333	ICE	10666	FSR	11080	AEA	11314	ICE		
10212	VWC	10401	AEA	10667	OLS	11081	AEA	11315	ICE		
10213	PRE	10402	AEA	10675	FSR	11082	AEA	11316	ICE		
10214	AEA	10403	AEA	10680	FSR	11083	CAD	11317	ICE		
10215	DBS	10404	AEA	10682	OLS	11084	CAD	11318	ICE		
10216	AEA	10405	AEA	10683	FSR	11085	AEA	11319	ICE		
10217	VWC	10406	AEA	10688	FSR	11086	CAD	11320	ICE		
10219	FGW	10501	FSR	10689	FSR	11087	AEA	11321	ICE		
10223	AEA	10502	FSR	10690	FSR	11088	AEA	11322	ICE		
10225	FGW	10504	FSR	10693	FSR	11089	CAD	11323	ICE		
10226	DBS	10506	FSR	10698	OLS	11090	AEA	11324	ICE		
10228	AEA	10507	FSR	10699	FSR	11091	AEA	11325	ICE		
10229	AEA	10508	FSR	10703	FSR	11092	AEA	11326	ICE		
10230	CRW	10513	FSR	10706	FSR	11093	AEA	11327	ICE		
10231	OLS	10516	FSR	10710	DBS	11094	AEA	11328	ICE		
10232	FGW	10519	FSR	10714	FSR	11095	AEA	11329	ICE		
10233	DBS	10520	FSR	10718	FSR	11096	AEA	11330	ICE		
10235	DBS	10522	FSR	10719	FSR	11097	DBS	11401	ICE		
10236	CRW	10523	FSR	10722	FSR	11098	AEA	11402	ICE		
10237	DBS	10526	FSR	10723	FSR	11099	AEA	11403	ICE		
10240	OLS	10527	FSR	10729	VSO	11100	AEA	11404	ICE		
10241	OLS	10529	FSR	10731	DBS	11101	AEA	11405	ICE		
10242	CAD	10531	FSR	10733	OLS	11201	ICE	11406	ICE		
10245	CAD	10532	FGW	10734	VSO	11219	ICE	11407	ICE		
10246	CAD	10534	FGW			11229	ICE	11408	ICE		
10247	AEA	10540	DBS			11237	ICE	11409	ICE		
10249	ATW	10541	VSO	11006	OLS	11241	ICE	11410	ICE		
10250	DBS	10542	FSR	11007	VWC	11244	ICE	11411	ICE		
10253	OLS	10543	FSR	11011	OLS	11273	ICE	11412	ICE		
10255	CRW	10544	FSR	11013	DBS	11277	ICE	11413	ICE		
10256	OLS	10546	DBS	11018	VWC	11278	ICE	11414	ICE		
10257	DBS	10547	OLS	11019	DBS	11279	ICE	11415	ICE		
10259	ATW	10548	FSR	11021	AEA	11280	ICE	11416	ICE		
10260	OLS	10551	FSR	11026	OLS	11281	ICE	11417	ICE		
10300	ICE	10553	FSR	11027	DBS	11282	ICE	11418	ICE		
10301	ICE	10556	VSO	11029	DBS	11283	ICE	11419	ICE		
10302	ICE	10561	FSR	11030	DBS	11284	ICE	11420	ICE		
10303	ICE	10562	FSR	11031	DBS	11285	ICE	11421	ICE		
10304	ICE	10563	FGW	11033	DBS	11286	ICE	11422	ICE		
10305	ICE	10565	FSR	11039	DBS	11287	ICE	11423	ICE		
10306	ICE	10569	VSO	11040	DBS	11288	ICE	11424	ICE		
10307	ICE	10580	FSR	11041	DBS	11289	ICE	11425	ICE		
10308	ICE	10584	FGW	11044	DRS	11290	ICE	11426	ICE		
10309	ICE	10588	CAD	11046	DBS	11291	ICE	11427	ICE		
10310	ICE	10589	FGW	11048	VWC	11292	ICE	11428	ICE		
10311	ICE	10590	FGW	11052	DBS	11293	ICE	11429	ICE		
10312	ICE	10594	FGW	11054	DBS	11294	ICE	11430	ICE		
10313	ICE	10596	OLS	11058	DBS	11295	ICE				
10314	ICE	10597	FSR	11064	CAD	11298	ICE	11998	ICE		
10317	ICE	10598	FSR	11065	CAD	11299	ICE	11999	ICE		
				11066	AEA						

Data Tables

No.		No.		No.		No.		No.	
12005	AEA	12094	CAD	12201	ICE	12406	ICE	12478	ICE
12008	OLS	12095	OLS	12202	ICE	12407	ICE	12480	ICE
12009	AEA	12097	AEA	12203	ICE	12409	ICE	12481	ICE
12011	VWC	12098	AEA	12204	ICE	12410	ICE	12483	ICE
12012	AEA	12099	AEA	12205	ICE	12411	ICE	12484	ICE
12013	AEA	12100	FGW	12206	ICE	12414	ICE	12485	ICE
12014	CRW	12101	OLS	12207	ICE	12415	ICE	12486	ICE
12015	AEA	12103	AEA	12208	ICE	12417	ICE	12488	ICE
12016	AEA	12105	AEA	12209	ICE	12419	ICE	12489	ICE
12017	CAD	12107	AEA	12210	ICE	12420	ICE	12513	ICE
12019	AEA	12108	AEA	12211	ICE	12421	ICE	12514	ICE
12021	AEA	12109	AEA	12212	ICE	12422	ICE	12515	ICE
12022	OLS	12110	AEA	12213	ICE	12423	ICE	12518	ICE
12024	AEA	12111	AEA	12214	ICE	12424	ICE	12519	ICE
12026	AEA	12114	AEA	12217	ICE	12425	ICE	12520	ICE
12027	AEA	12115	AEA	12218	ICE	12426	ICE	12522	ICE
12029	OLS	12116	AEA	12219	ICE	12427	ICE	12526	ICE
12030	AEA	12117	CRW	12220	ICE	12428	ICE	12533	ICE
12031	AEA	12118	AEA	12223	ICE	12429	ICE	12534	ICE
12032	AEA	12119	CAD	12224	ICE	12430	ICE	12538	ICE
12034	AEA	12120	AEA	12225	ICE	12431	ICE		
12035	AEA	12122	VWC	12226	ICE	12432	ICE	13306	WCR
12036	OLS	12124	CRW	12228	ICE	12433	ICE	13320	WCR
12037	AEA	12125	AEA	12229	ICE	12434	ICE	13321	WCR
12038	CAD	12126	AEA	12230	ICE	12436	ICE	13229	BOK
12040	AEA	12127	CRW	12231	ICE	12437	ICE	13230	BOK
12041	AEA	12129	AEA	12232	ICE	12438	ICE	13440	WCR
12042	AEA	12130	AEA	12300	ICE	12439	ICE	13508	RAF
12043	CAD	12131	CRW	12301	ICE	12440	ICE	13581	RRS
12045	OLS	12132	AEA	12302	ICE	12441	ICE	13583	RRS
12046	AEA	12133	VWC	12303	ICE	12442	ICE		
12047	OLS	12134	OLS	12304	ICE	12443	ICE	14007	SUP
12048	CRW	12137	AEA	12305	ICE	12444	ICE	14099	SUP
12049	AEA	12138	VWC	12307	ICE	12445	ICE		
12051	AEA	12139	AEA	12308	ICE	12446	ICE	16156	NYM
12053	DBR	12141	AEA	12309	ICE	12447	ICE		
12054	CRW	12142	OLS	12310	ICE	12448	ICE	17013	SUP
12056	AEA	12143	AEA	12311	ICE	12449	ICE	17015	RIV
12057	AEA	12144	OLS	12312	ICE	12450	ICE	17018	VTN
12059	CRW	12145	CRW	12313	ICE	12452	ICE	17019	SUP
12060	AEA	12146	AEA	12315	ICE	12453	ICE	17025	SUP
12061	AEA	12147	AEA	12316	ICE	12454	ICE	17041	SUP
12062	AEA	12148	AEA	12317	ICE	12456	ICE	17056	RIV
12063	OLS	12150	AEA	12318	ICE	12457	ICE	17077	RIV
12064	AEA	12151	AEA	12319	ICE	12458	ICE	17080	RAF
12065	OLS	12153	AEA	12320	ICE	12459	ICE	17090	VTN
12066	AEA	12154	AEA	12321	ICE	12460	ICE	17096	SUP
12067	AEA	12156	OLS	12322	ICE	12461	ICE	17102	WCR
12069	CRW	12158	OLS	12323	ICE	12462	ICE	17105	RIV
12072	CRW	12159	AEA	12324	ICE	12463	ICE	17159	DRS
12073	AEA	12160	OLS	12325	ICE	12464	ICE	17167	VSO
12078	VWC	12161	FGW	12326	ICE	12465	ICE	17168	WCR
12079	AEA	12163	OLS	12327	ICE	12466	ICE	17173	FGW
12081	AEA	12164	AEA	12328	ICE	12467	ICE	17174	FGW
12082	AEA	12166	AEA	12329	ICE	12468	ICE	17175	FGW
12083	OLS	12167	AEA	12330	ICE	12469	ICE		
12084	AEA	12169	CRW	12331	ICE	12470	ICE	18756	WCR
12087	OLS	12170	AEA	12400	ICE	12471	ICE	18767	WCR
12089	AEA	12171	AEA	12401	ICE	12472	ICE	18806	WCR
12090	AEA	12173	CRW	12402	ICE	12473	ICE	18808	WCR
12091	AEA	12174	CRW	12403	ICE	12474	ICE	18837	WCR
12092	OLS	12175	CRW	12404	ICE	12476	ICE	18862	WCR
12093	AEA	12200	ICE	12405	ICE	12477	ICE	18893	WCR

Data Tables

No.	Code	No.	Code	No.	Code	No.	Code	No.	Code
19208	WCR	40204	FGW	40747	OLS	41044	ICE	41120	ICE
		40205	FGW	40748	ICE	41045	FGW	41121	FGW
		40207	FGW	40749	EMT	41046	EMT	41122	FGW
21096	SUP	40208	OLS	40750	ICE	41051	FGW	41123	FGW
21224	RIV	40209	OLS	40751	EMT	41052	FGW	41124	FGW
21232	SUP	40210	FGW	40752	FGW	41055	FGW	41125	FGW
21236	SUP	40221	FGW	40753	EMT	41056	FGW	41126	FGW
21241	SRP	40228	OLS	40754	EMT	41057	EMT	41127	FGW
21245	RIV	40231	FGW	40755	FGW	41058	ICE	41128	FGW
21249	SUP	40402	DBS	40756	EMT	41059	FGW	41129	FGW
21252	MHR	40403	DBS	40757	FGW	41061	EMT	41130	FGW
21256	WCR	40416	DBS	40801	FGW	41062	EMT	41131	FGW
21266	WCR	40417	OLS	40802	FGW	41063	EMT	41132	FGW
21268	SUP	40419	DBS	40803	FGW	41064	EMT	41133	FGW
21269	RIV	40424	GTL	40805	ICE	41065	FGW	41134	FGW
21272	RIV	40425	OLS	40806	FGW	41066	ICE	41135	FGW
		40426	GTL	40807	FGW	41067	EMT	41136	FGW
34525	WCR	40433	GTL	40808	FGW	41068	EMT	41137	FGW
		40434	DBS	40809	FGW	41069	EMT	41138	FGW
35089	NYM	40700	EMT	40810	FGW	41070	EMT	41139	FGW
35185	SRP	40701	ICE	40811	FGW	41071	EMT	41140	FGW
35290	DBS	40702	ICE	40900	FGW	41072	EMT	41141	FGW
35317	SUP	40703	FGW	40901	FGW	41075	EMT	41142	FGW
35322	SUP	40704	ICE	40902	FGW	41076	EMT	41143	FGW
35329	SUP	40705	ICE	40903	FGW	41077	EMT	41144	FGW
35333	SUP	40706	ICE	40904	FGW	41079	EMT	41145	FGW
35407	WCR	40707	FGW			41081	FGW	41146	FGW
35449	SUP	40708	ICE	41003	FGW	41083	ICE	41147	FGW
35457	SUP	40709	OLS	41004	FGW	41084	EMT	41148	FGW
35459	WCR	40710	FGW	41005	FGW	41085	FGW	41149	FGW
35461	SUP	40711	ICE	41006	FGW	41086	FGW	41150	ICE
35463	SUP	40712	OLS	41007	FGW	41087	ICE	41151	ICE
35464	SUP	40713	FGW	41008	FGW	41088	ICE	41152	ICE
35465	SUP	40714	OLS	41009	FGW	41089	FGW	41153	FGW
35466	VSO	40715	FGW	41010	FGW	41090	ICE	41154	EMT
35468	SUP	40716	FGW	41011	FGW	41091	ICE	41155	FGW
35469	RIV	40717	OLS	41012	FGW	41092	ICE	41156	EMT
35470	SUP	40718	FGW	41015	FGW	41093	FGW	41157	FGW
35476	SUP	40720	ICE	41016	FGW	41094	FGW	41158	FGW
35486	SUP	40721	FGW	41017	FGW	41095	ICE	41159	ICE
35508	SUP	40722	FGW	41018	FGW	41096	FGW	41160	FGW
35517	SUP	40724	FGW	41019	FGW	41097	ICE	41161	FGW
35518	SUP	40725	FGW	41020	FGW	41098	ICE	41162	FGW
		40726	FGW	41021	FGW	41099	ICE	41163	FGW
40101	FGW	40727	FGW	41022	FGW	41100	ICE	41164	ICE
40102	FGW	40728	EMT	41023	FGW	41101	FGW	41165	ICE
40103	FGW	40730	EMT	41024	FGW	41102	FGW	41166	FGW
40104	FGW	40731	OLS	41026	AXC	41103	FGW	41167	FGW
40105	FGW	40732	EMT	41027	FGW	41104	FGW	41168	FGW
40106	FGW	40733	FGW	41028	FGW	41105	FGW	41169	FGW
40107	FGW	40734	FGW	41029	FGW	41106	FGW	41170	ICE
40108	FGW	40735	ICE	41030	FGW	41108	FGW	41176	FGW
40109	FGW	40736	FGW	41031	FGW	41109	FGW	41179	FGW
40110	FGW	40737	ICE	41032	FGW	41110	FGW	41180	FGW
40111	FGW	40738	FGW	41033	FGW	41111	EMT	41181	FGW
40112	FGW	40739	FGW	41034	FGW	41112	EMT	41182	FGW
40113	FGW	40740	ICE	41035	AXC	41113	EMT	41183	FGW
40114	FGW	40741	EMT	41037	FGW	41114	FGW	41184	FGW
40115	FGW	40742	ICE	41038	FGW	41115	ICE	41185	ICE
40116	FGW	40743	FGW	41039	ICE	41116	FGW	41186	FGW
40117	FGW	40744	FGW	41040	ICE	41117	EMT	41187	FGW
40118	FGW	40745	FGW	41041	EMT	41118	ICE	41189	FGW
40119	FGW	40746	EMT	41043	ICE	41119	FGW	41190	ICE

Data Tables

No.	Code	No.	Code	No.	Code	No.	Code	No.	Code
41191	FGW	42060	FGW	42131	EMT	42198	ICE	42267	FGW
41192	FGW	42061	FGW	42132	EMT	42199	ICE	42268	FGW
41193	AXC	42062	FGW	42133	EMT	42200	FGW	42269	FGW
41194	AXC	42063	ICE	42134	ICE	42201	FGW	42271	FGW
41195	AXC	42064	ICE	42135	EMT	42202	FGW	42272	FGW
41201	GTL	42065	ICE	42136	EMT	42203	FGW	42273	FGW
41202	GTL	42066	FGW	42137	EMT	42204	FGW	42275	FGW
41203	GTL	42067	FGW	42138	FGW	42205	EMT	42276	FGW
41204	GTL	42068	FGW	42139	EMT	42206	FGW	42277	FGW
41205	GTL	42069	FGW	42140	EMT	42207	FGW	42279	FGW
41206	GTL	42070	FGW	42141	EMT	42208	FGW	42280	FGW
42003	FGW	42071	FGW	42143	FGW	42209	FGW	42281	FGW
42004	FGW	42072	FGW	42144	FGW	42210	EMT	42283	FGW
42005	FGW	42073	FGW	42145	FGW	42211	FGW	42284	FGW
42006	FGW	42074	FGW	42146	ICE	42212	FGW	42285	FGW
42007	FGW	42075	FGW	42147	ICE	42213	FGW	42286	ICE
42008	FGW	42076	FGW	42148	EMT	42214	FGW	42287	FGW
42009	FGW	42077	FGW	42149	EMT	42215	ICE	42288	FGW
42010	FGW	42078	FGW	42150	ICE	42216	FGW	42289	FGW
42012	FGW	42079	FGW	42151	EMT	42217	FGW	42290	AXC
42013	FGW	42080	FGW	42152	EMT	42218	FGW	42291	FGW
42014	FGW	42081	FGW	42153	EMT	42219	ICE	42292	FGW
42015	FGW	42083	FGW	42154	ICE	42220	EMT	42293	FGW
42016	FGW	42085	FGW	42155	EMT	42221	FGW	42294	FGW
42019	FGW	42087	FGW	42156	EMT	42222	FGW	42295	FGW
42021	FGW	42089	FGW	42157	EMT	42224	FGW	42296	FGW
42023	FGW	42091	ICE	42158	ICE	42225	EMT	42297	FGW
42024	FGW	42092	FGW	42159	ICE	42226	ICE	42299	FGW
42025	FGW	42093	FGW	42160	ICE	42227	EMT	42300	FGW
42026	FGW	42094	FGW	42161	ICE	42228	ICE	42301	FGW
42027	FGW	42095	FGW	42163	ICE	42229	EMT	42302	FGW
42028	FGW	42096	FGW	42164	EMT	42230	EMT	42303	FGW
42029	FGW	42097	AXC	42165	EMT	42231	FGW	42304	FGW
42030	FGW	42098	FGW	42166	FGW	42232	FGW	42305	FGW
42031	FGW	42099	FGW	42167	FGW	42233	FGW	42306	ICE
42032	FGW	42100	EMT	42168	FGW	42234	AXC	42307	ICE
42033	FGW	42101	FGW	42169	FGW	42235	ICE	42308	FGW
42034	FGW	42102	FGW	42171	ICE	42236	FGW	42310	FGW
42035	FGW	42103	FGW	42172	ICE	42237	ICE	42315	FGW
42036	AXC	42105	FGW	42173	FGW	42238	ICE	42317	FGW
42037	AXC	42106	ICE	42174	FGW	42239	ICE	42319	FGW
42038	AXC	42107	FGW	42175	FGW	42240	ICE	42321	FGW
42039	FGW	42108	FGW	42176	FGW	42241	ICE	42322	ICE
42040	FGW	42109	ICE	42177	FGW	42242	ICE	42323	ICE
42041	FGW	42110	ICE	42178	FGW	42243	ICE	42325	FGW
42042	FGW	42111	EMT	42179	ICE	42244	ICE	42326	ICE
42043	FGW	42112	EMT	42180	ICE	42245	FGW	42327	EMT
42044	FGW	42113	EMT	42181	ICE	42247	FGW	42328	EMT
42045	FGW	42115	FGW	42182	ICE	42250	FGW	42329	EMT
42046	FGW	42116	ICE	42183	FGW	42251	FGW	42330	ICE
42047	FGW	42117	ICE	42184	FGW	42252	FGW	42331	EMT
42048	FGW	42118	FGW	42185	FGW	42253	FGW	42332	FGW
42049	FGW	42119	EMT	42186	ICE	42255	FGW	42333	FGW
42050	FGW	42120	EMT	42188	ICE	42256	FGW	42335	EMT
42051	AXC	42121	EMT	42189	ICE	42257	FGW	42337	EMT
42052	AXC	42123	EMT	42190	ICE	42258	FGW	42339	EMT
42053	AXC	42124	EMT	42191	ICE	42259	FGW	42340	ICE
42054	FGW	42125	EMT	42192	ICE	42260	FGW	42341	EMT
42055	FGW	42126	FGW	42193	ICE	42261	FGW	42342	AXC
42056	FGW	42127	ICE	42194	EMT	42263	FGW	42343	FGW
42057	ICE	42128	ICE	42195	FGW	42264	FGW	42344	FGW
42058	ICE	42129	FGW	42196	FGW	42265	FGW	42345	FGW
42059	ICE	42130	ICE	42197	FGW	42266	FGW	42346	FGW

Data Tables

No.		No.		No.		No.		No.	
42347	FGW	44018	FGW	44085	EMT	99534	VSO	6358	ICE
42348	FGW	44019	ICE	44086	FGW	99535	VSO	6359	ICE
42349	FGW	44020	FGW	44088	GTL	99536	VSO	6376	GBR
42350	FGW	44021	AXC	44089	GTL	99537	VSO	6377	GBR
42351	FGW	44022	FGW	44090	FGW	99539	VSO	6378	GBR
42352	ICE	44023	FGW	44091	FGW	99541	VSO	6379	GBR
42353	FGW	44024	FGW	44093	FGW	99543	VSO	6392	EMT
42354	ICE	44025	FGW	44094	ICE	99545	VSO	6395	EMT
42355	ICE	44026	FGW	44097	FGW	99546	VSO	6397	EMT
42356	FGW	44027	EMT	44098	ICE	99678	WCR	6398	EMT
42357	ICE	44028	FGW	44100	FGW	99679	WCR	6399	EMT
42360	FGW	44029	FGW	44101	FGW	99670	WCR	9393	ICE
42361	FGW	44030	FGW			99671	WCR	9394	ICE
42362	FGW	44031	ICE	45001	AXC	99672	WCR	9701	NRL
42363	ICE	44032	FGW	45002	AXC	99673	WCR	9702	NRL
42364	FGW	44033	FGW	45003	AXC	99674	WCR	9703	NRL
42365	FGW	44034	FGW	45004	AXC	99675	WCR	9708	NRL
42366	AXC	44035	FGW	45005	AXC	99676	WCR	9714	NRL
42367	AXC	44036	FGW	45018	WCR	99677	WCR		
42368	AXC	44037	FGW	45026	WCR	99680	WCR	72612	NRL
42369	AXC	44038	FGW	45029	DBS	99706	WCR	72616	NRL
42370	AXC	44039	FGW			99710	WCR	72630	NRL
42371	AXC	44040	FGW	80041	RIV	99712	WCR	72631	NRL
42372	AXC	44041	EMT	80042	RIV	99713	WCR	72639	NRL
42373	AXC	44042	FGW			99717	WCR		
42374	AXC	44043	FGW	99035	SUP	99718	WCR	80204	SUP
42375	AXC	44044	EMT	99040	SUP	99721	WCR	80217	SUP
42376	AXC	44045	ICE	99041	SUP	99722	WCR	80220	SUP
42377	AXC	44046	EMT	99080	SUP	99723	WCR	82101	VWC
42378	AXC	44047	EMT	99108	VTN	99782	SUP	82102	AEA
42379	AXC	44048	EMT	99120	SUP	99792	SUP	82103	AEA
42380	AXC	44049	FGW	99121	WCR	99884	WCR	82104	AEA
42381	FGW	44050	ICE	99125	WCR	99953	SUP	82105	AEA
42382	FGW	44051	EMT	99127	WCR	99966	WCR	82106	DBS
42383	FGW	44052	AXC	99128	WCR	99968	VSO	82107	AEA
42384	EMT	44054	EMT	99132	WCR	99969	VSO	82108	DBS
42401	GTL	44055	FGW	99193	WCR			82109	OLS
42402	GTL	44056	ICE	99194	WCR	99991	SUP	82110	DBS
42403	GTL	44057	ICE	99195	WCR	99995	SUP	82111	OLS
42404	GTL	44058	ICE	99241	SUP			82112	AEA
42405	GTL	44059	FGW	99304	WCR	**NPCCS Stock**		82113	DBS
42406	GTL	44060	FGW	99311	WCR	6260	NRL	82114	AEA
42407	GTL	44061	ICE	99312	SUP	6261	NRL	82115	NRL
42408	GTL	44063	ICE	99316	WCR	6262	NRL	82116	DBS
42409	GTL	44064	FGW	99317	WCR	6263	NRL	82118	AEA
		44065	GTL	99318	WCR	6264	NRL	82120	DBS
44000	FGW	44066	FGW	99319	WCR			82121	AEA
44001	FGW	44067	FGW	99326	WCR	6321	SIE	82122	DBS
44002	FGW	44068	FGW	99327	WCR	6322	SIE	82124	OLS
44003	FGW	44069	FGW	99328	WCR	6323	SIE	82125	OLS
44004	FGW	44070	EMT	99329	WCR	6324	SIE	82126	VWC
44005	FGW	44071	EMT	99348	WCR	6325	SIE	82127	AEA
44007	FGW	44072	AXC	99349	VTN	6330	FGW	82128	OLS
44008	FGW	44073	EMT	99350	WCR	6336	FGW	82129	OLS
44009	FGW	44074	FGW	99353	VTN	6338	FGW	82131	DBS
44010	FGW	44075	ICE	99354	WCR	6340	ICE	82132	AEA
44011	FGW	44076	FGW	99361	VTN	6344	ICE	82133	AEA
44012	AXC	44077	ICE	99371	WCR	6346	ICE	82136	AEA
44013	FGW	44078	FGW	99402	WCR	6348	FGW	82137	DBS
44014	FGW	44079	FGW	99405	SUP	6352	ICE	82138	DBS
44015	FGW	44080	ICE	99530	VSO	6353	ICE	82139	AEA
44016	FGW	44081	FGW	99531	VSO	6354	ICE	82140	OLS
44017	AXC	44083	FGW	99532	VSO	6355	ICE	82141	DBS

Data Tables

82143	AEA	94137	DBS	94431	DBS	96100	OLS	999605	NRL
82144	DBS	94147	DBS	94432	DBS	96139	OLS	999606	NRL
82145	OLS	94150	DBS	94433	DBS	96175	WCR		
82146	DBS	94153	DBS	94434	DBS	96181	OLS		
82148	DBS	94160	DBS	94435	DBS	96371	DBS		
82149	OLS	94166	DBS	94438	DBS	96372	DBS		
82150	DBS	94170	DBS	94440	DBS	96373	WAB		
82152	AEA	94176	DBS	94445	DBS	96374	DBS		
		94177	DBS	94451	DBS	96375	DBS		
82200	ICE	94191	DBS	94458	DBS				
82201	ICE	94192	DBS	94462	DBS	96602	OLS		
82202	ICE	94195	DBS	94463	DBS	96603	CAD		
82203	ICE	94197	DBS	94470	DBS	96604	CAD		
82204	ICE	94207	DBS	94479	DBS	96605	OLS		
82205	ICE	94208	DBS	94481	DBS	96606	OLS		
82206	ICE	94209	DBS	94482	DBS	96607	OLS		
82207	ICE	94213	DBS	94488	DBS	96608	OLS		
82208	ICE	94214	DBS	94490	DBS	96609	OLS		
82209	ICE	94217	DBS	94492	DBS				
82210	ICE	94221	DBS	94495	DBS	99666	NRL		
82211	ICE	94222	DBS	94497	DBS				
82212	ICE	94225	DBS	94498	DBS	**Service Stock**			
82213	ICE	94227	DBS	94499	DBS	930010	EMT		
82214	ICE	94229	DBS	94501	DBS	950001	NRL		
82215	ICE	94302	DBS	94504	DBS	960010	CRW		
82216	ICE	94303	DBS	94512	DBS	960014	CRW		
82217	ICE	94304	DBS	94514	DBS	960015	CRW		
82218	ICE	94306	DBS	94515	DBS	960201	NRL		
82219	ICE	94307	DBS	94518	DBS	960202	NRL		
82220	ICE	94308	DBS	94519	DBS	960301	CRW		
82222	ICE	94310	DBS	94520	DBS				
82223	ICE	94311	DBS	94521	DBS	971001	NRL		
82224	ICE	94313	DBS	94522	DBS	971002	NRL		
82225	ICE	94316	DBS	94525	DBS	971003	NRL		
82226	ICE	94317	DBS	94526	DBS	971004	NRL		
82227	ICE	94318	DBS	94527	DBS				
82228	ICE	94322	DBS	94528	DBS	975025	NRL		
82229	ICE	94323	DBS	94529	DBS	975081	NRL		
82230	ICE	94326	DBS	94530	DBS	975091	NRL		
82231	ICE	94331	DBS	94531	DBS	975280	NRL		
		94332	DBS	94532	DBS	975464	NRL		
82301	CRW	94333	DBS	94534	DBS	975486	NRL		
82302	CRW	94334	DBS	94536	DBS	975814	NRL		
82303	CRW	94335	DBS	94538	DBS	975984	NRL		
82304	CRW	94336	DBS	94539	DBS				
82305	CRW	94338	DBS	94540	DBS	977337	NRL		
82306	ATW	94340	DBS	94541	DBS	977868	NRL		
82307	ATW	94343	DBS	94542	DBS	977869	NRL		
		94344	DBS	94543	DBS	977969	NRL		
92114	NRL	94400	DBS	94544	DBS	977974	NRL		
92159	OLS	94406	DBS	94545	DBS	977983	NRL		
92203	DBS	94408	DBS	94546	DBS	977984	NRL		
92901	OLS	94410	DBS	94547	DBS	977985	NRL		
92904	VSO	94411	DBS	94548	DBS	977986	NRL		
92931	OLS	94412	DBS			977993	NRL		
92939	NRL	94413	DBS	95300	DBS	977994	NRL		
		94416	DBS	95301	DBS	977995	NRL		
94103	DBS	94420	DBS	95400	DBS	977996	PRE		
94104	DBS	94422	DBS	95410	DBS	977997	NRL		
94106	DBS	94423	DBS	95727	DBS				
94113	DBS	94427	DBS	95754	DBS	999508	NRL		
94116	DBS	94428	DBS	95761	DBS	999550	NRL		
94121	DBS	94429	DBS	95763	DBS	999602	NRL		

Data labels

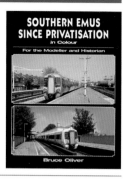
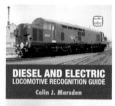